Collateral Management

Founded in 1807, John Wiley & Sons is the oldest independent publishing company in the United States. With offices in North America, Europe, Australia and Asia, Wiley is globally committed to developing and marketing print and electronic products and services for our customers' professional and personal knowledge and understanding.

The Wiley Finance series contains books written specifically for finance and investment professionals as well as sophisticated individual investors and their financial advisors. Book topics range from portfolio management to e-commerce, risk management, financial engineering, valuation and financial instrument analysis, as well as much more.

For a list of available titles, visit our Web site at www.WileyFinance.com.

Collateral Management

*A Guide to Mitigating
Counterparty Risk*

MICHAEL SIMMONS

WILEY

This edition first published 2019
© 2019 John Wiley & Sons, Ltd

Registered office
John Wiley & Sons Ltd, The Atrium, Southern Gate, Chichester, West Sussex, PO19 8SQ, United Kingdom

For details of our global editorial offices, for customer services and for information about how to apply for permission to reuse the copyright material in this book please see our website at www.wiley.com.

Wiley publishes in a variety of print and electronic formats and by print-on-demand. Some material included with standard print versions of this book may not be included in e-books or in print-on-demand. If this book refers to media such as a CD or DVD that is not included in the version you purchased, you may download this material at http://booksupport.wiley.com. For more information about Wiley products, visit www.wiley.com.

Designations used by companies to distinguish their products are often claimed as trademarks. All brand names and product names used in this book are trade names, service marks, trademarks or registered trademarks of their respective owners. The publisher is not associated with any product or vendor mentioned in this book.

Limit of Liability/Disclaimer of Warranty: While the publisher and author have used their best efforts in preparing this book, they make no representations or warranties with respect to the accuracy or completeness of the contents of this book and specifically disclaim any implied warranties of merchantability or fitness for a particular purpose. It is sold on the understanding that the publisher is not engaged in rendering professional services and neither the publisher nor the author shall be liable for damages arising herefrom. If professional advice or other expert assistance is required, the services of a competent professional should be sought.

Library of Congress Cataloging-in-Publication Data

Names: Simmons, Michael, author.
Title: Collateral management : a guide to mitigating counterparty risk / Michael Simmons.
Description: Chichester, West Sussex, United Kingdom : John Wiley & Sons, 2019. |
    Series: Wiley finance series | Includes bibliographical references and index. |
Identifiers: LCCN 2018043094 (print) | LCCN 2018044295 (ebook) | ISBN
    9781119377108 (Adobe PDF) | ISBN 9781119377122 (ePub) | ISBN 9780470973509
    (hardcover)
Subjects: LCSH: Collateralised debt obligations. | Credit derivatives. | Security (Law)
Classification: LCC HG6024.A3 (ebook) | LCC HG6024.A3 S556 2019 (print) | DDC
    332.64/5—dc23
LC record available at https://lccn.loc.gov/2018043094

A catalogue record for this book is available from the British Library.

ISBN 978-0-470-97350-9 (hardback)
ISBN 978-1-119-37710-8 (ePDF)
ISBN 978-1-119-37712-2 (ePub)
ISBN 978-1-119-37717-7 (obook)

10 9 8 7 6 5 4 3 2 1

Cover Design: Wiley
Cover Images: © KJ_Photography/Shutterstock; © agsandrew/Shutterstock; © Alex Staroseltsev/
Shutterstock; © ESB Professional/Shutterstock

Set in 10/12pt Times by Aptara, New Delhi, India
Printed in Great Britain by TJ International Ltd, Padstow, Cornwall, UK

For Allyson, Keir and Freya

Contents

CHAPTER 48
OTC Derivatives and Collateral – Regulatory Change and the Future of
Collateral – Non-Centrally Cleared Trades   **629**

Foreword

The collateral management processes rapidly developed during the past decade; after the financial crisis of 2008 there was a significantly greater need to reduce counterparty credit risk in a more efficient way. Not only the market participants but also the regulators expressed this requirement. The G20 summit held in Pittsburgh in 2009 focused on the financial markets and world economy, following which a range of major new regulations were drafted. These were implemented in several phases and are better known as Dodd-Frank and EMIR regulations.

The main reason for a firm to implement a collateral management process is to reduce counterparty credit risk via the exchange of collateral; this is generally achieved via cash or securities. This hasn't changed in essence since the financial crisis; however, the frequency, processes and products covered have changed. The regulations have had a huge impact on the used applications and processes, from additional trade reporting, trade reconciliations, daily margining, lower minimum transfer amounts, same day settlement, through to the exchange of initial margin with central counterparties.

As an industry expert I've experienced these developments directly, this is also the reason why I would like to share my personal view in this Foreword. Where ten years ago the process was executed by almost every market participant in Excel and Access on a weekly to monthly basis, the financial crisis was definitely the catalyst for change. Software vendors started to build systems supporting the gathering and storing of the most crucial information. This developed further to workflow systems with a high STP rate, often connected to trading systems. Connections were established via APIs, S.W.I.F.T. or SFTP with internally used systems, and with banks, custodians and other service software providers. Alongside such developments new systems assisting the workflow became part of the collateral architectural landscape; some generally accepted systems are triResolve and MarginSphere. (These additional applications will become of considerable benefit to the global collateral environment once adopted by a significant portion of market participants.)

Some years ago the collateral process was mainly focused on bilateral OTC Derivatives, with some additional Repo collateralisation. Now we see many different products subject to collateral, all supported by their own legal documents. Examples of the most frequently traded products in addition to those above are Centrally Cleared Derivatives, Mortgage-Backed Securities and Securities Lending. Additionally, the number of parties now required to exchange collateral has drastically increased due to greater regulation.

As author of this book, Michael Simmons has combined his industry knowledge, training experience and work experience with his enthusiastic interest in collateral management. This book will become essential reading for everyone working within collateral management (whether focused on repo, or securities lending, or derivatives – or all three topics), as it touches the necessary level of detail to gain a broad understanding of the products requiring collateral, as well as the collateral management process itself.

Guido Verkoeijen
Team Manager Cash & Collateral Management
APG Asset Management, The Netherlands

Acknowledgements

Once it became clear that the profile and importance of collateral management had risen significantly following the 2008 Global Financial Crisis, I sensed there was a growing need for a significantly greater understanding of collateral management amongst operations (and other) personnel working within the financial services industry.

In order to understand the subject to enable me to write such a book, I needed access to those that had insight on the subject.

In particular, I would like to thank Guido Verkoeijen for his explanations of both concepts and detailed points, and for his care and patience in reviewing a significant portion of the text.

I would also like to thank Hasse R. Brandt for his expertise and perspective on a range of topics, as well as time spent reviewing my draft chapters.

Other people that have contributed significantly are:

- Arthur Thelen
- Neil Schofield
- Quentin Gabriel
- Simon Lee

for which I thank them greatly.

Michael Simmons

About the Author

Michael (Mike) Simmons is an operations specialist, having spent his entire career focused on hands-on tasks, management and education relating to the various post-trade execution processes. Having spent over 20 years within a blue chip investment bank (S.G. Warburg and Warburg Securities) where he was the manager of Fixed Income (Bond) Operations, Mike then began writing and delivering training courses on behalf of a number of organisations, including the International Capital Market Association (ICMA). He is the author of two previous books, namely *Securities Operations* and *Corporate Actions* (both published by Wiley).

Mike's interest in Collateral Management arose as a result of the Global Financial Crisis in 2008, where it became very apparent that the profile of the topic had increased dramatically, compared with pre-crisis. In addition to existing collateral-related transaction types such as repo and securities lending, the introduction of mandatory central clearing for OTC derivatives in all jurisdictions globally meant there was suddenly a hugely increased focus on collateral which impacts both buy-side and sell-side firms, and other organisation types such as central securities depositories, custodians, management consultants and software providers. Under such circumstances, Mike felt there was a real need for education of operations and other personnel in the topic of collateral management.

Today, as a freelance trainer and consultant based in the UK, Mike delivers training courses on a range of operational topics both in the UK and overseas. Courses include collateral management, the securities (equity and bond) trade lifecycle, corporate actions, repo, securities lending & borrowing, and OTC derivatives incorporating both centrally cleared and non-centrally cleared trades. He also wrote and frequently delivers the 5-day Operations Certificate Programme (a 5-day multi-subject examined qualification) for ICMA Executive Education.

Observations on the style and content of this book can be conveyed to the author by email to info@mike-simmons.com.

Introduction

Note: within the main text throughout this book, terms and phrases in *bold/italics* are explained within the Glossary of Terms.

Within the financial services industry, on a daily basis cash and securities are lent to borrowers on a temporary basis. In order to *mitigate* (reduce) the lender's risk of the borrower failing to return the lent cash or securities, other assets of value are given by the borrower to the lender. Such other assets are generically known as '*collateral*'.

Additionally, collateral plays a major role in mitigating counterparty risk associated with *OTC derivative* transactions, in products such as *interest rate swaps* and *credit default swaps*.

Transactions including cash lending, securities lending and OTC derivatives are executed by *buy-side* firms (including pension funds, insurance companies, asset managers and other corporate entities) and *sell-side* firms (including *investment banks* and *brokers*). Consequently, collateral is relevant to both the buy side and the sell-side of the business.

For a number of years prior to the autumn of 2008, collateral had been used for OTC derivatives with the passing of collateral between trading parties occurring, in some cases, weekly or every 2 weeks or even monthly. Up to that point in time, usually only the larger financial services firms identified *exposures* and then gave or received collateral as frequently as daily.

Then came the *Global Financial Crisis* and the financial industry turmoil in October/November 2008. Both during and since the downfall of Lehman Brothers, the profile of collateral management has risen dramatically, and firms of all sizes are now actively using collateral to mitigate exposures as a primary *counterparty risk* mitigation measure, on a daily basis.

The degree of complication within operations departments has consequently multiplied greatly. Successful processing of collateral within an organisation requires knowledgeable staff who understand the component parts that lead to safe and secure processing, and awareness of the pitfalls that can result in unacceptable exposures. The efficient and successful collateral department within a financial services firm demands a highly unusual mixture of knowledge and know-how of a number of connected financial services operational disciplines.

The combination of new players in and the increased frequency of collateral management around the globe means that basic knowledge of the subject is in short supply and in big demand: many of the positions advertised currently by financial services firms are collateral management jobs. Risk management professionals need an excellent understanding of this topic in order to appreciate whether counterparty risk is in fact being mitigated. Lawyers negotiating legal documentation necessary to be signed prior to trading should ideally understand the overall collateral process. Those working within *central securities depositories* and *custodians* should appreciate the topic if they are to understand and comply with the securities and cash movements instructed by their clients. Consulting firms also need to understand the subject if they are to provide expertise into financial services firms. Software firms need to become aware of the topic if they are to provide collateral management systems that meet their clients' collateral objectives.

Collateral management is applicable to financial institutions globally.

TARGET AUDIENCE

This book is targeted towards those wishing to gain an all-round understanding of collateral management, from an *operations* (processing) perspective. Therefore, those that will find this book of value include:

- those that are entirely new to collateral management
- those currently working within a collateral department and who wish to gain an all-round understanding of collateral processes
- existing operations personnel that wish to broaden their all-round knowledge
- staff who instruct the movement of cash and securities collateral
- recipients of instructions to effect the movements of cash and securities assets
- trade confirmation personnel
- static data workforce
- corporate actions personnel
- reconciliation analysts
- risk managers
- credit controllers
- legal document negotiators
- management consultants
- business analysts
- software engineers.

This book describes the essential day-to-day and detailed practices that 1) a collateral professional requires, and 2) are necessary for a firm to achieve counterparty risk mitigation in a secure fashion and without introducing further risks.

Furthermore, this book is designed to enable readers to make a very positive connection between the conceptual need to minimise counterparty risk, and what must be done in practice in order to achieve counterparty risk mitigation.

OBJECTIVES AND STRUCTURE OF THE BOOK

The objective of this book is to demystify the subject of collateral management by breaking the subject into logical components, explaining the issues relating to each component and at the same time conveying the accumulated effect and the overall picture.

In order to aid the reader's understanding, approximately 150 diagrams are contained within the text. Furthermore, the text contains example calculations to facilitate the reader's complete understanding.

Towards the end of the book, the reader will find an extensive Glossary of Terms containing over 600 words and phrases relating to the subject of collateral management.

The book is structured to be read chapter-by-chapter, from the beginning to the end. However, in recognition that some readers may prefer to target certain parts of the book (e.g. Part 3: Securities Lending & Borrowing and Collateral), each Part has been written as a standalone topic.

The book is divided into four parts. Part 1 begins with a number of fundamental but important concepts; firstly, an explanation of elementary collateral principles, following which the features relating to types of collateral are described.

Thereafter, the three main transaction types which necessitate collateral are described, namely:

- Part 2: Sale & Repurchase (Repo) Trades and Collateral
- Part 3: Securities Lending & Borrowing and Collateral
- Part 4: OTC Derivatives and Collateral

Part 4 is significantly larger than Parts 2 and 3, consequently there are three sections to Part 4:

- Part 4a introduces the subject of derivatives in general, OTC derivatives in particular, examples of OTC derivative transaction types, and important characteristics of OTC derivative-related collateral
- Part 4b refers to the legal documentation pertaining to OTC derivatives
- Part 4c explains the OTC derivative-related regulatory requirements which were introduced following the 2008 Global Financial Crisis, and in particular the impact on collateral management.

I have written this book entirely independently; the views expressed within are my own and not the views of any organisation with whom I have been associated, whether as an employee or as a trainer or as a consultant.

Although every effort has been made to remove errors from the text, any errors that remain belong to me. If readers have comments on the content and style of the book, I would welcome such comments; I can be emailed at info@mike-simmons.com.

Michael Simmons

Introductory Elements

CHAPTER **1**

Fundamental Collateral Concepts

> *This chapter is designed to provide an overview of many of the essential aspects of collateral and of collateral management – each topic will be expanded and explained fully within the relevant chapter.*

What is collateral? Collateral refers to an asset of value that is given by one entity or firm (party A) as security for an amount owed to another entity or firm (party B).

The purpose of collateral is to provide assurance to party B that, in the event that party A does not fulfil its legal and **contractual obligations** relating to an underlying transaction, party B may legally sell the collateral in order to recover the full value owed by party A.

The generic and commonly used terms for such parties are *collateral giver* or *transferor* (party A) and *collateral taker* or *transferee* (party B).

For the collateral taker to be properly secured, the collateral asset must be of recognisable value in the open market place and be highly *liquid*, thereby enabling the collateral taker to quickly and easily convert the collateral to ready cash (should the need arise).

The underlying transactions that give rise to the giving and taking of collateral are many and varied, and in everyday life include, for example, mortgages on residential properties where the lending entity (e.g. a bank) lends cash to the homebuyer with the lender's legal right to take possession of the property should the homebuyer fail to abide by the terms of the mortgage agreement and make the necessary repayments. In this situation, the property itself is the collateral which the lender can sell in order to recover the cash it originally lent plus interest owed.

In the world of financial services, the underlying transaction types that give rise to the giving and taking of collateral fall into two main categories (note: the transaction types listed below are described fully within later chapters):

1. <u>Transaction Types Involving Loaning of Assets</u>
   The common theme in this category is the lending of assets by one party to its *counterparty*, where the lender has an immediate risk of not having the lent asset

returned. To *mitigate* the lender's risk, collateral is given by the asset borrower. Such transaction types include:

- *sale & repurchase (repo)* transactions
- *securities lending & borrowing* transactions.

2. Transaction Types That Accumulate Value Over Time

The common theme in this category is that two parties enter into a *derivative* transaction that typically has a duration of many years – up to 50 years is possible. This means that each party has *exposure* to its counterparty on an ongoing basis throughout the transaction's lifetime. It is important to understand the nature of each transaction type in order to appreciate the associated risks, and the role collateral plays. Although each such transaction begins with equal value to both parties, as time passes the value of a transaction at a particular point in time will fall to the advantage of one party and therefore to the disadvantage of the other party. As time progresses, the transaction value can fluctuate significantly, where on a particular day party A will have the advantage and the next day party B will have the advantage. For these transaction types, the disadvantaged (non-exposed) party is required to provide collateral to the advantaged (exposed) party, in recognition of the risk that should the disadvantaged party go out of business during the lifetime of the transaction, the advantaged party will (it is assumed) need to replace the original transaction at 'current' market rates, thereby incurring greater costs compared with the original transaction. Such transaction types are generically known as *OTC derivatives* and include:

- interest rate derivative transactions (e.g. *interest rate swaps*)
- credit derivative transactions (e.g. *credit default swaps*)
- foreign exchange transactions (e.g. *foreign exchange swaps* and *cross-currency swaps*).

OTC Derivative trades have historically been executed directly between the two trading firms, and are said to have been traded on a *bilateral* basis. Another way of describing such transactions is to state they have been *privately negotiated*, rather than being executed via a derivative exchange (as occurs with *exchange-traded derivatives*).

Common to all the above-mentioned transaction types is the fact that collateral is given and/or taken. The type of collateral that may be given and taken is usually documented in a legal agreement between the two trading parties, ideally finalised (signed by both parties) before trading commences. The form that collateral normally takes is cash or *bonds* (debt securities), as such assets are subject to either zero fluctuation in value (cash) or limited fluctuation in value (highly rated bonds). *Equity* securities (shares) are less commonly used as collateral due to their fluctuating and sometimes unpredictable values.

A party that has given cash collateral normally earns an agreed rate of interest on the cash (assuming a *positive interest rate* environment), from the collateral taker.

Both bonds and equity are classified as *securities* which, when given as collateral are usually subject to a *haircut*; having established the *current market value* of a security, the relevant haircut percentage is deducted in order to identify the security's *collateral value*. Conversely, major currencies given as collateral usually have no haircut applied and therefore usually retain 100% of their 'market' value.

It is in a firm's own interest to monitor collateral values on an adequate frequency in order to determine whether a current *exposure* exists; for example, a bond received as collateral yesterday and whose value yesterday covered the lender's risk, may today have a value which is below the value of the lent asset, and the lender now has an exposure. The lender's exposure must be mitigated by the lender requesting additional collateral (a process known as a *margin call*) from the borrower. Conversely, should the value of collateral rise relative to the value of the lent asset, the borrower has an exposure (i.e. too much collateral with the lender) and should make a margin call to request the lender to return the excess collateral.

Securities collateral currently held by the collateral taker may today have been sold by the collateral giver. The collateral giver requires return of the original collateral so as to facilitate settlement of its sale on its due date (*value date*). Under such circumstances the collateral giver usually has the right to substitute the original collateral with one or many replacement pieces of collateral with either securities or cash (dependent upon the transaction type). The collateral taker must ensure it does not become exposed by returning the original collateral without simultaneous receipt of replacement collateral. This process is known as *collateral substitution*.

Securities collateral currently held by the collateral taker may have an *income* payment becoming due; this is known as a *coupon payment* in the case of a bond, and a *dividend payment* in the case of equity. The legal agreement between the two parties usually states that an equivalent payment must be made by the collateral taker to the collateral giver, when the payment falls due.

As exposure will have ceased upon termination of the underlying transaction, any collateral outstanding at that time must be returned to the collateral giver. With this in mind, it is important to appreciate that the tenure (duration) of a transaction can vary significantly dependent upon the transaction type; see the descriptions earlier in this chapter. For example:

1. Transaction Types Involving Loaning of Assets – *repo* transactions and *securities lending & borrowing* transactions are typically short-term, with a usual lifetime of a matter of days or weeks
2. Transaction Types That Accumulate Value Over Time – *OTC derivative* transactions are typically long term, with a lifetime of multiple years in many cases.

For its own protection, a firm involved in any and all such transactions must be prepared to 1) identify exposures and 2) mitigate exposures, at the relevant frequency, through the process of collateral management.

CHAPTER 2

The Nature and Characteristics of Collateral Types

This chapter is targeted at readers that have had no exposure or limited exposure as to how cash and bond assets are handled within the financial services industry. The chapter is designed to provide an overview of the two primary collateral types, namely cash and bonds. In particular, the nature of bonds must be understood in order to appreciate their behaviour as collateral. Furthermore, the way that cash is paid and received and the way that bonds are delivered and received must be well understood in order for a firm to avoid incurring exposures.

The two most common types of collateral used within financial services are cash and bonds.

2.1 CASH COLLATERAL: OVERVIEW

2.1.1 Introduction

The most commonly accepted currencies as collateral are US Dollars (USD), Euros (EUR) and British Pounds (GBP).

If a firm's exposure is in for example USD, and USD cash collateral is taken from the *counterparty*, there is no *foreign exchange* (FX) *risk*, as there is no conversion to be made between currencies. Conversely, if that same firm has the same USD exposure, but receives another currency (e.g. EUR) as collateral, the firm is exposed to FX currency rate movements thereafter and this could result in collateral taken having a lower value than the firm's exposure. Should such exposure occur, the exposed firm would need to make a *margin call* on its counterparty in order to cover the shortfall and *mitigate* its exposure.

To clarify, either the original *collateral giver* or the *collateral taker* could be exposed due to exchange rate movements.

2.1.2 Eligible Collateral

The legal documentation signed between the two trading parties (preferably in advance of executing the first trade between the parties) should specify the currencies acceptable as collateral to each party. Generically, acceptable collateral is known as *eligible collateral*.

If a firm that needs to give collateral attempts to remit a currency outside of the legally documented eligible currencies, the taking firm is not obliged to accept that currency and is within their rights to refuse acceptance.

2.1.3 Haircut

Providing cash given/taken is in an eligible currency, no *haircut* should be applied. For example, if party B has an exposure of USD 5,000,000.00, party A should pay USD 5,000,000.00 of cash collateral, meaning 100% of the exposure amount and no more than that amount should be paid (because zero haircut is applicable).

Therefore, the *market value* of a major currency cash amount is equal to its *collateral value*, providing the exposure and the collateral are in the same currency. (Note: other currencies may be classified as eligible collateral, but the involved parties may have agreed that a certain percentage haircut is to be applied.)

2.1.4 Settlement

Generically, cash payments are made by a firm by initially appointing a *cash correspondent* (or *nostro*) for a particular currency, then issuing a *settlement instruction* to that nostro for individual cash payments.

Deadlines are applied by nostros for the receipt of settlement instructions relative to the due date (or *value date*) of payment. The firm must ensure it meets such deadlines in order to make payment on time. If the deadline is missed, the counterparty (payee) will not receive payment on time; for cash collateral, a late payment means 1) that the exposed party's risk has not been mitigated, and 2) that the legal agreement will have been breached.

In order to facilitate the payment of cash to a counterparty, it is common practice for *standing settlement instructions* (SSIs) to be stored within a firm's *static data repository*. SSIs are a generic name for bank account details, which are effectively standing orders provided by each counterparty to facilitate cash payments; they avoid the paying firm needing to contact the counterparty each time a payment needs to be made. When needing to make a payment, the paying firm simply instructs its nostro for payment to be made to the counterparty's nostro according to the SSI information held within the paying firm's static data.

The issuance of settlement instructions is a highly risky aspect of settlement; if instructions are not issued by a secure mechanism the risk exists that a third party could fraudulently effect payments out of a firm's bank account. The global standard for issuance of secure settlement instructions is *S.W.I.F.T.* which, for those firms that subscribe, provide high levels of message *encryption* designed to prevent third-party deciphering of secret coding structures intended for use only by sender and recipient of settlement instructions.

Note: to avoid any confusion as to the purpose and use of a standing settlement instruction, as opposed to the purpose and use of a settlement instruction:

- a standing settlement instruction is a piece of information containing bank account details and which is held within a firm's static data repository. A firm needs to hold its own bank account details for a particular currency (known as 'our SSI'), as well as bank account details for a particular currency for each of its counterparties (known as 'their SSI'). Such SSI information is used to generate individual settlement instructions in an efficient and (usually) electronic manner
- a settlement instruction is issued to a paying firm's nostro for payment of a particular cash amount, and which needs to contain currency, amount, value date, in addition to 'our SSI' and 'their SSI' (both of which are copied from the payer's static data repository).

It is important to note that the payment and receipt of cash requires no pre-matching of settlement instructions between payer and payee, before payment is actually made. Therefore the risk exists that, should a payer make a mistake when creating a settlement instruction (e.g. cash amount of EUR 10,000,000.00 rather than the correct amount of EUR 1,000,000.00), the payment of the incorrect amount will be made, assuming that adequate balance is held within the payer's account at its nostro. The firm should have internal procedures in place that identify such errors at source and before the settlement instruction is transmitted to its nostro, and post-payment reconciliation that verifies cash amounts that should have been paid versus actual amounts paid by the firm's nostro. It is not recommended that a firm relies on its counterparties to advise them that such errors have occurred.

When a firm is due to receive a payment from a counterparty, its nostro may require the firm to issue a funds preadvice, which advises the nostro to expect receipt of a specific cash amount on a particular value date. Should a payment be made by a counterparty to a firm, but the firm fails to issue a funds preadvice to its nostro (where the nostro requires such advices), although the nostro will have received the funds on value date on behalf of the firm, the nostro is unlikely to credit the funds on value date, and instead apply 'next day' value. This means the receiving firm will 1) not have their exposure mitigated on time, and 2) suffer a loss of interest on those funds for 1 night as a minimum; if the payment due date were a Friday, a minimum of 3 nights' interest will be lost. Under these circumstances, the paying counterparty will not be in breach of the legal documentation as they paid on the due date. It is also important to note that those nostros requiring receipt of funds preadvices for incoming cash also apply deadlines to the receipt of such preadvices.

2.2 BOND COLLATERAL: OVERVIEW

2.2.1 Introduction

AUTHOR'S COMMENT

This sub-section describes a number of important factors that must be taken into account when receiving and delivering bond collateral.

PART 1

Bonds are classified as *securities* (along with *equity*) and have the following character-istics:

- bonds raise temporary capital for the *issuer* (the issuing entity)
- issuing entities include:
  - governments (e.g. US Treasury, German Government, UK Government)
  - government agencies (e.g. Federal National Mortgage Association)
  - supranational organisations (e.g. World Bank, EBRD, Asian Development Bank), and
  - corporations (e.g. Siemens A.G., IBM, Qantas)
- the issuer borrows cash from investors (*bondholders*)
- the issuer typically pays a *fixed rate* of interest to bondholders as the cost of bor-rowing capital
- bonds have *maturity dates* typically up to 30 years
- investors typically include:
  - some individuals
  - *institutional investors* (e.g. mutual funds, pension funds)
  - corporations and
  - *investment banks*
- individual *bond issues* are issued:
  - by a particular issuer
  - to raise a specified cash amount (e.g. USD 1,000,000,000.00)
  - for a fixed* annual *coupon rate* (e.g. 4.75%)
  - with coupons payable on specified dates either annually (e.g. 1st October) or semi-annually (e.g. 1st October and 1st April)*
  - for a specified period of time (e.g. 20 years) at which point the bond matures and the issuer repays the capital to the bondholders
  - with the price upon issue at (or close to) 100%
  - with capital repayment at (or close to) 100% of original capital borrowed by the issuer

2.2.2 Types of Bond

The type of bond referred to in Sub-section 2.2.1 is commonly known as a *fixed rate bond*. The characteristics of such bonds can be summarised as:

- *Fixed Rate Bonds*
  - bonds issued with a defined (fixed) coupon rate
  - the bond's price will fluctuate according to the laws of supply and demand: please refer to Sub-section 2.2.5 'Market Value of Bonds' within this chapter
  - fixed rate bonds provide investors with a known and unchanging coupon rate throughout the bond's lifetime, as shown in Figure 2.1
  - the issuer determines the coupon payment frequency of a particular fixed rate issue, typically either *annually* or *semi-annually*
  - the first coupon payment date is usually 1 year after the bond is issued (in the case of an annual paying bond), or 6 months after the bond is issued (in the case of a semi-annual paying bond)

---

* exceptions exist – see later

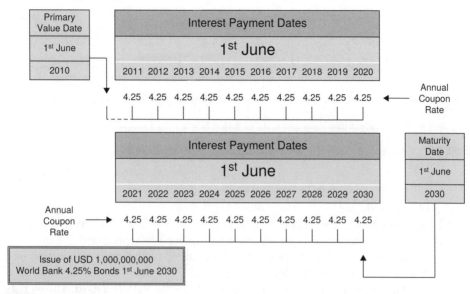

FIGURE 2.1 Example of fixed rate bond showing its coupon payment dates and coupon rates profile

Other types of bond which may be used as collateral are:

- *Floating Rate Notes (FRN)*
  - bonds issued with coupon rates based upon a defined *floating benchmark* rate (e.g. *Libor*)
  - FRNs provide investors with an alternative to fixed rate bonds, as FRNs reflect current interest rates in some cases, and rates of inflation in other cases
  - the benchmark rate is subject to constant change, consequently the FRN's coupon rate will change accordingly as shown in Figure 2.2: for example, the Libor benchmark rate reflects the average borrowing rate as stated by a number of UK-based banks
  - the issuer determines the coupon payment frequency of a particular FRN issue, for example monthly, quarterly, semi-annually
  - usual practice is for coupon payments to be made whenever the coupon rate changes (refixed), although this is not always the case (e.g. monthly rate refixes with quarterly coupon payments)
  - the terms of a particular FRN issue may state that a fixed margin (or spread) percentage is applied to the benchmark rate in order to determine the actual coupon rate: for example, the benchmark rate for a particular period is announced as 2.62%, but to this rate the fixed margin of 0.50% must be added to determine the coupon rate, which in total is 3.12%
  - for a particular FRN issue, the actual coupon rate payable by the issuer is determined and announced by the issuer (or its agent) at the appropriate frequency during the FRN's lifetime. Due to the fluctuating nature of the benchmark rate, there is every possibility that the coupon rate for a particular period is unique and is not repeated for any other coupon period during the FRN's lifetime.

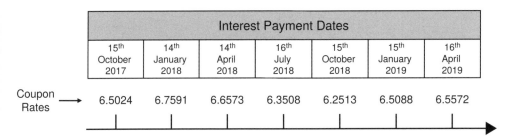

Interest Payment Dates						
15th October 2017	14th January 2018	14th April 2018	16th July 2018	15th October 2018	15th January 2019	16th April 2019

Coupon Rates → 6.5024   6.7591   6.6573   6.3508   6.2513   6.5088   6.5572

FIGURE 2.2 Example of floating rate note coupon payment dates and varying coupon rates

- *Zero Coupon Bonds*
  - bonds issued with repayment of capital at *par* (100%) and no payments of interest
  - unlike most other bond types, this is a non-interest-bearing bond
  - such bonds are issued at a price deeply discounted from par, in recognition of the fact that no coupon is payable; see Figure 2.3
  - following issuance and as time passes, the bond's market price gradually increases towards *redemption* at par on the bond's maturity date

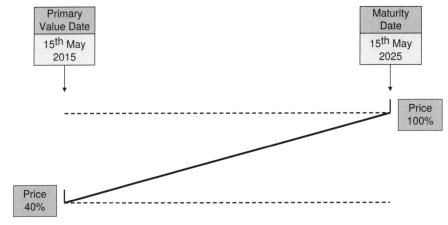

FIGURE 2.3 Example of zero coupon bond price profile, from issue date to maturity date

- *Convertible Bonds*
  - bonds that pay a fixed coupon but with an additional feature: they are issued with the *bondholders'* option to convert the bond (typically) into the issuer's underlying equity on specified conversion terms (e.g. every USD 20,000.00 bonds may be converted into 694 shares)
  - such bonds are often regarded as being hybrid securities, as they have the characteristics of bonds but their market value is influenced by the price of the underlying equity

- *Exchangeable Bonds*
    - bonds with a very similar basic structure to convertible bonds, but following a decision to convert/exchange, the bondholder receives equity of an entity associated with the bond issuer (rather than equity of the issuer itself as occurs in conversion of a convertible bond)
- *Mortgage-Backed Securities (MBS)*
    - securities (not necessarily classified as a true bond) issued by a cash lender to investors
    - cash is lent by an entity to homebuyers (e.g. for residential mortgages) with the homebuyers having a commitment to repay the cash borrowing via scheduled regular payments of a fixed cash amount (typically monthly) which is made up of a combination of capital and interest
    - the cash lending entity issues a security that mirrors the scheduled cashflows of interest and capital due from the mortgagees; investors in the bond will receive the same cashflows mirroring the cash receipts from the mortgagees
    - the term given to such MBS are *pass through securities*. A vitally important aspect of such securities is that of *prepayment*: mortgagees are typically allowed to make unscheduled repayments of capital at any time, which impacts the amount of capital outstanding on the security, and which is represented by an adjusting number known as a *pool factor*.

Additional characteristics of bonds include:

- bonds with a call option
    - the right for the issuer to redeem the bonds prior to the bond's maturity date. In some cases a time restriction is placed on the option, so that the bond cannot be called prior to a specified date. Also known as *callable bonds*
- bonds with a put option
    - the right for the bondholder to force the issuer to redeem the bonds prior to the bond's maturity date. Also known as *puttable bonds*
- bonds with graduated coupon rates
    - fixed rate bonds with a different coupon rate for each of two or more specified periods of time during the bond's lifetime. Also known as step up bonds.

2.2.3 Bond Identifiers

The millions of securities (both bonds and equity) that exist around the globe give rise to the possibility of confusion as to which particular security 1) has been traded, and 2) requires delivery.

Particularly in the case of bonds (rather than equity), some issuers have numerous concurrent issues with very similar details. For example, the World Bank (formal name: International Bank for Reconstruction and Development, or 'IBRD'), may have two concurrent bond issues with the same coupon rate and the same maturity date; however, these two bonds are distinguished by their currencies, for example one being issued in USD, the other in GBP. Consequently, there is scope for confusion between two trading parties as to which of these two bonds has been traded and requires delivery.

In order to overcome such potential confusion, a unique code number is allocated to every security in existence and has become the accepted global standard; this code is known as an **ISIN** (International Securities Identification Number). For example, the following bond issue 'International Bank for Reconstruction and Development 1.375% Notes September 20th 2021' was allocated the ISIN '*US459058FP39*'.

In addition to the ISIN code for a particular security, a national code exists. For example, for the same World Bank bond issue mentioned earlier, a **CUSIP** code (used in the USA and Canada) of '*459058FP3*' was allocated. Note: as can be seen, the national code is a constituent part of the ISIN code.

Other national codes are, for example:

- Germany: WKN (Wertpapierkennnummer)
- Switzerland: Valor
- UK: Sedol.

The responsibility for the allocation of ISIN codes is the country's National Numbering Agency (NNA).

In order for a firm to manage the processing of all transactions which relate to securities (including collateral-related transactions) in the most efficient manner, it is essential that securities static data is set up for each individual security, inclusive of ISIN and national codes.

2.2.4 Bond Denominational Values

Currency notes (also known as bills) are issued in multiple denominations. For example:

- USD notes are denominated in $1, $2, $5, $10, $20, $50 and $100
- EUR notes are denominated in €5, €10, €20, €50, €100, €200 and €500, and
- GBP notes are denominated in £1, £5, £10, £20, £50 and £100.

Similarly, bonds are issued in specified denominations, known as **denomination values**. For each bond issue, the issuer decides the number and size of denominations. For example, a particular bond issue has a single denomination of USD 10,000, whereas a different bond issue may have a single denomination, or 2 denominations (e.g. EUR 20,000 and EUR 50,000) or 3 denominations (e.g. GBP 5000, GBP 50,000 and GBP 100,000).

From a collateral management perspective, the significance of bond denominational values is that the only valid bond quantities that are deliverable (from collateral giver to collateral taker and vice versa) are a minimum of the smallest denomination, and multiples of the smallest denomination. For example, if a bond has its smallest denomination as EUR 20,000, it is simply not possible for a lesser quantity (e.g. EUR 8,500) to be delivered.

Issuance of a **settlement instruction** containing an invalid bond denominational value will be rejected by the recipient (whether **central securities depository** or **custodian**). The reason for rejection: bond quantity is undeliverable.

The primary internal control which should be adopted by a firm in order to prevent issuance of such invalid settlement instructions is as follows. Upon original setting up of the bond within the firm's **static data repository**, the denominational value(s) of the particular bond must be identified and set up. Bond denominational values can be found within the *prospectus* of the particular bond issue. The recording of the required collateral movement within the firm's books & records should utilise the bond denominational values information held within the firm's static data repository; this control should therefore trigger an acceptance or a rejection of the intended delivery quantity.

Note: bond denominational values are applicable to bonds issued in (the current) *global note* form, as well as those issued in (the historic) *bearer* form.

2.2.5 Market Value of Bonds

As mentioned earlier, interest-bearing bonds are typically issued at a price of 100%, and capital is typically repaid at 100% on the bond's maturity date. During the time between issuance and repayment of capital, bond values will fluctuate based upon market forces of supply and demand.

If a cash investor can earn (for example) 4% in the money market, but can earn 4.75% by investing in a particular bond, the bond will be in greater demand and its price is likely to increase beyond 100% (the bond is said to be trading at a premium to par [par = 100%]). If money market rates are above 4.75%, the opposite is probable and the bond's price is likely to fall below 100% (the bond is said to be trading at a discount to par).

However, the actual or perceived *creditworthiness* of the bond issuer may also impact bond prices.

An investor that buys a bond when the bond is first issued is said to have traded in the *primary market*. Once the bond has been issued, it may be bought and sold between market participants in the *secondary market*. Trades executed in interest-bearing bonds in the secondary market attract *accrued interest*, which is the market mechanism by which a seller is compensated for interest earned since the previous *coupon payment date*, up to the *value date* of the trade.

Note: for a full description of the steps involved in the calculation of accrued interest, please refer to *Securities Operations: a Guide to Trade and Position Management* by the same author (ISBN: 978-0-471-49758-5).

From a collateral management perspective, it is important to note that when *interest bearing bonds* are given or taken as collateral, the *current market value* of such a bond includes the current value of accrued interest. Consequently, a collateral giver that fails to take account of accrued interest on interest-bearing bonds will be unknowingly under-valuing the collateral, and therefore at risk of over-collateralisation; that is, delivering a greater market value and collateral value of bonds than is truly necessary to mitigate the counterparty's risk.

It is also important to note that the value of accrued interest associated with a particular bond quantity can be very significant. For example, a bond quantity of EUR 100,000,000.00 with an annual paying coupon and a *coupon rate* of 5% will, towards the end of the coupon year, have an accrued interest value approaching EUR 5,000,000.00.

2.2.6 Bond Holding Locations

Historically, most securities (both bonds and equity) were held in *certificated* form in the offices of *investment banks* and *institutional investors*: see Figure 2.4. Under these circumstances, movements of securities between firms were achieved by physical delivery of certificates between the offices of those firms.

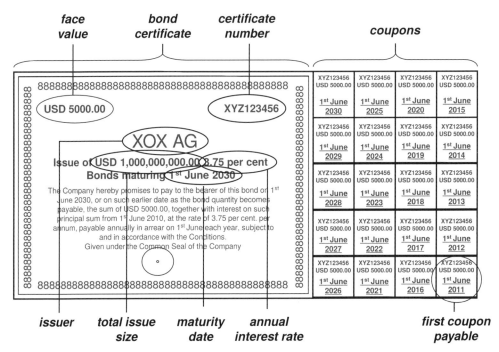

FIGURE 2.4   Representative example of a bond certificate, with coupons attached

By comparison, today securities are typically represented electronically and held at securities 'warehouses' known as ***central securities depositories*** (CSDs). Some firms choose to become direct members of one or more CSD. When a member firm requires to receive or to deliver securities at a CSD, the firm must issue a ***settlement instruction*** to the CSD. Before ***settlement*** can occur, it is common practice for the member firm's settlement instruction to be matched by the counterparty's settlement instruction. Once the instructions are matched, and the ***value date*** has been reached, and the deliverer has an adequate quantity of the securities available to achieve delivery, the CSD will effect settlement by a mechanism known as ***electronic book entry***, which results in the deliverer's securities balance being reduced by the appropriate quantity of securities, whilst the receiver's securities balance is increased by the same quantity. At the close of business each day, the CSD produces statements of securities holdings for each member firm in order to facilitate ***reconciliation*** by the member firm against their internal ***books & records***.

Therefore, the primary location where bonds are held on behalf of investors are CSDs. Bondholders such as ***investment banks*** typically have securities accounts directly with CSDs, in which their bonds are held.

Two types of CSD exist:

- ***National CSDs*** (NCSDs) typically provide services relating to securities issued by ***issuers*** based in the relevant country; usually a country will have one CSD only. Most NCSDs were originally set up for the holding of equity assets following trade execution via the national stock exchange, but in many cases the NCSD has expanded its range of securities products to include bonds

■ *International CSDs* typically provide services relating to *eurobonds* and other types of international securities. Servicing of national securities is also achievable in some cases through electronic links with some NCSDs.

CSDs are located in all the major financial centres around the globe. Table 2.1 lists examples of national CSDs located in various financial centres, while Table 2.2 lists the two international CSDs:

TABLE 2.1   Examples of national central securities depositories

Examples of National CSDs	
Country	CSD Name
Abu Dhabi	Abu Dhabi Securities Exchange
Argentina	Caja de Valores
Australia	CHESS (Clearing House Electronic Subregister System)
Brazil	CBLC (Brazilian Clearing & Depository Corporation)
Dubai	Dubai Financial Market
France	Euroclear France
Germany	Clearstream Banking Frankfurt
Hong Kong	CCASS (Central Clearing & Settlement System)
Italy	Monte Titoli
Japan	JASDEC (Japan Securities Depository Center)
Korea	KSD (Korea Securities Depository)
Kuwait	KCC (Kuwait Clearing Company)
Mexico	Indeval
Netherlands	Euroclear Netherlands
New Zealand	NZCSD
Russia	National Settlement Depository
Saudi Arabia	Securities Depository Center
Singapore	CDP (Central Depository Pte. Ltd)
Switzerland	SIX Group (SIX)
UK & Ireland	Euroclear UK and Ireland
USA	DTC (Depository Trust Company)

TABLE 2.2   The names and locations of the two international central securities depositories

International CSDs	
Location	CSD Name
Brussels	Euroclear Bank
Luxembourg	Clearstream International

The range of services provided by all CSDs to their account holders typically includes:

- the safekeeping of securities
- deliveries in/out of securities upon receipt of valid *settlement instructions*
- deliveries in/out of securities against payment/receipt of cash
- deliveries in/out of securities against nil cash (applicable to *margin calls*)
- updating of securities and cash account balances resulting from deliveries
- collection of *income* and processing of *corporate action* events.

Specifically relating to cash, although settlement of purchases and sales means that cash balances will be created on an intraday basis, at some NCSDs overnight cash balances are not allowed and must be zeroised prior to the NCSDs' close of business each day. Conversely, both ICSDs permit overnight cash balances in over 50 currencies.

In addition, both ICSDs provide an automated *securities lending and borrowing* service.

Not all securities investors choose to hold accounts directly with CSDs. Bondholders such as *institutional investors* more often have accounts held with *custodians*, who in turn have accounts at CSDs. Under these circumstances, in order to achieve settlement of 1) securities trades and 2) margin calls using securities collateral, such investors must issue settlement instructions to their custodian. In turn, the custodian will issue its own settlement instruction over the custodian's appropriate account at the relevant CSD; note that the custodian may operate a range of accounts at each CSD, typically for *withholding tax* purposes (due to the various domiciles of the custodian's clients). Figure 2.5 depicts multiple participants with holdings of a particular security at a CSD:

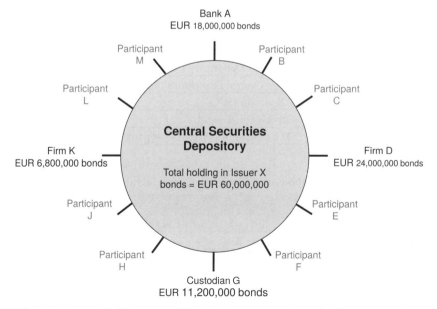

FIGURE 2.5 Participants' holdings at a CSD, including a custodian's holding. (Greyed-out participants have zero holding in Issuer X bonds.)

From a collateral management perspective, where a firm holds its securities has a direct impact on the deadlines by which a firm must operate regarding the issuance of settlement instructions. CSDs publish the deadline by which they must receive settlement instructions from their account holders. If a firm utilises a custodian (rather than a CSD), the custodian's published deadlines will be somewhat earlier than the CSD's deadlines. Collateral Management Departments must remain conscious of such deadlines if mistakes are to be avoided; a failure to deliver collateral on its due date will mean a breach of the contractual arrangements between the firm and its counterparty.

2.2.7 Acceptable Bond Collateral

In the world of collateral management, the types of assets (including bonds) that are generally acceptable as collateral are commonly referred to as *eligible collateral*.

From the perspective of the *exposed* party, whatever the nature of the collateral it is imperative that the collateral received is of sufficient quality and quantity to guarantee that the exposure is fully covered, in the event that the collateral must be *liquidated* due to the counterparty defaulting on its *contractual obligations*.

Consequently, the characteristics of bond collateral that impact perceived quality are those which relate to the likelihood of the bond issuer being able to comply with the terms of the bond issue, particularly *capital repayment* and the payment of *coupons* when falling due. Therefore, such characteristics include:

- issuer type: e.g. government, government agency, supranational, corporate
- issuer rating: e.g. whether the issuer is rated AAA, A or BBB (see Table 2.4)
- asset type: e.g. fixed rate coupon, floating rate note, zero coupon
- *residual maturity*: the length of time from 'today' until the bond's maturity date (the greater the residual maturity, the greater the perceived risk).

In parallel with cash collateral, the legal documentation signed between the two trading parties will specify the bond types which qualify as eligible collateral. For example:

- the highest quality of bond collateral may be defined as bonds issued by:
  - governments and central banks of Canada, France, Germany, the Netherlands, UK and USA – issued in GBP, EUR, USD, CAD
- the next highest quality of bond collateral may be defined as bonds issued by:
  - governments and central banks of Australia, Austria, Belgium, Denmark, Finland, Ireland, Italy, Japan, Luxembourg, New Zealand, Norway, Portugal, Slovenia, Spain, Sweden, Switzerland – issued in domestic currency or GBP, EUR, USD
  - major international institutions, issued in GBP, EUR, USD, CAD, including:
    - African Development Bank
    - Asian Development Bank
    - Council of Europe Development Bank
    - European Bank for Reconstruction and Development
    - European Financial Stability Facility
    - European Investment Bank
    - European Stability Mechanism
    - European Union

- Inter-American Development Bank
- International Bank for Reconstruction and Development
- International Finance Corporation
- Islamic Development Bank
- Nordic Investment Bank.

Note: the above list should be regarded as examples of eligible bond collateral at the time of writing, and is subject to change.

If a firm that needs to give collateral attempts to deliver a bond outside of the legally documented eligible bond types, the taking firm is within its legal rights to refuse acceptance.

2.2.8 Haircut and Bond Collateral Value

The term 'haircut' refers to a percentage differential between an asset's **market value** in order to derive the asset's **collateral value**: a firm's exposure is adequately collateralised if the asset's collateral value is no less than the **exposure** amount.

The purpose of a haircut is to provide a cushion of monetary value, in favour of the exposed party, in the event that the collateral 1) falls in value, or 2) must be sold to cover the exposed party's loss.

Imagine that Firm A has lent a cash amount of USD 10,000,000.00 to Firm B, for one week; Firm B is required to provide bond collateral to **mitigate** Firm A's risk (exposure) of not having the cash amount repaid by Firm B. Firm B chooses to provide collateral by delivering to Firm A a quantity of USD 11,000,000.00 World Bank bonds; Firm B needs to ensure that the collateral value of this bond will cover Firm A's exposure, for which Firm B takes the following steps (please read the following in conjunction with Table 2.3):

- identify the current market price of the bond (98.76%)
- identify the current number of accrued days (282) from which the current value of accrued interest is derived
- the total of the above provides the total market value
- identify the applicable percentage haircut (10%)
- deduct the haircut percentage from the total market value from which the bond's total collateral value is derived.

TABLE 2.3 The impact of haircut on market value to derive collateral value

Calculating Bond Collateral Values		
USD 11,000,000 World Bank 4.15% Bonds 15th April 2025		
Component	Example	Example Calculation
Current Market price	98.76%	USD 10,863,600.00
add Accrued Interest	282 days	+ USD 357,591.67
Total Market Value		USD 11,221,191.67
deduct Haircut	10%	-USD 1,122,119.17
Total Collateral Value		**USD 10,099,072.50**

As can be seen from the above example, Firm B (the *collateral giver*) is required to *over-collateralise* the exposure of Firm A (the *collateral taker*) by the value of the haircut percentage. Application of the correct haircut is a valid over-collateralisation.

(For different transaction types, instead of 'haircut' the terms 'margin' or 'initial margin' may be used, although all such terms refer to the differential stated above; such terminology will be highlighted at the relevant points within subsequent chapters.)

Deriving the specific percentage of haircut deductible from the security's market value can involve a range of factors, including:

- issuer type: e.g. government, government agency, supranational, corporate
- issuer rating: e.g. whether the issuer is rated AAA, A or BBB (see later)
- asset type: e.g. fixed rate coupon, floating rate note, zero coupon
- *residual maturity*: the length of time from 'today' until the bond's maturity date (the greater the residual maturity, the greater the perceived risk).

In general terms, bond collateral issued by stable governments with a short time to maturity date is considered to be of low risk; the lower the perceived risk, the lower the haircut percentage.

Opinions regarding an issuer's ability to fulfil its *contractual obligations* relating to individual bond issues are made by *ratings agencies* such as Fitch Ratings, Standard & Poor's and Moody's Investors Service. Part of the criteria for calculating the haircut applicable to a particular bond is the current rating; it is important to note that *ratings downgrades* and *ratings upgrades* do occur, so it is essential that all firms have access to current ratings. Example ratings and their meaning are shown in Table 2.4:

TABLE 2.4 Typical published ratings classes

Moody's	S&P	Description
Aaa	AAA	Best quality bonds: extremely strong ability to repay
Aa	AA	High quality bonds: very strong ability to repay
A	A	Upper medium grade bonds: strong repayment ability
Baa	BBB	Medium grade bonds: adequate repayment ability
Ba, B	BB, B	Lower medium grade bonds: repayment ability uncertain
Caa/Ca/C	CCC/CC/C	Poor grade bonds: vulnerable to non-payment

Should the incorrect haircut be calculated on a piece of bond collateral, the collateral giver is at risk of delivering that collateral with a collateral value calculated to be lower than its true collateral value. This miscalculation will result in a greater quantity of bonds being delivered (than is necessary) to cover the counterparty's exposure; therefore the collateral giver is at risk of (invalid) over-collateralisation.

2.2.9 Settlement

The settlement of purchases and sales of bonds requires the exchange of securities for cash, and are settled in one of two ways, either:

- *Delivery versus payment* (DvP)
- *Free of payment* (FoP).

By far the most favoured settlement method of securities trades (buying and selling) is DvP, as this is the simultaneous exchange of assets between seller and buyer, wherein each party is protected from loss of its asset:

- from the seller's perspective, they will not have the securities removed from their CSD/custodian account until the cash is available to be paid by the buyer
- from the buyer's perspective, they will not have the cash removed from their CSD/custodian account until the securities are available for delivery by the seller.

DvP requires **settlement instructions** issued by the buyer and the seller to be matched before settlement can occur. Such instructions are frequently unmatched due to a difference in one (or more) trade component, such as bond quantity, net cash value and *value date*.

Less favoured is FoP as a settlement method, as settlement is non-simultaneous between buyer and seller, typically requiring one party to make the first move and to go on-risk, by (when selling) delivering its securities prior to receipt of the sale proceeds, or (when buying) remitting the purchase cost prior to receipt of the bonds.

From a collateral management perspective, the nature of the transaction usually determines whether the DvP or FoP settlement method is used. For example:

- *Sale & Repurchase (Repo) trades* (refer to Part 2 for a detailed description):
  - settlement of the *opening leg* of a repo is typically effected on a DvP basis, as both the cash lender and the cash borrower are at risk and the simultaneous exchange aspect of DvP *mitigates* the risk for both parties
- *Securities Lending & Borrowing* (SL&B) *trades* (refer to Part 3 for a detailed description):
  - the settlement method of the opening leg of an SL&B transaction largely depends whether cash collateral or securities collateral is given by the securities borrower
  - if cash collateral, DvP is the usual settlement method
  - if securities collateral, FoP is the normal settlement method.

During the lifetime of a collateral-related transaction, either of the two involved parties could become exposed requiring the **exposed party** to issue a **margin call** to its counterparty. Assuming the **non-exposed party** agrees the margin call, they will decide whether to settle the call with cash or securities (dependent upon the **eligible collateral** stated in the legal documentation). It is important to understand that settlement of a margin call is directional (from the non-exposed party to the exposed party), therefore:

- margin call settled in cash:
  - requires issuance of a cash settlement instruction by the non-exposed party to its nostro
  - this method requires no matching of instructions prior to settlement
- margin call settled in securities:
  - requires issuance of an FoP securities settlement instruction by the non-exposed party to its *CSD* or *custodian*
  - this method requires an equivalent settlement instruction from the exposed party in order to match instructions prior to settlement.

Settlement of margin calls in this way is applicable to the following transaction types:

- OTC Derivatives
- Sale & Repurchase (Repo)
- Securities Lending & Borrowing (SL&B).

Once the giver's and the taker's securities settlement instructions are matched, should either of the parties cancel their instruction, the instruction that remains will revert to a status of 'unmatched'. Assuming that instructions remain matched, settlement is attempted (at the CSD) on *value date*, and not before.

In order for settlement to occur, 1) instructions must be matched, 2) value date must have been reached, and 3) the seller must have the bonds available for delivery. If steps 1 and 2 have been satisfied, but not step 3, settlement will 'fail'. *Settlement failure* means that settlement is delayed, not cancelled. Should settlement failure occur, under these circumstances both the giver's instruction and the taker's instruction will be given a status of 'deliverer insufficient of bonds'; the status of the instructions will remain the same until the collateral giver's account at the CSD is in receipt of an adequate quantity of bonds for the delivery to the collateral taker to occur.

Once settlement has occurred, the CSD/custodian will apply a status of 'settled' to both the collateral giver's and the collateral taker's instructions. This means that a specified quantity of a specified bond has been delivered from one account (the collateral giver's) to another account (the collateral taker's) on a particular *settlement date*.

At this point the collateral giver's obligation to settle the margin call and to deliver collateral to the collateral taker has been fulfilled.

Note: for a full description of the steps involved in the settlement of bonds, please refer to *Securities Operations: a Guide to Trade and Position Management* by the same author (ISBN: 978-0-471-49758-5).

2.2.10 Bond Interest Payments

Bond interest payment dates, commonly known as *coupon payment dates*, are normally scheduled at the point when the bond is first brought to the marketplace, meaning that both the interest rate (on *fixed rate bonds* and *convertible bonds*) and the coupon payment dates are scheduled throughout the bond's life.

Following the purchase of a bond, the **bondholder** (e.g. **investment bank** or **institutional investor**) will normally have their bonds held in safekeeping by a **central securities depository** (CSD) or a **custodian**. Within the **service level agreement** (SLA) signed between the CSD/custodian and its client, it is common practice for the CSD/custodian to include within its services to clients the collection of all income (i.e. **coupon** on bonds, **dividends** on equity), and the protection of clients' interests regarding other **corporate action** events, including:

- on bonds: **bond exchange offers, bond repurchase offers**
- on equity: **bonus issues, stock splits, rights issues**.

Therefore, an existing owner (e.g. a pension fund) of a quantity of USD 5,000,000.00 of a particular World Bank bond with a 4.5% annual paying coupon on 1st August each year until the year 2030, would expect to receive a coupon payment of USD 225,000.00 on (or very shortly after) 1st August each year. The pension fund's custodian will be holding these bonds on behalf of its client, and should be ensuring it receives payment from the relevant CSD (where the custodian has an account), and in turn the custodian should credit the account of the pension fund.

At a more granular level, CSDs typically operate a **record date** system for deciding which of its account holders to credit with the coupon proceeds; such a system of determining which account holders the CSD will pay is necessary due to deliveries of securities close to the coupon payment date. Imagine that a CSD holds a total quantity of USD 106,000,000.00 bonds of the World Bank issue mentioned earlier, and that as at close of record date there are six holders at that CSD, as shown in Table 2.5:

TABLE 2.5   Example of bondholdings at a CSD

Holder	Quantity
A	USD 5,000,000.00
B	USD 15,000,000.00
C	USD 8,000,000.00
D	USD 35,000,000.00
E	USD 25,000,000.00
F	USD 18,000,000.00
Total	*USD 106,000,000.00*

Assume the pension fund's custodian to be holder A. Two scenarios are possible relating to the holding of USD 5,000,000.00 bonds and subsequently the treatment of the coupon payment:

- scenario #1:
  - providing the bonds remain in the custodian's account and are not delivered out of the account prior to close of business on record date, the CSD will credit the custodian's account with USD 225,000.00 on (or shortly after) coupon payment date. The custodian will, in turn, credit the account of its client, the pension fund

■ scenario #2:

■ the pension fund executes a sale & repurchase (repo) transaction in which it borrows an amount of cash from Firm E, and is required to deliver bond collateral to that counterparty to mitigate the cash lender's risk. Both the pension fund and Firm E agree that a quantity of USD 2,000,000.00 of the World Bank bond covers Firm E's *exposure*, and the pension fund issues a *settlement instruction* to its custodian. This results in the following: on the *opening value date* of the repo transaction (assume that date to be the same as the record date), the USD 2,000,000.00 bonds are delivered out of the custodian's account (holder A) and into the account of Firm E. The close of record date position at the CSD will now appear as shown in Table 2.6:

TABLE 2.6   Example of bondholdings at a CSD following delivery of collateral

Holder	Quantity
A	USD 3,000,000.00
B	USD 15,000,000.00
C	USD 8,000,000.00
D	USD 35,000,000.00
E	USD 27,000,000.00
F	USD 18,000,000.00
Total	*USD 106,000,000.00*

Consequently, the CSD will credit the coupon payment amounts according to this (scenario #2) close of record date position, meaning that the custodian (on behalf of the pension fund) will be credited with the coupon on USD 3,000,000.00 bonds, and Firm E will be credited with the coupon on USD 27,000,000.00 bonds.

Scenario #2 clarifies who will be paid the coupon by the CSD, where delivery of bond collateral occurs prior to the close of record date. However, that scenario raises the following important question: *which party is entitled to the coupon payment on the USD 2,000,000.00 bonds given by the pension fund to Firm E as collateral?* The answer to this question is directly associated with the contents of the legal documentation signed by both parties prior to *trade execution*, and will be explained within the relevant chapters.

Note: the actions of 1) claiming coupon payments from collateral counterparties, 2) making payments of coupon, and 3) dealing with issues such as *withholding tax* differences on such coupon payments – are regarded by some firms as added complications which are best avoided. Consequently, where practical the two firms may agree to perform a *collateral substitution* in advance of the record date.

In the case of *eurobonds* which are typically held at the two *international central securities depositories* (namely *Euroclear Bank* in Brussels, and *Clearstream International* in Luxembourg), the record date is typically (but not always) the close of business on the business day prior to the coupon payment date.

Sale & Repurchase (Repo) Trades and Collateral

CHAPTER 3

Sale & Repurchase (Repo) Trades and Collateral – Introduction to Repo

This section is targeted at readers that have had no exposure to or limited exposure to the subject of repo.

Repo trades are a very popular and flexible mechanism by which cash is borrowed against securities collateral delivered to the cash lender.

Along with *securities lending & borrowing* trades, repo trades fall within the general grouping of transaction types known as *securities financing*.

This section describes the reasons for the lending and the borrowing of cash, the benefits to both lender and borrower, the various methods of trade execution and the role collateral plays in such trades.

3.1 INTRODUCTION TO REPO

Definition of a repo trade: the temporary loan of an asset, to a borrower, against receipt of collateral, for return at a specified later date.

A repo is a transaction in which one party lends cash to a borrower at an agreed interest rate, and the cash borrower immediately provides *collateral* in return in order to *mitigate* the cash lender's risk. At the close of the transaction those asset flows are reversed; the cash borrower repays the cash plus interest (in a *positive interest rate* environment), and the cash lender returns the collateral.

Alternatively, with the emphasis on the securities (as collateral), the transaction may be described as follows: the cash borrower sells the securities for immediate settlement against cash and simultaneously agrees to repurchase those same securities for settlement against the same cash amount, plus interest at an agreed rate, for *settlement* on a future *value date*.

Should the cash borrower (the *collateral giver*) default on its obligation to repay the borrowed cash at the close of the transaction, the cash lender (the *collateral taker*) may sell the collateral to recover the cash amount lent.

Investment banks that purchase and hold financial assets, in particular equity and bonds, typically do not possess adequate values of cash in order to pay for such purchases. Such firms need to borrow cash as cheaply as possible, in order to pay for their purchases; such firms are typically cash borrowers in repo transactions.

Firms that are 'long' of cash may choose to lend cash on a secured basis; such firms are the suppliers of cash in repo transactions.

The most commonly used security type in repo transactions are high quality bonds, although collateral in the form of equity is sometimes used.

The cost of borrowing any asset is minimised if the lender's risk (of not having the lent asset returned) is mitigated. The lender's risk is mitigated if the borrower provides an adequate value of high quality collateral to the lender. Generically speaking, such transactions are commonly known as *secured borrowing* or *collateralised borrowing*. Where cash borrowing transactions are executed under the protection of a sale & repurchase legal agreement (known as a *GMRA*), such transactions are called repo transactions.

Repo transactions are generally classified as *money market* transactions, due to their typically short-term nature of collateralised cash lending and borrowing. Therefore, a cash lender may view the execution of a repo trade as a cash loan, for which the lender's risk is mitigated through the receipt of collateral, and for which interest is earned (in a positive interest rate environment).

The interest rate charged by the cash lender is known as the *repo rate*, which is expressed as an annualised percentage and is calculated over the actual number of days over which the cash is lent. The creditworthiness of the bond *issuer* is a factor that influences the repo rate of a particular repo transaction. The cost of borrowing under a repo transaction is typically less than for an *unsecured borrowing*, due to the lender's risk being mitigated.

The type of collateral normally given by the cash borrower to the cash lender is government issued bonds; what constitutes *eligible collateral* in a repo transaction is defined within the legal documentation signed between the two trading parties. It is common to find that *fixed rate bonds*, *floating rate notes* and *zero coupon bonds* are acceptable as collateral.

There are two separate motivations for executing a repo trade; the need to borrow cash (*cash-based repo*), and the need to borrow securities (*stock-based repo*).

Note: some parties are of the opinion that repos should be treated as collateralised cash loans, whereas other parties regard repos as securities transactions.

3.2 PARTICIPANTS IN THE REPO MARKETPLACE

A variety of market participants utilise repo transactions, including investment banks, brokers, institutional investors, supranational organisations and central banks. Electronic trading platforms have also become popular methods by which repo trades are executed.

3.2.1 Institutional Investors

The term '*institutional investor*' is a collective term for organisations that invest in financial instruments (inclusive of equity and debt securities, foreign exchange and derivatives), but who are on the outside of the financial marketplace and must communicate with those on the inside of the marketplace in order to execute trades. Such firms are considered as 'end-users' of financial products, and a collective nickname for such firms is the *'buy-side'*.

Encompassed within this category of investor are firms whose business falls under the umbrella of financial services such as mutual funds, hedge funds, pension funds, insurance companies and regional banks. However, non-financial firms such as those large organisations within the textile or oil industries, who are proactive managers of their financial resources, may also be included under this heading.

Such firms need to borrow cash on occasions, and the repo market provides a highly flexible option for borrowing cash on terms tailored to the firm's specific needs. The repo market enables cash amounts ranging from the relatively small to the very large (in the hundreds of millions in USD, EUR and GBP terms), in a variety of currencies, to be borrowed at interest rates that are lower than borrowing on an *unsecured* basis, over periods of time lasting from overnight to many months. Such firms can utilise their existing holdings of high quality and highly *liquid* bonds in order to secure the cash lender's risk and thereby keeping borrowing costs at very competitive levels.

Those institutional investors that are 'long' of cash are able to lend cash on a secured basis, for periods of time that are tailored to suit the cash lender's requirement, receiving securities as collateral with, in many cases, a *current market value* of up to 105% of the cash amount lent.

In order to execute a repo trade, institutional investors are typically required to contact an investment bank (or broker), through whom the trade will be executed.

3.2.2 Supranational Organisations

A further type of buy-side institution that typically executes repo trades are *supranational organisations*. Such organisations are often cash long, and become cash lenders (and collateral takers) in repo trades.

3.2.3 Central Banks

The key objectives of national central banks are to control inflation and economic growth. In order to achieve such objectives, central banks typically execute repos via their *open market operations*, thereby applying control over short-term interest rates.

The repo market is the foremost mechanism by which many central banks put into operation their *monetary policy*, as repos are regarded as being a highly flexible transaction type which carries little *credit risk*.

3.2.4 Investment Banks

Generically speaking, investment banks are sometimes referred to as 'market professionals'. At the time of writing, such firms would include the investment banking division of, for example (in no particular order), Morgan Stanley, Credit Suisse, J.P. Morgan Chase, Nomura, Deutsche Bank, Goldman Sachs, Barclays, UBS and Bank of America Merrill Lynch. Such firms execute repo trades with 1) their clients (the institutional investor community), and with 2) other investment banks. Investment banks are regarded as the *'sell-side'* that provide services to buy-side firms.

Investment banks execute repo trades on a proprietary basis, meaning that they will, for example, borrow cash via repo in order to fund their inventory of securities (equity and bond) positions. Such firms may execute trades in securities with values far greater than the firm's capital, and therefore need to borrow cash at highly competitive rates in order to maximise trading profits and to minimise the negative impact of cash borrowing costs. Conversely, investment banks may choose to lend their excess cash via repo. A further motivation is to borrow specific securities via repo, in order to settle an underlying sale or other transaction.

Many firms operate a repo 'matched book', in which (for example) the cash they borrow from one counterparty via repo is then lent to a different counterparty via repo at a slightly higher repo rate, thereby making a profit on the repo interest differential.

3.2.5 Brokers

In the truest meaning of the term, a broker is an intermediary (or middleman) that having received an *order* from one party to buy or to sell, then attempts to find another party that's willing to fulfil that order which (if successful), results in *trade execution*.

In parallel with other areas within the financial services industry, brokers play a vital role in bringing together parties that have a particular requirement to fulfil, and those that can satisfy that requirement.

Brokers are the essential link between those with a demand and those that can supply the goods or services.

The consistent business model amongst broking firms is their desire to avoid taking a position in a particular asset, whether 'long' or 'short'. For example, taking a long position in a security (whether equity or bond) implies that position will need to be funded, which comes at a cost to the position holder. Furthermore, price volatility in the particular security means that *market risk* exists for the position holder.

In order to avoid such risk taking, brokers act in an *agency capacity* by facilitating transactions between two parties, and charging *commission* to the party placing the order. For repos specifically, their method of operation is typically by the provision of electronic trading platforms, over which firms that wish to execute repo transactions input their requirements (including currency and amount, repo rate, duration of trade and required collateral). Many of the largest firms utilise such platforms, enabling price comparison followed by trade execution.

3.2.6 Electronic Trading Platforms

Compared with the conventional method of executing repo trades (by telephone), automated repo trading platforms exist including:

- GC Pooling
- MTS Repo
- Brokertec.

The method of operation of one such platform, namely GC Pooling, will be explored within Chapter 7, 'Sale & Repurchase (Repo) Trades and Collateral – Repo Trade Variations'.

CHAPTER 4

Sale & Repurchase (Repo) Trades and Collateral – Classic Repo Trades

> *Definition of classic repo: the temporary loan of an asset to a borrower against receipt of collateral, for return at a later date, in return for cash interest.*

A classic repo is one form of repo in which one party executes a repo trade directly with another party, on a ***bilateral*** basis. Other forms of repo include:

- Buy/Sell-Backs
- Tri-Party Repo
- Delivery by Value
- GC Pooling, and
- RepoClear.

These forms of repo are described within Chapter 7 'Sale & Repurchase (Repo) Trades and Collateral – Repo Trade Variations'.

4.1 CASH-BASED CLASSIC REPO TRANSACTIONS

> *Definition of a cash-based classic repo: the temporary loan of a specific cash amount, to a borrower, against receipt of bond collateral, for return at a later date, in return for cash interest.*

This section focuses on one party's requirement to borrow cash (as opposed to securities); this is known as a cash-based repo.

All repos are two-legged transactions. In a cash-based repo, the opening leg involves the payment of cash from the cash lender to the cash borrower, with bond collateral passing in the opposite direction. The closing leg involves the return of the cash amount borrowed plus cash interest (assuming a *positive interest rate* environment), against return of the bond collateral. This is depicted in Figure 4.1:

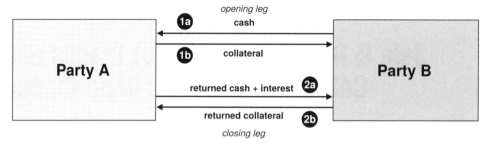

FIGURE 4.1   Repo asset flows on the opening and closing legs

- on the opening leg of the repo:
  - Step 1a: the cash lender pays cash to the cash borrower, and simultaneously
  - Step 1b: the cash borrower delivers bonds (as collateral) to the cash lender
- on the closing leg of the repo:
  - Step 2a: the cash borrower repays the borrowed cash, plus interest, to the cash lender, and simultaneously
  - Step 2b: the cash lender returns the bond collateral to the cash borrower.

Note that a range of terms are used to describe the legs in a repo transaction (see Table 4.1):

TABLE 4.1   Terminology used to describe each leg in a repo

Repo 'Leg' Terminology	
Opening Leg Also Known As	Closing Leg Also Known As
1st Leg	2nd Leg
Onside Leg	Offside Leg
Start Leg	End Leg
Near Leg	Far Leg
Purchase Leg	Repurchase Leg

Note: such a transaction is sometimes described from the primary perspective of the securities. For example, it may be stated that in the opening leg the bonds are sold against receipt of cash, and in the closing leg the bonds are repurchased against return of cash plus interest. In the author's view, it is more intuitive to regard the cash amount as the primary asset (and the primary motivation to execute the trade), with collateral (in the form of a bond) being given to the cash lender in order to *mitigate* the lender's risk.

Specific terms are popularly used to indicate the role of parties to a repo transaction. The cash borrower (and the ***collateral giver***) is said to have executed a '***repo***', whilst the cash lender (and ***collateral taker***) is said to have executed a '***reverse repo***'. To clarify the use of such terms, in one single repo transaction, one party executes a repo whilst its counterparty executes a reverse repo.

4.1.1 The Duration of a Classic Repo Transaction

In terms of tenure of a repo trade, two types exist:

- a repo executed for a fixed period of time, in which the ***closing value date*** is agreed on trade date, is known as a 'term' repo, whereas
- a repo executed without the parties agreeing (yet) to a closing value date is known as an 'on demand' (commonly known as an 'open') repo.

A term repo typically has the following basic components (from the cash borrower's perspective) as shown in Table 4.2:

TABLE 4.2   Primary components in a Term Repo

Term Repo	
Trade Component	**Trade Detail**
Transaction Type	Repo Cash Borrowing
Counterparty	Counterparty G
Currency Amount	USD 50,000,000.00
Repo Rate	3.15%
Trade Date	March 16th
Opening Value Date	March 17th
Closing Value Date	March 24th

Note that:

- the opening value date is also known as the ***purchase date***, and
- the closing value date is also known as the ***repurchase date***.

At the point of trade execution, the cash lender and the cash borrower agree the specific ***closing value date***; the fact that a closing value date has been agreed makes this repo a term repo. The two value dates indicate the dates that the cash (and the collateral) will be moved in either direction. In this trade, the cash is scheduled to be paid by the lender to the borrower on 17th March, and returned 7 days later on 24th March.

Note: since October 2014, the normal ***settlement cycle*** for repos executed in Europe is T+1; however, this may not suit all firms and so T+2 or T+3 may be negotiated between the two trading firms.

Conversely, an open repo typically has the following basic components (from the cash borrower's perspective) as shown in Table 4.3:

TABLE 4.3   Primary components in an Open Repo

Open Repo	
Trade Component	**Trade Detail**
Transaction Type	Repo Cash Borrowing
Counterparty	Counterparty G
Currency Amount	USD 50,000,000.00
Repo Rate	3.15%
Trade Date	March 16th
Opening Value Date	March 17th
Closing Value Date	Open

Unlike a term repo, at the point of trade execution, the cash lender and the cash borrower agree not to define the closing value date (yet). Each day the parties will agree to keep the repo rolling forward, until one of the parties needs to close the trade, at which point the counterparty is obliged to agree to a particular closing value date; such repos are said to be 'terminable on demand'. The party wishing to close an open repo must communicate their desire to close by an agreed daily deadline (e.g. 13:00 CET), in which case the closing value date will relate to that communication date, where delivery will usually occur either on the same date (T+0) or next day (T+1), dependent upon the market relating to the collateral. An open repo can be closed for its entire value, or for part of its value.

Cash-based repos may have a tenure of overnight (1 day), or any other duration agreed between the two parties. For example, periods of up to 3 months are common, and occasionally up to 6 months or one year can be agreed.

4.1.2 Classic Repo Legal Agreements

In parallel with other types of collateralised transaction (e.g. *securities lending & borrowing*, and *OTC derivatives*), before a firm executes a repo trade, for its own protection (and that of its counterparty) it is essential that an appropriate legal agreement is signed between the two trading parties. Once the legal agreement is in place, each individual repo trade is then executed between the two parties under the protection of the legal agreement.

Over a number of years, as the style and content of repo trades was shaped amongst the repo trading community, a common standard for the content of repo legal agreements was developed.

Today, that standard legal agreement for internationally traded repos is entitled the 'Global Master Repurchase Agreement', and is commonly known as the **GMRA**. Various versions of the GMRA have been produced over the years, the latest of which is the 2011 version (at the time of writing).

In essence, the purpose of legal agreements such as the GMRA is to clearly state *contractual obligations* and responsibilities pertaining to both parties. One very important feature of the GMRA is clearly defined *events of default*; if a firm's counter-party has defaulted (or becomes insolvent), the agreement permits obligations relating to all open trades falling under the agreement to be immediately terminated and *set off* against each other, and settled on a net basis. (The right of set off is invaluable to a firm, as without such a right 1) all payment obligations of a firm may be required to be made, without 2) simultaneous receipt of obligations due to the firm. In an insolvency situation, the latter can take an inordinate length of time, in some cases months or years.)

The GMRA additionally contains items such as:

- definitions of terms and phrases (e.g. deliverable securities, *equivalent securities*)
- content of *trade confirmations*
- method of settlement of opening and closing legs
- *margin call* conditions
- *collateral substitution* conditions
- the treatment of income payments (e.g. *coupons* and *dividends*).

Between two parties that intend executing repo trades with one another, the wording within the GMRA is typically not altered. Any specific arrangements between the two parties are documented within the GMRA Annex 1, entitled Supplemental Terms and Conditions, examples of which are:

- *eligible collateral*, whether cash only, securities only, or both are applicable
- for *bond collateral*, the issuer ratings and *haircut* percentages
- the deadline for the *exposed party* making a *margin call*
- whether *collateral substitution* is permitted, or not.

Legal ownership of the bonds is transferred from the *collateral giver* to the *collateral taker* for the duration of the repo trade. From an operational standpoint, however, the giver of the collateral has not sold the collateral, and as such retains all beneficial rights. Whilst the collateral taker is the legal owner, the collateral giver is the *beneficial owner*. Legal ownership is transferred because, under the GMRA, the legal basis on which the collateral is transferred is *title transfer*. The method of transfer of a securities purchase and sale is also title transfer, therefore the collateral taker in a repo has the same (unlimited) rights to the collateral as if that party had instead purchased the securities outright. Consequently, the collateral taker is free to choose whatever it wishes to do with the collateral, including:

- holding the collateral securely within the collateral taker's account at its *custodian*, or
- reusing the collateral in one (or more) of the following ways:
  - selling it, repoing it, lending it or delivering it to satisfy a margin call in (for example) an **OTC** *derivative* transaction.

Note that, due to title transfer, the collateral giver has no legal right to prevent the collateral taker from reusing the collateral. However, the collateral taker is obliged to return the *equivalent collateral* to the collateral giver, at the close of the repo trade. The collateral taker must remain aware of this fact, particularly if they have chosen to reuse the collateral.

Each set of legal documents (i.e. the GMRA plus Annex 1) a firm has with each of its repo counterparties is likely to contain different terms and conditions. It is therefore imperative that the repo operations staff carry out their day-to-day responsibilities according to the legal terms defined with each of their counterparties in the appropriate legal documents. If there is a failure to do so, the firm is likely to be at risk as, for example, the firm's exposures with counterparties may not be fully mitigated, and/or counterparty's exposures may be over-collateralised.

In order to view the content of the current GMRA, the complete 2011 version can be found in Chapter 8 'Sale & Repurchase (Repo) Trades and Collateral – The Global Master Repurchase Agreement'.

4.1.3 Collateral in a Classic Repo

In a classic repo trade, the bond collateral serves the purpose of mitigating the cash lender's risk. That risk is that the cash borrower fails to repay the borrowed cash.

From the perspective of the cash lender, at all times throughout the lifetime of a repo transaction, the *collateral value* of the bond must be no less than the cash amount lent. If, during the lifetime of the trade, the collateral value of the bond falls below the cash amount lent, the cash lender has an exposure and should make a *margin call* on the cash borrower for the difference.

Similarly, from the perspective of the cash borrower, at all times throughout the lifetime of a repo trade, if the collateral value of the bond increases beyond the cash amount borrowed, the cash borrower has an exposure and may make a margin call on the cash lender for the difference.

Therefore, the quality of collateral is an essential component of repo trades, from both the cash borrower's and the cash lender's perspectives. The commonly used term for acceptable collateral is 'eligible collateral'.

Eligible Collateral   Financial instruments generally considered as eligible collateral are:

- bonds issued by *creditworthy* institutions (such as governments, government agencies, supranational organisations and corporations), including:
  - *fixed rate bonds*
  - *floating rate notes*
  - *zero coupon bonds*
- equity, providing they form a marketplace's primary index, such as the UK's FTSE-100.

From the cash lender's perspective, the two most sought after attributes are that the collateral 1) retains its value due to the ongoing creditworthiness of the *issuer*, and 2) that the collateral is highly *liquid* thereby enabling rapid transformation of the collateral into cash in the event of *default* (non-repayment) by the cash borrower.

In terms of eligible collateral in a classic repo transaction, rather than utilising a predefined list of eligible collateral types, the two parties agree the specific terms of individual repo trades based upon the particular bond issuer and liquidity of the bond.

Eligible collateral is documented within Annex 1 (Supplemental Terms and Conditions) of the GMRA. Types of eligible bond may be listed, including US Government treasury securities, UK Government bonds (*gilts*), bonds issued by *supranational organisations* (e.g. World Bank, EBRD). Ineligible bonds may also be listed, such as Italian Government bonds in which the *withholding tax* on coupon payments makes the use of such bonds as collateral a particular challenge. The minimum credit rating level of bond issuers will also be listed, as will any margin (or haircut) levels; this topic is discussed in this chapter, within Sub-section 4.1.5 'Over-Collateralisation: Haircut and Initial Margin'.

Annex 1 may also define deadlines for the receipt of *margin call notifications* by the non-exposed party, following which the collateral giver will offer the exposed party collateral (e.g. a specific quantity of a particular bond), which may be accepted or rejected, as some agreements state that collateral must be 'mutually agreed'. The type of circumstance in which the offer of collateral is rejected occurs where the bond is eligible under Annex 1, but, for example, the issue may be relatively small with little liquidity.

In a classic repo trade, in order to satisfy the cash lender's risk a single bond may be given as collateral, or multiple bonds, providing all bonds meet the minimum collateral requirement as stated in the legal documentation.

Concentration Limits   Where a firm executes multiple repos concurrently, and where that firm is the cash lender, it is at risk of accepting a disproportionate quantity of the bonds of one single bond *issuer*. Should that issuer default on its financial commitments, the cash lender would be greatly exposed. It is therefore important that incoming collateral is monitored for over-concentration to a single issuer.

Firms should consider setting up internal ground rules for what the firm determines to be a limit to a particular issuer; a firm's actual exposure in this respect may encompass, for example, collateral received for exposures relating to a range of transaction types in addition to repos, including *securities lending* and *OTC derivatives*.

In general terms, firms should be wary of receiving collateral from a counterparty that is issued by that same counterparty.

Marking-to-Market   It is essential that all *non-cash collateral* is subject to frequent revaluation. Bond collateral is subject to daily price (and therefore value) movement, which may be in an upward or downward direction. This means that:

- the cash lender is at risk where bond collateral falls in value, as the cash amount lent is not fully covered by the collateral value
- the cash borrower is at risk where bond collateral rises in value, as the collateral value is in excess of the cash amount borrowed.

Consequently, for the protection of both cash lender and cash borrower, both parties should *mark-to-market* bond collateral at an agreed frequency, preferably daily.

Note that under volatile market conditions, the mark-to-market process may be conducted intraday.

In the mark-to-market process, it is imperative that a firm takes its bond prices from a neutral and independent source, otherwise resultant exposure calculations may prove to be inaccurate leading to disputes with counterparties when needing to mitigate exposures through the margin call process.

General Collateral and Special Collateral   In most repo transactions, the bonds in a *cash-based repo* are known as *general collateral* (GC), meaning the cash lender does not require any specific bond to be provided by the cash borrower, although the bonds must be of a certain quality as a minimum, otherwise the cash lender may be at risk. This is significant from the perspective of both parties, because as GC the bonds are solely in the role of providing security to the cash lender.

Conversely, should the cash lender specify a particular bond to be delivered by the cash borrower, the motivation for the transaction is no longer solely the borrowing of cash by the cash borrower, but in addition the cash lender has motivation as it wishes to borrow particular bonds (or equity); this is known as a *stock-based repo*. If the cash borrower is able to deliver the specific bond required by the cash lender, such circumstances mean that the cash borrower is in a position to further negotiate the terms of the transaction, and as a minimum reduce the repo rate. Where the market-wide demand for borrowing a particular security becomes significant, the collateral is said to be *special collateral*.

Consequently, for a GC repo, the repo rate is agreed based upon the quality of collateral being within a specified range, such as US Government-issued bonds with *residual maturity* of up to 5 years. Where a GC repo has been executed, the cash lender may not know from the outset which particular bond issue(s) they will receive from the cash borrower; conversely, the cash borrower must be certain that it can in fact deliver bonds classified as GC.

The repo rate on a special collateral repo is therefore typically lower than for a GC repo due to the higher demand for the particular bond or equity issue; the rates for special repos are issue-specific. From the cash borrower's perspective, giving bond collateral on which there is a greater demand compared with other bond collateral deserves the reward of a lower interest (repo) rate on the cash borrowing. From the cash lender's perspective, special collateral will be utilised beyond solely acting as collateral for the cash loan, and the cash lender is therefore willing to accept a lower rate of return on the lent cash. For example, the cash lender may have *short sold* a particular bond; a failure to deliver the sold bond to the buying counterparty will also mean a failure of the seller (i.e. the cash lender) to receive its sale proceeds at the earliest opportunity, resulting in a loss of cash interest. If the cash lender can (temporarily) acquire an adequate quantity of the same bond issue, that bond may be used (due to the previously mentioned *title transfer* and the change in *legal ownership*) to satisfy the delivery to the buying counterparty whilst simultaneously receiving the sale proceeds. Of course, the cash lender must return the *equivalent collateral* to the cash borrower on the closing leg of the repo transaction. This chain of events is illustrated in Figure 4.2:

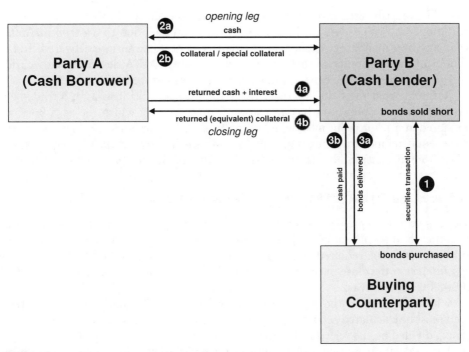

FIGURE 4.2   Example use of stock-based repo and special collateral

Step 1: Party B executes a (short) sale of a particular bond with a buying counterparty

Step 2a: Party B executes a stock-based repo transaction with Party A, in which a specified cash amount is lent by Party B, and simultaneously …

Step 2b: Party A delivers the specific bond to Party B as collateral for the cash borrowing

Step 3a: upon receipt of the bond from Party A, Party B on delivers the bond to the buying counterparty, and simultaneously …

Step 3b: Party B receives the sale proceeds from the buying counterparty

Step 4a: on the closing value date of the repo transaction, Party B must return equivalent collateral to Party A, and simultaneously …

Step 4b: Party A must return the borrowed cash, plus interest based upon the agreed repo rate.

The above-mentioned use of stock-based repo and special collateral is but one example; another example is the cash lender's requirement to deliver bonds to settle a *futures* contract.

Return of Bond Collateral   On the *closing value date* of the repo, the cash lender must return the same bond issue as was received on the opening value date; to clarify, the same *ISIN* must be returned if it still exists. Conversely, if the ISIN that was delivered on the opening value date no longer exists (for example, due to a *corporate action* event such as a mandatory exchange), the replacement ISIN must be delivered. To take account of the possibility of such an ISIN change, the GMRA describes the securities due to be returned on the closing value date as *equivalent securities*.

Assuming that the cash borrower owns the securities prior to a repo trade being executed, the cash borrower has a position in that security which the cash borrower purchased at a prior point in time. In a repo trade, the cash borrower loses possession of the bond temporarily, but does not lose *beneficial ownership*. Consequently, the same (or equivalent) ISIN must be returned to the cash borrower.

4.1.4 Repo Rate Format and Repo Interest Calculation Method

The repo rate is expressed as an annualised percentage (e.g. 3.15%), meaning that, given a cash amount lent of EUR 1,000,000.00 and a loan period of 12 months, the borrower would be required to pay EUR 31,500.00 (EUR 1,000,000.00 × 3.15%) of *repo interest* at the close of the borrowing period, in addition to the return of the EUR 1,000,000.00 borrowed.

Where the term of the repo is something less than 12 months, the cash interest owed must be calculated according to the actual number of days for which the cash was loaned, divided by the relevant divisor.

The calculation of repo interest utilises *money market* conventions as used in the calculation of *bank interest*; regardless of currency, the loan period is counted as actual (calendar) days, inclusive of weekends and public holidays. The divisor is based upon the currency in question (either 360 or 365); therefore, an amount of cash borrowed at the same repo rate over the same number of days will, for some currencies produce the same monetary amount of interest, and for other currencies will produce a different monetary amount. For example:

- EUR 1,000,000.00 at 3.15% for 10 days, divisor 360 = EUR 875.00
- USD 1,000,000.00 at 3.15% for 10 days, divisor 360 = USD 875.00
- GBP 1,000,000.00 at 3.15% for 10 days, divisor 365 = GBP 863.01
- AUD 1,000,000.00 at 3.15% for 10 days, divisor 365 = AUD 863.01.

In short, for repo interest the day count is always actual days, and the divisors are simply historic money market conventions; whether 360 or 365, based solely upon the currency in question. Note: the day count and divisor conventions used for the calculation of bank interest (including repo interest) should not be confused with the subject of bond *accrued interest*. To clarify, in a repo trade both bank interest and accrued interest are used:

- the bank interest calculation method is used to determine the amount of cash interest that's receivable/payable on the cash amount lent/borrowed
- the accrued interest calculation method is used (alongside the *clean price* of the bond) to determine the bond's current market value, from which the bond's current collateral value is derived, following deduction of the relevant haircut.

The calculation of repo interest is therefore:

■ (cash amount × repo rate / divisor) × days.

The days should be counted (*'day count'*) by including the 'from' date but excluding the 'to' date. This is because the first night the lender will be without the cash is the 'from' date (the borrower must start paying interest inclusive of that date), and the date that the lender repossesses the cash is the 'to' date (the borrower will stop paying interest on the 'to' date −1 inclusive). Example calculations are provided in Table 4.4:

TABLE 4.4   Repo interest calculation

Repo Interest Calculation					
Cash Amount	Repo Rate	Borrowing Period	Days of Borrowing	Divisor	Repo Interest
USD 5,000,000.00	2.75%	Mar 01 – Mar 02	1	360	USD 381.94
EUR 15,000,000.00	3.07%	Mar 01 – Apr 02	32	360	EUR 40,933.33
GBP 27,500,000.00	2.45%	Mar 01 – May 10	70	365	GBP 129,212.33

4.1.5 Over-Collateralisation: Haircut and Initial Margin

In repo trades, it is common practice for the market value of the bond collateral to exceed the value of cash by a particular amount. To clarify, the cash borrower is typically required to provide bond collateral that has a market value which is greater than the cash amount borrowed; in other words, the cash borrower is required to *over-collateralise*.

Note: over-collateralisation is common to all collateral-related transactions involving securities collateral, therefore including both *securities lending & borrowing*, and OTC *derivatives* in addition to repo.

The extent of over-collateralisation is dependent upon the risk to the cash lender, in particular the likely collateral value following *default* by the cash borrower. For example, the cash lender will be concerned over the volatility of the collateral's value during the period between agreeing a *margin call* and settlement of that call. Furthermore, a number of factors influence the extent of over-collateralisation, relating to the bond collateral itself and the issuer of the bond, for example:

■ type of bond issuer, such as government issuer or corporate issuer
■ credit rating: the opinion of the bond issuer's ability to comply with its financial obligations
■ residual maturity: the period of time between 'now' and the bond's maturity date
■ type of bond issue: such as fixed rate, floating rate, zero coupon.

There are two ways of expressing such over-collateralisation; as a *haircut*, or as an *initial margin*.

Although the calculations differ from one another, the resultant values are very similar (but not identical).

Haircut   Haircut is expressed as a percentage and as a low number, such as 2.5%. To determine the cash amount borrowable when a haircut is applicable, the calculation is:

market value of bond × (100% − Haircut percentage) = <u>cash amount borrowable</u>

If, for example, the market value of a bond is EUR 30,000,000.00, application of a 2.5% haircut means:

EUR 30,000,000.00 × (100% − 2.5%) = <u>EUR 29,250,000.00</u>

Further examples of differing haircut percentages used to derive cash amounts borrowable are depicted in Table 4.5:

TABLE 4.5   Haircut calculation

Haircut	Market Value of Bond	Cash Amount Borrowable
2.5%		EUR 29,250,000.00
6%	EUR 30,000,000.00	EUR 28,200,000.00
15%		EUR 25,500,000.00

Initial Margin   Initial Margin is also expressed as a percentage but as a high number, such as 102.5%. To determine the cash amount borrowable when an initial margin is applicable, the calculation is:

$$\frac{\text{market value of bond}}{(\text{Initial Margin}/100)} = \underline{\text{cash amount borrowable}}$$

If, for example, the market value of a bond is EUR 30,000,000.00, application of a 102.5% initial margin means:

$$\frac{\text{EUR } 30{,}000{,}000.00}{(102.5/100)} = \underline{\text{EUR} 29{,}268{,}292.68}$$

Further examples of differing initial margin percentages used to derive cash amounts borrowable are depicted in Table 4.6:

TABLE 4.6   Initial margin calculation

Initial Margin	Market Value of Bond	Cash Amount Borrowable
102.5%		EUR 29,268,292.68
106%	EUR 30,000,000.00	EUR 28,301,886.79
115%		EUR 26,086,956.52

Note that, although the resultant cash amounts borrowable are broadly similar, as can be seen, a 2.5% haircut does not produce exactly the same result as a 102.5% initial margin.

Haircut and initial margin can be agreed in advance of trading and may be recorded in the legal agreement between parties (i.e. in Annex I of the **GMRA**), or can be agreed ad hoc at the point of trade execution and recorded in the *trade confirmation*. Once agreed for a particular trade, the haircut or initial margin is fixed for the entire term of that trade.

As can be seen from the above examples, haircut and initial margin are usually in favour of the cash lender, where the cash borrower is required to over-collateralise. Under some circumstances however, where a firm has particular anxiety over a counterparty's credit status, application of haircut or initial margin results in under-collateralisation, meaning that the cash amount borrowed is greater than the market value of the bond collateral.

Impact of Haircut and Initial Margin   The usual impact of haircut and initial margin in a repo is that the cash borrower receives less cash than the market value of the bond given as collateral. This can result in either 1) the cash amount borrowed being dominant resulting in the bond quantity being increased to account for the haircut or initial margin being deducted from the bond's market value, or 2) the bond's market value being dominant resulting in the cash amount borrowed being reduced by the haircut or initial margin percentage. This concept is represented in Figure 4.3:

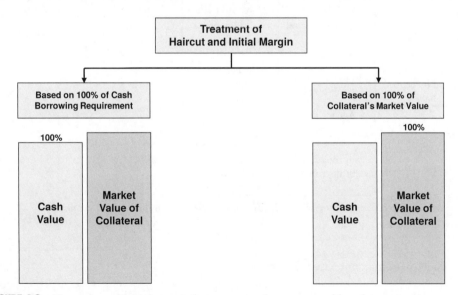

FIGURE 4.3   Treatment of initial margin/haircut on cash amount and bond quantity

The trading parties decide whether haircut or initial margin will be applied in subsequent repo trades (or not), and this is reflected either prior to trade execution within repo legal agreements (Annex 1), or for specific trades at the point of trade execution. The decision as to whether to apply a haircut/initial margin or not is a reflection of the relative creditworthiness of 1) the trading parties involved, and 2) the bond issuer. If the counterparty has a very good credit rating, and if the bond is of very good quality, then haircut/initial margin may not be applied. It is possible that, between a firm and its counterparty, for some trades a haircut is to be applied, and for other trades initial margin is applicable.

Where haircut/initial margin is applicable in a repo trade, it must be applied consistently including 1) at the opening value date, and 2) throughout the lifetime of the repo.

Example Method of Determining Haircut Percentage   To focus on haircut percentages at a more detailed level, the example of the European Central Bank (ECB) will be used, which implemented the following haircut regime, effective 1st January 2011. (Updates can be found at www.ecb.europa.eu/paym/coll/html/index.en.html). A number of factors must be considered to determine the appropriate percentage haircut for a given piece of securities collateral.

Firstly, the issuers of debt securities are structured into 5 categories, as shown in Table 4.7:

TABLE 4.7   Liquidity categories for marketable assets

Liquidity Categories for Marketable Assets				
Category I	**Category II**	**Category III**	**Category IV**	**Category V**
Central government debt instruments	Local & regional government debt instruments	Traditional covered bank bonds	Credit institution debt instruments (uncovered)	Asset backed securities
Debt instruments issued by central banks	Jumbo covered bank bonds	Structured covered bank bonds		
	Agency debt instruments	Multi-Cedulas		
	Supranational debt instruments	Debt instruments issued by corporate and other issuers		

Note: information listed is at summary level only – please refer to ECB for complete details

To explain the content of each category:

- Category I
  - Central government debt instruments
    - debt issuance by national governments
  - Debt instruments issued by central banks
    - debt issuance by central banks for monetary policy operations and/or for the development of financial markets (where there may be no government bonds in issue)

- Category II
  - Local & regional government debt instruments
    - debt issuance by municipalities, cities, counties/states for the financing of local and regional infrastructure
  - Jumbo covered bank bonds
    - debt issuance by banks in the form of collateralised mortgage bonds raising at least EUR 1,000,000,000 (1 billion)
  - Agency debt instruments
    - debt issuance by a national government agency, such as the Government National Mortgage Association (US), which may be guaranteed by the national government
    - debt issuance by government sponsored entities (US), such as the Federal National Mortgage Association, which are not openly guaranteed by the national government
  - Supranational debt instruments
    - debt issuance by organisations representing multiple countries, such as the International Bank for Reconstruction and Development, and the African Development Bank

- Category III
  - Traditional covered bank bonds
    - debt issuance by banks backed by a pool of assets that secures the issuer's bond commitments if the issuer becomes bankrupt, and which are backed by special laws
  - Structured covered bank bonds
    - as per traditional covered bank bonds, but are backed by general contractual laws
  - Multi-Cedulas
    - debt issuance of mortgages by Spanish regional banks that are pooled together
  - Debt instruments issued by corporate and other issuers
    - debt issuance by corporations for business expansion purposes

- Category IV
  - Credit institution debt instruments (uncovered)
    - debt issuance by banks and savings banks that are not secured by any underlying pool of assets

- Category V
  - Asset backed securities
    - financial instruments issued based upon a specific pool of underlying assets (generally unable to be sold in their own right) which are *securitised* and sold to investors.

In order to derive the appropriate haircut percentage, Table 4.7 (the liquidity category table) must be used in conjunction with Table 4.8 'Levels of haircut percentages applied to eligible market assets'.

PART 2

TABLE 4.8 Levels of haircut percentages applied to eligible market assets

Credit Quality	Residual Maturity (years)	Category I		Category II		Category III		Category IV		Category V
		Fixed Coupon	Zero Coupon	Fixed Coupon	Zero Coupon	Fixed Coupon	Zero Coupon	Fixed Coupon	Zero Coupon	All
AAA to A– (upper band)	0–1	0.5	0.5	1.0	1.0	1.5	1.5	6.5	6.5	16
	1–3	1.5	1.5	2.5	2.5	3.0	3.0	8.5	9.0	
	3–5	2.5	3.0	3.5	4.0	5.0	5.5	11.0	11.5	
	5–7	3.0	3.5	4.5	5.0	6.5	7.5	12.5	13.5	
	7–10	4.0	4.5	5.5	6.5	8.5	9.5	14.0	15.5	
	>10	5.5	8.5	7.5	12.0	11.0	16.5	17.0	22.5	
BBB+ to BBB– (lower band)	0–1	5.5	5.5	6.0	6.0	8.0	8.0	15.0	15.0	Not eligible
	1–3	6.5	6.5	10.5	11.5	18.0	19.5	27.5	29.5	
	3–5	7.5	8.0	15.5	17.0	25.5	28.0	36.5	39.5	
	5–7	8.0	8.5	18.0	20.5	28.0	31.5	38.5	43.0	
	7–10	9.0	9.5	19.5	22.5	29.0	33.5	39.0	44.5	
	>10	10.5	13.5	20.0	29.0	29.5	38.0	39.5	46.0	

The ECB's risk control framework for eligible marketable assets includes the following main elements:

- The haircuts are applied by deducting a certain percentage from the market value of the underlying asset. The haircuts applied to debt instruments included in categories I to IV differ according to the residual maturity and coupon structure of the debt instruments for eligible marketable fixed coupon and zero coupon debt instruments.
- Haircuts applicable to marketable debt instruments included in liquidity categories I to IV with variable rate coupons, excluding 'inverse floaters', will be those applicable to the 0–1 year maturity bucket of fixed coupon instruments in the corresponding liquidity and credit category.
- The assets are subject to daily valuation. On a daily basis, national central banks calculate the required value of underlying assets taking into account changes in outstanding credit volumes and the required valuation haircuts.
- The ECB may at any time decide to remove individual debt instruments from the published list of eligible marketable assets.
- (With effect from 1st January 2011, marketable debt instruments denominated in currencies other than the Euro (i.e. USD, GBP, JPY) and issued in the euro area, will no longer be eligible as collateral.)

Source: ECB (note: the above is not an exhaustive list of all elements quoted by ECB)

For a given piece of securities collateral, in order to determine its collateral value the relevant category must be determined. For example, assume that a firm wishes to give collateral in the form of EUR 10,000,000 nominal (quantity) of a bond issued in 1993 by the International Bank for Reconstruction & Development (also known as the World Bank), that has a 4.75% fixed coupon and a maturity date of 1st August 2023. Also assume that today is 8th May 2017, and the current *clean* price of this bond is 99.1875%. As the World Bank is a supranational organisation, the issuer falls within Category II.

Then, utilising the relevant parts of Table 4.8 ('Levels of haircut percentages applied to eligible market assets'), determine the relevant haircut percentage (from which the collateral value will be derived) by following these steps:

1. the higher the credit rating, the lower the haircut percentage – using the issuer's current credit rating in association with the Credit Quality column, determine the relevant banding. If the issuer's credit rating is A– or higher, utilise the upper of the two bands, and if the credit rating is between BBB+ and BBB–, utilise the lower band
   a. as the World Bank has a AAA credit rating, the upper band is applicable
2. the shorter the *residual maturity*, the lower the haircut percentage – the number of years between 'today' and the bond's maturity date is known as the residual maturity, and by applying the appropriate number of years to the Residual Maturity column, determine the relevant sub-band
   a. as the residual maturity of this bond is just over 6 years (May 2017 until August 2023), the residual maturity sub-band of 5–7 years is applicable
3. *Fixed coupon bonds* and *floating rate notes* will generally demand a lower percentage haircut compared with *zero coupon bonds* of the same issuer, credit rating and residual maturity
   a. as this bond has a fixed coupon, and World Bank falls within Category II, the haircut percentage of 4.5% is applicable.

The haircut percentage of 4.5% will now be used in Table 4.9 to calculate the collateral value:

TABLE 4.9   Example haircut calculation

Example Haircut Calculation		
		Resultant Cash Value
Bond Quantity EUR 10,000,000.00	Current Market Price 99.1875%	EUR 9,918,750.00
Accrued Days →	+279	
Accrued Interest → (30/360 basis)	EUR 368,125.00	+ EUR 368,125.00
	Current Market Value	**EUR 10,286,875.00**
Less Haircut	4.5%	(EUR 462,909.38)
	Current Collateral Value	**EUR 9,823,965.62**

Note: the current market value of interest-bearing debt instruments must include the current value of *accrued interest*, if the instrument is not to be undervalued. If the price is exclusive of accrued interest, the price is said to be a *clean price*, and if inclusive the price is said to be a *dirty price*.

In order to prove the readers' understanding of the above-mentioned concepts, the following 3 scenarios require calculation of current collateral values:

Scenario 1   On 19th March 2016, a national central bank enters into a repurchase transaction with Counterparty V, in which the national bank purchases EUR 35.0 million of an agency issued bond with a 4.25% coupon maturing 30th April 2024, rated AA. The current market dirty price of this bond is 97.81%.

Question 1: what is the collateral value of the asset?

Answer: Category II, upper band, 7–10 year sub-band, fixed coupon = haircut 5.5%. EUR 35,000,000.00 × 97.81% = EUR 34,233,500.00, less 5.5% = EUR 1,882,842.50, collateral value = EUR 32,350,657.50.

Scenario 2   On 6th July 2018, a national central bank enters into a repurchase transaction with Counterparty G, in which the national bank purchases EUR 75,000,000 of an A-rated European company's zero coupon bonds maturing on 15th February 2020. The current market price of this bond is 82.75%.

Question 2: what is the collateral value of the asset?

Answer: Category III, upper band, 1–3 year sub-band, zero coupon = haircut 3.0%. EUR 75,000,000.00 × 82.75% = EUR 62,062,500.00, less 3.0% = EUR 1,861,875.00, collateral value = EUR 60,200,625.00.

Scenario 3   On 25th October 2017, a national central bank enters into a repurchase transaction with Counterparty M, in which the national bank purchases EUR 55,000,000 of a BBB rated credit institution's uncovered bond with a 4.95% coupon maturing on 1st December 2023. The current market dirty price of this bond is 103.064%.

Question 3: what is the collateral value of the asset?

Answer: Category IV, lower band, 5–7 year sub-band, fixed coupon = haircut 38.5%. EUR 55,000,000.00 × 103.064% = EUR 56,685,200.00, less 38.5% = EUR 21,823,802.00, collateral value = EUR 34,861,398.00.

Where bonds are to be delivered to mitigate the cash lender's exposure, the bond quantity requiring delivery to the counterparty must take account of *bond denominational values*. Just like currency notes (USD notes are issued in denominations of $1, $5, $10, $20, $50, $100 and EUR in denominations of €5, €10, €20, €50, €100, €200, €500), bonds have historically been issued in specified denominations, for example, in a single denomination for a particular issue of USD 10,000.00, and for a different issue in multiple denominations of USD 50,000.00 and USD 100,000.00. Bonds are deliverable only in multiples of their denominational values; attempts to deliver (by issuance of a *settlement instruction*) an amount less than the minimum denomination, or an amount not in multiples of the minimum denomination, will result in the settlement instruction being rejected by the firm's *CSD* or *custodian*.

When needing to collateralise an exposure amount by use of bond collateral, the following example scenario suggests an approach to the calculation of bond quantity; this must be a precise quantity that (when current market price and haircut percentage are factored in) results in the collateral value being no less than the exposure amount:

Example Scenario Counterparty B borrows EUR 85 million cash from a national central bank on 6th January 2018, and owns a central government bond with variable rate coupon payments maturing 15th February 2027, rated A). The market dirty price of this bond is 98.15%.

Question: what quantity of bonds (to the nearest €100,000.00) must be delivered to cover the cash borrowing?

The recommended calculation method is depicted in Table 4.10:

TABLE 4.10 Calculating deliverable bond quantities

Calculating Deliverable Bond Quantities			
Step		Cash Value	Bond Quantity
1	**Calculate Collateral Value of €100,000 bonds**		
	€100,000 bonds × current market price (€ 100,000 × 98.15%)	€98,150.00	
	Deduct haircut percentage* (0.5%)	(€490.75)	
	Collateral value of € 100,000 bonds	**€97,659.25**	
2	**Derive Pre-Rounded Bond Quantity**		
	Divide exposure amount by collateral value of €100,000 bonds (€85,000,000 / 0.9765925)		**€87,037,326.21**
	Pre-Rounded Bond Quantity		**€87,037,326.21**
3	**Derive Deliverable Bond Quantity**		
	Round up pre-rounded bond quantity (€87,037,326.21 rounded up to nearest €100,000)		**€87,100,000.00**
	Deliverable Bond Quantity		**€87,100,000.00**

* Haircut percentage calculation: Category I, upper band, 7–10 year sub-band, floating rate note = haircut 0.5%.

This calculation reveals that a quantity of EUR 87,100,000.00 bonds would be needed to cover the exposure of EUR 85,000,000.00. To prove this bond quantity is adequate, the calculation shown in Table 4.11 can be performed:

TABLE 4.11   Example haircut calculation

Example Haircut Calculation		
		Resultant Cash Value
Bond Quantity EUR 87,100,000.00	Current Market Price 98.15%	EUR 85,488,650.00
Accrued Days →	(included in price)	
Accrued Interest → (30/360 basis)	(included in price)	-
	Current Market Value	**EUR 85,488,650.00**
Less Haircut	0.5%	(EUR 427,443.25)
	Current Collateral Value	**EUR 85,061,206.75**

This calculation shows that the correct bond quantity is EUR 87,100,000.00, and that the collateral value of a bond quantity of EUR 87,000,000.00 or less would be insufficient to cover the exposure amount of EUR 85,000,000.00.

The following 3 scenarios require calculation of a bond quantity in order to cover an amount of exposure:

Scenario 4   Counterparty L borrows EUR 45 million cash from a national central bank on 15th May 2018, and owns a credit institution debt instrument with a 5.35% coupon maturing 1st September 2019, rated BBB+. The market dirty price of this security is 102.73%.

Question 4: what quantity of bonds (to the nearest €100,000.00) must be delivered to cover the cash borrowing?

Answer: collateral value of EUR 100,000 bonds = EUR 100,000 × 102.73% = EUR 102,730.00, less 27.5% haircut (Category IV, lower band, 1-3 years, fixed coupon) = EUR 28,250.75 = EUR 74,479.25. Divide EUR 45,000,000 by 0.7447925 = Pre-rounded bond quantity of EUR 60,419,512.82. Round up to nearest EUR 100,000 bonds = bond quantity of EUR 60,500,000.00.

To prove that figure: bond quantity of EUR 60,500,000.00 × 102.73% = EUR 62,151,650.00, less 27.5% haircut (EUR17,091,703.75) = collateral value of EUR 45,059,946.25.

Scenario 5   Counterparty N borrows EUR 70 million cash from a national central bank on 17th August 2017, and owns a zero coupon bond issued by a municipality, maturing 15th January 2029, rated AA. The market price of this security is 67.92%.

Question 5: what quantity of bonds (to the nearest €100,000.00) must be delivered to cover the cash borrowing?

Answer: collateral value of EUR 100,000 bonds = EUR 100,000 × 67.92% = EUR 67,920.00, less 12.0% haircut (Category II, upper band, >10 years, zero coupon) = EUR 8,150.40 = EUR 59,769.60 Divide EUR 70,000,000 by 0.5976960 = Pre-rounded bond quantity of EUR 117,116,393.62. Round up to nearest EUR 100,000 bonds = bond quantity of EUR 117,200,000.00.

To prove that figure: bond quantity of EUR 117,200,000.00 × 67.92% = EUR 79,602,240.00, less 12.0% haircut (EUR 9,552,268.80) = collateral value of EUR 70,049,971.20.

Scenario 6 Counterparty P borrows EUR 110 million cash from a national central bank on 26th September 2018, and owns a bond issued by the European Bank for Reconstruction and Development with a 4.85% coupon maturing 15th June 2025, rated AA+. The market dirty price of this security is 100.07%.

Question 6: what quantity of bonds (to the nearest €100,000.00) must be delivered to cover the cash borrowing?

Answer: collateral value of EUR 100,000 bonds = EUR 100,000 × 100.07% = EUR 100,070.00, less 4.5% haircut (Category II, upper band, 5–7 years, fixed coupon) = EUR 4503.15 = EUR 95,566.85. Divide EUR 110,000,000 by 0.9556685 = Pre-rounded bond quantity of EUR 115,102,674.20. Round up to nearest EUR 100,000 bonds = bond quantity of EUR 115,200,000.00.

To prove that figure: bond quantity of EUR 115,200,000.00 × 100.07% = EUR 115,280,640.00, less 4.5% haircut (EUR5,187,628.80) = collateral value of EUR 110,093,011.20.

Haircut must be applied when bond collateral is first given at the start of a transaction, and on all subsequent days that exposure exists.

4.1.6 Repo Trade Settlement Cycle

In Europe, prior to October 2014, the standard (or default) number of days between a repo trade's trade date and the opening value date (known as the ***settlement cycle***) was 2 days, commonly referred to as T+2. Until that date, the securities 'cash' market – the market in which execution of outright buying and selling of bonds and equity occurs – was in many cases T+3. Therefore, a firm could buy securities on a Monday, with a value date of Thursday, and then execute a repo on Tuesday so as to borrow cash for value date Thursday, in order to cover the purchase cost.

On 6th October 2014, the vast majority of markets in Europe reduced the settlement cycle for 'cash' trades to T+2, as part of the European Commission's objective of harmonising settlement cycles across Europe, prior to the introduction of ***Target2-Securities*** (T2S) in 2015. The introduction of T+2 for 'cash' markets in Europe had the impact of the settlement cycle for repo trades reducing to T+1.

The pre-October 2014 repo trade settlement cycle of T+2 meant that firms had one whole business day between trade date and value date to resolve any differences with counterparties that were discovered as a result of the ***trade confirmation*** checking process. The move to T+1 meant a dramatic decrease in the available time to 1) identify a discrepancy, then 2) to investigate it, and 3) to rectify it; all such situations mean that checking of repo trade details between the two trading firms must be conducted on trade date if the trade is to settle on its due date (the opening value date).

4.1.7 Repo Trade Confirmation and Affirmation

When any trade is executed directly with a counterparty on an ***over-the-counter*** (OTC) basis rather than via an electronic exchange, the risk exists that one or the other party (or both parties) will fail to record accurately the components that comprise the trade as executed. This risk is applicable across multiple financial products that are traded on an OTC basis, including foreign exchange, OTC derivatives, bonds and repo markets.

If it is not known whether a firm's individual record of a trade is agreed by the counterparty or not, the firm is at risk of discovering, at a later point in time, that a difference exists. Dependent upon how much later in time that discrepancy is discovered, both monetary loss and reputational loss could result.

Conscious of the existence of such risks, it is imperative that the firm is very proactive in discovering, as quickly as possible following trade execution, whether its trade details are the same or different from the counterparty's trade details. This is particularly important given the current T+1 settlement cycle for repo trades.

The process by which trade details are compared is the act of *trade agreement*. The medium by which trade details are agreed is commonly known as *trade confirmation*, whereby a dealer trading with an *institutional investor* is required to communicate its trade details to the client, typically within an agreed time frame following trade execution, as part of the service required by the client. Where a dealer trades with another dealer, trade confirmation is just as important.

To clarify, as part of the service provided by *investment banks* to institutional investors, investment banks are required to act proactively in communicating trade details to their *buy-side* clients; conversely, buy-side firms are typically passive in this regard and await receipt of trade confirmations from the investment bank with whom they have traded. Of course, when a buy-side firm receives a trade confirmation from an investment bank, they are required to check it without delay. Due to the passive nature of buy-side firms in this regard, this process is sometimes referred to as *trade affirmation* (meaning 'to affirm' – to agree with details presented to you).

An example of the content of a repo trade confirmation is as follows, in which Firm A issues a trade confirmation to Party G:

TABLE 4.12 Repo trade confirmation #1

Repo Trade Confirmation	
From	Firm A, London
To	Party G, New York
As principal, we hereby confirm the following transaction:	
Trade Component	**Trade Detail**
Our Trade Reference	R0059397
Transaction Type	Classic Repo
Legal Agreement Type	GMRA
Term or Open	Term
Cash Borrower/Bond Seller	Firm A, London
Cash Lender/Bond Buyer	Party G, New York
Trade Date	June 7th 2017
Opening Value Date *(Purchase Date)*	June 8th 2017
Closing Value Date *(Repurchase Date)*	June 15th 2017
Repo Interest Rate *(Pricing Rate)*	2.42%
Repo Interest Payer	Firm A, London
Haircut	2.50%
Haircut Payer	Firm A, London

Opening Value Date (Purchase Date)			
	Security Description	Issuer ABC 4.35% Bonds August 1st 2030	
	Security Identifier	ISIN: XX1234567891	
	Quantity	USD 30,000,000.00	
	Price	99.95%	
	Gross Value		USD 29,985,000.00
Accrued Days	plus Accrued Interest	307	USD 1,112,875.00
	Market Value		USD 31,097,875.00
Haircut Percentage	less Haircut Value	2.5%	(USD 777,446.88)
Cash Amount Receivable/Payable *(Purchase Price)*			USD 30,320,428.12
Closing Value Date (Repurchase Date)			
Cash Amount (from Opening Value Date)			USD 30,320,428.12
Days of Repo Interest		7	
Repo Interest Amount			USD 14,267.45
Cash Amount Receivable/Payable			**USD 30,334,695.57**
Settlement Details			
	Ours	CSD T, account 66627	
	Yours	CSD T, account 99034	
	Settlement Method	Delivery versus payment	

Note: within the table, text in *italics* are terms used within the GMRA

Any of the trade components could unfortunately prove to be different from that which the counterparty has captured, including incorrect counterparty, correct counterparty but incorrect office location (e.g. London office rather than New York office), cash borrower is stated the wrong way round, the repo rate is incorrect, etc.

Upon receipt of the trade confirmation from a firm and upon comparison with its own records, should the counterparty discover a discrepancy it is imperative this is communicated to the firm, without delay, following which investigation and rectification must occur. This includes components that are trader-related, such as counterparty, opening and closing value dates, repo rate; the trader must be requested to verify that its firm's details are correct. Non-trade-related components are primarily the settlement details (shown at the end of the trade confirmation), where for example, the counterparty's custodian account details may not be stated accurately; such components are typically the responsibility of the **Operations Department** (or in some firms, the **Middle Office**) to investigate and resolve.

The medium by which trade confirmations are transmitted directly between two trading parties includes **S.W.I.F.T.**, which requires both sender and receiver to be subscribers to the S.W.I.F.T. network.

Many firms utilise repo trade matching services, whereby post-execution, trade details are submitted to a central platform that automatically compares individual trade details submitted by trading parties. Following the comparison process, a status is applied to each trade, whether 'matched' or 'unmatched'; such statuses are viewable by the involved parties, and trades having a status of unmatched must be investigated and resolved without delay. Any delay in the resolution of such a discrepancy is highly likely to result in delayed settlement of the repo's opening leg; this in turn will mean that the cash borrower will not receive the cash on the due date, and the cash lender will not receive the collateral on the due date. One such trade matching service is *Omgeo's* *CTM* (Central Trade Manager).

Once a firm is certain that its trade details are agreed by the counterparty, it is safe to proceed to the settlement of the opening leg of the repo.

4.1.8 Repo Trade Settlement

The normal method of settling repo trades between the two trading parties is dependent upon which stage in the repo lifecycle the trade has reached, whether:

- at the opening value date, or
- during the lifetime of the repo, or
- at the closing value date.

Note: the trading parties need to remain conscious of any maximum quantity of securities (applicable to settlement instructions); such quantity restrictions are imposed by the CSD through which settlement is due to occur. For example, the maximum valid bond quantity of a settlement instruction at the *Fedwire* (USA) is USD 50,000,000.00. This means that for a trade of (for example) USD 150,000,000.00, three settlement instructions of USD 50,000,000.00 each would need to be transmitted. Clients of local custodians or global custodians may find that their custodian generates the appropriate settlement instructions on their clients' behalf.

Opening Value Date   It is in the interests of both trading parties not to put their assets at risk whilst attempting to exchange cash for securities at the start of the repo trade.

From the cash lender's perspective, they are at risk of paying the cash without certainty of receipt of the bond collateral at the same time. Conversely, from the cash borrower's perspective, they are at risk if they allow the bond collateral to leave their control without certainty of receipt of the borrowed cash at the same time.

The predicament of which party 'makes the first move' is overcome where the place of settlement (i.e. the *Central Securities Depository* where the exchange of assets is due to occur) practises truly simultaneous exchange of cash for securities via *Delivery versus payment* (DvP).

In order for a firm to act safely regarding the release of its assets when settling a repo trade, it must transmit a securities *settlement instruction* containing the details of both the securities and the cash to be settled, including the relevant field that signifies 'DvP'. To clarify, the DvP settlement instruction issued by both parties must contain:

- the full cash amount receivable or payable (whichever is appropriate) on the opening value date:
  - in the previously mentioned example trade (see Table 4.12), USD 30,320,428.12, and
- the full quantity of bonds deliverable or receivable (whichever is appropriate) on the opening value date:
  - in the previously mentioned example trade (see Table 4.12), USD 30,000,000.00.

Upon receipt of such an instruction by the CSD or custodian, 'DvP' is a direct instruction not to release the outgoing asset from the firm's account without having 100% certainty that the counterparty's asset is incoming to the firm's account, <u>simultaneously</u>. The CSD/custodian must follow the instruction received from the firm, otherwise it is putting the firm's assets at risk.

Once the instruction has been received by the CSD/custodian, the following must take place in order for settlement to occur:

1. the firm's instruction and the counterparty's instruction must match
2. the opening value date must be reached
3. the cash borrower must have the appropriate quantity of bonds available in its account
4. the cash lender must have the means to pay, whether a) the account is in credit, or b) the cash lender has a *credit line* which is supported by an adequate value of collateral.

If all such items are in a state of readiness, the exchange of securities and cash should occur on value date, in which case settlement will have occurred on the due date, the opening value date.

Alternatively, instructions may be matched and value date may have been reached, but if (for example) the cash borrower has an insufficient quantity of bonds available in its account, the CSD/custodian is not able to deliver the bonds, triggering valid non-payment of cash from the cash lender's account, in turn meaning that the cash borrower will not receive the borrowed cash on the due date. However, the settlement instructions will remain matched, and therefore, if the cash borrower can acquire (e.g. through buying or borrowing) the missing quantity of bonds later on the opening value date or possibly the next day, settlement should then occur.

Under the circumstances stated above, the cash borrower will have incurred a loss through the failure to receive the cash on time; however, the cash borrower caused the delayed settlement and would not therefore be able to validly issue an *interest claim* to the cash lender.

Note: the normal alternative to 'DvP' is settlement on a *Free of payment* (FoP) basis. FoP results in either 1) cash only being paid, or 2) securities only being delivered. This is highly risky to the firm giving the asset, as there is no dependency in the release of the asset to the counterparty, as there is with DvP.

During the Lifetime of the Repo   Assuming a repo trade has a term of, for example, one week, on all the days which follow settlement of the opening leg the current value of the bond must be compared with the current value of the borrowed cash in order to ascertain whether any *exposure* exists. This comparison should be performed by each party for their own protection. Due to fluctuations in the market price of the bond, this is likely to result in an exposure for one of the parties to the trade, from which *margin calls* may be issued to its counterparty.

Where a firm issues a margin call to its counterparty (and assuming the counterparty agrees the calculation and direction of the margin call), the counterparty may have a choice as to whether to settle the call in cash or bonds, dependent upon the previously documented legal arrangements.

Because margin calls represent the exposure of one party (not both parties) to the trade, the movement of assets in settlement of a margin call is in one direction only, from the *non-exposed party* to the *exposed party*; therefore, there is no two-way exchange of assets in settlement of a margin call as there is in settlement of the opening leg.

Should the counterparty choose to provide cash collateral, settlement requires the counterparty to instruct its cash correspondent to make payment of the required currency and amount, on the due date, to the exposed party's nostro account. Cash payments are 'one-sided' payments; unlike securities settlement instructions, there is no requirement to match cash-only settlement instructions prior to payment occurring. (However, the cash recipient may be required to issue a *funds preadvice* to its CSD/custodian in order to receive 'good value' on the incoming funds. Failure to issue a funds preadvice where necessary is likely to result in the funds not being credited to the recipient's account until the following business day, thereby incurring loss of interest.)

Should the counterparty choose to provide bond collateral, settlement requires each party to transmit an FoP securities settlement instruction to their respective CSD/custodian; as a safety measure the instructions must match prior to settlement, otherwise a 'one-sided' instruction could result in the securities being delivered to the account of a third party in error (and the exposed party's risk not being mitigated). The following must take place in order for settlement to occur:

1. the firm's instruction and the counterparty's instruction must match
2. the value date of the movement must be reached
3. the bond deliverer must have the appropriate quantity of bonds available in its account.

Closing Value Date   On the closing value date both:

- the original cash amount borrowed, plus repo interest must be remitted to the cash lender, and
- the *equivalent securities* must be returned to the cash borrower
  - in the GMRA, the term 'equivalent' securities is used, as the bond originally received by the cash lender may or may not still exist as at the closing value date of the repo. If it does exist, the same ISIN (as originally received) must be returned to the collateral giver. If it no longer exists (due to a *corporate action* which has resulted in the original ISIN being replaced), then the replacement assets must be delivered to the collateral giver.

In order to achieve this, both parties are required to issue DvP settlement instructions containing:

- the full cash amount plus repo interest receivable or payable (whichever is appropriate) on the closing value date:
  - in the previously mentioned example trade (see Table 4.12), USD 30,334,695.57, and
- the full quantity of bonds deliverable or receivable (whichever is appropriate)
  - in the previously mentioned example trade (see Table 4.12), USD 30,000,000.00.

Note: for repo trades executed on a 'term' basis, closing leg settlement instructions could be issued at any time following trade execution; the earlier the better, as this enables resolution of any unmatched instructions well in advance of the closing value date.

Separately (and assuming that settlement of the closing value date occurred on its due date), as no exposure exists any assets given or taken due to margin calls during the lifetime of the repo must be returned to the original owner. Such assets include cash and securities collateral.

4.1.9 Portfolio Reconciliation

When a firm determines that it has an exposure and then issues a margin call to its counterparty, there is no guarantee that the counterparty will agree either 1) the monetary amount of the exposure, or 2) the direction of the exposure (whether the firm or the counterparty is exposed).

Such disagreements between a firm and its counterparty can be caused by differences in the trade population; for example, a firm has correctly excluded from its lists of trades a repo trade that had a closing value date of 'yesterday', whereas the counterparty incorrectly continues to list that trade as remaining live 'today'.

The possibility of such discrepancies is minimised if a proactive comparison of trades is made between firms, prior to margin calls being issued. A third-party *portfolio reconciliation* service exists that automatically compares files of repo trades received from a firm with the equivalent from its various counterparties. That service is triOptima's *triResolve* system.

4.1.10 Marking-to-Market

It is common practice for the collateral in a repo trade to be *marked-to-market* (revalued) from a reliable external source, at the close of business on the business day preceding the potential date of the margin call. In some cases the agreed source of prices may be documented in the GMRA Annex 1 in an attempt to avoid valuation disputes. It is also usual to use the *mid-price* (as opposed to the bid or offer price) to value the collateral.

In line with other collateral-related transactions (including *securities lending & borrowing*, and **OTC** *derivatives*), under volatile market conditions the parties to a repo trade may agree to perform intraday marking-to-market, which may result in intraday margin calls.

4.1.11 Exposure Calculation

In order for a firm to determine whether it, or its counterparty, has an exposure during the lifetime of a repo trade, it is necessary to calculate:

- the current value of the cash amount lent or borrowed, versus
- the current value of the bond collateral.

whilst also taking into account the current value of any existing collateral resulting from prior margin calls.

PART 2

By way of an example repo trade from which example calculations can be illustrated, imagine that the following trade (see Table 4.13) has been executed:

TABLE 4.13 Repo trade confirmation #2

Repo Trade Confirmation		
From	Firm A, London	
To	Party G, New York	
As principal, we hereby confirm the following transaction:		
Trade Component	**Trade Detail**	
Our Trade Reference	R0059397	
Transaction Type	Classic Repo	
Legal Agreement Type	GMRA	
Term or Open	Term	
Cash Borrower/Bond Seller	Firm A, London	
Cash Lender/Bond Buyer	Party G, New York	
Trade Date	June 7th 2017	
Opening Value Date *(Purchase Date)*	June 8th 2017	
Closing Value Date *(Repurchase Date)*	June 15th 2017	
Repo Interest Rate *(Pricing Rate)*	2.42%	
Repo Interest Payer	Firm A, London	
Haircut	2.50%	
Haircut Payer	Firm A, London	
Opening Value Date (Purchase Date)		
	Security Description	Issuer ABC 4.35% Bonds August 1st 2030
	Security Identifier	ISIN: XX1234567891
	Quantity	USD 30,000,000.00
	Price	99.95%
	Gross Value	USD 29,985,000.00
Accrued Days	plus Accrued Interest 307	USD 1,112,875.00
	Market Value	USD 31,097,875.00
Haircut Percentage	less Haircut Value 2.5%	(USD 777,446.88)
Cash Amount Receivable/Payable *(Purchase Price)*		**USD 30,320,428.12**
Closing Value Date (Repurchase Date)		
Cash Amount (from Opening Value Date)		USD 30,320,428.12
Days of Repo Interest	7	
Repo Interest Amount		USD 14,267.45
Cash Amount Receivable/Payable		**USD 30,334,695.57**
Settlement Details		
Ours	CSD T, account 66627	
Yours	CSD T, account 99034	
Settlement Method	Delivery versus payment	

Current Value of Cash   To derive the current value of the cash amount lent or borrowed, it is necessary to add 1) the original cash amount lent or borrowed, to 2) repo interest to date.

In the example trade, imagine that today is 9th June 2017, and that the opening leg of the trade did settle on the opening value date of 8th June. Therefore, Party G parted with the cash amount of USD 30,320,428.12 on 8th June, and therefore Firm A received that cash amount the same date; Firm A has today (9th June) had possession of the cash amount for one day (note: bank interest is calculated on an overnight basis). As mentioned earlier in this chapter (within Sub-section 4.1.4 'Repo Rate Format and Repo Interest Calculation Method'), the calculation of repo interest is:

- (cash amount × repo rate / divisor) × days

Therefore, for this trade, repo interest for each day is calculated as:

- (USD 30,320,428.12 × 2.42% / 360) × 1 day = USD 2038.21.

As at 9th June therefore, the current value of the cash is as reflected in Table 4.14:

TABLE 4.14   Current value of cash #1

Current Value of Cash as at Friday, June 9th 2017	
Cash Amount Lent/Borrowed	USD 30,320,428.12
Repo Interest To Date (1 Day)	USD 2038.21
Current Value of Cash	**USD 30,322,466.33**

As each day progresses through the lifetime of the repo trade, the same concepts will need to be applied, therefore as reflected in Table 4.15:

TABLE 4.15   Current value of cash #2

Current Value of Cash between June 12th and 15th 2017			
Date	Days of Repo Interest	Interest Amount	Current Value of Cash
Monday June 12th	4	USD 8152.83	USD 30,328,580.95
Tuesday June 13th	5	USD 10,191.03	USD 30,330,619.15
Wednesday June 14th	6	USD 12,229.24	USD 30,332,657.36
Thursday June 15th	7	USD 14,267.45	USD 30,334,695.57

As can be seen, the current value of cash on 15th June in the above table is the same as is stated in the Repo Trade Confirmation under the cash amount receivable/payable on the closing value date.

Current Value of Bond Collateral   To derive the current value of the bond collateral, it is necessary to 1) apply the current market price to the bond quantity, 2) add the current value of accrued interest (if clean price), and 3) apply any haircut or initial margin.

In the example trade, imagine that today is 9th June 2017. As at close of business 'yesterday' (8th June), the bond's current market (clean) price of 99.32% was provided by an independent and trusted source. As at 9th June therefore, the current value of the bond collateral is as reflected in Table 4.16:

TABLE 4.16   Current value of bond

Current Value of Bond Collateral as at Friday, June 9th 2017		
Component		Detail
	Security Description	Issuer ABC 4.35% Bonds August 1st 2030
	Security Identifier	ISIN: XX1234567891
	Quantity	USD 30,000,000.00
	Price	99.32%
	Gross Value	USD 29,796,000.00
Accrued Days	plus Accrued Interest	308	USD 1,116,500.00
	Current Market Value	USD 30,912,500.00
Haircut Percentage	less Haircut Value	2.5%	(USD 772,812.50)
Current Collateral Value		USD 30,139,687.50

Gross Exposure Amount   The difference between 1) the current value of cash, and 2) the current value of bond collateral, is the gross exposure amount. Where there is a difference in such values:

- if the current value of cash is greater than the current value of collateral, the cash lender is exposed, and
- if the current value of cash is less than the current value of collateral, the cash borrower is exposed.

Table 4.17 reflects the current values of the cash and the bond collateral:

TABLE 4.17   Gross exposure amount

Gross Exposure Amount as at Friday, June 9th 2017	
Current Value of Cash	USD 30,322,466.33
Current Value of Bond Collateral	USD 30,139,687.50
Gross Exposure Amount	**USD 182,778.83**

This calculation reveals that, as the current value of cash is greater than the current value of the bond collateral, it is the cash lender (Party G) that is exposed.

Note: the *net exposure* amount is the result of applying 1) any existing collateral resulting from prior margin calls, 2) any *threshold amount*, and/or 3) any *minimum transfer amount*; please refer to the next section for items 2) and 3). Should a net exposure amount exist after taking account of such amounts, the exposed party should issue a margin call to its counterparty.

4.1.12 Threshold and Minimum Transfer Amount

A *threshold* is an amount of unsecured exposure that one party (or both parties) allows its counterparty.

For example, a fixed threshold of USD 1,000,000.00 means that an exposure of USD 900,000.00 should not be called by the exposed party, whereas an exposure of USD 1,100,000.00 is subject to a valid margin call. Where a threshold is applicable between two trading parties, it must be agreed whether the entire amount may be called (in the example above, that amount is USD 1,100,000.00), or only the amount that exceeds the threshold (in the example above, that amount is USD 100,000.00).

Similarly a *minimum transfer amount* (MTA), if applicable between two parties, exists in order to avoid the administrative burden of mitigating relatively small exposure amounts.

On a case-by-case basis, threshold amounts and MTA may or may not be formally recorded within the GMRA annex; however, where not formally recorded, parties may still agree such amounts, albeit on an unofficial basis.

4.1.13 Making & Receiving Margin Calls

Following calculation of exposures, preferably on a daily basis by both parties in a repo trade, the *exposed party* must make a *margin call* by issuance of a margin call notification. This is typically effected by email, and must arrive with the counterparty by the deadline stated within the legal documentation, typically 14:00 *CET*.

If the non-exposed party receives the margin call beyond the deadline, the counterparty is under no obligation to act on it that day. However, many counterparties do not adhere strictly to the deadline and will endeavour to process the call as though it were received by the official deadline. Nevertheless, the exposed party should recognise late issuance of collateral demands as a risk to itself, as there is no guarantee it will be honoured by the counterparty; consequently, the firm's exposure may not be fully mitigated within the normal time frame.

Assuming the margin call is received by the deadline, the non-exposed party must now verify that the call amount is valid. The exposure amount calculated by both parties is unlikely to be precisely the same; therefore, a form of tolerance is applied.

Assuming the call amount is agreed, the non-exposed party must now choose whether to give cash collateral or bond collateral (assuming the legal documentation allows that choice). That decision must be communicated to the exposed party as proposed collateral, typically by email. In turn, the exposed party must validate the collateral proposed by the counterparty; particularly in the case of securities collateral, it is important that the exposed party checks the eligibility of the proposed *ISIN*(s). Should the exposed party reject the eligibility of the securities collateral, that party must inform its counterparty as quickly as possible.

Clearly, it is in the exposed party's interests to ensure it acts within deadlines and within reasonable time frames, in order to maximise the probability of their exposure being mitigated as soon as possible.

PART 2

4.1.14 Settlement of Margin Calls

Once the proposed collateral is agreed by the exposed party, the transfer of assets from the non-exposed party to the exposed party must occur.

In terms of the value date applicable to the settlement of margin calls:

- if cash collateral, normal market practice is for payment to be made on a same day (T+0) basis, and
- if bond collateral, normal market practice is for delivery to be made on a T+1 or T+2 basis.

Procedure for Settlement of Cash Collateral From the perspective of the non-exposed party, in order to make payment of the exposure amount, they must issue a *settlement instruction* to their appropriate *cash correspondent* (or '*nostro*'), instructing:

- debiting to its particular account number
- the currency and cash amount
- the value date, and
- the recipient's cash correspondent and its account number.

In order for payment to be made on time, the settlement instruction must be received by the applicable deadline quoted by the non-exposed party's cash correspondent. Providing that deadline is met, and an adequate cash balance or *credit line* exists within the non-exposed party's account, payment should be made on time and as instructed.

From the perspective of the exposed party, they may need to take no action in order for the cash collateral to be received on its due date. Conversely, some cash correspondents require their account holder to communicate an instruction to receive cash, known as a *funds preadvice*. The purpose of the funds preadvice is to forewarn the nostro to expect receipt of the incoming amount (i.e. currency, amount, value date), to enable the nostro to factor the receipt of such funds into their overall monetary position for that value date. Where preadvising is required by the nostro, issuance of a funds preadvice by the exposed party ensures that the funds will be received with 'good value', meaning that the cash will be credited to the exposed party's account at the nostro on the value date of the payment. Conversely, a failure to issue a preadvice is likely to result in delayed credit of cash to the exposed party's account at the nostro; this effectively means that the exposed party's risk has not been mitigated at the earliest opportunity.

Procedure for Settlement of Bond Collateral The normal method of settling a margin call with bond collateral is by both parties issuing *free of payment* (FoP) instructions to their respective CSD or custodian.

The non-exposed party is required to instruct for the delivery of the agreed quantity of the particular *ISIN*(s), whilst the exposed party instructs for the receipt of the same; it is normal market practice that the instructions must achieve a status of 'matched', prior to settlement occurring. The matching of instructions is considered to be a safety measure to ensure the securities are delivered to the exposed party's correct

CSD or custodian account; despite the possibility that FoP deliveries can be made on a non-matching basis (dependent upon the particular CSD's procedures), the risk, for both deliverer and receiver, is that a mistake is made on the recipient's account number resulting in the bonds being delivered to an account owned by someone other than the exposed party.

If the details on the two instructions differ for any reason, the instructions will be 'unmatched' and, if this status persists as at the value date, settlement of the margin call will be delayed. It is imperative that both parties monitor the current status of their instruction, and where 'unmatched', investigate and correct the instruction without delay.

Whether settlement of the margin call is due by the receipt of cash collateral or bond collateral, the exposed party must monitor their cash accounts or custodian accounts (as appropriate), to ensure that cash or bonds have in fact been received. A failure to receive timely settlement of a margin call can be treated as an *event of default* according to the GMRA; what action the exposed party actually takes is a decision only they can make.

4.1.15 Holding Collateral Received

As mentioned earlier in Sub-section 4.1.2 'Classic Repo Legal Agreements', under the GMRA the legal basis under which repo trade collateral is transferred from cash borrower to cash lender, is *title transfer*.

Title transfer provides the same legal rights to the *collateral taker*, as if that party had executed an 'outright' purchase. Therefore, legally, the collateral taker can choose to do with the collateral received, whatever it chooses to do, including:

- holding the collateral safely and securely within its account at a CSD or custodian, or
- reusing the collateral in the following ways:
  - selling
  - repoing
  - lending (as in *securities lending & borrowing*), or
  - delivering as collateral to satisfy a margin call (such as, in relation to an *OTC derivative* trade).

By signing the GMRA with the counterparty, the *collateral giver* (the cash borrower in a repo) has contractually agreed that the collateral taker becomes the *legal owner* of the bonds; consequently the collateral taker is free to choose its course of action relating to reuse (or otherwise) of the collateral. However, the collateral giver remains the *beneficial owner* of the bonds, meaning that any rights accruing (e.g. *coupon payments*) on the bonds belong to the collateral giver.

Should the collateral taker choose not to reuse the bonds, but to hold the collateral within its account at a CSD or custodian, in order to avoid accidental reuse the bonds could be held within a segregated account (rather than in its main account where the collateral taker's own securities are held).

Conversely, should the collateral taker choose to reuse the bonds, they must remain conscious of the contractual requirement to return *equivalent securities* to the collateral giver, on the closing value date of the repo.

4.1.16 Updating Books & Records

A crucial action by any firm involved in repos is to ensure its *books & records* fully reflect the current situation regarding the ownership of and the whereabouts of its assets.

From a legal perspective, for bonds that are given as collateral under the GMRA, ownership is transferred (via *title transfer*) to the cash lender, but the cash borrower remains the *beneficial owner* and is entitled to any income falling due during the term of the repo.

From an operational perspective however, ownership is retained as there has been no outright sale of the bonds, but possession is temporarily lost until the repo's *closing leg*. Before the repo is executed bonds are (usually) held by a firm's custodian, but following repo *trade execution* the process of settling the *opening leg* results in the transfer of bonds to the counterparty's custodian.

The updating of a firm's books & records is an essential step for a number of reasons; one of those reasons is *income* events (*coupon payments* on bonds) and other forms of *corporate action* (e.g. *bond exchange offers*). If the firm's books & records are not accurate at all times, the firm is at risk of failing to recognise cash that it is owed in a coupon payment, and at risk of failing to take advantage of an investment opportunity (as can arise through the corporate actions process).

The following text describes the pre-repo and post-repo (opening leg) books & records situation for both the cash borrower and cash lender. Note: the use of *double entry bookkeeping* within a firm's books & records is critically important, as this discipline enables proper control of assets to be maintained and *reconciliation* to be performed successfully.

Cash Borrower's Perspective   Assume that, before a repo trade is executed, Firm A owns (from a prior purchase) a quantity of USD 20,000,000 Issuer DEF 3.95% bonds, maturing 15th February 2031; within Firm A, the internal owner is a particular *trading book*. Also assume that the entire quantity of bonds is held by the firm's custodian, and that no trades are outstanding with counterparties. This situation is reflected within Table 4.18:

TABLE 4.18   Books & records #1

Firm A's Books & Records			
Issuer DEF 3.95% Bonds 15th February 2031			
Ownership		Location	
Trading Book K	+20,000,000	−20,000,000	Custodian T
	+20,000,000	−20,000,000	

Then Firm A decides to borrow cash via repo, and provides the cash lender (Counterparty L) with a quantity of USD 15,000,000 Issuer DEF 3.95% bonds, maturing 15th February 2031, as collateral for the cash borrowing. Upon settlement of the repo trade's opening leg, the firm's books & records must be updated to reflect the facts, as per Table 4.19:

TABLE 4.19   Books & records #2

Firm A's Books & Records			
Issuer DEF 3.95% Bonds 15th February 2031			
Ownership		Location	
Trading Book K	+20,000,000	−5,000,000	Custodian T
		−15,000,000	Counterparty L (Repo)
	+20,000,000	−20,000,000	

Firm A's books & records now reveal that the firm (specifically Trading Book K) is still the owner of USD 20,000,000 bonds, but that only USD 5,000,000 bonds are held by the firm's custodian, whilst the balance of USD 15,000,000 are in the possession of the repo counterparty. The accuracy of the firm's books & records must be proven via the process of reconciliation, preferably on a daily basis.

(Note: it is essential that the firm's books & records tell the truth of the situation and are in no way misleading. If the repo'd securities [USD 15,000,000 Issuer DEF 3.95% bonds] had been shown within Firm A's books & records as reducing the ownership position to USD 5,000,000 bonds, the risk of doing so is that, for example, if a coupon pays whilst the bonds are with Counterparty L, then Firm A will believe that they are entitled to the coupon on only the remaining USD 5,000,000 bonds (based upon their books & records), rather than the original quantity of USD 20,000,000 bonds, to which Firm A is, in fact, entitled.)

As well as the movement of bond collateral, the cash amount borrowed plus repo interest (both of which are payable to the cash lender) must be reflected within the firm's books & records.

Whatever collateral is given or taken in settlement of *margin calls* must also be reflected within the firm's books & records, as must the return of collateral on the *closing value date*.

Cash Lender's Perspective   For the same repo trade as described under 'Cash Borrower's Perspective', the cash lender will need to maintain accurate books & records.

Assume that, before the particular repo trade is executed, Firm A's counterparty ('Counterparty L') does not own any of Issuer DEF 3.95% bonds, maturing 15th February 2031. This situation is reflected within Table 4.20:

TABLE 4.20   Books & records #3

Counterparty L's Books & Records			
Issuer DEF 3.95% Bonds 15th February 2031			
Ownership		Location	
	0	0	
	0	0	

Then, following the receipt of USD 15,000,000 Issuer DEF 3.95% bonds, maturing 15th February 2031, as collateral for the cash loan to Firm A, Counterparty L updates its books & records as shown in Table 4.21:

TABLE 4.21   Books & records #4

Counterparty L's Books & Records		
Issuer DEF 3.95% Bonds 15th February 2031		
Ownership	Location	
0	−15,000,000	Custodian G
	+15,000,000	Firm A (Repo)
0	0	

Counterparty L's books & records now reveal that the firm is still not the owner of any of the particular bonds (because they have not purchased them outright), although it does have possession of USD 15,000,000 bonds, received from Firm A and owed back to Firm A upon closure of the repo. Again, the accuracy of the firm's books & records must be proven via the process of reconciliation, preferably on a daily basis.

(Note: it is essential that the firm's books & records tell the truth of the situation and are in no way misleading. If the receipt of the repo'd securities [USD 15,000,000 Issuer DEF 3.95% bonds] had been shown within Counterparty L's books & records as increasing the ownership position to USD 15,000,000 bonds, the risk of doing so is that, for example if a coupon pays whilst the bonds are with Counterparty L, then Counterparty L will believe that they are entitled to the coupon on those USD 15,000,000 bonds (based upon their books & records), whereas in fact Counterparty L is not entitled to the coupon. When the coupon pays, Custodian G will credit the account of Counterparty L who in turn must remit the equivalent cash value of the coupon to the beneficial owner, Firm A.)

4.1.17 Collateral Substitution

For a GC (*general collateral*) repo, the possibility exists that the cash borrower will want to replace the original bond collateral with other collateral during the lifetime of the repo. (Note that substitution is not applicable in a *stock-based repo*, as the original collateral is very much the reason why the cash lender was prepared to execute the trade.)

At the outset of the repo trade, the particular piece of eligible collateral will be selected from the cash borrower's inventory of securities, to be delivered to the cash lender as collateral against the borrowing of cash. The cash borrower will select a particular piece of collateral based upon internal understanding that there is currently no intention to sell the bond or to use it in any other transaction. The bond is then delivered as collateral in the repo trade. Subsequently, the cash borrower's bond trader decides to sell the bond, which is currently in possession of the cash lender. The cash borrower now needs the bond to be returned by the cash lender (so as to settle the sale and thereby receive the sale proceeds on value date), and the cash borrower must provide *replacement collateral* to the cash lender.

For all of the above to occur, at execution of the repo trade the cash borrower must request a Right of Substitution (RoS) from the cash lender. If an RoS is agreed at trade execution, this gives the cash borrower the power to request the cash lender to return the equivalent collateral in exchange for replacement collateral; this right exists at any time between the opening value date and the closing value date. Such an RoS usually requires the cash borrower to pay a higher repo rate, which is likely to increase further dependent upon the number of rights required by the cash borrower. For the avoidance of doubt between the two trading parties, any RoS agreed at trade execution should be documented within the ***trade confirmation***, the maximum number of permitted substitutions should be recorded, and the number of available (unused) substitutions monitored by both parties throughout the lifetime of the repo trade.

The underlying reasons for collateral substitution include, from the cash borrower's perspective, that the bond is required for use in a different transaction, whether sold, lent, or used as collateral. From the cash lender's perspective, where the bond issuer has suffered a ***credit rating downgrade***, replacement collateral will be sought from the cash borrower. Furthermore, both parties normally wish to avoid the difficulties surrounding ***withholding tax*** (payable on some bond types) relating to coupon payments.

The replacement collateral may be one bond (i.e. a single ***ISIN***), or multiple bonds (i.e. multiple ISINs). If a ***haircut*** or ***initial margin*** has been applied to the original collateral for the opening value date, the same is normally applied to any replacement collateral.

Substitution Settlement   As the cash lender continues to have an ***exposure*** to the cash borrower (to the value of the lent cash), the cash lender should ensure it remains collateralised at all times during a collateral substitution. The cash lender will experience exposure if it returns the original collateral prior to receiving the replacement collateral from the cash borrower. For the cash lender to avoid such exposure, the cash borrower is likely to be required to deliver the replacement collateral prior to receiving delivery of the original collateral.

Historically, the deliveries of the two securities have been effected by each party issuing 2 × ***free of payment*** settlement instructions, which must match prior to settlement occurring. Historically at ***CSDs***, there has been no means of linking the two sets of settlement instructions, consequently delivery of both the original collateral and the replacement collateral has been achieved independently of one another, so it is possible that:

1. both deliveries settle on ***value date***
2. only one delivery settles on value date, while the other delivery fails to settle, or
3. neither delivery settles on value date.

The immediate result of scenario 2 above, is that one of the parties will experience a significant exposure, as they will possess neither the original collateral nor the replacement collateral.

Figure 4.4 illustrates the typical substitution flow:

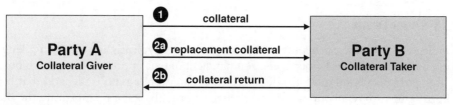

FIGURE 4.4   Collateral substitution

Where the cash borrower initiates substitution, the sequence of events is as follows:

- the cash borrower checks to confirm that substitutions are permitted under the terms of the repo trade, and if so:
- the cash borrower contacts the cash lender (typically by email), requesting substitution, stating the detail of the repo trade, the original collateral and the proposed replacement collateral
- the cash lender checks to confirm that substitutions are permitted under the terms of the repo trade, and if so:
- the cash lender validates the eligibility of the proposed replacement collateral
- if validated, for the replacement collateral both parties must issue free of payment (FoP) settlement instructions, which must match, prior to delivery being effected, from the cash borrower to the cash lender, on the agreed value date.
- for the original collateral, at the same time and for the same value date (as for the replacement collateral), both parties must issue FoP settlement instructions, which must match, prior to delivery being effected from the cash lender to the cash borrower, on the agreed value date.

Note that matching FoP settlement instructions are necessary as a precaution to ensure that bonds are delivered to the correct account.

In order for firms to avoid exposures when settling collateral substitutions (i.e. where only one (not both) securities are successfully delivered on the due date), the ideal mechanism by which collateral substitution is effected is by *delivery versus delivery* (DvD), the simultaneous exchange of one security (the original collateral) with another security (the replacement collateral), with no cash amount involved. DvD has historically not been available amongst many central securities depositories, but (in 2016) is available through the *Target2-Securities* (T2S) settlement facility, whereby two sets of matched FoP settlement instructions can be linked by either of the instructing parties, following which the settlement of one delivery will trigger settlement of the other delivery simultaneously (and conversely, the lack of available securities which are to be delivered in one direction will prevent delivery of the other security in the opposing direction). This T2S facility can be described as *effective DvD*, as the ideal future scenario is that parties are able to issue a single settlement instruction containing the details (and required delivery direction) of both the original collateral and the replacement collateral. (Note: in addition to its usefulness for collateral substitution, a DvD (or effective DvD) settlement mechanism will also be of value for *securities lending* and *securities borrowing* versus securities collateral.)

The value date of bond deliveries pertaining to substitutions is usually based upon agreement between the two parties, but can be same day, next day or next day + 1.

4.1.18 Income Events

As indicated previously, firms that execute repo trades typically try to avoid giving or taking bonds as collateral when a coupon payment date is approaching on such bonds.

If a particular bond has been delivered as collateral in a repo trade, and that bond is shortly due to pay a coupon, the two parties normally agree to substitute the bond with a different bond.

Typical bond types that are *interest bearing* include *fixed rate bonds*, *floating rate notes* and *convertible bonds*; *zero coupon bonds* do not pay coupons. Coupon payments on interest-bearing bonds are scheduled events; the *prospectus* of an individual bond issue clearly defines the coupon payment dates throughout the bond's lifetime. In the case of floating rate notes, the coupon frequency is clearly defined (as is the basis for calculating the rate for a particular coupon period). For the bonds that they trade, firms set up the details of individual bond issues internally within their *static data* (also known as 'reference data') *repository*, including coupon payment dates and coupon frequency. This means that static data can be used as a form of diary in order to highlight upcoming coupon payment dates, thereby triggering the need for *collateral substitution*, where necessary. However, a firm may not have previously traded in a bond which they now receive as collateral in a repo trade, meaning that the relevant information about the bond (e.g. coupon payment dates) needs to be identified and set up within the firm's static data. If the firm does not have access to the issue prospectus (the original source document for any bond issue), the types of organisation that can supply such information include *central securities depositories* (CSDs), *custodians* and *data vendors*.

The primary and overriding principle regarding coupon payments on collateral relating to repo trades, is that the cash borrower should be paid the equivalent value of the coupon payment made by the issuer, as would have occured if the collateral been held by the cash borrower's custodian (and had not been given as collateral).

If a coupon payment falls due on a bond being held as repo collateral by the cash lender (the *legal owner*) at its custodian, the cash lender's account at the custodian will be credited with the coupon proceeds either on (or very shortly following) the coupon payment date. Specifically, whichever account holders at the CSD hold the bonds as at a specified date known as the *record date*, those parties will be credited with the coupon proceeds. The cash lender's *Corporate Actions* Department should be monitoring such situations, and (if the cash lender's *books & records* are fully updated and *reconciled*) will identify that the cash lender is not the *beneficial owner* of the bonds, that they are beneficially owned by the cash borrower, and therefore the value of the coupon payment must be paid in the same currency to the cash borrower, in accordance with the *GMRA*. Table 4.22 provides an example of the cash lender's books & records as at record date of a coupon payment, showing zero ownership for the cash lender, and showing that the custodian has a record date position which is owed to firm A (the cash borrower):

TABLE 4.22 Books & records #5

Cash Lender's Books & Records		
Issuer DEF 3.95% Bonds 15th February 2031		
Ownership	Location	
0	−15,000,000	Custodian G
	+15,000,000	Firm A (Repo)
0	0	

By the same token, the Corporate Actions Department of the cash borrower will identify from their books & records that they are the owner of the bond, but they do not have possession of their total ownership position as at record date; therefore, the coupon proceeds must be remitted by the cash lender, in accordance with the GMRA. Table 4.23 provides an example of the cash borrower's books & records as at record date of a coupon payment, showing a positive ownership position of 20,000,000 bonds, 25% of which are held at the cash borrower's custodian, and the remaining 75% of which are held by the cash lender ('Counterparty L'):

TABLE 4.23   Books & records #6

Cash Borrower's Books & Records			
Issuer DEF 3.95% Bonds 15th February 2031			
Ownership		Location	
Trading Book K	+20,000,000	−5,000,000	Custodian T
		−15,000,000	Counterparty L (Repo)
	+20,000,000	−20,000,000	

The cash borrower must ensure it receives the coupon on its total ownership position. For the portion of its holding which is held by its custodian, the cash borrower will expect credit of coupon proceeds to its custodian account, on the *coupon payment date*. For the coupon proceeds on the portion of bonds held as collateral by the cash lender, the cash lender is obligated to remit the equivalent value of the coupon payment to the account of the cash borrower's choosing.

The above-mentioned scenario, in which the cash lender holds the bond as collateral as at record date of the coupon payment, is depicted in Figure 4.5:

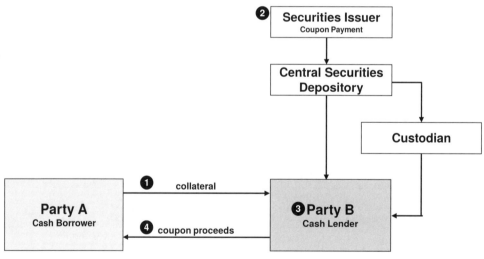

FIGURE 4.5   Coupon payment flow; cash lender has not reused the collateral

The diagram is explained as follows:

Step 1: the cash borrower provides bond collateral to the cash lender, who holds the bonds within its account at a CSD or custodian

Step 2: a coupon payment falls due, and the coupon proceeds are paid by the bond issuer to the CSD who in turn either credits the account of the custodian or pays directly to the account of the cash lender

Step 3: the cash lender is credited with the coupon proceeds by its CSD or custodian

Step 4: the cash lender remits the equivalent cash value of the coupon payment to the cash borrower.

To summarise, where the cash lender is holding the bond collateral in its account at the CSD or custodian (and had not therefore reused the collateral):

- the cash borrower should be paid the equivalent value of the coupon payment (from the cash lender), and should not suffer financially in any way
  - overall net effect to cash borrower (Party A) = in credit (the same as would have occurred had they not entered into the repo trade)
- the cash lender (Party B) will not benefit financially or be disadvantaged financially, as they will have received the coupon payment from their custodian and have remitted the same value to the cash borrower (Party A)
  - overall net effect to cash lender = zero.

Conversely, if the cash lender has reused the bonds, the cash borrower will still look to the cash lender to provide the coupon proceeds. This is depicted in Figure 4.6:

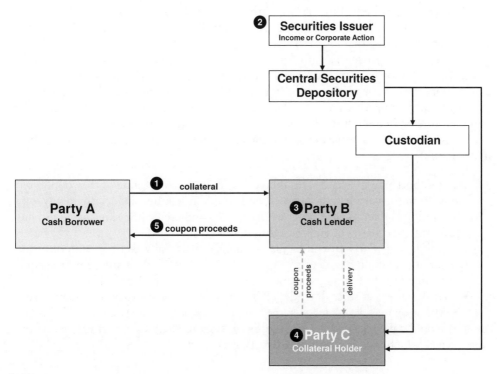

FIGURE 4.6   Coupon payment flow; cash lender has reused the collateral

The diagram is explained as follows:

Step 1: the cash borrower provides bond collateral to the cash lender, who utilises the bonds in another transaction, such as another repo trade

Step 2: a coupon payment falls due, and the coupon proceeds are paid by the bond issuer to the CSD who in turn either credits the account of the collateral holder directly or pays a custodian who then credits the collateral holder's account. It is important to note that the collateral holder may or may not be obliged to pass on the coupon proceeds to the cash lender, dependent upon the transaction type executed between Party B and Party C; if the bond collateral was delivered by Party B to Party C in settlement of a sale, Party C will be entitled to the coupon proceeds (and therefore will not pass the coupon proceeds to the cash lender). If, instead, the bond was used as collateral in a collateralised transaction (e.g. securities lending or repo), then Party C is obliged to remit the coupon proceeds to Party B.

Step 3: if the bonds were used by Party B to settle a sale to Party C, the coupon proceeds are not due to be paid by Party C. In a situation where the bonds were used as collateral, Party B will receive the credit of the equivalent value of the coupon payment from Party C

Step 4: Party C remits the equivalent value of the coupon payment to Party B

Step 5: Party B remits the equivalent value of the coupon payment to Party A.

To clarify, regardless of the nature of the transaction executed between Party B and Party C, Party B will owe the coupon proceeds to Party A. Therefore, in the situation where Party B utilised the bonds to settle a sale with Party C, the cash lender will need to pay the coupon proceeds, out of its own funds, to the cash borrower (a *manufactured coupon*). However, where Party B's transaction with Party C was a collateralised transaction, the cash lender's receipt of coupon proceeds from Party C will be used to satisfy the coupon proceeds owed to Party A; under these circumstances the cash lender will therefore be in a neutral position regarding the coupon proceeds.

To summarise, in a situation where the cash lender (Party B) had reused the bond in a sale to Party C:

- the cash borrower (Party A) should receive the equivalent value of the coupon payment (from the cash lender Party B), and should not suffer financially in any way
  - overall net effect to cash borrower (Party A) = in credit (the same as would have occurred had they not entered into the repo trade)
- the cash lender (Party B) will be disadvantaged financially, as they will not be able to claim the coupon payment from Party C, but Party B must still remit the equivalent value of the coupon payment to the cash borrower (Party A)
  - overall net effect to cash lender (Party B) = in deficit (as they must pay Party A without being able to recover the coupon payment from Party C). Note: Party B would have received the *accrued interest* from Party C as part of the sale proceeds, which will partially offset Party B's deficit

- the Buyer (Party C) will gain a financial advantage as they are entitled to the full coupon payment, although they would have paid a certain value of accrued interest to Party B upon settlement of their purchase
  - overall net effect to buyer (Party C) = in credit.

To summarise, in a situation where the cash lender (Party B) had reused the bond in a collateralised transaction with Party C:

- the cash borrower (Party A) should receive the equivalent value of the coupon payment (from the cash lender Party B), and should not suffer financially in any way
  - overall net effect to cash borrower (Party A) = in credit (the same as would have occurred had they not entered into the repo trade)
- the cash lender (Party B) will not benefit financially or be disadvantaged financially, as they are able to claim the coupon payment from Party C, and Party B must remit the equivalent value of the coupon payment to the cash borrower (Party A)
  - overall net effect to cash lender (Party B) = zero
- assuming that Party C is holding the collateral in their account at their custodian, they will not benefit financially or be disadvantaged financially, as they will have received the coupon payment from their custodian and remit the same value to Party B
  - overall net effect to Party C = zero.

4.1.19 Additional Aspects of Repo

In addition to the various aspects of classic bilateral repos described within this chapter, the following activities should be noted:

Processing of Individual Repo Trades versus a Portfolio of Repo Trades Within this chapter, examples of repo trades have typically been referred to as an individual trade with a particular counterparty. Where a firm has multiple concurrently live repo trades with a particular counterparty, in practice exposure is calculated on all such trades, on a daily basis, and any margin calls relate to the total exposure.

Single Repo Trade: Failed Settlement followed by Cash Pair-Off A repo trade has been executed on the following terms:

- Firm A executes a *reverse repo* trade with Firm B:
  - Opening Leg: Firm A is due to receive the bond collateral and pay cash to Firm B, on a DvP basis
  - Closing Leg: Firm A is due to return the bond collateral versus cash on a DvP basis, to Firm B.
- however, it transpires that Firm B is short of bonds to deliver on the opening leg value date. If this situation continues throughout the lifetime of the repo trade, Firm A will not be in possession of the bond collateral (and therefore it is not applicable for Firm A to return the bond collateral to Firm B)
  - under these circumstances, Firm A and Firm B may agree to execute a 'pair-off', meaning that both parties will cancel their *settlement instructions* (for both the *opening leg* and the *closing leg*). Additionally, the cash values are paired-off, resulting in the net cash difference (equivalent to the repo interest for the entire trade) being settled via a pure cash payment; in this example Firm B would pay Firm A.

Two (or more) Repo Trades: Closing Leg versus Opening Leg Cash Pair-Off   Cash pair-offs can arise where two (or more) repo trades have been executed 'back-to-back' between the same two parties; under such circumstances the first repo trade is said to have been 'rolled' into a second repo trade. Such a pair-off opportunity arises where the closing value date of the first repo trade is the same as the opening value date of the second repo trade. For example:

A repo trade has been executed on the following terms:

- Firm S executes a repo trade (Trade #1) with Firm T:
  - Opening Leg, value date 1st March: this leg of the repo has settled on the opening value date, resulting in Firm S receiving the cash and Firm T receiving the bond collateral, on a DvP basis
  - Closing Leg, value date 8th March: Firm S is due to return the cash (plus/minus repo interest) and Firm T is due to return the bond collateral, on a DvP basis.

Assume 'today' to be 7th March; the closing value date has not yet been reached. On 7th March a second repo trade is executed between the same two parties, involving the same bond collateral:

- Firm S executes a repo trade (Trade #2) with Firm T:
  - Opening Leg, value date 8th March: Firm S is due to receive the cash amount and Firm T is due to receive the bond collateral, on a DvP basis
  - Closing Leg, value date 15th March: Firm S is due to return the cash (plus/minus repo interest) and Firm T is due to return the bond collateral, on a DvP basis.

Firm S is due to receive its bond collateral from Firm T on 8th March (the closing value date of Trade #1), but is also due to redeliver the same bond collateral to Firm T on 8th March (the opening value date of Trade #2).

Under these circumstances, instead of settling both trades on 8th March in the usual (DvP) manner, Firm S and Firm T may agree to execute a 'pair-off', resulting in payment of the cash differential.

Settlement of the closing leg of Trade #2 will need to occur in the normal (DvP) manner, unless a further repo trade is executed between the two firms thereby providing a further pair-off opportunity.

To clarify, pair-offs can be executed only 1) between the same two firms, and 2) for the same bond collateral, and 3) in most cases for the same value date. It is also possible that a pair-off is agreed due to *settlement failure*.

Failure to Deliver on Repo Trades with Negative Repo Rates   Within this book, examples of repo trades have typically been referred to as having a *positive interest* (repo) *rate*, in which the cash borrower (collateral giver) pays repo interest to the cash lender (collateral taker) at the close of the trade. However, repo trades can be executed with a *negative interest rate*, whereby the cash borrower receives repo interest from the cash lender.

In a situation in which the repo rate of a trade is negative, and if the cash borrower (collateral giver) fails to deliver the bond collateral on the opening value date or later, the recommendation by the *International Capital Market Association* (ICMA) is that the repo rate should be set to zero for every day that the cash borrower fails to deliver the bond collateral.

Adoption of ICMA's recommendation will impact pair-off cash values which will need to be adjusted appropriately; please refer to the prior sections on pair-offs.

Compensation for Delivery Failure   Where repos are executed using US Treasury securities as collateral (for settlement within the *Fedwire* system), should the cash borrower (collateral giver) fail to deliver the securities collateral on the opening value date, the cash lender (collateral taker) is able to claim interest from its counterparty.

This interest claim mechanism is designed to incentivise timely settlement and was created in the USA by the Treasury Market Practices Group; the procedure is known as 'TMPG Claims'.

The claimable amount is based upon the trade's cash value; USD 500.00 is the minimum claimable amount. For example, a repo with an opening leg cash value of USD 100,000,000.00 which fails to settle for 3 days can result in an interest claim issued against the responsible party of USD 41,666.67 (USD 100,000,000.00 × 5% / 360 × 3 days).

CHAPTER 5

Sale & Repurchase (Repo) Trades and Collateral – The Repo Trade Lifecycle

This chapter illustrates the sequential and day-to-day steps in the Repo Trade Lifecycle, in which each step relates to concepts described earlier in Part 2 of the book. An example trade will be used for this purpose, specifically a cash-based classic repo trade.

INTRODUCTION

The Repo Trade Lifecycle is a series of logical and sequential steps which should be practised in order for a firm to process repo trades in a safe and secure fashion.

The following 'roadmap' diagram will be used to enable identification of 1) how far through the overall trade lifecycle a particular topic is, and 2) how many steps remain:

The Repo Trade Lifecycle

1	Pre-Trading
2	Trade Execution
3	Pre-Settlement
4	Settlement of Opening Leg
5	Throughout Lifetime of Trade
6	Settlement of Closing Leg

The following pages depict one repo trade in which Firm A is the cash borrower and the *collateral giver*, including calculations of cash values and bond quantities, and the actions necessary for *settlement* and *exposure mitigation* to occur in a timely fashion.

5.1 PRE-TRADING

The following should ideally be in place prior to repo *trade execution* (viewed from the perspective of Firm A):

Legal Documentation

- *GMRA* and applicable Annex signed by Firm A and its *counterparty*, Party G

Standing Settlement Instructions

- *SSIs* are exchanged between Firm A and Party G

Static Data

- Firm A sets up within its *static data repository*:
  - Party G as a counterparty, plus
  - particular attributes of legal documentation impacting *collateral management*, including:
    - *eligible collateral*
    - the frequency of *exposure* calculation
    - the source of securities collateral pricing
    - any *minimum transfer amount*
    - the deadline for receipt of *margin calls*
  - repo SSI details for Party G.

5.2 TRADE EXECUTION

The following three steps are usually taken immediately prior to execution of a repo trade (viewed from the perspective of Firm A):

Determine Cash Borrowing Requirement

- in order to fund its inventory of *bonds*, Firm A has a borrowing requirement for a particular amount of currency, for a specified period of time, namely:
  - USD 60,000,000.00, for a period of one week

Identify Bond Collateral

- in order to secure the cash lender's risk, Firm A selects a bond from its inventory of assets held at its custodian, namely:
  - Issuer ABC 4.35% Bonds 1st August 2030

Pre-Execution

- Firm A chooses to borrow cash via repo, and contacts Party G

Trade Execution

- Firm A executes a classic repo with Party G, and ...
  - sells ...
  - on a specific *trade date*
  - for *opening leg* settlement on a specific *value date* (*purchase date*)
  - for *closing leg* settlement on a specific future value date (*repurchase date*)
  - a specific quantity
  - of a specific bond
  - to a specific counterparty
  - at a specific *market price*
  - at a specific *repo rate*
  - at an agreed *haircut* or *initial margin*.

5.3 PRE-SETTLEMENT

The following steps occur immediately following execution of a repo trade; therefore, on trade date (viewed from the perspective of Firm A, unless stated otherwise):

Trade Capture

- trade details are captured internally by Firm A's repo trader (see Table 5.1)
- Firm A's books & records are updated as a result.

TABLE 5.1   Repo trade capture

Repo Trade Capture				
Trade Component		**Trade Detail**		
Transaction Type		Term Classic Repo Cash Borrowing		
Trade Reference		R0059397		
Counterparty		Party G, New York		
Security	ISIN	Issuer ABC 4.35% August 1st 2030	XX1234567891	
Quantity		USD 30,000,000.00		
Price (clean)		99.95%		
Repo Rate	Payer	2.42%	Ourselves	
Trade Date		June 7th 2017		
Opening Value Date		June 8th 2017		
Closing Value Date		June 15th 2017		
Haircut/Initial Margin	Rate	Payer	Haircut	2.50%	Ourselves

Trade Enrichment

- Firm A's static data has been used to calculate accrued days and accrued interest
  - Issuer ABC 4.35% Bonds 1st August 2030 pays interest annually on 1st August

- trade details are enriched with SSI information from Firm A's static data:
  - Firm A wishes to settle over its account 66627 at the relevant CSD
  - Party G wishes to settle over its account 99034 at the relevant CSD.

Trade Confirmation

- Firm A issues a trade confirmation to Party G (see Table 5.2), including ...
  - the original trade details, plus
  - the settlement method (DvP), plus
  - CSD account details for both parties

TABLE 5.2　Repo trade confirmation

Repo Trade Confirmation		
From	Firm A, London	
To	Party G, New York	
As principal, we hereby confirm the following transaction:		
Trade Component	**Trade Detail**	
Our Trade Reference	R0059397	
Transaction Type	Classic Repo	
Legal Agreement Type	GMRA	
Term or Open	Term	
Cash Borrower/Bond Seller	Firm A, London	
Cash Lender/Bond Buyer	Party G, New York	
Trade Date	June 7th 2017	
Opening Value Date *(Purchase Date)*	June 8th 2017	
Closing Value Date *(Repurchase Date)*	June 15th 2017	
Repo Interest Rate *(Pricing Rate)*	2.42%	
Repo Interest Payer	Firm A, London	
Haircut	2.50%	
Haircut Payer	Firm A, London	
Opening Value Date (Purchase Date)		
	Security Description	Issuer ABC 4.35% Bonds August 1st 2030
	Security Identifier	ISIN: XX1234567891
	Quantity	USD 30,000,000.00
	Price	99.95%
	Gross Value	USD 29,985,000.00
Accrued Days	plus Accrued Interest　307	USD 1,112,875.00
	Market Value	USD 31,097,875.00
Haircut Percentage	less Haircut Value　2.5%	(USD 777,446.88)
Cash Amount Receivable/Payable *(Purchase Price)*		USD 30,320,428.12

(continued)

TABLE 5.2   Repo trade confirmation *(continued)*

Closing Value Date (Repurchase Date)	
Cash Amount (from Opening Value Date)	USD 30,320,428.12
Days of Repo Interest	7
Repo Interest Amount	USD 14,267.45
Cash Amount Receivable/Payable	**USD 30,334,695.57**
Settlement Details	
Ours	CSD T, account 66627
Yours	CSD T, account 99034
Settlement Method	Delivery versus Payment

- Party G compares Firm A's trade confirmation with its own *books & records*, to discover the details match.

Opening Leg Settlement Instructions

- on *trade date*, for the *opening leg* of the repo, Firm A issues a *DvP* settlement instruction to the CSD (see Table 5.3):

TABLE 5.3   Settlement instruction: opening leg

Settlement Instruction	
Component	**Detail**
From	Firm A, London
To	CSD T
Date	June 7th 2017
Subject	**Settlement Instruction**
Our Reference	R0059397
Our Account Number	66627
Receive / Deliver	Deliver
Quantity	USD 30,000,000.00
ISIN	XX1234567891
Cash Countervalue	USD 30,320,428.12
Value Date	June 8th 2017
Settlement Method	DvP
Counterparty Account Number	99034

Note: the direction ('Deliver' in this example) of a securities settlement instruction always refers to the securities, rather than the cash.

- Firm A's instruction is matched by Party G's instruction.

5.4 SETTLEMENT OF OPENING LEG

The following two steps occur at the CSD, followed by internal steps, all of which should occur on the value date of the opening leg (viewed from the perspective of Firm A, unless stated otherwise):

Settlement

- timely settlement at the CSD requires all the following to be actioned:
    - settlement instructions to be matched
    - value date to be reached
    - seller to have securities available in its account
    - buyer to have cash (or credit line) available in its account
- the opening leg of the repo trade settles on its due date (the opening leg value date).

Advice of Settlement

- the CSD transmits an advice of settlement to Firm A (see Table 5.4)
    - advising that the bonds were successfully delivered against receipt of cash on the opening leg value date

TABLE 5.4   Advice of settlement: opening leg

Advice of Settlement	
Component	Detail
From	CSD T
To	Firm A, London
Date	June 8th 2017

(continued)

TABLE 5.4   Advice of settlement: opening leg *(continued)*

Subject	Advice of Settlement
Your Reference	R0059397
Your Account	66627
Receive / Deliver	Deliver
Quantity	USD 30,000,000.00
ISIN	XX1234567891
Cash Countervalue	USD 30,320,428.12
Settlement Date	June 8th 2017
Settlement Method	DvP
Counterparty Account	99034

Note: the CSD reports the fact that settlement has occurred by use of the term *'settlement date'*.

Receipt of the Advice of Settlement triggers the following actions internally within Firm A:

Updating of Books & Records

- internally, Firm A updates the relevant trade record, showing …
  - cash was received and bonds were delivered on the opening value date, as reflected in Table 5.5:

TABLE 5.5   Current cash & collateral balances

	Cash			Bond Collateral (Quantity)		
Date	Taken	Given	Balance	Taken	Given	Balance
June 8th	+USD 30,320,428.12	0	+USD 30,320,428.12	0	−USD 30,000,000	−USD 30,000,000

Current Cash & Collateral Balances – Firm A's Perspective

Reconciliation

- Firm A successfully conducts two reconciliations:
  - a ***depot reconciliation*** (comparison of books & records versus CSD's statement of securities holdings) showing that the bonds are no longer in Firm A's securities account at the CSD
  - a ***nostro reconciliation*** (comparison of books & records versus CSD's statement of cash balances) showing that the cash is in Firm A's cash account at the CSD.

5.5 THROUGHOUT LIFETIME OF TRADE

After settlement of the opening leg, a number of risk mitigation activities occur on a daily basis; the following is viewed from the perspective of Firm A (unless stated otherwise):

EVENING OF THURSDAY 8TH JUNE 2017

Marking-to-Market

- identify the *current market price* of the bond collateral, as at close-of-business (see Table 5.6).

TABLE 5.6   Marking-to-market

Bond Collateral	M2M Date (Close-of-Business)	Current Market (Clean) Price
Issuer ABC 4.35% Bonds August 1st 2030	June 8th 2017	99.32%

Portfolio Reconciliation

- to confirm that the trade population is the same between the two firms:
  - Firm A transmits details of all currently open repo trades with Party G, to the triResolve *portfolio reconciliation* service
  - Party G transmits its list of repo trades to triResolve
- triResolve advises Firm A and Party G that the lists match one another.

MORNING OF FRIDAY 9TH JUNE 2017

Calculation of Exposure

- identify the current value of bond collateral (see Table 5.7) ...
  - current M2M price (clean or dirty), plus
  - (if clean price) current value of accrued interest
  - less haircut or initial margin

TABLE 5.7 Calculation of exposure #1

Calculation of Exposure #1: Bond Collateral		
Component	**Detail**	
Security Description	Issuer ABC 4.35% Bonds August 1st 2030	
Security Identifier	ISIN: XX1234567891	
Quantity	USD 30,000,000.00	
Current Market (Clean) Price	99.32%	
Gross Value		US29,796,000.00
Accrued Days	plus Accrued Interest	308	USD 1,116,500.00
Current Market Value		USD 30,912,500.00
Haircut Percentage	less Haircut Value	2.5%	(USD 772,812.50)
Current Collateral Value		USD 30,139,687.50

- identify the current value of cash amount borrowed (see Table 5.8) ...
  - original cash amount borrowed, plus
  - repo interest to date

TABLE 5.8 Calculation of exposure #2

Calculation of Exposure #2: Cash Lent or Borrowed	
Component	**Detail**
Repo Interest Rate	2.42%
Days of Repo Interest To Date	1
Repo Interest Payer	Firm A, London
Cash Amount Borrowed	USD 30,320,428.12
Repo Interest Value To Date	USD 2038.21
Current Value of Cash Amount Borrowed	USD 30,322,466.33

- the difference in 1) the current value of bond collateral, and 2) the current value of cash, is the *gross exposure* amount (see Table 5.9)
- if any threshold or minimum transfer amount has been agreed between Firm A and Party G, the gross exposure amount must exceed those values, if a valid margin call is to be made by either party

TABLE 5.9   Gross and net exposure

Determining Gross and Net Exposure, and Margin Call Direction			
Component		Detail	
Current Value of Cash Amount Borrowed			USD 30,322,466.33
less Current Collateral Value			USD 30,139,687.50
Exposed Party	Gross Exposure	Party G, New York	USD 182,778.83
Minimum Transfer Amount		(USD 150,000.00)	No impact
Exposed Party	Net Exposure	Party G, New York	USD 182,778.83

- as the current value of collateral is less than the current value of cash amount borrowed, Party G is the *exposed party*.

Issuance/Receipt of Margin Call

- Party G communicates their *margin call* to Firm A
  - which must be received by the predefined deadline
- Firm A checks the accuracy of the margin call, and agrees.

Proposing Margin Call Settlement Method

- Firm A decides in which form to satisfy the margin call, and chooses to provide cash
- Firm A communicates their decision to settle the margin call in cash
- Party G verifies that cash is acceptable, by reference to the legal documentation.

Issuance of Settlement Instruction to Settle Margin Call

- Firm A issues a cash *settlement instruction* to its USD *cash correspondent*
  - by the cash correspondent's daily deadline (does not require matching by counterparty).

Settlement

- on value date of the margin call payment:
  - settlement will occur if Firm A has adequate means to pay at their cash correspondent (whether credit cash balance or collateralised overdraft facility)
- Firm A's USD cash correspondent makes payment as instructed by Firm A
- Firm A's cash correspondent updates Firm A's bank account as a result of the payment.

Advice of Settlement

- Firm A's cash correspondent issues a bank statement to Firm A, or Firm A accesses the statement electronically
- Firm A can thereby verify that the payment was made by their cash correspondent, as instructed.

Updating of Books & Records

- Firm A updates its books & records to reflect the fact that cash was paid to Party G in settlement of the margin call
- Firm A's running balance for this repo trade is as reflected in Table 5.10:

TABLE 5.10 Current cash & collateral balances

Date	Current Cash & Collateral Balances – Firm A's Perspective					
	Cash			Bond Collateral (Quantity)		
	Taken	Given	Balance	Taken	Given	Balance
June 8th	+USD 30,320,428.12	0	+USD 30,320,428.12	0	–USD 30,000,000	–USD 30,000,000
June 9th	0	USD 182,778.83	+USD 30,137,649.29	0	0	–USD 30,000,000

Reconciliation

- Firm A successfully conducts a *nostro reconciliation* by comparing its books & records versus its cash correspondent's statement.

At this point in time the exposed party's net exposure has been mitigated.

The above-mentioned activities are repeated at the frequency stated in the legal documentation.

EVENING OF FRIDAY 9TH JUNE 2017

Marking-to-Market

- identify the current market price of the bond collateral, as at close-of-business (see Table 5.11).

TABLE 5.11 Marking-to-market

Bond Collateral	M2M Date (Close-of-Business)	Current Market (Clean) Price
Issuer ABC 4.35% Bonds August 1st 2030	June 9th 2017	99.71%

Portfolio Reconciliation

- to confirm that the trade population is the same between the two firms:
  - Firm A transmits details of all currently open repo trades with Party G, to the triResolve portfolio reconciliation service
  - Party G transmits its list of repo trades to triResolve
- triResolve advises Firm A and Party G that the lists match one another.

MORNING OF MONDAY 12TH JUNE 2017

Calculation of Exposure

- identify the current value of bond collateral (see Table 5.12) …
  - current M2M price (clean or dirty), plus
  - (if clean price) current value of accrued interest
  - less haircut or initial margin.

TABLE 5.12　Calculation of exposure #1

Calculation of Exposure #1: Bond Collateral		
Component	**Detail**	
Security Description	Issuer ABC 4.35% Bonds August 1st 2030	
Security Identifier	ISIN: XX1234567891	
Quantity	USD 30,000,000.00	
Price	99.71%	
Gross Value		USD 29,913,000.00
Accrued Days　plus Accrued Interest	311	USD 1,127,375.00
Current Market Value		USD 31,040,375.00
Haircut Percentage　less Haircut Value	2.5%	(USD 776,009.38)
Current Collateral Value		**USD 30,264,365.62**

- identify the current value of cash amount borrowed (see Table 5.13) …
  - original cash amount borrowed, plus
  - repo interest to date

TABLE 5.13　Calculation of exposure #2

Calculation of Exposure #2: Cash Lent or Borrowed Including Value of Cash Settled Margin Calls	
Component	**Detail**
Repo Interest Rate	2.42%
Days of Repo Interest To Date	4
Repo Interest Payer	Firm A, London
Cash Amount Borrowed	USD 30,320,428.12
plus Repo Interest Value To Date	USD 8152.83
less Margin Calls Settled in Cash To Date	(USD 182,778.83)
Current Value of Cash Amount Borrowed	**USD 30,145,802.12**

- the difference in 1) the current value of bond collateral, and 2) the current value of cash, is the gross exposure amount (see Table 5.14)
- if any threshold or minimum transfer amount has been agreed between Firm A and Party G, the gross exposure amount must exceed those values, if a valid margin call is to be made by either party

TABLE 5.14   Gross and net exposure

Determining Gross and Net Exposure, and Margin Call Direction			
Component		Detail	
Current Value of Cash Amount Borrowed		USD 30,145,802.12	
less Current Collateral Value		USD 30,264,365.62	
Exposed Party	Gross Exposure	Firm A, London	USD 118,563.50
Minimum Transfer Amount		(USD 150,000.00)	Impact
Exposed Party	**Net Exposure**	**Firm A, London**	**No Call**

- although on this day Firm A has an exposure of USD 118,563.50, Firm A cannot issue a valid margin call to Party G as the exposure amount is less than the *minimum transfer amount*. Firm A contacts Party G to confirm that no margin call is applicable on this day.

Updating of Books & Records

- as no margin call is applicable on this day, Firm A records zero transfer of assets in its record of running balance, as reflected in Table 5.15:

TABLE 5.15   Current cash & collateral balances

Current Cash & Collateral Balances – Firm A's Perspective						
Date	Cash			Bond Collateral (Quantity)		
	Taken	Given	Balance	Taken	Given	Balance
June 8th	+USD 30,320,428.12	0	+USD 30,320,428.12	0	–USD 30,000,000	–USD 30,000,000
June 9th	0	USD 182,778.83	+USD 30,137,649.29	0	0	–USD 30,000,000
June 12th	0	0	+USD 30,137,649.29	0	0	–USD 30,000,000

At this point in time the exposed party's net exposure has validly not been mitigated, due to the minimum transfer amount.

The above-mentioned activities are repeated at the frequency stated in the legal documentation.

EVENING OF MONDAY 12TH JUNE 2017

Marking-to-Market

- identify the current market price of the bond collateral, as at close-of-business (see Table 5.16):

TABLE 5.16 Marking-to-market

Bond Collateral	M2M Date (Close-of-Business)	Current Market (Clean) Price
Issuer ABC 4.35% Bonds August 1st 2030	June 12th 2017	100.09%

Portfolio Reconciliation

- to confirm that the trade population is the same between the two firms:
  - Firm A transmits details of all currently open repo trades with Party G, to the triResolve portfolio reconciliation service
  - Party G transmits its list of repo trades to triResolve
- triResolve advises Firm A and Party G that the lists match one another.

MORNING OF TUESDAY 13TH JUNE 2017

Calculation of Exposure

- identify the current value of bond collateral (see Table 5.17) ...
  - current M2M price (clean or dirty), plus
  - (if clean price) current value of accrued interest
  - less haircut or initial margin

TABLE 5.17 Calculation of exposure #1

Calculation of Exposure #1: Bond Collateral			
Component		Detail	
	Security Description	Issuer ABC 4.35% Bonds August 1st 2030	
	Security Identifier	ISIN: XX1234567891	
	Quantity	USD 30,000,000.00	
	Price	100.09%	
	Gross Value		USD 30,027,000.00
Accrued Days	plus Accrued Interest	312	USD 1,131,000.00
	Current Market Value		USD 31,158,000.00
Haircut Percentage	less Haircut Value	2.5%	(USD 778,950.00)
Current Collateral Value			USD 30,379,050.00

- identify the current value of cash amount borrowed (see Table 5.18) ...
  - original cash amount borrowed, plus
  - repo interest to date

TABLE 5.18   Calculation of exposure #2

Calculation of Exposure #2: Cash Lent or Borrowed Including Value of Cash Settled Margin Calls	
Component	Detail
Repo Interest Rate	2.42%
Days of Repo Interest To Date	5
Repo Interest Payer	Firm A, London
Cash Amount Borrowed	USD 30,320,428.12
plus Repo Interest Value To Date	USD 10,191.03
less Margin Calls Settled in Cash To Date	(USD 182,778.83)
Current Value of Cash Amount Borrowed	**USD 30,147,840.32**

- the difference in 1) the current value of bond collateral, and 2) the current value of cash, is the gross exposure amount (see Table 5.19)
- if any threshold or minimum transfer amount has been agreed between Firm A and Party G, the gross exposure amount must exceed those values, if a valid margin call is to be made by either party

TABLE 5.19   Gross and net exposure

Determining Gross and Net Exposure, and Margin Call Direction			
Component		Detail	
Current Value of Cash Amount Borrowed			USD 30,147,840.32
less Current Collateral Value			USD 30,379,050.00
Exposed Party	Gross Exposure	Firm A, London	USD 231,209.68
	Minimum Transfer Amount	(USD 150,000.00)	No impact
Exposed Party	**Net Exposure**	**Firm A, London**	**USD 231,209.68**

- as the current value of collateral is in excess of the current value of cash amount borrowed, Firm A is the exposed party.

Issuance/Receipt of Margin Call

- Firm A communicates their margin call to Party G
  - which must be received by the predefined deadline
- Party G checks the accuracy of the margin call, and agrees.

Proposing Margin Call Settlement Method

- Party G decides in which form to satisfy the margin call, and chooses to provide cash
- Party G communicates their decision to settle the margin call in cash
- Firm A verifies that cash is acceptable, by reference to the legal documentation.

Issuance of Settlement Instruction to Settle Margin Call

- Party G issues a cash settlement instruction to its USD cash correspondent
  - by the cash correspondent's daily deadline (does not require matching by counterparty)
- Firm A issues a *funds preadvice* to its USD cash correspondent, in an attempt to ensure it receives good value on the incoming funds.

Settlement

- on value date of the margin call payment:
  - settlement will occur if Party G has adequate means to pay at their cash correspondent (whether credit cash balance or collateralised overdraft facility)
- Party G's USD cash correspondent makes payment as instructed by Party G
- Party G's cash correspondent updates Party G's bank account as a result of the payment
- Firm A's USD cash correspondent receives payment (as expected), and credits the account of Firm A.

Advice of Settlement

- Firm A's cash correspondent issues a bank statement to Firm A, or Firm A accesses the statement electronically
- Firm A can thereby verify that the payment was received by their cash correspondent.

Updating of Books & Records

- Firm A updates its books & records to reflect the fact that cash was received from Party G in settlement of the margin call
- Firm A's running balance for this repo trade is as reflected in Table 5.20:

TABLE 5.20   Current cash & collateral balances

	Current Cash & Collateral Balances – Firm A's Perspective					
Date	**Cash**			**Bond Collateral (Quantity)**		
	Taken	Given	Balance	Taken	Given	Balance
June 8th	+USD 30,320,428.12	0	+USD 30,320,428.12	0	−USD 30,000,000	−USD 30,000,000
June 9th	0	USD 182,778.83	+USD 30,137,649.29	0	0	−USD 30,000,000
June 12th	0	0	+USD 30,137,649.29	0	0	−USD 30,000,000
June 13th	+USD 231,209.68	0	+USD 30,368,858.97	0	0	−USD 30,000,000

Reconciliation

- Firm A successfully conducts a nostro reconciliation by comparing its books & records versus its cash correspondent's statement.

At this point in time the exposed party's net exposure has been mitigated.

The above-mentioned activities are continued until the business day prior to the closing value date.

Regarding the margin calls described in this part of the repo trade lifecycle, it should be noted that:

- rather than issuing margin calls for an exact amount of net exposure (as is shown within this chapter), it is common practice to apply *rounding* (either rounding up or down to a round cash value, such as USD 50,000.00) to the net exposure amount
- as cash has been used to settle the particular margin calls, a *rebate rate* will usually be negotiated between Firm A and Party G, in which:
  - the recipient of the cash margin will reinvest that cash with the intention of earning the current money market interest rate
  - the payer of the cash will receive the rebate rate from its counterparty
- if the recipients of margin calls had chosen to settle by delivery of bonds (rather than cash), and assuming that the legal documentation permitted such a choice:
  - the relevant quantity of bonds would need to be identified taking account of the appropriate *bond deliverable quantity*
- the bonds would need to be marked-to-market each day, as part of the assessment of current collateral values.

5.6 SETTLEMENT OF CLOSING LEG

The Repo Trade Lifecycle

1. Pre-Trading
2. Trade Execution
3. Pre-Settlement
4. Settlement of Opening Leg
5. Throughout Lifetime of Trade
6. Settlement of Closing Leg

In order to facilitate timely settlement of the *closing leg* of the repo trade, the following step should occur prior to the closing value date (viewed from the perspective of Firm A, unless stated otherwise):

Closing Leg Settlement Instructions

- no later than two days prior to the closing value date, for the closing leg of the repo, Firm A issues a DvP settlement instruction to the CSD (see Table 5.21), covering
  - the cash amount borrowed, plus repo interest, versus the original bond quantity
- *to verify the content of the closing leg settlement instruction, please refer to the trade confirmation within the 'Pre-Settlement' section of The Repo Trade Lifecycle*

TABLE 5.21 Settlement instruction: closing leg

Settlement Instruction	
Component	Detail
From	Firm A, London
To	CSD T
Date	June 12th 2017
Subject	Settlement Instruction
Our Reference	R0059397
Our Account	66627
Receive / Deliver	Receive
Quantity	USD 30,000,000.00
ISIN	XX1234567891
Cash Countervalue	USD 30,334,695.57
Value Date	June 15th 2017
Settlement Method	DvP
Counterparty Account	99034

- Firm A's instruction is matched by Party G's instruction.

Note: the return to the original owner of any cash or bonds received as a result of margin calls during the repo trade's lifetime is actioned separately.

The following two steps occur at the CSD, followed by internal steps, all of which should occur on the value date of the closing leg (viewed from the perspective of Firm A, unless stated otherwise).

Settlement

- timely settlement at the CSD requires all the following to be actioned:
    - settlement instructions to be matched
    - value date to be reached
    - seller to have securities available in its account
    - buyer to have cash (or credit line) available in its account
- the closing leg of the repo trade settles on its due date (the closing leg value date).

Advice of Settlement

- the CSD transmits an advice of settlement to Firm A (see Table 5.22)
    - advising that the bonds were successfully received against payment of cash on the closing leg value date

TABLE 5.22   Advice of settlement: closing leg

Advice of Settlement	
Component	Detail
From	CSD T
To	Firm A, London
Date	June 15th 2017
Subject	Advice of Settlement
Your Reference	R0059397
Your Account	66627
Receive / Deliver	Receive
Quantity	USD 30,000,000.00
ISIN	XX1234567891
Cash Countervalue	USD 30,334,695.57
Settlement Date	June 15th 2017
Settlement Method	DvP
Counterparty Account	99034

Note: the CSD reports the fact that settlement has occurred by use of the term 'settlement date'.

Receipt of the Advice of Settlement triggers the following actions internally within Firm A:

Updating of Books & Records

- internally, Firm A updates the relevant trade record, showing …
- cash was paid & bonds were received on the closing value date.

Reconciliation

- Firm A successfully conducts two reconciliations:
  - a depot reconciliation (comparison of books & records versus CSD's statement of securities holdings) showing that the bonds have been returned to Firm A's securities account at the CSD
  - a nostro reconciliation (comparison of books & records versus CSD's statement of cash balances) showing that the cash has been paid from Firm A's cash account at the CSD.

Once any cash or securities received as a result of margin calls have been returned to their original owner, the repo trade is fully settled with no remaining counterparty exposure.

PART 2

Sale & Repurchase (Repo) Trades and Collateral – Stock-Based Classic Repo Trades

> *Definition of a stock-based classic repo trade: the temporary loan of a specific quantity of a specific security, to a borrower, against receipt of cash, for return at a later date.*

This section focuses on one party's requirement to borrow securities (as opposed to cash); this is known as a ***stock-based repo***.

This transaction type is still regarded as a classic repo transaction, but the motivation for executing the trade is for one party (the securities borrower) to temporarily borrow a specific quantity of a particular security; such a motivation is identical to a securities borrowing transaction, apart from the governing legal document is a repo legal agreement (***GMRA***), rather than a securities lending & borrowing agreement (***GMSLA***).

The normal underlying motivation for a firm that wishes to borrow securities is the need for that firm to satisfy an existing delivery commitment. For example, a firm may have sold securities which the firm cannot (yet) settle, meaning that 1) there will be a delay in the firm receiving the sale proceeds, and/or 2) that the buyer is a client of the firm that requires timely settlement of its purchases, and/or 3) the buying counterparty may be threatening to take the ultimate measure relating to delivery failures, which is to effect a '***buy-in***'.

Although the normal method of executing a borrowing of securities is via the transaction type of ***securities lending & borrowing***, if a repo legal agreement exists between two firms then securities borrowing can be negotiated in the form of a stock-based repo.

The motivation to execute most repo trades is the fact that one party needs to borrow cash, whilst its counterparty is long of cash and is looking to earn repo interest on a collateralised basis; therefore, cash-based repo trades are executed under the protection (for both parties) of the GMRA. The same GMRA may be used for stock-based repo trades, as the assets involved are the same as for a cash-based repo, namely 1) securities, and 2) cash.

Cash-based repo trades are synonymous with the term **general collateral**, where the cash lender accepts any **eligible collateral**, providing it satisfies the previously documented quality criteria; in other words, the cash lender does not specify a particular ISIN or a particular quantity of the particular ISIN. In contrast, the borrower in a stock-based repo does require a particular quantity of a particular ISIN, as that is what the borrower requires to satisfy a delivery commitment.

For cash-based repo trades, the repo rate reflects the nature of general collateral. By comparison, for stock-based repo trades the repo rate is appreciably lower than the general collateral repo rate, reflecting the fact that the cash lender must pay for the privilege of borrowing the securities, therefore the cash borrower pays less of a repo rate on the cash received.

The parties in a stock-based repo are:

- the securities lender/seller/cash borrower:
  - the deliverer of the lent securities
  - the taker of cash
- the securities borrower/buyer/cash lender:
  - the receiver of the borrowed securities
  - the giver of cash.

If a particular security is in high demand (by potential borrowers) but short supply, the repo rate will reflect the demand and will be forced substantially lower than the repo rate for general collateral; this is known as a **special repo**. If the demand is exceptionally high, securities borrowers will accept a lower and lower repo rate with the possibility that the repo rate will go into negative territory.

In order to focus on the reasons for lending and borrowing securities, and many other characteristics of this subject, please refer to Part 3 'Securities Lending & Borrowing and Collateral'.

CHAPTER 7

Sale & Repurchase (Repo) Trades and Collateral – Repo Trade Variations

In addition to classic repo trades executed on a *bilateral* basis, a range of options exist as to 1) how repo trades can be executed, and/or 2) the method of administering the operational aspects of a repo trade following trade execution.

Within this chapter, the following options are described:

- Buy/Sell-Backs
- Tri-Party Repo
- Delivery by Value
- Repo Central Clearing
- GC Pooling, and
- RepoClear.

7.1 BUY/SELL BACKS (OVERVIEW)

Another form of repo (beside classic repo) are buy/sell backs (BSB) which may be documented (as per a classic repo) or undocumented. Undocumented BSBs are described in this part of the book.

Fundamental differences between classic repos and undocumented BSBs are that:

- classic repos:
  - are executed under the protection of the *GMRA*
  - are single trades comprising two legs, namely the *opening leg* and the *closing leg*
  - maintain a link between their opening leg and closing leg throughout the trade's lifetime, and consequently the daily *mark-to-market* process gives rise to *exposures* and resultant *margin calls*,

- buy/sell backs:
  - comprise two legally independent trades in which the opening and closing legs, which are traded at the same time, are also treated operationally as two separate trades from the outset
  - has no link between the two legs and as a result the mark-to-market process and margin calls are not applicable.

The motivation for undertaking BSB trades is usually the same as for classic repo trades. In terms of cash calculations, BSBs are similar, but not identical, to classic repos; see Sub-section 7.1.1 'Trade Monetary Calculations'.

In terms of trade direction, the following terminology may be used:

- Buy/Sell Back: the trade direction is stated from the cash lender's perspective, where bonds are being purchased in the opening leg, and sold back in the closing leg
- Sell/Buy Back: the trade direction is stated from the cash borrower's perspective, where bonds are being sold in the opening leg, and bought back in the closing leg.

The former terminology (buy/sell back) is used in this book.

7.1.1 Trade Monetary Calculations

In a BSB, the opening leg is calculated in the same way as for a classic repo. In a particular classic repo trade, assume that the opening leg value of a bond, inclusive of accrued interest (without margin or haircut applied) is USD 30,071,791.67, calculated as in Table 7.1:

TABLE 7.1 Repo trade capture

Repo Trade Capture	
Trade Component	**Trade Detail**
Transaction Type	Classic Repo Securities Sale
Counterparty	Party M
Trade Date	June 10th
Opening Value Date	June 11th
Closing Value Date	June 18th
Repo Rate	3.42%
Collateral	
Issue	Issuer ABC 4.35% Bonds August 1st 2030
Quantity	USD 29,000,000.00
Price	99.95%
Gross Value	USD 28,985,500.00
Accrued Days	310
plus Accrued Interest	USD 1,086,291.67
Net Value	**USD 30,071,791.67**

The closing leg of this classic repo would amount to a payment to the cash lender of USD 30,091,789.41, the components of which are:

- original borrowed cash: USD 30,071,791.67
- plus repo interest: USD   19,997.74
- **total:**   **USD 30,091,789.41**

To take the same trade, but to treat it as a BSB:

- opening leg cash value:
  - original borrowed cash: USD 30,071,791.67
- closing leg cash value:
  - bond price: 99.934374%   USD 28,980,968.58
  - accrued days: 317
  - accrued interest: USD   1,110,820.83
  - **total:**   **USD 30,091,789.41**

The closing leg cash value calculation is determined by adding the repo interest (USD 19,997.74) to the original cash amount borrowed (USD 30,071,791.67), which produces the final settlement amount of USD 30,091,789.41. Then, from that figure is to be deducted the value of accrued interest to the closing value date (USD 1,110,820.83), leaving a result being USD 28,980,968.58; that figure must be divided by the bond quantity (USD 29,000,000) in order to derive the clean price (99.934374%) of the closing leg.

In summary, although the closing leg cash settlement amount in a BSB is the same as for a classic repo, it is represented differently as the closing leg is expressed as a percentage (clean) price plus accrued interest. Furthermore, repo interest is not shown as a separate component and is factored into the closing leg clean price, and the accrued interest on the bond is calculated to the closing value date.

7.1.2 Other Characteristics of Buy/Sell Backs

In addition to those aspects mentioned earlier, the particular features of BSB compared to classic repos are as follows:

- only 'term' trades are applicable ('open' BSB trades are not possible) due to the nature of the closing leg which is traded at a specific price for a specified closing value date
- because BSBs are two standalone trades, there is no link between the opening and closing legs and consequently there is no requirement for marking-to-market or to make margin calls or to give or to take collateral
- as the opening leg and closing leg are disassociated trades, *collateral substitution* is not relevant. However, the parties may agree to close-out the existing trade, and to replace that trade with a new trade on the same basic terms (repo rate and closing date) using the new collateral

- if, during the lifetime of the BSB, the bond pays a coupon, the closing leg cash amount is adjusted by the value of the coupon payment. (The value of the coupon payment is not paid to the cash borrower on coupon payment date, as it is in a classic repo)
- as for classic repo, a margin or haircut may be included in a BSB trade.

From a legal documentation perspective, Annex 1 of the GMRA (2011 version), allows inclusion or exclusion of BSBs.

In conclusion, some firms execute BSBs because they are operationally simpler than classic repos, due to the fact the two legs are treated as distinct buy and sell trades, and without concerns regarding open trades, marking-to-market, margin calls and collateral movements.

PART 2

7.2 TRI-PARTY REPO (OVERVIEW)

Classic repos involve two trading parties; such repos may be labelled 'bilateral' or 'bi-party' repos. A particular variation of a classic repo is the inclusion of a third party known as a *tri-party agent*, being one of the parties in a *tri-party repo*.

A tri-party repo is a classic repo in which the two trading parties employ the services of a third party whose role is to administer the operational aspects of the repo during its lifetime.

In a bilateral repo, the two trading parties are directly responsible for carrying out a range of operational duties, including:

- payment of cash lent
- delivery of securities *collateral*
- *marking-to-market*
- applying current value of *accrued interest*
- applying *haircut* or *initial margin*
- determining *exposures*
- making or receiving *margin calls*
- settling margin calls
- *collateral substitution*, and
- making or receiving payments of *coupon*.

In a tri-party repo, it is those operational tasks that become the responsibility of the tri-party agent.

For some firms that wish to execute repo trades, the administrative task of managing multiple concurrent repo trades, with each repo having one or many pieces of collateral, on a day-to-day basis, requires a significant extent of operational effort and therefore cost. Such firms may need a large number of experienced repo staff in order to manage such a sizeable task, and specifically designed systems need to be utilised.

Two parties that wish to execute a repo trade choose whether to administer the trade on a bilateral or a tri-party basis. Where tri-party, a three-way contract must be put in place (before execution of a trade) between the two trading parties and the tri-party agent; this contract is specifically a *service level agreement* (SLA) that defines the service the agent will provide to both trading parties. The agent remains completely neutral at all times.

7.2.1 Tri-Party Trade Processing

The steps involved in a tri-party repo are depicted in Figure 7.1:

PART 2

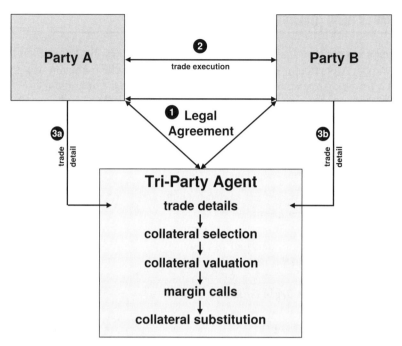

FIGURE 7.1 Tri-party repo processing

Step 1: a legal agreement is signed between the two trading parties and the tri-party agent

Step 2: a repo trade is executed directly between two trading parties, who agree to administer the trade as a tri-party repo

Step 3: both trading parties transmit their trade details to the tri-party agent, following which:

- the agent must ensure that trade details are fully matched
- the agent captures details of the trade internally
- the agent ensures the cash lender has adequate cash to remit to the cash borrower
- the agent ensures the cash borrower has an adequate quantity of *eligible collateral*
- the agent effects movement of cash and bonds on the opening value date, typically on a *delivery versus payment* basis
- during the lifetime of the repo, the agent:
  - revalues (via mark-to-market) the collateral at the agreed frequency and determines whether either party has exposure, and
  - automatically processes margin calls (by adding or deducting collateral) in order to rebalance the collateral versus the current value of cash borrowed, and
  - can normally identify whether bonds (currently utilised as collateral) are required for use by the cash borrower in a different transaction, through the receipt of

settlement instructions from the cash borrower. Consequently, the agent is able to determine when collateral substitution is necessary and to effect substitution automatically.

It is important to note that the cash lender is typically able to define which grouping of collateral is to be regarded as eligible collateral; such groupings are often known as *collateral baskets*. For example, the credit rating limits of bond issuers may be defined (e.g. no lower than a rating of AA), and margin or haircut levels can be stated.

7.2.2 Advantages of Tri-Party Repo

As well as the savings in administrative effort, tri-party repo provides additional benefits (compared with bilateral repo), including:

- optimal use of securities inventory; in some cases, the tri-party agent can select collateral automatically ('auto-select') from the cash borrower's inventory, or the cash borrower may choose to select the collateral itself
- reduced counterparty risk, as the collateral is held by a neutral agent rather than the counterparty to the trade
- outsourced risk control, as marking-to-market, exposure management and the settlement of margin calls are the responsibility of the tri-party agent.

7.2.3 Tri-Party Agents

Amongst those firms that offer tri-party repo services are the two *international central securities depositories*, namely *Euroclear Bank* (Brussels) and *Clearstream Banking* (Luxembourg).

Additionally, custodian banks such as BNY Mellon and J.P. Morgan offer tri-party services.

7.2.4 Updating Books & Records

From the cash borrower's perspective, the securities given as collateral in a tri-party repo are actually removed from the cash borrower's account.

Consequently (and in parallel with cash and collateral movements in bilateral repos), it is recommended that the cash borrower's books & records are updated with:

- on the opening value date: the incoming cash and the outgoing movement of collateral
- during the lifetime of the repo: any incoming or outgoing movement of cash collateral or securities collateral, and
- on the closing value date: the outgoing cash and the return of the collateral

immediately upon being informed of such movements by the tri-party agent.

PART 2

7.3 DELIVERY BY VALUE (OVERVIEW)

One specific type of repo is known as a 'DBV', meaning *delivery by value*. This term means that a securities delivery will be made according to, and in exchange for, a specified cash value.

DBVs are specific to the *Crest* system, which is operated by Euroclear UK & Ireland, the *central securities depository* for the UK, Ireland, Jersey, Guernsey and the Isle of Man.

Following the normal daily trade processing within Crest, a firm may have a cash deficit within its Crest account. At the same time, other firms may have a cash surplus. DBVs are a mechanism used by firms to swap cash on a collateralised basis, within a short time frame. Note: Crest operates cash accounts in EUR and USD as well as in GBP.

7.3.1 DBV Trade Execution

Two Crest participants, one being short of cash in a particular currency, the other being long of cash, agree to execute a DBV directly whereby the cash lender will instruct Crest to pay cash and to receive securities as collateral by DBV, whilst its counterparty will instruct Crest to receive cash and to deliver securities by DBV.

The terms of the trade include:

- currency and cash amount
- trade date
- opening value date
- closing value date (may be 'overnight' or 'term')
- repo rate
- margin (if applicable)
- collateral eligibility criteria.

7.3.2 Post-Execution Process

Following trade execution, each party inputs to Crest a specific DBV *settlement instruction* (to settle either *DvP* or *FoP*), for the particular cash amount lent or borrowed, including the collateral category as agreed at trade execution. Collateral categories are known as *DBV Baskets*, for example all equities, *FTSE-100* only, all *gilts*. Crest compares the instructions to ensure they match.

At the appropriate time, Crest automatically selects the relevant collateral from the cash borrower's securities account, according to the selected DBV Basket, as depicted in Figure 7.2. Because the timing of the DBV process occurs after normal settlement processing, securities in the cash borrower's Crest account will not be used for other purposes on that day, and are therefore safe to use as collateral in the DBV.

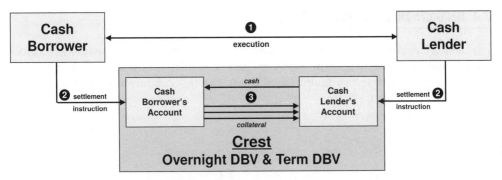

FIGURE 7.2   Overnight DBV and Term DBV

The cash and collateral are moved immediately, and in the case of an *Overnight DBV*, the DBV is automatically closed the next business day at which point the cash and securities assets are returned to their original owner.

7.3.3 Term DBVs

Prior to July 2011, the only form of DBV has been the overnight type. However since that date, Crest has introduced an additional form of DBV known as a *Term DBV*, where it is possible to state a future closing value date (other than overnight) up to two years forward. Under Term DBVs, the collateral remains with the cash lender throughout the lifetime of the DBV (unless *collateral substitution* is necessary). The introduction of Term DBVs removes the historic requirement to rekey term transactions in the form of Overnight DBVs on a daily basis.

Where two trading firms agree to execute a term borrowing over (say) 1 month, they have a choice of using the Overnight DBV facility, or the Term DBV facility. Even though the Term DBV may be a more obvious choice to administer a term collateralised borrowing, some parties may prefer to use the overnight DBV. The fact that an overnight DBV is automatically closed each day enables the collateral to be 'refreshed' each day, meaning that Crest selects collateral anew each day which may suit some firms.

Under a Term DBV, whenever Crest receives an instruction to deliver securities out of the Crest participant's account (e.g. following a sale), Crest checks whether the securities in question are being used as collateral in a Term DBV. If so, Crest effects collateral substitution automatically.

7.3.4 Changes to Cash or Collateral

Should a Term DBV user wish to change the cash amount or the collateral during the DBV's lifetime, Crest caters for this via input to Crest of a particular type of instruction known as a Term DBV Adjustment.

7.4 REPO CENTRAL CLEARING (OVERVIEW)

For *over the counter* (OTC) products, which result in a firm having outstanding trades directly with market participant counterparties on a bilateral basis, the firm has ongoing *counterparty risk* with a multitude of counterparties, concurrently. Such a situation is represented by Figure 7.3:

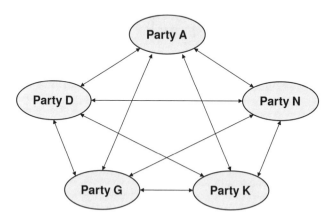

FIGURE 7.3   Bilateral trading and ongoing counterparty credit risk

Such counterparty credit risk requires active monitoring and, for some products (e.g. *repos*, *securities lending & borrowing*, *OTC derivatives*), collateral is given or taken in order to mitigate counterparty credit risk. Under such circumstances, a huge amount of work for all firms is necessary on a daily basis in order to keep risks to a minimum and to maintain proper control over a firm's assets and *exposures*.

Such a situation in those markets can be overcome by use of central clearing via a single *central counterparty* (CCP), as per Figure 7.4:

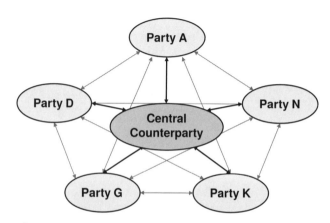

FIGURE 7.4   Central counterparty

CCPs become the seller to every buyer, and the buyer to every seller; the primary risk which CCPs seek to address is counterparty risk. The CCP therefore sits between two market participants, one of whom has sold whilst the other has purchased. A firm's true counterparty is the CCP; whether a firm knows the identity of the original market participant or not, the CCP becomes the counterparty and will remain the firm's counterparty for the lifetime of the transaction. The legal process of reassigning a trade executed bilaterally between Firm A and Firm B, in which the CCP is interposed between the two firms, is *novation.*

The CCP must remain *market risk neutral* at all times, meaning that they must maintain a zero position in terms of both cash and securities. The CCP therefore sits between both original parties to a trade.

Where a member of the CCP has executed multiple trades which are novated to the CCP, the CCP will attempt to reduce multiple trades in their original state (gross trades) through its netting process, which will result in a net settlement obligation (NSO) to be settled. Therefore, the single NSO represents all the gross exposures; consequently, once the net settlement obligation has settled, that has in effect settled all the gross trades to which it relates.

By way of an example, imagine that Firm A has executed:

- 5 repos in Bond X with a variety of bilateral counterparties, requiring delivery of a total quantity of USD 50,000,000 bonds versus USD 60,000,000.00 cash, and
- 4 *reverse repos* in the same bond with a variety of bilateral counterparties, requiring receipt of a total quantity of USD 40,000,000 bonds versus USD 51,000,000.00 cash.

These 9 trades executed by Firm A are represented in the first 5 columns of Table 7.2:

TABLE 7.2   Example of multilateral clearing via a central counterparty

Example of Multilateral Clearing via a Central Counterparty						
Trade #	Firm	Counterparty	Bonds Receivable (millions)	Bonds Deliverable (millions)	New Counterparty	Net (millions)
1a		B	-	USD 10		
2a		C	-	USD 10		
3a		E	-	USD 10		
4a		B	-	USD 10		
5a	A	E	-	USD 10	Central Counterparty	– USD 10
6a		D	USD 10	-		
7a		C	USD 10	-		
8a		E	USD 10	-		
9a		D	USD 10	-		
1b	B	A	USD 10	-		+ USD 20
4b		A	USD 10	-		

(continued)

TABLE 7.2 Example of multilateral clearing via a central counterparty (*continued*)

Trade #	Firm	Counterparty	Bonds Receivable (millions)	Bonds Deliverable (millions)	New Counterparty	Net (millions)
Example of Multilateral Clearing via a Central Counterparty						
2b	C	A	USD 10	-	Central Counterparty	0
7b	C	A	-	USD 10		
6b	D	A	-	USD 10		–USD 20
9b	D	A	-	USD 10		
3b	E	A	USD 10	-		+ USD 10
5b	E	A	USD 10	-		
8b	E	A	-	USD 10		
					Total Net at CCP	0

(Note: Table 7.2 reflects only the bond quantity in each repo trade; in reality, the cash values of each repo trade will also be factored into the netting process.)

Without these trades being novated to a CCP, all 9 trades would have been cleared on a bilateral basis between Firm A and their respective counterparties; under such circumstances, there would be a possibility of bilateral netting (that is, only for the trades executed by Firm A with each of the counterparties). Without any bilateral netting, risk management on all 9 trades would have been necessary, with potential margin calls to be made and settled with each counterparty until the closing value date of each repo trade.

However, if all 9 trades are novated to a CCP (as shown in columns 6 and 7), the CCPs multilateral netting process will reduce as many gross trades as possible to net positions, as shown in column 7 specifically). For Firm A, multilateral netting will reduce 9 gross repo trades to a net settlement obligation consisting of an outgoing delivery quantity of USD 10,000,000 bonds versus an incoming cash amount of USD 9,000,000.00.

Central clearing has been in place for many years in some countries and for some financial products. For example, in many electronic *stock exchanges*, the execution of an equities trade by a stock exchange member firm automatically results in the member firm's counterparty being the central counterparty (sometimes known as the *clearing house*). Central clearing has also been a standard feature of trading in *exchange-traded derivatives*, such as *futures* and *options*. There is a continuing trend away from the conventional bilateral model in favour of the central clearing model. For example, as a result of the 2008 *Global Financial Crisis*, trades in *standardised OTC derivatives* must be centrally cleared; see Part 4C 'OTC Derivatives and Collateral: Regulatory Change and The Future of Collateral' for details.

The most fundamental of benefits of the central clearing model are:

- reduced counterparty risk
    - instead of a firm having traditional counterparty risk with a normal bilateral counterparty, the firm's counterparty is (or becomes via novation) the CCP, which is required to operate under stringent regulation
- multilateral netting
    - from a purely settlement perspective, netting of multiple gross trades has always been regarded as a benefit (cheaper and more efficient), as settlement of the resultant net values of securities and cash in a single settlement effectively settles all the original (gross) trades
    - from a risk management perspective, once netting has occured, risk management is able to be applied to the single net position rather than to the original (gross) trades
    - although bilateral netting between a firm and its bilateral counterparty is regarded as beneficial in comparison with settlement of trades on a gross basis, it does not have the reach that multilateral netting has, as the latter involves two or more parties.

In Europe, existing CCPs (at the time of writing) for repo include:

- BME Clearing (formerly MEFF) for repos in Spanish Government bonds
- CC&G (Cassa di Compensazione e Garanzia) for repos in Italian Government bonds
- Eurex Clearing for repos in a variety of European Government and corporate bonds
- LCH SA RepoClear for repos in French, Italian and Spanish Government bonds
- RepoClear Ltd for repos in a range of European Government bonds.

In summary:

- without central clearing of trades, each individual repo trade remains open with a particular market counterparty, and exposures per counterparty must be mitigated through the giving or taking of collateral on a daily basis, until settlement of the closing leg
- with central clearing, bilateral counterparty risk disappears and each party provides collateral to (or receives from) the CCP daily, based upon that party's net exposure.

7.5 GC POOLING (OVERVIEW)

GC Pooling is a particular repo and collateral management service provided by *Eurex Repo*, *Eurex Clearing* and *Clearstream Banking*.

The GC Pooling service covers trading, clearing and settlement of cash-driven *general collateral* (GC) in standardised *collateral baskets* of *bonds* and *equity* tradable in EUR, USD, GBP and CHF. At the time of writing, over 100 banks and other institutions are GC Pooling members.

Firms are required to participate in the clearing process at Eurex Clearing, either:

- as a member (directly), or by
- utilising the services of a member (indirectly).

7.5.1 The GC Pooling Trading/Clearing/Settlement Process

The service provides anonymous repo trading, clearing via a *central counterparty*, and settlement via a *central securities depository*; the trading to settlement flow is represented in Figure 7.5:

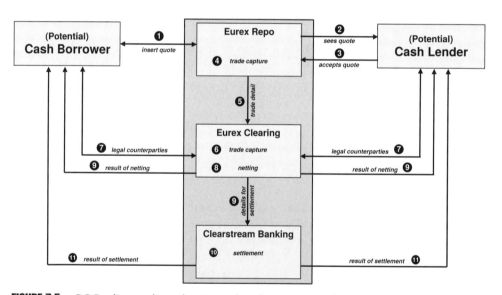

FIGURE 7.5   GC Pooling trading, clearing and settlement processing

Step 1: a party requiring to borrow or to lend cash via repo enters its requirements into the Eurex Repo trading platform, stating:

- they wish to borrow (or to lend)
- currency & amount

- term, for example:
  - Overnight (opening value date same day, closing value date next day)
  - Tom Next (opening value date next day, closing value date next day + 1)
  - Spot Next (opening value date next day + 1, closing value date next day + 2)
- required repo rate
- required collateral basket

Step 2: Eurex Repo allows its members to view the requirements anonymously

Step 3: a member accepts the cash borrower's terms, and becomes the cash lender

Step 4: Eurex Repo captures the details of both trades (cash borrower to counterparty Eurex Clearing, and cash lender to counterparty Eurex Clearing)

Step 5: Eurex Repo passes the trade details to *Eurex Clearing*

Step 6: Eurex Clearing captures the details of both trades

Step 7: Eurex Clearing is *central counterparty* (CCP) to both cash borrower and cash lender

Step 8: Eurex Clearing carries out netting for both parties and produces a net settlement obligation for each party

Step 9: Eurex Clearing passes details of the net settlement obligation to Clearstream Banking

Step 10: Clearstream Banking carries out settlement of the net settlement obligation on a *delivery versus payment* (DvP) basis

Step 11: Clearstream Banking reports the result of settlement to both cash borrower and cash lender.

Note: the role of a central counterparty, clearing and netting are all described in Section 7.4 'Repo Central Clearing (Overview)'.

To clarify, the counterparty to a firm that executes a trade over GC Pooling is Eurex Clearing, which acts in the role of central counterparty. Eurex Clearing is the immediate counterparty as they are an original party to the trade; consequently, there is no *novation* process from a conventional counterparty to Eurex Clearing, and it is not possible to discover the identity of the 'real' counterparty on the other side of the transaction.

The collateral that may be used in a GC Pooling repo is the combined assets held by the GC Pooling participant within Clearstream Banking Luxembourg and Clearstream Banking Frankfurt. More specifically, standardised fixed income and equity baskets may be used to collateralise cash borrowings.

During the lifetime of the repo, GC Pooling manages both margin calls and collateral substitution.

Additionally, where trades are executed bilaterally (and not in the way described earlier), participants are able to centrally clear such bilateral trades via Eurex Clearing, following novation.

7.6 REPOCLEAR (OVERVIEW)

RepoClear is part of the LCH.Clearnet group, and provides central clearing for repos. (See Section 7.4 'Repo Central Clearing (Overview)' within this chapter.)

Repo trades are executed on a bilateral basis, directly between two trading parties, either over the telephone or via trading screens; both trade execution methods are accepted by RepoClear.

Central clearing for repos is not mandatory, therefore it is important to note that the two trading parties may choose to centrally clear a trade, or not to. A reason why a firm may wish for a particular repo trade to be centrally cleared is that they may have concerns over the creditworthiness of the counterparty. A reason for a firm not to centrally clear a particular trade is that they have little or no concern as to the counterparty's credit standing, and to avoid the cost of central clearing. Within a firm and from an operational perspective, the repo trader must indicate whether the trade is to be centrally cleared, or not.

One route by which repo trades (which are to be centrally cleared) are received by RepoClear is as follows: details of trades executed bilaterally are submitted to the *ETCMS* system, and once a match of trade details has been achieved in ETCMS, the trade details are forwarded automatically to RepoClear. Following validation by RepoClear, the trade is novated to LCH.Clearnet Ltd which becomes the central counterparty to both the original trading parties.

Another route by which repo trades (destined for central clearing) are received by RepoClear are where trades originate within an automated trading system (e.g. Brokertec), and which are transmitted automatically to RepoClear. It is important to note that trades executed via automated trading systems are traded anonymously and therefore the counterparty to such trades is the CCP (as the original party to the trade); trades executed in this way are therefore not novated to the CCP.

As the central counterparty, RepoClear provides settlement netting whereby, for a particular firm, multiple (gross) repo trades in the same currency and with the same closing value date, are subject to the CCP's netting process in order to derive the net settlement obligation. Such netting activity can result in a bond delivery obligation against a cash amount, and in other cases a zero bond quantity but with a cash balance requiring payment to or from a party.

The overall trade flow is reflected in Figure 7.6:

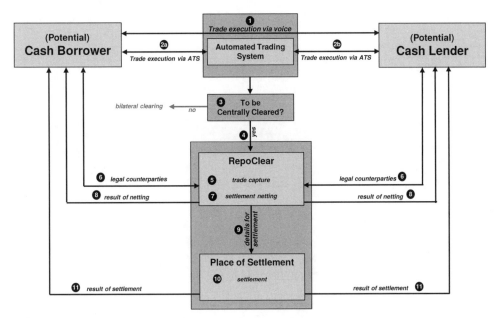

FIGURE 7.6   RepoClear processing

Step 1: a repo trade is executed directly (bilaterally) between cash lender and cash borrower

Step 2: alternatively, a repo trade is executed anonymously via an automated trading system

Step 3: the trade is assessed as to whether it is to be bilaterally or centrally cleared

Step 4: if the trade is to be centrally cleared the trade details are sent to RepoClear (e.g. by ETCMS)

Step 5: RepoClear captures the terms of the trade

Step 6: LCH Ltd becomes the counterparty to both trading parties

Step 7: RepoClear carries out settlement netting of trades in the same currency and with the same closing value date

Step 8: RepoClear makes the result of netting available to both trading parties

Step 9: RepoClear sends details of the net settlement obligation to the appropriate place of settlement

Step 10: settlement of the net settlement obligation occurs at the place of settlement

Step 11: both parties are advised once the net settlement obligation has settled.

CHAPTER 8

Sale & Repurchase (Repo) Trades and Collateral – The Global Master Repurchase Agreement

To enable readers to relate the content of the five chapters commencing with Chapter 3 'Sale & Repurchase (Repo) Trades and Collateral – Introduction to Repo' to Chapter 7 'Sale & Repurchase (Repo) Trades and Collateral – Repo Trade Variations', the text which follows this page within this chapter contains a complete version of the Global Master Repurchase Agreement (GMRA) 2011.

The GMRA has been reproduced with the express permission of ICMA and SIFMA in 2017.

Securities Industry and Financial Markets Association
New York • Washington
www.sifma.org

International Capital Market Association
Talacker 29, 8001 Zurich, Switzerland
www.icmagroup.org

2011 version

Global Master Repurchase Agreement

Dated as of _____

Between:

_____ (**"Party A"**)

and

_____ (**"Party B"**)

1.   **Applicability**

(a)   From time to time the parties hereto may enter into transactions in which one party, acting through a Designated Office, ("Seller") agrees to sell to the other, acting through a Designated Office, ("Buyer") securities or other financial instruments ("Securities") (subject to paragraph 1(c), other than equities and Net Paying Securities) against the payment of the purchase price by Buyer to Seller, with a simultaneous agreement by Buyer to sell to Seller Securities equivalent to such Securities at a date certain or on demand against the payment of the repurchase price by Seller to Buyer.

(b)   Each such transaction (which may be a repurchase transaction ("Repurchase Transaction") or a buy and sell back transaction ("Buy/Sell Back Transaction")) shall be referred to herein as a "Transaction" and shall be governed by this Agreement, including any supplemental terms or conditions contained in Annex I and any annex specified in Annex I, unless otherwise agreed in writing.

(c)   If this Agreement may be applied to -

(i)   Buy/Sell Back Transactions, this shall be specified in Annex I hereto, and the provisions of the Buy/Sell Back Annex shall apply to such Buy/Sell Back Transactions;

April 2011

    (ii)   Net Paying Securities, this shall be specified in Annex I hereto and the provisions of Annex I, paragraph 1(b) shall apply to Transactions involving Net Paying Securities.

2.   **Definitions**

(a)   "Act of Insolvency" shall occur with respect to any party hereto upon -

    (i)   its making a general assignment for the benefit of, or entering into a reorganisation, arrangement, or composition with, creditors; or

    (ii)   a secured party taking possession of, or carrying out other enforcement measures in relation to, all or substantially all assets of such party, provided the relevant process is not dismissed, discharged, stayed or restrained within 15 days; or

    (iii)   its becoming insolvent or becoming unable to pay its debts as they become due or failing or admitting in writing its inability generally to pay its debts as they become due; or

    (iv)   its seeking, consenting to or acquiescing in the appointment of any trustee, administrator, receiver or liquidator or analogous officer of it or any material part of its property; or

    (v)   the presentation or filing of a petition in respect of it (other than by the other party to this Agreement in respect of any obligation under this Agreement) in any court or before any agency or the commencement of any proceeding by any Competent Authority alleging or for the bankruptcy, winding-up or insolvency of such party (or any analogous proceeding) or seeking any reorganisation, arrangement, composition, re-adjustment, administration, liquidation, dissolution or similar relief under any present or future statute, law or regulation, such petition not having been stayed or dismissed within 15 days of its filing (except in the case of a petition presented by a Competent Authority or for winding-up or any analogous proceeding, in respect of which no such 15 day period shall apply); or

    (vi)   the appointment of a receiver, administrator, liquidator, conservator, custodian or trustee or analogous officer of such party or over all or any material part of such party's property; or

    (vii)   the convening of any meeting of its creditors for the purpose of considering a voluntary arrangement as referred to in section 3 of the Insolvency Act 1986 (or any analogous proceeding);

(b)   "Agency Transaction", the meaning specified in paragraph 1 of the Agency Annex to this Agreement as published by ICMA;

(c)   "Applicable Rate", in relation to any sum in any currency:

sifma

    (i)   for the purposes of paragraph 10, the rate selected in a commercially reasonable manner by the non-Defaulting Party;

    (ii)   for any other purpose, the rate agreed by the parties acting in a commercially reasonable manner;

(d)   "Appropriate Market", the meaning specified in paragraph 10;

(e)   "Base Currency", the currency indicated in Annex I;

(f)   "Business Day" means -

    (i)   in relation to the settlement of a Transaction or delivery of Securities under this Agreement through a settlement system, a day on which that settlement system is open for business;

    (ii)   in relation to the settlement of a Transaction or delivery of Securities under this Agreement otherwise than through a settlement system, a day on which banks are open for business in the place where the relevant Securities are to be delivered and, if different, the place in which the relevant payment is to be made; and

    (iii)   in relation to the payment of any amount under this Agreement not falling within (i) or (ii) above, a day other than a Saturday or a Sunday on which banks are open for business in the principal financial centre of the country of which the currency in which the payment is denominated is the official currency and, if different, in the place where any account designated by the parties for the making or receipt of the payment is situated (or, in the case of a payment in euro, a day on which TARGET2 operates).

(g)   "Cash Equivalent Amount" has the meaning given in paragraph 4(h);

(h)   "Cash Margin", a cash sum paid or to be paid to Buyer or Seller in accordance with paragraph 4;

(i)   "Competent Authority", a regulator, supervisor or any similar official with primary insolvency, rehabilitative or regulatory jurisdiction over a party in the jurisdiction of its incorporation or establishment or the jurisdiction of its head office;

(j)   "Confirmation", the meaning specified in paragraph 3(b);

(k)   "Contractual Currency", the meaning specified in paragraph 7(a);

(l)   "Defaulting Party", the meaning specified in paragraph 10;

(m)   "Default Market Value", the meaning specified in paragraph 10;

(n)   "Default Notice", a written notice served by the non-Defaulting Party on the Defaulting Party under paragraph 10(b) designating a day as an Early Termination Date;

(o)   "Deliverable Securities", the meaning specified in paragraph 10;

(p)   "Designated Office", a branch or office which is specified as such in Annex I or such other branch or office as may be agreed in writing by the parties;

(q)   "Distribution(s)", the meaning specified in sub-paragraph (y) below;

(r)   "Early Termination Date", the date designated as such in a Default Notice or as otherwise determined in accordance with paragraph 10(b);

(s)   "Electronic Messaging System", an electronic system for communication capable of reproducing communication in hard copy form, including email;

(t)   "Equivalent Margin Securities", Securities equivalent to Securities previously transferred as Margin Securities;

(u)   "Equivalent Securities", with respect to a Transaction, Securities equivalent to Purchased Securities under that Transaction. If and to the extent that such Purchased Securities have been redeemed, the expression shall mean a sum of money equivalent to the proceeds of the redemption (other than Distributions);

(v)   Securities are "equivalent to" other Securities for the purposes of this Agreement if they are: (i) of the same issuer; (ii) part of the same issue; and (iii) of an identical type, nominal value, description and (except where otherwise stated) amount as those other Securities, provided that -

    (A)   Securities will be equivalent to other Securities notwithstanding that those Securities have been redenominated into euro or that the nominal value of those Securities has changed in connection with such redenomination; and

    (B)   where Securities have been converted, subdivided or consolidated or have become the subject of a takeover or the holders of Securities have become entitled to receive or acquire other Securities or other property or the Securities have become subject to any similar event other than a Distribution, the expression "equivalent to" shall mean Securities equivalent to (as defined in the provisions of this definition preceding the proviso) the original Securities together with or replaced by a sum of money or Securities or other property equivalent to (as so defined) that receivable by holders of such original Securities resulting from such event;

(w)   "Event of Default", the meaning specified in paragraph 10;

(x)   "Forward Transaction", the meaning specified in paragraph 2(c)(i) of Annex I;

(y)   "Income", with respect to any Security at any time, all interest, dividends or other distributions thereon, including distributions which are a payment or repayment of principal in respect of the relevant securities ("Distribution(s)");

(z)   "Income Payment Date", with respect to any Securities, the date on which Income is

paid in respect of such Securities or, in the case of registered Securities, the date by reference to which particular registered holders are identified as being entitled to payment of Income;

(aa) "Margin Percentage", with respect to any Margin Securities or Equivalent Margin Securities, the percentage, if any, agreed by the parties acting in a commercially reasonable manner;

(bb) "Margin Ratio", with respect to a Transaction, the Market Value of the Purchased Securities at the time when the Transaction was entered into divided by the Purchase Price (and so that, where a Transaction relates to Securities of different descriptions and the Purchase Price is apportioned by the parties among Purchased Securities of each such description, a separate Margin Ratio shall apply in respect of Securities of each such description), or such other proportion as the parties may agree with respect to that Transaction;

(cc) "Margin Securities", in relation to a Margin Transfer, Securities of the type and value (having applied Margin Percentage, if any) reasonably acceptable to the party calling for such Margin Transfer;

(dd) "Margin Transfer", any, or any combination of, the payment or repayment of Cash Margin and the transfer of Margin Securities or Equivalent Margin Securities;

(ee) "Market Value", with respect to any Securities as of any time on any date, the price for such Securities (after having applied the Margin Percentage, if any, in the case of Margin Securities) at such time on such date obtained from a generally recognised source agreed by the parties or as otherwise agreed by the parties (and where different prices are obtained for different delivery dates, the price so obtainable for the earliest available such delivery date) having regard to market practice for valuing Securities of the type in question plus the aggregate amount of Income which, as at such date, has accrued but not yet been paid in respect of the Securities to the extent not included in such price as of such date, and for these purposes any sum in a currency other than the Contractual Currency for the Transaction in question shall be converted into such Contractual Currency at the Spot Rate prevailing at the time of the determination;

(ff) "Net Exposure", the meaning specified in paragraph 4(c);

(gg) the "Net Margin" provided to a party at any time, the excess (if any) at that time of (i) the sum of the amount of Cash Margin paid to that party (including accrued interest on such Cash Margin which has not been paid to the other party) and the Market Value of Margin Securities transferred to that party under paragraph 4(a) (excluding any Cash Margin which has been repaid to the other party and any Margin Securities in respect of which Equivalent Margin Securities have been transferred or a Cash Equivalent Amount has been paid to the other party) over (ii) the sum of the amount of Cash Margin paid to the other party (including accrued interest on such Cash Margin which has not been paid by the other party) and the Market Value of Margin Securities

transferred to the other party under paragraph 4(a) (excluding any Cash Margin which has been repaid by the other party and any Margin Securities in respect of which Equivalent Margin Securities have been transferred or a Cash Equivalent Amount has been paid by the other party) and for this purpose any amounts not denominated in the Base Currency shall be converted into the Base Currency at the Spot Rate prevailing at the time of the determination;

(hh) "Net Paying Securities", Securities which are of a kind such that, were they to be the subject of a Transaction to which paragraph 5 applies, any payment made by Buyer under paragraph 5 would be one in respect of which either Buyer would or might be required to make a withholding or deduction for or on account of taxes or duties or Seller might be required to make or account for a payment for or on account of taxes or duties (in each case other than tax on overall net income) by reference to such payment;

(ii) "Net Value", the meaning specified in paragraph 10;

(jj) "New Purchased Securities", the meaning specified in paragraph 8(a);

(kk) "Price Differential", with respect to any Transaction as of any date, the aggregate amount obtained by daily application of the Pricing Rate for such Transaction to the Purchase Price for such Transaction (on a 360 day, 365 day or other day basis in accordance with the applicable market convention, unless otherwise agreed between the parties for the Transaction) for the actual number of days during the period commencing on (and including) the Purchase Date for such Transaction and ending on (but excluding) the date of calculation or, if earlier, the Repurchase Date;

(ll) "Pricing Rate", with respect to any Transaction, the per annum percentage rate for calculation of the Price Differential agreed to by Buyer and Seller in relation to that Transaction;

(mm) "Purchase Date", with respect to any Transaction, the date on which Purchased Securities are to be sold by Seller to Buyer in relation to that Transaction;

(nn) "Purchase Price", on the Purchase Date, the price at which Purchased Securities are sold or are to be sold by Seller to Buyer;

(oo) "Purchased Securities", with respect to any Transaction, the Securities sold or to be sold by Seller to Buyer under that Transaction, and any New Purchased Securities transferred by Seller to Buyer under paragraph 8 in respect of that Transaction;

(pp) "Receivable Securities", the meaning specified in paragraph 10;

(qq) "Repurchase Date", with respect to any Transaction, the date on which Buyer is to sell Equivalent Securities to Seller in relation to that Transaction;

(rr) "Repurchase Price", with respect to any Transaction and as of any date, the sum of the Purchase Price and the Price Differential as of such date;

(ss) "Spot Rate", where an amount in one currency is to be converted into a second currency on any date, unless the parties otherwise agree

  (i) for the purposes of paragraph 10, the spot rate of exchange obtained by reference to a pricing source or quoted by a bank, in each case specified by the non-Defaulting Party, in the London inter-bank market for the purchase of the second currency with the first currency at such dates and times determined by the non-Defaulting Party; and

  (ii) for any other purpose, the latest available spot rate of exchange obtained by reference to a pricing source or quoted by a bank, in each case agreed by the parties (or in the absence of such agreement, specified by Buyer), in the London inter-bank market for the purchase of the second currency with the first currency on the day on which the calculation is to be made or, if that day is not a day on which banks are open for business in London, the spot rate of exchange quoted at close of business in London on the immediately preceding day in London on which such a quotation was available;

(tt) "TARGET2", the Second Generation Trans-European Automated Real-time Gross Settlement Express Transfer System, or any other system that replaces it;

(uu) "Term", with respect to any Transaction, the interval of time commencing with the Purchase Date and ending with the Repurchase Date;

(vv) "Termination", with respect to any Transaction, refers to the requirement with respect to such Transaction for Buyer to sell Equivalent Securities against payment by Seller of the Repurchase Price in accordance with paragraph 3(f), and reference to a Transaction having a "fixed term" or being "terminable upon demand" shall be construed accordingly;

(ww) "Transaction Costs", the meaning specified in paragraph 10;

(xx) "Transaction Exposure", with respect to any Transaction at any time during the period from the Purchase Date to the Repurchase Date (or, if later, the date on which Equivalent Securities are delivered to Seller or the Transaction is terminated under paragraph 10(h) or 10(i)) the amount "E" determined in accordance with (A) or (B) below as specified in Annex I (or as agreed by the parties with respect to particular transactions):

  (A) the result of formula $E = (R \times MR) - MV$, where:

    R =   the Repurchase Price at such time

    MR =   the applicable Margin Ratio

    MV =   the Market Value of Equivalent Securities at such time

    and so that where the Transaction relates to Securities of more than one description or to which different Margin Ratios apply, E shall be determined by

multiplying the Repurchase Price attributable to Equivalent Securities of each such description by the applicable Margin Ratio and aggregating the results and for this purpose the Repurchase Price shall be attributed to Equivalent Securities of each such description in the same proportions as those in which the Purchase Price was apportioned among the Purchased Securities.

If E is greater than zero, Buyer has a Transaction Exposure equal to E and if E is less than zero, Seller has a Transaction Exposure equal to the absolute value of E; provided that E shall not be greater than the amount of the Repurchase Price on the date of the determination; or

(B)   the result of the formula $E = R - V$, where:

R   =   the Repurchase Price at such time

V   =   the Adjusted Value of Equivalent Securities at such time or, where a Transaction relates to Securities of more than one description or to which different haircuts apply, the sum of the Adjusted Values of the Securities of each such description.

For this purpose the "Adjusted Value" of any Securities is their value determined on the basis of the formula, $(MV(1 - H))$, where:

MV   =   the Market Value of Equivalent Securities at such time

H   =   the "haircut" for the relevant Securities, if any, as agreed by the parties from time to time, being a discount from the Market Value of the Securities.

If E is greater than zero, Buyer has a Transaction Exposure equal to E and if E is less than zero, Seller has a Transaction Exposure equal to the absolute value of E; and

(yy)   except in paragraphs 14(b)(i) and 18, references in this Agreement to "written" communications and communications "in writing" include communications made through any Electronic Messaging System agreed between the parties.

3.   Initiation; Confirmation; Termination

(a)   A Transaction may be entered into orally or in writing at the initiation of either Buyer or Seller.

(b)   Upon agreeing to enter into a Transaction hereunder Buyer or Seller (or both), as shall have been agreed, shall promptly deliver to the other party written confirmation of such Transaction (a "Confirmation").

The Confirmation shall describe the Purchased Securities (including CUSIP or ISIN or other identifying number or numbers, if any), identify Buyer and Seller and set forth -

(i)   the Purchase Date;

(ii) the Purchase Price;

(iii) the Repurchase Date, unless the Transaction is to be terminable on demand (in which case the Confirmation shall state that it is terminable on demand);

(iv) the Pricing Rate applicable to the Transaction;

(v)   in respect of each party the details of the bank account(s) to which payments to be made hereunder are to be credited;

(vi) where the Buy/Sell Back Annex applies, whether the Transaction is a Repurchase Transaction or a Buy/Sell Back Transaction;

(vii) where the Agency Annex applies, whether the Transaction is an Agency Transaction and, if so, the identity of the party which is acting as agent and the name, code or identifier of the Principal; and

(viii) any additional terms or conditions of the Transaction;

and may be in the form of Annex II or may be in any other form to which the parties agree.

The Confirmation relating to a Transaction shall, together with this Agreement, constitute prima facie evidence of the terms agreed between Buyer and Seller for that Transaction, unless objection is made with respect to the Confirmation promptly after receipt thereof. In the event of any conflict between the terms of such Confirmation and this Agreement, the Confirmation shall prevail in respect of that Transaction and those terms only.

(c)   On the Purchase Date for a Transaction, Seller shall transfer the Purchased Securities to Buyer or its agent against the payment of the Purchase Price by Buyer in accordance with paragraph 6(c).

(d)   Termination of a Transaction will be effected, in the case of on demand Transactions, on the date specified for Termination in such demand, and, in the case of fixed term Transactions, on the date fixed for Termination.

(e)   In the case of on demand Transactions, demand for Termination shall be made by Buyer or Seller, by telephone or otherwise, and shall provide for Termination to occur after not less than the minimum period as is customarily required for the settlement or delivery of money or Equivalent Securities of the relevant kind.

(f)   On the Repurchase Date, Buyer shall transfer to Seller or its agent Equivalent Securities against the payment of the Repurchase Price by Seller (less any amount then payable and unpaid by Buyer to Seller pursuant to paragraph 5).

PART 2

4.   **Margin Maintenance**

(a)   If at any time either party has a Net Exposure in respect of the other party it may by notice to the other party require the other party to make a Margin Transfer to it of an aggregate amount or value at least equal to that Net Exposure.

(b)   A notice under sub-paragraph (a) above may be given orally or in writing.

(c)   For the purposes of this Agreement a party has a Net Exposure in respect of the other party if the aggregate of all the first party's Transaction Exposures plus any amount payable to the first party under paragraph 5 but unpaid less the amount of any Net Margin provided to the first party exceeds the aggregate of all the other party's Transaction Exposures plus any amount payable to the other party under paragraph 5 but unpaid less the amount of any Net Margin provided to the other party; and the amount of the Net Exposure is the amount of the excess.   For this purpose any amounts not denominated in the Base Currency shall be converted into the Base Currency at the Spot Rate prevailing at the relevant time.

(d)   To the extent that a party calling for a Margin Transfer has previously paid Cash Margin which has not been repaid or delivered Margin Securities in respect of which Equivalent Margin Securities have not been delivered to it or a Cash Equivalent Amount has not been paid, that party shall be entitled to require that such Margin Transfer be satisfied first by the repayment of such Cash Margin or the delivery of Equivalent Margin Securities but, subject to this, the composition of a Margin Transfer shall be at the option of the party making such Margin Transfer.

(e)   Any Cash Margin transferred shall be in the Base Currency or such other currency as the parties may agree.

(f)   A payment of Cash Margin shall give rise to a debt owing from the party receiving such payment to the party making such payment.   Such debt shall bear interest at such rate, payable at such times, as may be specified in Annex I in respect of the relevant currency or otherwise agreed between the parties, and shall be repayable subject to the terms of this Agreement.

(g)   Where Seller or Buyer becomes obliged under sub-paragraph (a) above to make a Margin Transfer, it shall transfer Cash Margin or Margin Securities or Equivalent Margin Securities within the minimum period specified in Annex I or, if no period is there specified, such minimum period as is customarily required for the settlement or delivery of money, Margin Securities or Equivalent Margin Securities of the relevant kind.

(h)   Where a party (the "Transferor") becomes obliged to transfer Equivalent Margin Securities and, having made all reasonable efforts to do so, is, for any reason relating to the Securities or the clearing system through which the Securities are to be transferred, unable to transfer Equivalent Margin Securities then

(i)   the Transferor shall immediately pay to the other party Cash Margin at least

equal to the Market Value of such Equivalent Margin Securities (and, unless the parties otherwise agree, such Cash Margin shall not bear interest in accordance with paragraph 4(f)); and

(ii) if the failure is continuing for two Business Days or more the other party may by notice to the Transferor require the Transferor to pay an amount (the "Cash Equivalent Amount") equal to the Default Market Value of the Equivalent Margin Securities determined by the other party in accordance with paragraph 10(f) which shall apply on the basis that references to the non-Defaulting Party were to the other party and references to the Early Termination Date were to the date on which notice under this paragraph is effective.

(i) The parties may agree that, with respect to any Transaction, the provisions of sub-paragraphs (a) to (h) above shall not apply but instead that margin may be provided separately in respect of that Transaction in which case -

(i) that Transaction shall not be taken into account when calculating whether either party has a Net Exposure;

(ii) margin shall be provided in respect of that Transaction in such manner as the parties may agree; and

(iii) margin provided in respect of that Transaction shall not be taken into account for the purposes of sub-paragraphs (a) to (h) above.

(j) The parties may agree that any Net Exposure which may arise shall be eliminated not by Margin Transfers under the preceding provisions of this paragraph but by the repricing of Transactions under sub-paragraph (k) below, the adjustment of Transactions under sub-paragraph (l) below or a combination of both these methods.

(k) Where the parties agree that a Transaction is to be repriced under this sub-paragraph, such repricing shall be effected as follows -

(i) the Repurchase Date under the relevant Transaction (the "Original Transaction") shall be deemed to occur on the date on which the repricing is to be effected (the "Repricing Date");

(ii) the parties shall be deemed to have entered into a new Transaction (the "Repriced Transaction") on the terms set out in (iii) to (vi) below;

(iii) the Purchased Securities under the Repriced Transaction shall be Securities equivalent to the Purchased Securities under the Original Transaction;

(iv) the Purchase Date under the Repriced Transaction shall be the Repricing Date;

(v) the Purchase Price under the Repriced Transaction shall be such amount as shall, when multiplied by the Margin Ratio applicable to the Original Transaction, be equal to the Market Value of such Securities on the Repricing Date;

(vi)   the Repurchase Date, the Pricing Rate, the Margin Ratio and, subject as aforesaid, the other terms of the Repriced Transaction shall be identical to those of the Original Transaction;

(vii)   the obligations of the parties with respect to the delivery of the Purchased Securities and the payment of the Purchase Price under the Repriced Transaction shall be set off against their obligations with respect to the delivery of Equivalent Securities and payment of the Repurchase Price under the Original Transaction and accordingly only a net cash sum shall be paid by one party to the other. Such net cash sum shall be paid within the minimum period specified in sub-paragraph (g) above.

(l)   The adjustment of a Transaction (the "Original Transaction") under this sub-paragraph shall be effected by the parties agreeing that on the date on which the adjustment is to be made (the "Adjustment Date") the Original Transaction shall be terminated and they shall enter into a new Transaction (the "Replacement Transaction") in accordance with the following provisions -

(i)   the Original Transaction shall be terminated on the Adjustment Date on such terms as the parties shall agree on or before the Adjustment Date;

(ii)   the Purchased Securities under the Replacement Transaction shall be such Securities as the parties shall agree on or before the Adjustment Date (being Securities the aggregate Market Value of which at the Adjustment Date is substantially equal to the Repurchase Price under the Original Transaction at the Adjustment Date multiplied by the Margin Ratio applicable to the Original Transaction);

(iii)   the Purchase Date under the Replacement Transaction shall be the Adjustment Date;

(iv)   the other terms of the Replacement Transaction shall be such as the parties shall agree on or before the Adjustment Date; and

(v)   the obligations of the parties with respect to payment and delivery of Securities on the Adjustment Date under the Original Transaction and the Replacement Transaction shall be settled in accordance with paragraph 6 within the minimum period specified in sub-paragraph (g) above.

5.   **Income Payments**

Unless otherwise agreed -

(a)   where: (i) the Term of a particular Transaction extends over an Income Payment Date in respect of any Securities subject to that Transaction; or (ii) an Income Payment Date in respect of any such Securities occurs after the Repurchase Date but before Equivalent Securities have been delivered to Seller or, if earlier, the occurrence of an Early Termination Date or the termination of the Transaction under paragraph 10(i)

then Buyer shall on the date such Income is paid by the issuer transfer to or credit to the account of Seller an amount equal to (and in the same currency as) the amount paid by the issuer;

(b)   where Margin Securities are transferred from one party ("the first party") to the other party ("the second party") and an Income Payment Date in respect of such Securities occurs before Equivalent Margin Securities are transferred or a Cash Equivalent Amount is paid by the second party to the first party, the second party shall on the date such Income is paid by the issuer transfer to or credit to the account of the first party an amount equal to (and in the same currency as) the amount paid by the issuer;

and for the avoidance of doubt references in this paragraph to the amount of any Income paid by the issuer of any Securities shall be to an amount paid without any withholding or deduction for or on account of taxes or duties notwithstanding that a payment of such Income made in certain circumstances may be subject to such a withholding or deduction.

6.   **Payment and Transfer**

(a)   Unless otherwise agreed, all money paid hereunder shall be in immediately available freely convertible funds of the relevant currency. All Securities to be transferred hereunder (i) shall be in suitable form for transfer and shall be accompanied by duly executed instruments of transfer or assignment in blank (where required for transfer) and such other documentation as the transferee may reasonably request, or (ii) shall be transferred through any agreed book entry or other securities clearance system or (iii) shall be transferred by any other method mutually acceptable to Seller and Buyer.

(b)   Unless otherwise agreed, all money payable by one party to the other in respect of any Transaction shall be paid free and clear of, and without withholding or deduction for, any taxes or duties of whatsoever nature imposed, levied, collected, withheld or assessed by any authority having power to tax, unless the withholding or deduction of such taxes or duties is required by law. In that event, unless otherwise agreed, the paying party shall pay such additional amounts as will result in the net amounts receivable by the other party (after taking account of such withholding or deduction) being equal to such amounts as would have been received by it had no such taxes or duties been required to be withheld or deducted.

(c)   Unless otherwise agreed in writing between the parties, under each Transaction transfer of Purchased Securities by Seller and payment of Purchase Price by Buyer against the transfer of such Purchased Securities shall be made simultaneously and transfer of Equivalent Securities by Buyer and payment of Repurchase Price payable by Seller against the transfer of such Equivalent Securities shall be made simultaneously.

(d)   Subject to and without prejudice to the provisions of sub-paragraph 6(c), either party may from time to time in accordance with market practice and in recognition of the practical difficulties in arranging simultaneous delivery of Securities and money waive

in relation to any Transaction its rights under this Agreement to receive simultaneous transfer and/or payment provided that transfer and/or payment shall, notwithstanding such waiver, be made on the same day and provided also that no such waiver in respect of one Transaction shall affect or bind it in respect of any other Transaction.

(e)   The parties shall execute and deliver all necessary documents and take all necessary steps to procure that all right, title and interest in any Purchased Securities, any Equivalent Securities, any Margin Securities and any Equivalent Margin Securities shall pass to the party to which transfer is being made upon transfer of the same in accordance with this Agreement, free from all liens (other than a lien granted to the operator of the clearance system through which the Securities are transferred), claims, charges and encumbrances.

(f)   Notwithstanding the use of expressions such as "Repurchase Date", "Repurchase Price", "margin", "Net Margin", "Margin Ratio" and "substitution", which are used to reflect terminology used in the market for transactions of the kind provided for in this Agreement, all right, title and interest in and to Securities and money transferred or paid under this Agreement shall pass to the transferee upon transfer or payment, the obligation of the party receiving Purchased Securities or Margin Securities being an obligation to transfer Equivalent Securities or Equivalent Margin Securities.

(g)   Time shall be of the essence in this Agreement.

(h)   Subject to paragraph 10, all amounts in the same currency payable by each party to the other under any Transaction or otherwise under this Agreement on the same date shall be combined in a single calculation of a net sum payable by one party to the other and the obligation to pay that sum shall be the only obligation of either party in respect of those amounts.

(i)   Subject to paragraph 10, all Securities of the same issue, denomination, currency and series, transferable by each party to the other under any Transaction or hereunder on the same date shall be combined in a single calculation of a net quantity of Securities transferable by one party to the other and the obligation to transfer the net quantity of Securities shall be the only obligation of either party in respect of the Securities so transferable and receivable.

(j)   If the parties have specified in Annex I that this paragraph 6(j) shall apply, each obligation of a party under this Agreement (the "first party") (other than an obligation arising under paragraph 10) is subject to the condition precedent that none of the events specified in paragraph 10(a) (Events of Default) shall have occurred and be continuing with respect to the other party.

7.   **Contractual Currency**

(a)   All the payments made in respect of the Purchase Price or the Repurchase Price of any Transaction shall be made in the currency of the Purchase Price (the "Contractual Currency") save as provided in paragraph 10(d)(ii). Notwithstanding the foregoing, the

payee of any money may, at its option, accept tender thereof in any other currency, provided, however, that, to the extent permitted by applicable law, the obligation of the payer to pay such money will be discharged only to the extent of the amount of the Contractual Currency that such payee may, consistent with normal banking procedures, purchase with such other currency (after deduction of any premium and costs of exchange) for delivery within the customary delivery period for spot transactions in respect of the relevant currency.

(b)   If for any reason the amount in the Contractual Currency received by a party, including amounts received after conversion of any recovery under any judgment or order expressed in a currency other than the Contractual Currency, falls short of the amount in the Contractual Currency due and payable, the party required to make the payment will, as a separate and independent obligation, to the extent permitted by applicable law, immediately transfer such additional amount in the Contractual Currency as may be necessary to compensate for the shortfall.

(c)   If for any reason the amount in the Contractual Currency received by a party exceeds the amount of the Contractual Currency due and payable, the party receiving the transfer will refund promptly the amount of such excess.

8.   **Substitution**

(a)   A Transaction may at any time between the Purchase Date and Repurchase Date, if Seller so requests and Buyer so agrees, be varied by the transfer by Buyer to Seller of Securities equivalent to the Purchased Securities, or to such of the Purchased Securities as shall be agreed, in exchange for the transfer by Seller to Buyer of other Securities of such amount and description as shall be agreed ("New Purchased Securities") (being Securities having a Market Value at the date of the variation at least equal to the Market Value of the Equivalent Securities transferred to Seller).

(b)   Any variation under sub-paragraph (a) above shall be effected, subject to paragraph 6(d), by the simultaneous transfer of the Equivalent Securities and New Purchased Securities concerned.

(c)   A Transaction which is varied under sub-paragraph (a) above shall thereafter continue in effect as though the Purchased Securities under that Transaction consisted of or included the New Purchased Securities instead of the Securities in respect of which Equivalent Securities have been transferred to Seller.

(d)   Where either party has transferred Margin Securities to the other party it may at any time before Equivalent Margin Securities are transferred to it under paragraph 4 request the other party to transfer Equivalent Margin Securities to it in exchange for the transfer to the other party of new Margin Securities having a Market Value at the time at which the exchange is agreed at least equal to that of such Equivalent Margin Securities. If the other party agrees to the request, the exchange shall be effected, subject to paragraph 6(d), by the simultaneous transfer of the Equivalent Margin Securities and new Margin Securities concerned. Where either or both of such

transfers is or are effected through a settlement system in circumstances which under the rules and procedures of that settlement system give rise to a payment by or for the account of one party to or for the account of the other party, the parties shall cause such payment or payments to be made outside that settlement system, for value the same day as the payments made through that settlement system, as shall ensure that the exchange of Equivalent Margin Securities and new Margin Securities effected under this sub-paragraph does not give rise to any net payment of cash by either party to the other.

9.   **Representations**

Each party represents and warrants to the other that -

(a)   it is duly authorised to execute and deliver this Agreement, to enter into the Transactions contemplated hereunder and to perform its obligations hereunder and thereunder and has taken all necessary action to authorise such execution, delivery and performance;

(b)   it will engage in this Agreement and the Transactions contemplated hereunder (other than Agency Transactions) as principal;

(c)   the person signing this Agreement on its behalf is, and any person representing it in entering into a Transaction will be, duly authorised to do so on its behalf;

(d)   it has obtained all authorisations of any governmental or regulatory body required in connection with this Agreement and the Transactions contemplated hereunder and such authorisations are in full force and effect;

(e)   the execution, delivery and performance of this Agreement and the Transactions contemplated hereunder will not violate any law, ordinance, charter, by-law or rule applicable to it or any agreement by which it is bound or by which any of its assets are affected;

(f)   it has satisfied itself and will continue to satisfy itself as to the tax implications of the Transactions contemplated hereunder;

(g)   in connection with this Agreement and each Transaction -

(i)   unless there is a written agreement with the other party to the contrary, it is not relying on any advice (whether written or oral) of the other party, other than the representations expressly set out in this Agreement;

(ii)   it has made and will make its own decisions regarding the entering into of any Transaction based upon its own judgment and upon advice from such professional advisers as it has deemed it necessary to consult;

(iii)   it understands the terms, conditions and risks of each Transaction and is willing to assume (financially and otherwise) those risks; and

(h)   at the time of transfer to the other party of any Securities it will have the full and unqualified right to make such transfer and that upon such transfer of Securities the other party will receive all right, title and interest in and to those Securities free of any lien (other than a lien granted to the operator of the clearance system through which the Securities are transferred), claim, charge or encumbrance.

On the date on which any Transaction is entered into pursuant hereto, and on each day on which Securities, Equivalent Securities, Margin Securities or Equivalent Margin Securities are to be transferred under any Transaction, Buyer and Seller shall each be deemed to repeat all the foregoing representations. For the avoidance of doubt and notwithstanding any arrangements which Seller or Buyer may have with any third party, each party will be liable as a principal for its obligations under this Agreement and each Transaction.

10.   **Events of Default**

(a)   If any of the following events (each an "Event of Default") occurs in relation to either party (the "Defaulting Party", the other party being the "non-Defaulting Party") whether acting as Seller or Buyer -

(i)   Buyer fails to pay the Purchase Price upon the applicable Purchase Date or Seller fails to pay the Repurchase Price upon the applicable Repurchase Date; or

(ii)   if the parties have specified in Annex I that this sub-paragraph shall apply, Seller fails to deliver Purchased Securities on the Purchase Date or Buyer fails to deliver Equivalent Securities on the Repurchase Date, in either case within the standard settlement time for delivery of the Securities concerned; or

(iii) Seller or Buyer fails to pay when due any sum payable under sub-paragraph (h) or (i) below; or

(iv)   Seller or Buyer fails to:

(A)   make a Margin Transfer within the minimum period in accordance with paragraph 4(g) or, in the case of an obligation to deliver Equivalent Margin Securities, either to deliver the relevant Equivalent Margin Securities or to pay Cash Margin in accordance with paragraph 4(h)(i) or to pay the Cash Equivalent Amount in accordance with paragraph 4(h)(ii);

(B)   where paragraph 4(i) applies, to provide margin in accordance with that paragraph; or

(C)   to pay any amount or to transfer any Securities in accordance with paragraphs 4(k) or (l); or

(v)   Seller or Buyer fails to comply with paragraph 5; or

(vi)   an Act of Insolvency occurs with respect to Seller or Buyer; or

(vii) any representations made by Seller or Buyer are incorrect or untrue in any material respect when made or repeated or deemed to have been made or repeated; or

(viii) Seller or Buyer admits to the other that it is unable to, or intends not to, perform any of its obligations hereunder or in respect of any Transaction; or

(ix) Seller or Buyer being declared in default or being suspended or expelled from membership of or participation in, any securities exchange or suspended or prohibited from dealing in securities by any Competent Authority, in each case on the grounds that it has failed to meet any requirements relating to financial resources or credit rating; or

(x) Seller or Buyer fails to perform any other of its obligations hereunder and does not remedy such failure within 30 days after notice is given by the non-Defaulting Party requiring it to do so,

then sub-paragraphs (b) to (g) below shall apply.

(b) If at any time an Event of Default has occurred and is continuing the non-Defaulting Party may, by not more than 20 days' notice to the Defaulting Party specifying the relevant Event of Default, designate a day not earlier than the day such notice is effective as an Early Termination Date in respect of all outstanding Transactions. If, however, "Automatic Early Termination" is specified in Annex I with respect to the Defaulting Party, then an Early Termination Date in respect of all outstanding Transactions will occur at the time immediately preceding the occurrence with respect to the Defaulting Party of an Act of Insolvency which is the presentation of a petition for winding-up or any analogous proceeding or the appointment of a liquidator or analogous officer of the Defaulting Party.

(c) If an Early Termination Date occurs, the Repurchase Date for each Transaction hereunder shall be deemed to occur on the Early Termination Date and, subject to the following provisions, all Cash Margin (including interest accrued) shall be repayable and Equivalent Margin Securities shall be deliverable and Cash Equivalent Amounts shall be payable, in each case on the Early Termination Date (and so that, where this sub-paragraph applies, performance of the respective obligations of the parties with respect to the delivery of Securities, the payment of the Repurchase Prices for any Equivalent Securities, the repayment of any Cash Margin and the payment of Cash Equivalent Amounts shall be effected only in accordance with the provisions of sub-paragraph (d) below).

(d) (i) The Default Market Values of the Equivalent Securities and any Equivalent Margin Securities to be transferred, the amount of any Cash Margin (including the amount of interest accrued) to be transferred and the Repurchase Prices and Cash Equivalent Amounts to be paid by each party shall be established by the non-Defaulting Party for all Transactions as at the Early Termination Date;

(ii) on the basis of the sums so established, an account shall be taken (as at the Early Termination Date) of what is due from each party to the other under this Agreement (on the basis that each party's claim against the other in respect of the transfer to it of Equivalent Securities or Equivalent Margin Securities under this Agreement equals the Default Market Value therefor and including amounts payable under paragraphs 10(g) and 12) and the sums due from one party shall be set off against the sums due from the other and only the balance of the account shall be payable (by the party having the claim valued at the lower amount pursuant to the foregoing). For the purposes of this calculation, all sums not denominated in the Base Currency shall be converted into the Base Currency at the Spot Rate; and

(iii) as soon as reasonably practicable after effecting the calculation above, the non-Defaulting Party shall provide to the Defaulting Party a statement showing in reasonable detail such calculations and specifying the balance payable by one party to the other and such balance shall be due and payable on the Business Day following the date of such statement provided that, to the extent permitted by applicable law, interest shall accrue on such amount on a 360 day, 365 day or other day basis in accordance with the applicable market convention (or as otherwise agreed by the parties), for the actual number of days during the period from and including the Early Termination Date to, but excluding, the date of payment.

(e) For the purposes of this Agreement, the "Default Market Value" of any Equivalent Securities or Equivalent Margin Securities shall be determined by the non-Defaulting Party on or as soon as reasonably practicable after the Early Termination Date in accordance with sub-paragraph (f) below, and for this purpose -

(i) the "Appropriate Market" means, in relation to Securities of any description, the market which is the most appropriate market for Securities of that description, as determined by the non-Defaulting Party;

(ii) "Deliverable Securities" means Equivalent Securities or Equivalent Margin Securities to be delivered by the Defaulting Party;

(iii) "Net Value" means at any time, in relation to any Deliverable Securities or Receivable Securities, the amount which, in the reasonable opinion of the non-Defaulting Party, represents their fair market value, having regard to such pricing sources (including trading prices) and methods (which may include, without limitation, available prices for Securities with similar maturities, terms and credit characteristics as the relevant Equivalent Securities or Equivalent Margin Securities) as the non-Defaulting Party considers appropriate, less, in the case of Receivable Securities, or plus, in the case of Deliverable Securities, all Transaction Costs which would be incurred or reasonably anticipated in connection with the purchase or sale of such Securities;

(iv) "Receivable Securities" means Equivalent Securities or Equivalent Margin Securities to be delivered to the Defaulting Party; and

(v) "Transaction Costs" in relation to any transaction contemplated in paragraph 10(e) or (f) means the reasonable costs, commissions, fees and expenses (including any mark-up or mark-down or premium paid for guaranteed delivery) incurred or reasonably anticipated in connection with the purchase of Deliverable Securities or sale of Receivable Securities, calculated on the assumption that the aggregate thereof is the least that could reasonably be expected to be paid in order to carry out the transaction.

(f) If -

(i) on or about the Early Termination Date the non-Defaulting Party has sold, in the case of Receivable Securities, or purchased, in the case of Deliverable Securities, Securities which form part of the same issue and are of an identical type and description as those Equivalent Securities or Equivalent Margin Securities (regardless as to whether or not such sales or purchases have settled), the non-Defaulting Party may elect to treat as the Default Market Value -

(A) in the case of Receivable Securities, the net proceeds of such sale after deducting all reasonable costs, commissions, fees and expenses incurred in connection therewith (provided that, where the Securities sold are not identical in amount to the Equivalent Securities or Equivalent Margin Securities, the non-Defaulting Party may, acting in good faith, either (x) elect to treat such net proceeds of sale divided by the amount of Securities sold and multiplied by the amount of the Equivalent Securities or Equivalent Margin Securities as the Default Market Value or (y) elect to treat such net proceeds of sale of the Equivalent Securities or Equivalent Margin Securities actually sold as the Default Market Value of that proportion of the Equivalent Securities or Equivalent Margin Securities, and, in the case of (y), the Default Market Value of the balance of the Equivalent Securities or Equivalent Margin Securities shall be determined separately in accordance with the provisions of this paragraph 10(f)); or

(B) in the case of Deliverable Securities, the aggregate cost of such purchase, including all reasonable costs, commissions, fees and expenses incurred in connection therewith (provided that, where the Securities purchased are not identical in amount to the Equivalent Securities or Equivalent Margin Securities, the non-Defaulting Party may, acting in good faith, either (x) elect to treat such aggregate cost divided by the amount of Securities sold and multiplied by the amount of the Equivalent Securities or Equivalent Margin Securities as the Default Market Value or (y) elect to treat the aggregate cost of purchasing the Equivalent Securities or Equivalent Margin Securities actually purchased as the Default Market Value of that proportion of the Equivalent Securities or Equivalent Margin Securities,

and, in the case of (y), the Default Market Value of the balance of the Equivalent Securities or Equivalent Margin Securities shall be determined separately in accordance with the provisions of this paragraph 10(f));

(ii)   on or about the Early Termination Date the non-Defaulting Party has received, in the case of Deliverable Securities, offer quotations or, in the case of Receivable Securities, bid quotations in respect of Securities of the relevant description from two or more market makers or regular dealers in the Appropriate Market in a commercially reasonable size, using pricing methodology which is customary for the relevant type of security (as determined by the non-Defaulting Party) the non-Defaulting Party may elect to treat as the Default Market Value of such Securities -

(A)   the price quoted (or where a price is quoted by two or more market makers, the arithmetic mean of such prices) by each of them for, in the case of Deliverable Securities, the sale by the relevant market maker or dealer of such Securities or, in the case of Receivable Securities, the purchase by the relevant market maker or dealer of such Securities provided that such price or prices quoted may be adjusted in a commercially reasonable manner by the non-Defaulting Party (x) to reflect accrued but unpaid coupons not reflected in the price or prices quoted in respect of such securities and (y) in respect of any Pool Factor Affected Security, to reflect the realisable value of such Security, taking into consideration the Pool Factor Distortion (and for this purpose, "Pool Factor Affected Security" means a security other than an equity security in respect of which the decimal value of the outstanding principal divided by the original principal balance of such Security is less than one (as indicated by any pool factor applicable to such security), such circumstance a "Pool Factor Distortion");

(B)   after deducting, in the case of Receivable Securities, or adding, in the case of Deliverable Securities the Transaction Costs which would be incurred or reasonably anticipated in connection with such a transaction; or

(iii)   if, acting in good faith the non-Defaulting Party either -

(A)   has endeavoured but been unable to sell or purchase Securities in accordance with sub-paragraph (i) above or to obtain quotations in accordance with sub-paragraph (ii) above (or both); or

(B)   has determined that it would not be commercially reasonable to sell or purchase Securities at the prices bid or offered or to obtain such quotations, or that it would not be commercially reasonable to use any quotations which it has obtained under sub-paragraph (ii) above,

the non-Defaulting Party may determine the Net Value of the relevant Equivalent Securities or Equivalent Margin Securities (which shall be specified) and may treat such Net Value as the Default Market Value of the relevant Equivalent Securities or Equivalent Margin Securities.

(g)   The Defaulting Party shall be liable to the non-Defaulting Party for the amount of all reasonable and legal and other professional expenses incurred by the non-Defaulting Party in connection with or as a consequence of an Event of Default, together with interest thereon at the Applicable Rate or, in the case of an expense attributable to a particular Transaction, the Pricing Rate for the relevant Transaction if that Pricing Rate is greater than the Applicable Rate.

(h)   If Seller fails to deliver Purchased Securities to Buyer on the applicable Purchase Date Buyer may -

    (i)   if it has paid the Purchase Price to Seller, require Seller immediately to repay the sum so paid;

    (ii)   if Buyer has a Transaction Exposure to Seller in respect of the relevant Transaction, require Seller from time to time to pay Cash Margin at least equal to such Transaction Exposure;

    (iii)   at any time while such failure continues, terminate the Transaction by giving written notice to Seller. On such termination the obligations of Seller and Buyer with respect to delivery of Purchased Securities and Equivalent Securities shall terminate and Seller shall pay to Buyer an amount equal to the excess of the Repurchase Price at the date of Termination over the Purchase Price.

(i)   If Buyer fails to deliver some or all Equivalent Securities to Seller on the applicable Repurchase Date Seller may -

    (i)   if it has paid the Repurchase Price to Buyer, require Buyer immediately to repay the sum so paid;

    (ii)   if Seller has a Transaction Exposure to Buyer in respect of the relevant Transaction, require Buyer from time to time to pay Cash Margin at least equal to such Transaction Exposure;

    (iii)   at any time while such failure continues, by written notice to Buyer declare that that Transaction or part of that Transaction corresponding to the Equivalent Securities that have not been delivered (but only that Transaction or part of Transaction) shall be terminated immediately in accordance with sub-paragraph (c) above (disregarding for this purpose references in that sub-paragraph to transfer of Cash Margin, delivery of Equivalent Margin Securities and payment of Cash Equivalent Amount and as if references to the Repurchase Date were to the date on which notice was given under this sub-paragraph).

(j)   The provisions of this Agreement constitute a complete statement of the remedies

available to each party in respect of any Event of Default.

(k) Subject to paragraph 10(l), neither party may claim any sum by way of consequential loss or damage in the event of a failure by the other party to perform any of its obligations under this Agreement.

(l) (i) Subject to sub-paragraph (ii) below, if as a result of a Transaction terminating before its agreed Repurchase Date or a Forward Transaction terminating before its Purchase Date under paragraphs 10(b), 10(h)(iii) or 10(i)(iii), the non-Defaulting Party, in the case of paragraph 10(b), Buyer, in the case of paragraph 10(h)(iii), or Seller, in the case of paragraph 10(i)(iii), (in each case the "first party") incurs any loss or expense in entering into replacement transactions or in otherwise hedging its exposure arising in connection with a Transaction so terminating, the other party shall be required to pay to the first party the amount determined by the first party in good faith and without double counting to be equal to the loss or expense incurred in connection with such replacement transactions or hedging (including all fees, costs and other expenses) less the amount of any profit or gain made by that party in connection with such replacement transactions or hedging; provided that if that calculation results in a negative number, an amount equal to that number shall be payable by the first party to the other party.

    (ii) If the first party reasonably decides, instead of entering into such replacement transactions, to replace or unwind any hedging transactions which the first party entered into in connection with the Transaction so terminating, or to enter into any replacement hedging transactions, the other party shall be required to pay to the first party the amount determined by the first party in good faith to be equal to the loss or expense incurred in connection with entering into such replacement or unwinding (including all fees, costs and other expenses) less the amount of any profit or gain made by that party in connection with such replacement or unwinding; provided that if that calculation results in a negative number, an amount equal to that number shall be payable by the first party to the other party.

(m) Each party shall immediately notify the other if an Event of Default, or an event which, upon the service of a notice or the lapse of time, or both, would be an Event of Default, occurs in relation to it.

(n) Any amount payable to one party (the Payee) by the other party (the Payer) under paragraph 10(d) may, at the option of the non-Defaulting Party, be reduced by its set off against any amount payable (whether at such time or in the future or upon the occurrence of a contingency) by the Payee to the Payer (irrespective of the currency, place of payment or booking office of the obligation) under any other agreement between the Payee and the Payer or instrument or undertaking issued or executed by one party to, or in favour of, the other party. If an obligation is unascertained, the non-Defaulting Party may in good faith estimate that obligation and set off in respect of the

estimate, subject to accounting to the other party when the obligation is ascertained. Nothing in this paragraph shall be effective to create a charge or other security interest. This paragraph shall be without prejudice and in addition to any right of set off, combination of accounts, lien or other right to which any party is at any time otherwise entitled (whether by operation of law, contract or otherwise).

11. **Tax Event**

(a) This paragraph shall apply if either party notifies the other that -

   (i) any action taken by a taxing authority or brought in a court of competent jurisdiction (regardless of whether such action is taken or brought with respect to a party to this Agreement); or

   (ii) a change in the fiscal or regulatory regime (including, but not limited to, a change in law or in the general interpretation of law but excluding any change in any rate of tax),

   has or will, in the notifying party's reasonable opinion, have a material adverse effect on that party in the context of a Transaction.

(b) If so requested by the other party, the notifying party will furnish the other with an opinion of a suitably qualified adviser that an event referred to in sub-paragraph (a)(i) or (ii) above has occurred and affects the notifying party.

(c) Where this paragraph applies, the party giving the notice referred to in sub-paragraph (a) may, subject to sub-paragraph (d) below, terminate the Transaction with effect from a date specified in the notice, not being earlier (unless so agreed by the other party) than 30 days after the date of the notice, by nominating that date as the Repurchase Date.

(d) If the party receiving the notice referred to in sub-paragraph (a) so elects, it may override that notice by giving a counter-notice to the other party. If a counter-notice is given, the party which gives the counter-notice will be deemed to have agreed to indemnify the other party against the adverse effect referred to in sub-paragraph (a) so far as relates to the relevant Transaction and the original Repurchase Date will continue to apply.

(e) Where a Transaction is terminated as described in this paragraph, the party which has given the notice to terminate shall indemnify the other party against any reasonable legal and other professional expenses incurred by the other party by reason of the termination, but the other party may not claim any sum by way of consequential loss or damage in respect of a termination in accordance with this paragraph.

(f) This paragraph is without prejudice to paragraph 6(b) (obligation to pay additional amounts if withholding or deduction required); but an obligation to pay such additional amounts may, where appropriate, be a circumstance which causes this paragraph to apply.

12. **Interest**

To the extent permitted by applicable law, if any sum of money payable hereunder or under any Transaction is not paid when due, interest shall accrue on the unpaid sum as a separate debt at the greater of the Pricing Rate for the Transaction to which such sum relates (where such sum is referable to a Transaction) and Applicable Rate on a 360 day basis or 365 day basis in accordance with the applicable market convention (or as otherwise agreed by the parties), for the actual number of days during the period from and including the date on which payment was due to, but excluding, the date of payment.

13. **Single Agreement**

Each party acknowledges that, and has entered into this Agreement and will enter into each Transaction hereunder in consideration of and in reliance upon the fact that all Transactions hereunder constitute a single business and contractual relationship and are made in consideration of each other. Accordingly, each party agrees (i) to perform all of its obligations in respect of each Transaction hereunder, and that a default in the performance of any such obligations shall constitute a default by it in respect of all Transactions hereunder, and (ii) that payments, deliveries and other transfers made by either of them in respect of any Transaction shall be deemed to have been made in consideration of payments, deliveries and other transfers in respect of any other Transactions hereunder.

14. **Notices and Other Communications**

(a)   Any notice or other communication to be given under this Agreement -

     (i)   shall be in the English language, and except where expressly otherwise provided in this Agreement, shall be in writing;

     (ii)   may be given in any manner described in sub-paragraphs (b) and (c) below;

     (iii)   shall be sent to the party to whom it is to be given at the address or number, or in accordance with the electronic messaging details, set out in Annex I.

(b)   Subject to sub-paragraph (c) below, any such notice or other communication shall be effective -

     (i)   if in writing and delivered in person or by courier, on the date when it is delivered;

     (ii)   if sent by facsimile transmission, on the date when the transmission is received by a responsible employee of the recipient in legible form (it being agreed that the burden of proving receipt will be on the sender and will not be met by a transmission report generated by the sender's facsimile machine);

     (iii)   if sent by certified or registered mail (airmail, if overseas) or the equivalent (return receipt requested), on the date that mail is delivered or its delivery is attempted; or

(iv)   if sent by Electronic Messaging System, on the date that electronic message is received;

except that any notice or communication which is received, or delivery of which is attempted, after close of business on the date of receipt or attempted delivery or on a day which is not a day on which commercial banks are open for business in the place where that notice or other communication is to be given shall be treated as given at the opening of business on the next following day which is such a day.

(c)   If -

(i)   there occurs in relation to either party an Event of Default; and

(ii)   the non-Defaulting Party, having made all practicable efforts to do so, including having attempted to use at least two of the methods specified in sub-paragraph (b)(ii), (iii) or (iv) above, has been unable to serve a Default Notice by one of the methods specified in those sub-paragraphs (or such of those methods as are normally used by the non-Defaulting Party when communicating with the Defaulting Party),

the non-Defaulting Party may sign a written notice (a "Special Default Notice") which -

(A)   specifies the relevant event referred to in paragraph 10(a) which has occurred in relation to the Defaulting Party;

(B)   specifies the Early Termination Date designated in the Default Notice;

(C)   states that the non-Defaulting Party, having made all practicable efforts to do so, including having attempted to use at least two of the methods specified in sub-paragraph (b)(ii), (iii) or (iv) above, has been unable to serve a Default Notice by one of the methods specified in those sub-paragraphs (or such of those methods as are normally used by the non-Defaulting Party when communicating with the Defaulting Party); and

(D)   specifies the date on which, and the time at which, the Special Default Notice is signed by the non-Defaulting Party.

On the signature of a Special Default Notice the Early Termination Date shall occur as designated in the Default Notice. A Special Default Notice shall be given to the Defaulting Party as soon as practicable after it is signed.

(d)   Either party may by notice to the other change the address or facsimile number or Electronic Messaging System details at which notices or other communications are to be given to it.

15.   **Entire Agreement; Severability**

This Agreement shall supersede any existing agreements between the parties containing general terms and conditions for Transactions. Each provision and

PART 2

agreement herein shall be treated as separate from any other provision or agreement herein and shall be enforceable notwithstanding the unenforceability of any such other provision or agreement.

16. **Non-assignability; Termination**

(a) Subject to sub-paragraph (b) below, neither party may assign, charge or otherwise deal with (including without limitation any dealing with any interest in or the creation of any interest in) its rights or obligations under this Agreement or under any Transaction without the prior written consent of the other party. Subject to the foregoing, this Agreement and any Transactions shall be binding upon and shall inure to the benefit of the parties and their respective successors and assigns.

(b) Sub-paragraph (a) above shall not preclude a party from assigning, charging or otherwise dealing with all or any part of its interest in any sum payable to it under paragraph 10(c) or (g) above.

(c) Either party may terminate this Agreement by giving written notice to the other, except that this Agreement shall, notwithstanding such notice, remain applicable to any Transactions then outstanding.

(d) All remedies hereunder shall survive Termination in respect of the relevant Transaction and termination of this Agreement.

(e) The participation of any additional member State of the European Union in economic and monetary union after 1 January 1999 shall not have the effect of altering any term of the Agreement or any Transaction, nor give a party the right unilaterally to alter or terminate the Agreement or any Transaction.

17. **Governing Law**

This Agreement and any non-contractual obligations arising out of or in connection with this Agreement shall be governed by, and interpreted in accordance with, the laws of England.

The English courts shall have exclusive jurisdiction in relation to all disputes (including claims for set-off and counterclaims) arising out of or in connection with this Agreement including, without limitation disputes arising out of or in connection with: (i) the creation, validity, effect, interpretation, performance or non-performance of, or the legal relationships established by, this Agreement; and (ii) any non-contractual obligations arising out of or in connection with this Agreement. For such purposes, Buyer and Seller hereby irrevocably submit to the jurisdiction of the English courts and waive any objection to the exercise of such jurisdiction.

Party A hereby appoints the person identified in Annex I as its agent to receive on its behalf service of process in such courts. If such agent ceases to be its agent, Party A shall promptly appoint, and notify Party B of the identity of, a new agent in England. If

Party A fails to appoint such an agent, Party A agrees that Party B shall be entitled to appoint one on behalf of Party A at the expense of Party A.

Party B hereby appoints the person identified in Annex I as its agent to receive on its behalf service of process in such courts. If such agent ceases to be its agent, Party B shall promptly appoint, and notify Party A of the identity of, a new agent in England. If Party B fails to appoint such an agent, Party B agrees that Party A shall be entitled to appoint one on behalf of Party B at the expense of Party B.

Each party shall deliver to the other, within 30 days of the date of this Agreement in the case of the appointment of a person identified in Annex I or of the date of the appointment of the relevant agent in any other case, evidence of the acceptance by the agent appointed by it pursuant to this paragraph of such appointment.

18. **No Waivers, etc.**

No express or implied waiver of any Event of Default by either party shall constitute a waiver of any other Event of Default and no exercise of any remedy hereunder by any party shall constitute a waiver of its right to exercise any other remedy hereunder. No modification or waiver of any provision of this Agreement and no consent by any party to a departure herefrom shall be effective unless and until such modification, waiver or consent shall be in writing and duly executed by both of the parties hereto. Without limitation on any of the foregoing, the failure to give a notice pursuant to paragraph 4(a) hereof will not constitute a waiver of any right to do so at a later date.

19. **Waiver of Immunity**

Each party hereto hereby waives, to the fullest extent permitted by applicable law, all immunity (whether on the basis of sovereignty or otherwise) from jurisdiction, attachment (both before and after judgment) and execution to which it might otherwise be entitled in any action or proceeding in the Courts of England or of any other country or jurisdiction, relating in any way to this Agreement or any Transaction, and agrees that it will not raise, claim or cause to be pleaded any such immunity at or in respect of any such action or proceeding.

20. **Recording**

The parties agree that each may electronically record all telephone conversations between them.

21. **Third Party Rights**

No person shall have any right to enforce any provision of this Agreement under the Contracts (Rights of Third Parties) Act 1999.

[Name of Party]   [Name of Party]

By _____   By _____

Title _____   Title _____

Date _____   Date _____

ANNEX I

Supplemental Terms or Conditions

Paragraph references are to paragraphs in the Agreement.

1.   The following elections shall apply -

[(a)   paragraph 1(c)(i). Buy/Sell Back Transactions [may/may not]   be effected under this Agreement, and accordingly the Buy/Sell Back Annex [shall/shall not]   apply.]*

[(b)   paragraph 1(c)(ii). Transactions in Net Paying Securities [may/may not]   be effected under this Agreement, and accordingly the following provisions [shall/shall not]   apply.

    (i)   The phrase "other than equities and Net Paying Securities" shall be replaced by the phrase "other than equities".

    (ii)   In the Buy/Sell Back Annex the following words shall be added to the end of the definition of the expression "IR": "and for the avoidance of doubt the reference to the amount of Income for these purposes shall be to an amount paid without withholding or deduction for or on account of taxes or duties notwithstanding that a payment of such Income made in certain circumstances may be subject to such a withholding or deduction".]*

[(c)   Agency Transactions [may/may not]   be effected under this Agreement, and accordingly the Agency Annex [shall/shall not]   apply.]*

[(d)   The following Annex(es) shall apply in respect of specified Transactions -

    for _____ Transactions, the _____ annex shall apply,

    for _____ Transactions, the _____ annex shall apply.]*

(e)   paragraph 2(e). The Base Currency shall be: _____.

(f)   paragraph 2(p). [list Buyer's and Seller's Designated Offices]

    _____

    _____

(g)   paragraph 2(xx): Transaction Exposure method [A]* [B]*

(h)   paragraph 3(b). [Seller/Buyer/both Seller and Buyer]*   to deliver Confirmation.

---

* Delete as appropriate

(i)   paragraph 4(f). Interest rate on Cash Margin to be _____% for _____ currency.
                                                            _____% for _____ currency.

        Interest to be payable [payment intervals and dates] _____.

(j)   paragraph 4(g). Delivery period for margin calls to be: _____.

[(k)   paragraph 6(j). Paragraph 6(j) shall apply.]*

[(l)   paragraph 10(a)(ii). Paragraph 10(a)(ii) shall apply.]*

[(m)   paragraph 10(b). Automatic Early Termination shall apply with respect to
        [Party A] [Party B]   ]*

(n)   paragraph 14. For the purposes of paragraph 14 of this Agreement -

        (i)   Address for notices and other communications for Party A -

                Address: _____
                Attention: _____
                Telephone: _____
                Facsimile: _____
                Electronic Messaging System: _____
                Answerback: _____
                Other:

        (ii)   Address for notices and other communications for Party B -

                Address: _____
                Attention: _____
                Telephone: _____
                Facsimile: _____
                Electronic Messaging System: _____
                Answerback: _____
                Other:

---

* Delete as appropriate

[(o)   paragraph 17. For the purposes of paragraph 17 of this Agreement -

(i)   Party A appoints _____ as its agent for service of process;

(ii)   Party B appoints _____ as its agent for service of process.]*

2.   The following supplemental terms and conditions shall apply -

[Existing Transactions

(a)   The parties agree that this Agreement shall apply to all transactions which are subject to the Global Master Repurchase Agreement between them dated _____ and which are outstanding as at the date of this Agreement so that such transactions shall be treated as if they had been entered into under this Agreement, and the terms of such transactions are amended accordingly with effect from the date of this Agreement.]*

[Negative rate transactions

(b)   In the case of Transactions in which the Pricing Rate will be negative, the parties agree that if Seller fails to deliver the Purchased Securities on the Purchase Date then -

(i)   Buyer may by notice to Seller terminate the Transaction (and may continue to do so for every day that Seller fails to deliver the Purchased Securities); and

(ii)   for every day that Seller fails to deliver the Purchased Securities the Pricing Rate shall be zero.]*

[Forward Transactions

(c)   The parties agree that Forward Transactions (as defined in sub-paragraph (i)(A) below) may be effected under this Agreement and accordingly the provisions of sub-paragraphs (i) to (iv) below shall apply.

(i)   The following definitions shall apply -

(A)   "Forward Transaction", a Transaction in respect of which the Purchase Date is at least [three] Business Days after the date on which the Transaction was entered into and has not yet occurred;

(B)   "Forward Repricing Date", with respect to any Forward Transaction the date which is such number of Business Days before the Purchase Date as

---

* Delete as appropriate

is equal to the minimum period for the delivery of margin applicable under paragraph 4(g).

(ii)   The Confirmation relating to any Forward Transaction may describe the Purchased Securities by reference to a type or class of Securities, which, without limitation, may be identified by issuer or class of issuers and a maturity or range of maturities. Where this paragraph applies, the parties shall agree the actual Purchased Securities not less than two Business Days before the Purchase Date and Buyer or Seller (or both), as shall have been agreed, shall promptly deliver to the other party a Confirmation which shall describe such Purchased Securities.

(iii)   At any time between the Forward Repricing Date and the Purchase Date for any Forward Transaction the parties may agree either -

(A)   to adjust the Purchase Price under that Forward Transaction; or

(B)   to adjust the number of Purchased Securities to be sold by Seller to Buyer under that Forward Transaction.

(iv)   Where the parties agree to an adjustment under paragraph (iii) above, Buyer or Seller (or both), as shall have been agreed, shall promptly deliver to the other party a Confirmation of the Forward Transaction, as adjusted under paragraph (iii) above.

(d)   Where the parties agree that this paragraph shall apply, paragraphs 2 and 4 of the Agreement are amended as follows.

(i)   Paragraph 2(xx) is deleted and replaced by the following -

"(xx)   "Transaction Exposure" means -

(i)   with respect to any Forward Transaction at any time between the Forward Repricing Date and the Purchase Date, the difference between (A) the Market Value of the Purchased Securities at the relevant time and (B) the Purchase Price;

(ii)   with respect to any Transaction at any time during the period (if any) from the Purchase Date to the date on which the Purchased Securities are delivered to Buyer or, if earlier, the date on which the Transaction is terminated under paragraph 10(h), the difference between (A) the Market Value of the Purchased Securities at the relevant time and (B) the Repurchase Price at the relevant time;

(iii)   with respect to any Transaction at any time during the period from the Purchase Date (or, if later, the date on which the Purchased Securities

are delivered to Buyer or the Transaction is terminated under paragraph 10(h)) to the Repurchase Date (or, if later, the date on which Equivalent Securities are delivered to Seller or the Transaction is terminated under paragraph 10(i)), the difference between (A) the Repurchase Price at the relevant time multiplied by the applicable Margin Ratio (or, where the Transaction relates to Securities of more than one description to which different Margin Ratios apply, the amount produced by multiplying the Repurchase Price attributable to Equivalent Securities of each such description by the applicable Margin Ratio and aggregating the resulting amounts, the Repurchase Price being for this purpose attributed to Equivalent Securities of each such description in the same proportions as those in which the Purchase Price was apportioned among the Purchased Securities) and (B) the Market Value of Equivalent Securities at the relevant time.

In each case, if (A) is greater than (B), Buyer has a Transaction Exposure for that Transaction equal to the excess, and if (B) is greater than (A), Seller has a Transaction Exposure to Buyer equal to the excess."

(ii)   In paragraph 4(c) -

(aa)   the words "any amount payable to the first party under paragraph 5 but unpaid" are deleted and replaced by "any amount which will become payable to the first party under paragraph 5 during the period after the time at which the calculation is made which is equal to the minimum period for the delivery of margin applicable under paragraph 4(g) or which is payable to the first party under paragraph 5 but unpaid"; and

(bb)   the words "any amount payable to the other party under paragraph 5 but unpaid" are deleted and replaced by "any amount which will become payable to the other party under paragraph 5 during the period after the time at which the calculation is made which is equal to the minimum period for the delivery of margin applicable under paragraph 4(g) or which is payable to the other party under paragraph 5 but unpaid".]*

---

* Delete as appropriate

ANNEX II

Form of Confirmation

To: _____

From: _____

Date: _____

Subject: [Repurchase] [Buy/Sell Back]*   Transaction
            (Reference Number: _____)

Dear Sirs,

The purpose of this [letter] [facsimile] , a "Confirmation" for the purposes of the Agreement, is to set forth the terms and conditions of the above repurchase transaction entered into between us on the Contract Date referred to below.

This Confirmation supplements and forms part of, and is subject to, the Global Master Repurchase Agreement as entered into between us as of _____ as the same may be amended from time to time (the "Agreement"). All provisions contained in the Agreement govern this Confirmation except as expressly modified below. Words and phrases defined in the Agreement and used in this Confirmation shall have the same meaning herein as in the Agreement.

1.   Contract Date: _____

2.   Purchased Securities [state type[s] and nominal value[s]]:

      _____

3.   CUSIP, ISIN or other identifying number[s]: _____

4.   Buyer: _____

5.   Seller: _____

6.   Purchase Date: _____

7.   Purchase Price: _____

8.   Contractual Currency: _____

[9.   Repurchase Date]:* _____

[10. Terminable on demand]:* _____

* Delete as appropriate

11.   Pricing Rate: _____

[12.   Sell Back Price]:* _____

13.   Buyer's Bank Account[s] Details:

14.   Seller's Bank Account[s] Details:

[15.   The Transaction is an Agency Transaction.   [Name of Agent]   is   acting
       as agent for   [name or identifier of Principal]   ]:*

[16.   Additional Terms]:*

Yours faithfully,

_____

* Delete as appropriate

Securities Lending & Borrowing and Collateral

CHAPTER 9

Securities Lending & Borrowing and Collateral – Introduction to SL&B

> *This part of the book is targeted at readers that have had no exposure to or limited exposure to the subject of securities lending & borrowing.*

Securities lending & borrowing* trades are a very popular and flexible mechanism by which *securities* are lent against receipt of either *cash collateral* or *non-cash collateral* (*securities*) provided by the securities borrower.

Along with *repo* trades, securities lending & borrowing trades fall within the general grouping of transaction types known as *securities financing*.

This part of the book (Part 3) describes the reasons for the lending and the borrowing of securities, the benefits to both lender and borrower, the various methods of lending and borrowing, and the role collateral plays in such trades.

As the motivations differ considerably behind a firm wishing to 1) lend securities, and to 2) borrow securities, these subjects are described separately and in that sequence.

9.1 INTRODUCTION TO SECURITIES LENDING

> *Definition of securities lending: the temporary loan of a specific quantity of a specific share or bond, to a borrower, against receipt of collateral, for return at a later date.*

For those institutions that purchase *equity* and *bonds*, once those purchases are settled, those securities will remain within their account at their *central securities depository* (CSD) or *custodian*, until sold or utilised in a different transaction; the term given to securities held within such a CSD or custodian account is a *settled securities position*. From this point forward, accounts held within either a CSD or a custodian will be referred to generically as a custodian account.

Whether a firm lends its securities or not is a decision for the firm itself. Some firms choose to lend all or some of their securities, but others choose not to lend at all. There is no regulatory requirement for a firm to lend its securities.

The primary reason for a firm to lend its securities is to optimise use of its existing assets, by increasing its revenue over and above income payments (*dividends* on equity and *coupon payments* on bonds) and increases in price which in turn increases capital value. Secondary reasons are 1) additional income earned by reinvesting cash collateral received from the borrower, and 2) *safe custody* charges imposed by custodians for holding securities will be avoided if the securities are lent and are therefore removed from the lender's custodian account.

Should a firm choose to lend its securities (whether bonds or equity, or both), the basic structure of the transaction is as depicted in Figure 9.1:

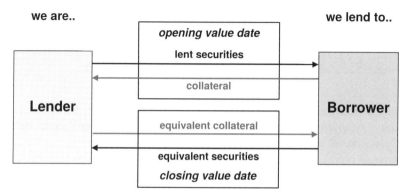

FIGURE 9.1   Basic securities lending trade structure

The dates associated with such a transaction are as follows:

- trade date
  - the date of *trade execution*
- *opening value date* (also known as 'start value date', 'onside value date' or 'first leg value date'):
  - the date the lent security is intended to be delivered to the securities borrower, and
  - the date the collateral is due to be received by the securities lender
- *closing value date* (also known as 'end value date', 'offside value date' or 'second leg value date'):
  - the date the lent security is intended to be returned by the securities borrower, and
  - the date the collateral is due to be returned by the securities lender.

With specific regard to the closing value date, trades can be executed with a fixed closing value date ('term' basis), or on an 'open' basis. Regarding the latter, upon execution of the trade, if neither party has decided at that point in time the date the securities are to be returned, the closing value date will be recorded as 'open' (or 'on demand'). This means that the trade continues day after day, until such time as the lender requires the return of the lent securities, or the borrower wishes to return the borrowed securities to the lender. On that decision day, the party wishing to close the transaction will contact its **counterparty** and the actual closing value date will be agreed; as a result, internally within both firms the trade details will need to be amended to reflect the fact that the 'open' closing value date now has an actual value date applied to it.

Term loans provide the securities lender with greater certainty regarding their lending fees, but at the cost of less flexibility as such loans are usually not able to be recalled (by the securities lender) prior to the previously agreed closing value date. For flexibility reasons therefore, most trades are executed on an 'open' basis; the securities lender has the legal right to '*recall*' the lent securities from the borrower, and the securities borrower has the legal right to '*return*' the borrowed securities to the lender – at any time.

Collateral can be provided in the form of cash or securities (typically highly rated bonds); the value of collateral required by the securities lender is the market value of the lent security, plus an agreed margin percentage. (In securities lending & borrowing, 'margin' has the equivalent meaning of 'haircut' in a repo; both terms refer to the requirement for the borrowing party to **over-collateralise**.) The form of the securities lending fee charged by the lender to the borrower is dependent upon the nature of the collateral:

- cash collateral:
  - the securities lender reinvests the cash received as collateral, and commits to paying an interest rate known as a **rebate rate** to the securities borrower (assuming a **positive interest rate** environment). For cash collateral therefore, the lending fee is the differential between the **reinvestment rate** of interest earned by the securities lender, versus the rebate rate of interest payable by the securities lender to the securities borrower.
- securities collateral:
  - the securities borrower pays a cash fee based upon an agreed percentage of the market value of the lent security; the agreed percentage is usually expressed in **basis points per annum** (bppa).

In order to protect its interests from a legal standpoint, securities lenders will normally enter into a standard and marketwide legal agreement with each of its borrowing counterparties; this agreement is the **Global Master Securities Lending Agreement** (GMSLA). The GMSLA contains the rights and responsibilities of both lenders and borrowers in relation to both the lent security and the collateral, and (should either party **default** on its **contractual obligations**) the legal courses of action open to the non-defaulting party.

Note: it should not be assumed that a party wishing to lend its securities will always be able to identify a borrower that 1) has a matching borrowing requirement, and 2) is prepared to borrow on the terms (e.g. the duration of the loan) required by the borrower.

9.1.1 Securities Lenders

Each firm that buys, holds and sells securities may choose to lend none, some or all of their securities.

Those that are typical major lenders of securities include institutional investors (*buy-side firms*) such as:

- *pension funds*
- *mutual funds*
- *insurance companies*
- national investment authorities.

The common factor amongst buy-side firms is that they are in possession of large pools of funds received from their underlying sources (e.g. many individual investors placing relatively small sums of cash in the hands of a mutual fund). Those funds are used to buy *equity* and *bonds* to increase capital growth and/or to receive income, such as *dividends* on equity and *coupon payments* on bonds. Because buy-side firms typically buy and hold securities over the longer term, the *portfolio* of securities held by such firms means that they are ideal lenders. However, some buy-side firms that possess extremely large inventories of securities choose not to lend their securities at all; the decision is for the individual firm to make. To clarify the term 'buy-side', such firms typically buy and hold securities over the longer term, but they also sell securities.

Additionally, *sell-side firms* including investment banks that hold *proprietary positions* in equity and bonds may choose to lend such securities.

Securities lenders are often referred to as the *beneficial owner* of the lent securities, as opposed to the *legal owner* (the securities borrower).

9.2 INTRODUCTION TO SECURITIES BORROWING

Definition of Securities Borrowing: the temporary borrowing of a specific quantity of a specific share or bond, from a lender, against payment/delivery of collateral, for return at a later date.

The reasons for lending securities may be relatively straightforward, whereas the reasons for borrowing securities are usually more involved.

When selling any goods, it is natural that the seller wishes to receive the sale proceeds at the earliest opportunity; due to the normal method of settling securities trades (i.e. *delivery versus payment* (DvP)), any delay in the seller's ability to deliver the securities also results in delayed receipt of sale proceeds and a negative interest impact on the seller's bank account (assuming a *positive interest rate* environment).

When securities (*equity* and *bonds*) are sold, a *value date* is agreed between buyer and seller; value date (otherwise known as *contractual settlement date*) is the intended date of settlement of the sale. In each securities market, a standard number of days exists between trade date and value date, commonly known as the *settlement cycle*; at the time of writing, the following settlement cycles apply:

- T+1 for US and UK government bonds, and
- T+2 for European equity, US equity and for *Eurobonds*.

Sales and purchases of securities are normally settled on value date, as a result of the seller having the securities available for delivery and the buyer having the means to pay; however, in some securities markets *settlement failure* is an everyday occurrence. Settlement failure means that settlement is delayed resulting in the seller not receiving its cash at the earliest opportunity. When settlement failure occurs, the primary cause is the seller not having the securities available in its custodian account, for delivery on value date; on a minority of occasions, settlement failures are caused by the buyer not having the cash available in its custodian account.

In a situation where a firm has sold securities, but it does not have possession of those securities in its custodian account in order to effect delivery, the seller has two choices, either:

- do nothing, in which case the seller is guaranteed not to receive the sale proceeds at the earliest opportunity, thereby incurring an interest loss, or
- borrow the securities, in which case such securities will be used to settle the sale and receive the sale proceeds simultaneously (providing the buyer has the cash available to pay).

A further reason for a seller choosing to borrow securities is to guard against the threat of the buyer enforcing settlement, a process known as *buy-in*. When the buyer is in urgent need of the securities, the failure of the seller to deliver the securities may cause the buyer to invoke the buy-in procedure. In most, if not all markets, the buyer may choose to force the seller to deliver securities via use of the buy-in market mechanism. The rules within each market state the number of days following value date when the buy-in process can be initiated; in some cases this is just one day.

As there is a cost to borrowing securities, the borrower must ensure that borrowing is financially viable; the borrowing cost must be compared with the benefit derived from receiving the sale proceeds. For example, if the borrowing cost is 1.1% and the receipt of the sale proceeds enables that cash to be lent at 3%, most firms would say that borrowing is beneficial.

Should a firm choose to borrow securities, the basic structure of the transaction is as depicted in Figure 9.2:

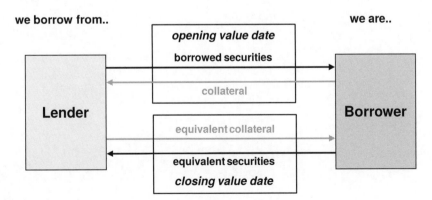

FIGURE 9.2   Basic securities borrowing trade structure

The signing of the *GMSLA* is as important for securities borrowers as it is for securities lenders. Securities borrowers are required to provide collateral in order to *mitigate* the securities lender's risk; the market value of the collateral given is greater (due to the previously mentioned margin that is applied) than the market value of the borrowed securities and therefore it is of paramount importance to the borrower that the terms of such arrangements are documented in a formal legal agreement.

Note: it should not be assumed that a party wishing to borrow securities will always be able to find a lender that 1) has the required securities, 2) has the required quantity of such securities, and 3) is prepared to lend on the terms (e.g. the fee) required by the borrower.

9.2.1 Securities Borrowers

The type of organisation that typically chooses to borrow equity and bonds are those firms that have a securities delivery commitment that cannot (at present) be fulfilled.

Such firms are typically investment banks and hedge funds. Providing that the borrowing of securities is beneficial (i.e. the cost of borrowing is less than the benefit derived from settling the delivery commitment), and that a lender can be identified, such firms will normally enter into a securities borrowing trade.

PART 3

CHAPTER 10

Securities Lending & Borrowing and Collateral – Principles of SL&B

In the first chapter of Part 3, the principles of 1) securities lending, 2) securities borrowing, and 3) the participants in the marketplace, are described. The collateral aspects of securities lending & borrowing (SL&B) are introduced within this chapter.

Note #1: For readers that are new to this subject, it is strongly recommended that the prior chapter (Chapter 9 'Securities Lending & Borrowing and Collateral – Introduction to SL&B') is read first.

Note #2: A variety of methods exist by which SL&B trades can be executed. However, to enable readers' understanding of fundamental principles, in this chapter the trade characteristics and market practices are intentionally described from a generic (bilateral) perspective. A number of SL&B trade execution methods are described within Chapter 12 'Securities Lending & Borrowing and Collateral – Accessing the SL&B Marketplace'.

10.1 PRINCIPLES OF SECURITIES LENDING

The particular circumstances giving rise to securities lending include:

- increasing the return on investment
- reducing the cost of holding securities, and
- reducing taxation through arbitrage strategies.

It is important to remember that throughout the period of any SL&B trade, the securities lender retains an investment (or economic) interest in the particular security; consequently, the securities lender remains *exposed* to fluctuations in price and value (despite the fact that the security is no longer in the possession of the securities lender).

10.1.1 Increasing Return on Investment

Having purchased *equity* and *bonds*, the holder could choose to keep their securities safely and securely in the hands of the *central securities depository* (CSD) or *custodian*. By so doing, the investor can benefit from 1) increases in price (capital growth), 2) receipt of *income* payments, and 3) receipts of advantageous forms of *corporate action*.

Should the investor be prepared to lend some or all of its securities, *beneficial ownership* is retained by the securities lender; this means that capital growth, income and corporate actions are also retained by the lending investor.

But in addition, the securities lender earns fees for lending its securities.

When securities are lent, under normal circumstances the securities are delivered to the securities borrower and are therefore no longer under the direct control of the investor, although beneficial ownership is retained by the securities lender. Some investors contemplating the lending of their securities may feel that losing direct control of their assets is too much of a risk; however, potential lenders should consider the fact that it is standard practice for the securities borrower to provide collateral, the value of which covers the market value of the lent securities, plus an agreed margin percentage. Furthermore, common practice is for the securities lender and the securities borrower to sign legal documentation, designed to protect the interests of both parties; once signed, all individual securities lending & borrowing (SL&B) trades fall under the terms and conditions of the legal documentation.

In summary, the key motivation for a firm to lend its securities is to optimise the return on its existing assets.

10.1.2 Reducing the Cost of Holding Securities

When purchased securities are settled, the securities are held on behalf of the investor either 1) directly at a *CSD*, or 2) at a *custodian*. Whilst such shareholdings or bondholdings exist, the CSD or custodian will charge the investor *securities safekeeping fees*.

Such fees can become significant, and can be based upon a range of factors, including:

- asset type: whether equity or bonds, and
- average value of holdings.

Because lent securities are usually delivered to the securities borrower, safekeeping fees will be reduced and the securities lender will therefore benefit financially.

In summary, although such safekeeping fee reductions may not be a key factor in an investor's decision whether to lend its securities or not, the investor does gain some benefit through avoiding safekeeping costs.

10.1.3 Arbitrage Strategies

In generic terms, arbitrage is the simultaneous purchase and sale of an asset in order to profit from price differences that exist in different markets.

Two examples of arbitrage strategies are:

- dividend reinvestment plan arbitrage, and
- dividend tax arbitrage.

Disclaimer: the two arbitrage strategies described in this section are stated as examples of reasons why securities are lent other than to increase returns on investment or to reduce the cost of holding securities. The author's intention is to explain the procedure, but not to offer an opinion regarding such practices; note that such practices may be unlawful in some jurisdictions.

Dividend Reinvestment Plan Arbitrage A dividend reinvestment plan (DRiP) is a type of dividend that is paid by an equity issuer, to *registered shareholders*, in the form of cash or securities. This is known as an *optional corporate action*, in which the shareholder can choose whether to take cash or securities; normally, the shareholder will be given the default outcome of cash, unless the shareholder opts for securities. If the shareholder opts for securities, the cash value of the dividend (share quantity x dividend rate per share) is used by the issuer to supply the resultant shares to the investor at a discount to the *current market price*.

Some types of investor may be required to accept cash in a DRiP, as they are prevented from opting for securities. For example, *index tracking funds* cannot deviate from defined securities weightings as their holdings would become greater than their investment guidelines permit and are therefore restricted to taking cash in a DRiP; the index tracking fund must therefore miss out on the opportunity to opt for the securities. However, such funds have an obligation to maximise returns for their investors.

A dividend reinvestment plan arbitrage involves the lending of securities by the beneficial owner, to a borrower that is able to accept the securities offered in a DRiP. By executing such an SL&B trade, both the securities lender and the securities borrower gain a benefit. Providing the borrower takes possession of the borrowed securities prior to the *record date* of the dividend, the borrower will opt for securities and the resultant shares will then be sold in the open market. The benefit gained from this overall transaction is the difference between the cash value of the DRiP and the proceeds from the sale of the shares acquired through the DRiP; the benefit is shared between the securities lender and the securities borrower. This series of steps is illustrated in Figure 10.1:

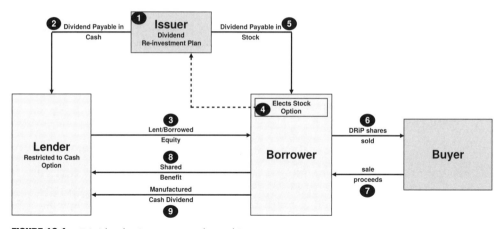

FIGURE 10.1   Dividend reinvestment plan arbitrage

The steps in the diagram are explained as follows:

Step 1: the issuer announces a dividend in the form of a DRiP

Step 2: the existing holder is restricted to taking cash only

Step 3: the existing holder lends the equity to a borrower – delivery needs to occur prior to the record date of the dividend

Step 4: the borrower communicates to the issuer that it wishes to take the stock option (rather than the cash option)

Step 5: the issuer provides stock to the borrower

Step 6: the borrower sells the stock arising from the DRiP

Step 7: the borrower delivers the DRiP shares to the buyer and receives the sale proceeds from the buyer

Step 8: the benefit derived (the difference between the cash value of the DRiP and the proceeds from the sale of the shares acquired through the DRiP) is shared between borrower and lender

Step 9: the cash dividend amount is 'manufactured' by the borrower and is paid to the lender – the lender thereby receives the dividend as originally expected, plus their share of the benefit.

Note: unlike the usual reason for borrowing securities (to fulfil a delivery commitment) in which the borrower on-delivers the borrowed securities, this strategy results in the borrower holding the borrowed securities, albeit temporarily.

Dividend Tax Arbitrage   Income payable on most equity (as dividends) and some bonds (as coupon) is subject to *withholding tax* (WHT). The tax authority within the issuer's country demands that the issuer deducts WHT from payments to investors at the appropriate rate, the choice of which can be:

- the statutory rate, for example 25%:
  - this is the basic rate of WHT deductible from income payable to investors that do not fall within either of the following two categories
  - also known as the 'non-treaty rate'
- the treaty rate, for example 15%:
  - governments of many countries enter into *double taxation agreements* (also known as 'treaties') with other national governments. When income is paid by an issuer to an investor resident in a treaty country, the applicable rate of WHT is the 'treaty rate', a lower rate of WHT compared with the 'non-treaty rate'
- the exempt rate, that is 0%:
  - some countries allow shareholders that are qualified pension funds and charities which are resident in other countries to be exempt from WHT.

Note that where WHT is applicable, the WHT is deducted (withheld) from income payments made by the issuer; the investor is therefore credited with the net proceeds of the income. The issuer must remit the WHT to its national tax authority.

Dividend tax arbitrage is the lending/borrowing of securities on which income is payable imminently, in order for both lender and borrower to benefit financially, where a difference exists in the withholding tax rates payable by the securities lender and the securities borrower. It is the practice of temporarily exploiting the differences in WHT rates between the issuer's country and the countries of residence of investors.

In situations where the shareholder's or bondholder's rate of withholding tax is the non-treaty rate (for example 25%), the holder may choose to lend the relevant security to a borrower that is resident in a treaty country and whose applicable withholding tax rate is considerably lower (for example 15%). Once the SL&B trade has been executed, the transfer of the lent/borrowed security must occur no later than the *record date* of the income payment, to facilitate the lower rate of WHT being deducted from the payment made by the issuer to the securities borrower. The differential (in the above example 10%) is shared between the securities lender and the securities borrower. Figure 10.2 represents the sequence of steps.

Explanation of diagram:

Step 1: the existing holder is subject to 25% WHT on the income due

Step 2: the security is lent to a borrower that is subject to a lower WHT rate (e.g. 15%)

Step 3: the issuer pays the borrower after deduction of the lower WHT rate

Step 4: lender and borrower share the benefit gained (in this case 10%).

Note: unlike the usual reason for borrowing securities (to fulfil a delivery commitment) in which the borrower on-delivers the borrowed securities, this strategy results in the borrower holding the borrowed securities, albeit temporarily.

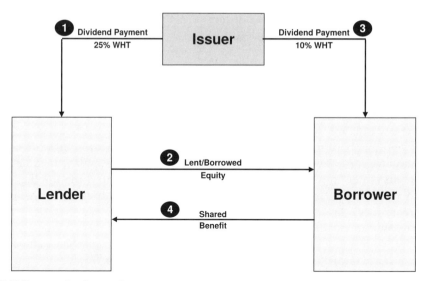

FIGURE 10.2 Dividend tax arbitrage

10.2 PRINCIPLES OF SECURITIES BORROWING

The particular circumstances giving rise to securities borrowing include the need:

- to fulfil a delivery commitment
- to deliver high quality collateral.

10.2.1 Fulfilling Delivery Commitments

Typically, the reasons why some firms borrow securities when they have an obligation to deliver securities is due to 1) a technical short position, and 2) *short selling*.

When a firm sells securities, the following motivating factors are normally at play:

- receiving the sale proceeds at the earliest opportunity:
    - the earliest opportunity is the *value date* of the sale, and
    - in order to receive the sale proceeds, the seller must deliver the securities to the buyer, assuming the settlement method is *delivery versus payment* (DvP)
- settling the client's purchase on value date:
    - where an *investment bank* has sold securities to a *buy-side* counterparty, the buyer expects the securities to be delivered on value date
    - from a client service perspective, it is important that such deliveries are made on time
- avoiding the buyer enforcing settlement:
    - if the buyer is in urgent need of the securities, the ultimate measure that the buyer can take is to enforce settlement by invoking the market's *buy-in* procedure.

Technical Short   A firm may purchase securities and immediately sell them. If settlement of the firm's purchase occurs on its due date (value date), then it is expected that the firm's sale will also settle on its value date; if this is the case, there is no requirement to borrow the securities. This is because the timely settlement of a firm's purchase will facilitate settlement of the firm's sale.

However, the failure to settle a purchase on its due date provides the firm with the opportunity to settle its sale before the purchase, and to benefit financially. (The *settlement failure* of a firm's purchase is usually due to the seller having an insufficient quantity of securities available for delivery.)

Assume the firm XYZ Securities has executed a purchase with one counterparty, and an equal and opposite sale with a different counterparty; also assume that all components of the two trades are identical, as listed in Table 10.1:

TABLE 10.1   Executed trades

Trades Executed by XYZ Securities		
001	*Trade Number*	002
Party D	*Counterparty*	Party K
Buy*	*Operation*	Sell*
5th June	*Trade Date*	5th June
7th June	*Value Date*	7th June
1,000,000	*Quantity*	1,000,000
M&S Shares	*Security*	M&S Shares
GBP 3.26	*Price*	GBP 3.26
DvP	*Settlement Method*	DvP

* Note: 'Buy' means that XYZ Securities buys from the counterparty, and 'sell' means that XYZ Securities sells to the counterparty

Both the purchase and sale by XYZ Securities are due to settle on a delivery versus payment (DvP) basis.

If on value date Party D is able to deliver the securities to XYZ Securities and XYZ Securities makes payment to Party D, that will in turn allow XYZ Securities to deliver the securities to Party K and to receive the sale proceeds. This means that both trades have successfully settled on value date; consequently, there is no opportunity for XYZ Securities to make profit through securities borrowing.

Instead, when value date is reached, if Party D fails to deliver the securities, then this will prevent XYZ Securities from settling its sale and receiving its sale proceeds at the earliest opportunity, as depicted in Figure 10.3.

FIGURE 10.3   Technical short situation, due to settlement failure of the purchase

However, under the circumstances in which Party D cannot deliver the securities to XYZ Securities on value date, XYZ Securities may choose to borrow securities in order to settle its sale and thereby receive its sale proceeds (before having paid Party D), as depicted in Figure 10.4.

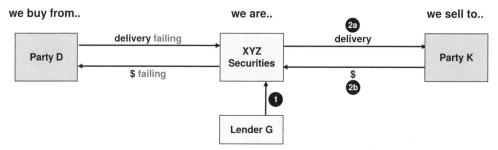

FIGURE 10.4   Technical short situation, post-borrowing

Following settlement failure on value date of its purchase:

Step 1: XYZ Securities executes a securities borrowing trade with Lender G, on an 'open' basis, resulting in Lender G delivering the securities to XYZ Securities

Step 2a: XYZ Securities now delivers the borrowed securities to Party K, on a DvP basis

Step 2b: simultaneously, XYZ Securities receives the sale proceeds from Party K.

Note: the borrowing of securities by XYZ Securities from Lender G was executed on an 'open' basis, which contractually permits XYZ Securities to close the trade with Lender G at any time.

At a later point in time (potentially days or weeks later), Party D delivers the securities it sold to XYZ Securities. The securities received by XYZ Securities should now be returned to Lender G and to close the securities borrowing trade, as depicted in Figure 10.5:

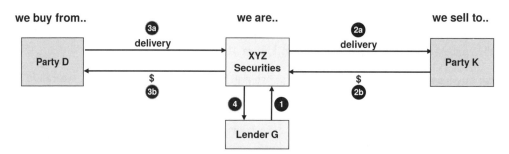

FIGURE 10.5   Technical short situation, post-settlement of purchase

Steps 1, 2a and 2b are as per Figure 10.4 above

Steps 3a and 3b: at a later date, Party D delivers its sold securities to XYZ Securities, on a DvP basis

Step 4: the securities received by XYZ Securities from its purchase are now used to reimburse the securities lender (Lender G), following which the securities borrowing trade has been closed.

Under the circumstances described above, in summary, the buyer with a failing purchase may choose to borrow the securities in order to settle its sale, thereby 1) receiving the sale proceeds at the earliest opportunity, 2) keeping the client happy (where the buyer is a buy-side firm), and 3) avoiding a buy-in.

Short Selling   The sale of a security that the seller does not own is said to be a ***short sale***, meaning that the first trade executed by a firm in a particular security is a sale (rather than a purchase); another way of representing this situation is that the seller has taken a ***negative trading position***. Such trades are executed by a firm's trader in the expectation and hope that the security's price will fall in the coming days or weeks or months. If the trader's initial decision proves to be correct, the securities will be purchased at a lower price at a later date, thereby generating profit for the trader and the firm.

Historically, a trader may have executed a short sale without first ensuring the securities can be borrowed; this is known as a ***naked short*** which is no longer allowed by regulation (at least in some markets). Conversely, a short sale executed only after the trader ensures the securities can be borrowed, is said to be a ***covered short***; in some markets today, regulation permits this type of short selling of equity and government bonds.

Figure 10.6 depicts the situation for a firm that has executed a short sale, prior to borrowing:

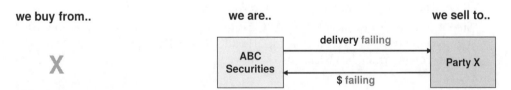

FIGURE 10.6   Short selling situation, pre-borrowing

The diagram illustrates that firm ABC Securities cannot deliver the securities to settle its sale, as it owns none of the particular securities and it has not (yet) purchased such securities; consequently, ABC Securities will suffer a delay in the receipt of the sale proceeds, if no action is taken.

PART 3

ABC Securities now borrows the securities to settle its sale; Figure 10.7 illustrates this situation:

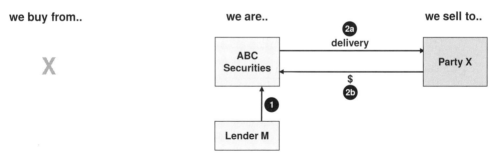

FIGURE 10.7   Short selling situation, post-borrowing

Step 1: ABC Securities executes a securities borrowing transaction with Lender M, resulting in Lender M delivering the securities to ABC Securities

Step 2a: ABC Securities now delivers the borrowed securities to Party X on a DvP basis

Step 2b: simultaneously, ABC Securities receives the sale proceeds from Party X.

At a later point in time, ABC Securities purchases the securities in the marketplace resulting in ABC Securities receiving delivery of the securities, in turn facilitating the closure of the securities borrowing transaction, as depicted in Figure 10.8:

Steps 1, 2a and 2b are as per Figure 10.7 above

Steps 3a and 3b: at a later date, ABC Securities purchases the securities from Party S who then delivers the securities to ABC Securities, on a DvP basis

Step 4: the securities received by ABC Securities from its purchase are now used to reimburse the securities lender (Lender M), following which the securities borrowing trade has been closed.

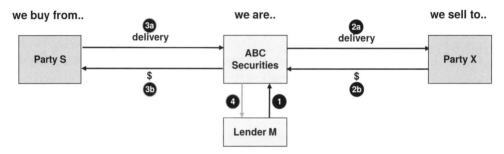

FIGURE 10.8   Short selling situation, post-purchase

In a short selling situation, in summary, the seller is usually obliged to arrange the borrowing of securities prior to execution of a short sale, following which that sale will be settled, thereby 1) receiving the sale proceeds at the earliest opportunity, 2) keeping the client happy (where the buyer is a buy-side firm), and 3) avoiding a buy-in.

Delivering High Quality Collateral   The 2008 *Global Financial Crisis* triggered regulators to demand the *mitigation* of firms' risks in financial transactions, through the provision of *collateral*. Such regulatory requirements are most noticeable in relation to the mitigation of exposures associated with trades in *OTC derivatives*; the regulation in Europe is known as the *European Market Infrastructure Regulation* (EMIR), and in the USA is the *Dodd-Frank Act*.

Mitigation of exposures in OTC derivative trades is usually achieved by the giving or taking of cash collateral or of highly rated government bonds; the latter is known as *high quality liquid assets* (HQLA). However, the choice of giving either cash collateral or HQLA is not always available to the collateral giver. This is because the introduction of *mandatory central clearing* (via *central counterparties* – CCPs) of *standardised OTC derivative* trades brings with it strict regulation as to the type of collateral that may be provided to CCPs in order to mitigate exposures.

For some organisations that engage in OTC derivative trades, the nature of their business means that they do not necessarily possess the (collateral) asset types that are CCP-eligible. This situation means that such organisations need to borrow HQLA so as to comply with *margin calls* received from CCPs.

This topic is described further within Part 4c 'OTC Derivatives and Collateral: Regulatory Change and The Future of Collateral'.

10.3 LENDABLE AND BORROWABLE ASSETS

The types of securities that are typically required by securities borrowers (and are therefore lendable by securities lenders) include:

- equity:
  - *global equity*
  - *American Depository Receipts* (ADRs)
  - *Global Depository Receipts* (GDRs)
  - *Exchange-Traded Funds(ETFs)*
- bonds, issued by:
  - central governments
  - *supranational entities*
  - *agencies*
  - corporations
- other types of security:
  - *mortgage-backed securities*.

10.4 PARTICIPANTS IN THE SECURITIES LENDING & BORROWING MARKETPLACE: INTRODUCTION

The typical parties that are involved in the lending and borrowing of securities are primarily the following.

10.4.1 Securities Lenders

The types of organisation that are active in securities lending are those that are classified as *institutional investors*, many of which have significant assets provided by their underlying members or investors. Such organisations have the nickname of '*buy-side*', because they are often long-term investors in *equity* and *bonds*; consequently, they are ideally suited to enhance their returns through their preparedness to lend the securities they own.

The following types of firm are amongst the buy-side community:

- pension funds
- mutual funds
- investment funds
- exchange-traded funds
- sovereign wealth funds
- endowment funds
- private foundations
- insurance companies.

Some types of fund operate within very competitive environments, where their investment performance is compared against their rivals; therefore having a means to increase their returns (via securities lending) becomes a critical component of their ongoing performance. Other buy-side firms may view securities lending revenues as a means of reducing their costs, such as *securities safekeeping fees* charged by *CSDs* and *custodians*.

Some of the larger buy-side firms may choose to manage their securities lending activity by themselves, where the parties to an SL&B trade are the securities lender and the securities borrower, with no intermediary involved.

Conversely, many buy-side firms utilise the securities lending services provided by intermediary firms, some of which are known as *lending agents*; see 'Intermediaries' later in this section of this chapter.

10.4.2 Securities Borrowers

The normal borrowers of securities include the following:

Broker-Dealers

- *market makers* form part of the Securities Trading Department of investment banks or *broker-dealers*, and are required to quote prices at which they are prepared to buy and to sell specific securities for which they choose to make a market; as

market makers, they are obliged to execute purchases and sales of such securities, at their quoted prices
- when a market maker sells, they may or may not own the share quantity they are selling. In situations in which the market maker is selling short (i.e. taking a *negative trading position*), their ability to borrow securities in order to effect delivery of such sales is of paramount importance in fulfilling their role as a market maker.
- the Trading Department of broker-dealers (which includes market making) buy and sell equity and bonds. On many occasions, the broker-dealer's ability to settle their sale on the value date of the trade is dependent upon their purchase settling first
  - where settlement of the broker-dealer's purchase is delayed (i.e. *settlement failure*), it is in the broker-dealer's interest to settle the sale without delay; borrowing securities under such circumstances enables the broker-dealer to effect the delivery to the buyer, thereby:
    - receiving the sale proceeds at the earliest opportunity
    - satisfying the securities delivery required by buy-side buyers, and
    - avoiding a *buy-in* (enforcement of settlement) by the buyer.

Hedge Funds
- amongst a variety of trading strategies employed by *hedge funds*, such firms utilise short selling; consequently, there is a need for securities borrowing in order to settle such short sales. Many hedge funds utilise various services provided by *prime brokers*, including facilitating the borrowing of securities to settle short sales executed by hedge funds.

In general terms, as time passes there is an increasing need for firms of all types to provide collateral for their various financial transactions. For example, a firm:

- may have borrowed equity or a bond, for which the securities lender requires high quality securities collateral
- may have executed a repo trade in which the firm wishes to borrow cash and needs to provide high quality securities collateral to the cash lender
- may have executed an *OTC derivative* trade in which the *central counterparty* (under *EMIR* or *Dodd-Frank*) is calling the firm to provide high quality securities collateral
  - in all three cases above, if the firm does not possess the necessary securities collateral, it is likely that the firm will choose to borrow the securities.

10.4.3 Intermediaries
As mentioned earlier, some of the larger buy-side firms choose to lend their securities directly to borrowers, whereas other buy-side firms opt to utilise the services provided by securities lending & borrowing intermediaries.

PART 3

Amongst the types of firm that fall within the category of intermediary are:

- international central securities depositories
- global custodians
- trading platforms and associated central counterparties, and
- non-custodial lending agents.

The role that intermediaries play is depicted in Figure 10.9:

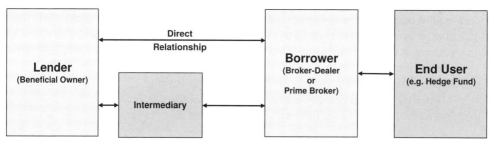

FIGURE 10.9   The role of the intermediary in securities lending & borrowing

International Central Securities Depositories   A *central securities depository* (CSD) is the ultimate storage location of *securities* within a financial centre, in which securities are held by the CSD in *safe custody* and on behalf of the securities holder, within one or more securities accounts; similarly, cash accounts are maintained.

The record of ownership is typically maintained electronically, and the settlement of trades is usually conducted by *electronic book-entry* on a *delivery versus payment* (DvP) basis or on a *free of payment* (FoP) basis.

Today, CSDs are present in most (if not all) major financial centres around the globe, usually on a per-country basis; these are known as *national central securities depositories* (NCSDs). Commonly, within a country one NCSD exists for domestic equity and bonds, although in some cases separate NCSDs exist for (say) equity as opposed to government bonds. At the time of writing, in China three NCSDs exist; one for equity, another for government bonds, and a third for corporate bonds.

In addition to numerous NCSDs globally, two *international central securities depositories* (ICSDs) exist, namely **Clearstream International** (Luxembourg) and **Euroclear Bank** (Brussels). Both ICSDs manage 1) international securities as well as 2) domestic securities, the latter usually being achieved via electronic links with certain NCSDs. Furthermore, both ICSDs are multi-currency environments, in which currency balances can be held overnight (as opposed to being zeroised each day as occurs in some NCSDs).

Both ICSDs offer automated and anonymous securities lending and securities borrowing programmes to their members. For further details as to the role of ICSDs in securities lending & borrowing, please refer to Chapter 12 'Securities Lending & Borrowing and Collateral – Accessing the SL&B Marketplace'.

Note: *Target2 Securities* (T2S) is a pan-European project in which trade settlement (which has historically been actioned within the relevant NCSDs) will instead be actioned within the T2S settlement platform, in *central bank money*.

Global Custodians   Generically speaking, custodians are organisations that provide services to securities holders that do not have direct accounts at NCSDs or ICSDs. Many *buy-side* firms choose not to become direct members of CSDs, and instead become clients of either a *local custodian* in a particular marketplace, or of a *global custodian* that provides access to multiple markets around the globe.

The custodian usually has one or more accounts at the relevant CSD, in which their various clients' securities are held. Note that the clients of such custodian organisations have a relationship directly with the custodian, and not with the CSD.

Global custodians (GCs) usually operate a network of sub-custodians that hold such assets on behalf of the GC; in turn the GC holds the securities on behalf of its client. The benefit in a firm utilising the services provided by global custodians is that it is a single point of contact for multiple markets around the globe.

A number of global custodians offer securities lending & borrowing services to their members.

For further details as to the securities lending & borrowing services provided by global custodians, please refer to Chapter 12 'Securities Lending & Borrowing and Collateral – Accessing the SL&B Marketplace'.

Central Counterparties   Trading platforms are software systems which facilitate the act of *trade execution* between two members of the system.

Central counterparties (CCPs) are firms that are situated between a buyer and a seller; the CCP is the buyer to every seller and the seller to every buyer. CCPs minimise counterparty risk, as the bilateral counterparty does not apply. The CCP becomes a party to a trade by one of two routes, either:

- immediately upon trade execution, where trading is anonymous and where the counterparty to both the end-buyer and end-seller is the CCP, or
- trade execution occurs directly between the two member firms and is subsequently assigned to the CCP by the process of *novation*.

Eurex is a Germany-based organisation which offers both trade execution capability and CCP services via its clearing house Eurex Clearing. Amongst its various services, securities lending & borrowing trades are executed bilaterally, then novated to Eurex Clearing as CCP.

For further details as to the role of CCPs in securities lending & borrowing, please refer to Chapter 12 'Securities Lending & Borrowing and Collateral – Accessing the SL&B Marketplace'.

Non-Custodial Third Party Lending Agents   Many *buy-side* firms choose to lend their securities via non-custodial lending agents, whereby the beneficial owner uses the lending agent as the conduit to securities borrowers.

The primary role of third party lending agents is to negotiate the terms of securities lending with borrowers, and to manage such arrangements on an ongoing basis, on

PART 3

behalf of the beneficial owner of the securities. 'Non-custodial' refers to this type of lending agent being a firm that does not have direct possession of the beneficial owner's securities assets (unlike a CSD or global custodian).

For further details as to the role of non-custodial third party lending agents, please refer to Chapter 12 'Securities Lending & Borrowing and Collateral – Accessing the SL&B Marketplace'.

10.5 SECURITIES LENDING & BORROWING: LEGAL DOCUMENTATION

Because a securities lending & borrowing (SL&B) trade is executed over a period of time, risks and *exposures* arise for both lender and borrower.

In parallel with other types of collateralised transaction (e.g. *repo* and *OTC derivatives*), before a firm executes an SL&B trade, for its own protection (and that of its *counterparty*) it is essential that an appropriate legal agreement is signed between the two trading parties. Once the legal agreement is in place, each individual SL&B trade is then executed between the two parties with reference to and under the protection of the legal agreement.

10.5.1 Background

Over a number of years, as the style and content of trades were shaped amongst the SL&B trading community, a common standard for the content of SL&B legal agreements was developed.

Today, that standard legal agreement is entitled the 'Global Master Securities Lending Agreement' and is commonly known as the *GMSLA*. Various versions of the GMSLA have been produced over the years, the latest of which is the 2010 version (at the time of writing).

10.5.2 GMSLA: Overview

In essence, the purpose of legal agreements such as the GMSLA is to clearly state contractual rights for both parties, and their *contractual obligations*.

One very important feature of the GMSLA is clearly defined *events of default*; if a firm's counterparty has defaulted (or becomes insolvent), the agreement permits obligations relating to all open trades falling under the agreement to be immediately terminated and *set off* against each other, and settled on a net basis. The right of set-off is invaluable to a firm, as without such a right 1) all payment obligations of a firm may be required to be made, without 2) simultaneous receipt of obligations due to the firm. In an insolvency situation, the latter can take an inordinate length of time, in some cases months or years. Due to *over-collateralisation* given by the securities borrower over and above the market value of the lent security, it is expected that the securities lender normally holds adequate collateral to repurchase the lent securities in the market, via utilisation of cash collateral held or by selling securities collateral held.

The GMSLA additionally contains terms and conditions covering areas such as:

- the *beneficial owner* and *legal owner* of the lent/borrowed security
- the beneficial owner and legal owner of securities collateral
- the value of collateral that must be given relative to the value of the lent/borrowed securities
- whether a margin is to be applied
- the method of settlement of the opening and closing legs
- the procedure for closing 'open' trades
- conditions under which *margin calls* can be made
- *collateral substitution* conditions
- the treatment of *income* payments (e.g. *coupons* and *dividends*)
- the securities that must be returned upon trade closure.

Between two parties that intend executing SL&B trades with one another, the wording within the GMSLA is typically not altered. Any specific arrangements between the two parties are documented within the Schedule to the GMSLA.

10.5.3 Ownership and Reuse of Securities

Specifically, regarding ownership of the lent/borrowed security and of securities collateral:

- the lent/borrowed security:
  - legal ownership of the lent securities is transferred from the securities lender to the securities borrower for the duration of the SL&B trade. From an operational standpoint, however, the lender has not sold the lent security, and as such retains beneficial rights. Whilst the securities borrower is the *legal owner*, the securities lender is the *beneficial owner*. Legal ownership is transferred because, under the GMSLA, the legal basis on which the securities are lent/borrowed is *title transfer*
- securities collateral:
  - in parallel with the above, legal ownership of securities collateral is transferred from the securities borrower (collateral giver) to the securities lender (collateral taker) for the duration of the SL&B trade. From an operational standpoint, however, the securities borrower has not sold the securities collateral, and as such retains beneficial rights. Whilst the securities lender (collateral taker) is the legal owner of the securities collateral, the securities borrower (collateral giver) is the beneficial owner. Legal ownership is transferred because, under the GMSLA, the legal basis on which securities collateral is given/taken is title transfer.

The method of transfer of a securities purchase and sale is also title transfer, therefore the securities borrower and the securities collateral taker in an SL&B trade have the same unlimited rights to the securities as if those parties had instead purchased the securities. Consequently, both parties are free to choose whatever they wish to do with the securities, including:

- for the securities borrower:
  - on-delivering in order to fulfil a delivery commitment, or
  - holding the securities safely within the borrower's account at its custodian (where the securities have been borrowed for a different purpose than on-delivering)
- for the securities lender (collateral taker):
  - holding the securities collateral safely within the lender's account at its custodian, or
  - reusing the securities collateral in one (or more) of the following ways: selling it, repoing it, lending it, or delivering it to satisfy a margin call in (for example) an *OTC derivative* transaction.

Note that, due to title transfer, neither the securities lender nor the securities borrower (collateral giver) has the legal right to prevent its counterparty from reusing the collateral. However, at the close of the SL&B trade, each party is obliged to return to its counterparty the *equivalent security* or the *equivalent collateral* (as appropriate). Each party must remain aware of this fact, particularly if:

- the securities borrower has chosen to on-deliver the borrowed securities, or
- the securities lender has chosen to reuse the securities collateral.

10.5.4 Uniqueness of Legal Documentation

Specifically, from a *collateral management* perspective, it is important to note that each set of legal documents (i.e. the GMSLA plus the Schedule) a firm has with each of its SL&B counterparties is likely to contain different terms and conditions and unique characteristics.

It is therefore imperative that the SL&B operations personnel carry out their day-by-day responsibilities according to the legal terms defined with each of their counterparties in the appropriate legal documents. If there is a failure to do so, the firm is likely to be at risk as, for example, the firm's exposures with counterparties may not be fully mitigated, and/or counterparty's exposures may be over-collateralised.

In order to view the content of the current GMSLA, the complete 2010 version can be found in Chapter 13 'Securities Lending & Borrowing and Collateral – The Global Master Securities Lending Agreement'.

10.6 SECURITIES LENDING & BORROWING AND COLLATERAL

In this section, further concepts of securities lending & borrowing are described, incorporating the principles of cash and securities collateral.

10.6.1 Risks and Risk Mitigation

Upon delivery of the lent securities to the borrower, the lender has a definite and immediate risk: the risk that the borrower will fail to return the lent securities. The following *mitigating* actions are usually taken by the securities lender:

- a securities lending & borrowing legal agreement (GMSLA) should be signed
- trades are executed on an 'open' (as opposed to 'term') basis, thereby allowing the securities lender to *recall* the lent securities at any time and at very short notice
- collateral must be provided by the securities borrower to the securities lender
- collateral must be of an adequate value* so as to cover the repurchase cost of the lent securities, in the event of the securities borrower's insolvency
- collateral acceptable to the securities lender is defined so as to make certain that only *liquid securities* are eligible
- the required value of collateral incorporates a margin (*over-collateralisation*) given by the securities borrower.

Similarly, the borrower is at risk of not having its collateral returned by the securities lender. The GMSLA is designed to protect the interests of both parties.

10.6.2 Purpose and Use of Collateral

Following execution of a securities lending & borrowing (SL&B) trade, the lender will deliver the securities to the borrower. The lender of securities bears the risk that the borrower will fail to return the lender's securities.

In order to mitigate that risk, it is common practice for the lender to receive collateral from the borrower. The form of collateral acceptable to the lender is agreed prior to executing a securities lending & borrowing trade, within a legal agreement.

If the lender is to avoid going on-risk and having an exposure, the value of collateral given by the securities borrower must be no less than the market value of the lent securities, plus the applicable margin, throughout the lifetime of the securities loan. Because the value of the lent securities will fluctuate and does not remain static, both securities lender and borrower must recalculate the value of the lent securities at the agreed frequency, normally on a daily basis. During the lifetime of the SL&B trade and on a day-to-day basis, this may result in the need for the borrower to provide further collateral, or for the securities lender to return some of the existing collateral; such activity is the result of *margin calls* which are made by the party with the current *exposure*.

When the lender delivers the lent security, in order to mitigate the lender's risk (of not having their asset returned) the borrower is required to provide collateral simultaneously. Likewise, at the close of the trade, when the borrowed securities are returned

---

*At a particular point in time during the lifetime of a trade, the securities lender may consider that it is in possession of an adequate value of collateral following settlement of its latest margin call; however, between that date and the point at which the collateral is liquidated, the possibility remains that securities price movements may cause the 'current' collateral value to become inadequate.

to the lender the collateral must be returned to the borrower simultaneously. This is illustrated in Figure 10.10:

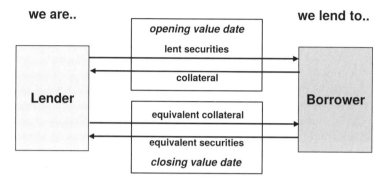

FIGURE 10.10   Securities lending trade structure, including collateral

Because (under normal circumstances) a securities borrower executes a borrowing trade due to a delivery commitment that it cannot otherwise fulfil, a securities borrower will take possession of the borrowed securities from the lender and immediately on-deliver the borrowed securities to another party. Any delay between the receipt of the borrowed securities and the on-delivery is likely to result in the securities borrower incurring unnecessary borrowing costs. This, therefore, means that (under normal circumstances) the borrower does not have possession of the borrowed securities throughout the lifetime of the borrowing, although it does have a legal commitment to return to the lender *equivalent securities*; the word 'equivalent' is used in recognition of the possibility that, during the lifetime of the SL&B trade, the original lent/borrowed security could be cancelled and replaced by a new *ISIN* (as a result of a *corporate action* event). If no such event has occurred, the borrower is required to return to the lender the same quantity of the same ISIN, upon closure of the SL&B trade.

10.6.3 Eligible Collateral

The form of collateral eligible (acceptable) to the lender must be documented within the legal documentation.

Typically, and per trade, eligible collateral will be either cash (in one or more specified currencies) or securities. Where securities are eligible, it must also be stated whether, for example, equity is eligible. Bonds are usually acceptable, providing they are issued by highly rated governments, government agencies, *supranational organisations* and corporations.

As mentioned earlier in this chapter (within Section 10.2 'Principles of Securities Borrowing'), high quality liquid assets (HQLA) are in great demand as collateral relating to, for example, *OTC derivative* exposures; consequently, securities borrowers are seeking to utilise other collateral assets wherever possible for their SL&B trades, thereby saving HQLA for when they are the only form of collateral acceptable to a counterparty.

Whether cash or securities collateral, the securities lender must have certainty that, should the securities borrower fail to return the lent security, the market value of its lent security is recoverable by liquidating the collateral it holds. This means 1) for cash collateral, becoming the owner of the cash it holds, and 2) for securities collateral, selling the securities and taking ownership of the sale proceeds.

Whether cash or securities collateral, it is common practice for a margin to be applied over and above the current value of the lent/borrowed security; 'margin' is the terminology used in SL&B for a valuation percentage. To clarify, margin has the effect of increasing the current market value of a lent/borrowed security in order to derive the required value of collateral which the borrower must provide to mitigate the securities lender's risk; in other words, the borrower is required to *over-collateralise*. This is depicted in Table 10.2:

TABLE 10.2　Required collateral value

Required Collateral Value			
Trade #	Lent Security Current Market Value	Margin	Required Collateral Value
1	EUR 20,000,000.00	2%	EUR 20,400,000.00
2	USD 16,000,000.00	5%	USD 16,800,000.00

10.6.4 Over-Collateralisation (Margin)

In SL&B trades, it is common practice to apply a risk adjusted value over and above the market value of the lent/borrowed security; this risk adjusted value is expressed in percentage terms and is known as 'margin' (the equivalent of '*haircut*' in a *repo* trade).

Margin provides an additional cushion of value to the securities lender, its purpose being to mitigate the risk of adverse movements in the value of collateral relative to the value of the lent security.

The value of collateral required by the securities lender is the sum of 1) the market value of the lent security, and 2) the value of the margin percentage. The margin therefore denotes the extent to which the securities borrower is required to over-collateralise the value of the borrowed securities. This is represented in Figure 10.11:

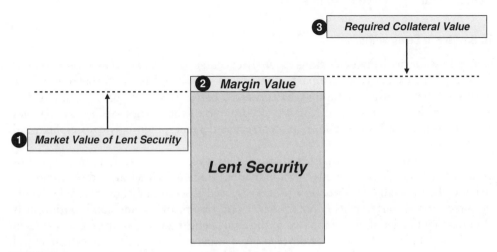

FIGURE 10.11　Deriving the required collateral value

Table 10.3 provides a monetary example:

TABLE 10.3   Calculation of required collateral value

	Currency	Cash Value
Market Value of Lent Securities	EUR	7,500,000.00
Margin Value (2%)	EUR	150,000.00
Required Collateral Value (102%)	**EUR**	**7,650,000.00**

Margin impacts the securities lender positively, as they will receive a greater value of collateral than the market value of the lent security. However, the securities borrower is impacted negatively, for the same reason.

It is important to note that margin is applicable not only to settlement of the *opening leg*, but it must be maintained throughout the lifetime of the SL&B trade as part of daily exposure management.

For reasons of standardisation and to facilitate automation, in the past it has been market practice to apply standard margin percentages of:

- 102%, where the lent security and collateral are in the same currency
- 105%, where the currencies of the lent security and collateral are different, and
- c.110%, where equity collateral is used.

Although such fixed percentages can still be applied today, a recent trend has been for firms to negotiate margin percentages according to factors including the particular parties involved and the specific type of collateral provided.

Whatever are the agreed margin percentages between two firms, they are documented within the schedule to the GMSLA.

10.6.5 Trade Confirmation

Where any form of financial transaction is executed on an *over-the-counter* (OTC) basis and directly between two parties, including securities lending & borrowing, the risk exists that a misunderstanding has occurred between the two parties, and/or that transaction details are recorded incorrectly by one of the parties. Such discrepancies may well lead to settlement failure or incorrect settlement, potentially causing financial loss to one or both parties.

Consequently, it is essential for all parties involved in OTC trading to adopt procedures that identify that details of an individual trade are either agreed or disagreed. Generically, the trade confirmation process is used to communicate the trade details captured by one party, to its counterparty. Upon receipt of a trade confirmation, it is essential that the details are compared to the equivalent trade within the recipient's own records. If details are found to be different, it is imperative that this is investigated and resolved without delay. This is depicted in Figure 10.12:

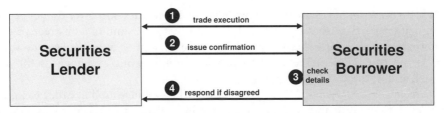

FIGURE 10.12   Steps in confirming OTC trades

Step 1: the SL&B trade is executed directly between securities lender and borrower

Step 2: one (or both) parties issues the terms of the trade to its counterparty

Step 3: without delay, the recipient of the trade confirmation should compare its details against internal records

Step 4: if there is any aspect that disagrees, the recipient must contact the counterparty immediately, in order to investigate and resolve the discrepancy without delay.

Trade confirmations should include, as a minimum, all basic trade details. Ideally, full trade cash values (including their line-by-line breakdown), plus the firm's and its counterparty's *standing settlement instructions* (SSIs) should also be included.

10.6.6 Giving and Taking Collateral

Where there is a choice of *eligible collateral*, the securities borrower must communicate to the securities lender the collateral it proposes to provide, in order to secure the lender's exposure. The collateral must fall within the specific terms of the agreement between the two parties concerned, in terms of its eligibility and any margin calculations. It is therefore important for both lenders and borrowers to have direct access to their respective SL&B agreements database, for each of their respective counterparties.

From the securities lender's perspective, they will be exposed if the lent security is delivered to the borrower without simultaneous receipt (from the borrower) of an asset of at least equivalent collateral value. Similarly, the securities borrower would be exposed if they provided collateral to the lender without simultaneous receipt of the borrowed security.

The delivery of a lent security can be made against receipt of collateral in the form of cash or securities, according to the legal agreement between the two parties. This is depicted in Figure 10.13:

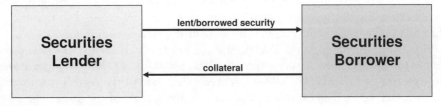

FIGURE 10.13   Initial exchange of lent/borrowed security and collateral

Whichever form of collateral is provided by the securities borrower to the securities lender, neither party wishes to part with its asset without simultaneous receipt of the counterparty's asset. But whether simultaneous exchange is achievable is dependent upon 1) the capability of the *CSD* to provide simultaneous exchange of the assets involved, and 2) the form of collateral.

Delivery versus payment (DvP) is the standard procedure used in order to mitigate *securities delivery risk* and *cash payment risk* in settlement of the purchase and sale of securities. The alternative to DvP is *free of payment* (FoP) settlement, which is in common use for delivering the lent/borrowed security FoP, and the securities collateral FoP, entirely independently of one another. It should be noted that under FoP, both securities lender and securities borrower are at risk of making a delivery of a security without simultaneous receipt of the counterparty's asset, unless one of the parties agrees to going on-risk by delivering or paying their asset first (known as pre-delivery and pre-pay respectively).

Cash Collateral   Where the securities borrower chooses to provide collateral in the form of cash, the exchange (on the *opening value date*) of the lent/borrowed security and the cash collateral is normally achieved simultaneously by DvP. Note: truly simultaneous exchange of assets is achievable only if the CSD practices true DvP settlement; that is, with no delay between the movement of one asset (i.e. the lent securities) and the movement of the contra asset (i.e. the cash collateral).

If DvP settlement is not available or applicable (for whatever reason), the securities borrower is usually required to go on-risk and to make payment of the cash prior to receipt of the borrowed security (known as 'pre-pay').

CASH COLLATERAL EXAMPLE (PART 1)

Note: this example will be continued throughout a number of subsequent sections.
   Party L lends Party B 2,000,000 Issuer P shares at an agreed fee, on an open basis. On this date, the market price of the security is EUR 15.37 per share, giving a market value of EUR 30,740,000.00.
   In order to secure the exposure of Party L, Borrower B chooses to provide cash collateral. According to the terms of the SL&B agreement, cash collateral must have a minimum value of 102% of the market value of the lent securities, in this example being EUR 31,354,800.00.

Party L refers to its SL&B database to discover that the cash collateral proposed by Party B does fall within the agreement's collateral eligibility criteria, and that the value of the collateral is acceptable taking into account the margin requirement.

Prior to the opening value date (ideally on trade date), each party issues a DvP settlement instruction, the lender requesting delivery of the 2,000,000 Issuer P shares, against receipt of EUR 31,354,800.00, with a value date of the trade's opening value date, on a DvP basis. The borrower instructs for the receipt of the same. The instructions must match (at the CSD) prior to settlement occurring.

Securities Collateral   Where the securities borrower chooses to provide collateral in the form of securities (typically bonds), the exchange (on the opening value date) of the lent/borrowed security and the securities collateral is achieved on a non-simultaneous basis, by FoP. This means that 1) the lender is required to deliver the lent securities on the opening value date without knowing whether the collateral will be received at the same time; similarly, 2) the borrower is required to deliver the securities collateral on the opening value date without knowing whether the borrowed securities will be received at the same time. Historically, simultaneous exchange of securities (i.e. *delivery versus delivery*, or DvD) has generally not been available within CSDs, consequently two-way FoP settlement has been necessary, although not without risk to both parties. Note: *Effective DvD* is available within *Target2 Securities*.

Under some circumstances, the securities borrower may be required to provide securities collateral one day in advance of the opening value date; should the collateral fail to arrive, the lender has time to cancel the delivery of the lent security and avoid going on-risk. This can occur in a *daylight exposure* situation where the lent security is to be delivered in one time zone (e.g. European), and the collateral is to be delivered in a different time zone (e.g. American).

In order to effect delivery of the lent/borrowed security and the collateral security, *settlement instructions* must be issued by each party to their respective CSD or custodian. It is important to note that all CSDs and custodians publicise deadlines for the receipt of instructions, relative to value date. If deadlines are missed, exposures will not be mitigated at the earliest opportunity.

Securities settlement instructions can be issued using various methods, but amongst the most popular is *S.W.I.F.T.* due to its inbuilt security levels and structured message formats. Use of S.W.I.F.T. requires subscription by both message sender and receiver. Security of settlement instructions is paramount for both lender and borrower if fraud is to be prevented. Other secure methods are the CSD's or custodian's proprietary systems. Fax is an alternative but is not recommended as it is generally considered to be insufficiently secure. Figure 10.14 represents how one party (in this example the securities borrower) communicates its settlement instruction via S.W.I.F.T.:

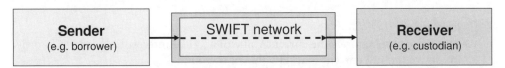

FIGURE 10.14   Issuance of settlement instructions via S.W.I.F.T.

Note: S.W.I.F.T. has a defined set of messages specifically for collateral purposes.

SECURITIES COLLATERAL EXAMPLE (PART 1)

Note: this example will be continued throughout a number of subsequent sections.
   Party L2 lends to Party B2 800,000 Issuer M shares at an agreed fee, on an open basis. On this date, the market price of the security is USD 21.25 per share, giving a market value of USD 17,000,000.00.

(continued)

(continued)

In order to secure the exposure of Party L2, Party B2 chooses to provide securities collateral. According to the terms of the SL&B agreement, securities collateral must have a minimum value of 105% of the market value of the lent securities, in this example being USD 17,850,000.00.

Party B2 communicates that it wishes to provide a quantity of USD 18,000,000 US Treasury 4.5% bonds, maturing 15th August 2030, currently priced at 97.55%. The current market value of this bond is shown in Table 10.4:

TABLE 10.4   Collateral value calculation

Example Securities (Bond) Collateral Value Calculation		
Component	**Calculation**	**Cash Value**
Principal	USD 18,000,000 × 97.55%	USD 17,559,000.00
Accrued Interest	USD 18,000,000.00 × 4.5% / 368 × 133 days	USD 292,744.56
	Current Market Value	USD 17,851,744.56

As can be seen from the table, the current market value of this bond is not less than the market value of the lent security, plus the margin.

It is important to note that, for interest-bearing bonds, the bond's current market value and current collateral value must include the current value of *accrued interest*. Failure to take account of accrued interest will mean that the collateral giver is in danger of undervaluing the collateral, thereby *over-collateralising* and delivering collateral with a true value greater than the giver has calculated. The topic of accrued interest is explained fully within this author's book, *Securities Operations: A Guide to Trade and Position Management* (ISBN 0471497584). Bond prices can be quoted in two ways, namely:

- 'clean' price:
    - this price type requires the current value of accrued interest to be added in order to derive the full current market value of the bond
    - in the example trade above, the price of 97.55% is a clean price
- 'dirty' price:
    - this price type is an 'all-in' price, in which the current value of accrued interest is incorporated within the price
    - in the example trade above, the dirty price is 99.17635% (current market value divided by bond quantity).

Party L2 refers to its SL&B database to discover that the collateral proposed by Party B2 does fall within the agreement's eligibility criteria, and that the current market value of the collateral is acceptable, taking into account the margin requirement.

Each party inputs two settlement instructions (1 × delivery, 1 × receipt) for the movement of the lent/borrowed securities and of the securities collateral, on an FoP basis; each instruction is required to be matched prior to settlement occurring (but with no dependency between the two sets of instructions). Once 1) the instructions are matched, and 2) the *opening value date* has been reached, the lent/borrowed security is transferred at the CSD between the accounts of the two involved parties; similarly, on the same date, the securities collateral is transferred in the opposite direction. Party L2 receives a settlement advice from its custodian, which reflects delivery of the lent securities, and receipt of the securities collateral. Likewise, Party B2's custodian issues a settlement advice to Party B2 reflecting the receipt of the borrowed securities, and the outgoing delivery of the securities collateral. Furthermore, the resultant securities balances are reflected within *depot statements* issued by the custodians of both firms, which then facilitates *depot reconciliation* by both firms.

10.6.7 Interest on Cash Collateral

Collateral given in the form of cash is usually subject to interest payable by the *collateral taker* (i.e. the securities lender) to the securities borrower. The interest rate is agreed between securities lender and borrower at *trade execution*; this rate is commonly known as a *rebate rate*.

An important aspect of securities lending is that the lender should profit from cash collateral received, and that the collateral giver earns a return on its cash. It is common practice for the securities lender to reinvest the cash collateral in the *money market* for the duration of the transaction, in order to earn interest at a greater rate than the rebate rate; this interest rate is known as the *reinvestment rate*. It is in the securities lender's interest to negotiate as high an interest rate as possible when placing the cash in the money market, as the rebate rate agreed with the collateral giver must be deducted from the reinvestment rate earned by the securities lender.

Following the close of the SL&B transaction, the agreed rate is paid to the securities borrower, whilst the remainder is retained by the securities lender, as illustrated in Figure 10.15:

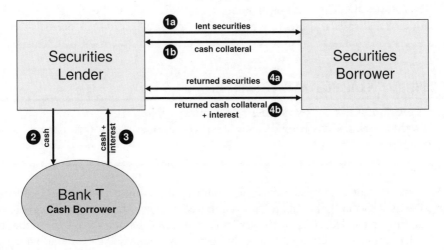

FIGURE 10.15   Treatment of cash collateral and rebate interest

Step 1a: on the opening leg of an SL&B transaction, the securities lender delivers the lent security to the securities borrower

Step 1b: the securities borrower provides cash collateral to the securities lender

Step 2: the securities lender lends the cash collateral to a bank, at an agreed interest rate.

At the close of the SL&B transaction:

Step 3: the cash loan is terminated with the bank; both the capital sum lent and the interest due is paid by the bank to the securities lender

Step 4a: the lent securities are returned to the securities lender by the securities borrower

Step 4b: capital plus rebate interest is remitted by the securities lender to the securities borrower.

Reinvestment of cash collateral is a risk for the securities lender, as they have entered into a contractual agreement to pay the securities borrower the rebate rate regardless of the rate at which the securities lender reinvests. Should money market interest rates fall below the rebate rate, the securities lender is at risk of suffering a loss on the securities loan trade. Similarly, if instead of reinvesting the cash in the money market, the securities lender invests the cash collateral in a financial product which is subject to price fluctuation (for example, *mortgage-backed securities*), the risk of loss remains.

CASH COLLATERAL EXAMPLE (PART 2)

(Continuation of previous cash collateral example.)

The rebate rate agreed at trade execution is 0.85%; the cash interest earned by the collateral giver is EUR 740.32 per day. (Calculation: EUR 31,354,800.00 × 0.85% / 360 × 1). The total cash interest earned by the collateral giver for the duration of the trade will be known only after the SL&B trade has been closed.

SECURITIES COLLATERAL EXAMPLE (PART 2)

(Continuation of previous securities collateral example.)

As the borrower has provided securities collateral, interest on cash collateral is not applicable.

Note: if the lent/borrowed security is in short supply but high demand (sometimes referred to as a 'special'), the rebate rate negotiated between the two parties can go negative, resulting in the securities borrower (collateral giver) paying the rebate to the securities lender. Under such circumstances, the securities lender will earn rebate income as well as reinvestment income.

10.6.8 Exposure Management During the Lifetime of the Trade

Following the initial exchange of lent securities and collateral on the opening value date, both parties to the trade remain at risk. If, during the lifetime of the trade, the fluctuating value of the lent security plus margin:

- is greater than the current collateral value:
    - the securities lender is at risk as they are holding an insufficient value of collateral
- is less than the current collateral value:
    - the securities borrower is at risk due to excess collateral being held by the securities lender.

Usually every day during the lifetime of the SL&B trade, in order to determine 1) whether any *exposure* exists, 2) the value of such exposure, and 3) which party (securities lender or securities borrower) is exposed, it is necessary to revalue via the *mark-to-market* process.

Marking-to-market (MTM or M2M) is a generic term used throughout the financial services industry for a variety of revaluation purposes. MTM is the act of gathering the *current market price* of an asset from an external source, and applying that price to current trades and positions, including securities lent/borrowed and to securities collateral; it is essential that the price source is truly independent in order to prevent valuation inaccuracies.

Under any circumstances, the lent/borrowed security (whether equity or bond) is very likely to fluctuate in value, consequently it must be marked-to-market. Whether the collateral needs to be marked-to-market is dependent upon the nature of the collateral:

- if cash collateral:
    - cash retains 100% of its value from one day to the next (unless devaluation occurs)
    - as cash does not fluctuate in value, there is no requirement to mark-to-market
- if securities collateral:
    - as per the lent/borrowed security, securities collateral will fluctuate in value and must therefore be marked-to-market.

Consequently, the following situations can arise. Where cash collateral applies, the current market value of the lent/borrowed security can rise or fall or remain the same relative to the (static) value of cash collateral. Where securities collateral applies, it is possible that the current market value of the collateral and of the lent/borrowed security rise together (but unlikely to rise by the same value), or one asset rises in value while the other asset falls in value, or both assets fall in value (albeit unlikely to fall by the same value). In summary, numerous possibilities exist as to how exposures can arise in SL&B trades.

In terms of timing, mark-to-market is conducted following the close of business on the business day prior to the exposure calculation day; in other words, for 'today's' valuation, mark-to-market is performed as at close of business 'yesterday', providing that day is a business day.

Today, it is very common for the larger *sell-side* and *buy-side* firms to have externally sourced prices fed to them electronically by subscription to *data vendors*, with such prices updating various internal systems (for a variety of purposes) electronically, including collateral systems. Data vendors typically collect prices from a variety of sources.

Marking-to-market is depicted in Figure 10.16, where each party may well be subscribing to different data vendors:

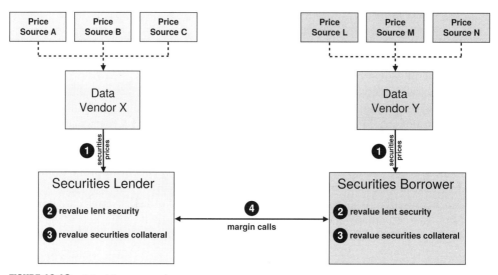

FIGURE 10.16   Marking-to-market

Step 1: independently, the securities lender and the securities borrower gather prices from their respective data vendors

Step 2: the lent/borrowed security is revalued by both parties

Step 3: the securities collateral is revalued by both parties (not applicable to cash collateral)

Step 4: the party with the exposure makes the margin call.

Note: it is possible that the securities lender and the securities borrower will agree to obtain current market prices from the same external source; this is designed to ensure that margin call disputes are minimised.

Should the current collateral value fall short of the current value of the lent security, the securities lender will make a *margin call* on the securities borrower for additional collateral to be posted. Conversely, if the current collateral value exceeds the current market value of the lent security, the securities borrower would make the margin call and request the return of the excess collateral.

However, there is a difference in treatment dependent upon the type of collateral.

Cash Collateral   Assume a securities loan is made, and the current market value of the lent securities is USD 25,000,000.00 at the outset of the transaction. Also assume the securities lender is given cash collateral of USD 25,500,000.00 which covers the lender's exposure, including a 2% margin.

The nature of equities and bonds means that the lent security will fluctuate in value; however, the value of cash collateral remains static and will not fluctuate. Therefore, when cash collateral has been given or taken, only the increasing and decreasing value of the lent security gives rise to margin calls.

CASH COLLATERAL EXAMPLE (PART 3)

(Continuation of previous cash collateral example.)
On opening value date plus 1, the lent/borrowed 2,000,000 Issuer P shares are marked-to-market to a price of EUR 16.05, giving a new market value of EUR 32,100,000.00. The 2% margin brings the required collateral value to EUR 32,742,000.00.

The existing collateral (EUR 31,354,800.00 cash) is inadequate to cover the lender's current exposure. A margin call is made by the securities lender to the securities borrower, who agrees the call and makes payment of EUR 1,387,200.00 to cover the lender's shortfall.

SECURITIES COLLATERAL EXAMPLE (PART 3)

(Continuation of previous securities collateral example.)
On value date plus 1, the lent security (800,000 Issuer M shares) is marked-to-market to a price of USD 21.50, giving a new value of USD 17,200,000.00. The 5% margin brings the required collateral value to USD 18,060,000.00.

The existing collateral (USD 18,000,000 US Treasury 4.5% bonds, maturing 15th August 2030) is today priced at 97.45%; inclusive of accrued interest (134 days), the total market value is USD 17,835,945.65, as per the following calculation:

Example Securities (Bond) Collateral Value Calculation		
Component	Calculation	Cash Value
Principal	USD 18,000,000 × 97.45%	USD 17,541,000.00
Accrued Interest	USD 18,000,000.00 × 4.5% / 368 × 134 days	USD 294,945.65
	Current Market Value	USD 17,835,945.65

Party L2 (the securities lender) therefore has an exposure of USD 224,054.35. A margin call is made by Party L2 to the securities borrower, who delivers additional collateral (in the form of cash or securities) to make up the shortfall.

The mark-to-market process should continue on a daily basis, for the duration of the loan.

10.6.9 Portfolio Reconciliation

When a firm determines that it has an exposure and then issues a margin call to its counterparty, there is no guarantee that the counterparty will agree either 1) the direction of the exposure (whether the firm or the counterparty is exposed), or 2) the size of the exposure.

Such disagreements between a firm and its counterparty can be caused by differences in the trade population; for example, a firm has correctly excluded from its lists of trades an SL&B trade that had a closing value date of 'yesterday', whereas the counterparty continues to list that trade as remaining live 'today'.

The possibility of such discrepancies is minimised if a proactive comparison of trades is made between firms, prior to margin calls being issued. A third party *portfolio reconciliation* service exists that automatically compares files of SL&B trades received from a firm with the equivalent from its various counterparties. That service is triOptima's *triResolve* system.

10.6.10 Securities Collateral: Holding and Reuse

As described earlier in this chapter (within Section 10.5 'Securities Lending & Borrowing: Legal Documentation'), under the **GMSLA**, the legal basis on which securities collateral is given/taken is *title transfer*, which means that the securities lender (collateral taker) has the legal right to do with the securities collateral whatever it chooses.

The choices for the securities collateral taker are to:

- hold the securities collateral safely within the securities lender's account at its custodian, or
- reuse the securities collateral in one (or more) of the following ways: selling it, repoing it, lending it or delivering it to satisfy a margin call in (for example) an **OTC** *derivative* transaction.

Holding the Securities Collateral   If the securities lender (collateral taker) chooses to act cautiously and to not reuse the securities collateral, such securities will need to be held within the collateral taker's account at the relevant CSD or at its custodian.

However, the collateral taker must decide whether 1) to *commingle* the securities collateral within its account containing its own securities, or 2) to hold the securities collateral within a segregated and dedicated 'incoming collateral' (or similarly named) account.

The risk in holding the securities collateral in a commingled manner is that the securities lender may apply insufficient internal control to prevent accidental reuse. Conversely, the advantage in the collateral taker adopting the segregated account method is that when it becomes time to return the securities collateral to the securities borrower at the close of the SL&B trade, the securities should definitely be available.

Reusing the Securities Collateral   Should the collateral taker choose to reuse the securities collateral, whether the collateral taker is able to return the securities collateral to the securities borrower on the closing value date of the SL&B trade is dependent upon the nature of the (reuse) trade executed by the securities lender:

- if the securities lender has sold the securities collateral, there will be no return (to the securities lender) of the security by the buyer
  - this situation will require the securities lender to source the securities elsewhere in order to return the securities collateral to the securities borrower on the *closing value date* of the SL&B trade, in order to avoid *settlement failure*
- if instead the securities lender has lent, repo'd or delivered the securities collateral to satisfy another collateral delivery obligation, there will be a return of the security by the counterparty
  - this situation will require the securities lender to ensure that the closing value date of such a trade is no later than the closing value date of the original SL&B trade, in order to avoid settlement failure.

In summary, at the close of the SL&B trade, the securities lender (collateral taker) must ensure that it is able to return the securities collateral (described as *equivalent collateral* within the GMSLA) to the securities borrower (collateral giver).

10.6.11 Collateral Substitution

Where securities collateral has been given, in the event that the securities borrower (collateral giver):

- sells the securities collateral that is currently in the possession of the securities lender, or
- requires the securities collateral for delivery within a different transaction (e.g. *repo*), or
- wishes to avoid processing difficulties associated with *income* events or *corporate action* events on the securities collateral

the existing collateral should be substituted for *replacement collateral*. This is depicted in Figure 10.17:

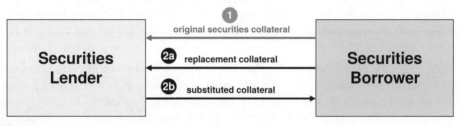

FIGURE 10.17   Collateral substitution

PART 3

Step 1: the original securities collateral is delivered to the securities lender

Step 2: the replacement collateral is provided to the securities lender

Step 3: the substituted collateral is returned to the securities borrower.

Note: collateral substitution is applicable only to collateral given in the form of securities; it is not applicable to the lent/borrowed security (as for the lender to request substitution of the lent security would completely defeat the borrower's objective in taking delivery of the particular *ISIN*).

The *GMSLA* states that collateral may be substituted, providing the replacement collateral meets the eligibility criteria. However, the need for collateral substitution may or may not arise during the lifetime of a securities loan.

The securities lender must ensure it does not become exposed within the collateral substitution process; exposure will occur if the original (now substituted) collateral is returned to the securities borrower prior to receipt of the replacement collateral.

It is possible that the securities borrower will substitute one piece of securities collateral with two or more pieces, or give cash collateral instead.

CASH COLLATERAL EXAMPLE (PART 4)

(Continuation of previous cash collateral example.)

As the borrower has provided cash collateral, substitution is not applicable. (However, it is possible that cash collateral could be replaced by securities collateral.)

SECURITIES COLLATERAL EXAMPLE (PART 4)

(Continuation of previous securities collateral example.)

Party B2 (the securities borrower) has now sold the US Treasury bond collateral and, one week into the SL&B transaction, contacts Party L2 to request collateral substitution, advising that it wishes to provide replacement collateral of GBP 15,000,000.00 UK Government 4.1% Bonds maturing 15th February 2028. Party L2 refers to its SL&B database to discover that the collateral proposed by Party B2 does fall within the agreement's eligibility criteria, and that the current market value of the collateral is acceptable, taking into account the margin requirement.

Due to a lack of *delivery versus delivery* (DvD) capability within *CSDs*, substitution of securities collateral has historically been achieved by two-way *free of payment* (FoP) deliveries; that is 1) the delivery of the *replacement collateral* by the securities borrower on an FoP basis, and 2) the return of the original collateral by the securities lender on an FoP basis. The $2 \times$ FoP settlements have not been linked historically, therefore simultaneous exchange has not been possible; consequently, the delivery of one of the securities can occur whilst delivery of the opposing security fails, thereby leaving one of the parties exposed. The ideal method of settling a collateral substitution is by DvD, meaning the simultaneous exchange will occur providing both securities are available for delivery, and therefore settlement is prevented unless both securities are available for delivery. However, *effective DvD* is available within *Target2 Securities*.

Following the transmission of FoP settlement instructions to their respective custodians, and subsequent matching, on the agreed date the *replacement collateral* in the form of the UK Government bonds is delivered to Party L2's custodian account, and the original US Treasury collateral is returned to the custodian account of Party B2. In this case a current GBP/USD exchange rate will need to be used to calculate collateral values in USD.

From this point forward until the closure of the trade, as part of the mark-to-market process, the value of the new collateral will be calculated and compared against the value of the lent/borrowed security (unless a further collateral substitution occurs).

10.6.12 Treatment of Income

Income on securities is regarded as being dividends on equity and coupon payments on bonds.

In general terms:

- dividend payments on equity are not predictable in advance and are announced by the *issuer*, following a decision by the issuer's board of directors
- coupon payments on bonds are predictable as their payment dates and amounts are known at the time of issue launch (with the exception of *floating rate notes*), and can be found in the issue *prospectus*.

Income payments may or may not arise during the lifetime of a securities lending/borrowing trade.

Income on Lent/Borrowed Securities   Should an income payment fall due on the lent/borrowed security during the lifetime of an SL&B trade, the securities borrower must make an equivalent payment to the securities lender, so the lender suffers no financial disadvantage and therefore receives the income as though the securities had never been lent.

It is expected that, in most (but not all) situations the securities borrower will have on-delivered the borrowed securities in order to satisfy a delivery commitment; under such circumstances, as the borrower is not holding the security in its account at its custodian as at *record date*, the borrower will therefore not receive the income from the issuer. However, the borrower must then make the equivalent income payment to the securities lender, from its own funds; such payments are commonly known as a *manufactured dividend* or a *manufactured coupon*. The exception to this rule arises where the securities borrower is able to validly claim the income from the counterparty to whom it on-delivered the securities, but this is achievable only where the securities borrower has itself lent the securities or has used the securities as collateral.

Conversely, in a situation in which the securities borrower is holding the borrowed securities in its account at a CSD or custodian (as is likely to occur in an arbitrage situation such as those described in this chapter within Sub-section 10.1.3 'Arbitrage Strategies'), the borrower will be credited with the income by their CSD or custodian.

The borrower is then required to make the equivalent payment to the securities lender. Note: such a scenario does not involve a manufactured dividend or manufactured coupon, as the securities borrower receives the payment and then remits the equivalent value to the securities lender. In other words, there is no requirement to manufacture a payment.

Income on Securities Collateral   Income payments may or may not arise on securities collateral during the lifetime of an SL&B trade.

   If an income payment falls due on the securities collateral whilst in the possession of the securities lender, the securities lender must make an equivalent payment to the securities borrower, so the securities borrower receives the income as though the securities collateral had never left the possession of the securities borrower. This situation is depicted in Figure 10.18:

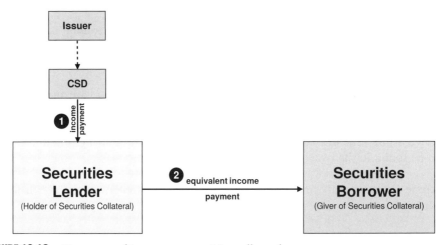

FIGURE 10.18   Treatment of income on securities collateral

   It is important to note the possibility that the securities lender has *reused* the securities collateral received, in settlement of a separate transaction; under the GMSLA, because the method of transfer of securities collateral is *title transfer* the securities lender has the legal right to reuse the securities collateral, as it sees fit. However, under all circumstances, at the close of the SL&B trade the securities lender must return the same *ISIN* as received from the securities borrower, providing that the ISIN still exists (i.e. it has not been replaced by a different ISIN, as a result of a *corporate action*). Should the securities lender choose to reuse the collateral, and should an income payment fall due on that security, the securities lender is obliged to remit the equivalent value to the securities borrower; whether the securities lender will itself receive an equivalent payment from the counterparty to the separate transaction depends upon the nature of that transaction. For example, if the securities collateral received by the securities lender has been reused as collateral in the separate transaction (e.g. a *repo*), then the securities lender will be legally due to receive the income from the repo counterparty, and that cash value can then be remitted to the securities borrower. Conversely, if the securities lender has sold the securities collateral received from the securities borrower, the securities lender will not validly be able to claim the income proceeds from the buyer (as the buyer will be entitled to the income payment); under these circumstances the securities lender will be required to pay the securities borrower from their own funds (known as a *manufactured payment*).

Note that *withholding tax* is usually deducted from dividend payments and certain coupon payments, at a rate decided by the issuer's national tax authority. Withholding tax is an involved subject; for further detail refer to this author's book, *Corporate Actions: A Guide to Securities Event Management* (ISBN 0470870664).

Many lenders and borrowers prefer to avoid the administrative burden of and/or tax issues associated with the handling income on securities collateral, and instead opt to effect a collateral substitution in advance of the *record date* of the income payment.

CASH COLLATERAL EXAMPLE (PART 5)

(Continuation of previous cash collateral example.)
   As the borrower has provided cash collateral, securities income payments are not applicable.

SECURITIES COLLATERAL EXAMPLE (PART 5)

(Continuation of previous securities collateral example.)
   Three weeks after the collateral substitution, both lender and borrower are alerted to the fact that the upcoming coupon payment (on the GBP 15,000,000.00 UK Government 4.1% Bonds 15th February 2028) is scheduled to occur within the next 2 weeks. It is agreed that a further collateral substitution will be effected prior to the record date of the coupon payment. This substitution results in the securities borrower providing equity collateral in the form of 200,000 Issuer X USD 1.00 Common Stock.

10.6.13 Corporate Actions

Corporate actions are applicable to the lent/borrowed security and to securities collateral. Corporate actions are events that are typically announced by an *issuer* of a security that affect holdings in that security.

The issuer may decide to invoke a specific type of corporate action to achieve a specific aim; for example, a *stock split* is designed to reduce the share price in the market, and a *rights issue* is designed to raise further capital for the issuer.

Events are classified as mandatory, optional or voluntary, where:

- for mandatory events, the terms of the event are applicable to all position holders, participation is compulsory with no choice of outcome, therefore requiring no decision by the holder
    - e.g. *bonus issue, stock split*

PART 3

- for optional events, the terms of the event are applicable to all position holders, participation is compulsory with a choice of outcome, requiring the holder to select an option provided by the issuer unless the default option is required
  - e.g. *currency option dividend*
- for voluntary events, the terms of the event are applicable to all position holders, participation is not compulsory, requiring the holder to decide whether to participate or not
  - e.g. *share buy-back, rights issue*.

For both optional events and voluntary events, in which the shareholder or bondholder is required to make an investment decision, it is important to note that deadlines (imposed by the issuer) are applicable. For example:

- in a currency option dividend, the issuer will pay the shareholder the default currency, unless the shareholder communicates (to the issuer) no later than the issuer's stated deadline, that the alternative currency is required, and
- in a rights issue, if the shareholder chooses to subscribe to the offer of additional shares, payment must be received by the issuer no later than the issuer's stated deadline.

If such deadlines are missed, the beneficial owner incurs the risk that its investment decision will be null and void.

Important Note: the issuer's deadline (as referred to above) is cascaded through the layers of parties as follows: the CSD's deadline applicable to its membership is typically 1 or 2 days in advance of the issuer's deadline, similarly the custodian's deadline applicable to its clients is typically 1 or 2 days in advance of the CSD's deadline. Furthermore, the Corporate Actions Department of a *buy-side* or *sell-side* firm is highly likely to await an investment decision from the ultimate beneficial owner, for which a deadline will need to be imposed which is 1 or 2 days earlier than the custodian's deadline.

Corporate Actions on Lent/Borrowed Securities   Corporate actions on lent/borrowed securities may or may not arise during the lifetime of a securities loan.

Where an optional or voluntary corporate action event has been announced, should the *beneficial owner* (the securities lender) require a certain action to be taken, this must be communicated in writing to the counterparty (the securities borrower) within a reasonable time frame prior to the latest decision deadline.

If the securities lender is concerned regarding the outcome of a corporate action, and if the SL&B trade has been executed on an 'open' basis, the securities lender may decide to execute a *recall* and to terminate the trade as soon as possible. This will enable the beneficial owner to handle the processing of the corporate action event under its direct control.

Corporate Actions on Securities Collateral   Corporate actions on securities collateral may or may not arise during the lifetime of a securities loan.

Where an optional or voluntary event has been announced, should the *beneficial owner* of the securities collateral (the securities borrower) require a certain action to be taken, this must be communicated in writing to the counterparty within a reasonable time frame prior to the latest decision deadline.

In parallel with income events, many lenders and borrowers prefer to avoid the administrative burden of handling corporate actions on securities collateral, and instead opt to effect a *collateral substitution* in advance of the *record date* of the corporate action.

CASH COLLATERAL EXAMPLE (PART 6)

(Continuation of previous cash collateral example.)

As the borrower has provided cash collateral, corporate actions are not applicable.

SECURITIES COLLATERAL EXAMPLE (PART 6)

(Continuation of previous securities collateral example.)

Eighteen days after Party L2 takes delivery of the 200,000 Issuer X USD 1.00 Common Stock, the issuer announces a stock split. From an equity holder's perspective, stock splits result in the complete replacement of the original security with a new security of the same issuer, the current market price being reduced and offset by a pro-rata increase in the share quantity, but with no change in the current market value; stock splits are mandatory events.

On the effective date of the stock split, Issuer X USD 1.00 Common Stock is trading at a price of USD 140.00 per share. A holding of 200,000 shares would have a (pre-split) market value of USD 28,000,000.00. The issuer announces a 2:1 stock split, where 200,000 shares are cancelled and replaced by 400,000 Issuer X USD 0.50 Common Stock, with a market price of USD 70.00 per share. As the post-stock split market value remains at USD 28,000,000.00, no exposure is created for either the securities lender or securities borrower.

Income and corporate actions events are very detailed topics; to understand this topic further, refer to this author's book, *Corporate Actions: A Guide to Securities Event Management* (ISBN: 0470870664).

10.6.14 Voting Rights

Voting rights are applicable to both the lent/borrowed security and to securities collateral.

Under the GMSLA, legal title to the lent/borrowed securities passes from the lender to the borrower for the period of the loan; consequently, the beneficial owner temporarily loses the right to vote. (However, all the lender's rights are protected regarding events such as *dividends* on equity and *coupon payments* on bonds.) Note that voting opportunities occur on both equities and bonds.

For any voting opportunity on lent/borrowed securities, the borrower is not obliged to vote in accordance with the beneficial owner's wishes.

Because voting rights are transferred, some beneficial owners avoid lending some or all of their securities. But should the beneficial owner prefer to lend, the GMSLA provides a solution to the loss of voting rights due to the lender's right to *recall* the lent securities and to terminate the trade, where an SL&B trade has been executed on an 'open' basis.

Similarly, where securities collateral has been provided, the borrower's voting rights are transferred to the securities lender. A solution for the borrower that wishes to vote is to effect a *collateral substitution* in advance of the voting date.

10.6.15 Recalls and Returns

Following closure of the SL&B trade, collateral must be returned to the collateral giver. However, closure of the trade will arise according to whether the trade has been executed on a fixed-term basis, or on an 'open' basis.

Fixed-Term Loans   Where an SL&B trade has been executed on a fixed-term basis, the lent/borrowed security and the collateral must be returned to their original owners, on the *closing value date*.

'Open' Loans   Where an SL&B trade has been executed on an 'open' basis, both the securities lender and the securities borrower have the legal right to close out the trade (as stated within the GMSLA): following trade execution, the trade remains open and is rolled forward daily, until either the securities lender or the securities borrower needs to close the trade.

The closure of an open SL&B trade from the viewpoint of the securities lender is known as a securities loan '*recall*'. Typical reasons for recalls include the need:

- to fulfil a delivery commitment (relating to, for example, a sale or a *repo*)
- to vote in, for example, an *annual general meeting*
- to closely manage a challenging and risky event, for example, a *voluntary corporate action*.

By comparison, the closure of an open SL&B trade from the viewpoint of the securities borrower is known as a securities borrowing '*return*'. Typical reasons for returns include:

- a previously failing purchase has now been settled
- a previously executed *short sale* is no longer short.

In both of the securities borrower examples above, securities received in settlement of the purchases should now be used to reimburse the securities lender. Unless the securities borrower actively searches for opportunities to terminate such open SL&B trades, the securities borrower stands the risk of continuing to pay securities borrowing fees unnecessarily.

In some markets, the return of the lent security and the return of the collateral must be actioned simultaneously. In other markets, in order to mitigate the lender's risk (at the expense of the borrower's risk) the lent securities are returned to the securities lender prior to the collateral being returned to the securities borrower. This is illustrated in Figure 10.19:

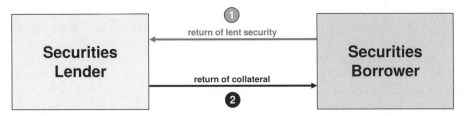

FIGURE 10.19　Return of collateral following return of lent security

In order to maintain control internally, it is essential that within internal books & records, SL&B trades that were originally recorded as being 'open' are now updated with the agreed *closing value date.* By so doing, the firm's *books & records* reflect reality and the true status of the trade with the counterparty; once the required movements of the lent/borrowed security and of the collateral have been settled, books & records must be updated again thereby showing that the trade is no longer open with the counterparty.

CASH COLLATERAL EXAMPLE (PART 7)

(Continuation of previous cash collateral example.)

Three weeks after trade execution, Party L (the securities lender) sells the lent securities. Party L's books & records reveal that these securities are currently being lent. Party L contacts Party B (the securities borrower), to advise their requirement to close the transaction and to recall the lent securities; the closing value date is agreed. Party L issues a confirming communication to Party B. Each party updates their respective trade record from 'open' to the agreed closing value date.

Party L issues a DvP settlement instruction to its CSD or custodian to receive the lent securities against payment of the outstanding cash collateral; Party B issues an equivalent settlement instruction. The instructions match prior to the closing value date. Once a settlement advice has been received from their CSD or custodian, each party updates its books & records to show that the trade is now fully settled. Additionally, the cash rebate amount is payable by the 10th of the following month.

SECURITIES COLLATERAL EXAMPLE (PART 7)

(Continuation of previous securities collateral example.)

Seven weeks after trade execution, Party B2 (the securities borrower) receives delivery of securities in settlement of a purchase from a counterparty. Party B2's books & records reveal that these same securities are currently being borrowed from Party L2. Party B2 contacts Party L2, to advise their requirement to close the SL&B transaction by returning the equivalent borrowed securities; the closing value date is agreed. Party B2 issues a confirming communication to Party L2. Each party updates their respective trade record from 'open' to the agreed closing value date.

Party L2 issues 1) an FoP settlement instruction to its CSD or custodian to receive the lent securities, and 2) an FoP settlement instruction for the delivery of the securities collateral. Party B2 issues two equivalent settlement instructions. Both sets of instructions match prior to the closing value date. Once 2 × settlement advices have been received from their CSD or custodian, each party updates its books & records to show that the trade is now fully settled. Additionally, the securities borrowing fee is payable by the 10th of the following month.

10.6.16 Fees and Rebates

The form in which fees are received by a securities lender is dependent upon the nature of the collateral provided by the securities borrower:

- cash collateral:
  - securities borrower's perspective:
    - at trade execution, when the borrower states that it wishes to provide cash collateral, an interest ('*rebate*') rate is negotiated between the two parties. The rebate rate is payable by the lender to the borrower (assuming a *positive interest rate* environment). The cost to the borrower is the difference between current interest rates (at which it is assumed that the cash has been borrowed) and the rebate rate received from the securities lender
  - securities lender's perspective:
    - the lender reinvests (e.g. in the *money market*) the cash collateral received from the securities borrower with the expectation of earning a greater return than the rebate rate payable to the securities borrower. The fee the lender earns in the SL&B trade is therefore the differential between the reinvestment income and the rebate payable
  - rebate amounts are payable (by the securities lender) no later than the 10th business day of the month following the calendar month in which a securities loan was open
  - note: no separate fee is payable
- securities collateral:
  - securities borrower's perspective:
    - where securities collateral is to be provided by the securities borrower, the cost of borrowing is a negotiated percentage (expressed in *basis points per annum* – bppa) of the market value of the borrowed security

- securities lender's perspective:
  - the fee the lender earns is the negotiated percentage of the lent security's market value
  - fee amounts are payable (by the securities borrower) no later than the 10th business day of the month following the calendar month in which a securities loan was open.

For cash collateral, to calculate the rebate amount, the standard *money market divisor* conventions for cash in the particular currency must be used; for USD and EUR = 360, for GBP = 365. An example follows:

- if the value (including margin) of the lent security is USD 20,000,000.00, and if the rebate rate is 0.35%, and if the securities are lent for 12 days, the calculation would be USD 20,000,000.00 × 0.35% / 360 × 12 = USD 2,333.33 payable to the securities borrower, and
- for the same trade, if the reinvestment rate is 0.68%, the securities lender would earn USD 4533.33, thereby profiting by USD 2200.00.

For securities collateral, to calculate the fee amount, the same money market divisor conventions must be used for cash in the particular currency. A number of calculation examples are shown in Table 10.5:

TABLE 10.5   Fee amount calculation

Securities Collateral: Fee Amount Calculation			
Market Value of Lent/Borrowed Securities	Fee	Loan/Borrow Duration	Fee Amount
EUR 34,000,000.00	28 bppa	3 days	EUR 793.33
GBP 14,100,000.00	24 bppa	13 days	GBP 1205.26
USD 21,250,000.00	32 bppa	22 days	USD 4155.56

Note that the examples given above may imply that the fee is payable on the initial market value of the lent security; in reality, the fee is payable on the fluctuating market value of the lent/borrowed security throughout the lifetime of the SL&B trade.

Fee/Rebate Payment Processing   The procedure that results in payment of fees and rebates is known as the 'billing' process. Based upon trading activity in a particular month, it is common practice for:

- the securities lender to determine rebate amounts payable to securities borrowers, and
- the securities borrower to determine fee amounts payable to securities lenders.

The party that is owed the payment then issues an invoice, typically including a breakdown of trade details, to enable the recipient to compare and reconcile prior to making payment.

Some firms utilise software systems that perform reconciliation of SL&B fees and rebates, in which securities lenders and securities borrowers submit trade details electronically, for the appropriate billing period. The system then automatically compares trade details and identifies either matched or unmatched items utilising customised tolerances.

10.7 CONCLUSION

Today, securities lending & borrowing is an integral and essential component of the securities industry, which, in terms of value of lent/borrowed securities, is estimated to exceed USD 2 trillion globally.

Established securities markets benefit from securities lending & borrowing through the support of trading and increased settlement efficiency.

As part of optimising use of their financial assets, many firms benefit from lending their portfolio of equities and bonds. Furthermore, many firms take advantage of other parties' lendable securities by borrowing such securities in order to facilitate timely settlement of sales.

Together with legal agreements, collateral plays a vital role in mitigating the securities lenders' risk; without collateral, firms would be highly unlikely to lend.

PART 3

CHAPTER 11

Securities Lending & Borrowing and Collateral – The SL&B Trade Lifecycle

This chapter illustrates the day-by-day and step-by-step activities necessary to successfully process an SL&B trade, by use of cash collateral. Both pre- and post-trade execution actions are covered, including the application of margin, exposure calculation, margin calls, settlement of margin calls and settlement of cash rebate.

The Securities Lending & Borrowing Trade Lifecycle

❶	Pre-Trading
❷	Trade Execution
❸	Pre-Settlement
❹	Settlement of Opening Leg
❺	Throughout Lifetime of Trade
❻	Recall/Return of Securities
❼	Settlement of Closing Leg
❽	Settlement of Fees & Rebates

Note #1: The contents of this chapter relate directly to the concepts described within the prior chapter, namely Chapter 10 'Securities Lending & Borrowing and Collateral – Principles of SL&B'; it is strongly recommended that readers firstly familiarise themselves with that chapter, so as to be able to successfully follow each step within this chapter.

Note #2: A variety of methods exist by which SL&B trades can be executed. However, to enable readers' understanding of fundamental principles, in this chapter the trade characteristics and market practices are intentionally described from a generic (bilateral) perspective. A number of SL&B trade execution methods are described within Chapter 12 'Securities Lending & Borrowing and Collateral – Accessing the SL&B Marketplace'.

11.1 PRE-TRADING

The actions that should be performed prior to *trade execution* are:

Background

■ Institution C (a *buy-side* firm) and Bank K (a *sell-side* firm) are planning on executing securities lending & borrowing (SL&B) trades with each other in the near future.

Legal Documentation

■ following a brief period of negotiation, the following legal documents are signed by both parties:
  ■ the *Global Master Securities Lending Agreement* (GMSLA)
  ■ the Schedule, including the characteristics listed in Table 11.1:

TABLE 11.1 Characteristics of the schedule

Component	Agreed and Documented Characteristics
Base Currency	GBP
Eligible Collateral	Currencies GBP, USD, EUR
Exposure Calculation Frequency	Daily
Threshold	GBP 250,000.00 (or currency equivalent) Bilateral
Minimum Transfer Amount	GBP 50,000.00 Bilateral
Margin Call Notification Deadline	13:00 UK time

Standing Settlement Instructions

- the *standing settlement instructions* (SSIs) of each firm are exchanged.

Static Data

In order to facilitate repeated use of the above-mentioned data, and for efficiency in trade processing:

- the details contained in the signed Schedule are set up within the SL&B collateral management system of both firms
- each firm's own SSIs, and those of the *counterparty*, are set up within the *static data repository* of both firms.

11.2 TRADE EXECUTION

The actions that should be performed immediately prior to and during trade execution are:

Determining Securities Available for Lending

- in order to maximise its revenues, Institution C identifies the specific securities it is prepared to lend, with the associated quantity.

Communicating Lendable Securities

- Institution C communicates its lendable securities to particular counterparties, including Bank K.

Determining Securities Borrowing Requirement

- in order to settle an existing delivery commitment, Bank K identifies a borrowing requirement for a particular quantity of a specific security.

Pre-Execution

- Bank K finds a match of its borrowing requirement with the list of lendable securities provided by Institution C, and contacts Institution C.

Trade Execution

- a trade is executed between lender & borrower on a *bilateral* and *OTC* basis
- trade execution details are as shown in Table 11.2:

TABLE 11.2   Trade execution details

Trade Component	Execution Details
Lender	Institution C
Borrower	Bank K
Lent Security	Rolls-Royce Holdings shares
Lent Quantity	2,950,000
Market Price	GBP 7.045
Margin Percentage	2%
Collateral	GBP Cash
Rebate Rate	45 bppa
Trade Date	October 28th
Opening Value Date	October 29th
Closing Value Date	Open

11.3 PRE-SETTLEMENT

The actions that should be performed during and following trade execution are described below and illustrated in Tables 11.3 to 11.5:

TRADE DATE: 28TH OCTOBER

Trade Capture

- all the above-listed execution details are captured internally by both parties
- additionally, the following cash values are calculated and captured by both parties:

TABLE 11.3 Trade capture

Component	Cash Value
Lent Security's Market Value on October 28th	GBP 20,782,750.00
Value of Margin on Lent Security on October 28th	GBP 415,655.00
Required Collateral Value on October 28th	GBP 21,198,405.00

- additionally, the securities lender negotiates a reinvestment rate of 68 bppa with a cash borrower, Bank S.

Trade Enrichment

- both parties must identify and capture the place of settlement and the settlement account numbers of lender and borrower:
  - place of settlement is determined by the market in which the security is held & traded
  - settlement account numbers are obtained from SSIs held within static data
    - Institution C wishes to settle over its account 77098 at CSD M
    - Bank K wishes to settle over its account 54003 at CSD M.

Trade Confirmation

- the borrower (Bank K) issues a trade confirmation to the lender (Institution C) by S.W.I.F.T. MT516 (Loan Confirmation), as follows:

TABLE 11.4   Trade confirmation

Securities Lending/Borrowing Trade Confirmation		
From	*Bank K*	
To	*Institution C*	
We confirm the following transaction:		
Trade Component		**Trade Detail**
Our Trade Reference	*SLB0059397*	
Transaction Type	*Securities Borrowing*	
Securities Lender	*Institution C*	
Securities Borrower	*Bank K*	
Security	*ISIN*	*Rolls-Royce Holding Shares*	*GB00B63H8491*
Quantity	*2,950,000*	
Current Market Price	*GBP7.045*	
Margin Percentage	*2.0%*	
Collateral Type	*GBP Cash*	
Rebate Rate	*45 bppa*	
Trade Date	*October 28th*	
Opening Value Date	*October 29th*	
Closing Value Date	*Open*	
Opening Value Date Cash Values		
Current Market Value		*GBP 20,782,750.00*
Margin Value		*GBP 415,655.00*
Required Collateral Value		*GBP 21,198,405.00*
Settlement Details		
Our Depot/Nostro	*CSD M, account 54003*	
Your Depot/Nostro	*CSD M, account 77098*	
Settlement Method	*Delivery versus Payment*	

- Institution C compares the trade confirmation details to its internal records to find that all the details match. If not the same, the lender must immediately advise the borrower in order to investigate and resolve the issue as quickly as possible.

Opening Leg Settlement Instructions

- each party issues a settlement instruction either directly to the relevant CSD or to their custodian
- the settlement instruction transmission method is the choice of each firm, but is usually either S.W.I.F.T. or the CSD's or custodian's proprietary system
- the content of the lender's opening leg settlement instruction is as follows:

PART 3

TABLE 11.5   Settlement instruction: opening leg

Settlement Instruction	
Component	Detail
From	Institution C
To	CSD M
Date	October 28th
Subject	Settlement Instruction
Our Reference	SecL7079014
Our Account	77098
Receive / Deliver	Deliver
Quantity	2,950,000
ISIN	GB00B63H8491
Cash Countervalue	GBP 21,198,405.00
Value Date	October 29th
Settlement Method	DvP
Counterparty Account	54003

- Note: in a DvP settlement instruction, the 'Receive/Deliver' direction always pertains to the required direction of the securities (rather than the cash).

Opening Leg Settlement Instructions Statuses

- following issuance of their respective settlement instructions ...
  - both parties receive advices that their instructions are matched by the counterparty's instruction.

11.4 SETTLEMENT OF OPENING LEG

OPENING VALUE DATE: 29TH OCTOBER

At CSD M:

- the lender's account held an adequate quantity of the relevant security, thereby enabling delivery to the borrower's account to occur
  - the securities quantity was removed from the lender's account and added to the borrower's account on this day (*settlement date*)
- the borrower's account held either 1) an adequate cash balance or 2) sufficient credit line and collateral, thereby enabling payment to the lender's account to occur
  - the cash amount was removed from the borrower's account and added to the lender's account on this day (settlement date)
- the above exchange of assets occurred on a simultaneous exchange (DvP) basis, as instructed by both parties.

Advice of Settlement of Opening Leg

- both parties receive an advice of settlement from CSD M to confirm that their respective settlement instruction had settled on the due date.

Updating of Books & Records

- internally, both parties update their internal *books & records*, showing ...
  - for Institution C:
    - 2,950,000 Rolls-Royce shares were delivered 29th October
    - GBP 21,198,405.00 was received 29th October
  - for Bank K
    - 2,950,000 Rolls-Royce shares were received 29th October
    - GBP 21,198,405.00 was paid 29th October.

PART 3

Reconciliation

- following internal updating of their books & records, each party conducts the following reconciliations …
  - for Institution C:
    - a *depot reconciliation* proving that internal books & records correctly show that 2,950,000 shares are no longer in their securities account at CSD M, and
    - a *nostro reconciliation* proving that internal books & records correctly show GBP 21,198,405.00 has been received at CSD M
  - for Bank K:
    - a depot reconciliation proving that internal books & records correctly show that 2,950,000 shares have been received in their securities account at CSD M, and
    - a nostro reconciliation proving that internal books & records correctly show GBP 21,198,405.00 has been paid from their account at CSD M.

Updating of Collateral Record

- following settlement of the opening leg, each party updates their record of collateral for the particular trade (see Tables 11.6 and 11.7):

TABLE 11.6 Collateral balance #1

Current Collateral Balance – Institution C's Perspective			
Date	Cash Collateral		
	Taken	Given	Balance
October 29th	GBP 21,198,405.00		+ GBP 21,198,405.00

TABLE 11.7 Collateral balance #2

Current Collateral Balance – Bank K's Perspective			
Date	Cash Collateral		
	Taken	Given	Balance
October 29th		GBP 21,198,405.00	− GBP 21,198,405.00

On-Delivery by the Securities Borrower

- as a consequence of Bank K receiving delivery, the securities were on-delivered to Bank K's counterparty on this day, thereby fulfilling Bank K's delivery commitment and the purpose in Bank K executing the borrowing of securities
- note: securities are sometimes borrowed for reasons other than fulfilling a delivery commitment; for example, to satisfy an arbitrage opportunity. For details, please refer to Chapter 10 'Securities Lending & Borrowing and Collateral – Principles of SL&B'.

Cash Reinvestment by the Securities Lender

- as a consequence of Institution C receiving the cash collateral, the same cash amount was paid to Bank S on this day, in order to settle the opening leg of the cash loan arranged the previous day; please refer to Section 11.3 'Pre-Settlement' in this chapter. From Institution C's perspective, this is *cash collateral reinvestment*.

11.5 THROUGHOUT LIFETIME OF TRADE

The Securities Lending & Borrowing Trade Lifecycle

1. Pre-Trading
2. Trade Execution
3. Pre-Settlement
4. Settlement of Opening Leg
5. Throughout Lifetime of Trade
6. Recall/Return of Securities
7. Settlement of Closing Leg
8. Settlement of Fees & Rebates

OPENING VALUE DATE +1: 30TH OCTOBER

The following tasks are actioned on this day:

Marking-to-Market

- following the close-of-business 'yesterday' (29th October), both parties independently gather the current market price of the lent/borrowed security:
  - current mid-market price is GBP 6.873.

Calculation of Exposure

- following the mark-to-market process, both parties independently determine whether exposure exists (see Table 11.8):

TABLE 11.8   Exposure calculation #1

Component		Cash Value
Lent Security's Market Value at c-o-b on October 29th		GBP 20,275,350.00
Value of Margin on Lent Security on October 30th		GBP 405,507.00
Required Collateral Value on October 30th		**GBP 20,680,857.00**
Existing Cash Collateral		– GBP 21,198,405.00
Exposed Party: Bank K	**Exposure Amount**	GBP 517,548.00

- the calculation reveals that the securities borrower (Bank K) has too much collateral in the hands of the securities lender.

Issuance of Margin Call Notification

- following the calculation of exposure, Bank K issues a margin call, so the non-exposed party receives the notification by the documented deadline.

Validation of Margin Call

- following receipt of the *margin call notification* by the deadline, Institution C (the non-exposed party) agrees the margin call.

Settlement of Margin Call

- following validation of the margin call, Institution C remits payment of the *exposure* amount (GBP 517,548.00) to Bank K's GBP *cash correspondent* (from the *SSI* held within static data), by issuance of a cash only (non-matching) settlement instruction to its own cash correspondent, with value date of 'today'
- note: although Institution C has chosen to settle the margin call by payment of GBP, the legal documentation additionally permits settlement of margin calls in USD and EUR.

Issuance of Funds Preadvice

- in order for Bank K to receive 'good value' on the receipt of the funds, its cash correspondent (or 'nostro') may require Bank K to send the cash correspondent a *funds preadvice*. If such a communication is required by the cash correspondent, a deadline for receipt will be stated. Where a preadvice is required, but Bank K fails to issue it, Bank K will be taking the risk that the funds will be credited with a later value date: under these circumstances, Bank K's exposure will not be *mitigated* at the earliest opportunity.

Advice of Settlement

- both securities lender and securities borrower now monitor their nostro accounts to ensure payment has been 1) made by the non-exposed party and 2) received by the exposed party.

Updating of Books & Records

- both parties now update their respective internal *books & records* to formally reflect the fact that payment has been made/received on the *settlement date*.

Reconciliation

- following internal updating of their books & records, each party conducts the following reconciliations …
  - for Institution C:
    - a nostro reconciliation proving that internal books & records correctly show GBP 517,548.00 has been paid

- for Bank K:
  - a nostro reconciliation proving that internal books & records correctly show GBP 517,548.00 has been received.

Updating of Collateral Record

- following settlement of the margin call, each party updates their record of collateral for the particular trade (see Tables 11.9 and 11.10):

TABLE 11.9   Collateral balance #3

Current Collateral Balance – Institution C's Perspective			
Date	Cash Collateral		
	Taken	Given	Balance
October 29th	GBP 21,198,405.00		+ GBP 21,198,405.00
October 30th		GBP 517,548.00	+ GBP 20,680,857.00

TABLE 11.10   Collateral balance #4

Current Collateral Balance – Bank K's Perspective			
Date	Cash Collateral		
	Taken	Given	Balance
October 29th		GBP 21,198,405.00	– GBP 21,198,405.00
October 30th	GBP 517,548.00		– GBP 20,680,857.00

OPENING VALUE DATE +2: 31ST OCTOBER

The following tasks are actioned on this day (see Tables 11.11 to 11.13):

Marking-to-Market

- following the close-of-business 'yesterday' (30th October), both parties independently gather the current market price of the lent/borrowed security:
  - current mid-market price is GBP 6.762.

Calculation of Exposure

- following the mark-to-market process, both parties independently determine whether exposure exists:

TABLE 11.11   Exposure calculation #2

Component		Cash Value
Lent Security's Market Value at c-o-b on October 30th		GBP 19,947,900.00
Value of Margin on Lent Security on October 31st		GBP 398,958.00
Required Collateral Value on October 31st		**GBP 20,346,858.00**
Existing Cash Collateral		– GBP 20,680,857.00
Exposed Party: Bank K	**Exposure Amount**	GBP 333,999.00

- the calculation reveals that the securities borrower (Bank K) has too much collateral in the hands of the securities lender.

Issuance of Margin Call Notification

- following the calculation of exposure, Bank K issues a margin call, so the non-exposed party receives the notification by the documented deadline.

All of the following actions must now be performed, as per the previous day:

<u>Validation of Margin Call</u>
<u>Settlement of Margin Call</u>
<u>Issuance of Funds Preadvice</u>
<u>Advice of Settlement</u>
<u>Updating of Books & Records</u>
<u>Reconciliation</u>
<u>Updating of Collateral Record</u>

- following settlement of the margin call, each party updates their record of collateral for the particular trade:

TABLE 11.12   Collateral balance #5

Current Collateral Balance – Institution C's Perspective			
Date	Cash Collateral		
	Taken	Given	Balance
October 29th	GBP 21,198,405.00		+ GBP 21,198,405.00
October 30th		GBP 517,548.00	+ GBP 20,680,857.00
October 31st		GBP 333,999.00	+ GBP 20,346,858.00

TABLE 11.13   Collateral balance #6

Current Collateral Balance – Bank K's Perspective			
Date	Cash Collateral		
	Taken	Given	Balance
October 29th		GBP 21,198,405.00	− GBP 21,198,405.00
October 30th	GBP 517,548.00		− GBP 20,680,857.00
October 31st	GBP 333,999.00		− GBP 20,346,858.00

OPENING VALUE DATE +3: 1ST NOVEMBER

The following tasks are actioned on this day (see Tables 11.14 to 11.16):

Marking-to-Market

- following the close-of-business 'yesterday' (31st October), both parties independently gather the current market price of the lent/borrowed security:
  - current mid-market price is GBP 6.819.

Calculation of Exposure

- following the mark-to-market process, both parties independently determine whether exposure exists:

TABLE 11.14 Exposure calculation #3

Component		Cash Value
Lent Security's Market Value at c-o-b on October 31st		GBP 20,116,050.00
Value of Margin on Lent Security on November 1st		GBP 402,321.00
Required Collateral Value on November 1st		**GBP 20,518,371.00**
Existing Cash Collateral		– GBP 20,346,858.00
Exposed Party: Institution C	Exposure Amount	GBP 171,513.00

- the calculation reveals that the securities lender (Institution C) holds insufficient collateral to cover its exposure.

Issuance of Margin Call Notification

- following the calculation of exposure, Institution C issues a margin call, so the non-exposed party receives the notification by the documented deadline.

Validation of Margin Call

- following receipt of the margin call notification by the deadline, the non-exposed party attempts to validate the detail, however, because the exposure amount is within the documented Threshold of GBP 250,000.00, the margin call is rejected
  - no margin is transferred on this day.

Updating of Collateral Record

- as no margin call occurred on this day, the following was recorded by each party:

TABLE 11.15 Collateral balance #7

Date	Current Collateral Balance – Institution C's Perspective		
	Cash Collateral		
	Taken	Given	Balance
October 29th	GBP 21,198,405.00		+ GBP 21,198,405.00
October 30th		GBP 517,548.00	+ GBP 20,680,857.00
October 31st		GBP 333,999.00	+ GBP 20,346,858.00
November 1st	Nil	Nil	+ GBP 20,346,858.00

TABLE 11.16   Collateral balance #8

Current Collateral Balance – Bank K's Perspective			
Date	Cash Collateral		
	Taken	Given	Balance
October 29th		GBP 21,198,405.00	– GBP 21,198,405.00
October 30th	GBP 517,548.00		– GBP 20,680,857.00
October 31st	GBP 333,999.00		– GBP 20,346,858.00
November 1st	Nil	Nil	– GBP 20,346,858.00

OPENING VALUE DATE +4: 2ND NOVEMBER

The following tasks are actioned on this day (see Tables 11.17 to 11.19):

Marking-to-Market

- following the close-of-business 'yesterday' (1st November), both parties independently gather the current market price of the lent/borrowed security:
  - current mid-market price is GBP 6.963.

Calculation of Exposure

- following the mark-to-market process, both parties independently determine whether exposure exists:

TABLE 11.17   Exposure calculation #4

Component		Cash Value
Lent Security's Market Value at c-o-b on November 1st		GBP 20,540,850.00
Value of Margin on Lent Security on November 2nd		GBP 410,817.00
Required Collateral Value on November 2nd		**GBP 20,951,667.00**
Existing Cash Collateral		– GBP 20,346,858.00
Exposed Party: Institution C	**Exposure Amount**	**GBP 604,809.00**

- the calculation reveals that the securities lender (Institution C) holds insufficient collateral to cover its exposure.

Issuance of Margin Call Notification

- following the calculation of exposure, Institution C issues a margin call, so the non-exposed party receives the notification by the documented deadline.

All of the following actions must now be performed, as per previous days:

<u>Validation of Margin Call</u>
<u>Settlement of Margin Call</u>

Issuance of Funds Preadvice

Advice of Settlement

Updating of Books & Records

Reconciliation

Updating of Collateral Record

■ following settlement of the margin call, each party updates their record of collateral for the particular trade:

TABLE 11.18   Collateral balance #9

Current Collateral Balance – Institution C's Perspective			
Date	Cash Collateral		
	Taken	Given	Balance
October 29th	GBP 21,198,405.00		+ GBP 21,198,405.00
October 30th		GBP 517,548.00	+ GBP 20,680,857.00
October 31st		GBP 333,999.00	+ GBP 20,346,858.00
November 1st	Nil	Nil	+ GBP 20,346,858.00
November 2nd	GBP 604,809.00		+ GBP 20,951,667.00

TABLE 11.19   Collateral balance #10

Current Collateral Balance – Bank K's Perspective			
Date	Cash Collateral		
	Taken	Given	Balance
October 29th		GBP 21,198,405.00	– GBP 21,198,405.00
October 30th	GBP 517,548.00		– GBP 20,680,857.00
October 31st	GBP 333,999.00		– GBP 20,346,858.00
November 1st	Nil	Nil	– GBP 20,346,858.00
November 2nd		GBP 604,809.00	– GBP 20,951,667.00

PART 3

11.6 RECALL AND RETURN OF SECURITIES

The Securities Lending & Borrowing Trade Lifecycle

1. Pre-Trading
2. Trade Execution
3. Pre-Settlement
4. Settlement of Opening Leg
5. Throughout Lifetime of Trade
6. **Recall/Return of Securities**
7. Settlement of Closing Leg
8. Settlement of Fees & Rebates

This SL&B trade was executed on an 'open' (or 'on-demand' basis). Both the securities lender and the securities borrower have the legal right to terminate the trade at any time; this legal right is documented within the *GMSLA*.

Recall of Lent Securities

On 2nd November, Institution C's trader decides to sell all 2,950,000 Rolls Royce shares, to Party G, consequently:

- Institution C identifies (from its reconciled books & records) that the sale could not settle unless the lent securities were recalled from Bank K
- Institution C contacts Bank K in order to effect a recall of the lent securities
- the two parties agree the closing value date of 3rd November
- internally, both parties update the closing value date of their respective trade record from 'open' to '3rd November'
- Bank K issues an updated trade confirmation to Institution C
- upon receipt, Institution C compares Bank K's updated trade confirmation with its books & records, which agree.

Note: Bank K continued to have a securities borrowing requirement, and following the recall request from Institution C, Bank K arranged a securities borrowing from another securities lender, thereby facilitating settlement of the securities recall to Institution C.

As a result of the above, the following tasks are actioned on this day (see Table 11.20).

Closing Leg Settlement Instructions

- both parties are independently responsible for issuing their settlement instruction to the place of settlement:
  - the content of the lender's closing leg settlement instruction is as follows:

TABLE 11.20   Settlement instruction: closing leg

Settlement Instruction	
Component	**Detail**
From	Institution C
To	CSD M
Date	November 2nd
Subject	**Settlement Instruction**
Our Reference	SecL7079015
Our Account	77098
Receive / Deliver	Receive
Quantity	2,950,000
ISIN	GB00B63H8491
Cash Countervalue	GBP 20,951,667.00
Value Date	November 3rd
Settlement Method	DvP
Counterparty Account	54003

Closing Leg Settlement Instructions Statuses

- following issuance of their respective settlement instructions …
  - both parties receive advices that their instructions are matched by the counterparty's instruction.

PART 3

11.7 SETTLEMENT OF CLOSING LEG

The Securities Lending & Borrowing Trade Lifecycle

1. Pre-Trading
2. Trade Execution
3. Pre-Settlement
4. Settlement of Opening Leg
5. Throughout Lifetime of Trade
6. Recall/Return of Securities
7. Settlement of Closing Leg
8. Settlement of Fees & Rebates

CLOSING VALUE DATE: 3RD NOVEMBER

At CSD M:

- the borrower's account held an adequate quantity of the relevant security, thereby enabling successful return of the lent securities to the lender's account
  - the securities quantity was removed from the borrower's account and added to the lender's account on this day (*settlement date*)
- the lender's account held either 1) an adequate cash balance or 2) sufficient credit line and collateral, thereby enabling successful return of the current cash collateral balance to the borrower's account
  - the cash amount was removed from the lender's account and added to the borrower's account on this day (settlement date)
- the above exchange of assets occurred on a simultaneous exchange (DvP) basis, as instructed by both parties.

Advice of Settlement of Closing Leg

- both parties receive an advice of settlement from CSD M to confirm that their respective settlement instruction had settled on the due date.

Updating of Books & Records

- internally, both parties update their respective books & records, showing …
  - for Institution C:
    - 2,950,000 Rolls-Royce shares were received 3rd November
    - GBP 20,951,667.00 was paid 3rd November

- for Bank K:
  - 2,950,000 Rolls-Royce shares were delivered 3rd November
  - GBP 20,951,667.00 was received 3rd November.

Reconciliation

- following internal updating of their books & records, each party conducts the following reconciliations …
  - for Institution C:
    - a ***depot reconciliation*** proving that internal books & records correctly show that 2,950,000 shares have been returned to their securities account at CSD M, and
    - a ***nostro reconciliation*** proving that internal books & records correctly show GBP 20,951,667.00 has been paid at CSD M
  - for Bank K:
    - a depot reconciliation proving that internal books & records correctly show that 2,950,000 shares have been removed from their securities account at CSD M, and
    - a nostro reconciliation proving that internal books & records correctly show GBP 20,951,667.00 has been received into their account at CSD M.

Updating of Collateral Record

- following settlement of the closing leg, each party updates their record of collateral for the particular trade (see Tables 11.21 and 11.22):

TABLE 11.21   Collateral balance #11

Date	Current Collateral Balance – Institution C's Perspective		
	Cash Collateral		
	Taken	Given	Balance
October 29th	GBP 21,198,405.00		+ GBP 21,198,405.00
October 30th		GBP 517,548.00	+ GBP 20,680,857.00
October 31st		GBP 333,999.00	+ GBP 20,346,858.00
November 1st	Nil	Nil	+ GBP 20,346,858.00
November 2nd	GBP 604,809.00		+ GBP 20,951,667.00
November 3rd		GBP 20,951,667.00	Nil

TABLE 11.22   Collateral balance #12

Date	Current Collateral Balance – Bank K's Perspective		
	Cash Collateral		
	Taken	Given	Balance
October 29th		GBP 21,198,405.00	− GBP 21,198,405.00
October 30th	GBP 517,548.00		− GBP 20,680,857.00
October 31st	GBP 333,999.00		− GBP 20,346,858.00
November 1st	Nil	Nil	− GBP 20,346,858.00
November 2nd		GBP 604,809.00	− GBP 20,951,667.00
November 3rd	GBP 20,951,667.00		Nil

At this point the trade has been settled in full, apart from settlement of the rebate amount; please refer to Section 11.8 'Settlement of Fees & Rebates'.

11.8 SETTLEMENT OF FEES & REBATES

The Securities Lending & Borrowing Trade Lifecycle

❶ Pre-Trading
❷ Trade Execution
❸ Pre-Settlement
❹ Settlement of Opening Leg
❺ Throughout Lifetime of Trade
❻ Recall/Return of Securities
❼ Settlement of Closing Leg
❽ Settlement of Fees & Rebates

As this SL&B trade was collateralised with cash, at *trade execution* the parties to the trade negotiated a *rebate* rate, which is payable by the *collateral taker* (securities lender) to the *collateral giver* (securities borrower).

The rebate is the return earned by the collateral giver on cash collateral provided by the collateral giver, whereas the differential between the rebate rate and the *reinvestment rate* amounts to the securities lending fee earned by the securities lender. For this SL&B trade, the rebate rate is 45 *bppa*, and the reinvestment rate is 68 bppa.

The rebate rate is payable by a deadline of the 10th of the month following the month in which the SL&B trade was live and outstanding; this deadline is documented within the GMSLA. To clarify, where a trade's lifetime spans two or more calendar months, the relevant rebate amount due for each month should be paid to the borrower separately.

Note: the same deadline applies to the payment of fees by the securities borrower, where the SL&B trade has been collateralised with securities.

Calculation of Rebate Amount

- following each calendar month end in which the SL&B trade was outstanding, each party determines the rebate amount payable by the securities lender to the securities borrower
- the cash amount upon which the rebate rate is applied is the fluctuating market value of the lent/borrowed security, plus the margin (2%), as illustrated in Table 11.23:

TABLE 11.23   Calculation of rebate amount

Rebate Rate: 45 bppa				
Date	Collateral Value	Daily Rebate Amount	Monthly Rebate Amount (Calendar Month)	
			Accrued During	Payable By
October 29th	GBP 21,198,405.00	GBP 261.35	October GBP 767.17	November 10th
October 30th	GBP 20,680,857.00	GBP 254.97		
October 31st	GBP 20,346,858.00	GBP 250.85		
November 1st	GBP 20,346,858.00	GBP 250.85	November GBP 509.16	December 10th
November 2nd	GBP 20,951,667.00	GBP 258.31		
	Total Rebate Amount	GBP 1276.33		

Following each calendar month end relating to the trade, Bank K (the securities borrower) issues an invoice to the securities lender, thereby claiming the relevant rebate amounts.

Having received such invoices, Institution C compares the invoiced amounts to its internal calculations, to find that they agree; Institution C then makes payment of the rebate amounts no later than the 10th of the month following the month in which the rebate amount accrued.

11.9 ADDITIONAL FACTORS

Calculation of Securities Lender's Overall Profit

For the securities lender (Institution C), in order to determine their profit on this securities lending trade, the following needs to be considered:

- receivable and non-payable items:
  - receivable: *reinvestment* earnings at 68 bppa
  - non-payable: avoidance of *securities safekeeping fees* charged by the CSD or custodian
- payable items:
  - rebate at 45 bppa.

Calculation of Securities Borrower's Overall Benefit

As mentioned within Section 11.2 'Trade Execution' in this chapter, Bank K chose to borrow the securities in order to fulfil an existing delivery commitment. The underlying situation which caused Bank K to borrow the securities will impact the benefit of borrowing; two examples follow.

Example #1 – Technical Short Imagine that, for example, Bank K had bought from one counterparty and sold the same quantity of the same security to a different counterparty on identical terms (please refer to Figure 10.4 'Technical short situation, post-borrowing' within Chapter 10 'Securities Lending & Borrowing and Collateral – Principles of SL&B'). Then, on value date of the two trades, the purchase fails to settle; as Figure 10.4 indicates, Bank K could then choose to borrow the securities in order to settle the sale. The calculation of benefit to Bank K would consist of:

- firstly, zero trading profit or loss
  - the purchase and the sale were executed on identical terms
- the borrowing fee
  - Bank K will earn a rebate rate of 45 bppa on the cash collateral provided to Institution C
- the cost of providing cash collateral
  - if, for example, Bank K needed to borrow the cash (in the money market) to provide it as collateral to Institution C, the interest cost of that borrowing must be considered
  - if instead, Bank K was already in possession of the cash collateral (i.e. Bank K did not need to borrow the cash), then the theoretical credit interest which could have been earned on that cash must be considered
- the interest earned on the loan of the sale proceeds into the money market
  - it is assumed that when the sale settled (following borrowing of the securities), Bank K would lend the sale proceeds into the money market and earn interest on that cash (assuming a *positive interest rate* environment).

PART 3

In such a situation, assuming there is a monetary benefit in borrowing the securities for Bank K, the longer that Bank K's purchase takes to settle, the greater the monetary benefit to Bank K.

Example #2 – Short Sale　If, for example, Bank K had sold short, it is suggested that the cost of borrowing the securities plus other considerations need to be factored into the overall picture for the 'set' of trades executed by Bank K, which consists of:

- the price at which the shares were sold
  - that is, the short sale
- the borrowing fee
  - Bank K will earn a rebate rate of 45 bppa on the cash collateral provided to Institution C
- the cost of providing cash collateral
  - if, for example, Bank K needed to borrow the cash (in the money market) to provide it as collateral to Institution C, the interest cost of that borrowing must be considered
  - if instead, Bank K was already in possession of the cash collateral (i.e. Bank K did not need to borrow the cash), then the theoretical credit interest which could have been earned on that cash must be considered
- the interest earned on the loan of the sale proceeds into the money market
  - it is assumed that when the sale settled (following borrowing of the securities), Bank K would lend the sale proceeds into the money market and earn interest on that cash (assuming a *positive interest rate* environment)
- the price at which the shares were ultimately purchased
  - in order to close Bank K's short position.

Relevant to both earlier examples, other (possibly unquantifiable) factors which should be considered where the securities are <u>not</u> borrowed are:

- potential reputation loss of failing to settle the sales
  - particularly if the buyer is a *buy-side* firm (a client of Bank K)
- potential for a *buy-in* actioned against Bank K
  - although there is no guarantee that the buyer would invoke such an action.

Securities Collateral

As the reader will be aware, cash collateral has been used within this chapter in the example of an SL&B trade.

Had securities collateral been used instead, the differences (compared with cash collateral) would be:

- a greater margin is typically given on securities collateral
  - the securities borrower would be *over-collateralising* to a greater extent

PART 3

- greater settlement risk, as non-simultaneous exchange of assets exists on both the *opening value date* and the *closing value date* of the trade
  - *FoP* x2 settlement is the norm under these circumstances
    - as these two deliveries are not linked, simultaneous exchange is not possible
  - *DvP* settlement is not applicable
    - as no cash is involved
  - *DvD* settlement is not available
    - although *effective DvD* is available within *T2S*
- further effort throughout the lifetime of the trade, as marking-to-market is necessary on the securities collateral (as well as the lent/borrowed security)
  - including calculation of *accrued interest* (where *clean prices* are used)
- the possibility of *collateral substitution* exists
- the possibility of *income* events and *corporate action* events exists.

In addition, where a firm holds an inventory of securities at its custodian, as those securities are already owned by the securities borrower, there is no further cost in utilising those securities as collateral; in fact, use of such securities as collateral will reduce *securities safekeeping fees* for the *collateral giver*. Conversely, in order to provide cash collateral, a securities borrower may need to borrow such cash in the money market, thereby incurring a cash borrowing cost (in a *positive interest rate* environment).

Securities Lending & Borrowing and Collateral – Accessing the SL&B Marketplace

Within the Securities Lending & Borrowing (SL&B) part of this book, the three chapters which precede this chapter, namely:

- Chapter 9 'Securities Lending & Borrowing and Collateral – Introduction to SL&B'
- Chapter 10 'Securities Lending & Borrowing and Collateral – Principles of SL&B'
- Chapter 11 'Securities Lending & Borrowing and Collateral – The SL&B Trade Lifecycle'

all describe SL&B from the perspective of the securities being lent directly by the lender to the borrower. In addition to such a 'Direct Lender to Borrower' arrangement, other methods exist by which securities can be lent and borrowed, and related collateral can be managed. This chapter outlines those methods.

PART 3

Today, a number of methods exist for securities to be lent and borrowed, including:

- direct lender to borrower contact
- use of a lending agent, and
- use of an ICSD's failed trades management service.

Each of those SL&B methods is described within this chapter in Section 12.1 'Routes to Market'.

Furthermore, the management of collateral relating to the above-mentioned methods is described within Section 12.2 'Collateral Management'.

12.1 ROUTES TO MARKET

12.1.1 Direct Lender to Borrower Contact: Overview

This method involves direct communication between the *securities lender* and the *securities borrower*, therefore on a *bilateral* and *OTC* basis.

Securities Lender's Perspective   The first steps in being able to lend securities are:

- ensuring that the securities are in fact in the lender's *custodian* account
  - care needs to be taken where the lender has purchased securities, where that purchase has not yet *settled*; typically, this can be for either of two reasons, 1) the *value date* of the purchase is in the future, or 2) the value date has been reached but the selling *counterparty* has been unable to deliver the securities
- ensuring that the securities have not been sold or are not designated for use in another transaction type (e.g. *repo*, or delivery of *collateral* as required in an *OTC derivative* trade)
  - in order to discover whether the securities are available for lending or not, access is required to the firm's *books & records* containing all trades.

These questions are depicted in Figure 12.1:

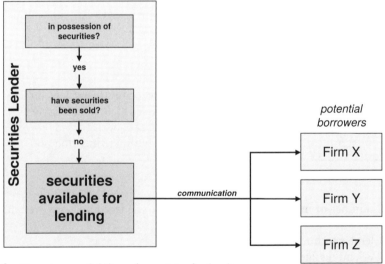

FIGURE 12.1   Ensuring availability of securities for lending

Once it is ascertained that the securities are available for lending, contact can be made with potential borrowers to establish whether the securities available for lending can be matched with the potential borrower's borrowing requirement. This could be actioned by telephone, or by issuing a communication by email, or by potential borrowers accessing the lender's website. Conversely, borrowers may initiate proceedings by contacting likely lenders.

Securities Borrower's Perspective   The first steps in wishing to borrow securities are to ensure there is a real borrowing requirement in order to avoid unnecessary borrowing costs, for example:

- avoiding acting prematurely; in a situation where securities have been bought and sold, where it is still possible for the purchase to settle on its value date, making the assumption that the purchase will not settle on value date, then borrowing securities based on that assumption creates the risk of unnecessary borrowing. (If the purchase does settle on value date, the sale can also be settled on value date, and borrowing costs can be avoided)
- securities held elsewhere; some securities are able to be traded and settled in two (or more) financial centres, and it is possible that securities purchased previously are held at a custodian in location X, and securities now sold are to be delivered in location Y. Under these circumstances, there is a risk that borrowing securities to complete delivery of the sale is unnecessary, as just a *free of payment* transfer of securities between location X and location Y is all that is necessary in order to effect settlement of the sale.

Once it is ascertained that there is a true borrowing requirement, contact can be made with potential lenders to ascertain whether the borrowing requirement can be satisfied by the lenders' available securities. This could be actioned by telephone, or by issuing a communication by email, or by access to the lender's website. Conversely, borrowers may initiate proceedings by contacting likely lenders. Such situations are reflected in Figure 12.2:

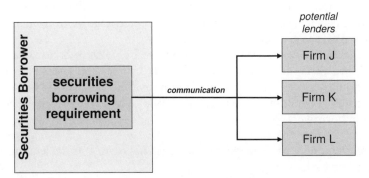

FIGURE 12.2   Ensuring a real borrowing requirement exists

Providing the lender and borrower agree terms (as described within prior Securities Lending & Borrowing chapters), a direct securities lending & borrowing trade will have been executed.

The types of financial institution that choose to manage the trade execution aspects of securities lending & borrowing directly with counterparties tend to be the larger *buy-side* and *sell-side* firms that possess the necessary resources. Many other financial institutions may choose to utilise services provided by a variety of intermediaries in the securities lending & borrowing marketplace; descriptions of such intermediaries follow.

The management of collateral relating to SL&B trades executed bilaterally is described within this chapter in Section 12.2 'Collateral Management'.

12.1.2 Agency Lending: Overview

Lending agents are intermediaries focused on providing specialist services to *beneficial owners* of securities, whereby the lending programme can be tailored to the requirements of each of the agent's clients.

The effort involved in a firm managing by itself every aspect of securities lending can be very significant. Consequently, rather than the beneficial owner lending securities to borrowing counterparties directly (see the prior chapters in Part 3 of the book), the beneficial owner effectively outsources the effort of finding borrowers to the lending agent. Lending agents typically have long established relationships with multiple securities borrowers.

Under such arrangements, the beneficial owner is able to dictate:

- to which borrowers it is prepared to lend its securities
- the level of securities lending fees required
- the nature of *eligible collateral* it will accept
- the level of *over-collateralisation* (margin) it requires
- the frequency of *exposure* calculation (*marking-to-market*).

In turn, the lending agent is required to operate to those parameters set by the beneficial owner in its negotiations with potential borrowers. Furthermore, the lending agent collects securities lending fees from borrowers and provides reporting to the beneficial owner of current loans and of lending fees earned.

Securities lending fees earned from borrowers are typically split between the lending agent and the beneficial owner at a pre-agreed percentage, with the beneficial owner usually being paid the greater portion.

Agency lending services are typically provided by *CSDs* and *custodian* banks and third party specialists, and some firms which fall under the latter category provide securities lending services on a non-custodial basis. This means that the lending agent is not responsible for holding the lender's portfolio of lendable securities. For collateral received from borrowers:

- *cash collateral* may be managed by the beneficial owner, or the lending agent or by a third party cash manager
- *securities* collateral will be held in a custody account, typically by a *tri-party agent*.

An example of a lending agent that is independent and provides tailored securities lending services is eSecLending (www.eseclending.com).

Once a beneficial owner has decided to utilise the services offered by a lending agent, two securities lending methods are normally available, namely a) exclusive lending, and b) discretionary lending.

Exclusive Lending via Lending Agents   Exclusive lending is the lending of an entire portfolio (or a subset) of assets owned by a beneficial owner, via a lending agent, to a specific borrower. An example of an exclusive lending service is as depicted in Figure 12.3:

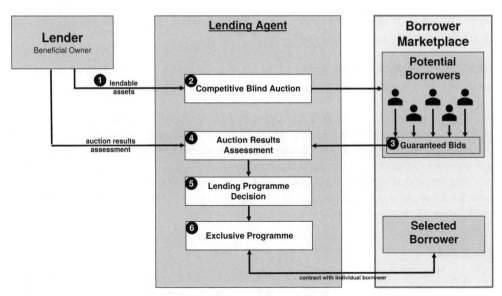

FIGURE 12.3   Agency lending; exclusive lending programme

The steps depicted in the diagram are explained below:

Step 1: at the beginning of the process, the beneficial owner provides its list of lendable assets to the lending agent. Such a list may comprise the beneficial owner's
entire portfolio of lendable assets, or a portion only

Step 2: the agent publishes the list of assets to pre-approved potential borrowers

Step 3: interested borrowers then place their bids simultaneously, without a bidder
able to see the bids of other firms (a *competitive blind auction*)

Step 4: the beneficial owner and the agent assess the bids received

Step 5: a decision is made as to which borrower will be awarded the contract

Step 6: the contract is put in place with the selected borrower for a defined duration, for example 12 months; the contract gives the borrower sole access to the
portfolio for the duration of the contract.

The advantage of this method to the beneficial owner is that they will receive guaranteed securities lending fees for the duration of the contract. Conversely, the borrower
is paying for sole access to the entire portfolio, whether it makes use of the securities
within the portfolio, or not.

Although under an exclusive arrangement the beneficial owner receives guaranteed
securities lending fees, during the period of the contract they must forego any opportunity for increased fees.

Should the beneficial owner choose to offer separate portions of its portfolio, this is
likely to result in multiple exclusive contracts with a variety of borrowers.

Lending agents typically indemnify the beneficial owner against the borrower's
default. Should such an event of default occur, the indemnity would normally cover the

return of either 1) the full quantity of the lent security, or 2) the current market value of the lent security payable in cash.

Discretionary Lending via Lending Agents   Discretionary lending is the lending of individual securities, by a lending agent on behalf of the beneficial owner, as and when a borrower requires such securities.

The details of each loan will be negotiated by the lending agent directly with the borrower; consequently, lending fees will fluctuate according to the supply and demand of the securities in question. As a result, the beneficial owner's returns on its discretionary securities lending activity are not guaranteed.

The beneficial owner's legal counterparty is the lending agent, and typically each beneficial owner signs an Agency Lending Agreement with the lending agent. In turn, the lending agent signs a *GMSLA* with each borrower.

Conclusion

Amongst the community of beneficial owners (including *pension funds, mutual funds* and *insurance companies*) that are prepared to lend their *equity* and *bonds*, utilising the services provided by lending agents is very popular.

Agency lenders specialise in providing securities lending services to *buy-side* beneficial owners, facilitating securities lending through methods such as 'exclusive' lending and 'discretionary' lending.

Whatever lending method is employed, the agent lender's role is to protect the interests of the beneficial owner, and to put into practice the requirements dictated by the beneficial owner in the lending agent's dealings with the various borrowers.

The management of collateral relating to SL&B trades executed by lending agents is described within this chapter in Section 12.2 'Collateral Management'.

12.1.3 ICSDs' Failed Trade Management: Overview

Two *international central securities depositories* (ICSDs) exist, namely *Clearstream International* (Luxembourg) and *Euroclear Bank* (Brussels).

Note: fundamental services provided by all central securities depositories, both national and international, are described within Chapter 2 'The Nature and Characteristics of Collateral Types'.

A significant volume and concentration of securities (particularly *Eurobonds*) are held by the two ICSDs, on behalf of their participants; consequently, both ICSDs are able to offer securities lending & borrowing services to those participants wishing to lend and to borrow. Specifically, the service referred to here addresses the issue of *settlement failure*.

At the ICSDs, thousands of participants located in numerous countries own one or many securities accounts. Upon initial opening of a participant's account, the ICSD will ask whether the participant would like to:

- lend their securities, and if so the parameters for such lending, for example:
  - whether all the participant's securities should be made available for lending, or
  - whether a specific category of securities (e.g. only GBP-denominated Eurobonds) should be lent, or

- whether a specific category of securities (e.g. only EUR-denominated Eurobonds) should be excluded from lending
- borrow securities, and if so the relevant parameters (as per the list above).

Participants wishing to lend or to borrow (or both) via their ICSD, are required to sign a legal agreement with their ICSD. The ICSD's role is to facilitate the lending and borrowing of securities (at individual settlement instruction level) on behalf of their SL&B participants. Furthermore such SL&B is anonymous; the lender will not discover the identity of the ultimate borrower, and vice versa. From a legal perspective, the lender has in fact lent to the ICSD and has exposure with the ICSD throughout the lending period; likewise, the borrower has in fact borrowed from the ICSD.

Note: there is no guarantee that lending or borrowing will occur. Just because a participant is willing to lend their securities does not guarantee that there are any borrowers that 'today' have a borrowing requirement. Conversely, a participant that needs to borrow securities may or may not be successful in borrowing, as there may be no availability from the lender community at the ICSD.

On any one business day, within the community of participants there will be those that are willing to lend their securities, and others wishing to borrow. Amongst many other services, the ICSDs facilitate securities lending by matching the lenders' willingness to lend with the borrowers' requirement to borrow. On an individual loan/borrowing basis, the trade is executed and processed as follows:

- assume that an ICSD participant (Firm M) has signed up to the securities borrowing programme, and that Firm M has purchased (from Firm G) and sold (to Firm P) the same quantity of the same security on the same value date
  - from the normal DvP instructions within Firm M's account, on value date of those instructions the ICSD can identify that an incoming securities delivery is failing because the delivering party (Firm G) is insufficient of securities
  - as a result, the ICSD can also identify that the delivery to Firm P will also fail unless the securities can be borrowed, therefore ...
- the ICSD now attempts to identify one (or more) lender(s) that have the necessary quantity of the specific securities (required by Firm M) available for lending ...
  - the ICSD identifies that Firm L has available for lending the relevant securities, and effectively transfers the securities:
    - from the account of Firm L to the ICSD, and immediately
    - from the ICSD to the account of Firm M
  - the arrival of the securities into Firm M's account will now cause the ICSD to deliver the securities to Firm P, thereby causing Firm M to receive the sale proceeds.

As a result of the above:

- the securities lender will now begin earning a securities lending fee from the ICSD (without loss of *beneficial ownership*)
- the securities borrower will now begin incurring a securities borrowing fee from the ICSD.

This form of securities lending & borrowing is commonly known as *ICSD auto-lending/borrowing*.

Recall of Lent Securities   Following the initial loan as described above, should the securities lender sell the securities (or require to deliver the securities for any other purpose), the ICSD's receipt of the lender's settlement instruction will cause the ICSD to automatically issue a recall notice to the borrower(s).

Return of Borrowed Securities   In the example set of trades listed above, assume that the delivery of securities from Firm G to Firm M occurs 5 days after *value date* of the trade. Under these circumstances, the ICSD will recognise that Firm M is borrowing securities, and therefore will automatically remove the securities from Firm M's account and return the same to Firm L (the securities lender).

    The above situations are depicted in Figure 12.4:

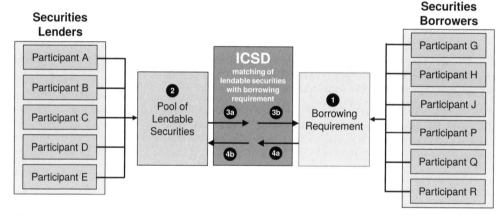

FIGURE 12.4   ICSDs – lenders, borrowers and anonymous lending and borrowing

      Step 1: the ICSD identifies a borrowing requirement from one or many potential borrowers

      Step 2: the ICSD identifies whether the relevant securities are available for lending

      Step 3a: the ICSD removes the securities from the (one or many) securities lenders' accounts, and

      Step 3b: the ICSD delivers the securities to the particular borrower(s) account, in turn resulting in settlement of the borrowers' delivery obligation

      Step 4a: at a later date, based on the lender's recall requirement or on the borrower's return requirement, once the borrower's account contains an adequate quantity of securities, the ICSD removes the borrowed quantity of securities from the borrower's account

      Step 4b: the ICSD facilitates the return of the lent securities to the lender.

Fees   The fees applicable to the auto-lending/borrowing programme at the ICSDs are based upon the type of security (for example, equity or domestic bonds or international bonds), and the currency involved.

Fees are calculated based upon the close-of-business *current market value* of the security in question; in the case of *interest-bearing bonds* the value of *accrued interest* is incorporated into the bond's market value.

Fees paid to lenders are less than fees charged to borrowers; for example, lenders receive 1.20% whilst borrowers are charged 1.75%. The ICSD takes the differential for the service provided to both parties.

Impacts Resulting from ICSD Auto-Lending/Borrowing

Once a securities loan has been executed, the resultant impacts are:

- from the lender's perspective:
  - securities are lent on an automatic basis, as and when the ICSD detects a borrowing requirement; no 'trading' effort is required by the securities lender
  - any delays in receiving recalled lent securities will result in supplemental fees being paid to the lender (and charged to the borrower) by the ICSD
  - in the event of the borrower failing to return the lent security to the ICSD, the ICSD provides a guarantee to the lender that 1) the securities will be returned, or 2) the cash equivalent will be paid
  - lending fees are credited on a monthly basis
  - no *securities safekeeping fees* are charged to the lender whilst the securities are being lent
  - the value of *income* and *redemption* payments are credited to the lender automatically
  - all operational/administrative effort is managed by the ICSD (not by the securities lender)
- from the borrower's perspective:
  - securities are borrowed on an automatic basis, as and when the ICSD detects a borrowing requirement; no 'trading' effort is required by the securities borrower
  - providing that borrowing is successful, outstanding delivery commitments will be settled automatically (as the receipt of borrowed securities into the borrower's ICSD account will automatically result in settlement of the outstanding delivery commitment)
  - any delays in delivering recalled borrowed securities will result in supplemental fees being charged to the borrower (and paid to the lender) by the ICSD
  - borrowing fees are charged on a monthly basis
  - all operational/administrative effort is managed by the ICSD (not by the securities borrower).

Conclusion

The lending and borrowing of securities via the automated service provided by both the ICSDs is a highly efficient mechanism by which borrowers can minimise the impact of failed trades, thereby also benefitting lenders.

The fact that the service is automated means that there is no effort required by the lending and borrowing firms on a day-to-day basis; once a firm has signed up to the ICSDs' service, lenders can simply run reports from the relevant ICSD which lists the securities currently being lent, likewise for borrowers.

PART 3

Collateral management relating to SL&B trades executed under the ICSDs' failed trade management service is described within this chapter in Section 12.2 'Collateral Management'.

12.2 COLLATERAL MANAGEMENT

Within this chapter, in Section 12.1 'Routes to Market', three methods of executing securities lending & borrowing (SL&B) trades were described, namely:

- direct lender to borrower contact
- use of a lending agent, and
- use of an ICSD's failed trades management service.

This section describes the collateral arrangements relating to those SL&B trading methods.

Regarding the direct method and the agency lending method, in both cases cash and non-cash (securities) are classified as *eligible collateral*. The ICSDs' failed trades SL&B service can be collateralised only with non-cash (securities). These arrangements are depicted in Figure 12.5:

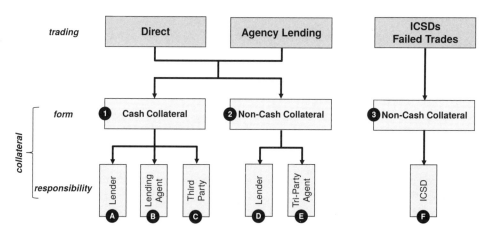

FIGURE 12.5   Collateral types and responsibilities

The following sub-sections elaborate on such collateral arrangements, making repeated reference to the diagram above.

12.2.1 Direct and Agency Lending Models

As mentioned above, both cash collateral and non-cash collateral (numbers 1 and 2 in Figure 12.5) are applicable to these two trade execution methods.

Whether cash collateral or non-cash collateral, the parties listed below are responsible for ensuring that an adequate value of collateral is given by the securities borrower, to cover the variable market value of the lent/borrowed security, plus margin, at the agreed frequency and throughout the lifetime of a trade. This therefore includes the daily *marking-to-market* of the lent/borrowed security and of any non-cash (securities) collateral.

Cash Collateral　It is possible for one of three parties to be responsible for managing the cash collateral received:

- the lender (party A in Figure 12.5) would have negotiated a *rebate rate* with the securities borrower. In order for the lender to make profit from the securities loan, they must reinvest the cash so as to earn a greater *reinvestment rate* than the rebate rate. The lender may choose to simply lend the cash into the *money market*
- alternatively, the *lending agent* (party B in Figure 12.5) must reinvest the cash collateral on behalf of the lender in order to generate profitable returns for the lender and for itself. The lending agent may choose to reinvest into an independently run cash fund or into suitable money market products
- a further option is for a third party (party C in Figure 12.5) to be given responsibility for management of cash collateral received from securities borrowers. Such firms are normally traditional fund managers that invest in cash products.

Non-Cash Collateral　Two options are available in terms of the responsibility for managing non-cash (securities) collateral received from securities borrowers:

- the lender (party D in Figure 12.5) will receive securities collateral from the securities borrower, and either 1) hold the collateral securely in its CSD account or custodian account, or 2) *reuse* the collateral to settle a delivery commitment in a separate transaction. (In choosing to reuse the collateral, the lender must remain conscious of the need to return to the securities borrower the same quantity of the same ISIN (or *equivalent collateral*), on the *closing value date* of the SL&B trade)
- a neutral *tri-party agent* (mutually acceptable to the securities lender and the securities borrower) may be appointed in order to manage all aspects of collateral.

Under the circumstances in which the *beneficial owner* utilises the services of a *lending agent* to execute securities loans on its behalf, a tri-party agent is typically appointed to manage non-cash (securities) collateral.

Agency Lending – Non-Cash Collateral　Before an SL&B trade is executed, the beneficial owner's assets are held by their usual custodian. Following trade execution between a lending agent and the securities borrower:

- the lending agent issues a *settlement instruction* to the beneficial owner's custodian, requesting delivery of the lent security to the borrower's account (by use of counterparty *standing settlement instructions* held within the lending agent's static data)
  - if securities collateral, settlement is by $2 \times FoP$
    - the securities borrower is required to *pre-collateralise*: the beneficial owner's lent assets are delivered following successful receipt of the borrower's collateral
      - in the majority of cases, securities collateral is held by a tri-party agent of the borrower's choice, within segregated accounts in the name of the lending agent and/or the beneficial owner
      - in the minority of cases, securities collateral is held by the beneficial owner's custodian.

PART 3

Following settlement of the opening leg, and throughout the lifetime of the SL&B trade:

- *exposure* calculations (including ***marking-to-market***) are performed on a daily basis by the lending agent (on behalf of the securities lender) and the securities borrower, following which ***margin calls*** are agreed between those two parties
  - where the beneficial owner is exposed, a settlement instruction is issued by the lending agent to the tri-party agent to receive additional assets from the securities borrower, following which the tri-party agent receives delivery in settlement
  - where the securities borrower is exposed, the borrower requests the tri-party agent to provide additional assets, following which the tri-party agent makes delivery.

Regarding settlement of the closing leg, for 'open' SL&B trades:

- *recalls* initiated by the lending agent
  - where the beneficial owner has sold (or otherwise utilised) the security currently on loan, the lending agent will identify such circumstances and will therefore request closure of the trade from the securities borrower
    - the lending agent then issues a settlement instruction (either DvP or FoP, as appropriate) to the tri-party agent which must match with the borrower's settlement instruction before settlement can occur
- *returns* initiated by the securities borrower
  - where the securities borrower wishes to close an open SL&B trade, the borrower requests closure from the lending agent
    - the lending agent then issues a settlement instruction (either DvP or FoP, as appropriate) to the tri-party agent which must match with the borrower's settlement instruction before settlement can occur.

ICSD Failed Trades – Non-Cash Collateral   Where securities have been lent and borrowed under the ICSD's auto-lending/borrowing programme:

- from the lender's perspective:
  - the ICSD provides a credit guarantee to the lender; no physical collateral is received by the lender
  - the lender retains the collateral value of the lent securities, therefore the lender's credit facility with the ICSD remains unaffected
  - reinvestment risk does not apply, as only securities (not cash) collateral is acceptable
- from the borrower's perspective:
  - upon transfer of borrowed securities to the borrower's account, collateral is made available to the ICSD simultaneously and irrevocably
  - to cover the borrower's obligation to return the borrowed securities, adequate collateral must be held (in either securities or cash, or in a combination of securities and cash) in the borrower's account at the ICSD to cover the market value

of the borrowed securities throughout the lifetime of the borrowing. (Whilst a securities borrowing exists, movement of assets out of the securities borrower's account will be prevented by the ICSD if that movement means that inadequate cover will remain)
- both lender's and borrower's perspectives:
  - collateral is not exchanged directly between lender and borrower
  - securities loans are revalued daily (incorporating *haircut*):
    - shortfalls in collateral are automatically taken from the borrower's ICSD account.

12.2.2 ICSDs' Tri-Party Collateral Management

An *ICSD* in the role of *tri-party agent* is a neutral third party appointed by the securities lender and securities borrower to administer securities lending & borrowing (SL&B) trades and their associated collateral, throughout the trades' lifetime. *Eligible collateral* under a tri-party arrangement at the ICSDs is non-cash (securities) collateral.

In an ICSDs' tri-party SL&B trade, the agreement to trade is executed outside of the tri-party agent, typically directly between the securities lender and the securities borrower. At trade execution, the parties agree whether the trade should be administered in the conventional *bilateral* fashion, or via a mutually acceptable ICSD tri-party agent.

The administration referred to above relates to all the primary tasks necessary to be applied to any SL&B trade throughout its lifetime, namely:

- post-execution agreement of basic trade details, including quantity of securities lent, the specific security lent, the lending fee, the duration of the loan (whether 'term' or 'open')
- eligible collateral, including security types, and related margin (*haircut*)
- exposure management via *marking-to-market* of both lent security and securities collateral
- carrying out *margin calls* when necessary
- executing *collateral substitutions* when necessary
- processing *income events* and *corporate action events*
- at close of the loan, the return of the lent securities and return of the collateral

and in general terms, the reporting to the involved parties to facilitate the monitoring of exposures.

Note: the role of the tri-party agent under an *agency lending* arrangement (see heading 'Agency Lending – Non-Cash Collateral' within Sub-section 12.2.1 'Direct and Agency Lending Models') is not the same as provided by the ICSDs' tri-party agent service. The agency lending tri-party agent's role is solely to hold the collateral, and not to provide the range of services provided by the ICSDs' tri-party service.

The relationship between the three parties, and the typical services provided by the tri-party agent are as represented in Figure 12.6:

PART 3

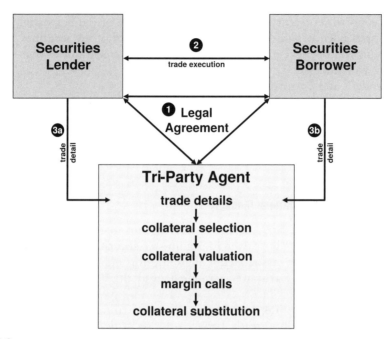

FIGURE 12.6 Tri-party arrangements – representative structure

The steps in the diagram are explained as follows:

Step 1: a legal agreement is signed between the two trading parties and the ICSD as tri-party agent

Step 2: an SL&B trade is executed directly between two trading parties, who agree to administer the trade on a tri-party basis

Step 3: both trading parties transmit their trade details to the tri-party agent, following which:
- the tri-party agent must ensure that trade details are fully matched
- the tri-party agent captures details of the trade internally
- the tri-party agent ensures the securities lender has the relevant quantity of the particular lent security to deliver to the borrower
- the tri-party agent ensures the securities borrower has an adequate quantity of eligible securities collateral (in accordance with the pre-documented eligible collateral), which either the securities borrower or the tri-party agent can select (as required by the securities borrower)
- the tri-party agent effects movement of lent/borrowed securities versus securities collateral on the opening value date. The borrower receives the securities into its account, and from there is able to on-deliver it or hold it, as required. The lender does not receive the securities collateral into its own account, instead it is held by the tri-party agent on behalf of the securities lender
- during the lifetime of the SL&B trade, the tri-party agent:
  - revalues the lent/borrowed security and securities collateral, taking account of margin – on a daily basis – and determines whether either party has exposure, and

- automatically processes margin calls (by adding or deducting collateral) in order to rebalance the 'current' value of the lent/borrowed security versus the 'current' value of the collateral, and
- can normally identify whether the lent security is required for use by the securities lender in a different transaction, or whether securities collateral is required for use by the securities borrower in a different transaction; this is possible through the receipt of settlement instructions from either party. Consequently the agent is able to determine when closure of the SL&B trade is necessary (from the securities lender's perspective), or when collateral substitution is necessary (from the securities borrower's perspective) and to effect such substitution automatically.

It is important to note that the securities lender is typically able to define which grouping of collateral is to be regarded as *eligible collateral*; such groupings are often known as *collateral baskets*. For example, the credit rating limits of bond issues may be defined (e.g. no lower than a rating of AA), and margin or haircut levels can be stated. Furthermore, securities lenders can dictate collateral *concentration limits*. Note that both 'term' and 'open' trades can be managed by the ICSD as tri-party agent. However, cash collateral is not accepted.

It is also important to note that the ICSDs as tri-party agent are not involved in the risk associated with the trade itself; in the event of default by one of the original parties to the trade (e.g. the securities borrower), the exposed party is that firm's counterparty (i.e. the securities lender), and not the ICSD as tri-party agent.

Conclusion

For firms wishing to lend their securities, or to borrow securities, or to do both, if such firms do not possess adequate human or IT resources to manage the administrative (operational) tasks themselves, a solution exists in the form of the ICSDs' tri-party SL&B collateral management.

The ICSDs' tri-party SL&B collateral management is an outsourced solution – use of tri-party agents has grown in popularity in recent years, as the demand for collateral has become more acute due to new regulatory requirements.

Securities lenders are completely able to mitigate exposures, as 1) they can dictate the quality of collateral they will accept from their borrowing counterparties, and 2) the tri-party agent will monitor 'live' exposures daily during the lifetime of the SL&B trade, and effect margin calls automatically. The need to close an 'open' securities loan is identifiable by the tri-party agent, and closure (recall) of a current loan is effected automatically.

Securities borrowers are able to borrow securities they need, and to give eligible collateral which can be selected by the tri-party agent, if required. The need to substitute collateral is identifiable by the tri-party agent, following which collateral substitution is effected automatically. Likewise, the need to close an 'open' securities borrowing is identifiable by the tri-party agent, and closure (return) of a current borrowing is effected automatically.

CHAPTER 13

Securities Lending & Borrowing and Collateral – The Global Master Securities Lending Agreement

PART 3

To enable readers to relate the content of the four chapters commencing with Chapter 9 'Securities Lending & Borrowing and Collateral – Introduction to SL&B' to Chapter 12 'Securities Lending & Borrowing and Collateral – Accessing the SL&B Marketplace', the text which follows this page within this chapter contains a complete version of the Global Master Securities Lending Agreement (GMSLA) 2010.

The GMSLA has been reproduced with the express permission of The International Securities Lending Association.

VERSION: JANUARY 2010

GLOBAL MASTER SECURITIES LENDING AGREEMENT

FRESHFIELDS BRUCKHAUS DERINGER

CONTENTS

PART 3

AGREEMENT

BETWEEN:

(*Party A*) a company incorporated under the laws of acting through one or more Designated Offices; and

(*Party B*) a company incorporated under the laws of acting through one or more Designated Offices.

1. APPLICABILITY

1.1 From time to time the Parties acting through one or more Designated Offices may enter into transactions in which one party (*Lender*) will transfer to the other (*Borrower*) securities and financial instruments (*Securities*) against the transfer of Collateral (as defined in paragraph 2) with a simultaneous agreement by Borrower to transfer to Lender Securities equivalent to such Securities on a fixed date or on demand against the transfer to Borrower by Lender of assets equivalent to such Collateral.

1.2 Each such transaction shall be referred to in this Agreement as a *Loan* and shall be governed by the terms of this Agreement, including the supplemental terms and conditions contained in the Schedule and any Addenda or Annexes attached hereto, unless otherwise agreed in writing. In the event of any inconsistency between the provisions of an Addendum or Annex and this Agreement, the provisions of such Addendum or Annex shall prevail unless the Parties otherwise agree.

1.3 Either Party may perform its obligations under this Agreement either directly or through a Nominee.

2. INTERPRETATION

2.1 In this Agreement:

Act of Insolvency means in relation to either Party:

(a) its making a general assignment for the benefit of, or entering into a reorganisation, arrangement, or composition with creditors; or

(b) its stating in writing that it is unable to pay its debts as they become due; or

(c) its seeking, consenting to or acquiescing in the appointment of any trustee, administrator, receiver or liquidator or analogous officer of it or any material part of its property; or

(d) the presentation or filing of a petition in respect of it (other than by the other Party to this Agreement in respect of any obligation under this Agreement) in any court or before any agency alleging or for the bankruptcy, winding-up or insolvency of such Party (or any analogous proceeding) or seeking any reorganisation, arrangement, composition, re-adjustment, administration, liquidation, dissolution or similar relief under any present or future statute, law or regulation, such petition not having been stayed or dismissed within 30 days of its filing (except in the case of a petition for winding-up or any analogous proceeding in respect of which no such 30 day period shall apply); or

(e)   the appointment of a receiver, administrator, liquidator or trustee or analogous officer of such Party over all or any material part of such Party's property; or

(f)   the convening of any meeting of its creditors for the purpose of considering a voluntary arrangement as referred to in Section 3 of the Insolvency Act 1986 (or any analogous proceeding);

Agency Annex means the Annex to this Agreement published by the International Securities Lending Association and providing for Lender to act as agent for a third party in respect of one or more Loans;

Alternative Collateral means Collateral having a Market Value equal to the Collateral delivered pursuant to paragraph 5 and provided by way of substitution in accordance with the provisions of paragraph 5.3;

Applicable Law means the laws, rules and regulations (including double taxation conventions) of any relevant jurisdiction, including published practice of any government or other taxing authority in connection with such laws, rules and regulations;

Automatic Early Termination has the meaning given in paragraph 10.1(d);

Base Currency means the currency indicated in paragraph 2 of the Schedule;

Business Day means:

(a)   in relation to Delivery in respect of any Loan, a day other than a Saturday or a Sunday on which banks and securities markets are open for business generally in the place(s) where the relevant Securities, Equivalent Securities, Collateral or Equivalent Collateral are to be delivered;

(b)   in relation to any payments under this Agreement, a day other than a Saturday or a Sunday on which banks are open for business generally in the principal financial centre of the country of which the currency in which the payment is denominated is the official currency and, if different, in the place where any account designated by the Parties for the making or receipt of the payment is situated (or, in the case of a payment in euro, a day on which TARGET operates);

(c)   in relation to a notice or other communication served under this Agreement, any day other than a Saturday or a Sunday on which banks are open for business generally in the place designated for delivery in accordance with paragraph 3 of the Schedule; and

(d)   in any other case, a day other than a Saturday or a Sunday on which banks are open for business generally in each place stated in paragraph 6 of the Schedule;

Buy-In means any arrangement under which, in the event of a seller or transferor failing to deliver securities to the buyer or transferee, the buyer or transferee of such securities is entitled under the terms of such arrangement to buy or otherwise acquire securities equivalent to such securities and to recover the cost of so doing from the seller or transferor;

Cash Collateral means Collateral taking the form of a transfer of currency;

Close of Business means the time at which the relevant banks, securities settlement systems or depositaries close in the business centre in which payment is to be made or Securities or Collateral is to be delivered;

Collateral means such securities or financial instruments or transfers of currency as are referred to in the table set out under paragraph 1 of the Schedule as being acceptable or any combination thereof as agreed between the Parties in relation to any particular Loan and which are delivered by Borrower to Lender in accordance with this Agreement and shall include Alternative Collateral;

Defaulting Party has the meaning given in paragraph 10;

Delivery in relation to any Securities or Collateral or Equivalent Securities or Equivalent Collateral comprising Securities means:

(a)   in the case of Securities held by a Nominee or within a clearing or settlement system, the crediting of such Securities to an account of the Borrower or Lender, as the case may be, or as it shall direct, or,

(b)   in the case of Securities otherwise held, the delivery to Borrower or Lender, as the case may be, or as the transferee shall direct of the relevant instruments of transfer, or

(c)   by such other means as may be agreed,

and *deliver* shall be construed accordingly;

Designated Office means the branch or office of a Party which is specified as such in paragraph 6 of the Schedule or such other branch or office as may be agreed to in writing by the Parties;

Equivalent or *equivalent to* in relation to any Loaned Securities or Collateral (whether Cash Collateral or Non-Cash Collateral) provided under this Agreement means Securities or other property, of an identical type, nominal value, description and amount to particular Loaned Securities or Collateral (as the case may be) so provided. If and to the extent that such Loaned Securities or Collateral (as the case may be) consists of Securities that are partly paid or have been converted, subdivided, consolidated, made the subject of a takeover, rights of pre-emption, rights to receive securities or a certificate which may at a future date be exchanged for Securities, the expression shall include such Securities or other assets to which Lender or Borrower (as the case may be) is entitled following the occurrence of the relevant event, and, if appropriate, the giving of the relevant notice in accordance with paragraph 6.7 and provided that Lender or Borrower (as the case may be) has paid to the other Party all and any sums due in respect thereof. In the event that such Loaned Securities or Collateral (as the case may be) have been redeemed, are partly paid, are the subject of a capitalisation issue or are subject to an event similar to any of the foregoing events described in this paragraph, the expression shall have the following meanings:

(a)   in the case of redemption, a sum of money equivalent to the proceeds of the redemption;

(b)   in the case of a call on partly-paid Securities, Securities equivalent to the relevant Loaned Securities or Collateral, as the case may be, provided that Lender shall have paid Borrower, in respect of Loaned Securities, and Borrower shall have paid to Lender, in respect of Collateral, an amount of money equal to the sum due in respect of the call;

(c)   in the case of a capitalisation issue, Securities equivalent to the relevant Loaned Securities or Collateral, as the case may be, together with the securities allotted by way of bonus thereon;

(d)   in the case of any event similar to any of the foregoing events described in this paragraph, Securities equivalent to the Loaned Securities or the relevant Collateral, as the case may be, together with or replaced by a sum of money or Securities or other property equivalent to that received in respect of such Loaned Securities or Collateral, as the case may be, resulting from such event;

Income means any interest, dividends or other distributions of any kind whatsoever with respect to any Securities or Collateral;

Income Record Date, with respect to any Securities or Collateral, means the date by reference to which holders of such Securities or Collateral are identified as being entitled to payment of Income;

Letter of Credit means an irrevocable, non-negotiable letter of credit in a form, and from a bank, acceptable to Lender;

Loaned Securities means Securities which are the subject of an outstanding Loan;

Margin has the meaning specified in paragraph 1 of the Schedule with reference to the table set out therein;

Market Value means:

(a)   in relation to the valuation of Securities, Equivalent Securities, Collateral or Equivalent Collateral (other than Cash Collateral or a Letter of Credit):

    (i)   such price as is equal to the market quotation for the mid price of such Securities, Equivalent Securities, Collateral and/or Equivalent Collateral as derived from a reputable pricing information service reasonably chosen in good faith by Lender; or

    (ii)   if unavailable the market value thereof as derived from the mid price or rate bid by a reputable dealer for the relevant instrument reasonably chosen in good faith by Lender,

in each case at Close of Business on the previous Business Day, or as specified in the Schedule, unless agreed otherwise or, at the option of either Party where in its reasonable opinion there has been an exceptional movement in the price of the asset in question since such time, the latest available price, plus (in each case):

PART 3

PART 3

(iii) the aggregate amount of Income which has accrued but not yet been paid in respect of the Securities, Equivalent Securities, Collateral or Equivalent Collateral concerned to the extent not included in such price,

provided that the price of Securities, Equivalent Securities, Collateral or Equivalent Collateral that are suspended or that cannot legally be transferred or that are transferred or required to be transferred to a government, trustee or third party (whether by reason of nationalisation, expropriation or otherwise) shall for all purposes be a commercially reasonable price agreed between the Parties, or absent agreement, be a price provided by a third party dealer agreed between the Parties, or if the Parties do not agree a third party dealer then a price based on quotations provided by the Reference Dealers. If more than three quotations are provided, the Market Value will be the arithmetic mean of the prices, without regard to the quotations having the highest and lowest prices. If three quotations are provided, the Market Value will be the quotation remaining after disregarding the highest and lowest quotations. For this purpose, if more than one quotation has the same highest or lowest price, then one of such quotations shall be disregarded. If fewer than three quotations are provided, the Market Value of the relevant Securities, Equivalent Securities, Collateral or Equivalent Collateral shall be determined by the Party making the determination of Market Value acting reasonably;

(b) in relation to a Letter of Credit the face or stated amount of such Letter of Credit; and

(c) in relation to Cash Collateral the amount of the currency concerned;

Nominee means a nominee or agent appointed by either Party to accept delivery of, hold or deliver Securities, Equivalent Securities, Collateral and/or Equivalent Collateral or to receive or make payments on its behalf;

Non-Cash Collateral means Collateral other than Cash Collateral;

Non-Defaulting Party has the meaning given in paragraph 10;

Notification Time means the time specified in paragraph 1.5 of the Schedule;

Parties means Lender and Borrower and *Party* shall be construed accordingly;

Posted Collateral has the meaning given in paragraph 5.4;

Reference Dealers means, in relation to any Securities, Equivalent Securities, Collateral or Equivalent Collateral, four leading dealers in the relevant securities selected by the Party making the determination of Market Value in good faith;

Required Collateral Value has the meaning given in paragraph 5.4;

Sales Tax means value added tax and any other Tax of a similar nature (including, without limitation, any sales tax of any relevant jurisdiction);

Settlement Date means the date upon which Securities are due to be transferred to Borrower in accordance with this Agreement;

Stamp Tax means any stamp, transfer, registration, documentation or similar Tax; and

Tax means any present or future tax, levy, impost, duty, charge, assessment or fee of any nature (including interest, penalties and additions thereto) imposed by any government or other taxing authority in respect of any transaction effected pursuant to or contemplated by, or any payment under or in respect of, this Agreement.

2.2 Headings

All headings appear for convenience only and shall not affect the interpretation of this Agreement.

2.3 Market terminology

Notwithstanding the use of expressions such as "borrow", "lend", "Collateral", "Margin" etc. which are used to reflect terminology used in the market for transactions of the kind provided for in this Agreement, title to Securities "borrowed" or "lent" and "Collateral" provided in accordance with this Agreement shall pass from one Party to another as provided for in this Agreement, the Party obtaining such title being obliged to deliver Equivalent Securities or Equivalent Collateral as the case may be.

2.4 Currency conversions

Subject to paragraph 11, for the purposes of determining any prices, sums or values (including Market Value and Required Collateral Value) prices, sums or values stated in currencies other than the Base Currency shall be converted into the Base Currency at the latest available spot rate of exchange quoted by a bank selected by Lender (or if an Event of Default has occurred in relation to Lender, by Borrower) in the London inter-bank market for the purchase of the Base Currency with the currency concerned on the day on which the calculation is to be made or, if that day is not a Business Day, the spot rate of exchange quoted at Close of Business on the immediately preceding Business Day on which such a quotation was available.

2.5

The Parties confirm that introduction of and/or substitution (in place of an existing currency) of a new currency as the lawful currency of a country shall not have the effect of altering, or discharging, or excusing performance under, any term of the Agreement or any Loan thereunder, nor give a Party the right unilaterally to alter or terminate the Agreement or any Loan thereunder. Securities will for the purposes of this Agreement be regarded as equivalent to other securities notwithstanding that as a result of such introduction and/or substitution those securities have been redenominated into the new currency or the nominal value of the securities has changed in connection with such redenomination.

2.6 Modifications etc. to legislation

Any reference in this Agreement to an act, regulation or other legislation shall include a reference to any statutory modification or re-enactment thereof for the time being in force.

PART 3

3. **LOANS OF SECURITIES**

Lender will lend Securities to Borrower, and Borrower will borrow Securities from Lender in accordance with the terms and conditions of this Agreement. The terms of each Loan shall be agreed prior to the commencement of the relevant Loan either orally or in writing (including any agreed form of electronic communication) and confirmed in such form and on such basis as shall be agreed between the Parties. Unless otherwise agreed, any confirmation produced by a Party shall not supersede or prevail over the prior oral, written or electronic communication (as the case may be).

4. **DELIVERY**

4.1 **Delivery of Securities on commencement of Loan**

Lender shall procure the Delivery of Securities to Borrower or deliver such Securities in accordance with this Agreement and the terms of the relevant Loan.

4.2 **Requirements to effect Delivery**

The Parties shall execute and deliver all necessary documents and give all necessary instructions to procure that all right, title and interest in:

(a)   any Securities borrowed pursuant to paragraph 3;

(b)   any Equivalent Securities delivered pursuant to paragraph 8;

(c)   any Collateral delivered pursuant to paragraph 5;

(d)   any Equivalent Collateral delivered pursuant to paragraphs 5 or 8;

shall pass from one Party to the other subject to the terms and conditions set out in this Agreement, on delivery of the same in accordance with this Agreement with full title guarantee, free from all liens, charges and encumbrances. In the case of Securities, Collateral, Equivalent Securities or Equivalent Collateral title to which is registered in a computer-based system which provides for the recording and transfer of title to the same by way of book entries, delivery and transfer of title shall take place in accordance with the rules and procedures of such system as in force from time to time. The Party acquiring such right, title and interest shall have no obligation to return or deliver any of the assets so acquired but, in so far as any Securities are borrowed by or any Collateral is delivered to such Party, such Party shall be obliged, subject to the terms of this Agreement, to deliver Equivalent Securities or Equivalent Collateral as appropriate.

4.3 **Deliveries to be simultaneous unless otherwise agreed**

Where under the terms of this Agreement a Party is not obliged to make a Delivery unless simultaneously a Delivery is made to it, subject to and without prejudice to its rights under paragraph 8.6, such Party may from time to time in accordance with market practice and in recognition of the practical difficulties in arranging simultaneous delivery of Securities, Collateral and cash transfers, waive its right under this Agreement in respect of simultaneous delivery and/or payment provided that no such waiver (whether by course of conduct or otherwise) in respect of one transaction shall bind it in respect of any other transaction.

4.4 Deliveries of Income

In respect of Income being paid in relation to any Loaned Securities or Collateral, Borrower (in the case of Income being paid in respect of Loaned Securities) and Lender (in the case of Income being paid in respect of Collateral) shall provide to the other Party, as the case may be, any endorsements or assignments as shall be customary and appropriate to effect, in accordance with paragraph 6, the payment or delivery of money or property in respect of such Income to Lender, irrespective of whether Borrower received such endorsements or assignments in respect of any Loaned Securities, or to Borrower, irrespective of whether Lender received such endorsements or assignments in respect of any Collateral.

5. COLLATERAL

5.1 Delivery of Collateral on commencement of Loan

Subject to the other provisions of this paragraph 5, Borrower undertakes to deliver to or deposit with Lender (or in accordance with Lender's instructions) Collateral simultaneously with Delivery of the Securities to which the Loan relates and in any event no later than Close of Business on the Settlement Date.

5.2 Deliveries through securities settlement systems generating automatic payments

Unless otherwise agreed between the Parties, where any Securities, Equivalent Securities, Collateral or Equivalent Collateral (in the form of securities) are transferred through a book entry transfer or settlement system which automatically generates a payment or delivery, or obligation to pay or deliver, against the transfer of such securities, then:

(a)   such automatically generated payment, delivery or obligation shall be treated as a payment or delivery by the transferee to the transferor, and except to the extent that it is applied to discharge an obligation of the transferee to effect payment or delivery, such payment or delivery, or obligation to pay or deliver, shall be deemed to be a transfer of Collateral or delivery of Equivalent Collateral, as the case may be, made by the transferee until such time as the Collateral or Equivalent Collateral is substituted with other Collateral or Equivalent Collateral if an obligation to deliver other Collateral or deliver Equivalent Collateral existed immediately prior to the transfer of Securities, Equivalent Securities, Collateral or Equivalent Collateral; and

(b)   the Party receiving such substituted Collateral or Equivalent Collateral, or if no obligation to deliver other Collateral or redeliver Equivalent Collateral existed immediately prior to the transfer of Securities, Equivalent Securities, Collateral or Equivalent Collateral, the Party receiving the deemed transfer of Collateral or Delivery of Equivalent Collateral, as the case may be, shall cause to be made to the other Party for value the same day either, where such transfer is a payment, an irrevocable payment in the amount of such transfer or, where such transfer is a Delivery, an irrevocable Delivery of securities (or other property, as the case may be) equivalent to such property.

PART 3

5.3   **Substitutions of Collateral**

Borrower may from time to time call for the repayment of Cash Collateral or the Delivery of Collateral equivalent to any Collateral delivered to Lender prior to the date on which the same would otherwise have been repayable or deliverable provided that at or prior to the time of such repayment or Delivery Borrower shall have delivered Alternative Collateral acceptable to Lender and Borrower is in compliance with paragraph 5.4 or paragraph 5.5, as applicable.

5.4   **Marking to Market of Collateral during the currency of a Loan on aggregated basis**

Unless paragraph 1.3 of the Schedule indicates that paragraph 5.5 shall apply in lieu of this paragraph 5.4, or unless otherwise agreed between the Parties:

(a)   the aggregate Market Value of the Collateral delivered to or deposited with Lender (excluding any Equivalent Collateral repaid or delivered under paragraphs 5.4(b) or 5.5(b) (as the case may be)) (*Posted Collateral*) in respect of all Loans outstanding under this Agreement shall equal the aggregate of the Market Value of Securities equivalent to the Loaned Securities and the applicable Margin (the *Required Collateral Value*) in respect of such Loans;

(b)   if at any time on any Business Day the aggregate Market Value of the Posted Collateral in respect of all Loans outstanding under this Agreement together with: (i) all amounts due and payable by the Lender under this Agreement but which are unpaid; and (ii) if agreed between the parties and if the Income Record Date has occurred in respect of any Non-Cash Collateral, the amount or Market Value of Income payable in respect of such Non-Cash Collateral exceeds the aggregate of the Required Collateral Values in respect of such Loans together with: (i) all amounts due and payable by the Borrower under this Agreement but which are unpaid; and (ii) if agreed between the parties and if the Income Record Date has occurred in respect of any securities equivalent to Loaned Securities, the amount or Market Value of Income payable in respect of such Equivalent Securities, Lender shall (on demand) repay and/or deliver, as the case may be, to Borrower such Equivalent Collateral as will eliminate the excess;

(c)   if at any time on any Business Day the aggregate Market Value of the Posted Collateral in respect of all Loans outstanding under this Agreement together with: (i) all amounts due and payable by the Lender under this Agreement but which are unpaid; and (ii) if agreed between the parties and if the Income Record Date has occurred in respect of any Non-Cash Collateral, the amount or Market Value of Income payable in respect of such Non-Cash Collateral falls below the aggregate of Required Collateral Values in respect of all such Loans together with: (i) all amounts due and payable by the Borrower under this Agreement but which are unpaid; and (ii) if agreed between the parties and if the Income Record Date has occurred in respect of Securities equivalent to any Loaned Securities, the amount or Market Value of Income payable in respect of such Equivalent Securities, Borrower shall (on demand) provide such further Collateral to Lender as will eliminate the deficiency;

(d)   where a Party acts as both Lender and Borrower under this Agreement, the provisions of paragraphs 5.4(b) and 5.4(c) shall apply separately (and without duplication) in respect of Loans entered into by that Party as Lender and Loans entered into by that Party as Borrower.

5.5   **Marking to Market of Collateral during the currency of a Loan on a Loan by Loan basis**

If paragraph 1.3 of the Schedule indicates this paragraph 5.5 shall apply in lieu of paragraph 5.4, the Posted Collateral in respect of any Loan shall bear from day to day and at any time the same proportion to the Market Value of Securities equivalent to the Loaned Securities as the Posted Collateral bore at the commencement of such Loan. Accordingly:

(a)   the Market Value of the Posted Collateral to be delivered or deposited while the Loan continues shall be equal to the Required Collateral Value;

(b)   if at any time on any Business Day the Market Value of the Posted Collateral in respect of any Loan together with: (i) all amounts due and payable by the Lender in respect of that Loan but which are unpaid; and (ii) if agreed between the parties and if the Income Record Date has occurred in respect of any Non-Cash Collateral, the amount or Market Value of Income payable in respect of such Non-Cash Collateral exceeds the Required Collateral Value in respect of such Loan together with: (i) all amounts due and payable by the Borrower in respect of that Loan; and (ii) if agreed between the parties and if the Income Record Date has occurred in respect of Securities equivalent to any Loaned Securities, the amount or Market Value of Income payable in respect of such Equivalent Securities, Lender shall (on demand) repay and/or deliver, as the case may be, to Borrower such Equivalent Collateral as will eliminate the excess; and

(c)   if at any time on any Business Day the Market Value of the Posted Collateral together with: (i) all amounts due any payable by the Lender in respect of that Loan; and (ii) if agreed between the parties and if the Income Record Date has occurred in respect of any Non-Cash Collateral, the amount or Market Value of Income payable in respect of such Non-Cash Collateral falls below the Required Collateral Value together with: (i) all amounts due and payable by the Borrower in respect of that Loan; and (ii) if agreed between the parties and if the Income Record Date has occurred in respect of Securities equivalent to any Loaned Securities, the amount or Market Value of Income payable in respect of such Equivalent Securities, Borrower shall (on demand) provide such further Collateral to Lender as will eliminate the deficiency.

5.6   **Requirements to deliver excess Collateral**

Where paragraph 5.4 applies, unless paragraph 1.4 of the Schedule indicates that this paragraph 5.6 does not apply, if a Party (the *first Party*) would, but for this paragraph 5.6, be required under paragraph 5.4 to provide further Collateral or deliver Equivalent Collateral in circumstances where the other Party (the *second Party*) would, but for this paragraph 5.6, also be required to or provide Collateral or deliver Equivalent Collateral under paragraph 5.4, then the Market Value of the Collateral or Equivalent Collateral deliverable by the first Party (*X*) shall be set off against the Market Value of the Collateral or Equivalent Collateral deliverable by the second

Party (*Y*) and the only obligation of the Parties under paragraph 5.4 shall be, where X exceeds Y, an obligation of the first Party, or where Y exceeds X, an obligation of the second Party to repay and/or (as the case may be) deliver Equivalent Collateral or to deliver further Collateral having a Market Value equal to the difference between X and Y.

5.7 Where Equivalent Collateral is repaid or delivered (as the case may be) or further Collateral is provided by a Party under paragraph 5.6, the Parties shall agree to which Loan or Loans such repayment, delivery or further provision is to be attributed and failing agreement it shall be attributed, as determined by the Party making such repayment, delivery or further provision to the earliest outstanding Loan and, in the case of a repayment or delivery up to the point at which the Market Value of Collateral in respect of such Loan equals the Required Collateral Value in respect of such Loan, and then to the next earliest outstanding Loan up to the similar point and so on.

5.8 **Timing of repayments of excess Collateral or deliveries of further Collateral**

Where any Equivalent Collateral falls to be repaid or delivered (as the case may be) or further Collateral is to be provided under this paragraph 5, unless otherwise provided or agreed between the Parties, if the relevant demand is received by the Notification Time specified in paragraph 1.5 of the Schedule, then the delivery shall be made not later than the Close of Business on the same Business Day; if a demand is received after the Notification Time, then the relevant delivery shall be made not later than the Close of Business on the next Business Day after the date such demand is received.

5.9 **Substitutions and extensions of Letters of Credit**

Where Collateral is a Letter of Credit, Lender may by notice to Borrower require that Borrower, on the third Business Day following the date of delivery of such notice (or by such other time as the Parties may agree), substitute Collateral consisting of cash or other Collateral acceptable to Lender for the Letter of Credit. Prior to the expiration of any Letter of Credit supporting Borrower's obligations hereunder, Borrower shall, no later than 10.30 a.m. UK time on the second Business Day prior to the date such Letter of Credit expires (or by such other time as the Parties may agree), obtain an extension of the expiration of such Letter of Credit or replace such Letter of Credit by providing Lender with a substitute Letter of Credit in an amount at least equal to the amount of the Letter of Credit for which it is substituted.

6. **DISTRIBUTIONS AND CORPORATE ACTIONS**

6.1 In this paragraph 6, references to an amount of Income *received* by any Party in respect of any Loaned Securities or Non-Cash Collateral shall be to an amount received from the issuer after any applicable withholding or deduction for or on account of Tax.

6.2 **Manufactured payments in respect of Loaned Securities**

Where the term of a Loan extends over an Income Record Date in respect of any Loaned Securities, Borrower shall, on the date such Income is paid by the issuer, or on such other date as the Parties may from time to time agree, pay or deliver to Lender such sum of money or property as is agreed between the Parties or, failing such agreement, a sum of money or property equivalent to (and in the same currency as) the type and amount of such Income that would be received by Lender in respect of such Loaned Securities assuming such Securities were not loaned to Borrower and were retained by Lender on the Income Record Date.

6.3   **Manufactured payments in respect of Non-Cash Collateral**

Where Non-Cash Collateral is delivered by Borrower to Lender and an Income Record Date in respect of such Non-Cash Collateral occurs before Equivalent Collateral is delivered by Lender to Borrower, Lender shall on the date such Income is paid, or on such other date as the Parties may from time to time agree, pay or deliver to Borrower a sum of money or property as is agreed between the Parties or, failing such agreement, a sum of money or property equivalent to (and in the same currency as) the type and amount of such Income that would be received by Lender in respect of such Non-Cash Collateral assuming Lender:

(a)   retained the Non-Cash Collateral on the Income Record Date; and

(b)   is not entitled to any credit, benefit or other relief in respect of Tax under any Applicable Law.

6.4   **Indemnity for failure to redeliver Equivalent Non-Cash Collateral**

Unless paragraph 1.6 of the Schedule indicates that this paragraph does not apply, where:

(a)   prior to any Income Record Date in relation to Non-Cash Collateral, Borrower has in accordance with paragraph 5.3 called for the Delivery of Equivalent Non-Cash Collateral;

(b)   Borrower has given notice of such call to Lender so as to be effective, at the latest, five hours before the Close of Business on the last Business Day on which Lender would customarily be required to initiate settlement of the Non-Cash Collateral to enable settlement to take place on the Business Day immediately preceding the relevant Income Record Date;

(c)   Borrower has provided reasonable details to Lender of the Non-Cash Collateral, the relevant Income Record Date and the proposed Alternative Collateral;

(d)   Lender, acting reasonably, has determined that such Alternative Collateral is acceptable to it and Borrower shall have delivered or delivers such Alternative Collateral to Lender; and

(e)   Lender has failed to make reasonable efforts to transfer Equivalent Non-Cash Collateral to Borrower prior to such Income Record Date,

Lender shall indemnify Borrower in respect of any cost, loss or damage (excluding any indirect or consequential loss or damage or any amount otherwise compensated by Lender, including pursuant to paragraphs 6.3 and/or 9.3) suffered by Borrower that it would not have suffered had the relevant Equivalent Non-Cash Collateral been transferred to Borrower prior to such Income Record Date.

6.5 **Income in the form of Securities**

Where Income, in the form of securities, is paid in relation to any Loaned Securities or Collateral, such securities shall be added to such Loaned Securities or Collateral (and shall constitute Loaned Securities or Collateral, as the case may be, and be part of the relevant Loan) and will not be delivered to Lender, in the case of Loaned Securities, or to Borrower, in the case of Collateral, until the end of the relevant Loan, provided that the Lender or Borrower (as the case may be) fulfils its obligations under paragraph 5.4 or 5.5 (as applicable) with respect to the additional Loaned Securities or Collateral, as the case may be.

6.6 **Exercise of voting rights**

Where any voting rights fall to be exercised in relation to any Loaned Securities or Collateral, neither Borrower, in the case of Equivalent Securities, nor Lender, in the case of Equivalent Collateral, shall have any obligation to arrange for voting rights of that kind to be exercised in accordance with the instructions of the other Party in relation to the Securities borrowed by it or transferred to it by way of Collateral, as the case may be, unless otherwise agreed between the Parties.

6.7 **Corporate actions**

Where, in respect of any Loaned Securities or any Collateral, any rights relating to conversion, sub-division, consolidation, pre-emption, rights arising under a takeover offer, rights to receive securities or a certificate which may at a future date be exchanged for securities or other rights, including those requiring election by the holder for the time being of such Securities or Collateral, become exercisable prior to the delivery of Equivalent Securities or Equivalent Collateral, then Lender or Borrower, as the case may be, may, within a reasonable time before the latest time for the exercise of the right or option give written notice to the other Party that on delivery of Equivalent Securities or Equivalent Collateral, as the case may be, it wishes to receive Equivalent Securities or Equivalent Collateral in such form as will arise if the right is exercised or, in the case of a right which may be exercised in more than one manner, is exercised as is specified in such written notice.

7. **RATES APPLICABLE TO LOANED SECURITIES AND CASH COLLATERAL**

7.1 **Rates in respect of Loaned Securities**

In respect of each Loan, Borrower shall pay to Lender, in the manner prescribed in sub-paragraph 7.3, sums calculated by applying such rate as shall be agreed between the Parties from time to time to the daily Market Value of the Loaned Securities.

7.2 **Rates in respect of Cash Collateral**

Where Cash Collateral is deposited with Lender in respect of any Loan, Lender shall pay to Borrower, in the manner prescribed in paragraph 7.3, sums calculated by applying such rates as shall be agreed between the Parties from time to time to the amount of such Cash Collateral. Any such payment due to Borrower may be set-off against any payment due to Lender pursuant to paragraph 7.1.

7.3 **Payment of rates**

In respect of each Loan, the payments referred to in paragraph 7.1 and 7.2 shall accrue daily in respect of the period commencing on and inclusive of the Settlement Date and terminating on and exclusive of the Business Day upon which Equivalent Securities are delivered or Cash Collateral is repaid. Unless otherwise agreed, the sums so accruing in respect of each calendar month shall be paid in arrears by the relevant Party not later than the Business Day which is the tenth Business Day after the last Business Day of the calendar month to which such payments relate or such other date as the Parties shall from time to time agree.

8. DELIVERY OF EQUIVALENT SECURITIES

8.1 Lender's right to terminate a Loan

Subject to paragraph 11 and the terms of the relevant Loan, Lender shall be entitled to terminate a Loan and to call for the delivery of all or any Equivalent Securities at any time by giving notice on any Business Day of not less than the standard settlement time for such Equivalent Securities on the exchange or in the clearing organisation through which the Loaned Securities were originally delivered. Borrower shall deliver such Equivalent Securities not later than the expiry of such notice in accordance with Lender's instructions.

8.2 Borrower's right to terminate a Loan

Subject to the terms of the relevant Loan, Borrower shall be entitled at any time to terminate a Loan and to deliver all and any Equivalent Securities due and outstanding to Lender in accordance with Lender's instructions and Lender shall accept such delivery.

8.3 Delivery of Equivalent Securities on termination of a Loan

Borrower shall procure the Delivery of Equivalent Securities to Lender or deliver Equivalent Securities in accordance with this Agreement and the terms of the relevant Loan on termination of the Loan. For the avoidance of doubt any reference in this Agreement or in any other agreement or communication between the Parties (howsoever expressed) to an obligation to deliver or account for or act in relation to Loaned Securities shall accordingly be construed as a reference to an obligation to deliver or account for or act in relation to Equivalent Securities.

8.4 Delivery of Equivalent Collateral on termination of a Loan

On the date and time that Equivalent Securities are required to be delivered by Borrower on the termination of a Loan, Lender shall simultaneously (subject to paragraph 5.4 if applicable) repay to Borrower any Cash Collateral or, as the case may be, deliver Collateral equivalent to the Collateral provided by Borrower pursuant to paragraph 5 in respect of such Loan. For the avoidance of doubt any reference in this Agreement or in any other agreement or communication between the Parties (however expressed) to an obligation to deliver or account for or act in relation to Collateral shall accordingly be construed as a reference to an obligation to deliver or account for or act in relation to Equivalent Collateral.

8.5 Delivery of Letters of Credit

Where a Letter of Credit is provided by way of Collateral, the obligation to deliver Equivalent Collateral is satisfied by Lender delivering for cancellation the Letter of Credit so provided, or where the Letter of Credit is provided in respect of more than one Loan, by Lender consenting to a reduction in the value of the Letter of Credit.

8.6   Delivery obligations to be reciprocal

Neither Party shall be obliged to make delivery (or make a payment as the case may be) to the other unless it is satisfied that the other Party will make such delivery (or make an appropriate payment as the case may be) to it. If it is not so satisfied (whether because an Event of Default has occurred in respect of the other Party or otherwise) it shall notify the other Party and unless that other Party has made arrangements which are sufficient to assure full delivery (or the appropriate payment as the case may be) to the notifying Party, the notifying Party shall (provided it is itself in a position, and willing, to perform its own obligations) be entitled to withhold delivery (or payment, as the case may be) to the other Party until such arrangements to assure full delivery (or the appropriate payment as the case may be) are made.

9.   FAILURE TO DELIVER

9.1   Borrower's failure to deliver Equivalent Securities

If Borrower fails to deliver Equivalent Securities in accordance with paragraph 8.3 Lender may:

(a)   elect to continue the Loan (which, for the avoidance of doubt, shall continue to be taken into account for the purposes of paragraph 5.4 or 5.5 as applicable); or

(b)   at any time while such failure continues, by written notice to Borrower declare that that Loan (but only that Loan) shall be terminated immediately in accordance with paragraph 11.2 as if (i) an Event of Default had occurred in relation to the Borrower, (ii) references to the Termination Date were to the date on which notice was given under this sub-paragraph, and (iii) the Loan were the only Loan outstanding. For the avoidance of doubt, any such failure shall not constitute an Event of Default (including under paragraph 10.1(i)) unless the Parties otherwise agree.

9.2   Lender's failure to deliver Equivalent Collateral

If Lender fails to deliver Equivalent Collateral comprising Non-Cash Collateral in accordance with paragraph 8.4 or 8.5, Borrower may:

(a)   elect to continue the Loan (which, for the avoidance of doubt, shall continue to be taken into account for the purposes of paragraph 5.4 or 5.5 as applicable); or

(b)   at any time while such failure continues, by written notice to Lender declare that that Loan (but only that Loan) shall be terminated immediately in accordance with paragraph 11.2 as if (i) an Event of Default had occurred in relation to the Lender, (ii) references to the Termination Date were to the date on which notice was given under this sub-paragraph, and (iii) the Loan were the only Loan outstanding. For the avoidance of doubt, any such failure shall not constitute an Event of Default (including under paragraph 10.1(i)) unless the Parties otherwise agree.

9.3   **Failure by either Party to deliver**

Where a Party (the *Transferor*) fails to deliver Equivalent Securities or Equivalent Collateral by the time required under this Agreement or within such other period as may be agreed between the Transferor and the other Party (the *Transferee*) and the Transferee:

(a)   incurs interest, overdraft or similar costs and expenses; or

(b)   incurs costs and expenses as a direct result of a Buy-in exercised against it by a third party,

then the Transferor agrees to pay within one Business Day of a demand from the Transferee and hold harmless the Transferee with respect to all reasonable costs and expenses listed in sub-paragraphs (a) and (b) above properly incurred which arise directly from such failure other than (i) such costs and expenses which arise from the negligence or wilful default of the Transferee and (ii) any indirect or consequential losses.

10.   **EVENTS OF DEFAULT**

10.1   Each of the following events occurring and continuing in relation to either Party (the *Defaulting Party*, the other Party being the *Non-Defaulting Party*) shall be an Event of Default but only (subject to sub-paragraph 10.1(d)) where the Non-Defaulting Party serves written notice on the Defaulting Party:

(a)   Borrower or Lender failing to pay or repay Cash Collateral or to deliver Collateral on commencement of the Loan under paragraph 5.1 or to deliver further Collateral under paragraph 5.4 or 5.5;

(b)   Lender or Borrower failing to comply with its obligations under paragraph 6.2 or 6.3 upon the due date and not remedying such failure within three Business Days after the Non-Defaulting Party serves written notice requiring it to remedy such failure;

(c)   Lender or Borrower failing to pay any sum due under paragraph 9.1(b), 9.2(b) or 9.3 upon the due date;

(d)   an Act of Insolvency occurring with respect to Lender or Borrower, provided that, where the Parties have specified in paragraph 5 of the Schedule that Automatic Early Termination shall apply, an Act of Insolvency which is the presentation of a petition for winding up or any analogous proceeding or the appointment of a liquidator or analogous officer of the Defaulting Party shall not require the Non-Defaulting Party to serve written notice on the Defaulting Party (*Automatic Early Termination*);

(e)   any warranty made by Lender or Borrower in paragraph 13 or paragraphs 14(a) to 14(d) being incorrect or untrue in any material respect when made or repeated or deemed to have been made or repeated;

(f)   Lender or Borrower admitting to the other that it is unable to, or it intends not to, perform any of its obligations under this Agreement and/or in respect of any Loan where such failure to perform would with the service of notice or lapse of time constitute an Event of Default;

(g)   all or any material part of the assets of Lender or Borrower being transferred or ordered to be transferred to a trustee (or a person exercising similar functions) by a regulatory authority pursuant to any legislation;

(h)   Lender (if applicable) or Borrower being declared in default or being suspended or expelled from membership of or participation in, any securities exchange or suspended or prohibited from dealing in securities by any regulatory authority, in each case on the grounds that it has failed to meet any requirements relating to financial resources or credit rating; or

(i)   Lender or Borrower failing to perform any other of its obligations under this Agreement and not remedying such failure within 30 days after the Non-Defaulting Party serves written notice requiring it to remedy such failure.

10.2   Each Party shall notify the other (in writing) if an Event of Default or an event which, with the passage of time and/or upon the serving of a written notice as referred to above, would be an Event of Default, occurs in relation to it.

10.3   The provisions of this Agreement constitute a complete statement of the remedies available to each Party in respect of any Event of Default.

10.4   Subject to paragraphs 9 and 11, neither Party may claim any sum by way of consequential loss or damage in the event of failure by the other Party to perform any of its obligations under this Agreement.

11.   CONSEQUENCES OF AN EVENT OF DEFAULT

11.1   If an Event of Default occurs in relation to either Party then paragraphs 11.2 to 11.7 below shall apply.

11.2   The Parties' delivery and payment obligations (and any other obligations they have under this Agreement) shall be accelerated so as to require performance thereof at the time such Event of Default occurs (the date of which shall be the *Termination Date*) so that performance of such delivery and payment obligations shall be effected only in accordance with the following provisions.

(a)   The Default Market Value of the Equivalent Securities and Equivalent Non-Cash Collateral to be delivered and the amount of any Cash Collateral (including sums accrued) to be repaid and any other cash (including interest accrued) to be paid by each Party shall be established by the Non-Defaulting Party in accordance with paragraph 11.4 and deemed as at the Termination Date.

(b)   On the basis of the sums so established, an account shall be taken (as at the Termination Date) of what is due from each Party to the other under this Agreement (on the basis that each Party's claim against the other in respect of delivery of Equivalent Securities or Equivalent Non-Cash Collateral equal to the Default Market Value thereof) and the sums due from one Party shall be set off against the sums due from the other and only the balance of the account shall be payable (by the Party having the claim valued at the lower amount pursuant to the foregoing) and such balance shall be payable on the next following Business Day after such account has been taken and such sums have been set off in accordance with this paragraph. For the purposes of this calculation, any sum not denominated in the Base Currency shall be converted into the Base Currency at the spot rate prevailing at such dates and times determined by the Non-Defaulting Party acting reasonably.

(c)   If the balance under sub-paragraph (b) above is payable by the Non-Defaulting Party and the Non-Defaulting Party had delivered to the Defaulting Party a Letter of Credit, the Defaulting Party shall draw on the Letter of Credit to the extent of the balance due and shall subsequently deliver for cancellation the Letter of Credit so provided.

(d)   If the balance under sub-paragraph (b) above is payable by the Defaulting Party and the Defaulting Party had delivered to the Non-Defaulting Party a Letter of Credit, the Non-Defaulting Party shall draw on the Letter of Credit to the extent of the balance due and shall subsequently deliver for cancellation the Letter of Credit so provided.

(e)   In all other circumstances, where a Letter of Credit has been provided to a Party, such Party shall deliver for cancellation the Letter of Credit so provided.

11.3   For the purposes of this Agreement, the **Default Market Value** of any Equivalent Collateral in the form of a Letter of Credit shall be zero and of any Equivalent Securities or any other Equivalent Non-Cash Collateral shall be determined in accordance with paragraphs 11.4 to 11.6 below, and for this purpose:

(a)   the **Appropriate Market** means, in relation to securities of any description, the market which is the most appropriate market for securities of that description, as determined by the Non-Defaulting Party;

(b)   the **Default Valuation Time** means, in relation to an Event of Default, the close of business in the Appropriate Market on the fifth dealing day after the day on which that Event of Default occurs or, where that Event of Default is the occurrence of an Act of Insolvency in respect of which under paragraph 10.1(d) no notice is required from the Non-Defaulting Party in order for such event to constitute an Event of Default, the close of business on the fifth dealing day after the day on which the Non-Defaulting Party first became aware of the occurrence of such Event of Default;

(c)   **Deliverable Securities** means Equivalent Securities or Equivalent Non-Cash Collateral to be delivered by the Defaulting Party;

(d)   **Net Value** means at any time, in relation to any Deliverable Securities or Receivable Securities, the amount which, in the reasonable opinion of the Non-Defaulting Party, represents their fair market value, having regard to such pricing sources and methods (which may include, without limitation, available prices for securities with similar maturities, terms and credit characteristics as the relevant Equivalent Securities or Equivalent Collateral)

PART 3

as the Non-Defaulting Party considers appropriate, less, in the case of Receivable Securities, or plus, in the case of Deliverable Securities, all Transaction Costs incurred or reasonably anticipated in connection with the purchase or sale of such securities;

(e)   *Receivable Securities* means Equivalent Securities or Equivalent Non-Cash Collateral to be delivered to the Defaulting Party; and

(f)   *Transaction Costs* in relation to any transaction contemplated in paragraph 11.4 or 11.5 means the reasonable costs, commissions (including internal commissions), fees and expenses (including any mark-up or mark-down or premium paid for guaranteed delivery) incurred or reasonably anticipated in connection with the purchase of Deliverable Securities or sale of Receivable Securities, calculated on the assumption that the aggregate thereof is the least that could reasonably be expected to be paid in order to carry out the transaction.

11.4   If between the Termination Date and the Default Valuation Time:

(a)   the Non-Defaulting Party has sold, in the case of Receivable Securities, or purchased, in the case of Deliverable Securities, securities which form part of the same issue and are of an identical type and description as those Equivalent Securities or that Equivalent Collateral, (and regardless as to whether or not such sales or purchases have settled) the Non-Defaulting Party may elect to treat as the Default Market Value:

     (i)   in the case of Receivable Securities, the net proceeds of such sale after deducting all Transaction Costs; provided that, where the securities sold are not identical in amount to the Equivalent Securities or Equivalent Collateral, the Non-Defaulting Party may, acting in good faith, either (A) elect to treat such net proceeds of sale divided by the amount of securities sold and multiplied by the amount of the Equivalent Securities or Equivalent Collateral as the Default Market Value or (B) elect to treat such net proceeds of sale of the Equivalent Securities or Equivalent Collateral actually sold as the Default Market Value of that proportion of the Equivalent Securities or Equivalent Collateral, and, in the case of (B), the Default Market Value of the balance of the Equivalent Securities or Equivalent Collateral shall be determined separately in accordance with the provisions of this paragraph 11.4; or

     (ii)   in the case of Deliverable Securities, the aggregate cost of such purchase, including all Transaction Costs; provided that, where the securities purchased are not identical in amount to the Equivalent Securities or Equivalent Collateral, the Non-Defaulting Party may, acting in good faith, either (A) elect to treat such aggregate cost divided by the amount of securities purchased and multiplied by the amount of the Equivalent Securities or Equivalent Collateral as the Default Market Value or (B) elect to treat the aggregate cost of purchasing the Equivalent Securities or Equivalent Collateral actually purchased as the Default Market Value of that proportion of the Equivalent Securities or Equivalent Collateral, and, in the case of (B), the Default Market Value of the balance of the Equivalent Securities

PART 3

or Equivalent Collateral shall be determined separately in accordance with the provisions of this paragraph 11.4;

(b) the Non-Defaulting Party has received, in the case of Deliverable Securities, offer quotations or, in the case of Receivable Securities, bid quotations in respect of securities of the relevant description from two or more market makers or regular dealers in the Appropriate Market in a commercially reasonable size (as determined by the Non-Defaulting Party) the Non-Defaulting Party may elect to treat as the Default Market Value of the relevant Equivalent Securities or Equivalent Collateral:

 (i) the price quoted (or where more than one price is so quoted, the arithmetic mean of the prices so quoted) by each of them for, in the case of Deliverable Securities, the sale by the relevant market marker or dealer of such securities or, in the case of Receivable Securities, the purchase by the relevant market maker or dealer of such securities, provided that such price or prices quoted may be adjusted in a commercially reasonable manner by the Non-Defaulting Party to reflect accrued but unpaid coupons not reflected in the price or prices quoted in respect of such Securities;

 (ii) after deducting, in the case of Receivable Securities or adding in the case of Deliverable Securities the Transaction Costs which would be incurred or reasonably anticipated in connection with such transaction.

11.5 If, acting in good faith, either (A) the Non-Defaulting Party has endeavoured but been unable to sell or purchase securities in accordance with paragraph 11.4(a) above or to obtain quotations in accordance with paragraph 11.4(b) above (or both) or (B) the Non-Defaulting Party has determined that it would not be commercially reasonable to sell or purchase securities at the prices bid or offered or to obtain such quotations, or that it would not be commercially reasonable to use any quotations which it has obtained under paragraph 11.4(b) above the Non-Defaulting Party may determine the Net Value of the relevant Equivalent Securities or Equivalent Collateral (which shall be specified) and the Non-Defaulting Party may elect to treat such Net Value as the Default Market Value of the relevant Equivalent Securities or Equivalent Collateral.

11.6 To the extent that the Non-Defaulting Party has not determined the Default Market Value in accordance with paragraph 11.4, the Default Market Value of the relevant Equivalent Securities or Equivalent Collateral shall be an amount equal to their Net Value at the Default Valuation Time; provided that, if at the Default Valuation Time the Non-Defaulting Party reasonably determines that, owing to circumstances affecting the market in the Equivalent Securities or Equivalent Collateral in question, it is not reasonably practicable for the Non-Defaulting Party to determine a Net Value of such Equivalent Securities or Equivalent Collateral which is commercially reasonable (by reason of lack of tradable prices or otherwise), the Default Market Value of such Equivalent Securities or Equivalent Collateral shall be an amount equal to their Net Value as determined by the Non-Defaulting Party as soon as reasonably practicable after the Default Valuation Time.

PART 3

Other costs, expenses and interest payable in consequence of an Event of Default

11.7   The Defaulting Party shall be liable to the Non-Defaulting Party for the amount of all reasonable legal and other professional expenses incurred by the Non-Defaulting Party in connection with or as a consequence of an Event of Default, together with interest thereon at such rate as is agreed by the Parties and specified in paragraph 10 of the Schedule or, failing such agreement, the overnight London Inter Bank Offered Rate as quoted on a reputable financial information service (**_LIBOR_**) as at 11.00 a.m., London time, on the date on which it is to be determined or, in the case of an expense attributable to a particular transaction and, where the Parties have previously agreed a rate of interest for the transaction, that rate of interest if it is greater than LIBOR. Interest will accrue daily on a compound basis.

Set-off

11.8   Any amount payable to one Party (the **_Payee_**) by the other Party (the **_Payer_**) under paragraph 11.2(b) may, at the option of the Non-Defaulting Party, be reduced by its set-off against any amount payable (whether at such time or in the future or upon the occurrence of a contingency) by the Payee to the Payer (irrespective of the currency, place of payment or booking office of the obligation) under any other agreement between the Payee and the Payer or instrument or undertaking issued or executed by one Party to, or in favour of, the other Party. If an obligation is unascertained, the Non-Defaulting Party may in good faith estimate that obligation and set off in respect of the estimate, subject to accounting to the other Party when the obligation is ascertained. Nothing in this paragraph shall be effective to create a charge or other security interest. This paragraph shall be without prejudice and in addition to any right of set-off, combination of accounts, lien or other right to which any Party is at any time otherwise entitled (whether by operation of law, contract or otherwise).

12.   TAXES

Withholding, gross-up and provision of information

12.1   All payments under this Agreement shall be made without any deduction or withholding for or on account of any Tax unless such deduction or withholding is required by any Applicable Law.

12.2   Except as otherwise agreed, if the paying Party is so required to deduct or withhold, then that Party (**_Payer_**) shall:

(a)   promptly notify the other Party (**_Recipient_**) of such requirement;

(b)   pay or otherwise account for the full amount required to be deducted or withheld to the relevant authority;

(c)   upon written demand of Recipient, forward to Recipient documentation reasonably acceptable to Recipient, evidencing such payment to such authorities; and

(d)   other than in respect of any payment made by Lender to Borrower under paragraph 6.3, pay to Recipient, in addition to the payment to which Recipient is otherwise entitled under this Agreement, such additional amount as is necessary to ensure that the amount actually received by Recipient (after taking account of such withholding or deduction) will equal the amount Recipient would have received had no such deduction or withholding been required; provided Payer will not be required to pay any additional amount to Recipient under this sub-paragraph (d) to the extent it would not be required to be paid but for the failure by Recipient to comply with or perform any obligation under paragraph 12.3.

12.3   Each Party agrees that it will upon written demand of the other Party deliver to such other Party (or to any government or other taxing authority as such other Party directs), any form or document and provide such other cooperation or assistance as may (in either case) reasonably be required in order to allow such other Party to make a payment under this Agreement without any deduction or withholding for or on account of any Tax or with such deduction or withholding at a reduced rate (so long as the completion, execution or submission of such form or document, or the provision of such cooperation or assistance, would not materially prejudice the legal or commercial position of the Party in receipt of such demand). Any such form or document shall be accurate and completed in a manner reasonably satisfactory to such other Party and shall be executed and delivered with any reasonably required certification by such date as is agreed between the Parties or, failing such agreement, as soon as reasonably practicable.

Stamp Tax

12.4   Unless otherwise agreed, Borrower hereby undertakes promptly to pay and account for any Stamp Tax chargeable in connection with any transaction effected pursuant to or contemplated by this Agreement (other than any Stamp Tax that would not be chargeable but for Lender's failure to comply with its obligations under this Agreement).

12.5   Borrower shall indemnify and keep indemnified Lender against any liability arising as a result of Borrower's failure to comply with its obligations under paragraph 12.4.

Sales Tax

12.6   All sums payable by one Party to another under this Agreement are exclusive of any Sales Tax chargeable on any supply to which such sums relate and an amount equal to such Sales Tax shall in each case be paid by the Party making such payment on receipt of an appropriate Sales Tax invoice.

Retrospective changes in law

12.7   Unless otherwise agreed, amounts payable by one Party to another under this Agreement shall be determined by reference to Applicable Law as at the date of the relevant payment and no adjustment shall be made to amounts paid under this Agreement as a result of:

(a)   any retrospective change in Applicable Law which is announced or enacted after the date of the relevant payment; or

(b)   any decision of a court of competent jurisdiction which is made after the date of the relevant payment (other than where such decision results from an action taken with respect to this Agreement or amounts paid or payable under this Agreement).

PART 3

13.   LENDER'S WARRANTIES

Each Party hereby warrants and undertakes to the other on a continuing basis to the intent that such warranties shall survive the completion of any transaction contemplated herein that, where acting as a Lender:

(a)   it is duly authorised and empowered to perform its duties and obligations under this Agreement;

(b)   it is not restricted under the terms of its constitution or in any other manner from lending Securities in accordance with this Agreement or from otherwise performing its obligations hereunder;

(c)   it is absolutely entitled to pass full legal and beneficial ownership of all Securities provided by it hereunder to Borrower free from all liens, charges and encumbrances; and

(d)   it is acting as principal in respect of this Agreement, other than in respect of an Agency Loan.

14.   BORROWER'S WARRANTIES

Each Party hereby warrants and undertakes to the other on a continuing basis to the intent that such warranties shall survive the completion of any transaction contemplated herein that, where acting as a Borrower:

(a)   it has all necessary licences and approvals, and is duly authorised and empowered, to perform its duties and obligations under this Agreement and will do nothing prejudicial to the continuation of such authorisation, licences or approvals;

(b)   it is not restricted under the terms of its constitution or in any other manner from borrowing Securities in accordance with this Agreement or from otherwise performing its obligations hereunder;

(c)   it is absolutely entitled to pass full legal and beneficial ownership of all Collateral provided by it hereunder to Lender free from all liens, charges and encumbrances;

(d)   it is acting as principal in respect of this Agreement; and

(e)   it is not entering into a Loan for the primary purpose of obtaining or exercising voting rights in respect of the Loaned Securities.

15.   INTEREST ON OUTSTANDING PAYMENTS

In the event of either Party failing to remit sums in accordance with this Agreement such Party hereby undertakes to pay to the other Party upon demand interest (before as well as after judgment) on the net balance due and outstanding, for the period commencing on and inclusive of the original due date for payment to (but excluding) the date of actual payment, in the same currency as the principal sum and at the rate referred to in paragraph 11.7. Interest will accrue daily on a compound basis and will be calculated according to the actual number of days elapsed. No interest shall be payable under this paragraph in respect of any day on which one Party endeavours to make a payment to the other Party but the other Party is unable to receive it.

16. TERMINATION OF THIS AGREEMENT

Each Party shall have the right to terminate this Agreement by giving not less than 15 Business Days' notice in writing to the other Party (which notice shall specify the date of termination) subject to an obligation to ensure that all Loans which have been entered into but not discharged at the time such notice is given are duly discharged in accordance with this Agreement.

17. SINGLE AGREEMENT

Each Party acknowledges that, and has entered into this Agreement and will enter into each Loan in consideration of and in reliance upon the fact that, all Loans constitute a single business and contractual relationship and are made in consideration of each other. Accordingly, each Party agrees:

(a)   to perform all of its obligations in respect of each Loan, and that a default in the performance of any such obligations shall constitute a default by it in respect of all Loans, subject always to the other provisions of the Agreement; and

(b)   that payments, deliveries and other transfers made by either of them in respect of any Loan shall be deemed to have been made in consideration of payments, deliveries and other transfers in respect of any other Loan.

18. SEVERANCE

If any provision of this Agreement is declared by any judicial or other competent authority to be void or otherwise unenforceable, that provision shall be severed from the Agreement and the remaining provisions of this Agreement shall remain in full force and effect. The Agreement shall, however, thereafter be amended by the Parties in such reasonable manner so as to achieve as far as possible, without illegality, the intention of the Parties with respect to that severed provision.

19. SPECIFIC PERFORMANCE

Each Party agrees that in relation to legal proceedings it will not seek specific performance of the other Party's obligation to deliver Securities, Equivalent Securities, Collateral or Equivalent Collateral but without prejudice to any other rights it may have.

20. NOTICES

20.1   Any notice or other communication in respect of this Agreement may be given in any manner set forth below to the address or number or in accordance with the electronic messaging system details set out in paragraph 6 of the Schedule and will be deemed effective as indicated:

(a)   if in writing and delivered in person or by courier, on the date it is delivered;

PART 3

(b)   if sent by facsimile transmission, on the date that transmission is received by a responsible employee of the recipient in legible form (it being agreed that the burden of proving receipt will be on the sender and will not be met by a transmission report generated by the sender's facsimile machine);

(c)   if sent by certified or registered mail (airmail, if overseas) or the equivalent (return receipt requested), on the date that mail is delivered or its delivery is attempted; or

(d)   if sent by electronic messaging system, on the date that electronic message is received,

unless the date of that delivery (or attempted delivery) or the receipt, as applicable, is not a Business Day or that communication is delivered (or attempted) or received, as applicable, after the Close of Business on a Business Day, in which case that communication shall be deemed given and effective on the first following day that is a Business Day.

20.2   Either Party may by notice to the other change the address or facsimile number or electronic messaging system details at which notices or other communications are to be given to it.

21.   ASSIGNMENT

21.1   Subject to paragraph 21.2, neither Party may charge, assign or otherwise deal with all or any of its rights or obligations hereunder without the prior consent of the other Party.

21.2   Paragraph 21.1 shall not preclude a party from charging, assigning or otherwise dealing with all or any part of its interest in any sum payable to it under paragraph 11.2(b) or 11.7.

22.   NON-WAIVER

No failure or delay by either Party (whether by course of conduct or otherwise) to exercise any right, power or privilege hereunder shall operate as a waiver thereof nor shall any single or partial exercise of any right, power or privilege preclude any other or further exercise thereof or the exercise of any other right, power or privilege as herein provided.

23.   GOVERNING LAW AND JURISDICTION

23.1   This Agreement and any non-contractual obligations arising out of or in connection with this Agreement shall be governed by, and shall be construed in accordance with, English law.

23.2   The courts of England have exclusive jurisdiction to hear and decide any suit, action or proceedings, and to settle any disputes or any non-contractual obligation which may arise out of or in connection with this Agreement (respectively, *Proceedings* and *Disputes*) and, for these purposes, each Party irrevocably submits to the jurisdiction of the courts of England.

23.3   Each Party irrevocably waives any objection which it might at any time have to the courts of England being nominated as the forum to hear and decide any Proceedings and to settle any Disputes and agrees not to claim that the courts of England are not a convenient or appropriate forum.

23.4   Each Party hereby respectively appoints the person identified in paragraph 7 of the Schedule pertaining to the relevant Party as its agent to receive on its behalf service of process in the courts of England. If such an agent ceases to be an agent of a Party, the relevant Party shall promptly appoint, and notify the other Party of the identity of its new agent in England.

24.   TIME

Time shall be of the essence of the Agreement.

25.   RECORDING

The Parties agree that each may record all telephone conversations between them.

26.   WAIVER OF IMMUNITY

Each Party hereby waives all immunity (whether on the basis of sovereignty or otherwise) from jurisdiction, attachment (both before and after judgement) and execution to which it might otherwise be entitled in any action or proceeding in the courts of England or of any other country or jurisdiction relating in any way to this Agreement and agrees that it will not raise, claim or cause to be pleaded any such immunity at or in respect of any such action or proceeding.

27.   MISCELLANEOUS

27.1   This Agreement constitutes the entire agreement and understanding of the Parties with respect to its subject matter and supersedes all oral communication and prior writings with respect thereto.

27.2   The Party (the **Relevant Party**) who has prepared the text of this Agreement for execution (as indicated in paragraph 9 of the Schedule) warrants and undertakes to the other Party that such text conforms exactly to the text of the standard form Global Master Securities Lending Agreement (2010 version) posted by the International Securities Lending Association on its website except as notified by the Relevant Party to the other Party in writing prior to the execution of this Agreement.

27.3   Unless otherwise provided for in this Agreement, no amendment in respect of this Agreement will be effective unless in writing (including a writing evidenced by a facsimile transmission) and executed by each of the Parties or confirmed by an exchange of telexes or electronic messages on an electronic messaging system.

27.4   The Parties agree that where paragraph 11 of the Schedule indicates that this paragraph 27.4 applies, this Agreement shall apply to all loans which are outstanding as at the date of this Agreement and which are subject to the securities lending agreement or agreements specified in paragraph 11 of the Schedule, and such Loans shall be treated as if they had been entered into under this Agreement, and the terms of such loans are amended accordingly with effect from the date of this Agreement.

27.5   The Parties agree that where paragraph 12 of the Schedule indicates that this paragraph 27.5 applies, each may use the services of a third party vendor to automate the processing of Loans under this Agreement and that any data relating to such Loans received from the other Party may be disclosed to such third party vendors.

27.6   The obligations of the Parties under this Agreement will survive the termination of any Loan.

27.7   The warranties contained in paragraphs 13, 14 and 27.2 and in the Agency Annex will survive termination of this Agreement for so long as any obligations of either of the Parties pursuant to this Agreement remain outstanding.

27.8   Except as provided in this Agreement, the rights, powers, remedies and privileges provided in this Agreement are cumulative and not exclusive of any rights, powers, remedies and privileges provided by law.

27.9   This Agreement (and each amendment in respect of it) may be executed and delivered in counterparts (including by facsimile transmission), each of which will be deemed an original.

27.10   A person who is not a party to this Agreement has no right under the Contracts (Rights of Third Parties) Act 1999 to enforce any terms of this Agreement, but this does not affect any right or remedy of a third party which exists or is available apart from that Act.

PART 3

EXECUTED by the **PARTIES**

SIGNED by   )
)
duly authorised for and   )
on behalf of   )

SIGNED by   )
)
duly authorised for and   )
on behalf of   )

SCHEDULE

1.   **COLLATERAL**

1.1   The securities, financial instruments and deposits of currency set out in the table below with a cross marked next to them are acceptable forms of Collateral under this Agreement.

1.2   Unless otherwise agreed between the Parties, the Market Value of the Collateral delivered pursuant to paragraph 5 by Borrower to Lender under the terms and conditions of this Agreement shall on each Business Day represent not less than the Market Value of the Loaned Securities together with the percentage contained in the row of the table below corresponding to the particular form of Collateral, referred to in this Agreement as the *Margin*.

Security/Financial Instrument/ Deposit of Currency	Mark "X" if acceptable form of Collateral	Margin (%)

1.3   Basis of Margin Maintenance:

Paragraph 5.4 (aggregation) shall not apply*   ☐

Paragraph 5.4 (aggregation) applies unless the box is ticked.

1.4   Paragraph 5.6 (netting of obligations to deliver
Collateral and redeliver Equivalent Collateral) shall not apply*   ☐

Paragraph 5.6 (netting) applies unless the box is ticked

1.5   For the purposes of Paragraph 5.8, Notification Time means by ☐ , London time.

1.6   Paragraph 6.4 (indemnity for failure to redeliver
Equivalent Non-Cash Collateral) shall not apply*   ☐

Paragraph 6.4 (indemnity for failure to redeliver Equivalent Non-Cash Collateral) applies unless the box is ticked.

---

*   Delete as appropriate.

*   Delete as appropriate.

*   Delete as appropriate.

2.   **BASE CURRENCY**

The Base Currency applicable to this Agreement is   provided that if that currency ceases to be freely convertible the Base Currency shall be [US Dollars] [Euro] [specify other currency]*

3.   **PLACES OF BUSINESS**

(See definition of Business Day.)

4.   **MARKET VALUE**

(See definition of Market Value.)

5.   **EVENTS OF DEFAULT**

Automatic Early Termination shall apply in respect of Party A   ☐

Automatic Early Termination shall apply in respect of Party B   ☐

6.   **DESIGNATED OFFICE AND ADDRESS FOR NOTICES**

(a)   **Designated office of Party A**:

Address for notices or communications to Party A:

Address:

Attention:

Facsimile No:

Telephone No:

Electronic Messaging System Details:

(b)   **Designated office of Party B**:

Address for notices or communications to Party B:

Address:

Attention:

Facsimile No:

Telephone No:

Electronic Messaging System Details:

7. (a)   **Agent of Party A for Service of Process**

Name:

Address:

(b)   **Agent of Party B for Service of Process**

Name:

Address:

8.   **AGENCY**

–   Party A [may][will always]* act as agent   ☐

–   Party B [may][will always]* act as agent   ☐

–   The Addendum for Pooled Principal Transactions
        may apply to Party A   ☐

–   The Addendum for Pooled Principal Transactions
        may apply to Party B   ☐

9.   **PARTY PREPARING THIS AGREEMENT**

Party A   ☐

Party B   ☐

10.   **DEFAULT INTEREST**

Rate of default interest:

11.   **EXISTING LOANS**

Paragraph 27.4 applies*   ☐

[Overseas Securities Lenders Agreement dated   ]*

[Global Master Securities Lending Agreements dated   ]*

12.   **AUTOMATION**

Paragraph 27.5 applies*   ☐

---

*   Delete as appropriate.

AGENCY ANNEX

1. TRANSACTIONS ENTERED INTO AS AGENT

1.1 Power for Lender to enter into Loans as agent

Subject to the following provisions of this paragraph, Lender may enter into Loans as agent (in such capacity, the *Agent*) for a third person (a *Principal*), whether as custodian or investment manager or otherwise (a Loan so entered into being referred to in this paragraph as an *Agency Loan*).

If the Lender has indicated in paragraph 8 of the Schedule that it may act as Agent, it must identify each Loan in respect of which it acts as Agent as an Agency Loan at the time it is entered into. If the Lender has indicated in paragraph 8 of the Schedule that it will always act as Agent, it need not identify each Loan as an Agency Loan.

1.2 [Pooled Principal transactions

The Lender may enter into an Agency Loan on behalf of more than [one] Principal and accordingly the addendum hereto for pooled principal transactions shall apply.]*

1.3 Conditions for Agency Loan

A Lender may enter into an Agency Loan if, but only if:

(a) it provides to Borrower, prior to effecting any Agency Loan, such information in its possession necessary to complete all required fields in the format generally used in the industry, or as otherwise agreed by Agent and Borrower (*Agreed Format*), and will use its best efforts to provide to Borrower any optional information that may be requested by the Borrower for the purpose of identifying such Principal (all such information being the *Principal Information*). Agent represents and warrants that the Principal Information is true and accurate to the best of its knowledge and has been provided to it by Principal;

(b) it enters into that Loan on behalf of a single Principal whose identity is disclosed to Borrower (whether by name or by reference to a code or identifier which the Parties have agreed will be used to refer to a specified Principal) either at the time when it enters into the Loan or before the Close of Business on the next Business Day after the date on which Loaned Securities are transferred to the Borrower in the Agreed Format or as otherwise agreed between the Parties; and

(c) it has at the time when the Loan is entered into actual authority to enter into the Loan and to perform on behalf of that Principal all of that Principal's obligations under the agreement referred to in paragraph 1.5(b) below.

Agent agrees that it will not effect any Loan with Borrower on behalf of any Principal unless Borrower has notified Agent of Borrower's approval of such Principal, and has not notified Agent that it has withdrawn such approval (such Principal, an *Approved Principal*), with both such notifications in the Agreed Format.

---

* Delete as appropriate.

Borrower acknowledges that Agent shall not have any obligation to provide it with confidential information regarding the financial status of its Principals; Agent agrees, however, that it will assist Borrower in obtaining from Agent's Principals such information regarding the financial status of such Principals as Borrower may reasonably request.

1.4   **Notification by Agent of certain events affecting any Principal**

Agent undertakes that, if it enters as agent into an Agency Loan, forthwith upon becoming aware:

(a)   of any event which constitutes an Act of Insolvency with respect to the relevant Principal; or

(b)   of any breach of any of the warranties given in paragraph 1.6 below or of any event or circumstance which results in any such warranty being untrue if repeated by reference to the then current facts,

it will inform Borrower of that fact and will, if so required by Borrower, furnish it with such additional information as it may reasonably request to the extent that such information is readily obtainable by Agent.

1.5   **Status of Agency Loan**

(a)   Each Agency Loan shall be a transaction between the relevant Principal and Borrower and no person other than the relevant Principal and Borrower shall be a party to or have any rights or obligations under an Agency Loan. Without limiting the foregoing, Agent shall not be liable as principal for the performance of an Agency Loan, but this is without prejudice to any liability of Agent under any other provision of this Annex; and

(b)   all the provisions of the Agreement shall apply separately as between Borrower and each Principal for whom the Agent has entered into an Agency Loan or Agency Loans as if each such Principal were a party to a separate agreement with Borrower in all respects identical with this Agreement other than this Annex and as if the Principal were Lender in respect of that agreement; provided that

(i)   if there occurs in relation to the Agent an Event of Default or an event which would constitute an Event of Default if Borrower served written notice under any sub-clause of paragraph 10 of the Agreement, Borrower shall be entitled by giving written notice to the Principal (which notice shall be validly given if given in accordance with paragraph 20 of the Agreement) to declare that by reason of that event an Event of Default is to be treated as occurring in relation to the Principal. If Borrower gives such a notice then an Event of Default shall be treated as occurring in relation to the Principal at the time when the notice is deemed to be given; and

(ii)   if the Principal is neither incorporated in nor has established a place of business in Great Britain, the Principal shall for the purposes of the agreement referred to in paragraph 1.5(b) above be deemed to have appointed as its agent to receive on its behalf service of process in the courts of England the Agent, or if the Agent is neither incorporated nor has established a place of business in Great Britain, the person appointed by the Agent for the purposes of this Agreement, or such other person as the Principal may from time to time specify in a written notice given to the other Party.

If Lender has indicated in paragraph 6 of the Schedule that it may enter into Loans as agent, the foregoing provisions of this paragraph do not affect the operation of the Agreement as between Borrower and Lender in respect of any Loans into which Lender may enter on its own account as principal.

1.6 **Warranty of authority by Lender acting as Agent**

Agent warrants to Borrower that it will, on every occasion on which it enters or purports to enter into a Loan as an Agency Loan, have been duly authorised to enter into that Loan and perform the obligations arising under such Loan on behalf of the Principal in respect of that Loan and to perform on behalf of the Principal all the obligations of that person under the agreement referred to in paragraph 1.5(b) above.

PART 3

ADDENDUM FOR POOLED PRINCIPAL AGENCY LOANS

1.   SCOPE

This addendum applies where the Agent wishes to enter into an Agency Loan on behalf of more than one Principal. The Agency Annex shall apply to such a Loan subject to the modifications and additional terms and conditions contained in paragraph 2 to 7 below.

2.   INTERPRETATION

2.1   In this addendum:

(a)   *Collateral Transfer* has the meaning given in paragraph 5.1 below;

(b)   if at any time on any Business Day the aggregate Market Value of Posted Collateral in respect of all Agency Loans outstanding with a Principal under the Agreement exceeds the aggregate of the Required Collateral Value in respect of such Agency Loans, Borrower has a *Net Loan Exposure* to that Principal equal to that excess; if at any time on any Business Day the aggregate Market Value of Posted Collateral in respect of all Agency Loans outstanding under the Agreement with a Principal falls below the aggregate of the Required Collateral Value in respect of such Agency Loans, that Principal has a *Net Loan Exposure* to Borrower for such Agency Loans equal to that deficiency;

(c)   *Pooled Principal* has the meaning given in paragraph 6(a) below; and

(d)   *Pooled Loan* has the meaning given in paragraph 6(a) below.

3.   MODIFICATIONS TO THE AGENCY ANNEX

3.1   Paragraph 1.3(b) of the Agency Annex is deleted and replaced by the following:

"it enters into that Loan on behalf of one or more Principals and at or before the time when it enters into the Loan it discloses to Borrower the identity and the jurisdiction of incorporation, organisation or establishment of each such Principal (and such disclosure may be made either directly or by reference to a code or identifier which the Parties have agreed will be used to refer to a specified Principal);".

3.2   Paragraph 1.3(c) of the Agency Annex is deleted and replaced by the following:

"it has at the time when the Loan is entered into actual authority to enter into the Loan on behalf of each Principal and to perform on behalf of each Principal all of that Principal's obligations under the Agreement".

4.   ALLOCATION OF AGENCY LOANS

4.1   The Agent undertakes that if, at the time of entering into an Agency Loan, the Agent has not allocated the Loan to a Principal, it will allocate the Loan before the Settlement Date for that Agency Loan either to a single Principal or to several Principals, each of whom shall be responsible for only that part of the Agency Loan which has been allocated to it. Promptly following such allocation, the Agent shall notify Borrower of the Principal or Principals (whether by name or reference to a code or identifier which the Parties have agreed will be used to refer to a specified Principal) to which that Loan or part of that Loan has been allocated.

4.2   Upon allocation of a Loan in accordance with paragraph 4.1 above or otherwise, with effect from the date on which the Loan was entered into:

(a)   where the allocation is to a single Principal, the Loan shall be deemed to have been entered into between Borrower and that Principal; and

(b)   where the allocation is to two or more Principals, a separate Loan shall be deemed to have been entered into between Borrower and each such Principal with respect to the appropriate proportion of the Loan.

4.3   If the Agent shall fail to perform its obligations under paragraph 4.2 above then for the purposes of assessing any damage suffered by Borrower (but for no other purpose) it shall be assumed that, if the Loan concerned (to the extent not allocated) had been allocated in accordance with that paragraph, all the terms of the Loan would have been duly performed.

5.   ALLOCATION OF COLLATERAL

5.1   Unless the Agent expressly allocates (a) a deposit or delivery of Posted Collateral or (b) a repayment of Cash Collateral or a redelivery of Equivalent Collateral (each a **Collateral Transfer**) before such time, the Agent shall, at the time of making or receiving that Collateral Transfer, be deemed to have allocated any Collateral Transfer in accordance with paragraph 6.3 below.

5.2 (a) If the Agent has made a Collateral Transfer on behalf of more than one Pooled Principal, that Collateral Transfer shall be allocated in proportion to Borrower's Net Loan Exposure in respect of each Pooled Principal at the Agent's close of business on the Business Day before the Collateral Transfer is made; and

(b)   if the Agent has received a Collateral Transfer on behalf of more than one Pooled Principal, that Collateral Transfer shall be allocated in proportion to each Pooled Principal's Net Loan Exposure in respect of Borrower at the Agent's close of business on the Business Day before the Collateral Transfer is made.

(c)   Sub-paragraphs (a) and (b) shall not apply in respect of any Collateral Transfer which is effected or deemed to have been effected under paragraph 6.3 below.

6.   POOLED PRINCIPALS: REBALANCING OF MARGIN

6.1   Where the Agent acts on behalf of more than one Principal, the Parties may agree that, as regards all (but not some only) outstanding Agency Loans with those Principals, or with such of those Principals as they may agree (**Pooled Principals**, such Agency Loans being **Pooled Loans**), any Collateral Transfers are to be made on an aggregate net basis.

6.2   Paragraphs 6.3 to 6.5 below shall have effect for the purpose of ensuring that Posted Collateral is, so far as is practicable, transferred and held uniformly, as between the respective Pooled Principals, in respect of all Pooled Loans for the time being outstanding under the Agreement.

6.3   At or as soon as practicable after the Agent's close of business on each Business Day on which Pooled Loans are outstanding (or at such other times as the Parties may from time to time agree) there shall be effected such Collateral Transfers as shall ensure that immediately thereafter:

(a)   in respect of all Pooled Principals which have a Net Loan Exposure to Borrower, the amount of Collateral then deliverable or Cash Collateral then payable by Borrower to each such Pooled Principal is equal to such proportion of the aggregate amount of Collateral then deliverable or Cash Collateral then payable, to all such Pooled Principals as corresponds to the proportion which the Net Loan Exposure of the relevant Pooled Principal bears to the aggregate of the Net Loan Exposures of all Pooled Principals to Borrower; and

(b)   in respect of all Pooled Principals to which Borrower has a Net Loan Exposure, the aggregate amount of Equivalent Collateral then deliverable or repayable by each such Pooled Principal to Borrower is equal to such proportion of the aggregate amount of Equivalent Collateral then deliverable or repayable by all such Pooled Principals as corresponds to the proportion which the Net Loan Exposure of Borrower to the relevant Pooled Principal bears to the aggregate of the Net Loan Exposures of Borrower to all Pooled Principals.

6.4   Collateral Transfers effected under paragraph 6.3 shall be effected (and if not so effected shall be deemed to have been so effected) by appropriations made by the Agent and shall be reflected by entries in accounting and other records maintained by the Agent. Accordingly, it shall not be necessary for payments of cash or deliveries of Securities to be made through any settlement system for the purpose of such Collateral Transfers. Without limiting the generality of the foregoing, the Agent is hereby authorised and instructed by Borrower to do all such things on behalf of Borrower as may be necessary or expedient to effect and record the receipt on behalf of Borrower of cash and Securities from, and the delivery on behalf of Borrower of cash and Securities to, Pooled Principals in the course or for the purposes of any Collateral Transfer effected under that paragraph.

6.5   Promptly following the Collateral Transfers effected under paragraph 6.3 above, and as at the Agent's close of business on any Business Day, the Agent shall prepare a statement showing in respect of each Pooled Principal the amount of cash Collateral which has been paid, and the amount of non-cash Collateral of each description which have been transferred, by or to that Pooled Principal immediately after those Collateral Transfers. If Borrower so requests, the Agent shall deliver to Borrower a copy of the statement so prepared in a format and to a timetable generally used in the market.

7.   WARRANTIES

7.1   The Agent warrants to Borrower that:

(a)   all notifications provided to Borrower under paragraph 4.1 above and all statements provided to the other party under paragraph 6.5 above shall be complete and accurate in all material respects;

(b)   at the time of allocating an Agency Loan in accordance with paragraph 4.1 above, each Principal or Principals to whom the Agent has allocated that Agency Loan or any part of that Agency Loan is duly authorised to enter into the Agency Loans contemplated by this Agreement and to perform its obligations thereunder; and

(c)   at the time of allocating an Agency Loan in accordance with paragraph 4.1 above, no Event of Default or event which would constitute an Event of Default with the service of a Default Notice or other written notice under paragraph 14 of the Agreement has occurred in relation to any Principal or Principals to whom the Agent has allocated that Agency Loan or any part of that Agency Loan.

OTC Derivatives and Collateral

CHAPTER 14

OTC Derivatives and Collateral – Transaction Types – Introduction

Part 4a of the book is targeted at those readers that are new to the subject of derivatives, or are familiar with one particular derivative product but not others. This chapter provides an introduction to the subject of derivatives, and to OTC derivatives, and to the role of collateral in OTC derivatives.

Derivatives are financial products whose values are derived from an *underlying* financial product. A derivative trade is a contract containing specific terms between one party and its *counterparty*; in the world of derivatives, the terms 'trade' and 'contract' are synonymous.

The particular characteristic that makes the buying and selling of derivatives distinct from buying and selling underlying financial products (e.g. *equity* or *bond*), is the following:

- purchasing an equity or bond requires the buyer to pay 100% of its market value, and selling an equity or bond means the seller will receive 100% of its market value
- purchasing a derivative (for example, where the underlying product is an equity or bond) requires the buyer to pay a fraction (e.g. 10%) of the market value of that underlying product.

Investing in a derivative provides access to an underlying product, but at a fraction of the cost. Providing the value of the underlying investment increases, the derivative investor's profits can be magnified greatly. Conversely, if the underlying investment decreases in value, the derivative investor can suffer very significant losses. This magnification of derivative profits and losses is commonly known as leverage or gearing.

Derivatives can be broadly placed into two main categories, namely *exchange-traded derivatives* and *OTC derivatives*.

PART 4a

14.1 EXCHANGE-TRADED DERIVATIVES

> *This section provides a high level introduction to the subject of exchange-traded derivatives, as a contrast to and comparison with OTC derivatives (which are described next).*

Within the global financial landscape are exchanges that provide the investor community with the ability to invest in certain types of derivative product. The particular characteristic of derivative exchanges (as distinct from **OTC derivatives**) is the fact that the exchange itself determines the particular attributes of the products available to investors.

When an investor executes a trade with a derivative exchange, the investor's counterparty is the exchange itself or the **clearing house** affiliated with the exchange. (This is the same concept as is applicable for many electronic **stock exchanges** where equity securities are traded). The exchange acts in the role of middleman or intermediary, by bringing together buyers and sellers. For example, a trade executed via the derivative exchange **Eurex** is automatically transferred to the affiliated clearing house **Eurex Clearing**, which becomes the true counterparty to both the buyer and the seller; the generic and common term for the clearing house is **central counterparty**.

Examples of derivative exchanges are:

- CME Group
- Eurex Exchange
- Intercontinental Exchange
- Nasdaq Derivatives Markets
- National Commodity and Derivatives Exchange (India)
- Sydney Futures Exchange (part of Australian Securities Exchange)
- Singapore Mercantile Exchange.

The types of financial product that are typically listed and available for trading on derivative exchanges are futures and options.

14.1.1 Futures: Overview

A futures contract is a trade executed between two parties, whereby the buyer has the <u>obligation to purchase</u> a specified quantity of a particular underlying asset at a price agreed on trade date, for settlement on a specified future **value date**. Similarly, the seller has the <u>obligation to deliver</u> a specified quantity of a particular underlying asset at a price agreed on trade date, for settlement on a future specified value date. The terms of futures contracts are standardised as they are specified by the derivatives exchange.

Figure 14.1 and the accompanying description illustrate a futures contract:

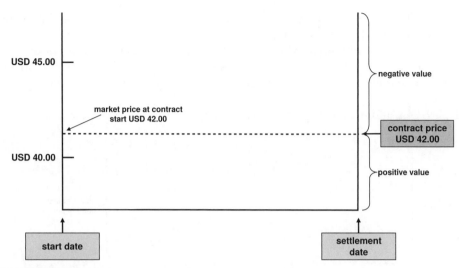

FIGURE 14.1   Example of a futures sale

Futures contract example: on 1st January, Investor A is an existing owner of 5,000 Company T shares for which the *current market price* is USD 42.00 per share. Believing that the value of the investment may fall in the coming months, Investor A enters into a futures contract with the <u>obligation to sell</u> the 5,000 shares at a fixed price of USD 42.00 per share, for settlement in 9 months' time. The futures contract buyer has an opposing view, believing that Company T shares are likely to rise to a level beyond USD 42.00 per share, within the next 9 months. One of two outcomes is possible at the time of settlement 9 months later:

1. the current market price has fallen to (for example) USD 39.00 per share. Under these circumstances, Investor A will benefit from entering into the futures contract (by USD 3.00 per share). Had Investor A chosen not to enter into the futures contract, a sale of the underlying shares executed 9 months later would have given Investor A only the lower market price of USD 39.00 per share. Conversely, this situation will be costly for the futures contract buyer, as he is obligated to pay USD 42.00 per share, for a stock now trading at USD 3.00 less in the market.
2. the current market price has risen to (for example) USD 46.00 per share. Under these circumstances, Investor A will not have benefitted from entering into the futures contract (by USD 4.00 per share). Conversely, this situation will be profitable for the futures contract buyer, as he is obligated to pay USD 42.00 per share, for a stock now trading at USD 4.00 higher in the market.

14.1.2 Options: Overview

An option contract is a trade executed between two parties, wherein the option holder has the <u>right, but not the obligation,</u> to *exercise* the option to buy (or to sell) a specified quantity of the underlying asset at a pre-agreed price, either during the term of the contract or on the final day (expiry date) of the contract. The right to buy the underlying asset is known as a ***call option***, whilst the right to sell the underlying is a ***put option***. The pre-agreed price is known as the ***strike price*** (also known as the exercise price). The terms of options contracts are standardised as they are specified by the derivatives exchange.

Figure 14.2 and the accompanying description illustrate an option contract:

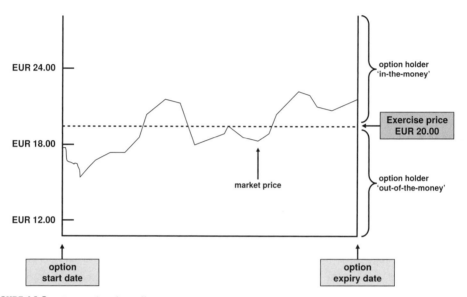

FIGURE 14.2 Example of a call option

Option contract example: Investor B enters into a call option to buy 1,000 Company X shares at a strike price of EUR 20.00 per share, prior to the option's expiry date in 3 months' time. Investor B is hoping that the price of the shares (the underlying product) will increase beyond EUR 20.00 per share, within the next 3 months. The cost of buying the option contract is the option premium (payable on trade date), which is typically a fraction of the cost of the underlying share. One of two outcomes is possible:

1. prior to the option expiry date, the share price increases above the strike price to (for example) EUR 24.50 per share. Under these circumstances Investor B will immediately exercise the option, and pay the exercise cost of EUR 20.00 per share; if the investor immediately sells the 1,000 shares at the market price of EUR 24.50, the investor will profit as follows: 1,000 × EUR 4.50 = EUR 4,500.00, less the option premium paid.
2. the share price has fallen beneath the strike price to (for example) EUR 18.75 per share, and it remains at this level through and beyond the option's expiry date. Under these circumstances Investor B will allow the option to lapse on the option expiry date, at which point the option is worthless. The investor will have made a loss due to the option premium paid.

In a put option (see Figure 14.3), the buyer hopes that the market price of the underlying product falls below the strike price; if that situation transpires, the buyer will exercise the option and receive the (higher) strike price, and buy the underlying in the market at the current market price. The differential is the buyer's profit, less the option premium. If instead the market price of the underlying remains above the strike price, the buyer will allow the option to lapse, at the cost of the option premium.

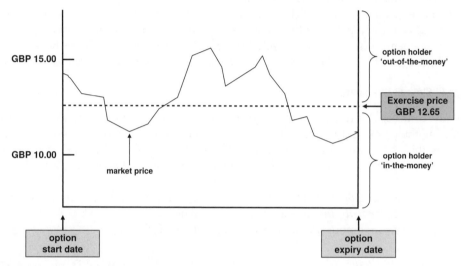

FIGURE 14.3   Example of a put option

A primary attribute of exchange-traded derivatives is the fact that the exchange dictates the features and characteristics of the derivative products it makes available for trading; these features and characteristics are documented within the product's **contract specification**. This creates product standardisation, meaning that the available products are typically highly **liquid**, thereby facilitating quick and efficient trading. Note: product standardisation is of paramount importance for risk management purposes and in general for the efficient operation of derivative markets.

Only members of the derivative exchange are permitted to execute trades on the exchange; such member firms (usually **sell-side** firms) are commonly known as **clearing members**. All non-members (typically **buy-side** firms) are required to appoint a clearing member through whom their trades are managed at the exchange's clearing house.

14.2 OTC DERIVATIVES

This section provides an introduction to the subject of OTC derivatives in order to provide a baseline of understanding prior to delving into the detail of these financial products, and the role collateral plays. In this book, significantly greater time will be spent focusing on OTC derivatives (rather than exchange-traded derivatives), due to the extent of collateral management activity associated with OTC derivatives.

PART 4a

Over-the-counter (OTC) derivative trades are financial contracts negotiated privately and directly (***bilaterally***) between two parties. Historically, OTC derivative trades have been tailored to meet the specific needs of the two parties involved, without the existence of standardised products (unlike exchange-traded derivatives). As no derivative exchange is involved in such trades, each trading party has direct ***counterparty risk*** for the lifetime of the contract. The duration of an individual contract can be many years, and each trading party must assess the various risks (particularly counterparty risk) on a regular (e.g. daily) basis and throughout the contract's duration. Parties involved in such trades can be a ***sell-side*** firm (e.g. an investment bank) trading with a ***buy-side*** firm (e.g. a pension fund), or a sell-side firm trading with another sell-side firm.

The primary types of OTC derivative product are commonly referred to as 'swaps':

14.2.1 Swaps: Overview

A swap contract is a trade executed directly between two parties on a ***bilateral*** basis, involving the agreement to exchange (swap) specific cashflows at one or more specified times within the duration of the contract. The ***underlying*** financial product to which the swap relates may be, for example, an interest rate, an exchange rate, a share or a bond.

Firms execute trades in OTC derivatives in order to protect themselves from a particular risk (i.e. for ***hedging*** purposes), or to speculate.

Types of swap (amongst a large choice) include the following:

- ***interest rate swaps***, which protect against rising or falling interest rates
- ***credit default swaps***, which protect against defaulting bond issuers
- ***foreign exchange swaps***, which protect against foreign exchange risk
- ***cross-currency swaps***, which enable cash borrowing in a non-natural currency.

Each of these swap products will be described in the chapters immediately following this chapter.

The common theme amongst ***OTC derivatives*** is that two parties enter into a trade that typically has a duration of years – for example up to 50 years, meaning that each party will have ***exposure*** to its ***counterparty*** on an ongoing basis throughout the trade's lifetime. It is important to understand the nature of each transaction type in order to appreciate the associated risks, and the role collateral plays.

The reason why collateral is necessary in OTC derivative trades is explained:

- to a medium level in Section 15.4 of Chapter 15 'OTC Derivatives and Collateral – Transaction Types – Generic Structural Aspects', and
- to a detailed level in Section 22.4 of Chapter 22 'OTC Derivatives and Collateral – Legal Protection – Credit Support Annex'.

14.3 EXCHANGE-TRADED DERIVATIVES VERSUS OTC DERIVATIVES: SUMMARY

The essential similarities and differences between exchange-traded derivatives and OTC derivatives are summarised as shown in Table 14.1:

TABLE 14.1   Similarities and differences between exchange-traded derivatives and OTC derivatives

Exchange-Traded Derivatives	OTC Derivatives
Traded with an exchange	Traded direct with a bilateral counterparty
Standardised contract terms	Tailor-made contract terms
Price transparency	Less transparent prices due to tailoring
Highly liquid products	Less liquid due to tailoring
Cleared via central counterparty	Cleared directly with bilateral counterparty

14.4 THE FUTURE OF OTC DERIVATIVES

It is important to note that, since the *global financial crisis* in 2008, new regulation is being introduced globally in an attempt to prevent a repeat of the dire events that occurred that year. The lack of mandatory *transaction reporting* of OTC derivatives meant that regulators were blind to the risks that caused some of the problems experienced during and following 2008.

In brief, the new regulation requires trades:

- in *standardised OTC derivatives* to be subject to clearing via *central counterparties*, and
- to be transaction reported to *trade repositories* (for regulatory scrutiny).

This regulation is intended to have OTC derivatives behaving much more like the desired model of exchange-traded derivatives.

The background to these regulatory changes is explained further, and the implications for both buy-side and sell-side institutions are explored within Part 4c 'OTC Derivatives and Collateral: Regulatory Change and the Future of Collateral'.

PART 4a

OTC Derivatives and Collateral – Transaction Types – Generic Structural Aspects

This chapter is designed to develop further fundamental aspects that are applicable to all OTC derivatives, prior to focusing on particular types of OTC derivative (which will be covered within the chapters immediately following this chapter).

15.1 OTC DERIVATIVE PRODUCTS

The term 'OTC derivative' is an umbrella term which describes a range of financial products, in each case relating to an *underlying* or associated financial product. However, and as will be explained subsequently, each OTC derivative product has distinct characteristics which differentiate one OTC derivative product from any other.

OTC derivative products include:

- interest rate swaps
- credit default swaps
- foreign exchange swaps
- cross-currency swaps

all of which are described to a detailed level in the following chapters.

Other types of OTC derivative product include:

- contracts for difference
- forward rate agreements
- non-deliverable forwards
- total return swaps, and
- variance swaps.

15.2 OTC DERIVATIVE TRADES – GENERIC TRADE COMPONENTS AND SUBSEQUENT ACTIONS

The generic components that are applicable to trades in all types of OTC derivative product include:

15.2.1 Parties

Typically, a trade begins with an *institutional investor* having an *exposure*, following which an appropriate OTC derivative trade is executed between the investor and an investment bank.

15.2.2 Term (Duration)

There is no officially defined minimum or maximum term of an OTC derivative trade. The duration of a trade is subject to negotiation between the two parties, but to provide an indication, up to 50 years is possible.

Whatever the term, each party to the trade has ongoing exposure to its counterparty for the entire duration of the trade. For such trades, of primary risk to each firm involved is whether the counterparty will comply with its *contractual obligations* throughout the entire lifetime of the trade. Due to such risk, it is common practice for each party to be legally protected by putting in place formal legal documentation; see Chapters 20–22.

Durations of multiple years make OTC derivative trades extremely different from *securities* trades. By comparison, trades in *equity* and *bonds* typically have a duration of a matter of just days. At the time of writing, the *settlement cycle* for European equity, US equity and Eurobond trades is 2 days. Providing such equity and bond trades settle on their *value date*, the counterparties to such trades have exposure to one another for just 2 days.

15.2.3 Notional Principal (also known as Notional Amount, Notional Quantity)

The quantity or value on which all trade calculations are based.

It is important to note that true derivative trades do not involve the up-front payment or receipt of the notional principal: it can therefore be described as a theoretical underlying quantity. The practice of not paying/receiving the notional principal reduces exposure between the two parties to the trade, but it does not negatively impact calculations of monies payable/receivable during the trade's lifetime.

To those readers that may be very familiar with settlement of equity and bond trades, where the full share quantity or bond quantity are delivered by the seller in order to receive the full sale proceeds, the fact that true OTC derivatives do not involve the payment or receipt of the notional principal may seem a very strange concept to grasp. An analogy from everyday life may help to understand this concept: imagine you have bought a car for the first time (cost of USD 10,000.00) and have arranged insurance, and that the agreement with the insurer is that you pay a fixed premium amount of USD 300.00 each year for the next 5 years. Neither you nor the insurer is required to pay the current value of the car (USD 10,000.00), but you are aware that the premium you are required to pay is impacted (to some extent) by the value of the car. Only in the event of total loss of the car would the USD 10,000.00 be paid, by the insurer to you.

Example #1: a trade in a particular type of OTC derivative product (a *credit default swap*) requires the payment of premium periodically by the buyer to the seller. For this trade, if the notional principal is USD 30,000,000.00, and the annual premium rate is 1.65%, the amount of premium payable each year is USD 495,000.00 (i.e. USD 30,000,000.00 × 1.65%). The notional principal of USD 30,000,000.00 is not paid by either party.

Example #2: a trade in a different type of OTC derivative product (an *interest rate swap*) requires the payment of interest periodically by one party to its counterparty. For this trade, if the notional principal is EUR 45,000,000.00, and the annual interest rate is 3.15%, the amount of interest payable each year is EUR 1,417,500.00 (i.e. EUR 45,000,000.00 × 3.15%). The notional principal of EUR 45,000,000.00 is not paid by either party.

15.2.4 Rates

Each OTC derivative trade contains some form of rate or price, for example:

- interest rate swaps contain an agreed fixed rate of interest versus an (as yet unknown) floating rate of interest
- credit default swaps contain a premium expressed in *basis points per annum*, which translates to a percentage, such as 1.65%.

As can be seen from the two examples under the heading of Notional Principal, such rates are directly involved in the calculation of cash payments and receipts.

15.2.5 Dates

The dates in an OTC derivative trade usually include:

- Trade Date:
  - the date of trade execution. The date that the two parties agreed on the terms of the trade, therefore the same meaning as for trade date in equity and bond trades
- Effective Date:
  - the date from which payment calculations commence
- Scheduled Maturity Date (also known as Termination Date):
  - the final date of the trade following which the trade is no longer live and in force.

15.2.6 Settlement

Trades in many types of OTC derivative product entail the payment or receipt of cash on numerous occasions during the contract's lifetime.

By comparison with securities settlement which usually occurs once only for equity and bond trades, OTC derivative trades typically require multiple settlements. For example:

- interest rate swaps:
  - involve a net payment to be made at an agreed frequency, such as every 6 months. The net payment is derived by comparing the fixed interest rate versus the floating interest rate for the period in question

- credit default swaps:
  - involve the buyer paying premium to the seller on specified dates each quarter. These quarterly dates are predefined and known around the globe.

For those readers that are familiar with securities settlement, another different aspect of OTC derivative settlement is the fact that, in most cases, settlement of an OTC derivative trade requires the payment or receipt of cash (only). In 99% of cases, settlement of equity and bond trades involves dependent securities delivery and dependent payment of cash (i.e. the seller will not deliver without simultaneous receipt of sale proceeds, and the buyer will not pay without simultaneous receipt of the securities); for settlement of OTC derivative trades there are usually no dependencies, the cash payer is expected to make a 'one-sided' payment on the due date. (If the payment is not made when falling due, the failing payer will have breached the legal agreement between the two parties.)

As for other financial products, efficient handling of OTC derivative settlement payments by a firm requires the payer to hold its counterparty's **standing settlement instructions** within the firm's **static data repository**.

15.2.7 Exiting

During the lifetime of an OTC derivative trade, a party to a trade that wishes to discontinue its involvement with the trade can choose to 'step out' of the trade whilst another party 'steps in'. This legal process is known as **novation**.

If and when novation occurs, it is essential that the **books & records** of the involved firms are immediately updated, otherwise the risk exists that 1) identified exposures do not in fact exist, 2) exposures that do in fact exist are not identified, 3) exposures will be shown against the incorrect counterparty, 4) settlement payments are made to the incorrect party, and 5) settlement payments are expected from the incorrect party.

The various methods of exiting an OTC derivative trade are explored within Chapter 37 'OTC Derivatives and Collateral – The Collateral Lifecycle – Throughout Lifetime of Trade – Post-Trade Execution Events – Introduction' and in the three subsequent chapters.

15.3 OTC DERIVATIVES: TRADE PROCESSING AND COLLATERAL PROCESSING

It is important to appreciate that the activities necessary to safely and securely process an OTC derivative trade primarily involve two parallel streams of operational activity, namely:

- trade processing, and
- collateral processing

as shown in Figure 15.1.

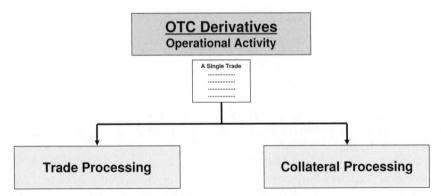

FIGURE 15.1   Single trade with two streams of operational activity

There is scope for confusion here as to what is included and excluded within each activity: to clarify:

- trade processing:
  - includes 1) the trade confirmation/affirmation process, and 2) settlement of OTC derivative trades, for example the payment of periodic interest in an interest rate swap, whilst
- collateral processing:
  - involves 1) the identification of counterparty *exposure*, 2) the *mitigation* of such exposures via the issuance or receipt of *margin calls*, and 3) the movement of assets to or from the counterparty to settle the margin calls. (For further detail, please refer to the next sub-section.)

In most organisations, these two activities are managed by separate *Operations Departments*, namely trade processing by the Derivative Operations Section/Department, and collateral processing by the Collateral Management Section/Department.
It is important to note that:

- the execution of a new trade triggers the need for both trade processing and collateral processing
- the closure of a trade triggers the need to cease both trade processing and collateral processing. Any collateral given or taken whilst the trade remained live must now be returned to the giver of such collateral. Trade closure can occur for a variety of reasons; these reasons will be explored in later chapters.

15.4 OTC DERIVATIVES: EXPOSURE AND COLLATERAL MANAGEMENT

Exposures to *counterparties* in all types of OTC derivative product, including:

- interest rate swaps
- credit default swaps

PART 4a

- foreign exchange swaps, and
- cross-currency swaps

(all of which will be covered in the following chapters) are identified by the comparison of 1) the rate/price agreed at trade execution, versus 2) the current rate/price which is also known as the *replacement cost*.

To explain further, imagine Firm A has entered into a 5-year-long contract in which Firm A has purchased a particular OTC derivative product at an agreed price of USD 100, from Firm B, and:

- the contract requires both parties to comply with the agreed *contractual commitments* for the entirety of the contract's 5-year lifetime
- a legal contract is drawn up which defines the responsibilities of each party, and the penalties for *defaulting* on the terms of the contract
- after 1 year, the current (market) cost of entering into the equivalent contract has risen to USD 120; this current cost is known as the replacement cost
- under such circumstances, the increase in the cost is regarded as an exposure for Firm A, for the following reason; if the contract with Firm B was to cease through no fault of Firm A (e.g. due to Firm B's *bankruptcy*) at any time prior to the scheduled maturity date of the contract, the original trade could no longer be fulfilled and it is assumed that Firm A would want to replace the trade immediately
- the differential between the original cost (USD 100) and the current (replacement) cost (USD 120), taking account of the remaining time to the contract's maturity date, is used to determine a monetary sum that represents Firm A's exposure
- that exposure monetary sum is claimed (in this example) by Firm A from Firm B in the form of a *margin call*
- providing Firm B agrees Firm A's margin call calculation, Firm B is required to deliver either cash collateral or bond collateral to Firm A in order to *mitigate* Firm A's exposure.

The legal contract states the frequency by which such exposures must be determined, which could be (for example) daily, weekly, monthly; this frequency is negotiable between the two parties up front, but once agreed (in advance of trade execution) it will be written into the legal contract and both parties must comply accordingly for the duration of the contract. If either firm fails to comply, they will be in default and this can trigger immediate closure of the trade (prior to reaching the contract's *scheduled maturity date*).

In the legal contract between Firm A and Firm B, assume the frequency of exposure calculation is (for example) weekly. As a continuation of the above example, the following is possible:

- one week later, the replacement cost has risen further to USD 128; this will require Firm A to issue a further margin call to Firm B, but Firm A must take account of the fact that it is holding a certain value of Firm B's collateral from the previous margin call (therefore, the exposure monetary sum that represents the difference between USD 120 and USD 128)

- one further week later, the replacement cost has fallen to USD 109; this will require Firm B to issue a margin call to Firm A, requesting the return of some of its collateral (the exposure monetary sum that represents the difference between USD 128 and USD 109)
- one further week later again, the replacement cost has fallen to USD 97; this will require Firm B to issue a margin call to Firm A, requesting the return of the remainder of its collateral still held by Firm A (the exposure monetary sum that represents the difference between USD 109 and USD 100), plus some of Firm A's own collateral (the exposure monetary sum that represents the difference between USD 97 and USD 100).

Note: a fully expanded explanation of how exposures arise in OTC derivative trades can be found in Section 22.4 'OTC Derivative Exposures' within Chapter 22 'OTC Derivatives and Collateral – Legal Protection – Credit Support Annex'.

As can be seen from the above example, *collateral processing* does not include OTC derivative *trade processing* activity, such as the payment/receipt of interest amounts in an *interest rate swap*, or the payment/receipt of premium in a *credit default swap*. This point will be emphasised and clarified in the chapters which follow.

CHAPTER 16

OTC Derivatives and Collateral – Transaction Types – Interest Rate Swaps

This chapter describes the purpose of and characteristics of interest rate swaps, one of the most popular types of OTC derivative product.

16.1 DEFINITION

An interest rate swap (IRS) is an *OTC derivative* contract in which two parties periodically exchange interest payments of different types, on a specified *notional principal*, during a set period of time.

IRS are part of a family of financial products known as *interest rate derivatives*.

16.2 PURPOSE

IRS (also known as plain vanilla swaps) are used to *mitigate* interest rate risk, specifically the risk that changes in future rates of interest will cause losses to be incurred.

Imagine that Firm X (a motor manufacturer) has an existing commitment to pay interest at a fixed rate of 4.0% for the next 5 years, to Party D, on a borrowing of EUR 30,000,000.00. Firm X chooses to compare that outgoing stream of fixed interest payments with an incoming stream of floating rate interest payments that are due from Party E, for the same cash amount and over the same 5-year period. Note: floating rate interest payments are representative of fluctuating money market interest rates. This situation is reflected in Figure 16.1, which is viewed from the perspective of Firm X:

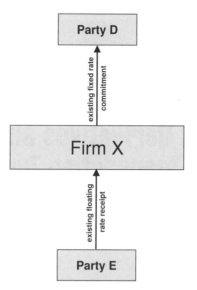

FIGURE 16.1   Firm X's situation prior to execution of the interest rate swap

Under those circumstances, Firm X is exposed to the possibility that, should current interest rates fall, there will be a widening and increasingly costly differential between the incoming (floating rate) of interest versus the outgoing (fixed rate) of interest. Conversely, if current interest rates rise beyond the 4.0% fixed rate, Firm X will benefit from the positive differential in rates.

Firm X decides to act cautiously and chooses to mitigate the potential *exposure* in case current interest rates fall. Firm X contacts an *investment bank* (Bank T), stating that it wishes to execute a *fixed-for-floating IRS*, for a notional principal of EUR 30,000,000.00, for a period of 5 years. Bank T is prepared to execute the IRS trade, and the trade terms are agreed, resulting in an IRS trade being executed.

Once *trade execution* of the IRS has been actioned:

- Firm X will receive from Bank T on a semi-annual basis, a fixed rate of 4.0% interest on a notional principal of EUR 30,000,000.00, until the *scheduled maturity date* of the IRS trade
  - Firm X will match this incoming fixed rate of 4.0% to the existing commitment to pay Party D a fixed rate of 4.0% on EUR 30,000,000.00
- Firm X will pay to Bank T, on a semi-annual basis, the floating rate of 6-month EUR *Libor* on a notional principal of EUR 30,000,000.00, until the *scheduled maturity date* of the IRS trade
  - Firm X will match this outgoing floating interest rate payment to the existing incoming floating rate receipt due from Party E on EUR 30,000,000.00.

Note: Libor (London Interbank Offered Rate) is a commonly used *floating benchmark* rate, therefore in Firm X's situation, the incoming floating rate from Party E will be matched against the outgoing floating (Libor) rate payable to Bank T.

To ensure clarity of understanding, the fixed rate remains constant throughout the entire lifetime of the IRS trade; however, the floating rate (in this case 6-month EUR Libor) is directly reflective of the changes in money market rates going forward in time. Although an individual or firm may speculate as to what will happen with money market interest rates in the future, the actual rates will be known only when the benchmark rate is officially set and announced at the relevant dates in the future. Libor rates are calculated and announced on a daily basis for 5 currencies, namely EUR, USD, GBP, CHF and JPY, for 7 maturity periods, namely overnight, 1 week, 1 month, 2 months, 3 months, 6 months and 12 months; the rates are provided by a number of contributor banks. (Note: at the time of writing, the organisation that is responsible for collating and announcing the average of the Libor benchmark rates received from contributor banks [including 6-month EUR Libor] is Intercontinental Exchange [ICE]).

When interest payments fall due (in the example trade above this is every 6 months), the cash amount payable is the net differential between the fixed rate versus the floating rate; that differential rate is then applied to the notional principal to determine the net cash amount payable by one or the other party. Example calculations are provided later in this chapter.

The overall situation (following execution of the IRS trade) is represented in Figure 16.2:

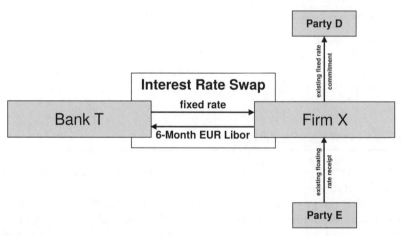

FIGURE 16.2   Interest rate swap contract

Commonly used terminology for each of the parties in a fixed-for-floating IRS is:

- the party that pays the fixed rate is known as the IRS 'payer'; this party is sometimes referred to as the 'buyer', and
- the party that receives the fixed rate is known as the IRS 'receiver'; this party is sometimes referred to as the 'seller'.

In summary, prior to the IRS trade being executed, the motor manufacturer had a direct exposure to the risk that current interest rates would fall, in which case a negative differential would exist between receivable interest (the floating rate due from Party E), and the fixed rate payable to Party D. Following IRS trade execution, the risk is effectively transferred to the motor manufacturer's counterparty (Bank T).

Note: beside fixed-for-floating IRS, other types of interest rate swap include floating-for-floating IRS, which is also known as a basis swap.

16.3 TRADE COMPONENTS

Once a firm has executed an IRS trade, it must be captured without delay. The trade components that must be captured include those listed in Table 16.1 (from Firm X's perspective):

TABLE 16.1   Trade capture: detail of an interest rate swap trade

Trade Component	Example Trade Detail
Transaction Type	Interest Rate Swap: Fixed-for-Floating
Notional Principal	EUR 30,000,000.00
Fixed Rate Payer	Bank T
Floating Rate Payer	Firm X
Fixed Rate	4.0% semi-annual
Floating Rate	6-month EUR Libor
Trade Date	1st November 2016
Effective Date	1st November 2016
Scheduled Maturity Date	1st November 2021

16.4 INTEREST PAYMENT CALCULATION

In order to understand how IRS interest payment amounts are determined, the above example trade detail will be used.

When the first interest payment is due (6 months after trade date), in order to determine the net interest payment amount, both parties to the trade need to utilise the fixed rate of 4.0% and the floating rate applicable to the particular 6-month period, which has been announced as 2.9764%. The differential between those rates is 1.0236%. It should be expected that when subsequent interest payments fall due, the floating rate will almost certainly differ from the initial rate of 2.9764%.

The calculation of the amount payable (or receivable) every 6 months involves the notional principal, the net interest rate, the relevant divisor (i.e. 360 for USD and EUR, and 365 for GBP) and the number of calendar days in the particular period, as shown in Figure 16.3:

Notional Principal × Net Interest Rate % / 360 or 365 × Actual Days in Quarter

FIGURE 16.3   Interest rate swap: interest payment calculation components

In order to count the number of calendar (actual) days in each 6-month period, include the previous interest payment date, and exclude the next interest payment date. For example, to determine the number of days relating to interest due on the first occasion for this trade, namely 1st May 2017 (6 months after trade date and effective date), count the calendar days from and including 1st November 2016 up to but excluding 1st May 2017; therefore 30 days in November, 31 days in December, 31 days in January, 28 days in February, 31 days in March, 30 days in April and zero days in May – a total of 181 calendar days. (Assume the year to be a non-leap year.)

The floating rate for the first interest payment date (due 1st May 2017) is normally determined on trade date, the same date as the effective date (namely 1st November 2016). The floating rate for an upcoming period is determined on the **_fixing date_**, commonly two days prior to the **_reset date_**. The reset date is the date at which the new rate becomes effective, and therefore the date from which calculations should commence for that new rate.

The interest due on the first occasion and for a number of subsequent occasions in Table 16.2 refers to the trade detailed in the Trade Capture table above. (Note: leap years are ignored for the purposes of this calculation example.)

TABLE 16.2 IRS interest payment calculation

Reset Date	Interest Payment Date	Fixed Rate Interest Calculation	6-Month EUR Libor Interest Calculation	Net Payment Amount (EUR)	
				Bank T Pays	Firm X Pays
1st Nov 2016	1st May 2017 *ED + 6 months	4.0% Notional × 4.0% /360 × 181d €603,333.33	2.9764% Notional × 2.9764% /360 × 181d €448,940.33	€154,393.00	×
1st May 2017	1st Nov 2017 ED + 12 months	4.0% Notional × 4.0% /360 × 184d €613,333.33	3.4781% Notional × 3.4781% /360 × 184d €533,308.67	€80,024.66	×
1st Nov 2017	1st May 2018 ED + 18 months	4.0% Notional × 4.0% /360 × 181d €603,333.33	3.9052% Notional × 3.9052% /360 × 181d €589,034.33	€14,299.00	×
1st May 2018	1st Nov 2018 ED + 24 months	4.0% Notional × 4.0% /360 × 184d €613,333.33	4.3179% Notional × 4.3179% /360 × 184d €662,078.00	×	€48,744.67
1st Nov 2018	1st May 2019 ED + 30 months	4.0% Notional × 4.0% /360 × 181d €603,333.33	4.0196% Notional × 4.0196% /360 × 181d €606,289.67	×	€2,956.34

*ED = Effective Date

PART 4a

The profile of interest payments over the lifetime of an IRS can therefore appear as in Figure 16.4:

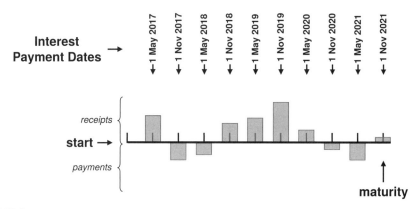

FIGURE 16.4   Interest rate swap example payment profile

Note: the number of calendar days for any combination of 6-monthly periods (within one year) will not be identical, therefore the actual interest amounts due will vary.

In some cases, an IRS trade may incorporate a margin, where (for example) the floating rate has an ever-present fixed margin of 0.25% deducted from (or added to) whatever is the currently applicable floating rate. For example, if an IRS is executed as '6-month EUR Libor+0.25% margin', a floating rate of 2.9764% would become 3.2264%, and that latter figure must be used for the calculation of floating interest for that 6-month period. The fixed margin of 0.25% would need to be added to all other 6-month EUR Libor rates for the remainder of the IRS contract.

16.5 IRS OPERATIONS ACTIVITY: OVERVIEW

From an operations perspective, both parties to an IRS trade must:

- calculate the net differential between the fixed interest rate and the floating interest rate for the period in question
- determine which party is responsible for making the net payment.

And, the paying party must ensure payment is made to the counterparty on the due date, whilst the receiving party ensures the payment is received from its counterparty when falling due.

These actions are represented in Figure 16.5:

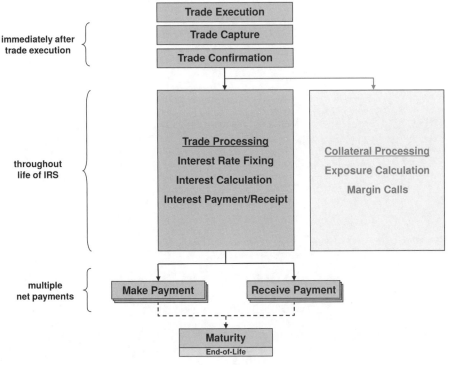

FIGURE 16.5 IRS trade processing actions

The trade processing operational activity for IRS is summarised in Table 16.3:

TABLE 16.3 IRS trade processing operational activity

Interest Rate Swaps	
Premium payable?	No
Exchange of notional principal?	No
Single/multiple currencies?	Single
Single/multiple settlements?	Multiple
Payments gross or net?	Net

16.6 IRS AND COLLATERAL MANAGEMENT

Regarding collateral management, after the IRS trade has been executed the current value of the IRS trade is calculated through the regular (normally daily) *mark-to-market* process.

The party having a *positive mark-to-market* has an exposure to its counterparty, and the non-exposed party must provide collateral (in the agreed form) to the exposed party. There are a significant number of steps in this process; please refer to Chapters 24–44, all of which fall under the heading of 'The OTC Derivative Collateral Lifecycle'.

CHAPTER 17

OTC Derivatives and Collateral – Transaction Types – Credit Default Swaps

This chapter describes the purpose of and characteristics of credit default swaps, one of the most popular types of OTC derivative product.

17.1 DEFINITION

A credit default swap (CDS) is an OTC derivative contract in which one party pays a periodic *premium* to its *counterparty*, in return for compensation for failure of a third party cash borrower to repay cash owed.

CDS are part of a family of financial products known as *credit derivatives*.

17.2 PURPOSE

Imagine that in April 2015 Firm A (a *mutual fund*) purchases a quantity of USD 10,000,000 Issuer X bonds maturing in October 2025, in the *secondary market*. The mutual fund's intention is to hold the bond until *maturity date*. In October 2015, the mutual fund becomes concerned as to the *creditworthiness* of Issuer X, which brings into question whether Issuer X will be able to comply with its *contractual obligations* relating to the bond; those obligations are 1) to repay capital invested (USD 10,000,000.00) on the bond's maturity date, and 2) to pay interest on the borrowing of cash via *coupon payments* when scheduled to occur.

Rather than selling the bond, the mutual fund considers that continuing to hold the bond is preferable, despite the risk of the issuer *defaulting* on its contractual obligations. However, in order to *mitigate* its risk, the mutual fund chooses to take out a form of insurance known as a credit default swap.

PART 4a

The mutual fund contacts an *investment bank* (Bank B), stating that it wishes to buy a CDS on Issuer X, for a notional principal of USD 10,000,000 (to match the quantity of bonds held), for a period of 10 years (to match the maturity date of the bond). Bank B is prepared to execute the CDS, and quotes a price of 132 *basis points per annum*; this means that the cost of the CDS to the mutual fund will be 1.32% of USD 10,000,000 per year (i.e. *premium* payments of USD 132,000.00 per year). The mutual fund obtains quotes from other banks, but decides to go ahead and execute the CDS trade with Bank B.

Once the CDS trade has been executed:

- the mutual fund is required to make payments of premium on a quarterly basis (approximately 25% of USD 132,000.00 each quarter) until the *scheduled maturity date* of the CDS trade
- in the event of default by Issuer X during the lifetime of the CDS contract, Bank B is required to remit the full notional principal (USD 10,000,000.00) to the mutual fund, following which the CDS contract will automatically terminate.

The overall situation is represented in Figure 17.1:

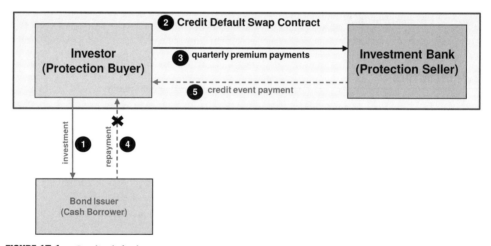

FIGURE 17.1 Credit default swap contract

Step 1: an investor (e.g. a mutual fund) invests in a bond for which the investor expects repayment of capital on the bond's maturity date and periodic receipt of coupon payments when falling due

Step 2: the investor becomes concerned as to the creditworthiness of the bond issuer, and executes a CDS contract with an investment bank

Step 3: the investor (*protection buyer*) is required to make payments of premium to the investment bank (*protection seller*) on a quarterly basis

Step 4: if the bond issuer defaults on its bond payment obligations, the investor will not receive the full repayment of capital from the bond issuer

Step 5: default by the bond issuer becomes a '***credit event***' which will trigger settlement of the CDS contract requiring the protection seller to remit the full value of the CDS contract to the protection buyer, following which the CDS contract ceases to exist.

It is important to note that Issuer X is not involved in the CDS trade at all. The CDS trade is a ***bilateral*** contract directly between the mutual fund and the investment bank. The price quoted by the investment bank (132 bppa) represents the bank's view of the likelihood of default by the issuer; this price remains constant for the duration of the CDS contract (in this case, 10 years).

In summary, prior to the CDS trade being executed, the mutual fund had a direct ***exposure*** to the risk of default by Issuer X. Following CDS trade execution, the risk of issuer default is transferred from the mutual fund (the ***protection buyer***) to the investment bank (the ***protection seller***). CDS are designed to mitigate the risk that the issuer of the underlying security (the ***reference entity***) will default on coupon payments or repayment of capital. The risk is assumed by the protection seller in exchange for payment of a premium from the protection buyer.

Note: the type of CDS referred to above is a ***single name credit default swap***, as the entity on which the CDS trade is based is the sole bond issuer. Other types of credit derivative exist and an example (basket default swaps) is summarised later in this chapter.

17.3 TRADE COMPONENTS

Once a firm has executed a CDS trade, it must be captured without delay. The trade components that must be captured include those listed in Table 17.1 (from Firm A's perspective):

TABLE 17.1   Trade capture: detail of a credit default swap trade

Trade Component	Example Trade Detail
Transaction Type	Credit Default Swap: Single Name
Reference Entity	Issuer X
Notional Principal	USD 10,000,000.00
Protection Buyer	Firm A
Protection Seller	Bank B
Premium	132 bppa
Premium Payment Frequency	Quarterly
Trade Date	October 18th, 2015
Settlement Date	October 20th, 2015
Scheduled Maturity Date	October 20th, 2025

In CDS terminology, the bond issuer is known as the 'reference entity', the particular underlying bond is known as the 'reference obligation' or the 'reference asset', and the premium is sometimes referred to as the 'coupon' (confusingly).

17.4 COST OF PROTECTION

The cost of a CDS to the protection buyer is the premium, a percentage rate agreed with the protection seller at the time of *trade execution*. This amount is expressed in *basis points per annum*, and is payable on specific quarterly dates, namely the 20th of each March, June, September and December throughout the lifetime of the contract: all CDS premium payments are payable on those dates. It is important to note that the premium remains constant and unchanged for the duration of the contract.

The amount payable (or receivable) each quarter involves the notional principal, the annual premium percentage, the relevant divisor (i.e. 360 for USD and EUR, and 365 for GBP) and the number of calendar days in the particular quarter, as shown in Figure 17.2:

Notional Principal × Annual Premium % / 360 or 365 × Actual Days in Quarter

FIGURE 17.2   Credit default swap: premium payment calculation components

Note: the premium of 132 bppa translates to 1.32% of the notional principal.

In order to count the number of calendar (actual) days in each quarter, include the previous premium payment date, and exclude the next premium payment date. For example, to determine the number of days relating to premium payable/receivable at quarter ending 20th June, count the calendar days from and including 20th March up to but excluding 20th June; therefore 12 days in March, 30 days in April, 31 days in May, 19 days in June – a total of 92 calendar days. (Assume the year to be a non-leap year.)

The Premium Payable in Table 17.2 refers to the trade detailed in Table 17.1.

TABLE 17.2   CDS premium payment calculation

Premium Payment Date	Days in Quarter	Premium Payable
20th March	90	USD 33,000.00
20th June	92	USD 33,733.33
20th September	92	USD 33,733.33
20th December	91	USD 33,366.67

As can be seen, due to the number of calendar days not being identical for all quarters, the actual premium payable varies.

17.5 CREDIT EVENTS

A credit event is a valid *event of default* by the bond issuer which triggers payout by a protection seller to a protection buyer.

In the past many disputes have occurred between CDS trade parties due to differences of opinion as to whether a credit event has or has not occurred. Such disputes have been largely overcome by the advent of *ISDA Regional Determination Committees*, whose role is to establish whether a credit event has or has not occurred, their decision being final and binding on *ISDA* members.

At the time of trade execution, the protection buyer and protection seller must agree exactly which events constitute a credit event, typically including:

- failure to pay interest and principal when falling due
- bankruptcy
- debt restructuring.

Generically speaking, there is no certainty at all that a credit event will occur during the lifetime of a CDS. Should no credit event occur for a particular CDS contract, premium payments must continue throughout the contract's lifetime, and the contract will cease on its *scheduled maturity date*. Conversely, if a credit event is triggered, once the protection seller has paid the protection buyer the notional principal of the contract, the CDS contract is terminated immediately and the CDS contract has thereby reached its end of life; consequently, no further premium is payable or receivable.

For an explanation of the impact of credit events on collateral management, please refer to Chapter 41 'OTC Derivatives and Collateral – The Collateral Lifecycle – Throughout Lifetime of Trade – Post-Trade Execution Events – Credit Events'.

17.6 CDS OPERATIONS ACTIVITY: OVERVIEW

From an operations perspective, a protection buyer must:

- make payments of premium to the protection seller on the quarterly payment dates, and
- should a credit event occur, claim payment of the notional principal from the protection seller.

A protection seller must:

- ensure receipt of premium from the protection buyer on the quarterly payment dates, and
- should a credit event occur, make payment of the notional principal to the protection buyer.

These actions are represented in Figure 17.3:

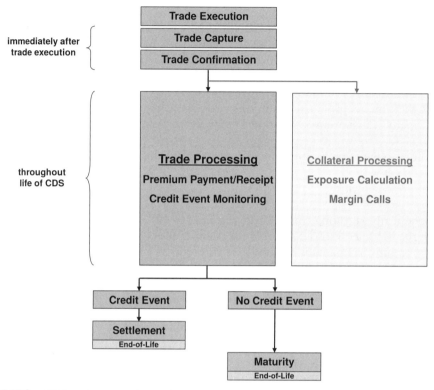

FIGURE 17.3   CDS trade processing actions

The trade processing operational activity for CDS are summarised in Table 17.3:

TABLE 17.3   CDS trade processing operational activity

Credit Default Swaps	
Premium payable?	Yes, at quarterly intervals
Exchange of notional principal?	No, unless a credit event occurs
Single/multiple settlements?	Multiple premium settlements
Payments gross or net?	Gross

17.7 SETTLEMENT FOLLOWING CREDIT EVENTS

If a credit event occurs, the trade may be settled in one of two ways, either *physical settlement* or *cash settlement*. In order to appreciate what's involved, it should be understood that normally, following a credit event, a bond retains some level of market value. The value of protection is intended to be identical under both settlement methods.

17.7.1 Physical Settlement

Physical settlement is defined as the delivery (by the protection buyer to the protection seller) of the notional principal of the bond in exchange for 100% of the notional principal in cash. This form of settlement is applicable where the protection buyer owns the underlying bonds. (Note that not all protection buyers are bond owners; please refer to Section 17.8 'The Protection Seller's Risk' later in this chapter.) This form of settlement is represented in Figure 17.4.

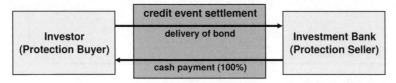

FIGURE 17.4 Physical settlement following credit event

Following physical settlement, the protection seller can be partially reimbursed for the cost of credit event settlement through selling the bonds in the market, providing the bonds retain some residual market value.

17.7.2 Cash Settlement

Cash settlement is defined as the payment of a 'free' cash amount by the protection seller to the protection buyer in full and final settlement of the CDS contract. This form of settlement is applicable where the protection buyer does not own the underlying bonds. This form of settlement is represented in Figure 17.5.

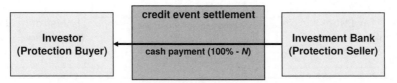

FIGURE 17.5 Cash settlement following credit event

Cash settlement involves the payment of 100% of the full notional principal, less the current market value of the bond.

17.8 THE PROTECTION SELLER'S RISK

Once a firm, as protection seller, has executed a CDS trade, it now has the risk that, should the bond issuer suffer a credit event, the firm will be contractually committed to remit the full notional principal of the trade to the protection buyer.

Such risks for the firm selling protection can be mitigated if an equal and opposite trade is executed with a different counterparty (trade #2), whereby the firm will be in the role of protection buyer (and will therefore be paying premium). Should a credit event occur the firm will receive the full value of the trade from the trade #2 counterparty. That cash would be used by the firm in order to settle trade #1.

17.9 CDS AND COLLATERAL MANAGEMENT

Regarding collateral management, after the CDS trade has been executed the current value of the CDS trade is calculated through the regular (normally daily) *mark-to-market* process.

The party having a *positive mark-to-market* has an exposure to its counterparty, and the non-exposed party must provide collateral (in the agreed form) to the exposed party. There are a significant number of steps in this process; please refer to Chapters 24–44, all of which fall under the heading of 'The OTC Derivative Collateral Lifecycle'.

17.10 CDS VARIATIONS

17.10.1 Basket Default Swaps

There exist a number of variations of CDS, one of which is basket default swaps.

Definition: an OTC contract in which one party (protection buyer) pays a periodic fee to another party (protection seller) in return for compensation for default (or similar credit event) by one (or more) reference entities in a collection of reference entities.

Purpose: basket default swaps (BDS) are designed to mitigate the risk that an issuer (out of a collection of issuers) of an underlying security will default on its payment obligations. The risk is assumed by another party (the protection seller) in exchange for payment of a premium from the protection buyer (see Figure 17.6).

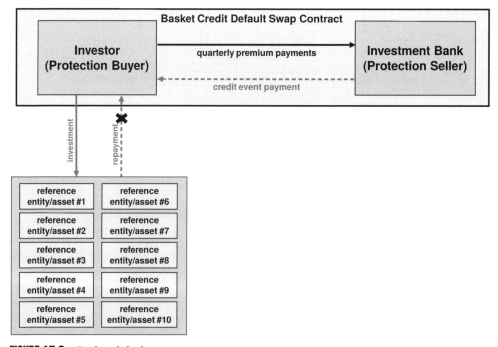

FIGURE 17.6 Basket default swap

The trigger for payout by the protection seller can be (for example):

- the First to Default, in which any of the reference entities to default will trigger payout, or
- the Second to Default, in which the first to default does not trigger payout, but the next does.

17.10.2 Loan Credit Default Swaps

In addition to providing protection against bond issuer default, CDS are used to provide protection against default of a cash borrower via Loan CDS.

CHAPTER 18

OTC Derivatives and Collateral – Transaction Types – Foreign Exchange Swaps

This chapter describes the purpose of and characteristics of foreign exchange swaps, one type of OTC derivative product. Also described are a number of fundamentally important concepts of foreign exchange settlement, with their associated risks.

18.1 DEFINITION

A foreign exchange swap (FXS) is an OTC derivative contract in which two parties exchange principal amounts in different currencies at the start of the trade (at one exchange rate), with the reverse exchange occurring at the close of the trade (at a different exchange rate).

FXS are part of a family of financial products known as *currency derivatives*.

FXS are also known as 'plain vanilla foreign exchange swaps', 'spot/forward fx swaps', and 'forex swaps'.

Note: in a foreign exchange swap, because the principal amounts are paid in full, the term 'notional' (meaning 'theoretical') is not applicable, consequently the terms 'principal' and 'principal amount' are used instead.

18.2 PURPOSE

FXS are used to mitigate foreign exchange risk.

Imagine that a firm needs to borrow a particular amount of a particular currency immediately, where the firm currently holds a different currency that the firm does not need immediately. An FXS trade is a temporary (therefore two-legged) exchange of the two currencies:

- in the first leg of the trade, the firm's existing currency known as the **base currency** [ccy #1] is paid to the **counterparty**, versus receipt of the equivalent value of the required currency or **quote currency** [ccy #2] – this part of the FXS is executed on **trade date** at the **spot exchange rate**
- in the second leg of the trade, the base currency [ccy #1] is repaid by the counterparty, versus payment of the equivalent value of the quote currency [ccy #2] – this part of the FXS is also executed on trade date, but at the **forward exchange rate**.

In order to appreciate how FXS work, it is firstly necessary to understand what is meant by 'spot' and 'forward'.

18.2.1 'Spot' Foreign Exchange

The execution of a normal foreign exchange trade is said to be traded for 'on-the-spot' settlement (hence 'spot'), meaning the normal **settlement cycle** between trade date and **value date**.

One FX trade involves each party selling one currency and buying the contra currency. This therefore involves the sale of a currency by each of the two involved parties; for the majority of the world's currencies 2 days is the historic period of time necessary for a firm to organise the payment of a currency amount to the firm's counterparty. This time period is due, at least in part, to time zone differences between currency banking centres. This situation is represented in Figure 18.1.

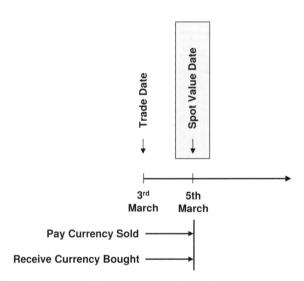

FIGURE 18.1   Profile and example of dates in a spot FX trade

Note: an exception to the 2-day rule exists for FX trades between USD/CAD, where spot is the business day following trade date.

At trade execution of an FX spot trade, an exchange rate is determined for the currency that a firm wishes to sell and the currency that firm is seeking to buy. Approximately 180 currencies exist around the globe, therefore many combinations of currencies are possible in a foreign exchange trade.

Spot FX trades involve the outright sale (not a loan) of the base currency against the outright purchase of a quote currency, at an agreed (spot) exchange rate, for settlement 2 business days following trade date. The components of a spot FX trade are as follows (written from the perspective of Party A):

TABLE 18.1 Example spot foreign exchange trade components

Spot Foreign Exchange	
Trade Component	**Example Trade Detail**
Transaction Type	Foreign Exchange Spot
Counterparty	Firm B
Trade Date	3rd March 2017
Spot Value Date	5th March 2017
Base Currency and Amount	USD 20,000,000.00
Quote Currency and Amount	GBP 16,032,064.13
Spot Exchange Rate	USD 1.2475/GBP 1.00
Base Currency Seller	Party A
Quote Currency Seller	Firm B

From a settlement perspective, the traditional method of settlement is for each party to the spot FX trade to issue a settlement instruction to its *cash correspondent* (or *nostro*) for the currency amount it is selling. Settlement instructions must be received by the deadline stated by each cash correspondent, relative to currency and the value date of the payment. Under the traditional settlement method, in the world of foreign exchange there is no matching of settlement instructions prior to settlement occurring. Focusing on the trade in Table 18.1, Party A needs to pay USD 20,000,000.00 to Firm B on 5th March 2017; Firm A's cash correspondent should comply with the settlement instruction received, providing firm A has adequate cash balance or overdraft facility. Firm A's settlement instruction must contain the account details of its counterparty, Firm B; from an operational efficiency perspective, such account details should already be held in Firm A's internal *static data repository*, in the form of a *standing settlement instruction*.

Regarding the currency that Firm A is due to receive following execution of this spot FX trade, Firm B must issue a settlement instruction to its GBP cash correspondent for the payment of the GBP 16,032,064.13 to Party A. Note: Firm A's GBP cash correspondent may require to be informed that a cash amount is due to be received. If that is the case, Firm A must issue a *funds preadvice* to its cash correspondent by the stated deadline, in order to ensure crediting of funds with *good value* (and to avoid incurring a delay in the receipt of the funds).

In this particular spot FX trade in which the currencies are GBP and USD, clearly there is a *time zone difference* between banking hours in London and New York; this is usually 5 hours. And, in the traditional method, settlement is *free of payment*, with no simultaneous exchange of the two currencies. Consequently, the party that pays first is the party that pays the more eastern currency first, and the party that takes the risk that payment of the eastern currency is made at a point in time when it is not (yet) known whether the contra currency has (or will be) received. Such a settlement risk is known as *Herstatt Risk* and cross-currency settlement risk.

An extreme (but realistic) example of Herstatt Risk would occur where one currency is very eastern and the other is very western, such as New Zealand dollars (NZD) versus USD; Wellington is 17 hours ahead of New York, so a seller (and payer) of NZD will not know for many hours whether the USD had been received by their USD cash correspondent.

However, Herstatt Risk can be overcome. *CLS Bank* began operations in 2002; it is designed to make payments from one member's account to another member's account on a simultaneous exchange basis, known as PvP (*payment-versus-payment*) – this is the cash/currency equivalent of *delivery-versus-payment* which is so popular for securities settlement (as described in Chapter 2 'The Nature and Characteristics of Collateral Types'. Note: for currencies not covered by CLS and for firms that have chosen not to use CLS, the traditional settlement method remains available for use.

Settlement of the aforementioned spot FX trade can be summarised as shown in Figure 18.2 (viewed from Party A's perspective):

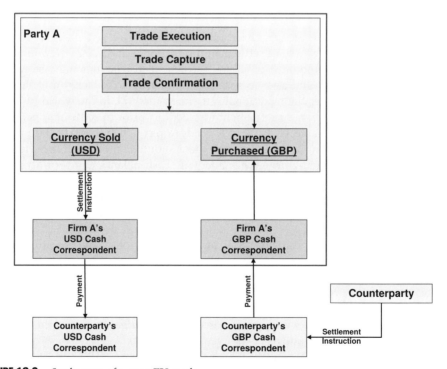

FIGURE 18.2   Settlement of a spot FX trade

18.2.2 'Forward' Foreign Exchange

Forward FX trades are used by firms to 'lock in' today the sale of one currency (base currency), and the purchase of a quote currency, for settlement at an agreed future date.

For example, a Singaporean furniture manufacturer (Firm G) is due to receive EUR 5,000,000.00 in 60 days' time, on 2nd May. If the firm takes no action and waits until the EUR payment arrives, the possibility exists that the SGD/EUR exchange rate will have moved against the firm, compared with today's exchange rate. In order to *mitigate* that risk, Firm G decides to execute a forward FX trade today with Bank K, with the result that the sale of the incoming EUR 5,000,000.00 in 60 days from now will provide a fixed amount of Singapore dollars, due to execution of the trade today at today's forward FX rate. This situation is represented in Figure 18.3.

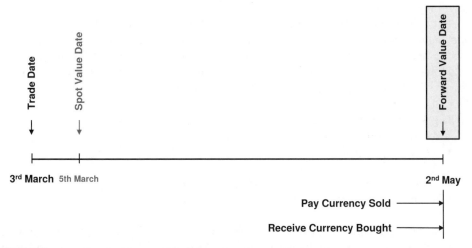

FIGURE 18.3   Profile of and example of dates in a forward FX trade

For this particular forward FX trade, the trade components captured by Firm G would appear as shown in Table 18.2:

TABLE 18.2   Example forward foreign exchange trade components

Forward Foreign Exchange	
Trade Component	**Example Trade Detail**
Transaction Type	Foreign Exchange Forward
Counterparty	Bank K
Trade Date	3rd March 2017
Forward Value Date	2nd May 2017
Base Currency and Amount	EUR 5,000,000.00
Quote Currency and Amount	SGD 7,661,000.00
Forward Exchange Rate	EUR 1.00/SGD 1.5322
Base Currency Seller	Firm G
Quote Currency Seller	Bank K

The similarities and differences between a spot FX trade and a forward FX trade can be summarised as follows:

- similarities: the trade is executed on trade date, and is an outright sale of one currency (base currency) against the outright purchase of a quote currency at an agreed exchange rate
- differences: the settlement cycle is extended beyond the standard 2 days to a mutually agreed future value date, and the exchange rate is typically at a premium or discount over the spot exchange rate.

18.2.3 Foreign Exchange 'Swaps'

As for spot and forward FX trades, foreign exchange swaps (FXS) are designed to mitigate foreign exchange risk.

But unlike spot and forward FX trades, FXS trades are used to borrow one currency against the loan of another currency, for a defined period of time; therefore, an FXS trade is not an outright sale of one currency and the purchase of another currency.

However, foreign exchange swaps incorporate the characteristics of both spot and forward FX trades, in a single transaction which has two legs:

- Leg 1 – on the spot value date:
  - receive Currency A
  - pay the equivalent spot value of Currency B
- Leg 2 – on the forward value date:
  - repay the same amount received of Currency A
  - receive the equivalent forward value of Currency B.

Note that the value of Currency A remains constant in both legs; this is known as the 'base' currency in a foreign exchange swap. Also note that no interest payments are applicable in a foreign exchange swap.

This situation is represented in Figure 18.4.

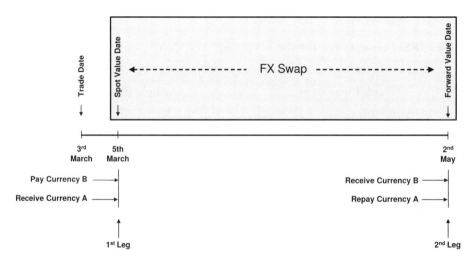

FIGURE 18.4 Profile and example of dates in a foreign exchange swap trade

Imagine that, for goods purchased from a US manufacturer (Manufacturer G), a European importer (Firm M) has committed to pay USD 10,000,000.00 in 2 business days from now. In turn, Firm M has contracted the goods to be onsold in 3 months' time; upon delivery of the goods, the buyer (Buyer T) will pay USD 10,000,000.00. Whilst Firm M's overall USD position in 3 months' time is netted to zero, there's a timing difference in cashflows. Firm M is therefore exposed to exchange rate movements over the 3-month period.

The following describes 1) what could occur if Firm M takes no action to mitigate the risk, and 2) what happens if an FXS is executed.

Firm M Takes No Action   If Firm M takes no action now, the exchange rate risk they face would be as follows:

- the amount of EUR Firm M will pay to Manufacturer G in 2 business days for the USD will depend on the exchange rate quoted for delivery that day
- the amount of EUR Firm M will receive in 3 months' time relating to the receipt of USD from Buyer T will depend on the exchange rate quoted 3 months from now. That exchange rate may be advantageous or disadvantageous to Firm M.

Regarding Firm M's payment of USD 10,000,000.00 to Manufacturer G in 2 days' time, assume the spot exchange rate is EUR 1.00/USD 1.1108. Firm M will pay EUR 9,002,520.71 (USD 10,000,000.00 / 1.1108).

If the EUR increases in value (relative to USD) during the next 3 months, the USD will become less valuable and as a consequence, in 3 months' time Firm M will receive a lesser amount of EUR when it comes time to exchange the USD received from Buyer T. Assume the exchange rate in 3 months' time is EUR 1.00/USD 1.1313, Firm M will receive EUR 8,839,388.31 (USD 10,000,000.00 / 1.1313).

These circumstances will result in a loss to Firm M of EUR 163,132.40 (EUR 9,002,520.71 – EUR 8,839,388.31).

If instead, the EUR decreases in value (relative to USD) during the next 3 months, the opposite outcome will occur and Firm M will receive more EUR. Assume the exchange rate in 3 months' time is EUR 1.00/USD 1.0896, Firm M will receive EUR 9,177,679.89 (USD 10,000,000.00 / 1.0896). This situation will result in a profit to Firm M of EUR 175,159.18 (EUR 9,002,520.71 – EUR 9,177,679.89).

As can be seen by the above example exchange rates, Firm M could make a profit if the fluctuating exchange rate falls in their favour, but equally Firm M could experience a loss if exchange rates go against them. Exchange rate fluctuations are influenced by many factors, most (if not all) of which are outside the control of Firm M. For firms that do not wish to gamble, FXS mitigate such risks.

Firm M Executes a Foreign Exchange Swap Trade   Firm M chooses not to take such a risk and executes an FXS trade with Bank Q:

- Leg 1: for spot value Firm M buys USD 10,000,000.00 (the base currency amount) with EUR 9,002,520.71, at an exchange rate of EUR 1.00/USD 1.1108, from Bank Q
- Leg 2: for forward value (3 months from now) Firm M sells USD 10,000,000.00 (the base currency amount) for EUR 9,031,791.91 at an exchange rate of EUR 1.00/USD 1.1072 to Bank Q.

The terms of the FXS are now final, meaning that Firm M has mitigated the risk and knows precisely the amounts payable and receivable over the next 3 months, regardless of the actual exchange rate in 3 months' time – both parties to the trade have locked in to both the spot and the forward rates. One important aspect of this situation is that, by executing an FXS trade, Firm M has peace of mind and thereby avoids the nagging concern as to what the exchange rate will be in 3 months' time. The cashflows applicable to this particular FXS trade are shown in Figure 18.5:

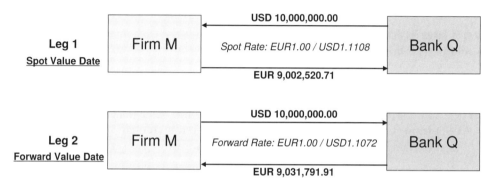

FIGURE 18.5   Example foreign exchange swap cashflows

PART 4a

Note: the difference between the spot rate and the forward rate is an adjustment factor known as the 'forward margin'; this relates to the difference in interest rates applicable to the two involved currencies. Each party has the use of a currency over the lifetime of the FXS trade, which the recipient can invest to earn a particular interest rate. The purpose of the adjustment factor is to equalise this interest rate differential and to compensate the relevant party for giving the higher interest-bearing currency.

The primary benefits in executing FXS are:

- flexibility, as firms can tailor trades to meet their specific requirements in terms of the currencies involved, start (spot) date, maturity (forward) date and duration
- certainty, as FXS trades allow firms to lock-in to exchange rates thereby removing the doubt as to how a firm will be impacted by fluctuating exchange rates.

As a technical comment, although many firms treat FX swap trades as OTC derivatives, they are not true derivatives because:

- there is no underlying product
- the full value of principal amounts is exchanged, and
- there is no payment uncertainty requiring to be managed.

18.3 TRADE COMPONENTS

Once a firm has executed an FXS trade, it must be captured without delay. The trade components that must be captured include those listed in Table 18.3 (from Firm M's perspective):

TABLE 18.3   Example foreign exchange swap trade components

Foreign Exchange Swap	
Trade Component	**Example Trade Detail**
Transaction Type	Foreign Exchange Swap
Counterparty	Bank Q
Trade Date	30th May 2017
Spot Value Date	1st June 2017
Forward Value Date	1st September 2017
Spot Payments	
Base Currency and Amount	USD 10,000,000.00
Quote Currency and Amount	EUR 9,002,520.71
Spot Exchange Rate	EUR 1.00 / USD 1.1108
Base Currency Buyer	Firm M
Quote Currency Buyer	Bank Q
Forward Payments	
Base Currency and Amount	USD 10,000,000.00
Quote Currency and Amount	EUR 9,031,791.91
Forward Exchange Rate	EUR 1.00 / USD 1.1072
Base Currency Buyer	Bank Q
Quote Currency Buyer	Firm M

18.4 FXS OPERATIONS ACTIVITY: OVERVIEW

From an operations perspective, each party to a trade must:

- make payments of currency amounts as and when they fall due, and
- monitor receipts of currency amounts when they fall due.

These actions are represented in Figure 18.6:

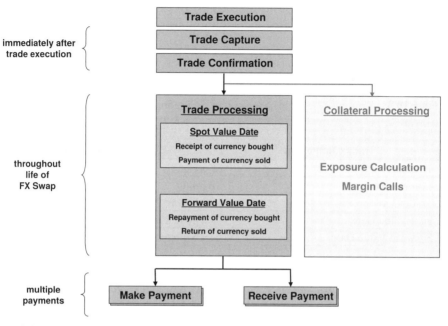

FIGURE 18.6   Foreign exchange swap processing actions

The trade processing operational activity for FXS is summarised in Table 18.4:

TABLE 18.4   FXS trade processing operational activity

Foreign Exchange Swaps	
Premium payable?	No – not applicable
Exchange of principal?	Yes – on both legs
Single/multiple currencies?	Multiple
Single/multiple settlements?	Multiple principal settlements
Payments gross or net?	Gross

18.5 FOREIGN EXCHANGE SWAPS AND COLLATERAL MANAGEMENT

Regarding collateral management, after the FXS trade has been executed the current value of the FXS trade is calculated through the regular (normally daily) *mark-to-market* process.

The party having a *positive mark-to-market* has an exposure to its counterparty, and the non-exposed party must provide collateral (in the agreed form) to the exposed party. There are a significant number of steps in this process; please refer to Chapters 24–44, all of which fall under the heading of 'The OTC Derivative Collateral Lifecycle'.

PART 4

18.6 FOREIGN EXCHANGE SWAP VARIATIONS

18.6.1 Forward/Forward Foreign Exchange Swap

Definition: a type of FXS in which both legs are forward transactions.
    For example, a '3/6 forward/forward swap' means:

- Buy 3 months swap (= sell spot, buy forward)
- Sell 6 months swap (= buy spot, sell forward)

    As both spot transactions offset each other (if done at same spot rate and same cash amount), the result of both transactions will be as follows:

- buy base currency 3 months forward, and
- sell base currency 6 months forward.

    Forward/forward FX swaps are also known as:

- forward swap
- forward start swap
- delayed start swap
- deferred start swap.

CHAPTER 19

OTC Derivatives and Collateral – Transaction Types – Cross-Currency Swaps

This chapter describes the purpose of and characteristics of cross-currency swaps, another type of OTC derivative product. A particular reason for covering this topic is to highlight the specific characteristics of cross-currency swaps, to enable comparison with the similar sounding product foreign exchange swaps (as covered within the previous chapter). Particularly for those readers that are unfamiliar with foreign exchange operations and settlement, it is recommended that the foreign exchange swaps chapter is read prior to reading this chapter, as fundamental concepts of foreign exchange are covered therein.

19.1 DEFINITION

A cross-currency swap (CCS) is an OTC derivative contract in which two parties exchange principal amounts in different currencies at the start of the trade, with the reverse exchange occurring at the close of the trade, and with the exchange of interest payments in different currencies periodically, during a set period of time.

CCS are part of a family of financial products known as *currency derivatives*.

CCS are also known as 'foreign currency swaps', 'plain vanilla foreign currency swaps', and 'back-to-back loans'.

Note: in a cross-currency swap, because the principal amounts are paid in full, the term 'notional' (meaning 'theoretical') is not applicable, consequently the terms 'principal' and 'principal amount' are used instead.

19.2 PURPOSE

CCS are used to borrow cash in currencies other than a firm's domestic currency, at lower interest rates not otherwise accessible. They are also used to *hedge* exposure to *exchange rate risk.*

Imagine that a British multinational company (Company T) wishes to expand its operations into Australia. Simultaneously, an Australian company (Company V) is seeking entrance into the UK market.

Financial problems that Company T will typically face stem from overseas banks' unwillingness to extend loans to international corporations. Therefore, in order to borrow cash in Australia, Company T might be subject to an unacceptably high interest rate.

Similarly, Company V is unlikely to be able to borrow GBP at a favourable interest rate in the UK market, and may therefore be facing prohibitively high interest rates.

While the cost of borrowing in the international market for both companies is unreasonably high, both companies enjoy an advantage when borrowing cash from their domestic banks. The UK-based Company T is currently able to borrow cash from a UK bank at (for example) 3%, and the Australia-based Company V can borrow from its local institutions at (for example) 4%. The reason for this discrepancy in lending rates is due to 1) the natural variations that occur between interest rates in different countries, and 2) the partnerships and ongoing relationships that domestic companies usually have with their local lending institutions.

Based on each company's *comparative advantage* of borrowing cash in their domestic markets at very competitive rates, a cross-currency swap is executed:

- for the funds required by Company V, Company T will borrow from a UK bank at 3%, and
- for the funds required by Company T, Company V will borrow from an Australian bank at 4%,

in both cases for a period of 4 years. Each company has effectively taken out a loan on behalf of its counterparty.

The exchange rate at the time of *trade execution* is AUD 1.5572 / GBP 1.00; Company T receives AUD 155,720,000.00 from its Australian counterparty in exchange for GBP 100,000,000.00, and vice versa for Company V.

19.2.1 Initial Exchange of Principal Amounts

As a first step in settlement of the CCS, the respective principal amounts are paid to the counterparty on the value date of the first leg, as shown in Figure 19.1.

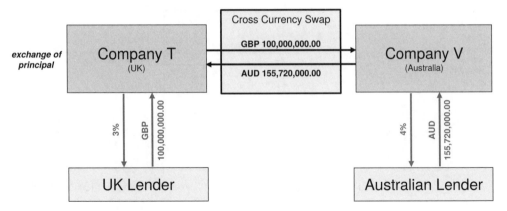

FIGURE 19.1   The initial exchange of principal in a cross-currency swap

The CCS satisfies the needs of both firms for funds receivable in the alternative currency at a reasonable rate of interest.

However, as in any other foreign exchange transaction type where the currencies involved are not in the same time zone, due to time zone differences between Australia and the UK, *Herstatt Risk* is applicable. Use of *CLS Bank* is the primary method of overcoming such settlement risk. (Refer to Chapter 18 'OTC Derivatives and Collateral – Transaction Types – Foreign Exchange Swaps' for an explanation of Herstatt Risk and CLS Bank.)

19.2.2 Periodic Exchange of Interest Payments

For both firms, when the cash borrowing was executed with their respective domestic bank (namely the UK lender for Company T and the Australian lender for Company V), a commitment was made for each company to pay interest to the lender on the cash borrowing, in the original currency, at an agreed interest rate and at an agreed frequency.

At intervals defined within the CCS trade terms (agreed at trade execution), interest payments on the respective principal amounts will be exchanged. If, for example, the terms are for annual interest payments, assume the first payment is to occur 1 year after trade execution.

Because Company T has borrowed AUD from the counterparty, it must remit interest based upon the AUD interest rate (agreed at trade execution) of 4.0%. Because Company V has borrowed GBP, it must remit interest based upon the GBP interest rate (agreed at trade execution) of 3.0% (see Figure 19.2).

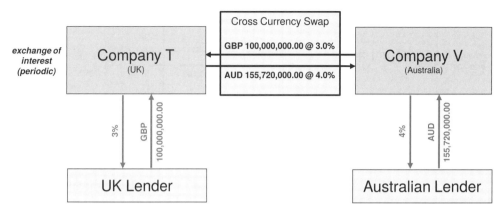

FIGURE 19.2   The periodic exchange of interest in a cross-currency swap

The annual interest amounts payable by each firm are shown in Table 19.1:

TABLE 19.1   Interest calculation

Firm	Principal Amount Borrowed (Swapped)	Interest Rate	Annual Interest Payable
Company T	AUD 155,720,000.00	4.0%	AUD 6,228,800.00
Company V	GBP 100,000,000.00	3.0%	GBP 3,000,000.00

This procedure must be followed at each interest payment date.

Note: if instead of annual interest payments, semi-annual payments had been nego-tiated at trade execution, the calculation of each interest payment would need to take account of 1) the date from which interest accrues, 2) the specific payment date, and 3) the relevant currency divisor (which for both GBP and AUD is 365).

In summary, each company has to pay interest on the original borrowed currency to their respective domestic lending banks, at the agreed frequency. Although Company T swapped GBP for AUD, it still must satisfy its obligation to the UK lender in GBP. Company V faces a similar situation with its domestic bank. As a result, both compa-nies will incur interest payments equivalent to their counterparty's cost of borrowing; this point forms the basis of the advantages that a currency swap provides.

19.2.3 Re-Exchange of Principal Amounts

As a final step, at the close of the cross-currency swap (usually also the date of the final interest payments), the parties are required to repay the original principal amounts, which remain unaffected by exchange rates (see Figure 19.3).

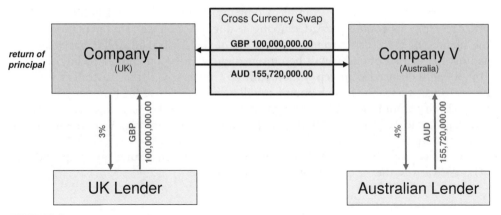

FIGURE 19.3   The return of principal in a cross-currency swap trade

Additionally, each company must repay the original cash lender at the maturity date of the borrowing.

Note: in a cross-currency swap, the exchange rate determined at trade execution (which is applied for payment of principal initially) is also applicable to the return of principal on the scheduled maturity date of the CCS. Primary distinguishing factors between cross-currency swaps and foreign exchange swaps are:

- the use of a single exchange rate in a cross-currency swap, as opposed to a spot exchange rate and a different forward exchange rate in a foreign exchange swap, and
- the application of periodic interest payments in a cross-currency swap, as opposed to no interest payments in a foreign exchange swap.

The primary benefits in executing CCS are:

- reduced costs of borrowing a particular currency; rather than borrowing directly from overseas cash lenders at an unacceptably high interest rate, each party borrows cash at domestic rates then lends to the counterparty at an agreed lower interest rate
- flexibility, as firms can tailor trades to meet their specific requirements in terms of the currencies involved, start date, interest rates, maturity date, and duration
- certainty, as CCS trades allow firms to lock in to the borrowing of an overseas currency at an agreed exchange rate and interest rate, thereby removing the doubt as to how a firm will be impacted by fluctuating exchange rates.

However, a risk exists for both parties; the original borrowed principal amount must be returned to the counterparty upon reaching the ***scheduled maturity date*** of

PART 4a

the cross-currency swap. For example, Company V must find GBP 100,000,000.00 in order to repay its counterparty, Company T; due to exchange rate fluctuation during the lifetime of the cross-currency swap trade, if the Australian dollar has weakened against the British pound it will be more expensive for Company V to buy the GBP 100,000,000.00 needed to repay Company T. Conversely, if the Australian dollar is now stronger versus the British pound, it will be less expensive for Company V to raise the necessary amount of GBP to repay Company T. A similar risk exists for Company T in raising the AUD 155,720,000.00 required to repay Company V on the scheduled maturity date.

As a technical comment, although many firms treat cross-currency swap trades as OTC derivatives, they are not true derivatives because:

- there is no underlying product
- the full value of principal amounts is exchanged, and
- there is no payment uncertainty requiring to be managed.

19.3 TRADE COMPONENTS

Once a firm has executed a CCS trade, it must be captured without delay. The trade components that must be captured include those shown in Table 19.2 (from Company T's perspective):

TABLE 19.2   Example cross-currency swap trade components

Cross-Currency Swap	
Trade Component	**Example Trade Detail**
Transaction Type	Cross-Currency Swap
Counterparty	Company V
Trade Date	15th July 2017
Effective Date (1st Leg Value Date)	17th July 2017
Scheduled Maturity Date (2nd Leg Value Date)	17th July 2021
Base Currency & Principal Amount	GBP 100,000,000.00
Quote Currency & Principal Amount	AUD 155,720,000.00
Exchange Rate	GBP 1.00 / AUD 1.5572
Base Currency Lender	Company T
Quote Currency Lender	Company V
Base Currency Interest Rate	3.0%
Quote Currency Interest Rate	4.0%
Base Currency Interest Payment Dates	17th July Annual
Quote Currency Interest Payment Dates	17th July Annual

19.4 CCS OPERATIONS ACTIVITY: OVERVIEW

From an operations perspective, each party to a trade must:

- make payment of the currency principal amount lent on the value date of the initial exchange
- ensure receipt of the currency principal amount borrowed on the value date of the initial exchange
- make payment of interest on the currency borrowed (repeated according to agreed frequency)
- ensure receipt of interest on the currency lent (repeated according to agreed frequency)
- make repayment of the currency principal amount borrowed on the scheduled maturity date
- ensure receipt of the currency principal amount lent on the scheduled maturity date.

These actions are represented in Figure 19.4:

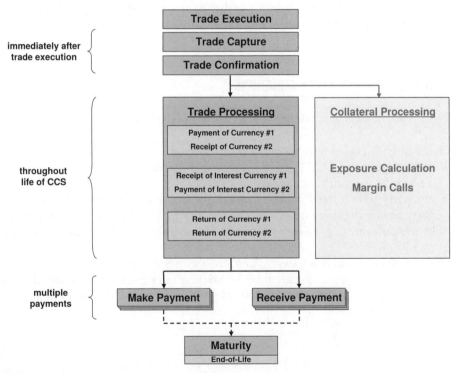

FIGURE 19.4   Cross-currency swap processing actions

The trade processing operational activity for CCS is summarised in Table 19.3:

TABLE 19.3   CCS trade processing operational activity

Cross-Currency Swaps	
Premium payable?	No – not applicable
Exchange of principal?	Yes – on both legs
Single/multiple currencies?	Multiple
Single/multiple settlements?	Multiple principal settlements & multiple interest settlements
Payments gross or net?	Gross – for both principal amounts & interest amounts

19.5 CROSS-CURRENCY SWAPS AND COLLATERAL MANAGEMENT

Regarding collateral management, after the CCS trade has been executed the current value of the CCS trade is calculated through the regular (normally daily) *mark-to-market* process.

The party having a *positive mark-to-market* has an exposure to its counterparty, and the non-exposed party must provide collateral (in the agreed form) to the exposed party. There are a significant number of steps in this process; please refer to Chapters 24–44, all of which fall under the heading of 'The OTC Derivative Collateral Lifecycle'.

19.6 CROSS-CURRENCY SWAP VARIATIONS

Different types of CCS exist along with a variety of labels, such as:

- 'Back-to-back currency swaps' and 'fixed-to-fixed currency swaps'
  - this is the type of CCS described within this chapter
- 'Fixed-for-floating currency swaps'
  - one party pays a fixed interest rate on one of the currencies while the counterparty pays a floating interest rate on the alternate currency, based on a floating benchmark rate (e.g. *Libor* or *Euribor*). Comparable to a 'fixed-for-floating interest rate swap'
- 'Floating/floating currency swaps' and 'cross-currency basis swaps'
  - one party will pay a specific form of floating interest rate (e.g. 1-month Libor) on one currency, while the counterparty will pay a different form of floating rate (e.g. 3-month Libor) on the alternate currency.

CHAPTER 20

OTC Derivatives and Collateral – Legal Protection – Introduction

This chapter introduces the legal documentation necessary to put in place before any trade in OTC derivatives is executed, and therefore prior to the requirement either to give or to receive collateral.

Please note that the contents of this chapter represent the author's own view of how the documentation produced by the International Swaps and Derivatives Association (ISDA) is normally used by financial institutions and is not an ISDA official guide of how to understand or to complete or to use such documentation. Readers are advised to take their own legal advice regarding the implementation and use of such documentation.

A trade executed in an *OTC derivative* product typically has a lifetime (or duration) of anything between a few weeks to many years; a single trade which has a lifetime of tens of years (e.g. 50 years) is not unheard of.

Whatever the duration of an OTC derivative trade, a party to that trade has on-going *counterparty risk* with its counterparty for the entire duration of the trade, until the trade's *scheduled maturity date*. For example, a firm (Entity A) executes an *interest rate swap* trade for a lifetime of 20 years, with Party B; the terms of the trade require settlement of interest payments every 6 months throughout the lifetime of the trade. This means that Entity A expects Party B (and vice versa) to comply with its *contractual obligations* agreed at *trade execution*, including the *settlement* of interest payments, for the entirety of the 20 years.

Because of the commitments entered into by both parties to the trade over such an extended period of time, normal market practice is to specify the ongoing commitments of both parties in legal documentation, which states the responsibilities of both parties and their legal rights in case of non-performance by the counterparty.

Note: readers that are familiar with **securities** (equity and bond) operations, but new to the world of OTC derivatives, may be wondering why such legal documentation is not applicable to the buying and selling of securities. The normal duration of trades (*settlement cycle*) in securities markets is expressed in numbers of days, ranging from (at the time of writing) T+0 (e.g. in Saudi Arabia), T+1 (e.g. for US Treasuries and UK Gilts), to T+2 in Europe and in the USA. The vast majority of securities trades settle on schedule, on their **value date**; however, **settlement failure** (delayed settlement) occurs in many markets, but most failed trades will settle within a few days following their value date. Consequently, the duration of a very high percentage of securities trades is a matter of days, rather than months and years as is the case with OTC derivative trades; therefore, counterparty risk is very short-lived in most securities trades and, as a result, there has been no reason for the kind of legal documentation necessary for OTC derivatives.

The normal starting point for putting in place the legal documentation between two parties that intend to execute OTC derivative trades with one another, is the *ISDA™ Master Agreement*. The *International Swaps and Derivatives Association* (ISDA)[1] is the principal global trade organisation for the OTC derivatives marketplace.

When trading in (what are now known as) OTC derivatives first became popular in the early 1980s, the firms executing such trades would assess their risks and create legal documentation according to the terms of each trade. But much of the wording within such documentation for each trade remained the same, apart from the specific terms of an individual trade. As trading volumes increased and the popularity of OTC derivatives grew, there was a growing need to make the production of legal documentation less time-consuming and more efficient. In the mid-1980s, ISDA was formed; ISDA was instrumental in creating the first ISDA master agreement, a legal document containing standardised terms and conditions for use by all users of OTC derivatives. Periodically, over the years ISDA has produced updated versions of the ISDA master agreement, for example the 1992 ISDA Master Agreement and the 2002 ISDA Master Agreement.

For its own protection, it is essential that a firm that wishes to enter into an OTC derivative trade does so only after having signed the necessary legal documentation (usually the ISDA master agreement and its associated documents) prior to trade execution.

The following chapters describe the content and use of the ISDA master agreement, and its related documents.

---

[1] ISDA is the registered trademark of the International Swaps and Derivatives Association.

CHAPTER 21

OTC Derivatives and Collateral – Legal Protection – Master Agreement and Schedule

This chapter describes the purpose of and role played by the OTC derivative-related master agreement, and the associated schedule to the master agreement, covering the circumstances under which such legal documents are utilised between two trading parties.

Please note that the contents of this chapter represent the author's own view of how the documentation produced by the International Swaps and Derivatives Association (ISDA) is normally used by financial institutions and is not an ISDA official guide of how to understand or to complete or to use such documentation. Readers are advised to take their own legal advice regarding the implementation and use of such documentation.

21.1 INTRODUCTION

The *ISDA Master Agreement* (IMA) is a commonly used standard for documenting the legal arrangements between two parties that intend trading with one another in a variety of *OTC derivative* product types, such as *interest rate swaps* and *credit default swaps*. The IMA is produced by the *International Swaps and Derivatives Association*

(ISDA) and is designed for use by all organisations that trade in OTC derivatives, around the globe.

Generically, IMAs have been developed and refined over many years to reflect the typically agreed legal terms and conditions that govern *bilateral* trading relationships in OTC derivatives.

OTC derivatives are used by thousands of companies based in all regions, in a variety of industries, in order to *mitigate* the *exposures* that arise from their business activities. The types of organisation that use OTC derivatives, and therefore the ISDA master agreement, include:

- governments
- supranational organisations
- corporations
- mutual funds
- pension funds
- insurance companies
- asset managers
- investment banks, and
- regional banks

thereby encompassing both *buy-side* and *sell-side* firms.

ISDA master agreements are used as a starting point for documenting legal arrangements between two trading firms; furthermore, a set of documents are signed (including the IMA) which together form a structured document framework covering all aspects of the legal relationship. The set of documents is:

- the <u>ISDA Master Agreement</u>: this is the key document which defines the essential responsibilities of both parties, using predefined and standard terms and conditions (and which is typically <u>not</u> tailored to record particular arrangements between the two specific parties)
  - two versions of the IMA are still in use today, namely the 1992 ISDA Master Agreement and the 2002 ISDA Master Agreement
- the <u>Schedule</u>: this is the second legal document (after the IMA) and is used to record the particular arrangements desired by both organisations, over and above the content of the ISDA master agreement
- the <u>Credit Support Annex</u> (CSA): this is the third legal document and is used to record the particular arrangements relating specifically to the posting of OTC derivative-related *collateral* between the two parties.

The OTC derivative structured document framework is represented in Figure 21.1:

Step 1: the master agreement is used as a starting point for negotiation between two parties

Step 2: the Schedule contains agreed amendments to the master agreement

Step 3: the CSA contains the collateral terms applicable when exposures arise.

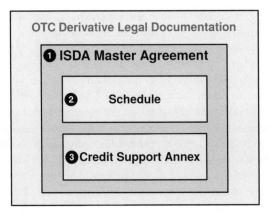

FIGURE 21.1   Relationship between ISDA Master Agreement, Schedule and Credit Support Annex

It is important to note that despite the Schedule and the CSA being separate documents from the IMA, both fall under and within the terms and conditions of the ISDA Master Agreement. The IMA can therefore be considered to be the 'umbrella' document under which the Schedule and CSA fit.

The process of the two trading parties signing the set of documents can take a significant length of time, due to the preferences of the individual firms which will ultimately be reflected within the two tailored documents, namely the Schedule and the CSA. This is a negotiation process which can involve many iterations and can last many months before agreement is reached, typically conducted by a firm's Legal Department or specialist lawyers appointed by the firm.

Once negotiation has been completed and both parties have applied their signatures, each of the documents will 1) state the names of the two organisations, and 2) be dated. This means that there is a real possibility that a set of legal documents put in place by Party A, with its counterparty Firm B, will be unique in terms of the content. To be clear on this point, although the IMA is not amended, both the Schedule and the CSA will be tailored to reflect the specific requirements of both parties. Consequently, if an organisation has (for example) 50 or 100 counterparties with whom it executes OTC derivative trades, the real probability exists that no two sets of legal documents are exactly the same. This probability has knock-on consequences for *collateral management*, as each CSA an organisation has in place with its various counterparties is highly likely to contain unique features; and collateral management of OTC derivatives must be conducted according to the parameters stated within each CSA, otherwise exposures may not be mitigated in the manner recorded within the legal documentation. (The purpose and content of the CSA are detailed within Chapter 22 'OTC Derivatives and Collateral – Legal Protection – Credit Support Annex'.)

Once the document framework has been signed by both parties, all OTC derivative trades executed between the parties fall under the umbrella of the framework. An exception to this can be where trades are executed in newly created OTC derivative products that have been traded after the document framework had been put in place.

Because some organisations have been executing trades in OTC derivatives for many years, the possibility exists that a set of legal documents that a firm has with a particular counterparty may have been signed many years ago, and no longer reflects the preferences (terms and conditions) that are required 'today'. Under such circumstances, an organisation may agree with a particular counterparty to renegotiate the set of legal documents; once the new set is signed by both parties, the new terms and conditions will apply and effectively override the original set of documents.

Immediately following trade execution, a **trade confirmation** is required to be issued by one party to its counterparty; the trade confirmation is intended to reflect the specific details of an individual trade. A trade confirmation is also a legal document and is in addition to the set of documents signed prior to the first trade being executed. The trade confirmation falls under the terms and conditions of the ISDA master agreement.

21.2 CONTENT OF THE ISDA MASTER AGREEMENT

When an organisation executes an OTC derivative trade, as mentioned previously the duration of the trade can range from a matter of months to tens of years. During the lifetime of the trade, both parties to the trade are expected to fulfil their **contractual obligations**; such obligations differ amongst the various OTC derivative product types.

Amongst a range of clauses, the IMA states terms and conditions defining what constitutes **default** (by either party) on its contractual obligations. For example, if a firm's counterparty becomes bankrupt, such an occurrence (under the heading of an **Event of Default** in the IMA) triggers the termination of live (open) OTC derivative trades between the two firms.

AUTHOR'S COMMENT AND DISCLAIMER

The events listed within this chapter are 1) the author's interpretation of a selection of terms and conditions contained within an ISDA master agreement, and are 2) the author's explanation of such events in plain English and non-legal language so as to be meaningful to the target audience for this book, and are 3) intended to convey the general nature of the master agreement and are in no way intended to be an exhaustive list of all terms and conditions contained within an ISDA master agreement.

21.2.1 Events of Default

An event of default is an occurrence of a documented event within the IMA, caused by either of the parties to the IMA, that results in all trades with the counterparty to be terminated without delay and prior to their **scheduled maturity date**.

Such events, which are applicable to both parties, include:

- ▪ Failure to Pay or Deliver: failure to 1) remit cash or 2) to deliver securities to the counterparty, when falling due and failing to be made within a specified number of days that follow

- <u>Breach of Agreement</u>: failure to act on any aspect (except payment or delivery) of the IMA or associated document and failing to act within a specified number of days following
- <u>Collateral Default</u>: failure to act on any collateral-related aspect of the Credit Support Annex and failing to act within a specified grace period that follows. This event of default falls under the heading of *Credit Support Default* within the IMA
- <u>Bankruptcy</u>: if a party to the agreement is declared bankrupt, or is incapable of paying its debts when falling due, or is the subject of an insolvency or liquidation decision
- <u>Merger</u>: if a party to the agreement merges with another organisation, and the new combined entity fails to assume the legal obligations of the original party.

Should any such event of default arise, a Right to Terminate Following Event of Default is invoked, resulting in *early termination* of the underlying trades (beyond which no further requirement to give or to take collateral exists).

21.2.2 Termination Events

A termination event, similar to an event of default, is an occurrence of a documented event within the IMA, except the cause of the event is not associated with either of the parties to the IMA; however, the outcome is the same, as all trades between the two parties are terminated prior to their *scheduled maturity date*.

Such events, which are applicable to both parties, include:

- <u>Change in Law</u>: following trade execution, should a new law be enacted, or should an existing law be reinterpreted, which makes cash payments and/or receipts, and securities deliveries and/or receipts unlawful, pertaining to the transaction and the collateral. This termination event falls under the heading of *Illegality* within the IMA
- <u>Change in Tax Law</u>: following trade execution, should a law be passed that requires either party to pay a tax amount or an additional tax amount pertaining to the transaction and the collateral. This termination event falls under the heading of *Tax Event* within the IMA.

Should any such termination event arise, a Right to Terminate Following Termination Event is invoked, resulting in early termination of the underlying trades (beyond which no further requirement to give or to take collateral exists).

21.2.3 Other Terms and Conditions

Many more terms and conditions are listed within the ISDA master agreement, including:

- the deadline by which certain notices must be issued; for example, in the case of an event of default, the non-defaulting party is required to issue a written communication to the defaulting party by a specified deadline in order to propose an *early termination date*

- the requirement of either party to notify the counterparty of a termination event as soon as possible, listing all impacted transactions
- following early termination, the requirement of both parties to calculate amounts payable or receivable and to formally notify its counterparty of such calculations and the account into which the receiving party requires payment to be made
- the date that payment following early termination becomes payable, and that interest is payable (if applicable) and how such interest is to be calculated
- the method of communicating notifications between the parties, such as on paper and delivered in person, by fax (where permitted), or electronically, plus when the notice becomes effective (dependent upon transmission method)
- should legal actions be brought by either party, the authority of the court, dependent upon whether the agreement is made under English law or New York law.

21.2.4 Close Out Netting

For an event of default, early termination within the IMA provides for all outstanding trades to be closed and resultant cash owed by both parties to be settled on a net basis, through a single payment. This procedure is known as *close out netting*.

By way of an example, assume that Party A and Party B have executed 5 separate OTC derivative trades in the past 3 years, all of which have a scheduled termination date in the future, and which are outstanding today, at which point an event of default occurs. Party B is the party in default. In order to effect close out netting in such situations, the close out value (replacement value) of each trade must be assessed, as depicted in Table 21.1:

TABLE 21.1   Close out netting

Close Out Netting			
Net Payment Calculation			
Trade Number	Trade Replacement Cost	In Favour of...	
1	USD 3,200,000.00		Party B
2	USD 650,000.00	Party A	
3	USD 4,100,000.00	Party A	
4	USD 3,750,000.00		Party B
5	USD 475,000.00		Party B
	Total per Party	USD 4,750,000.00	USD 7,425,000.00
	Net Payable		USD 2,675,000.00

Without close out netting written in to the IMA, closure of trades following an event of default is required to be managed on a gross (trade-by-trade) basis. In this example Party A would be required to remit a total of USD 7,425,000.00 to the *defaulting party*, without delay. And whilst Party B would owe a total of USD 4,750,000.00 to Party A, the bankruptcy process may cause a significant delay in payment, and furthermore, the amount ultimately paid on behalf of the defaulting party may well be significantly short of the full amount owed.

With close out netting forming part of the terms and conditions of the ISDA Master agreement, closure of trades following an event of default is required to be managed on a net basis. In this example early termination requires the non-defaulting party (Party A) to remit the net cash amount of USD 2,675,000.00 to the defaulting party. Had the situation been reversed and the net cash amount been payable by the defaulting party, Party A would become a general creditor from Party B's perspective.

In summary, close out netting provides both parties, in relation to an event of default, with the power to close out multiple gross trades, by a single net payment. This concept prevents the bankrupt firm's liquidator from choosing 1) to demand immediate payment on trades in favour of the bankrupt firm (Party B), and 2) to delay payment on trades in favour of the non-defaulting party (Party A).

Furthermore, where Party A (the non-defaulting party) is owed the net close out value by Party B (the defaulting party), and if Party A holds collateral previously given by Party B, such collateral may be sold by Party A in order to realise the cash value it is owed.

21.3 CONTENT OF THE SCHEDULE TO THE MASTER AGREEMENT

Following agreement of specific terms and conditions mutually agreed by both parties, the schedule to the master agreement is the document that is used to formally record any such amendments to the IMA.

Examples of such specific terms are:

- whether a particular provision does or does not apply to a particular party or to both parties
- whether, in relation to a particular event (e.g. a termination event), an additional provision applies.

The schedule is also used to record, for example:

- specified documents (e.g. tax certificates) that are to be delivered, the party responsible for doing so and the associated deadline
- recipient addresses (regarding notifications), contact names, email addresses and telephone numbers for both parties
- details of the document detailing collateral arrangements, namely the *Credit Support Annex*
- the governing law applicable to the IMA (usually a choice between English law and New York law)
- whether recorded telephone conversations between the two parties are permitted and, if so, whether permitted for use within any legal proceedings.

The finalised schedule must be signed and dated by both parties.

21.4 NEGOTIATING AND SIGNING THE DOCUMENT FRAMEWORK

Reaching the target of the two involved firms signing the document framework can be a quite lengthy process, in some cases lasting a number of months.

The reason for such a time frame is most commonly associated with the iterative process of negotiating details of amendments that are ultimately documented within the schedule to the master agreement.

A firm's Legal Department are central to this process; for those firms without such a department, it is essential that external lawyers are hired for the purpose of protecting the firm's interests and ensuring the finally agreed document framework adequately covers the firm's perceived risks.

21.5 TRADING FOLLOWING SIGNING OF DOCUMENT FRAMEWORK

Once the set of documents has been agreed and signed, trading can commence between the two parties.

As the intention is that all trades are executed under the umbrella of the document framework, following **trade execution** there is no requirement other than for the involved parties to exchange details of individual trades to ensure accuracy of trades captured within each firm's **books & records**.

This is achieved by a process commonly known as **trade confirmation** or simply 'confirmation'; see the next section.

Agreed trade details in turn ensures both parties have the same foundation from which operational actions can occur correctly throughout the trade's lifetime. For example, payments of **premium** from a **trade processing** perspective, and **exposure** calculations from a **collateral processing** perspective.

21.6 TRADE CONFIRMATION

Following trade execution and **trade capture**, significant risks exist at this point for both parties.

For example, an **IRS** trade executed by a firm for a **notional principal** of USD 10,000,000 could in error be captured by one of the parties to the trade as USD 1,000,000 or as USD 100,000,000. It is imperative that errors such as this are identified and rectified immediately following trade execution. If such errors fail to be detected and corrected immediately, any subsequent action relating directly to the trade will (in this example where the notional principal is different) result in an underpayment or overpayment, and calculation of exposures (following which collateral will be given or taken) will be ten times too great or too small.

Due to the risks involved it is paramount for the involved parties to verify the details of every OTC derivative trade through the trade confirmation process. This process involves each party communicating their trade details for comparison, resulting in either 1) immediate agreement, or 2) identification of a discrepancy which then must be investigated and corrected without delay.

Trade confirmation is achieved either manually or electronically, largely dependent upon the particular OTC derivative product.

This subject is covered in detail within Chapter 29 'OTC Derivatives and Collateral – The Collateral Lifecycle – Post-Trading – Trade Confirmation/Affirmation'.

21.7 SUMMARY

The legal document framework for bilateral trading of OTC derivatives encompasses the ISDA Master Agreement, the Schedule to the master agreement and the Credit Support Annex.

From an individual firm's perspective, the primary purpose of such documents is to set out terms and conditions that protect the firm under a variety of circumstances, and which are legally enforceable should such circumstances arise.

Although the mutual signing of such documents is frequently a lengthy process, ideally trading with the particular counterparty should be prevented until signing has been completed, in order for a firm to avoid the risks associated with having inadequate legal protection.

PART 4a

OTC Derivatives and Collateral – Legal Protection – Credit Support Annex

This chapter describes the purpose of the Credit Support Annex (CSA), its impact on collateral management, its typical content and its use on a day-to-day basis. This chapter is targeted at readers that have had no exposure or limited exposure to the legal documentation relating to OTC derivative trades. The CSA is the primary document used by collateral professionals on a day-to-day basis regarding margin calls resulting from exposures on OTC derivative trades.

Please note that the contents of this chapter represent the author's own view of how the documentation produced by the International Swaps and Derivatives Association (ISDA) is normally used by financial institutions and is not an ISDA official guide of how to understand or to complete or to use such documentation. Readers are advised to take their own legal advice regarding the implementation and use of such documentation.

22.1 INTRODUCTION

A Credit Support Annex (CSA) is an addendum to the legal documentation signed between two parties that intend to execute OTC derivative trades with each other; it is effectively a procedural rulebook for the management of collateral between the two firms.

Its specific purpose is to document the terms and conditions under which the posting of collateral is to occur between the two parties. In most cases, such terms and conditions are applicable to both parties; this is known as a **bilateral CSA**. In other cases, where there is a difference in the credit rating of the two parties, a strongly rated party may be unwilling to post collateral, consequently the lesser rated party is the only party required to provide collateral; this is known as a *one-way CSA*.

The CSA is not a standalone document. It is directly associated with the ISDA master agreement and schedule which are also signed by the two parties. The relationship between such legal documentation and collateral is depicted in the diagram below, as are the fundamental steps necessary to utilise the CSA:

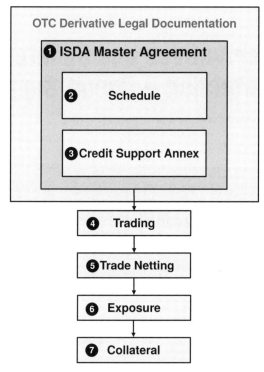

FIGURE 22.1 Relationship between legal documentation, trading, netting, exposure and collateral

The diagram is explained as follows:

Step 1: the master agreement is used as a starting point for negotiation between two parties

Step 2: the schedule contains agreed amendments to the master agreement

Step 3: the CSA contains the terms regarding the posting of collateral, when exposures arise

Step 4: once the legal documentation is in place, trading in OTC derivatives can commence

Step 5: trading may result in trade netting, where the same OTC derivative product has been traded previously with the same counterparty

Step 6: *exposures* arise from trading in OTC derivatives

Step 7: *collateral* must be given to the *exposed party*, according to the terms and conditions stated in the CSA.

22.2 SIGNING OF CSA AND TRADE EXECUTION

It is normal practice for a CSA to be signed at the same time that the master agreement and schedule are signed. It is also highly desirable that such documents are fully signed and in place prior to execution of the first trade between the two concerned parties. If this is practised, any trade executed subsequently will be subject to the terms and conditions contained within the CSA; an exception to this rule may arise if a trade is executed in an OTC derivative product that is not covered by the CSA.

If trades are executed prior to the CSA being put in place, alternative and specific collateral arrangements will need to be agreed and documented on a trade-by-trade basis. Such arrangements are reflected in a communication issued by a firm to its counterparty, known as a *Long Form Confirmation*.

Within an organisation, multiple stakeholders are involved and are required to give their approval prior to signing the legal documentation with the counterparty. Such stakeholders include Trading, Risk Management, Portfolio Management, the Legal Department and the *Operations Department*.

22.3 NEW VERSUS OLD CSAs

For an individual firm that has been in business for a number of years, some of its current CSAs with its various counterparties may well have been negotiated, in some cases, many years ago, whilst other of the firm's CSAs may have been negotiated quite recently. Consequently, the content of a firm's CSAs with its various counterparties may vary significantly.

Today, the firm may regard the content of some of the older CSAs as being out-of-date and ideally in need of renegotiation with the counterparty. Renegotiation of CSA content with a counterparty involves a firm's Legal Department or the hiring of external lawyers and is a process that can take weeks and months to complete; consequently such 'legacy' CSAs may remain live and valid even though a firm may prefer to update the contents. However, as an alternative to renegotiation, amendments to CSAs are possible, where a particular CSA may contain multiple amendments.

22.4 OTC DERIVATIVE EXPOSURES

Exposures arise on OTC derivative trades as follows. (Note: a generic description of how such exposures arise is covered within Chapter 15 'OTC Derivatives Trades – Transaction Types – Generic Structural Aspects', Section 15.4 'OTC Derivatives: Exposure and Collateral Management'.)

On trade date of an OTC derivative trade such as an *interest rate swap* (IRS) or a *credit default swap* (CDS), the value to both trading parties is zero; this means that the two parties have agreed a rate or price which is equitable, with neither party having a financial advantage over the other at the onset of a trade. The reason for such an equitable rate or price is that the trade must be fair to both parties, which can only be achieved through negotiating a zero (or neutral) value. Note that profits and losses will emerge as rates evolve during the lifetime of the trade.

PART 4a

Following *trade execution* however, at any one point in time (during the lifetime of the trade) and as a result of the *mark-to-market* (M2M) process, the trade is deemed to be profitable to one of the trading parties due to movements in market rates or prices, in comparison to the rate or price at which the trade was executed on trade date. The party currently in profit is said to have a *positive mark-to-market* or *positive exposure* (and the opposite for the counterparty).

Although good news for the party currently in profit, that party also has *counterparty risk*; if their counterparty goes out of business 'today', all future contractual commitments relating to the trade will not be fulfilled.

Under these circumstances, it is assumed that the remaining (non-defaulting) party will want to replace the original trade, in which case the replacement trade will be executed at the (less favourable) current market rate or price. In other words, such an exposure to the non-defaulting party is said to be the trade's *replacement cost*. In the normal course of events and on a daily basis (where neither party has defaulted), in order to *mitigate* the risk that the cost of replacement is greater than the cost of the original trade, under the terms of the specific CSA between the two parties, the party with the positive exposure will issue a *margin call* to its counterparty (the party with the *negative exposure)* who is then required to satisfy the margin call by delivering collateral (usually cash or bonds, as per the specific CSA) in order to mitigate the exposed party's risk.

However, it is essential to appreciate that, from a firm's perspective, such counterparty risk occurs:

1. when a counterparty defaults, <u>and if</u>
2. the trade is profitable for the firm (the non-defaulting party).

In other words, from the firm's perspective only profitable trades carry counterparty risk; non-profitable trades do not carry counterparty risk. For example, imagine that Party A is a protection buyer in a *credit default swap* executed (say) 18 months ago, at 115 *basis points per annum* (bppa), with Party B. The current price is 122 bppa, which means that the trade is currently profitable for Party A who, under these circumstances, has counterparty risk. Conversely, if the current market price is instead 109 bppa, the trade is currently loss-making for Party A and as a result Party A has no counterparty risk because if Party B defaults, Party A would simply execute a replacement trade in the market at the current rate or price (which is currently a more advantageous rate or price for Party A, compared with the original 115 bppa). However, in such a loss-making situation for Party A, if the counterparty defaults Party A would need to settle the outstanding debt by payment to the counterparty; in this scenario, there is no counterparty risk from Party A's perspective as they are not owed money by the counterparty.

To confirm and to clarify, the key principles regarding exposures in OTC derivative trades are:

- the initial value of an OTC derivative trade is zero
- as rates evolve the trade/position will reveal a profit or a loss
- the in-profit party has counterparty risk to the extent of the replacement cost
- counterparty risk for the in-profit party is mitigated through issuance of margin calls and receipt of collateral from the counterparty.

An example of how exposures arise in OTC derivatives is depicted by use of a credit default swap trade, in which end-of-day prices are used (note that *fixed coupons* are ignored for ease of explanation and illustration):

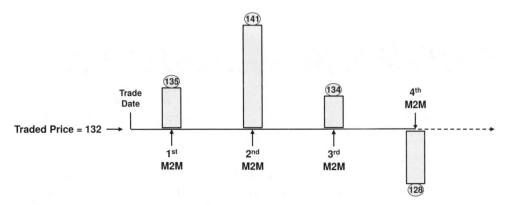

FIGURE 22.2　How exposures arise in OTC derivative trades

Figure 22.2 is explained as follows:

The trade is executed on trade date at a price of 132 basis points per annum (bppa).

Step 1: the first mark-to-market (M2M) reveals that the current cost (replacement cost) of executing a CDS trade on the same bond issuer (reference entity) is now 135 bppa. The protection buyer has a positive mark-to-market but also a counterparty exposure, and as a result issues a margin call to the counterparty for the exposure amount, that is the monetary value of 3 bppa (the difference between 135 bppa and 132 bppa). The protection seller chooses to pay cash collateral to the protection buyer in settlement of the margin call. This situation is reflected in Table 22.1:

TABLE 22.1　Identification of exposure #1

M2M	Exposure Amount (bppa)	Party With Positive Exposure	Margin Call	Collateral Status
1	135 – 132 = 3	Protection Buyer = +3	PS pays PB 3	Protection Buyer = +3 Protection Seller = −3

Note: the monetary value is calculated as follows. For example, in a CDS trade with a USD 10,000,000.00 notional principal and a *residual maturity* of 5 years to its scheduled maturity date, the monetary value of 3 bppa is determined as follows: USD 10,000,000.00 × 0.03% = USD 3,000.00 per annum for the remaining 5 years. In order to derive its value 'today', its *present value* must be determined to take account of the *time value of money*, which is also known as the *discount factor*. Further note: this example calculation is designed to indicate to readers the general principles of the calculation, and the complete calculation components fall outside the scope of this text.

Step 2: the 2nd M2M reveals that the current market price has risen to 141 bppa. Again, the protection buyer has a positive mark-to-market and an increased counterparty exposure, and as a result issues a margin call to the counterparty for the exposure amount, namely the monetary value of 141 bppa–132 bppa, whilst also taking account of the cash collateral the protection buyer is holding from the previous margin call. In summary, the margin call would be the monetary value of 9 bppa less 3 bppa cash collateral = 6 bppa. The protection seller again chooses to pay cash collateral to the protection buyer in settlement of the margin call. This situation is reflected in Table 22.2:

TABLE 22.2   Identification of exposure #2

M2M	Exposure Amount (bppa)	Party With Positive Exposure	Margin Call	Collateral Status
1	135 − 132 = 3	Protection Buyer = +3	PS pays PB 3	Protection Buyer = +3 Protection Seller = −3
2	141 − 132 = 9	Protection Buyer = +9	PS pays PB 6	Protection Buyer = +9 Protection Seller = −9

Step 3: the 3rd M2M reveals that the current market price has fallen (compared with the previous M2M) to 134 bppa. Again, the protection buyer has a positive mark-to-market on the trade therefore it still has a counterparty exposure, but the exposure has decreased (compared with the previous M2M). As a result, the protection seller now has an exposure to the excess collateral, because it has a greater value of collateral (held by the protection buyer) than is necessary to mitigate the protection buyer's exposure. The protection seller issues a margin call to the protection buyer, requesting the return of collateral to the monetary value of 141 bppa–134 bppa. In summary, this margin call would be the monetary value of 7 bppa; the protection buyer now has an exposure of 2 bppa (134 bppa–132 bppa) which is mitigated by the protection buyer continuing to hold 2 bppa of cash collateral previously paid by the protection seller. The protection buyer returns the relevant amount of cash collateral to the protection seller in settlement of the margin call. This situation is reflected in the Table 22.3:

TABLE 22.3   Identification of exposure #3

M2M	Exposure Amount (bppa)	Party With Positive Exposure	Margin Call	Collateral Status
1	135 − 132 = 3	Protection Buyer = +3	PS pays PB 3	Protection Buyer = +3 Protection Seller = −3
2	141 − 132 = 9	Protection Buyer = +9	PS pays PB 6	Protection Buyer = +9 Protection Seller = −9
3	134 − 132 = 2	Protection Buyer = +2	PB pays PS 7	Protection Buyer = +2 Protection Seller = −2

Step 4: the 4th M2M reveals that the current market price has fallen further (compared with the previous M2M) to 128 bppa. The protection buyer no longer has a positive mark-to-market; for the first time it is the protection seller that has the positive mark-to-market and therefore has a counterparty exposure. From the protection seller's perspective, it has two parts to its exposure: 1) it needs to reclaim all of the remaining collateral that the protection buyer is still holding, which is the monetary value of 2 bppa (134 bppa–132 bppa), plus it needs to claim the positive exposure amount which is the monetary value of 4 bppa (128 bppa–132 bppa). The protection buyer pays the relevant amount of cash collateral to the protection seller in settlement of the margin call. This situation is reflected in Table 22.4:

TABLE 22.4   Identification of exposure #4

M2M	Exposure Amount (bppa)	Party With Positive Exposure	Margin Call	Collateral Status
1	135 – 132 = 3	Protection Buyer = +3	PS pays PB 3	Protection Buyer = +3 Protection Seller = –3
2	141 – 132 = 9	Protection Buyer = +9	PS pays PB 6	Protection Buyer = +9 Protection Seller = –9
3	134 – 132 = 2	Protection Buyer = +2	PB pays PS 7	Protection Buyer = +2 Protection Seller = –2
4	128 – 132 = 4	Protection Seller = +4	PB pays PS 6*	Protection Buyer = –4 Protection Seller = +4

*Note that, under these circumstances where existing collateral is returned by one party and that same party is additionally required to provide its own collateral to satisfy a margin call, it is common practice to treat the two amounts separately rather than to net them by payment of a single cash amount. Therefore, in Table 22.4, M2M #4 would realistically be treated as stated in Table 22.5:

TABLE 22.5   Treatment of margin call

M2M	Margin Call	Margin Call Amount	Margin Call Reason	Collateral Status
4	A	PB pays PS 2	Return of Existing Collateral	Protection Buyer = 0 Protection Seller = 0
	B	PB pays PS 4	New Collateral	Protection Buyer = –4 Protection Seller = +4

It is important to note that such exposures are normally bilateral; both trading parties are subject to exposures based upon the changing values of OTC derivative contracts over a period of time. It is therefore essential to appreciate that the value of an OTC derivative contract can change significantly from day to day, requiring the giving and taking of collateral on a daily basis between the two parties. For instance, the extent of exposure yesterday (e.g. USD 4,000,000.00) in favour of Party B can today quite feasibly become (for example):

- USD 5,000,000.00 in favour of Party B, in which case more collateral will need to be given by Party A, or
- USD 1,000,000.00 in favour of Party A, in which case Party B will need to return the USD 4,000,000.00 of collateral, plus provide USD 1,000,000.00 of its own collateral to mitigate Party A's exposure.

Consequently, exposures on OTC derivatives are regarded as very fluid and subject to considerable change on a day-by-day basis. Such exposures must be mitigated by the giving and taking of collateral.

PART 4a

22.5 CSA LEGAL STRUCTURES

The legal structure of a CSA signed between two trading parties determines whether a taker of securities collateral is legally permitted to utilise *securities* collateral in a separate transaction. Whether permitted or not, there are operational implications.

There are three main types of CSA, namely:

- the English Law Credit Support Annex
- the New York Law Credit Support Annex, and
- the English Law Credit Support Deed.

The term 'reuse' refers to the collateral taker's legal right to utilise (redeliver) securities collateral received in another transaction, whether selling the security, lending the security, repoing the security or delivering the security as collateral for another transaction, such as an OTC derivative trade.

Note: cash collateral is unaffected, as it is considered a *fungible* financial instrument.

One of the most important aspects of a CSA is the legal standing of the securities collateral, in particular whether the collateral giver or the collateral taker has *legal title* (or not) whilst the collateral is in possession of the collateral taker. The legal terms used are as follows:

- *title transfer* basis; full legal title to the securities collateral passes from the collateral giver to the collateral taker, consequently reuse is permitted automatically
  - the English Law CSA is a title transfer document
- *security interest* basis (also known as a *pledge*); the collateral remains in the legal interest of the collateral giver, however permission to use the collateral in another transaction may be granted by the collateral giver. Note: such use under a security interest arrangement is known as *rehypothecation* (not 'reuse')
  - both the New York Law CSA and the English Law Credit Support Deed operate on a *security interest* basis,

Whether a firm has signed a title transfer CSA or a security interest CSA with a particular counterparty has implications on whether a firm and its counterparty is permitted to reuse or to rehypothecate securities collateral received, or not. That in turn will determine how a firm should hold collateral received at a *central securities depository* (CSD) or at a *custodian*, whether in its own account or in a segregated account.

The subjects of reuse under a title transfer arrangement, and of rehypothecation under a security interest arrangement, are explored further within Chapter 36 'OTC Derivatives and Collateral – The Collateral Lifecycle – Throughout Lifetime of Trade – Holding Collateral'.

22.6 RESPONSIBILITIES UNDER THE CSA: OVERVIEW

The CSA states the responsibilities of both parties, pertaining to exposures and collateral. At the required frequency, both parties are required to:

- calculate exposures on trades, and

- calculate the current value of any collateral currently held, and:
  - where the collateral value exceeds the exposure
    - some or all of the existing collateral must be returned to the collateral giver
  - where the exposure exceeds the collateral value
    - the collateral taker must call for further collateral
  - where the exposure and collateral value are very similar
    - no action is required by either party.

In addition, and before actioning a collateral movement, each party must take account of CSA items that impact the margin call amount, including whether the CSA is one-way or two-way and whether items such as the following are applicable: *independent amount, threshold, minimum transfer amount* and *rounding*. These items are described within Section 22.8 'CSA Components' within this chapter.

Then, having taken account of such items, if a margin call is made by the *exposed party* and if the margin call amount is agreed by the *counterparty*, the *collateral giver* must then decide which collateral type to provide (according to the CSA with the particular counterparty), for example, whether cash collateral or securities collateral. Having selected the collateral, the giver must apply a *haircut* percentage, if applicable, and ensure the resultant collateral value is no less than the exposed party's margin call amount. These items are also described in the 'CSA Components' section within this chapter.

Besides those terms listed above, generic terminology within a CSA typically includes terms such as:

- Base Currency: the currency into which exposures and collateral are converted
- Credit Support: collateral that *mitigates* exposures
- Delivery Amount: the collateral amount paid to or delivered to the exposed party
- Eligible Credit Support: the type of collateral acceptable in mitigation of exposures, for example cash or bonds
- Exchanges: securities collateral currently held by the exposed party may be required by the non-exposed party to be returned and to be replaced by other eligible collateral – a process commonly known as *collateral substitution*.
- Exposure: the monetary value of the difference between a trade's original cost and its current *replacement cost*, taking account of the current value of any existing collateral
- Return Amount: the collateral value held by the exposed party in excess of the current exposure value, which will be returned to the non-exposed party
- Transferee: the party in receipt of collateral, the collateral taker, the exposed party
- Transferor: the party delivering collateral, the collateral giver, the non-exposed party.

Such terms reflect the legal nature of the CSA which must be understood by a collateral professional, in order to appreciate its parameters so as to mitigate risk in the most efficient manner, and without introducing further risks.

PART 4a

22.7 DAY-TO-DAY USE OF THE CSA

From the perspective of an individual company, whether a *buy-side* firm or *sell-side* firm, on a day-to-day basis the Collateral Department must operate according to the terms and conditions within the relevant CSA for each of the firm's counterparties. This is providing that:

- currently live and valid OTC derivative trades exist between the firm and its counterparty
- such trades are covered by the CSA
- an exposure exists (for either the firm or the counterparty).

The Collateral Department may not need daily access to the signed CSA document itself but will need access to a database containing the component parts of the CSA with each counterparty. In general terms, such information forms part of a firm's collateral management system, although such data could be set up within a firm's master data applications in order to make the information accessible to the entire organisation.

The following three topics need to be referenced on a day-to-day basis, alongside of the CSA.

22.7.1 Product Coverage

In order for a firm and its counterparty to be certain of the particular OTC *derivative* products covered by a CSA, the legal documentation will state either:

- all products classified as OTC derivatives are covered, or
- specific types of OTC derivative are covered, which should be listed within the CSA.

Exposures on all trades executed in such products will be collateralised, therefore a firm must take care to ensure that all relevant products are covered by the legal documentation, otherwise the risk exists that exposures on trades falling outside of the listed products will not be collateralised and exposures relating to such products may not be mitigated.

Typical financial products covered by the legal documentation are OTC derivative products traded on a *bilateral* basis, including:

- interest rate swaps*
- interest rate options
- forward rate agreements
- foreign exchange forwards
- foreign exchange swaps*
- cross-currency swaps*
- credit default swaps*
- total return swaps
- equity options
- variance swaps.

Note: products with an asterisk* are described within Chapters 16–19, all of which fall under the heading of 'OTC Derivatives – Transaction Types'.

At any one point in time, the legal documentation can cover only those derivative products whose characteristics are well established within the financial services industry. Therefore, where a firm has legal documentation in place before a new product becomes established in the market place and its characteristics are yet to become well known amongst the OTC derivative community, a firm must remain conscious that any trades executed in such products may fall outside of the protection provided by the legal documentation. Under the circumstances where a firm wishes to trade in such a new product, the (post-trade execution) *trade confirmation* needs to state that the trade falls under the scope of the existing legal documentation. Alternatively, the specific trade may be executed with collateral provisions that are pertinent only to the individual trade in the particular product, and which are managed separately from trades in products listed within the legal documentation with the same counterparty. A further alternative is for the firm to delay trade execution and to renegotiate or amend the legal documentation with the counterparty, so as to include trades executed in the new product.

A highly significant characteristic of trades executed in OTC derivative products (such as those listed earlier), is the existence of counterparty credit risk. Since OTC derivatives typically involve an exchange of cashflows, potentially both parties to the trade could have credit risk at different times during the lifetime of the trade. This is illustrated in Figure 22.2 which shows the protection buyer has credit risk for the first 3 positive mark-to-markets. Note however, that the fourth mark-to-market results in the switching of credit risk to the protection seller. The maturity of such trades can be for any length of time from a number of months to many years, potentially up to 50 years, although no formal upper limit exists.

Other products that are typically not included within the legal documentation are those whose lifetime is a number of days and where a firm has no ongoing contract with its counterparty. For example, buy and sell trades in securities (*equity* and *bonds*) are not collateralised as their lifetime is relatively short; at the time of writing the default *settlement cycle* for European equity (including the UK), US equity and Eurobonds is trade date plus 2 business days (T+2). Once a buy or sell securities trade is fully settled, that is, securities and cash have been exchanged between buyer and seller, there is no ongoing counterparty exposure. *Spot* foreign exchange trades are another example of a product with a short lifetime and with no ongoing counterparty exposure; the standard settlement period is 2 days after trade date. For the avoidance of doubt, products that are to be intentionally excluded may be listed within the negotiated CSA as products that are not to be collateralised.

With a negotiated CSA in place, regular exposure calculations between a firm and its counterparty must include all open trades in all of the included products. Care must be taken to ensure that open trades are truly currently open, as for example, an OTC derivative trade executed 2 years ago with a 10-year life with Party T, may now be fully terminated, partially terminated, or open with a different counterparty due to one or more *post-trade execution events*. Please refer to Chapter 37 'OTC Derivatives and Collateral – The Collateral Lifecycle – Throughout Lifetime of Trade – Post-Trade Execution Events – Introduction' and the three subsequent chapters. However, to mitigate the risk of a firm calculating exposures on trades which are no longer open with a particular counterparty, it is common practice for firms to conduct frequent *reconciliation* with its counterparties; please refer to Chapter 31 'OTC Derivatives and Collateral – The Collateral Lifecycle – Throughout Lifetime of Trade – Portfolio Reconciliation'.

Table 22.6 provides examples of product coverage within three of a firm's negotiated CSAs with counterparties:

TABLE 22.6   Examples of negotiated CSA content – product coverage

Product Coverage		
CSA #1	CSA #2	CSA #3
interest rate swaps forward rate agreements foreign exchange forwards credit default swaps total return swaps variance swaps	interest rate swaps interest rate options forward rate agreements cross-currency swaps credit default swaps total return swaps equity options variance swaps	interest rate swaps cross-currency swaps credit default swaps total return swaps

22.7.2 Collateral Direction (Two-Way and One-Way CSAs)

Where a negotiated CSA requires that the posting of collateral is mutual between the two parties, the CSA is said to be 'two-way'. This is likely to be the case where the parties have an equal credit rating. Under such circumstances whichever party has a *positive exposure* will call for collateral from its counterparty.

However, negotiated CSAs may be 'one-way', requiring the firm posting collateral to deliver the required assets where the OTC derivative position is currently profitable for their stronger rated counterparty. However, in the opposite situation, where the position is profitable for the weaker rated firm, they will not be able to issue a valid *margin call* to the counterparty. Such CSAs may arise where, for example, an investment bank trades with **supranational organisations** (e.g. World Bank, European Bank for Reconstruction & Development, Asian Development Bank) and **sovereigns** (central governments), where the investment bank has a weaker credit rating.

Table 22.7 provides examples of the direction of collateral listed within three of a firm's negotiated CSAs with counterparties:

TABLE 22.7   Examples of negotiated CSA content – collateral direction

Collateral Direction		
CSA #1	CSA #2	CSA #3
Bilateral (two-way)	Unilateral (in favour of counterparty)	Unilateral (in favour of firm)

22.7.3 Standing Settlement Instructions

Generically speaking, whenever cash is to be paid or received, and whenever securities are to be delivered or received, it is important for a firm to know in advance:

1. when paying cash:
   - the firm's own bank account number from which payment will be made
   - the counterparty's bank account number to which payment will be made

and vice versa when receiving cash, particularly where the firm's *cash correspondent* requires receipt of a *funds preadvice*, and

2. when delivering securities (*bonds* and *equity*):
   ▪ the firm's own *custodian* account number from which delivery will be made
   ▪ the counterparty's custodian account number and settlement location to which delivery will be made

and vice versa when receiving securities. Securities collateral movements usually require the mandatory matching of giver's and taker's *settlement instructions*, before delivery can occur.

Superficially, this may seem obvious. However, as many investment banks operate the business of multiple entities within their group, and similarly many buy-side firms operate the business of multiple clients (e.g. in the case of a mutual fund, multiple funds), such firms are likely to have multiple bank accounts and multiple custodian accounts from which cash collateral is to be paid and received, and securities collateral is to be delivered and received. Under any circumstances, it is essential that the correct bank and custodian accounts are identified whenever collateral must be given or taken.

Such accounts are commonly known as *standing settlement instructions*, as the intention, by both parties, is to treat such accounts as standing orders for payment and delivery, until further notice. The common abbreviation for standing settlement instructions is *SSI*. SSIs are:

1. swapped with counterparties (ideally prior to executing the first trade),
2. stored internally within a firm's *static data repository*, then
3. utilised whenever necessary, in order to avoid repeatedly contacting the counterparty.

Within a firm's static data repository, SSIs are usually set up within *counterparty static data* so as to facilitate the automated generation of cash payment/receipt instructions and securities delivery/receipt instructions. Please note that the subject of static data is covered within Chapter 23 'OTC Derivatives and Collateral – Static Data'.

Failure to store SSIs increases the risk of delayed issuance of settlement instructions, potentially leading to delayed settlement of collateral, and consequently the firm's or counterparty's exposures failing to be mitigated on the due date.

In the case of securities collateral, SSIs relate to both the original collateral and to any collateral substitutions.

Table 22.8 provides examples of the SSIs listed within three of a firm's negotiated CSAs with counterparties:

PART 4a

TABLE 22.8   Examples of negotiated CSA content – standing settlement instructions

Standing Settlement Instructions		
CSA #1	**CSA #2**	**CSA #3**
Firm's EUR Cash: Bank X Account 12345 Cpty's EUR Cash: Bank G, Account 98765 Firm's International Bonds: Custodian G, Account ABC06 Cpty's International Bonds: Custodian G, Account 34076	Firm's USD Cash: Bank Y Account 60335 Cpty's USD Cash: Bank T, Account 55562 *(plus SSIs for EUR and GBP for each party)*	Firm's GBP Cash: Bank Z Account 88827 Cpty's GBP Cash: Bank P, Account 00769 Firm's International Bonds: Custodian G, Account ABC06 Cpty's International Bonds: Custodian G, Account HH909

22.8 CSA COMPONENTS

Particular components of the CSA are listed here, incorporating a description of the component and its specific purpose and use.

AUTHOR'S COMMENT AND DISCLAIMER

The components listed within this chapter are 1) the author's interpretation of the most commonly used attributes of a CSA that impact day-to-day collateral management activity, and are 2) the author's explanation of such components in plain English and non-legal language so as to be meaningful to the target audience for this book, and are 3) intended to convey the general nature of the CSA and are in no way intended to be an exhaustive list of all terms and conditions contained within a CSA.

Additionally, within each component three examples of negotiated CSAs are provided (within a table) so as to enable the reader to appreciate the typical content of each component and example variations of such content. Note that such examples are as applicable to sell-side firms as they are to buy-side firms.

22.8.1 Base Currency

In order to ensure that exposure calculations are performed by both trading parties in the same currency, that currency is stated within the CSA and is referred to as the *base currency*.

Base currency is necessary to avoid one party calculating exposure in one currency (e.g. USD) and the counterparty calculating exposure in a different currency (e.g. EUR), where use of an exchange rate would be necessary in order to compare exposure calculations on a like-for-like basis.

For example, if a firm had current open OTC derivative trades denominated in a variety of currencies, with the same counterparty, the single base currency requires both the firm and its counterparty to convert such multi-currency exposures into that base currency prior to the exposed party making a ***margin call***. Table 22.9 represents a firm's multi-currency exposures with one counterparty, which when converted reveals the exposure amount, and the direction of exposure, in the base currency (USD in this example):

TABLE 22.9   Multi-currency exposures

Multi-Currency Exposures with a Firm's Counterparty – Converted to Base Currency				
Currency of OTC Derivative Trades	Exposure in Currency of Trade		Exchange Rate	Base Currency Equivalent (USD)
	In Favour of Firm	In Favour of Counterparty		
GBP	GBP 7,800,000.00		GBP 1.00/USD 1.25	+ USD 9,750,000.00
EUR		EUR 5,900,000.00	EUR 1.00/USD 1.10	– USD 6,490,000.00
USD	USD 3,500,000.00		n/a	+ USD 3,500,000.00
			Net Exposure in Base Currency	+ USD 6,760,000.00

Note: the exchange rates used in this table are approximate exchange rates at the time of writing.

In a multi-currency exposure situation as depicted in the table above, the post-conversion exposure amount is referred to as the ***base currency equivalent*** within the CSA.

Table 22.10 provides examples of base currency within three of a firm's negotiated CSAs with counterparties:

TABLE 22.10   Examples of negotiated CSA content – base currency

Base Currency		
CSA #1	CSA #2	CSA #3
EUR	USD	GBP

22.8.2 Eligible Currency

The currencies that are acceptable as cash collateral are listed within the CSA and are referred to as ***eligible currency***.

Whereas base currency is designed to ensure that exposure calculations between the two parties are comparable and on a like-for-like basis, once the exposure amount and direction are agreed, the collateral giver that chooses to give cash (as opposed to securities) collateral must provide such collateral in the stated collateral currency (or currencies).

For example, utilising Table 22.9 within the Base Currency section above, assume that the counterparty agrees the net exposure figure of USD 6,760,000.00 in favour of the firm. If the CSA states that, for example, USD is the sole eligible currency then the counterparty must pay the USD exposure amount. Alternatively, if the CSA states that, for example, USD and EUR are the eligible currencies, then the counterparty has a choice as to which currency to provide as collateral; in this example, should the counterparty choose to pay EUR cash collateral, the net exposure amount in USD would need to be converted to EUR at the current exchange rate.

Note: calculation differences between firms can arise where base currency differs from an eligible currency, due to exchange rate differences. For example, although Party A has used the same source of exchange rates as Party B, the exchange rate utilised by Party A was taken hours earlier compared with when Party B gathered the exchange rate.

Table 22.11 provides examples of eligible currency within three of a firm's negotiated CSAs with counterparties:

TABLE 22.11   Examples of negotiated CSA content – eligible currency

Eligible Currency		
CSA #1	CSA #2	CSA #3
EUR	USD, EUR, GBP	GBP

22.8.3 Eligible Collateral

The primary purpose of collateral is, in the event of default by its counterparty, to enable a firm to liquidate the collateral held so as to recover the full value of its exposure. It is therefore essential that the type of collateral receivable by a firm provides surety of and immediate *liquidation* of such collateral.

This section of the CSA, under the heading of Eligible Credit Support, defines the type of collateral acceptable to one of the parties (one-way CSA), or to both parties (two-way CSA), whether:

- cash only, in one or more specified currencies (i.e. eligible currency)
- cash and securities (whether *bonds* and/or *equity*), or
- securities only.

Eligible collateral is likely to be listed in one or more appendix to the CSA.

Table 22.12 provides examples of the types of eligible collateral listed within three of a firm's negotiated CSAs with counterparties:

TABLE 22.12   Examples of negotiated CSA content – eligible credit support

Eligible Credit Support		
CSA #1	CSA #2	CSA #3
EUR cash G10 Government Securities	USD cash EUR cash GBP cash	GBP cash G10 Government Securities Corporate Bonds

Regarding cash that's acceptable as collateral, this is typically restricted to the major western currencies, namely USD, EUR and GBP. In many cases, a negotiated CSA will define just one currency as eligible cash collateral, but in other negotiated CSAs more than one stipulated currency is acceptable, with non-major currencies usually being subject to a *haircut* (see Sub-section 22.8.4).

Regarding eligible securities, historically bonds have been the more popular choice due to their typical lack of volatility in price movement and therefore their value.

Amongst the vast choice of bonds available globally, a popular category of bonds listed within a CSA are likely to be *G-7* and *G-10* government bonds, as these have historically been regarded as highly creditworthy. However, other bond categories may be used for collateral purposes; these are described within Sub-section 22.8.4 'Haircut and Valuation Percentage'.

With regard to the use of equity as collateral, it is likely that only the equity comprising a main equity index within their country of listing will be acceptable as collateral. Examples of such indices are the All Ordinaries (Australia), Bovespa (Brazil), DAX (Germany), Hang Seng (Hong Kong), Nikkei-225 (Japan), AEX-Index (the Netherlands), FTSE-100 (UK) and NASDAQ-100 (US). Equity collateral is likely to have a haircut rate which takes into account its historic volatility and is likely to attract a greater haircut than highly rated bond issues.

22.8.4 Haircut and Valuation Percentage

All eligible collateral is (potentially) subject to a percentage reduction in its value; this reduction is commonly known as a *haircut* and is normally a low percentage, for example 2.5%. The remainder (i.e. 100% – 2.5% = 97.5%) is known as a 'valuation percentage'.

The haircut reflects the perceived risk of holding the asset as collateral; the greater the perceived risk, the higher the percentage haircut. Haircuts provide a certain amount of risk *mitigation* for the *exposed party*, in case the collateral suffers a fall in value or it needs to be liquidated in a *stressed market*.

Haircut results in the *collateral value* of the asset being less than its *market value*. Imagine that a firm had an exposure of USD 1,000,000.00; the elementary effect that different collateral types have on collateral values is reflected in Table 22.13.

TABLE 22.13   Impact of haircut

Impact of Haircut			
	Collateral Asset Type		
	USD Cash	G-10 Government Bonds	Corporate Bonds
Market Value of Asset	USD 1,000,000.00	USD 1,000,000.00	USD 1,000,000.00
Applicable Haircut Percentage	0%	1%	5%
Cash Value of Haircut	0.00	USD 10,000.00	USD 50,000.00
Collateral Value of Asset	USD 1,000,000.00	USD 990,000.00	USD 950,000.00

The table indicates:

1. that collateral in the form of cash may be subject to a zero haircut (particularly in the major currencies); where this is the case, the asset's collateral value remains the same as its market value
2. that government bonds issued by stable governments have historically been considered a good credit risk; consequently the haircut percentage on such assets is typically very low

3. that bonds issued by corporations have, in some cases, been considered a higher credit risk; consequently the haircut percentage on such assets is typically greater than for government bonds.

Note that in examples 2 and 3, the firm's exposure of USD 1,000,000.00 is not fully covered by the collateral value of the asset, therefore additional assets will need to be provided by the *collateral giver* in order to cover the exposure. This can be achieved by the non-exposed party delivering a greater quantity (therefore a greater value) of the same bond.

A common feature within negotiated CSAs is the detailed listing of haircut percentages to be applied 1) to bond issuers and 2) to the number of years from 'today' until the bond's maturity date (known as *residual maturity*) of the issuer's bonds. Time is a risk factor in the repayment of capital on bonds; the longer the residual maturity, the greater the perceived risk, therefore the higher the haircut percentage. Examples of such haircut percentages are depicted in Table 22.14:

TABLE 22.14   Example haircut percentages

Issuer & Issue Type	Residual Maturity	Example Haircut Percentage
Issuer XYZ USD-denominated Fixed Rate bonds	<1 year	0.5%
	1–2 years	1%
	2–3 years	1.5%
	3–5 years	2.5%
	5–7 years	3.5%
	7–10 years	4.5%
	10–20 years	6%
	>20 years	8%

The above table and descriptions are intended to be at an introductory level, targeted at those readers that are new to such concepts. In reality, the determination of haircut percentages can be significantly more involved. For further detail of the parameters that can be involved in the determination of haircut percentages, please refer to Chapter 4 'Sale & Repurchase (Repo) Trades and Collateral – Classic Repo Trades'.

An example of how valuation percentages might appear within a negotiated CSA are depicted as shown in Table 22.15:

TABLE 22.15   Example valuation percentages

Eligible Credit Support	Party A	Party B	Example Valuation Percentage
Cash in an Eligible Currency	√	√	100%
Negotiable debt obligations issued by the Government of *country X* having an original maturity at issuance of not more than one year	√	√	99.0%
Negotiable debt obligations issued by the Government of *country X* having an original maturity at issuance of more than one year but no more than 10 years	√	√	96.0%

This table shows that all the stated valuation percentages are applicable to both parties.

Valuation percentages are typically stated alongside the eligible collateral listed in one or more appendices to the CSA.

In some cases, the CSA negotiated between the two firms is completed with types of bond issue and their credit ratings. Where a *bond issue downgrade* occurs, the negotiated CSA defines the resultant decrease in valuation percentage. For example, for the same issuer, two valuation percentages may be stated for the same residual maturity. For instance:

- for Issuer X with a credit rating of at least A+, the valuation percentage of 98.5% applies, and
- for Issuer X with a credit rating of at least A–, the valuation percentage of 97.5% applies.

In the case of a government issuer, all bonds issued by that issuer will be downgraded. This approach to completing the CSA between two firms facilitates 'future-proofing' to some extent, thereby requiring fewer amendments in future should unforeseen aspects of creditworthiness arise.

Table 22.16 provides examples of the types of eligible collateral listed within three of a firm's negotiated CSAs with counterparties, and their associated valuation percentages:

TABLE 22.16   Examples of negotiated CSA content – valuation percentage

Valuation Percentage					
CSA #1		CSA #2		CSA #3	
EUR cash	VP = 100%	USD cash	VP = 100%	GBP cash	VP = 100%
G10 Government Securities	VP = 99%	EUR cash	VP = 100%	G10 Government Securities	VP = 99%
		GBP cash	VP = 100%	Corporate Bonds	VP = 95%

22.8.5 Independent Amount

In the case of OTC derivatives, the amount of *exposure* requiring to be collateralised between two trading parties is the current *replacement cost* of all the current *open trades*.

An independent amount is a cash amount that remains outside of a firm's exposure amount relating to its open trades. In other words, if a firm has a *positive exposure* relating to its open trades of, for example USD 6,000,000, but a fixed independent amount of USD 3,000,000 had been negotiated in favour of the firm (and recorded within the CSA), the firm would be owed collateral by its counterparty for a total of USD 9,000,000.

The purpose of an independent amount is to create a protective layer of additional collateral for one of the involved parties, as a means of mitigating risk over and above the movement of collateral based purely upon *current market value* exposures.

Independent amounts are typically in place where one of the parties has a stronger credit rating than its counterparty, but may also be used on an individual trade if the trade is considered to be of greater risk than is normal.

Independent amount may or may not be applicable between the two parties; where it is applicable, it will relate to one of the parties, not both. Where it has been negotiated, its nature can be:

- a fixed monetary sum in a specified currency; for example, USD 5 million, or EUR 10 million
- a fixed percentage of the **notional principal** of a trade; for example, an independent amount of 6% on an **interest rate swap** with a notional principal of USD 80,000,000 would require collateral of USD 4,800,000.

Whether a fixed monetary sum or a fixed percentage of notional, independent amount can be applied to individual trades or to the sum of all open trades between the two parties.

Its effect is to increase the overall collateral value that the weaker rated party is required to deliver.

An independent amount can be combined (netted) with the exposure amount and paid or received as a single net payment, or (where the independent amount is not linked with the exposure amount) it can be kept separate from the exposure amount resulting in two separate payments or receipts.

Table 22.17 provides examples of whether independent amount is relevant, and if so the types of independent amount listed within three of a firm's negotiated CSAs with counterparties:

TABLE 22.17   Examples of negotiated CSA content – independent amount

Independent Amount		
CSA #1	CSA #2	CSA #3
Independent amount in firm's favour, for a fixed sum of EUR 10 million for all open trades	No independent amount applicable	Independent amount in counterparty's favour, at 5% of notional principal for individual trades

22.8.6 Threshold

A threshold is an uncollateralised exposure amount.

The purpose of a threshold is for one (or both) parties to take a calculated and specified level of credit risk on an unsecured basis, up to the level of the threshold. For exposures beyond the threshold level, collateral is required.

If a threshold is documented within a negotiated CSA, for example USD 1 million and where the threshold is two-way, for whichever of the parties has an exposure below USD 1 million, that party must not make a margin call and there is no requirement for the non-exposed party to provide collateral to the exposed party. Under the same negotiated CSA, where the exposure amount is, for example, USD 2.5 million, the value of collateral requiring to be given to the exposed party is the difference between the exposure amount and the threshold amount.

Thresholds can be negotiated on a two-way or a one-way basis. In a one-way threshold in which Party B is the stronger party, Party A is the weaker party and the threshold amount is USD 2,000,000, Party A cannot call for collateral below USD 2,000,000. However, Party B can call for collateral for any exposure amount, for example USD 1,500,000 or USD 750,000. Such arrangements are known as asymmetrical thresholds (see Figure 22.3).

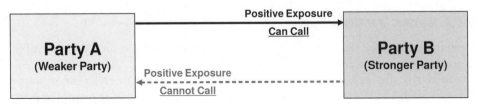

FIGURE 22.3   Asymmetrical threshold

Threshold may or may not be applicable between the two parties. Where it has been negotiated, its nature can be:

- a fixed monetary sum in a specified currency; for example, USD 1 million, or EUR 2 million
- a monetary sum that is subject to change if and when a party's credit rating changes.

The effect of threshold is to decrease the overall collateral value that a particular party is required to deliver.

From the perspective of any particular party, independent amounts and thresholds provide opposing credit risk impacts:

- a firm that is required to provide an independent amount to a particular counterparty is highly unlikely to also have a threshold in place that has the effect of decreasing collateral to be given
- a firm that is required to receive an independent amount from a particular counterparty is highly unlikely to also have a threshold in place that has the effect of decreasing collateral to be received
- a firm that has a threshold in place that has the effect of decreasing collateral to be given to a particular counterparty is highly unlikely to be required to also provide an independent amount
- a firm that has a threshold in place that has the effect of decreasing collateral to be received from a particular counterparty is highly unlikely to be required to also receive an independent amount.

Consequently, it should be expected that amongst a firm's negotiated CSAs with its various counterparties, either independent amount or threshold (but not both) will be listed, although it is also entirely possible that, for some firms, neither independent amount nor threshold is listed.

Table 22.18 provides examples of whether threshold is relevant, and if so the types of threshold listed within three of a firm's negotiated CSAs with counterparties:

TABLE 22.18 Examples of negotiated CSA content – threshold

Threshold		
CSA #1	CSA #2	CSA #3
No threshold applicable	Two-way threshold for a fixed sum of USD 1 million for all open trades	No threshold applicable

22.8.7 Minimum Transfer Amount

A minimum transfer amount (MTA) is the smallest collateral value that is payable or receivable, relating to daily exposures between two parties.

To clarify, any exposure beneath the MTA is not subject to collateral movement, therefore such amounts remain *unsecured* from the perspective of the *exposed party*.

The purpose of an MTA is to avoid the cost and administrative burden of transferring relatively small values of collateral. For example, if an MTA is listed within a negotiated CSA as being USD 500,000, an exposure of USD 450,000 would require no collateral to be delivered, whereas an exposure amount of USD 550,000 would require delivery of collateral for its full value.

Threshold (where applicable), must also be factored in when determining collateral movements. For example, if an MTA is listed within the CSA as being USD 500,000, and:

- a current exposure amount is USD 1,400,000, with a threshold of USD 1,000,000, the remaining amount of USD 400,000 would result in no collateral being moved as this amount is less than the MTA
- a current exposure amount is USD 1,600,000, with a threshold of USD 1,000,000, the remaining amount of USD 600,000 would result in collateral needing to be delivered as this amount is greater than the MTA.

MTAs may be applicable to one party only, for example Party A is required to deliver collateral above USD 250,000 to Party B, but Party B has zero MTA. Alternatively, the same MTA amount may be applicable to both parties (two-way), or different MTA amounts may be applicable to each party.

Table 22.19 provides examples of whether MTA is relevant, and if so the nature of the MTAs listed within three of a firm's negotiated CSAs with counterparties:

TABLE 22.19 Examples of negotiated CSA content – minimum transfer amount

Minimum Transfer Amount		
CSA #1	CSA #2	CSA #3
Two-way MTA of EUR 500,000	Two-way MTA of USD 100,000	MTA of GBP 250,000 when we call. MTA of GBP 500,000 when counterparty calls

22.8.8 Rounding

Rounding refers to a rule documented within a negotiated CSA, regarding the treatment of odd exposure values between the two trading parties. The rounding rule is to either round up, or to round down, to the ***nearest integer***, in order to avoid transfer of odd collateral values, the effect being the transfer of an even (rounded) value of collateral.

For example, rather than giving collateral to cover an exposure amount of USD 4,116,806.92, a 'round up to the nearest USD 100,000' rounding rule will result in a deliverable collateral value of USD 4,200,000.00.

Where rounding rules apply, they may be applicable not only to the original delivery of collateral, but also to the return of collateral. Rules such as:

- round up the delivery amount, round up the return amount
- round down the delivery amount, round down the return amount
- round up the delivery amount, round down the return amount

may be listed within a negotiated CSA. Where rounding is applicable, the rounding rule must state the value that must be applied (e.g. to the nearest EUR 10,000 or USD 50,000 or EUR 100,000).

In a situation in which a negotiated CSA contains multiple ***eligible currencies***, common practice is to extend the agreed rounding rule to all such currencies, rather than solely to the base currency. This is to avoid a situation where, for example, a USD exposure remains unrounded because the negotiated CSA has an EUR base currency, and other eligible currencies (including USD) are not subject to the rounding rule.

Rounding rules are normally applicable to both parties.

Table 22.20 provides examples of whether rounding is relevant, and if so the nature of the rounding rules listed within three of a firm's negotiated CSAs with counterparties:

TABLE 22.20   Examples of negotiated CSA content – rounding

Rounding		
CSA #1	CSA #2	CSA #3
Round up the delivery amount, round down the return amount to the nearest EUR 50,000	No rounding applicable	Round down the delivery amount, round down the return amount to the nearest GBP 10,000

22.8.9 Valuation and Timing: Introduction

Valuation within the CSA refers to the action of valuing ***open trades*** in relevant OTC derivative products, and any previously delivered collateral.

This action is commonly known as ***marking-to-market*** (frequently abbreviated to M2M or MTM), involving discovery of the ***current market price*** of a particular product from an external and independent source. Marking-to-market is a broad term used within financial services referring to the valuing of all types of financial product. For OTC derivatives in particular, the current market price of a trade represents the current exposure which will be a ***positive exposure*** for one party, and a ***negative exposure*** for their ***counterparty***. The former is the at-risk party, requiring the party with the negative exposure (the ***non-exposed party***) to mitigate its counterparty's risk by the payment of ***cash collateral*** or the delivery of ***securities*** collateral.

Note that of the three common price types available for any financial product (i.e. bid, offer, mid), when valuing assets for collateral purposes it is normal practice for the ***mid price*** to be applied.

PART 4a

It is important to note that where cash collateral has been provided previously, valuation of only the applicable OTC derivative trade(s) will need to be performed, as cash collateral does not fluctuate in value (provided the currency of cash collateral is the same as the base currency). Conversely, where securities (*bond* or *equity*) collateral has been provided previously, valuation of both the applicable OTC derivative trade(s) and the collateral will need to be performed. This difference in valuation of collateral is depicted in the Tables 22.21 and 22.22. Firstly, using cash collateral:

TABLE 22.21   Exposure amount versus cash collateral

Exposure Amount versus Cash Collateral			
	Day 1	Day 2	Day 3
Exposure Amount →	USD 7.5m	USD 7.5m	USD 7.8m
Cash Collateral Received →	USD 7.5m	USD 7.5m	USD 7.5m +USD 0.3m

The above table is explained as follows:

- Day 1: valuation of the underlying trade(s) reveals an exposure amount of USD 7.5m, which is mitigated by the receipt of USD 7.5m cash collateral
- Day 2: valuation of the underlying trade(s) reveals the exposure is the same as Day 1, requiring no further collateral to mitigate the exposure. Note: the existing cash collateral has not changed in value
- Day 3: valuation of the underlying trade(s) reveals the exposure has increased to USD 7.8m, which is mitigated by the receipt of a further USD 300,000.00 cash collateral. Note: the existing cash collateral has not changed in value.

Secondly, using securities collateral:

TABLE 22.22   Exposure amount versus securities collateral

Exposure Amount versus Securities (Bond) Collateral			
	Day 1	Day 2	Day 3
Exposure Amount →	USD 7.5m	USD 7.5m	USD 7.8m
Bond Collateral Value Received →	USD 7.5m	USD 7.1m +USD 0.4m	USD 7.6m +USD 0.2m

This table is explained as follows:

- Day 1: valuation of the underlying trade(s) reveals an exposure amount of USD 7.5m, which is mitigated by the receipt of bonds with a collateral value of USD 7.5m, inclusive of the applicable *haircut*
- Day 2: valuation of the underlying trade(s) reveals the exposure is the same as Day 1, but valuation of the bond collateral reveals its value has fallen by USD 400,000.00, requiring additional collateral of that amount to *mitigate* the exposure

- Day 3: valuation of the underlying trade(s) reveals the exposure has increased to USD 7.8m, and valuation of the bond collateral reveals its value has risen to USD 7.6m, requiring additional collateral of USD 200,000.00 to mitigate the exposure.

In summary (providing there are no additional (new) trades to be included in the valuation and no trades that should have been excluded (e.g. trades having reached their scheduled maturity date)):

- cash collateral (in a currency that does not attract a haircut) retains its value from one day to the next, so only the valuation of the open OTC derivative trades will cause exposure to alter from the previous day, whereas
- securities collateral is highly likely to fluctuate in value from one day to the next, therefore the fluctuating values of both the open OTC derivative trades and the collateral will cause exposure to alter from the previous day.

22.8.10 Valuation Agent

Valuation agent within the CSA refers to the party (or parties) responsible for carrying out valuation of open trades in relevant OTC derivative products and any previously delivered collateral.

Either of the two parties to the negotiated CSA may be listed as valuation agent, or a third party agent may be specified. In some negotiated CSAs, no valuation agent is specified; under these circumstances the party with the *positive exposure* (that calls the *counterparty* for collateral) is regarded as the valuation agent. Where an *investment bank* has a comparatively small *buy-side* firm as its counterparty, it is common practice for the investment bank to take the role of valuation agent.

It should be noted that any party to a trade has the right to dispute a valuation.

Table 22.23 provides examples of whether a valuation agent is stated, and if so the specific agent listed within three of a firm's negotiated CSAs with counterparties:

TABLE 22.23　Examples of negotiated CSA content – valuation agent

Valuation Agent		
CSA #1	**CSA #2**	**CSA #3**
No valuation agent specified; the party making the margin call will be regarded as the agent	The counterparty will be the valuation agent, subject to agreement by the firm	The firm will be the valuation agent, subject to agreement by the counterparty

22.8.11 Valuation Date

Within the CSA, valuation date refers to the regularity of valuation, whether daily, weekly, bi-weekly, monthly, etc.

Historically, particularly for smaller firms, valuation may have been performed, for example, weekly, bi-weekly or monthly. Since the *global financial crisis* in the autumn of 2008, one of the most significant realisations for all firms trading in OTC derivatives is that even large investment banks can go out of business, and a firm's true exposures are unlikely to be identified or mitigated if valuations are not performed daily. A firm wishing to increase the frequency of valuation would need to renegotiate or amend its CSAs with its various counterparties. Note: some of the larger financial institutions, both *sell-side* and *buy-side*, perform intraday valuations as a risk mitigation measure.

Valuations can only be performed on business days, therefore where the parties to a trade are located in different cities or countries, the negotiated CSA must contain reference to business days in the applicable location of each party.

Table 22.24 provides examples of the nature of valuation date listed within three of a firm's negotiated CSAs with counterparties:

TABLE 22.24   Examples of negotiated CSA content – valuation date

Valuation Date		
CSA #1	CSA #2	CSA #3
Every business day in London	Every Wednesday in London and Paris	Each local business day in London and New York

22.8.12 Valuation Time

Within the CSA, valuation time refers to the time of day, on the valuation date, that the *valuation agent* is required to value *open trades* and any existing securities collateral. This action will reveal whether a *margin call* or a return of collateral is needed.

Where both parties are performing valuations, it is clearly important that such valuations are conducted at approximately the same time of day, if valuation and exposure mismatches are to be avoided. The normal valuation time listed within a negotiated CSA is at close of business on valuation date −1 business day. Today, because the normal frequency of valuation is daily, the normal valuation time is following the close of business each day.

Table 22.25 provides examples of the specific valuation times listed within three of a firm's negotiated CSAs with counterparties:

TABLE 22.25   Examples of negotiated CSA content – valuation time

Valuation Time		
CSA #1	CSA #2	CSA #3
Close of business on valuation date −1 business day	Close of business on valuation date −1 business day	Close of business on valuation date −1 business day

22.8.13 Notification Time

Following valuation, Notification Time within the CSA refers to the latest hh/mm deadline, within the applicable timezone, by which:

- the *valuation agent* must communicate valuations to the relevant party (or parties), and
- the *exposed party* must communicate their *margin call* to their counterparty.

Normally, this deadline is 1:00pm in any particular financial centre, but this must be meaningful and achievable for both parties where they are located in different time zones. Where a third party valuation agent is involved, an earlier deadline for the communication of valuations is desirable to allow adequate time for a margin call notification to be generated and transmitted to the counterparty by the margin call deadline.

From the perspective of the recipient of a margin call notification, they are obliged to act (by providing collateral) if the notification has been received prior to the documented deadline. Where a margin call has been received beyond the deadline, there is no legal obligation for the receiving party to act that day; however, in the longer term interests of both parties, many firms do choose to act on a best-efforts basis, although under such circumstances settlement may be delayed by one business day. An example of a consciously soft approach towards such situations is where an *investment bank* has traded with a *buy-side* firm; the buy-side firm is a client of the investment bank, and as such it is sensible that the bank protects the interests of its client wherever possible in order to retain the client's business on an ongoing basis.

Table 22.26 provides examples of the specific communication deadlines listed within three of a firm's negotiated CSAs with counterparties:

TABLE 22.26　Examples of negotiated CSA content – notification time

Notification Time		
CSA #1	CSA #2	CSA #3
1:00pm London time	2:00pm Central European Time	1:00pm London Time

22.8.14 Collateral Substitution

Collateral substitution occurs when securities, which have been previously given as collateral, are required to be returned to the *collateral giver* in exchange for *replacement collateral*, which may be either other eligible securities or eligible cash. This action is under the heading of 'Exchange Date' within the CSA.

Collateral substitution is depicted in Figure 22.4:

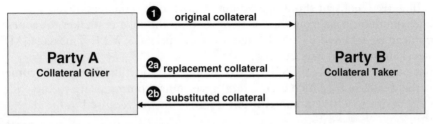

FIGURE 22.4　Collateral substitution

Step 1: the collateral giver delivers securities collateral to the collateral taker

Step 2a: at a later date, the collateral giver delivers replacement collateral (securities or cash)

Step 2b: the collateral taker returns the original securities collateral which has now been substituted.

Securities are usually substituted when the collateral giver either:

* has executed a different transaction (e.g. a sale) requiring delivery of the specific securities in question, or
* wishes to avoid tax issues relating to income payments that become payable on the securities.

The replacement collateral must be *eligible collateral* under the terms listed within the particular CSA negotiated between the two parties. Substituted securities collateral does not need to be replaced by other securities; the collateral giver can choose the form of the replacement collateral (e.g. whether cash or securities), according to the terms documented within the negotiated CSA. Where a negotiated CSA permits use of cash collateral in a single eligible currency, substitution is not relevant as cash in any particular currency is fully *fungible*. Conversely, where a negotiated CSA contains two or more eligible currencies (e.g. EUR, GBP, USD), existing USD cash collateral can be substituted with either EUR or GBP.

The *exposed party* (the collateral taker) should ensure they have no *uncollateralised exposure* when processing a substitution, by ensuring the substituted collateral is not returned to the *collateral giver* prior to receipt of the *replacement collateral*.

The collateral giver must communicate to the collateral taker that it wishes to effect a substitution, by providing details of:

* the particular securities to be substituted and the relevant quantity of that security, and
* the proposed replacement collateral, and (in the case of bonds or equity) the quantity of that security, and
* the required *value date* of the substitution.

This information allows the collateral taker to assess the eligibility of the replacement collateral and its *current market value* and its *current collateral value*, following which (if agreed) consent should be communicated to the collateral giver.

The communication from the collateral giver to the collateral taker to request substitution can be achieved by email, alternatively a specific *S.W.I.F.T.* message (MT 505 Collateral Substitution) may be used.

Within the negotiated CSA, the Exchange Notification Time is documented; this is the deadline by which a collateral giver must communicate to the collateral taker its desire to effect a substitution, relative to the required value date of the substitution.

Table 22.27 provides examples of the specific collateral substitution communication deadlines listed within three of a firm's negotiated CSAs with counterparties:

TABLE 22.27   Examples of negotiated CSA content – collateral substitution communication deadline

Collateral Substitution Communication Deadline		
CSA #1	CSA #2	CSA #3
1:00pm London time	2:00pm London time	1:00pm London time

The subject of collateral substitution is explored further with Chapter 42 'OTC Derivatives and Collateral – The Collateral Lifecycle – Throughout Lifetime of Trade – Collateral Substitution'.

22.8.15 Valuation and Calculation Differences

The party that is in receipt of a valuation from a valuation agent, or a margin call notification from a counterparty, may not agree with the figures contained therein. The procedure for resolving such situations is covered within the CSA under the heading of *Dispute Resolution*.

Differences can arise from *marking-to-market* and *exposure* calculation relating to 1) OTC derivative trades, and 2) existing collateral.

The procedure requires:

- the recipient of the valuation or margin call to communicate its disagreement to the valuation agent or counterparty respectively, by the latest the close of business on the day following receipt. Common practice is to communicate a dispute as soon as possible
- settlement of the *undisputed amount* by close of business on the day following receipt of the margin call notification, if settled in cash; for example, if a margin call states a call amount of USD 6,000,000.00, but the recipient calculates the call amount to be USD 5,000,000.00, the recipient is required to deliver collateral of the latter amount, as that amount is not in dispute
- the involved parties to communicate with each other in an attempt to resolve the *disputed amount* by the stated resolution time; in general, because valuations are typically daily, the two firms will compare their valuation methods which may result in the disappearance of the disputed amount
- should the involved parties fail to resolve the disputed amount between them, then 1) that the valuation agent recalculate, and 2) that the valuation agent be required to gather *mid-market quotations* from four *market-makers* relating to the disputed amount and calculate their arithmetic average
- that the valuation agent notify the involved parties of the recalculation result (which is binding on both parties), following which the relevant party must deliver the appropriate collateral value.

Figure 22.5 represents the dispute resolution procedure relating to valuations of OTC derivative trades:

PART 4a

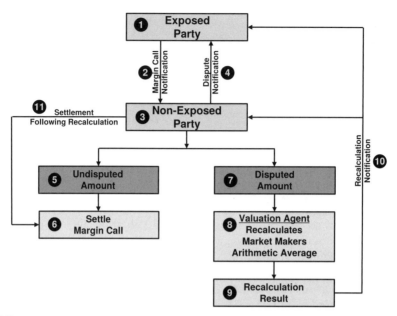

FIGURE 22.5 Dispute resolution procedure for exposure calculation

Step 1: following revaluation by both parties, the exposed party calculates the exposure

Step 2: the exposed party issues a margin call to its counterparty

Step 3: upon receipt of the margin call, the non-exposed party identifies a discrepancy

Step 4: the non-exposed party issues a dispute notification to the exposed party

Step 5: the undisputed amount is identified by the non-exposed party

Step 6: the undisputed amount is settled via cash or securities collateral

Step 7: the disputed amount is identified by the non-exposed party

Step 8: the valuation agent will attempt recalculation, obtaining prices from at least two market makers from which the arithmetic average is derived

Step 9: the recalculated exposure amount is identified

Step 10: the valuation agent notifies the two trading parties of the recalculation result

Step 11: following receipt of an updated margin call notification from the exposed party, the non-exposed party must settle the margin call.

A negotiated CSA lists the deadline by which the two trading parties must attempt to resolve any disputed amounts, following which the valuation agent's dispute-related responsibilities begin. This deadline falls under the heading of Resolution Time and is normally 25 hours after the Notification Time.

Table 22.28 provides examples of the dispute resolution deadlines listed within three of a firm's negotiated CSAs with counterparties:

TABLE 22.28 Examples of negotiated CSA content – dispute resolution deadline

Dispute Resolution Deadline		
CSA #1	CSA #2	CSA #3
1:00pm London time on the business day following the date of dispute notification	1:00pm London time on the dispute notification date	2:00pm London time on the third business day following the date of dispute notification

22.8.16 Interest on Cash Collateral

Where a party chooses to deliver collateral in the form of cash, it is common practice for interest to be paid by the collateral taker to the collateral giver (unless *negative interest rates* apply).

The rate payable is usually a commonly known interest 'reference' rate applicable to particular currencies; these are rates that change frequently based upon actual lending rates in the respective *money market*. Such reference rates are usually defined within each negotiated CSA and would typically be as listed in Table 22.29:

TABLE 22.29 Interest on cash collateral: example reference rates

Interest on Cash Collateral		
Currency	Reference Rate Name/Acronym	Reference Rate Description
USD	Effective Federal Funds	The Federal Reserve Bank of New York sets the rate based upon overnight lending between depository institutions.
EUR	EONIA	European Overnight Index Average. A weighted average of overnight lending rates; the standard reference rate for EUR loans.
GBP	SONIA	Sterling Overnight Index Average. A weighted average of overnight lending rates; the standard reference rate for GBP overnight loans.

The 'Reference Rate Name/Acronym' column in the above table states 'flat' rates. It is also possible to negotiate a 'spread', in which the reference rate has a fixed rate component, such as Effective Federal Funds rate minus 10 *basis points*, or EONIA minus 8 basis points.

The timing as to when such interest becomes payable is also listed within the negotiated CSA and is usually documented as being on a valuation date (refer to Sub-section 22.8.11 'Valuation Date' earlier in this chapter), normally 5 business days following calendar month end.

When interest rates in a particular currency are very low, rates may go lower still resulting in negative interest rates, where a payer of cash collateral is also the payer of the interest amount due on that cash. A firm may have many of its older negotiated CSAs referring only to positive interest rates, in which the receiver of the cash pays the interest due; that firm may choose to effect amendments to such negotiated CSAs with their relevant counterparties to ensure negative interest rate situations are covered.

The money market day count and divisor convention for the calculation of cash interest is:

- for USD and EUR – actual (calendar) days / 360
- for GBP – actual (calendar) days / 365.

For example:

- cash collateral of USD 5,000,000.00 given throughout the month of July, earning an Effective Federal Funds rate of 3.02% would earn USD 13,002.78 for the collateral giver. (The calculation is USD 5,000,000.00 × 3.02% / 360 × 31 days)
- cash collateral of EUR 8,500,000.00 given between 10th – 26th November, earning an EONIA rate of 1.64% would earn EUR 6,195.56 for the collateral giver. (The calculation is EUR 8,500,000.00 × 1.64% / 360 × 16 days)
- cash collateral of GBP 11,750,000.00 given throughout the month of February in a non-leap year, earning a SONIA rate of 0.92% would earn GBP 8,292.60 for the collateral giver. (The calculation is GBP 11,750,000.00 × 0.92% / 365 × 28 days.)

Table 22.30 provides examples of reference interest rates relating to cash collateral listed within three of a firm's negotiated CSAs with counterparties:

TABLE 22.30   Examples of negotiated CSA content – interest on cash collateral

Interest on Cash Collateral		
CSA #1	CSA #2	CSA #3
EUR – EONIA -2bp	USD – Fed Effective –10bp EUR – EONIA -4bp GBP – SONIA -6bp	GBP – SONIA -8bp

The remainder of this chapter refers to important impacts of giving and taking collateral, relating to OTC derivative trades.

22.9 OWNERSHIP OF COLLATERAL

Under the version of the CSA known as the *English Law CSA* (refer to Section 22.5 'CSA Legal Structures' earlier within this chapter), outright legal ownership of securities collateral passes from *transferor* to *transferee*; the CSA also states that the transferor retains no legal claim to the collateral. In legal parlance such a claim is known as a *security interest*.

The transferee does, however, have a legal obligation to return the collateral to the transferor in future as a result of 1) the *exposed party* changing from transferee to transferor, or 2) through *collateral substitution*, or 3) when the underlying trade is terminated (at which point no exposure remains).

It must also be observed that, from a trading and an operations standpoint, and from the perspective of both parties:

1. the transferor:
   - has not sold the securities given as collateral and therefore ownership of the securities *trading position* is retained (although possession has been temporarily lost) – this party is known as the *beneficial owner*
   - will recover possession of the collateral at a future point in time (for the reasons stated in the previous paragraph)
2. the transferee:
   - has not purchased the securities received as collateral and therefore has no trading position in the securities (although possession has been temporarily gained) – this party is known as the *legal owner*
   - will give back possession of the collateral at a future point in time (for the reasons stated in the previous paragraph).

In order for both the transferor and the transferee to remain in proper control of its business, the *books & records* of both firms must accurately reflect these facts.

Regarding the return of securities collateral to the collateral giver, the same security (i.e. the same *ISIN*) must be returned; this is known as *equivalent collateral*. Only under the circumstances where the issuer of the security has replaced the originally delivered security with a replacement security (i.e. the original security no longer exists), would it be unavoidable to return a different security from the original security.

22.9.1 Income on Securities Collateral

In general terms, income is payable on securities in the form of *coupon payments* on bonds, and *dividend payments* on equity.

Coupon payments are usually predictable, as on most types of *interest-bearing bonds* both the *coupon rate* and *coupon payment dates* are known when the bond is issued. Dividend payments on normal equity issues are not predictable (they are announced to shareholders as and when the *issuer* chooses to make such a payment), as the decision to pay a dividend is normally dependent upon profits made within a specified trading period.

When income falls due on securities held as collateral, and where the transferee has a *record date* position at its *custodian*, the transferee's cash account will be credited at the custodian (usually on the income payment date) with the cash income amount. For example, an *exposed party* holding collateral in the form of USD 15,000,000.00 of International Bank for Reconstruction & Development bonds with a 4.25% coupon maturing 15th March 2030, with interest paying annually on 15th March, will receive a credit of USD 637,500.00 on 15th March (providing the *transferee* held the bonds in its custodian account on the record date, which is normally 1 day prior to coupon payment date).

PART 4a

The value of the income payment must be paid by the transferee (the party in possession of the collateral and the *legal owner*) to the transferor (the *beneficial owner* of the collateral). By receiving such a payment, the transferor will receive the income to which it is entitled.

It is also possible that, dependent upon the security type, *withholding tax* is deducted from the gross income amount received by the transferee. (Withholding tax is an involved subject in its own right and can become complex; therefore this subject is intentionally not covered here.)

In order to receive timely payment, the transferor may need to issue a coupon claim for the income amount to its counterparty. Conversely, the transferee should immediately recognise (from its own books & records) that it owes the transferor the income.

Some firms may consider such actions relating to income payments as significant extra work, and both the transferor and transferee may choose to avoid such situations by effecting a *collateral substitution* prior to the record date of the income event.

22.9.2 Corporate Actions on Securities Collateral

Corporate actions are events that occur to securities and which impact a securities holding. Although impacting bonds on some occasions, the majority of corporate actions relate to equity and, like dividends, are announced by the issuer as and when they arise.

The significance of corporate actions on collateral held by a transferee is that:

- the security may need to be removed and replaced by a different security, or
- the quantity of the holding may need to be increased or decreased, or
- cash may need to be paid by a deadline date.

An important consideration is whether the event is classified as mandatory, optional or voluntary:

- mandatory event: the holder has no choice of outcome, and many such events apply to holdings on a pro-rata basis
- optional event: the holder has a choice of outcome (e.g. cash or securities) – all holders will be impacted similarly dependent upon their choice
- voluntary event: the holder has a choice as to whether to subscribe or to convert, or to take no action.

Bond-related corporate actions include *restructuring events*, in which the issuer decides to replace one or many existing bond issues with one or more replacement securities, potentially a new bond plus equity. Another such event is the decision to convert a *convertible bond*, which may be at the bondholder's option or the issuer's option.

Equity corporate actions are also designed to meet an issuer's specific objective. Table 22.31 provides examples of popular equity corporate action types:

TABLE 22.31   Equity corporate actions

Equity Corporate Actions: Impact on Collateral Held			
Corporate Action Type	Description (issuer's objective)	Example	Impact
Bonus Issue (mandatory)	Issuance of new shares, on a pro-rata basis to existing shareholders, free of cost (to reward investors)	1:5 Bonus Issue – 1 new share for every 5 currently held	Existing shareholding increased, balanced by pro-rata decrease in share price
Rights Issue (voluntary)	Issuance of new shares, on a pro-rata basis to existing shareholders, at a cost to investors (to raise further capital)	3:7 Rights Issue – opportunity for investors to acquire 3 new shares for every 7 currently held at a cost of GBP 4.76 per new share	Existing shareholding increased, balanced by decrease in share price, taking account of the difference between market price of existing shares & subscription price of new shares
Stock Split (mandatory)	Issuance of new shares in replacement of existing shares (to reduce market price)	2:1 Stock Split – 2 shares in a new security in replacement of 1 share in cancelled old security	Existing shareholding cancelled, replaced by increased share quantity in new security balanced by pro-rata decrease in share price
Reverse Split (mandatory)	Issuance of new shares in replacement of existing shares (to increase market price)	1:15 Reverse Split – 1 share in a new security in replacement of 15 shares in cancelled old security	Existing shareholding cancelled, replaced by decreased share quantity in new security balanced by pro-rata increase in share price

Following such events, the course of action relating to collateral must be determined carefully, dependent upon the purpose and impact of the event:

- stock splits
  - assume collateral is transferred in the form of 100,000 Issuer ABC USD 1.00 Common Stock, with a current market price of USD 110.00 and a market value of USD 11,000,000.00. Two weeks later, the issuer announces a 2:1 stock split (a mandatory event), resulting in a replacement holding of 200,000 Issuer XYZ USD 0.50 Common Stock, with a new market price of USD 55.00 and a market value of USD 11,000,000.00. The issuer's objective in a stock split is to reduce the share price in the market place; in this example the share price is halved and the share quantity is doubled, but the market value remains unaffected. In a stock split, the removal of holdings in the original security and the replacement of holdings in the new security are effected simultaneously on the same date (the Effective Date). Consequently, from a collateral management perspective, there is no benefit in the transferee returning the securities to the transferor as that would leave the transferee uncollateralised.

PART 4a

■ rights issues

   ■ assume collateral is transferred in the form of 1,000,000 Issuer XYZ GBP 1.00 Ordinary Shares. Three weeks later, the issuer announces a 3:7 rights issue (a voluntary event) at a subscription cost of GBP 4.76 per new share. In this example, the beneficial owner has the opportunity to acquire 428,571 new shares, at a cost of GBP 2,039,997.96 (calculation 1,000,000 / 7 × 3 = 428,571 × GBP 4.76 = GBP 2,039,997.96). The beneficial owner (i.e. the transferor) must decide whether to subscribe, or not; the transferee is not the beneficial owner and is not empowered to decide whether to subscribe or not. If the transferee is holding the securities on the record date of the event, the transferor and transferee must communicate as to whether the transferor wishes to subscribe, or not. If the answer is yes (subscribe), payment of GBP 2,039,997.96 must be made to the transferee's custodian by the custodian's subscription deadline; if the deadline is missed, the opportunity has been lost. The transferee is unlikely to make the subscription payment (on behalf of the transferor) without first receiving the subscription cash from the transferor. Such complications and risks between transferor and transferee can be avoided if the collateral is returned to the transferor (as part of a *collateral substitution*) prior to the event's record date, following which the transferor will be directly responsible for paying the subscription cost to its custodian by that custodian's deadline.

In general terms, the processing of corporate actions is a specialist and risky aspect of securities processing, and great care must be taken particularly for optional and voluntary events. For further detail read this author's book, *Corporate Actions: a Guide to Securities Event Management* (ISBN 0-470-87066-4)).

22.10 EXAMPLE NEGOTIATED CSAs: OVERVIEW

At various points within Section 22.8 'CSA Components' earlier in this chapter, the contents of three example negotiated CSAs have been listed. For the reader's convenience, Table 22.32 brings together all the components of all three negotiated CSAs.

TABLE 22.32 Consolidated view of the content of three of a firm's negotiated CSAs with counterparties

Component	CSA #1	CSA #2	CSA #3
Product Coverage	interest rate swaps forward rate agreements foreign exchange forwards credit default swaps total return swaps variance swaps	interest rate swaps interest rate options forward rate agreements cross-currency swaps credit default swaps total return swaps equity options variance swaps	interest rate swaps cross-currency swaps credit default swaps total return swaps
Collateral Direction	Bilateral (two-way)	Unilateral (in favour of counterparty)	Unilateral (in favour of firm)
Standing Settlement Instructions	Firm's EUR Cash: Bank X Account 12345 Cpty's EUR Cash: Bank G, Account 98765 Firm's International Bonds: Custodian G, Account ABC06 Cpty's International Bonds: Custodian G, Account 34076	Firm's USD Cash: Bank Y Account 60335 Cpty's USD Cash: Bank T, Account 55562 *(plus SSIs for EUR and GBP for each party)*	Firm's GBP Cash: Bank Z Account 88827 Cpty's GBP Cash: Bank P, Account 00769 Firm's International Bonds: Custodian G, Account ABC06 Cpty's International Bonds: Custodian G, Account HH909
Base Currency	EUR	USD	GBP
Eligible Currency	EUR	USD, EUR, GBP	GBP
Eligible Credit Support	EUR cash G10 Government Securities	USD cash EUR cash GBP cash	GBP cash G10 Government Securities Corporate Bonds
Valuation Percentage	EUR cash — VP = 100% G10 Government Securities — VP = 99%	USD cash — VP = 100% EUR cash — VP = 100% GBP cash — VP = 100%	GBP cash — VP = 100% G10 Government Securities — VP = 99% Corporate Bonds — VP = 9.5%
Independent Amount	Independent amount in firm's favour, for a fixed sum of EUR 10 million for all open trades	No independent amount applicable	Independent amount in counterparty's favour, at 5% of notional principal for individual trades

(continued)

TABLE 22.32 Consolidated view of the content of three of a firm's negotiated CSAs with counterparties *(continued)*

Component	CSA #1	CSA #2	CSA #3
Threshold	No threshold applicable	Two-way threshold for a fixed sum of USD 1 million for all open trades	No threshold applicable
Minimum Transfer Amount	Two-way MTA of EUR 500,000	Two-way MTA of USD 100,000	MTA of GBP 250,000 when we call. MTA of GBP 500,000 when counterparty calls
Rounding	Round up the delivery amount, round down the return amount to the nearest EUR 50,000	No rounding applicable	Round down the delivery amount, round down the return amount to the nearest GBP 10,000
Valuation Agent	No valuation agent specified; the party making the margin call will be regarded as the agent	The counterparty will be the valuation agent, subject to agreement by the firm	The firm will be the valuation agent, subject to agreement by the counterparty
Valuation Date	Every business day in London	Every Wednesday in London and Paris	Each local business day in London and New York
Valuation Time	Close of business on valuation date –1 business day	Close of business on valuation date –1 business day	Close of business on valuation date –1 business day
Notification Time	1:00pm London time	2:00pm Central European Time	1:00pm London Time
Collateral Substitution Communication Deadline	1:00pm London time	2:00pm London time	1:00pm London time
Dispute Resolution Deadline	1:00pm London time on the business day following the date of dispute notification	1:00pm London time on the dispute notification date	2:00pm London time on the third business day following the date of dispute notification
Interest on Cash Collateral	EUR – EONIA -2bp	USD – Fed Effective –10bp EUR – EONIA -4bp GBP – SONIA -6bp	GBP – SONIA -8bp

22.11 PARTY LIQUIDATION: IMPACT ON COLLATERAL

The ISDA Master Agreement lists as Events of Default situations including (with reference to either party), bankruptcy, failure to pay or to deliver, failure to comply with a credit support requirement.

Clearly, such events do not occur on a day-by-day basis, unlike the majority of topics listed within this chapter. Should such an event occur, the legal documentation provides for the settlement of the combined result of:

- current transaction exposures, and
- current collateral held by the transferee.

Should the party in default owe the net settlement figure, any collateral held by the non-defaulting party may be used in settlement, and any remainder pursued as an *unsecured creditor*. Should the non-defaulting party owe the settlement figure, any collateral held by the defaulting party plus any other amounts owed by the defaulting party would be taken into account, and any remaining balance is payable to the defaulting party's administrator.

This process is known as *close out netting*, and within the CSA falls under the heading of Default.

22.12 CONCLUSION

From the perspective of any firm, whether *buy-side* or *sell-side*, a CSA defines the terms and conditions under which OTC derivative trade-related *exposures*, with a particular *counterparty*, are to be *mitigated*.

From the perspective of the operations and collateral professional, the day-to-day management of counterparty exposures in OTC derivative trades must be achieved with direct relevance to the currently valid legal documentation negotiated between the firm and its various counterparties.

Failure to manage the firm's counterparty exposures in accordance with the legal documentation is very likely to result in the firm's exposures failing to be mitigated fully.

PART 4a

CHAPTER 23

OTC Derivatives and Collateral – Static Data

This chapter describes what static data[1] is, how it is used for OTC derivative collateral, the benefits gained by its use and the protective measures needed to ensure such valuable data is not corrupted, moved or lost. Additionally, the way that software systems are used for collateral management purposes is described.

23.1 INTRODUCTION

Generically speaking, the use of *static data* (also known as reference data) is a significant factor in enabling a firm to process trades of all types in a highly efficient manner, and to achieve *Straight Through Processing* (STP).

Static data is an internal store of information that remains constant or changes infrequently; it facilitates automated and repeated use of essential information which must be added to the basic details of an individual trade.

If static data is present within the relevant systems of a firm, it enables immediate capture of an individual trade's details and subsequent enrichment of additional (but essential) information.

Different categories of static data are necessary, including:

- *trading entities* within the firm
- *counterparties* of the firm
- currencies
- derivative products, and
- *securities* (in a variety of roles, including when used as collateral)

and in each case, the necessary static data is explored within this chapter.

---

[1] Note: although strictly speaking the word 'data' is a plural in the English language, the author's preference is to refer to 'data' in the singular as that is how it is used in normal everyday language.

PART 4a

Such data can be held entirely manually (i.e. in handwritten form), or within a software system repository; how such information is held is entirely a matter for the firm itself. The use of static data is not confined to the Settlement Department, as other areas including **Risk Management, Reconciliation Department** and the **Corporate Actions** Department make active use of this information.

The word 'static' within the term 'static data' may imply that the information does not change; the majority of static data items are static and are not subject to change, however certain aspects of static data are subject to periodic change or updating, and such areas of static data are highlighted within this chapter.

The challenge for a firm is to:

- gather the relevant data
- store it securely
- update it when necessary
- utilise it appropriately

ensuring that for every individual trade, only the appropriate information is attached to the trade from the entire store of data. Typically, the amount of information held within a firm's static data repository is vast; large firms may be holding within their systems database hundreds of thousands of financial products, and hundreds (in some cases thousands) of counterparties. It is essential to select the correct information in a timely fashion if delays and costs are to be avoided.

In an automated environment in which a software system is central to the firm's operational processing needs, when a trade has been executed and captured by the trader within a dedicated trading system, the trade will be received by the operations processing system (via an interface) and will, at that point in time, typically contain only the basic (but essential) trade details. The actual information captured for an individual OTC derivative trade will depend upon the specific type of OTC derivative product. But, as a minimum, and for **credit default swaps** and **interest rate swaps**, the following must be captured:

- the particular OTC derivative product traded, for example:
  - a fixed-for-floating interest rate swap
  - a single name credit default swap
- the firm's own trading entity and location
- the **counterparty's** name and location
- the operation (trade direction) from the firm's perspective, for example:
  - in an interest rate swap, whether the fixed rate payer or fixed rate receiver
  - in a credit default swap, whether **protection buyer** or **protection seller**
- the trade date:
  - the date of trade execution
- the price or rate at which the trade was executed, for example:
  - in a fixed-for-floating interest rate swap, the specific fixed rate versus the floating benchmark rate (e.g. 6-month EUR Libor)
  - in a single name credit default swap, the premium rate (expressed in **basis points per annum**)

- the *notional principal*:
  - the theoretical quantity on which all cash values are calculated
- the *scheduled maturity date*:
  - the closing date of the trade, beyond which the trade is no longer live and valid.

However, for operational processing purposes, the trade requires enriching with additional and essential information.

For some firms, their systems structure will be as described above, that is the traders have a dedicated trading system which is interfaced with the (completely separate) operations processing system. Under such arrangements, each of the systems will need to utilise their own set of static data, which, if not maintained identically, is highly likely to cause mismatches. For example, a trade is successfully captured within the trading system but not captured in the operations processing system due to missing static data (e.g. a new counterparty). Consequently, additional reconciliation processes and controls around static data entry and amendment are often employed in organisations that use separate systems for trading and operations. The purpose of such controls is to mitigate the risk of static data not being synchronised and subsequently to reduce the probability of a trade being delayed in the daily operations flow, due to inaccuracies in static data held. Other firms may have a single system which caters for the needs of the traders and of the operations personnel; under this arrangement there is no possibility of a mismatch.

Fully functional operations systems not only hold the necessary static data, but also have the capability of automatically enriching trades with the appropriate data.

23.2 STATIC DATA AND NEW OTC DERIVATIVE TRADES

Where a firm executes a trade in an OTC derivative such as a credit default swap or an interest rate swap, the trade details can only be captured by the trader if the particular product is set up within the trading system's static data.

If that is not the case, the static data relating to the particular product will need to be set up as quickly as possible, following which the trade can be captured by the trader. Such a delay in setting up the relevant static data means that the firm's commitment is not (yet) recorded within the firm's *books & records*; such a situation can have negative consequences as:

- the firm's risk managers will not be aware of the *exposure* with the counterparty,
- the operations personnel will not be aware of the trade (and may advise a client that the firm has not traded with the client, when in fact the firm has executed the trade), and
- the Collateral Department will not be aware of the trade and are therefore unlikely to factor the trade into 1) their portfolio of trades with the counterparty, and consequently 2) their exposure calculations.

It is therefore important that traders and static data personnel work closely in order to identify situations where the product static data is not present, and then to act

PART 4a

as quickly as possible to set up the necessary data, without jeopardising the accuracy of data.

Similarly, where a trade has been executed with a new counterparty, and that counterparty has not (yet) been set up within static data, similar risks exist. However, in this particular circumstance, providing the product is set up within static data, a prudent measure is to capture the trade temporarily against a 'dummy' counterparty, pending the setting up of the real counterparty. This measure allows the aforementioned areas (i.e. risk management, operations and Collateral Department) to be aware that a trade has been executed, albeit with missing counterparty details. Once the real counterparty has been set up within static data, the trade booked to the dummy counterparty should be replaced by the trade booked against the real counterparty.

23.3 STATIC DATA AND COLLATERAL MANAGEMENT

From a purely *collateral management* perspective, the following two aspects are important:

1. whether the trade has been captured with all the correct details (as mentioned previously), and
2. whether the specific collateral-related information has been set up.

The particular collateral-related static data that is necessary to set up within a firm begins with details of each **Credit Support Annex** (CSA) with each counterparty, which should be held within an agreements database. Like any other static data system, this system must have restricted access in order to prevent unauthorised input, amendment and cancellation of data.

Then, the details contained within each CSA (i.e. per counterparty) should be input and held within the database; such details include:

- base currency
- products covered (e.g. IRS, CDS)
- whether collateral arrangements are 1-way (unilateral) or 2-way (bilateral)
- frequency of *mark-to-market* and collateral valuation
- *eligible collateral*
- applicable *haircuts*
- *independent amounts*
- *thresholds*
- *minimum transfer amounts*
- *rounding* rules
- notification times
- the counterparty's cash *standing settlement instructions* (SSIs)
- the counterparty's securities standing settlement instructions (SSIs).

Please refer to Chapter 22 'OTC Derivatives and Collateral – Legal Protection – Credit Support Annex' for further details regarding CSA content and its use.

Where eligible collateral within the particular CSA includes *bonds*, the details of each bond that may be given or received as collateral should be set up within static data. This is important if a firm wishes to automate the following: 1) calculation of current values of bond collateral, 2) the current value of *accrued interest*, and 3) the generation of securities *settlement instructions*.

Likewise, if a CSA includes *equity* collateral, the details of such securities that may be given or received as collateral should be set up within static data.

With regard to point 2) above, the *current market value* of *interest-bearing bonds* includes the current value of *accrued interest*, and correct calculation of accrued interest is dependent upon knowing:

- the *coupon rate* (e.g. 4.75%)
- the most recent *coupon payment date* (e.g. 15th October)
- the coupon frequency (e.g. semi-annual)
- the accrued interest *day count convention* (e.g. 30 days per month or actual days), and
- the accrued interest *divisor convention* (e.g. 360 or 365).

Additionally, for bonds and equity as collateral, external securities identifiers such as *ISIN* and the relevant national codes (e.g. *Sedol, CUSIP, WKN*) should be stored within static data for automation of securities settlement instructions, and for listing on collateral correspondence with counterparties (e.g. *collateral substitution* notification).

23.4 HOW SOFTWARE SYSTEMS HOLD COLLATERAL-RELATED STATIC DATA

A firm needs to hold, within its static data, appropriate information regarding the content of each of its CSAs with counterparties, as well as the detail of eligible securities (which may be given or taken as collateral relating to exposures in OTC derivative trades).

How the information is stored within modern systems is often dependent upon the main purpose of the system. For example, is the starting point a trading system that has evolved with *middle office* or operations functionality, or is it an operations system that has evolved with collateral management functionality throughout time? This means that the data relating to the legal agreement is held within:

- the trading/operations system and hence referenced internally, or
- a dedicated collateral management system, or
- a standalone master customer data system.

If the information is held in the trading/operations system, it is usually held as part of the party/counterparty static data in that same system; if instead the data is held in a standalone collateral management system, it is usually held together with the party/counterparty data, but the majority of the static data is held outside the collateral

PART 4a

management system, except for the data regarding the agreement which is then held in the collateral management system. If the data is recorded in the 'master customer data system', it is then referenced by the collateral management system via a common reference.

Common to all systems, regardless of their native purpose, is that they hold the data in the following way; Party/Counterparty –> Master Agreement –> CSA details. The details, regardless of system, are usually held in a matrix fashion, presenting the data to the end user in tables. This data is then available to the end user via a quick link; for example, if the end user is looking at the *margin call* monitor, clicking on a particular call enables viewing of both the call's details and the details of the appropriate CSA. Such 'single click' access has become the dominant access method in recent times, as the focus on collateral management in general and the accuracy of calculations in particular has increased significantly.

The approach of holding the CSA details under each agreement is observed to be the prevailing approach in systems delivered from vendors such as IBM, FIS and Lombard. The matrix approach under each CSA is very often used to provide the end user with an 'Excel'-like experience, facilitating a smooth and familiar system adaptation.

The specific details held in such systems are, in general terms:

- a list of *eligible collateral* (based on ISIN as the key to the instrument register), then
- a list of associated *haircut* values (please refer to Chapter 22 'OTC Derivatives and Collateral – Legal Protection – Credit Support Annex'), and then
- a number of fields for the *minimum transfer amount, threshold*, etc.

Usually, systems will show these details in a dashboard-like fashion, available in real time to the end user when working with daily *exposure* calculations.

In very mature systems, the end user will be able to jump from the overview page, to other relevant details to perform daily exposure calculation tasks. For example, the end user can often jump from the eligible collateral list to a portfolio overview that shows available securities holdings (including a proposed ISIN) to perform the posting of collateral. Some systems facilitate use of an algorithm to automatically select the instrument for collateral posting; such algorithms are linked to the CSA or the portfolio.

23.5 SOURCES OF STATIC DATA

The origin of static data depends upon the type of data, whether the CSA, counterparty or financial product data.

23.5.1 Credit Support Annex

The origin of the content of each *CSA* that a firm negotiates with its *counterparty* is the firm itself. Consequently, each of the components relating to a particular CSA originates from the firm itself, and as such the creation of CSA-related static data is in the firm's own hands.

23.5.2 Cash and Securities Standing Settlement Instructions

Prior to a firm trading with a particular counterparty for the first time, it is usual for the firm and the counterparty to exchange *cash correspondent* (or *nostro*) and account number details, per currency. Such data will be used (for example) for payments and receipts of *premium* in a *credit default swap*, and for payments and receipts of *cash collateral*. Where *securities* are included in the CSA as *eligible collateral*, securities *custodian* details will also be exchanged.

Such nostro and custodian details are commonly known as *standing settlement instructions*; the intention, from the perspective of both parties, is that the account details exchanged reflect the account numbers over which cash is to be paid and received, and securities are to be delivered and received, until further notice. Should, for example, the firm choose to set up a new nostro in place of the original nostro, the firm must ensure it communicates the details of such changes, including the effective date of the change, to all of its counterparties well before the effective date. If this is not actioned, the firm is at risk of receiving payments from its counterparties into the incorrect nostro, which may prove costly to the firm. Conversely, if the firm receives a communication from a counterparty stating that the counterparty is changing its nostro or custodian account details as at a specified date, the firm is at risk of failing to update the counterparty's SSI within the firm's own static data, or of failing to update the SSI as at the effective date. Any cash amounts due to be paid by the firm to the counterparty from the effective date are at risk of being made to the old SSI erroneously; if such errors are made by the firm, the counterparty may well claim for loss of interest from the firm.

A firm's nostro and custodian details should be regarded as private information; such information is therefore typically not freely available. Consequently, it is normal that only when it is agreed by two parties that they will trade with one another, will information such as nostro and custodian details be swapped.

23.5.3 Financial Product Data

Generically speaking, systems that handle financial products (whether trading systems or operational processing systems), are reliant upon coding methods in order to uniquely identify an individual product. This includes currencies, *securities* and *OTC derivatives*.

Currencies   For example, currencies are today recognised globally by use of a three-character coding system introduced by the International Organisation for Standardisation; the coding system is commonly known as *ISO Currency Codes* and is less commonly known as the 'ISO 4217 code list'. Each of the world's currencies is given such a code; Table 23.1 lists a selection of ISO currency codes, by country and currency name:

PART 4a

TABLE 23.1   ISO Currency Codes

Country	Currency	ISO Code
Argentina	Peso	ARS
Australia	Dollar	AUD
Brazil	Real	BRL
Canada	Dollar	CAD
China	Renminbi	CNY
Denmark	Krone	DKK
Hong Kong	Dollar	HKD
India	Rupee	INR
Indonesia	Rupiah	IDR
Japan	Yen	JPY
Korea (South)	Won	KRW
Kuwait	Dinar	KWD
Malaysia	Ringgit	MYR
New Zealand	Dollar	NZD
Mexico	Peso	MXN
Pakistan	Rupee	PKR
Russia	Ruble	RUB
Saudi Arabia	Riyal	SAR
Singapore	Dollar	SGD
South Africa	Rand	ZAR
Taiwan	New Dollar	TWD
Thailand	Baht	THB
UK	Pound	GBP
USA	Dollar	USD
Vietnam	Dong	VND

Table 23.2 lists those countries that utilise the Euro (EUR) as their currency, at the time of writing:

TABLE 23.2   Currency of 19 EU Member States

EUR: Currency of 19 EU Member States
Austria, Belgium, Cyprus, Estonia, Finland, France, Germany, Greece, Ireland, Italy, Latvia, Lithuania, Luxembourg, Malta, the Netherlands, Portugal, Slovakia, Slovenia and Spain

The ISO currency codes are recognised internationally and can therefore be used by, for example, a firm in Sweden that wishes to settle a *margin call* received from its counterparty based in the UK, in USD, by transmitting a cash *settlement instruction* to its cash correspondent in New York, without the need for interpretation of the currency in question by the receiving party.

Note: prior to the common adoption of ISO currency codes globally, the sender of such a settlement instruction could have used one of a range of symbols or abbreviations for USD, including United States Dollar, US Dollar, Dollar, US$, $; the recipient of such an instruction would then need to 'translate' the symbol received into a currency symbol that was meaningful to its organisation.

Securities   Where securities (*bonds* in particular) are eligible as collateral, in order to automate the processing of such collateral, firms need to hold within their static data the attributes and characteristics of individual bonds which facilitates, for example, accurate bond collateral value calculation.

Securities static data is publicly available data. Each security has specific and unique attributes that a firm must make itself aware of as, from a *collateral management* perspective, *over-collateralisation* or under-collateralisation may result if information is not held accurately, thereby leaving the firm exposed. Numerous types of bond exist with many bonds having significantly different features. However, it must also be noted that some individual bonds have almost identical characteristics to another individual bond; for example, two bonds may have been issued by the same *issuer* (e.g. International Bank for Reconstruction and Development), with the same coupon rate (e.g. 4.25%), with the same maturity date (e.g. 15th January 2030), with the distinguishing feature being the issued currency of the two bonds (e.g. one bond issued in EUR, the other in USD).

In order to facilitate unambiguous identification of securities, each individual security is given a unique identification code number.

The securities numbering convention that is used globally is *ISIN* (International Securities Identification Number), a 12-character code comprising the following:

- the first two characters are a country code relating to the country of the issuer
- the next nine characters are the national securities identification number, and
- the last character is a check digit (which verifies the code).

In addition to the ISIN code, securities identification numbers are given and used nationally within the world's financial centres. For example, in the US, *CUSIP* codes are used, whilst *Sedol* codes are used in the UK, *ASX* codes are used in Australia, *WKN* codes are used in Germany and *Quick* codes are used in Japan.

An individual bond may therefore have two valid identifier codes, both an ISIN and a national code; both codes should be held within a firm's static data. Securities identification code numbers are used for a variety of purposes, and from a collateral management perspective, uses include:

- the *marking-to-market* of bonds from *data vendors*
- the communication of proposed collateral by a firm to its *counterparty*
- the issue of settlement instructions to custodians.

Regarding use of both codes by a firm, for example the marking-to-market process may utilise the ISIN code, whilst the custodian requires the national code to be quoted on settlement instructions.

PART 4a

The primary source of static data for both bonds and equity is the issue *prospectus*, which is the origin of the detail of a security. For an individual issue, the issuer produces the prospectus which contains all the features, characteristics (and peculiarities) of the issue; there is a significantly greater chance of an unusual feature relating to a bond (for example, a *short first coupon* or a *long first coupon*), compared with equity.

However, many *buy-side* and *sell-side* firms source their securities information from organisations that specialise in gathering and distributing securities data, typically electronically; such organisations are known as *data vendors*. Examples of such organisations are: Bloomberg, ICE Data Services, Markit, SIX Financial Information and Thomson Reuters. Data vendors usually charge a subscription cost to supply their services to firms.

Furthermore, entities that utilise and publish securities static data include *stock exchanges*, *central securities depositories* and *custodian* organisations.

Note: although securities static data is publicly available information, it may or may not be free to use. Over the last decade, various companies in the financial sector have taken the role of maintaining publicly available securities data and are now demanding payment for various uses of that data. An example is the American CUSIP which is embedded in the ISIN. The issuance of the ISIN may be followed with a small fee, however, under the agreement with the Association of National Numbering Agencies (ANNA), this fee is intended to cover only the actual processing cost of the issuance of a new CUSIP number. The debate over charging for the use of securities static data is ongoing.

OTC Derivatives   In parallel with currencies and securities, OTC derivative products must also be uniquely identifiable.

In order for a firm to *mitigate* the risk that its *counterparty* believes a different product has been traded (from that captured by the firm), it is essential that both firms reference a uniquely identifiable OTC derivative product. The importance of this is seen following *trade execution*, in the areas of trade capture and the *trade confirmation* process.

For credit derivatives, the equivalent of an ISIN exists; this is known as the *Reference Entity Database* (RED), owned by Markit. This database combines the *reference entity* and associated *reference obligation* to form a unique alphanumeric code. For example:

- General Electric – the reference entity, represented by a unique 6-digit reference entity code (known as a CLIP), is combined with an individual bond, such as
- General Electric 3.95% bonds 15th February 2028 – a particular bond issued by General Electric, represented by its ISIN or CUSIP or Sedol code.

When these two components are brought together, a unique 9-digit alphanumeric Pair CLIP is formed. Where the same reference entity is combined with a different bond issued by the same entity, a different 9-digit Pair CLIP results; however, the first 6 digits (the reference entity code) will be the same, but the final 3 digits will differ according to the particular bond.

This is also necessary for a firm internally, so that two or more trades form a single position in the same product; in the case of a *single name credit default swap*, for example, a sale of a *notional principal* of USD 5,000,000 of Reference Entity XYZ with a *scheduled maturity date* of 20th June 2030 is able to be offset against an existing purchase of USD 20,000,000 of the same product, resulting in a net positive position of USD 15,000,000 of notional principal.

Note: regulatory authorities around the globe recognise the need for regulatory reporting of OTC derivative trades, and in order for such reporting to be executed effectively, common standards must be utilised. Please refer to Chapter 46 'OTC Derivatives and Collateral – Regulatory Change and the Future of Collateral – Introduction'.

23.6 SETTING UP OF AND MAINTENANCE OF STATIC DATA

The activity involved in static data management includes the maintenance of existing data and the insertion of new data.

23.6.1 Maintenance of Existing Data

For most firms, the existing data held within its internal *static data repository* (or repositories) has been accumulated over many years. Once in situ, such data is typically accessed thousands of times per day, for a variety of reasons. Consequently, the data is considered very precious, as gathering such data is the result of many years of work, and where subscription to *data vendors* has occurred, significant accumulated cost. If a total failure of static data systems occurred, such a circumstance is likely to prove very costly to the firm.

As a result, all data set up to date should be carefully guarded, with change capability limited to just those personnel that appreciate the impact of such changes, as mistakes may prove extremely costly in monetary and relationship terms.

23.6.2 Insertion of New Data

The firm should ensure, as far as entirely new data is concerned (e.g. new OTC derivative products, new bonds as collateral, SSIs of new counterparties), that firstly only verified data results in input to static data repositories. Secondly, where data has been input manually, such input is verified by a senior member of staff using the *four eyes principle*.

In general terms, the firm must take measures to ensure the integrity of its static data at all times.

23.7 CONCLUSION

For all financial services firms, the quality of static data held internally is of paramount importance; it is at the heart of a firm's ability to process trades, positions and associated tasks in a highly efficient manner, and is the key to a firm achieving *straight through processing* (STP).

However, having high quality static data is of limited use if the creation (input) of new or amended static data is not achieved in a timely fashion, as this will prevent STP and may jeopardise time-sensitive tasks, such as the issuance of trade confirmations to clients or the issuance of settlement instructions to the firm's cash correspondents and custodians.

The ideal is the combination of high quality static data and timely input of new or amended data. Furthermore, the personnel responsible for the maintenance of static data should ideally possess a good understanding of how their data is used, in order to appreciate the importance of their responsibilities.

CHAPTER 24

The OTC Derivative Collateral Lifecycle

This chapter introduces the multiple steps involved in the collateral processing lifecycle relating specifically to OTC derivatives. This entire section of the book covers the primary components impacting the successful management of OTC derivative-related collateral.

24.1 THE OTC DERIVATIVE COLLATERAL LIFECYCLE – INTRODUCTION

For each *OTC derivative* trade that a firm executes, two parallel streams of processing activity exist alongside one another (see Figure 24.1), and for the duration of the trade's lifetime, namely:

- trade processing, and
- collateral processing.

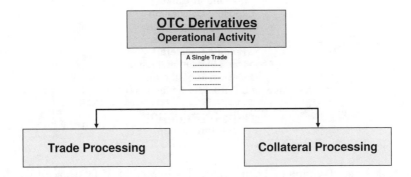

FIGURE 24.1 Single trade with two streams of operational activity

Each stream has a processing lifecycle; a series of logical and sequential steps through which the trade passes, albeit for differing ultimate purposes.

Both lifecycles begin from the same base, with areas such as pre-trading, trading and particularly post-trading activity being common to both. It is important to state that risks are introduced for a firm should a particular trade not follow the same path for both trade and collateral processing.

A common requirement amongst the management of all firms executing OTC derivative trades is that trades are processed in the most efficient manner possible, and this is reflected in their desire to achieve *straight through processing*; this is only achievable if the trade lifecycle is begun by recording the details of each trade in a timely and accurate fashion by the firm's traders, and is handled efficiently, cost effectively and within the various deadlines in the operational areas of the firm.

A problem created early on in the processing lifecycle will cost more to correct the further it flows through the operational process, the effect of the error being replicated and magnified.

The OTC derivative collateral lifecycle can be regarded as a series of logical steps, which are represented generically within the following diagram:

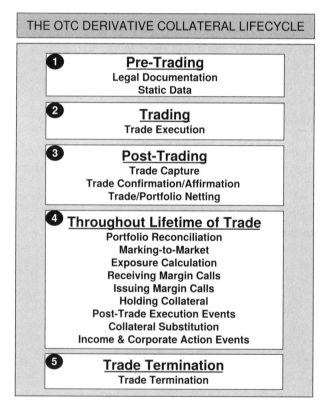

The following 20 chapters, beginning with Chapter 25 'OTC Derivatives and Collateral – The Collateral Lifecycle – Pre-Trading – Legal Documentation', and ending with Chapter 44 'OTC Derivatives and Collateral – The Collateral Lifecycle – Trade Termination', focus on each major step in the collateral lifecycle.

The chapters are structured so as to form a logical and progressive sequence of steps.

OTC Derivatives and Collateral – The Collateral Lifecycle – Pre-Trading – Legal Documentation

The Pre-Trading section of the OTC Derivative Collateral Lifecycle covers activities that should ideally be performed by a firm prior to execution of any OTC derivative trade with a particular counterparty.

This chapter reinforces the need for a firm trading in OTC derivatives to have legal documentation in place for its own protection, ideally prior to trade execution.

THE OTC DERIVATIVE COLLATERAL LIFECYCLE

❶ Pre-Trading
Legal Documentation
Static Data

❷ Trading
Trade Execution

❸ Post-Trading
Trade Capture
Trade Confirmation/Affirmation
Trade/Portfolio Netting

❹ Throughout Lifetime of Trade
Portfolio Reconciliation
Marking-to-Market
Exposure Calculation
Receiving Margin Calls
Issuing Margin Calls
Holding Collateral
Post-Trade Execution Events
Collateral Substitution
Income & Corporate Action Events

❺ Trade Termination
Trade Termination

If a firm decides to execute trades in any type of OTC derivative, it is imperative that it firstly puts in place the standard legal documentation, for its own protection. For further detail regarding the purpose and content of such documentation, please refer to:

- Chapter 20 'OTC Derivatives and Collateral – Legal Protection – Introduction', and to
- Chapter 21 'OTC Derivatives and Collateral – Legal Protection – Master Agreement and Schedule', and to
- Chapter 22 'OTC Derivatives and Collateral – Legal Protection – Credit Support Annex'.

The legal documentation is intended to cover all types of OTC derivative product in which the firm and its *counterparty* intend to trade. For example, the documentation which was signed by both parties two years ago may list both *interest rate swaps* and *credit default swaps*; therefore any trades in such products are covered under the protection of the legal documentation. For trades in such products between the two parties, following trade execution there is only the need to compare trade details to ensure all details are the same, via issuance of a *short form confirmation*.

However, with the same documentation in place, should the firm and the same counterparty choose to execute a trade in an OTC derivative product not covered by the legal documentation, the firm must take additional steps in order to protect itself. For example, if the firm executed a trade with the same counterparty in a *variance swap*, as this OTC derivative product is not covered by the existing legal documentation between the two parties, a *long form confirmation* should be issued by one of the parties and signed and returned by its counterparty.

Both short form and long form confirmations are discussed within Chapter 29 'OTC Derivatives and Collateral – The Collateral Lifecycle – Post-Trading – Trade Confirmation/Affirmation'.

Under such circumstances, if the firm and its counterparty feel that regular trading of variance swaps may ensue, they must together decide whether to amend the legal documentation so as to incorporate variance swaps alongside the existing OTC derivative products covered by the current documentation. If the parties choose not to amend the legal documentation, any trades executed in future in any OTC derivative product not falling under the umbrella of the legal documentation will mean that associated *exposure* calculations cannot form part of the normal daily exposure calculations relating to trades in products which are covered by the *credit support annex* (CSA) with the particular counterparty. Exposure calculations (and any subsequent *margin calls*) in products falling outside the CSA must be managed separately and according to the terms stated within the long form confirmation.

From a day-to-day *collateral management* perspective, all the characteristics of a particular CSA between a firm and its counterparty need to be easily accessible, whether held within a spreadsheet or within a dedicated collateral management system. Such access to the details of CSAs means that the collateral management personnel are able to perform their responsibilities in accordance with the firm's legal agreements with each of their counterparties. If access is more of a challenge for the collateral management personnel, the risk is introduced of actual exposure management being misaligned with the legal documentation.

Note: where a firm is intending to execute OTC derivative trades with a new counterparty, it should be expected that the process of agreeing legal documentation would occur following the '*counterparty onboarding*' process, involving *anti-money laundering* and *know your customer* procedures.

OTC Derivatives and Collateral – The Collateral Lifecycle – Pre-Trading – Static Data

This chapter describes the need for a firm to ensure it has set up its internal static (reference) data before trading commences, in order to ensure that all critical components of a trade are available for processing purposes, immediately following trade execution.

THE OTC DERIVATIVE COLLATERAL LIFECYCLE

1 Pre-Trading
Legal Documentation
Static Data

2 Trading
Trade Execution

3 Post-Trading
Trade Capture
Trade Confirmation/Affirmation
Trade/Portfolio Netting

4 Throughout Lifetime of Trade
Portfolio Reconciliation
Marking-to-Market
Exposure Calculation
Receiving Margin Calls
Issuing Margin Calls
Holding Collateral
Post-Trade Execution Events
Collateral Substitution
Income & Corporate Action Events

5 Trade Termination
Trade Termination

PART 4a

Further to the description of and use of static data within Chapter 23 'OTC Derivatives and Collateral – Static Data', this chapter emphasises the need for a firm to have all its static data set up, prior to execution of the very first trade with a *counterparty*.

If, prior to execution of the first trade, the following components of static data are set up within a firm's systems, then the associated actions are immediately achievable (stated in the indented row in each case):

- the specific OTC derivative product, facilitates:
  - immediate capture of the trade (one-off)
  - *marking-to-market* of the OTC derivative trade (ongoing)
  - identification of OTC derivative trade *exposures* (ongoing)
- the particular counterparty (legal entity), including its correct location, facilitates:
  - immediate capture of the trade (one-off)
  - identification of OTC derivative trade exposures (ongoing)
  - identification of existing collateral values (ongoing)
- trade confirmation/affirmation method, facilitates:
  - immediate post-trade communication of trade details to the counterparty or to a trade matching facility (one-off)
- CSA details facilitate:
  - identification of marking-to-market frequency (ongoing)
  - identification of exposures (ongoing)
  - issuance of *margin calls* to the counterparty (ongoing)
  - identification of *eligible collateral* to and from the counterparty (ongoing)
- cash (currency) *standing settlement instructions* for the firm, facilitate:
  - from which of the firm's *cash correspondents* (including account numbers) payments to the counterparty will be made, and vice versa (ongoing)
- cash (currency) standing settlement instructions for the counterparty facilitate:
  - to which of the counterparty's cash correspondents (including account numbers) payments will be made, and vice versa (ongoing)
- securities collateral details facilitate:
  - initial identification of *bond* deliverable quantities (ongoing)
  - marking-to-market of securities collateral given or taken (ongoing)
  - application of *haircut* (ongoing)
  - identification of upcoming bond *coupon payments* [re potential *collateral substitution*] (ongoing)
- securities standing settlement instructions for the firm facilitate:
  - from which of the firm's securities accounts at **CSD**s or *custodians* (including account numbers) deliveries to the counterparty will be made, and vice versa (ongoing)
- securities standing settlement instructions for the counterparty facilitate:
  - to which of the counterparty's securities accounts at CSDs or custodians (including account numbers) deliveries will be made, and vice versa (ongoing).

As can be seen from the above list, a significant amount of effort can be managed by systems providing 1) the static data is present, and 2) the system is able to utilise such static data in an automated fashion.

Having made reference above to static data from a systems perspective, of course all such data would absolutely be needed even if (hypothetically) a firm had no system and needed to operate entirely manually.

OTC Derivatives and Collateral –
The Collateral Lifecycle –
Trading – Trade Execution

The Trading section of the OTC Derivative Collateral Lifecycle covers the single activity of trade execution, which should ideally be performed only after pre-trading activities have been completed.

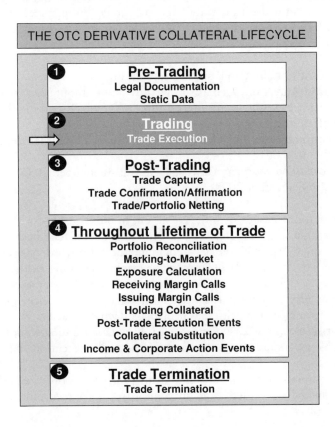

THE OTC DERIVATIVE COLLATERAL LIFECYCLE

1 **Pre-Trading**
Legal Documentation
Static Data

2 **Trading**
Trade Execution

3 **Post-Trading**
Trade Capture
Trade Confirmation/Affirmation
Trade/Portfolio Netting

4 **Throughout Lifetime of Trade**
Portfolio Reconciliation
Marking-to-Market
Exposure Calculation
Receiving Margin Calls
Issuing Margin Calls
Holding Collateral
Post-Trade Execution Events
Collateral Substitution
Income & Corporate Action Events

5 **Trade Termination**
Trade Termination

PART 4a

> *This chapter provides an overview as to how* OTC *derivative trades are executed, and the associated risks. From a collateral management perspective, trades executed accurately will result in a solid foundation from which exposure calculations and margin calls can be made successfully.*

From the perspective of any firm, the act of **trade execution** and the closely associated process of **trade capture** are absolutely critical to be performed accurately and in a timely fashion, in order for subsequent **trade processing** and **collateral processing** to be managed in an efficient and risk-free fashion.

27.1 TRADE EXECUTION: INTRODUCTION

Trade execution: the act of buying or selling (or lending and borrowing) a financial product, is performed at the very start of the processing lifecycle of an individual trade, including trades in **OTC derivative** products.

Trade execution is the responsibility of the firm's OTC derivative traders. OTC derivative trades have historically been executed directly between the two firms and are said to be 'privately negotiated' or traded on a '*bilateral*' basis. For <u>any</u> trade executed by a firm on a bilateral basis (including, but not limited to trades in OTC derivative products), risk exists for the firm at this very early stage. For instance, in the case of an *investment bank* executing trades on behalf of its client, misinterpretation of the client's requirements, for example:

- incorrect operation (direction) such as sell not buy
- undefined trade direction, such as stating 'buy' but without specifying which party is the buyer, for example in an *interest rate swap*, which party is the payer of the fixed rate of interest
- incorrect *notional principal* such as EUR 10,000,000.00 rather than the intended EUR 100,000,000.00
- incorrect *scheduled maturity date* such as 1st September 2034 rather than the intended 15th September 2034

can lead to reputational issues with the client and to monetary loss.

An example of how errors can arise when trading on a bilateral basis is in a situation where a client requests 'sell me'; the bank could interpret this wording as either 1) 'sell to me' (i.e. bank sells to client), or 2) 'sell for me' (i.e. bank buys from client). A further example occurs where, in a telephone conversation, one party states 'fifty'; this could quite easily be heard either as 'fifty' or 'fifteen'. Risk exists where such circumstances are not mitigated through clarifying immediately with the client exactly what is meant.

A similar risk exists for an investment bank when executing trades with another investment bank as counterparty; errors made at trade execution may well lead to monetary loss.

It should be noted that many *sell-side* firms prefer to record their telephone conversations conducted by traders (and in some cases such recording is a regulatory requirement). Taped conversations may be used in the event of dispute between two firms (e.g. regarding price or notional principal) in order to resolve differences.

The fact that the trade is being executed on an OTC basis immediately means that the method of trade execution (i.e. OTC rather than *exchange traded*) is subject to human error and is therefore considerably riskier than a trade executed via an exchange.

Note: providing that the input or orders to an electronic exchange is effected accurately, the resultant exchange trading means that trade execution details provided by the exchange are rarely incorrect, therefore the same level of risk does not normally exist between exchange-executed trades and OTC-executed trades. Further note: mandatory electronic trading of traditionally OTC-executed derivative products is being introduced as part of a suite of major and global changes due to come into effect as a result of the 2008 *Global Financial Crisis*; please refer to Chapter 46 'OTC Derivatives and Collateral – Regulatory Change and the Future of Collateral – Introduction', which describes such regulatory changes under the heading of the *Dodd-Frank Act* in the US and *EMIR* (European Market Infrastructure Regulation) in Europe.

Consequently, the firm's OTC derivative traders carry a large degree of responsibility to ensure that trades are 1) executed and 2) captured accurately. If trading is not carried out accurately at the first attempt, the extent of work required to both identify and to then rectify trade details can be very disproportionate to the profitability of the trade to the firm.

27.2 TRADE EXECUTION METHODS

Generically speaking, a range of methods are employed by firms that execute trades in OTC derivatives.

For example, for a variety of products including interest rate swaps and *credit default swaps*, many electronic execution facilities exist (e.g. the Barclays Bank BARX facility at 'www.barx.com') whereby account holders (including sell-side and *buy-side* firms) can view price quotes and execute trades electronically.

Where a buy-side firm (e.g. a corporate entity such as an airline company) wishes to trade in an OTC derivative product, trade execution usually begins with the client placing an *order* with an investment bank with which the client has an existing relationship. The client's order may be communicated to the bank by telephone or via an order management system (and in some cases, via the bank's own order management system). The client's point of contact within the investment bank is usually the *relationship manager* (also known as 'salesperson'), whose primary role is to both set up and to cultivate the bank's relationship with the client. The relationship manager typically has no power to execute trades, and therefore the client's order is forwarded to the bank's Trading Department; the relevant trader does have trade execution power and responsibility. Where the client wishes to sell, the bank may choose to:

- execute the trade and to take on the position from the client as a *trading position* (i.e. inventory), or to
- act as an intermediary and effectively buy from the client and sell to the market, without the investment bank taking a position; this is commonly known as *back-to-back trading*.

PART 4a

Where the client wishes to buy, the investment bank has the same two choices as above, although if the bank chooses to take on the position the bank will be left with a *negative trading position* (or 'short' position).

Under these circumstances, the investment bank must choose carefully whether to take a position (whether long or short). When an investor (including banks) holds a position in any financial product, the fundamental risk is that the price at which the position was acquired by the investor changes in a disadvantageous direction, thereby potentially causing the investor to incur a loss. Within investor institutions, the daily *mark-to-market* process is designed to highlight whether, at the *current market price*, the bank would make a profit or a loss if the position were to be liquidated 'now'; this is known as *unrealised profit and loss*. Profit and loss calculated after 1) a long position has been liquidated after a sale, or 2) after a short position has been liquidated following a purchase, is known as *realised profit and loss*.

Where the investment bank chooses to act as intermediary following receipt of an order from a client, common practice for the bank is to then place an order, either by telephone or electronically, with an *inter-dealer broker* (IDB), whose role is to find another dealer wishing to trade on the same terms. The intention of the IDB (e.g. ICAP, Creditex, Tullett Prebon) is to act in the neutral role of intermediary between two trading parties, with the aim of not taking a position. If another party cannot be found, usually no trade will have been executed by the IDB or the bank. The IDB makes its money by charging *commission* for trade execution, either to one or to both parties.

Note: following trade execution, the IDB does not remain an ongoing party to the transaction; the ongoing OTC derivative contract is directly between the two trading parties. At this point the trade is said to be 'done, subject to credit lines'; the possibility remains that following trade execution, when the bank discovers who its counterparty is, the bank has insufficient *credit lines* for the counterparty in question, in which case the trade must be cancelled.

27.3 TRADE EXECUTION, TRADE PROCESSING AND COLLATERAL PROCESSING

The impact of accurately performed trade execution is that there is a very high probability that the counterparty will agree the trade detail communicated between the two firms through the *trade confirmation* or *trade affirmation* process.

Such agreement of individual trade details means:

- from a *trade processing* perspective, that all actions that are scheduled to occur during the (multi-year) lifetime of the trade can be performed with confidence that the counterparty agrees the basis of calculation, for example:
  - in an interest rate swap, the calculation of the agreed fixed rate (e.g. 2.42%) versus the agreed floating rate basis (e.g. GBP 6-month Libor), using the agreed *notional principal*
  - in a credit default swap, the calculation of the agreed *premium* (e.g. 128 *basis points per annum*), using the agreed notional principal

- from a *collateral processing* perspective, that the actions documented within the **Credit Support Annex** can be performed with confidence that the counterparty agrees the basic trade terms which, when combined with the CSA content, should mean, for example:
  - in both an interest rate swap and in a credit default swap, that both parties perform *marking-to-market* and exposure calculations at the same frequency, at the same time of day, and utilising the agreed notional principal.

Conversely, failure to gain up-front agreement of basic trade detail between the two parties means that ongoing differences are highly likely to become apparent for both trade processing and collateral processing. Please refer to Chapter 29 'OTC Derivatives and Collateral – the Collateral Lifecycle – Post-Trading – Trade Confirmation/ Affirmation'.

27.4 TRADE EXECUTION AND FUTURE CASHFLOW DISCOUNTING

Many *buy-side* and *sell-side* financial institutions revalue their derivatives *portfolio* on a periodic basis, normally daily. The revaluation process requires all future cashflows to be discounted to today's terms (a process known as *present valuing*), and the choice of discount rate depends upon whether the trade is collateralised or not.

Note: OTC derivative trades executed with counterparties on an *uncollateralised* basis may exist due to, for example, long-term relationships between an investment bank and certain of its clients where such trades have not been collateralised historically, or possibly due to the client having insufficiently liquid assets to fund the required collateral. Such circumstances may not be ideal from a bank's perspective, and the bank must assess the risks and whether such relationships should continue on an uncollateralised basis.

If the deal is not collateralised, historically banks have applied a *Libor* rate as the discount rate. If the deal is collateralised with cash collateral, the discount rate will be based on an *overnight index swap* (OIS) rate, which is taken by the market to be the more appropriate rate (compared with Libor); the OIS rate is used in daily exposure calculations as it represents the overnight funding rate.

Interest on cash collateral has always been paid at the appropriate OIS rate, whereas traditionally all swaps were valued using Libor. This practice prevailed for many years, because the difference between Libor and OIS rates was negligible; however, since 2008, Libor increased dramatically relative to the OIS rate. This difference created an unacceptable mismatch between the value of the trade and the value of the collateral.

The market has now moved to adopt a consistent methodology (OIS), whereby the discount rate applied to collateralised swaps matches the interest rate paid on cash collateral.

The particular OIS rate used is dependent upon the currency of the cash collateral; for example:

- for USD cash collateral, the **Federal Funds Rate** is used
- for EUR cash collateral the Euro Overnight Index Average (**EONIA**) rate is used, and
- for GBP cash collateral the Sterling Overnight Index Average (**SONIA**) rate is used.

In relation to the use of Libor versus OIS in order to value collateralised swaps, the following simplified example outlines both the issue and the market's solution:

TABLE 27.1   Valuing a collateralised swap

VALUING A COLLATERALISED SWAP

THE ISSUE

Consider a legacy interest rate swap (IRS) in which Party A is paying a fixed rate of 2% to Firm B on an annually settled IRS, scheduled to mature 1 year from 'today'. The notional principal is USD 100,000,000.00.

Suppose that 1-year Libor rates fix at 2.5% for the final period. This means that the final net settlement due to Party A in 1 year's time will be a receipt of USD 500,000.00 (i.e. USD 100,000,000.00 × (2.5% − 2%)).

1. To protect against counterparty credit risk, Party A takes collateral equal to the present value of this amount. Based on Libor discounting, this amounts to:
   - *USD 500,000.00 / (1 + 2.5%) = USD 487,805.00.*
2. Is this adequate to cover Party A's risk with Firm B? Party A can reinvest the collateral at the OIS rate. Suppose that this is 1% (i.e. less than the Libor rate). How much will Party A receive 1 year from now when the swap is due to terminate? Is it enough to offset the loss in the event of Firm B's default?
   - *one year from now when Party A's reinvestment matures, Party A will receive USD 487,805.00 × (1 + 1%) = USD 492,683.00. Should Firm B default, this would result in Party A suffering a shortfall of USD 7317.00 (i.e. USD 500,000.00 − USD 492,683.00).*

THE SOLUTION

The correct amount of collateral to take from Firm B can be found by discounting at the OIS rate. How much collateral should Party A demand?

- *Answer: USD 500,000.00 / (1 + 1%) = USD 495,050.00. Reinvesting this amount at the OIS rate raises USD 495,050.00 × (1 + 1%) = USD 500,000.00 one year from now, which is the exact amount required to offset the potential loss in the event of Firm B's default.*

Such calculations suggest that the correct rate at which to discount the swap cashflows in order to mark the swap to market (to enable accurate calculation of the exposure) is the OIS rate. In summary, for collateralised swaps, discounting should be based on OIS rates rather than on Libor or Euribor rates.

However, in many cases the legal documentation (particularly the *Credit Support Annex*) that underpins the collateral relationship between two firms executing OTC derivatives states that bonds as well as cash are eligible collateral. At the time of

PART 4a

writing, the market has not yet derived a consensus as to which discount rate should be applied where firms have a choice of cash or bond collateral. However, in some cases, firms' calculations are based upon the ***cheapest to deliver*** asset, with discount calculations made either 1) at the time of trade execution only, or 2) periodically throughout the lifetime of the trade. The likely issue between trading firms regarding method 1) is that, at the time of trade execution, what is currently the cheapest to deliver may well not remain so throughout the lifetime of the trade.

The significance of this subject is that, at trade execution, the trader must apply discount rates based upon the currency of the collateral, whether cash or bonds.

For readers interested in a more detailed explanation of swap valuation relating to collateral on OTC derivatives, please refer to the following book: *Trading the Fixed Income, Inflation and Credit Markets* by Schofield and Bowler, ISBN 9780-470-74229-7.

27.5 CONCLUSION

Collateral processing can be managed positively and with confidence if trade execution is performed accurately.

Conversely, problems are likely to arise in the areas of exposure calculation if trades are not executed accurately and if there is a failure to identify and then correct trade details very soon following trade execution.

PART 4a

OTC Derivatives and Collateral –
The Collateral Lifecycle –
Post-Trading – Trade Capture

The Post-Trading section of the OTC Derivative Collateral Lifecycle covers one-off activities that should be performed by a firm following trade execution and prior to activities that must occur repeatedly throughout the lifetime of the trade.

THE OTC DERIVATIVE COLLATERAL LIFECYCLE

❶ Pre-Trading
Legal Documentation
Static Data

❷ Trading
Trade Execution

❸ Post-Trading
Trade Capture
Trade Confirmation/Affirmation
Trade/Portfolio Netting

❹ Throughout Lifetime of Trade
Portfolio Reconciliation
Marking-to-Market
Exposure Calculation
Receiving Margin Calls
Issuing Margin Calls
Holding Collateral
Post-Trade Execution Events
Collateral Substitution
Income & Corporate Action Events

❺ Trade Termination
Trade Termination

> *This chapter focuses on the requirement to capture individual trade details, and the associated risks. The management of collateral within a firm will be adversely impacted if executed trades are not captured accurately or in a timely fashion.*

All **OTC derivative** trades executed by a firm must be recorded formally, within the firm's **books & records**, without delay.

28.1 TRADE CAPTURE: INTRODUCTION

This critical step following **trade execution** is achieved by the firm's trader capturing (recording) the basic detail of each trade immediately. This is necessary in order to:

- record the firm's commitments without delay
- trigger operational **trade processing**
- initiate the **trade confirmation** or **trade affirmation** process with the **counterparty**
- prompt the **mark-to-market** process
- activate the **collateral management** process.

For example, an interest rate swap (IRS) trade will contain the details listed in Table 28.1:

TABLE 28.1 Trade capture: detail of an interest rate swap trade

Trade Component	Example Trade Detail
Transaction Type	Interest Rate Swap: Fixed-for-Floating
Notional Principal	GBP 15,000,000.00
Fixed Rate Payer	Bank T New York
Floating Rate Payer	Firm X Amsterdam
Fixed Rate	4.0% semi-annual
Floating Rate	6-month GBP Libor
Trade Date	1st November 2016
Effective Date	1st November 2016
Scheduled Maturity Date	1st November 2021

However, in attempting to capture the trade's details, there is a distinct risk that one or more errors are made. Any component of a trade could be captured incorrectly, from incorrect **counterparty** (e.g. Bank T rather than Bank Y), correct counterparty but incorrect office (e.g. Bank T New York rather than Bank T Milan), **notional principal** (e.g. GBP 15,000,000.00 rather than GBP 50,000,000.00), to **scheduled maturity date** (e.g. 1st November 2021 rather than 1st November 2031).

For *any* trade executed on an OTC basis (and beside many other reasons for capturing the trade's details immediately), it is essential for the firm to compare its captured trade details against the details captured by the counterparty as soon as possible; please refer to the next chapter (Chapter 29 'OTC Derivatives and Collateral – The Collateral

Lifecycle – Post-Trading – Trade Confirmation/Affirmation'). This is because time is an important factor when trade discrepancies exist; the longer a trade's details remain unchecked against the counterparty's details, the greater the risk of price (or rate) movement and a loss being incurred by either of the involved parties. The majority of trades are confirmed electronically where trade details are automatically compared immediately following trade execution.

28.2 TRADE CAPTURE WITHIN SEPARATE TRADING AND OPERATIONS SYSTEMS

Some firms utilise separate trading and operations OTC derivative processing systems, whilst others utilise a single combined system.

Where separate systems are used, trade capture within a dedicated trading system requires that the trade must be replicated within the operations processing system, otherwise the Operations Department may not become aware of the trade, thereby negatively impacting trade processing and potentially collateral management.

Common practice is for a systems interface to exist between the trading system and the operations system, with trades entered into the trading system being pushed through the interface at regular intervals. If an interface does not exist, manual trade capture into the operations processing system will need to be performed.

Risks exist for the firm at this early stage, as a trade successfully entered into the trading system does not in itself guarantee that the same trade is successfully captured within the operations processing system. Consequently, where an interface exists it should be monitored to ensure that trades sent by the trading system are actually received by the operations processing system. In order for the firm to know whether all trades captured within the trading system have also been received in the operations processing system, an internal but formal system-to-system *reconciliation* should be performed on a daily basis; this is known as the FO/BO (front office/back office) reconciliation.

Where such a reconciliation reveals a discrepancy, it is likely that trades will be missing from the operations processing system. A common reason for such missing trades is a lack of *static data* in the operations system. Separate systems may well be supported by separate repositories of static data, which (for example) can mean that a trade captured successfully in the trading system may have missing static data (e.g. missing counterparty) in the operations processing system. As operations processing systems are typically programmed to accept a minimum set of trade components (according to product type), any missing components will cause a trade capture failure; such failures need to be identified, analysed and rectified immediately if downstream actions (e.g. the trade confirmation process and the collateral management process) are not to be negatively impacted.

Where a trade has been executed and been captured within the trading system, it is dangerous practice to prevent the trade from being accepted by the operations processing system, without good reason. This is because if the trade cannot be seen by any of the firm's operations personnel due to the trade not having been captured (yet) within the operations processing system, any enquiry about the trade from a counterparty may be met by the firm's operations staff stating 'we have not executed that trade'. Furthermore, such a failure to capture a trade will negatively impact 1) the reporting of exposures and positions, 2) client reports, and 3) feeds to risk modules. From a collateral management perspective, if the executed trade has not yet been captured into the firm's collateral management system, this will cause discrepancies between the firm and its counterparty from a trade population perspective. Note: the *portfolio reconciliation* process is designed to ensure that, from a collateral management perspective, the population of trades between two trading parties is the same. Please refer to Chapter 31 'OTC Derivatives and Collateral – The Collateral Lifecycle – Throughout Lifetime of Trade – Portfolio Reconciliation'.

Besides the capture of newly executed trades, care must also be taken when amending or cancelling trades where a firm has separate trading and operations processing systems. The full detail of a trade will incorporate:

1. the 'economic' terms of the trade (e.g. buy/sell, notional principal, financial product, rate/price, counterparty) which are the responsibility of the trader, and
2. the 'non-economic' terms of the trade (e.g. counterparty *SSI*s) which are typically the domain of the Operations Department, or in some firms the *Middle Office*.

If a trade discrepancy is discovered between a firm and its counterparty, the firm's personnel that are handling the discrepancy should firstly ascertain the nature of the discrepancy. If the discrepancy is 'economic' in nature (e.g. difference in notional principal), the only party empowered to amend the trade's details is the trader; it is highly dangerous to permit non-trading staff to amend the economic details of a trade. The amendment should be made to the original trade by the trader, within the trading system, and the amendment should then flow (via the interface) to the operations processing system, from which the amended trade details should update the original trade captured within the operations processing system. Such a procedure *mitigates* the risk of the firm's trading system and operations system becoming unsynchronised, at an individual trade level.

Conversely, if the nature of the discrepancy is 'non-economic', such trade components are typically managed purely by operations, as under normal circumstances no financial aspects of the trade will be impacted by such changes to trade details.

In parallel with trade amendments that are economic in nature, the responsibility for outright cancellation of trades should fall within the domain of the trader.[1] Trade cancellations should be made within the trading system and should flow through to the operations processing system to effect full trade cancellation. This procedure is designed to ensure that trade population within the trading system remains synchronised within the trade population within the operations processing system.

28.3 TRADE CAPTURE WITHIN A SINGLE TRADING AND OPERATIONS SYSTEM

In contrast to separate trading and operations OTC derivative processing systems, some firms utilise a single 'front-to-back' or 'integrated' system.

---

[1] A number of attempted and successful frauds within financial services firms have revolved around the capture of fictitious trades, followed by cancellations of such trades. Consequently, a control employed by some firms is to disallow trade cancellations by the trader without prior approval by senior management.

PART 4a

An integrated system requires a single point of trade capture, from which all operations tasks are managed within the same system; such systems avoid the types of reconciliation issues that can arise with separate trading and operations processing systems (as described in the previous section).

28.4 TRADE REFERENCE NUMBERS

It is common practice for trading systems to apply a (preferably) unique trade reference number to a trade at the point of trade capture.

Where separate trading and operations processing systems exist within a firm, the trading system trade reference number should be held as part of the trade detail captured within the operations processing system; this is advantageous when it is necessary to reconstruct the history of a trade internally, within the firm. Upon receipt of the trade within the operations processing system, it is common practice for a separate trade reference number to be applied to the trade. When communicating trade details externally, such as to the counterparty, the operations processing system trade reference number is usually the primary reference number of the trade. For collateral management purposes, it is useful to know both the operations system trade reference number and its trading system equivalent; additionally, it may be preferable to maintain both trade reference numbers within both systems to facilitate use of either number for collateral purposes.

28.5 TRADE CAPTURE ERROR IDENTIFICATION

Even where the FO/BO reconciliation (see Section 28.2 'Trade Capture within Separate Trading and Operations Systems') reveals no discrepancy in trade population between trading and operations processing systems, unfortunately this does not guarantee that trade components (e.g. notional principal, rate, counterparty) within an individual trade are correct.

Proof that a firm's trade components are correct can only be achieved by comparison with the counterparty's details; the process of trade detail comparison is commonly known as *trade confirmation* or *trade affirmation*, which is described within the following chapter.

28.6 TRADE CAPTURE AND COLLATERAL MANAGEMENT

Collateral processing systems are typically separate systems (or modules) from either of a firm's trading system or operations processing system.

As described earlier in this chapter, at the very beginning of a trade's life potential issues exist regarding the capture of trades accurately and on a timely basis. Similarly, during a trade's lifetime events can occur which cause:

- the trade to terminate earlier than its scheduled maturity date (e.g. a *credit event* relating to a *credit default swap*), or
- a firm to be no longer involved in the trade (e.g. *novation*).

   Due to such possibilities during a trade's lifetime, rather than holding complete records of all OTC derivative trades on an ongoing basis, collateral systems are normally refreshed daily with exposures calculated in other internal systems, such as trading systems.

28.7 CONCLUSION

Errors made at the very beginning of the OTC derivative trade lifecycle can easily result in disproportionate operational effort in order to identify the problem and then to correct the problem.

   Traders should be encouraged to take adequate care in the capture of trade details, in order to minimise risk and cost for their firm.

   Unless trade details are captured accurately first time, or are corrected very quickly after trade capture, exposures calculated (as part of collateral processing) by a firm are highly likely to result in disagreement with the counterparty.

PART 4a

OTC Derivatives and Collateral – The Collateral Lifecycle – Post-Trading – Trade Confirmation/Affirmation

This chapter describes the essential process of formally agreeing trade details with the counterparty, following trade execution. A firm's trade detail which differs from the counterparty's trade detail will potentially create a failure to calculate exposures accurately and create uncertainty in the collateral management process.

THE OTC DERIVATIVE COLLATERAL LIFECYCLE

① **Pre-Trading**
Legal Documentation
Static Data

② **Trading**
Trade Execution

③ **Post-Trading**
Trade Capture
Trade Confirmation/Affirmation
Trade/Portfolio Netting

④ **Throughout Lifetime of Trade**
Portfolio Reconciliation
Marking-to-Market
Exposure Calculation
Receiving Margin Calls
Issuing Margin Calls
Holding Collateral
Post-Trade Execution Events
Collateral Substitution
Income & Corporate Action Events

⑤ **Trade Termination**
Trade Termination

PART 4a

Once a trade has been executed and its details captured within a firm's internal system(s), the next action to complete is the act of gaining formal agreement of the trade details with the *counterparty*.

29.1 TRADE CONFIRMATION/AFFIRMATION: INTRODUCTION

The act of trade confirmation/affirmation is necessary because, despite the fact that the firm and its counterparty may have executed the trade as required, there is no guarantee that the trade's details have been captured correctly by either party.

If, for an individual trade, a difference exists in a trade component (e.g. different fixed rate in an *interest rate swap*, or different *premium* in a *credit default swap*), this must be identified immediately and corrected by the party at fault. If, instead, the trade details go unchecked (or unconfirmed) between the firm and its counterparty, such a situation will cause discrepancies subsequently in both operational *trade processing* and in *collateral processing* during the lifetime of the trade. Dependent upon the particular trade component, differences will occur in the *mark-to-market* process which will in turn impact *exposure* calculations and the *collateral management* process, with the firm calculating one exposure figure and the counterparty a different figure, which will cause differences resulting from the issuance of *margin calls,* potentially leading to disputes.

Whilst trades remain unchecked, or checked but not agreed by the counterparty, the firm has a risk that its captured trades within its *books & records* are not an accurate representation of the firm's true commitments and obligations.

Generically speaking, trade agreement can be achieved through:

- the issuance of an outgoing trade confirmation to the counterparty
- the receipt of an incoming trade confirmation from the counterparty
- by electronic trade confirmation, or
- by electronic trade affirmation.

Today, for some OTC derivative products, third party electronic trade matching platforms are available; this is typically the preferred option for many firms, due to the speed and efficiency of such platforms.

Where an electronic platform is not available for the particular OTC derivative product, trade agreement is achieved either by the firm communicating the details of each trade directly to its counterparty, or vice versa; that communication is commonly known as a *trade confirmation*, and is an essential aspect of all trades executed on an **OTC** basis, including (but not limited to) OTC derivatives. The recipient of the trade confirmation is required to check the detail against the details captured internally, and either 1) if agreed, sign and return the confirmation to the sender, or 2) if disagreed, communicate the reason for disagreement to the sender, following which both parties must liaise, resulting in the party at fault amending its trade details, and where necessary an amended trade confirmation must be issued, then checked and signed by the recipient.

It is also possible that the counterparty does not recognise the trade at all, which implies the trade confirmation sender has either:

- captured the trade against the completely incorrect counterparty (e.g. traded with Counterparty A but the trade has been booked (captured) against Counterparty Z), or
- captured the trade against the correct counterparty group, but the incorrect entity or location (e.g. traded with Counterparty G, Paris but booked against Counterparty G, New York).

All such erroneous trade capture, unless identified and corrected without delay, will jeopardise counterparty risk mitigation and successful collateral processing (in addition to negatively impacting trade processing).

29.2 TRADE CONFIRMATION VERSUS TRADE AFFIRMATION

When two *sell-side* firms trade with one another, the post-trading communication is known as a trade confirmation. Trade confirmation implies that neither party is the client of the other; the two trading parties are considered equal.

When, instead, a sell-side firm executes a trade with a *buy-side* firm (or *institutional investor*), the sell-side is providing a service to the client. Amongst a number of service aspects (e.g. speed and competitiveness of *trade execution*), the sell-side firm is expected to 1) issue a communication containing the fully accurate trade terms, and 2) within the pre-agreed time frame (e.g. within 3 hours of trade execution). If the sell-side firm fails in these respects the client may well complain to the sell-side firm regarding the level of service, and ultimately may threaten to take their business to a rival sell-side firm if service levels do not improve.

Due to this client-to-service provider relationship, buy-side firms are typically passive regarding the issuance of trade confirmations. It is therefore the responsibility of the sell-side firm to issue a trade confirmation to the buy-side firm. Upon receipt of a trade confirmation, the buy-side firm should check the detail against their internal records and (assuming the details agree) advise the sell-side firm of their agreement. Because the client is passive in the issuance of the trade confirmation (their role is to check the trade details, and if correct, to affirm their agreement by advising the sell-side firm of their agreement), this sequential process is known as *trade affirmation*.

It should also be noted that, for buy-side firms having an underlying structure of multiple funds (e.g. a mutual fund), trades are often executed by sell-side firms at the 'block' level; for example, the sell-side firm sells the buy-side firm one block of USD 50,000,000 *notional principal* of an *interest rate swap*. Subsequent to trade execution, the buy-side firm allocates that block trade amongst a number of its funds, such as:

- USD 10,000,000 notional principal to Fund A
- USD 25,000,000 notional principal to Fund B
- USD 15,000,000 notional principal to Fund C.

PART 4a

The client must advise the sell-side firm of such allocations. Internally, the sell-side firm must in turn replace the original USD 50,000,000 notional principal 'block' trade with the allocations as advised by the mutual fund client, because each fund (Fund A, Fund B and Fund C) is a legal entity in its own right, and each requires an individual contract. A further reason is that each fund normally has its own (segregated) cash accounts from which, or to which, payments are made throughout the lifetime of the trade. Such payments will relate to both trade processing and to collateral processing.

29.3 ELECTRONIC TRADE CONFIRMATION/AFFIRMATION

Today, for certain types of OTC derivative products, electronic trade confirmation and affirmation platforms exist.

For trades in a range of OTC derivative products, MarkitSERV (www.markitserv .com) provides a confirmation matching service where user firms transmit trade details which MarkitSERV then compares and matches. Trades which do not match are reported as 'unmatched' to the two trading parties, requiring investigation, amendment and resubmission. Trade affirmation (as described earlier in this chapter) is also supported; therefore, both sell-side and buy-side firms are users of MarkitSERV.

The ICE Link platform (www.theice.com) provides trade affirmation services between sell-side firms and their buy-side clients. New trades are alleged electronically by sell-side firms, following which their clients are able to affirm such trades and also (where appropriate) supply details of allocations to their underlying funds.

29.4 CONCLUSION

Following trade execution and trade capture, the process of a firm gaining formal agreement of trade details with its counterparty is critically important as a risk mitigation measure for the firm.

Where a trade has been matched, both parties to a trade can proceed to trade processing and collateral processing with confidence; however, it is also true that (during the lifetime of an OTC derivative trade) a *post-trade execution event* may occur which can mean that the trade does not proceed to its *scheduled maturity date* either 1) at all, or 2) on the same terms that it began its life on trade date. See Chapter 37 'OTC Derivatives and Collateral – The Collateral Lifecycle – Throughout Lifetime of Trade – Post-Trade Execution Events – Introduction' and the subsequent four chapters for details.

Where a trade is currently unmatched due to a discrepancy in one or more trade details, it is essential that this is investigated and rectified immediately.

OTC Derivatives and Collateral – The Collateral Lifecycle – Post-Trading – Trade/Portfolio Netting

This chapter describes the possibility that a newly executed OTC derivative trade may be netted with an existing trade or position, providing all such trades have the same characteristics and are with the same bilateral counterparty. If netting does occur, this will reduce two or more gross trades to a net position, on which exposures will need to be calculated going forward in time, until the position's scheduled maturity date is reached or earlier termination occurs.

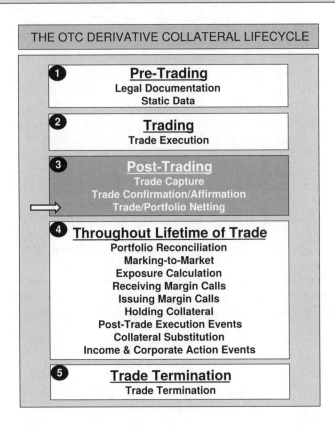

THE OTC DERIVATIVE COLLATERAL LIFECYCLE

1 **Pre-Trading**
Legal Documentation
Static Data

2 **Trading**
Trade Execution

3 **Post-Trading**
Trade Capture
Trade Confirmation/Affirmation
Trade/Portfolio Netting

4 **Throughout Lifetime of Trade**
Portfolio Reconciliation
Marking-to-Market
Exposure Calculation
Receiving Margin Calls
Issuing Margin Calls
Holding Collateral
Post-Trade Execution Events
Collateral Substitution
Income & Corporate Action Events

5 **Trade Termination**
Trade Termination

PART 4a

Following formal agreement of the trade details with the **counterparty**, it is generally accepted as beneficial to both parties if a trade can be netted with another trade or with an existing position. Such netting is applicable to both **buy-side** and **sell-side** firms.

30.1 INTRODUCTION

Trade/Portfolio netting is the process of offsetting trades that contain the same details as an existing position in the same **OTC derivative** product and updating that existing position to a new net position, whilst terminating (cancelling) the original trades. This netting process is commonly known as **portfolio compression**.

The holding of OTC derivative trades to their **scheduled maturity date**, especially when trades have a lifetime of up to 50 years, carries significant annual maintenance costs and risks, which can be either eliminated or minimised by reducing the number of trades to maintain, through the netting/compression process whereby 'unnecessary' trades are removed and/or replaced by a new trade which represents the original net position.

For example, imagine that a firm had no existing position in a particular OTC derivative product (a **credit default swap**) prior to 'today'. Then today, Firm A executes two trades with the same counterparty (Firm M):

- Trade #1: Firm A buys protection on a **notional principal** of EUR 30,000,000.00, and
- Trade #2: Firm A sells protection on a notional principal of EUR 10,000,000.00.

As well as the same counterparty, the same **reference entity** and the same scheduled maturity date are applicable to both trades.

Without netting/compressing these trades, both trades will remain live and active until their scheduled maturity date, requiring a significant amount of **trade processing** and **collateral processing** effort by both firms. Furthermore, firms are required to set aside capital (the **capital requirement**) based upon the outstanding notional principal; the larger the notional principal and the greater the length of time until the scheduled maturity date, the larger the capital requirement. Therefore, if the two example trades (above) were not netted/compressed, the combined notional principal would be EUR 40,000,000.00. Note: although the two trades are in opposing directions, the combined notional principal is achieved by always adding the 'gross' notional principals together.

If these trades are netted/compressed, then only the net position (Firm A buys protection on EUR 20,000,000.00 notional principal) will be carried forward. In other words, the netting/compression process results in the net position of EUR 20,000,000.00 representing the two original trades. Effectively, following netting/compression, both of the original trades can be considered to be terminated. Multiple gross trades and notional principals become a single net position between the two parties, containing precisely the same economic values as the original (gross) trades. Therefore, all future net cashflows (i.e. payments and receipts) are identical to the overall cashflows for the original trades.

Assume that Firm A and Firm M agree to net/compress those two trades, and as a result the net position of EUR 20,000,000.00 is carried forward.

To continue this example, three months after execution of those two trades, Firm A executes a further trade with Firm M:

■ Trade #3: Firm A sells protection on a notional principal of EUR 5,000,000.00.

The reference entity relating to the existing EUR 20,000,000.00 position is applicable to this trade, as is the scheduled maturity date. The firms agree to net/compress this trade with the existing position, resulting in a new notional principal of EUR 15,000,000.00. Consequently, the current net position of EUR 15,000,000.00 represents all three trades.

If further credit default swap trades are executed by Firm A in the same reference entity, for the same scheduled maturity date, and with the same counterparty, then such trades can also be merged into the current net position to produce a new net position.

Note that the following combinations of trade direction can be netted/compressed:

■ buy versus sale, for example:
  ■ buy of EUR 30,000,000.00 notional principal, and
  ■ sale of EUR 10,000,000.00 notional principal
    ■ producing a net buy position of EUR 20,000,000.00 notional principal
  ■ buy of EUR 60,000,000.00 notional principal, and
  ■ sale of EUR 60,000,000.00 notional principal
    ■ producing a net position of zero notional principal

■ buy versus buy, for example:
  ■ buy of EUR 45,000,000.00 notional principal, and
  ■ buy of EUR 10,000,000.00 notional principal, and
  ■ buy of EUR 25,000,000.00 notional principal
    ■ producing a net buy position of EUR 80,000,000.00 notional principal

■ sale versus sale, for example:
  ■ sale of EUR 15,000,000.00 notional principal, and
  ■ sale of EUR 35,000,000.00 notional principal
    ■ producing a net sale position of EUR 50,000,000.00 notional principal.

In addition to trades between two parties, firms can also benefit from netting/compression of trades between multiple parties. Figure 30.1 shows two trades executed between three parties, in which Party A has executed opposing interest rate swap (IRS) trades, one with Party B, the other with Party C, with differing notional principals.

PART 4a

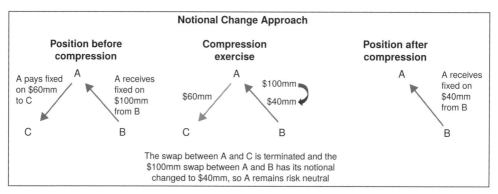

FIGURE 30.1   Example of compression methodology between three parties, using IRS

The 'compression exercise' reveals that:

- Party A will benefit as their original two trades are reduced to a single net position of USD 40,000,000 notional principal with Party B
- Party B will benefit as the notional principal on their trade will reduce from USD 100,000,000 to USD 40,000,000, and
- Party C will benefit as their trade with Party A will be terminated completely.

A key consideration of multilateral compression is that *all* parties need to remain *market risk neutral* as a result of the exercise. While the diagram depicts the scenario for Party A, the compression algorithm would also need to find a solution which proposed offsetting trade terminations for both Party B and Party C, in order for them to remain market risk neutral too. The compressed trades may be with any of the other participants in the compression event.

Note: the technical difference between the terms 'netting' and 'compression' is as follows: netting leaves the original trades legally intact, whereas compression results in the legal termination of the original trades.

30.2 BENEFITS OF TRADE/PORTFOLIO NETTING (PORTFOLIO COMPRESSION)

By entering into trade/portfolio netting (portfolio compression) with its various counterparties to the fullest extent, a firm will benefit (from reducing its gross notional principal exposures to net exposures) in the following areas:

- counterparty credit risk
  - the total number of outstanding gross trades can be significantly reduced
- exposure management
  - assessment of exposures is based on net positions rather than multiple gross trades
- capital requirements
  - capital charges are reduced where net positions replace gross trades

- operational risk
  - netting results in greater efficiency (and cost reduction) for both trade processing and collateral processing.
- administrative costs
  - costs apply to each gross trade, therefore netted positions equate to lower cost
  - netted positions result in lower reconciliation costs, where such costs are charged per trade.

30.3 THE TRADE/PORTFOLIO NETTING (PORTFOLIO COMPRESSION) PROCESS

Historically, whether to net/compress OTC derivative trades has been a choice of individual firms (although this is changing under the new regulatory regime – see Section 30.5).

For example, firms wishing to net/compress their trades may choose to use TriOptima's *triReduce* service, whereby trades are submitted to triReduce for matching and trades eligible for full or partial compression, plus any *replacement trades*, are presented by triReduce to the relevant firms as a compression proposal. Only after all participants have accepted the proposal will the compression cycle be declared legally binding. Execution occurs away from TriOptima and participants terminate trades and book replacement trades as required.

The effect of portfolio compression is illustrated by comparison of Figures 30.2 and 30.3, which reveal pre-compression and post-compression outcomes:

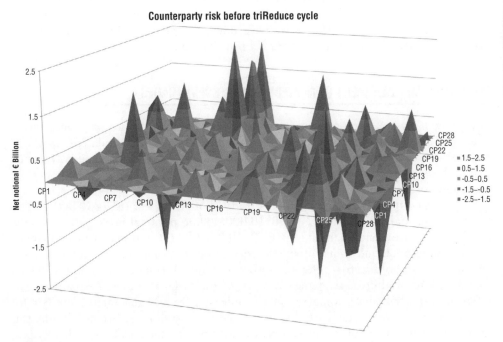

FIGURE 30.2   Counterparty risk before triReduce cycle

PART 4a

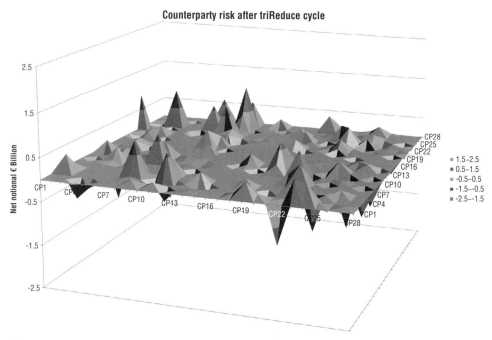

FIGURE 30.3 Counterparty risk after triReduce cycle

For the use of its services, portfolio compression providers such as triReduce charge per transaction, where every compressed trade incurs a cost, although the cost may differ according to the type of OTC derivative product. The charge can be based on a fixed price per transaction, or on size of notional principal, plus volume discounts.

30.4 INTERNAL TREATMENT OF NETTED (COMPRESSED) TRADES

Following successful compression, in which a firm's original trades have been terminated and replaced by a net position, the firm must immediately update its *books & records* in order to properly reflect these facts, and by doing so subsequently ensure that both trade processing and collateral processing are actioned on the correct current trade and position details.

Using the earlier example of Firm A's trades, both Trade #1 (EUR 30,000,000.00 notional principal) and Trade #2 (EUR 10,000,000.00 notional principal) must now be closed, with one net transaction (EUR 20,000,000.00 notional principal) being created using a unique transaction reference number. Common practice is for the closed trades to hold a cross-reference to the relevant net transaction, and for the net transaction to hold cross-references to each of the original trades. Regarding trade references, the triReduce compressions include a triReduce-generated identifier for each fully terminated trade, partially terminated trade and/or replacement trade; this identifier is made available in the compression proposal which is downloaded by participants from the triReduce website. Because compression execution occurs directly between participants (and not by the triReduce system), it is the participants that will attribute a trade reference of their choice.

Note: if Firm A's internal procedure is to utilise an internally generated reference number for the net position, it is suggested that the net transaction reference of the external portfolio compression service (e.g. triReduce) is cross-referenced on the net trade in the internal system.

It is clearly extremely important that, following the netting process, Firm A's staff are able to instantly identify that the original trades have a 'closed' (or similar) status and that they are no longer open with the counterparty, and that the net position has replaced the original trades and has a status of 'open' with the counterparty. This is essential as:

- all future trade processing activities (e.g. payment or receipt of net interest in an *interest rate swap*, or payment or receipt of *premium* in a credit default swap), and
- all future collateral processing activity (e.g. *portfolio reconciliation*, *marking-to-market*, and *exposure* calculation)

must be based on the current net position.

Note: 'today's' net position is subject to change as, if a further credit default swap trade is executed by Firm A in the future (with the same counterparty, for the same reference entity and with the same scheduled maturity date), the netting of that new trade with the existing EUR 20,000,000.00 notional principal position will result in a new net position.

30.5 THE FUTURE OF TRADE/PORTFOLIO NETTING (PORTFOLIO COMPRESSION)

The world's regulatory authorities have introduced a number of critically important structural reforms relating to OTC derivatives, following the *Global Financial Crisis* in 2008.

In acknowledgment of the value of portfolio compression from a risk *mitigation* viewpoint, one such international regulatory requirement is that firms are required to have business procedures in place and evaluate portfolio compression on a regular basis, in order to reduce *systemic risk* in the global financial system.

As defined in the regulators' rule on Confirmation, Portfolio Reconciliation, Portfolio Compression, and Swap Trading Relationship Documentation Requirements for Swap Dealers and Major Swap Participants, 77 Fed. Reg. 55904 (11th September 2012), a multilateral portfolio compression exercise is:

An exercise in which multiple swap counterparties wholly terminate or change the notional value of some or all of the swaps submitted by the counterparties for inclusion in the portfolio compression exercise and, depending on the methodology employed, replace the terminated swaps with other swaps whose combined notional value (or some other measure of risk) is less than the combined notional value (or some other measure or risk) of the terminated swaps in the compression exercise.

For further detail, please refer to Chapter 48 'OTC Derivatives and Collateral –
Regulatory Change and the Future of Collateral – Non-Centrally Cleared Trades', and
in particular Sub-section 48.6.4 'Portfolio Compression Regulations'.

30.6 CONCLUSION

Trade/portfolio netting (portfolio compression) has positive long-lasting effects in
terms of reduced risk and reduced costs, with no loss of the financial impact of trades
as originally traded.

OTC Derivatives and Collateral – The Collateral Lifecycle – Throughout Lifetime of Trade – Portfolio Reconciliation

The 'Throughout Lifetime of Trade' section of the OTC Derivative Collateral Life-cycle covers multiple activities that, in most cases, should be performed repeatedly by a firm following trade execution and post-trading activities, and throughout the trade's entire lifetime (unless the contract ceases to exist prior to its scheduled maturity date due to a post-trade execution event).

THE OTC DERIVATIVE COLLATERAL LIFECYCLE

❶ Pre-Trading
Legal Documentation
Static Data

❷ Trading
Trade Execution

❸ Post-Trading
Trade Capture
Trade Confirmation/Affirmation
Trade/Portfolio Netting

❹ Throughout Lifetime of Trade
Portfolio Reconciliation
Marking-to-Market
Exposure Calculation
Receiving Margin Calls
Issuing Margin Calls
Holding Collateral
Post-Trade Execution Events
Collateral Substitution
Income & Corporate Action Events

❺ Trade Termination
Trade Termination

> *This chapter explains the essential step of ensuring that a firm's view of the OTC derivative trades that are subject to collateralisation with a particular counterparty, are agreed by that counterparty, prior to the calculation of exposures.*

31.1 INTRODUCTION

At this point in the collateral lifecycle, a firm is likely to have multiple OTC derivative trades that are open with many of its counterparties.

At this early stage in the collateral lifecycle, the firm is at risk of calculating exposures on (for example) an incorrect population of underlying trades, or on out-of-date trade details. If a control is not utilised, exposure differences with the firm's various counterparties remain a distinct possibility and are not likely to come to light until later in the day when deadlines may be approaching. Any such discrepancies will cause valuable time to be lost whilst both parties attempt to resolve the cause of the discrepancy prior to the margin call deadline (as documented within the *credit support annex*).

That control is commonly known as portfolio reconciliation, which would ideally be conducted by a firm with each of its counterparties at the same frequency as exposure calculation, in most cases on a daily basis. The use of the term 'portfolio' in this context refers to all OTC derivative trades (executed by a firm with a particular counterparty) that are currently live and valid. Included within the portfolio therefore should be trades that:

- were executed in the past (in some cases years ago) and which have not yet reached their *scheduled maturity date*, plus
- trades that were executed up to and including 'yesterday', plus
- the result of any *post-trade execution events*, including:
  - *novation*
  - *unwind*
  - *offset*, and
  - *credit events* (on *credit default swaps*).

Note: the subject of post-trade execution events is covered within Chapter 37 'OTC Derivatives and Collateral – The Collateral Lifecycle – Throughout Lifetime of Trade – Post-Trade Execution Events – Introduction' and in the subsequent four chapters.

31.2 PURPOSE OF PORTFOLIO RECONCILIATION

Margin call notifications issued by a firm to its counterparty are the result of the following steps:

1. the list of currently open OTC derivative trades with the particular counterparty
2. the *marking-to-market* of such OTC derivative trades
3. utilising the content of the *CSA* (e.g. *Threshold*) with the particular counterparty
4. taking account of any existing *cash collateral* given or taken
5. the marking-to-market of any existing *securities* collateral given or taken.

As can be seen from the above list, the management of periodic (e.g. daily) OTC derivative exposures by a firm commences with the identification of the existing open OTC derivative trades with the particular counterparty.

Portfolio reconciliation is performed specifically for collateral management purposes, and it is designed to identify whether a firm's trade population with its various counterparties is the same or different from the list of trades each of the counterparties has.

Since exposure calculations are based on trade (portfolio) population, the identification of whether the portfolio of trades is the same or different between a firm and its counterparty is critically important. If such a reconciliation is not performed, receipt of a margin call notification is likely to be the earliest point at which a problem is identified.

Therefore, portfolio reconciliation is a pre-emptive action designed to streamline the process of verifying a margin call received from a counterparty (and vice versa).

31.3 REASONS FOR PORTFOLIO DISCREPANCIES

Amongst a variety of reasons for a firm to have differing lists of trades with its counterparties are:

- in error, the trades listed in exposure calculations by the firm (or its counterparty) include trades in transactions not covered by the *CSA* (with the specific counterparty). The legal documentation that a firm signs with a particular counterparty will list the specific OTC derivative transaction types the two firms have agreed to include up to that moment in time. For example, in the legal documentation signed 2 years previously with Counterparty X, the transaction types listed may include *interest rate swaps* and *credit default swaps*. If today, the firm executes a new trade with Counterparty X in a transaction type not previously traded and not covered by the legal documentation (for example a *foreign exchange swap*), such new transactions must not be listed in exposure calculations due to the fact that the CSA does not cover them. (Exposures relating to transaction types falling outside the current CSA with a counterparty must be handled separately.) If and when such circumstances arise, the two firms must decide whether to renegotiate and put in place a new CSA, or to make an amendment to the existing CSA. Note: it is possible that the two firms agree to include trades in all OTC derivative products by default, thereby avoiding amendments to, or renegotiation of, the legal documentation
- the trades listed in exposure calculations by the firm include trades which are no longer open with the particular counterparty. OTC derivative trades such as *IRS* and *CDS* may be subject to *novation* or *unwind* or *offset*, all of which are methods of exiting a contract. In an unwind, an existing trade is effectively reversed and closed-out by a new trade (in the opposite direction to the original trade) with the same counterparty, leaving differentials in cash amounts of the two trades to be settled; the result is that the firm has no open trade or position with the particular counterparty. An offset is similar to an unwind, apart from the counterparty involved not being the same as the counterparty with whom the firm originally traded. In a novation, a firm may choose to step out of an existing contract with a particular counterparty, by arranging for a third party to step in (with the consent of the original counterparty); the result is that the firm has no open trade or position with the original counterparty.

PART 4a

When novations occur, the three parties involved are impacted as follows:

- the 'remaining' party – must update its *books & records* to show the new (third and stepped-in) party as the counterparty with whom the remaining party now has an open trade
- the 'stepped-out' party – must update its books & records to show that it no longer has an open trade with the original counterparty
- the 'stepped-in' party – must update its books & records to show it now has an open trade with the remaining party

- the trades listed by a firm include trades which have been part of a portfolio compression cycle or have undergone some form of adjustment, such as would occur in a *partial unwind*, a method of partially exiting a contract. In a partial unwind, an existing trade (e.g. *notional principal* of USD 30 million) is reversed in part by a new trade (e.g. notional principal of USD 10 million) in the opposite direction with the original counterparty, leaving an adjusted open trade (e.g. notional principal of USD 20 million); the result is that the firm has an open trade with the particular counterparty, but for a reduced notional principal.

Other common reasons for portfolio discrepancies include:

- trades booked by both parties in the same direction; for example, in an IRS both parties state they are the fixed rate payer
- legal entity misbookings; this occurs when either the firm or its counterparty has recorded the trade in (or versus) the incorrect legal entity, but often to the correct parent entity. For example, an investment manager may have multiple funds and the firm or the counterparty can mistakenly register the trade to a sister fund, which belongs under a different CSA. Such misbookings will give rise to trade discrepancies
- incorrect trade attributes; for example, if a notional principal of an *amortising swap* is registered incorrectly in the source system at trade execution, this is likely to result in trade detail differences later in the trade's lifetime when the amortising event is scheduled to occur, which could be a year after the execution of the trade. Such a booking issue would impact the mark-to-market valuation as well as future payments.

31.4 ADVANTAGES AND DISADVANTAGES OF PORTFOLIO RECONCILIATION

The only disadvantage of portfolio reconciliation is that it takes time to conduct the reconciliation; however, in the author's opinion this is time very well spent. With modern technology, the time required to reconcile a portfolio has decreased radically. What was historically a manual and labour-intensive process is now a highly automated process, where firms only need to focus on and rectify the identified exceptions.

If portfolio reconciliation is not practised, the discovery of a discrepancy (via differences in exposure calculations) with a counterparty requires time to investigate the problem and time to rectify it. Those activities are most likely to be occurring while the margin call deadline is approaching.

The advantages of portfolio reconciliation are:

- it is part of a structured (rather than a haphazard) approach to *collateral management*
- it avoids discovery of a discrepancy with a counterparty later in the collateral day, at a critical time when margin call deadlines are approaching.

Portfolio reconciliation is used to *mitigate* risk and is mandated by a number of regulators. If portfolio reconciliation is not practised, the likelihood increases that a firm will experience numerous margin call disputes on a daily basis, dependent upon trade volumes. The advent of portfolio reconciliation came about due to the many disputes that arose historically between different parties. From a collateral management perspective, the specific purpose of portfolio reconciliation is to ensure that both parties have the same trade components, and the same trade population, as one another. If such reconciliation is performed with adequate frequency, any new discrepancies are likely to be small in number, thereby minimising both the number of margin call disputes and the time taken to investigate and resolve such disputes.

Note that early identification of portfolio discrepancies is of benefit to a firm (and its counterparty) beyond just collateral management, as a result of amendments to trade detail from which trade processing tasks will be actioned based upon agreed trade detail.

31.5 THE PORTFOLIO RECONCILIATION PROCESS

Portfolio reconciliation can be achieved by any method, whether manual or automated, that allows two trading parties to compare their trades.

However, as in any financial services reconciliation process, reconciliation is performed in the most efficient manner where files of information are compared electronically using predefined matching criteria, and with any non-matching items being immediately highlighted as exceptions. Exceptions (otherwise known as 'breaks') can then be investigated and corrections made without delay. Electronic reconciliation methods are adopted by many of the large *investment banks* and *buy-side* firms as it is far speedier and not error prone, as compared with manual reconciliation.

Globally, one dominant OTC derivative portfolio reconciliation service provider exists; it is a web-based system known as *triResolve*. This service is used by all major investment banks, many of the larger buy-side institutions and regional banks, as well as the major banks in the Asia-Pacific region. At the time of writing, triResolve reconciles more than 75% of *bilateral* OTC derivatives globally on a regular basis and more than 90% of the global bilateral collateralised OTC derivatives trade population.

Specifically, triResolve is designed to compare all OTC derivative trades executed under legal agreements between two parties, and to provide matching results and exception management workflow. The portfolio reconciliation process is based on a snapshot of the trade population as at the close of business 'yesterday', since this is the data on which *margin calls* are based. Files are securely uploaded during the morning hours to triResolve (typically via an automatic feed but manual uploads to the triResolve website are also possible). Immediately after the firm and the counterparty have uploaded their data, the triResolve comparison process commences. Results are typically available on the website within minutes after all data is received. Thus, parties that upload their data early have access to the results in the morning hours, well ahead of the normal margin call deadlines. Figure 31.1 summarises the generic information flow:

PART 4a

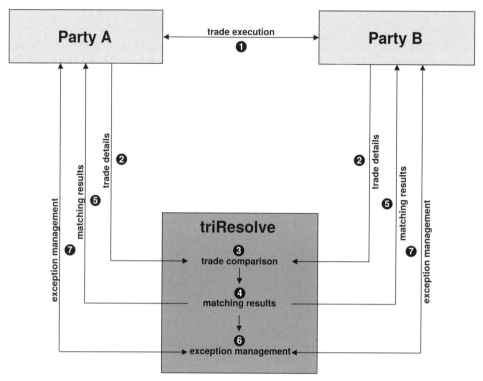

FIGURE 31.1 triResolve processing sequence

Note that triResolve requests firms to send their full portfolio in each submission, rather than just the new trades; it is this full portfolio of trades on which the *mark-to-market* calculations are based. This approach ensures that no trades are omitted due to synchronisation issues and it thus provides a much more stable and reliant mechanism when comparing trade populations. New results build on past results, so a cumulative picture is built over time and any changes from the last reconciliation are easily detected.

In terms of products covered, triResolve handles all types of OTC derivatives, ranging from normal OTC derivatives to highly *structured trades* across all asset classes (e.g. Interest Rate, Credit, Equity, FX, Precious Metal and Commodity/Energy).

The service provides a separate facility for reconciling those trades that do not fall under a CSA.

Firms can submit trade files securely through two options:

- manually via a file upload through the triResolve website
- automatically via a daily batch job via *Secure File Transfer Protocol* (SFTP).

With regard to the trade components requiring submission to triResolve, as a minimum the following must be supplied by a firm:

- unique trade reference
- counterparty
- product type
- trade date
- scheduled maturity date

- trade currency (second currency required for multi-currency trades)
- notional principal (second notional required for multi-currency trades)
- mark-to-market value,* and
- mark-to-market currency.*

In terms of data format requirements, triResolve can translate the firm's native data format into a standard format. As a result, there are few requirements on the actual data format in which files are submitted. As to the contents of the trade file, triResolve supports **ISDA**'s Minimum Market Standard fields plus a number of additional fields (100+ trade attributes are supported).

The matching engine utilises the submitted trade attributes and the key attributes for each asset class/product class are assigned a higher weight. The matching engine can also utilise additional information from external and internal confirmation platforms. For example, there is a direct feed from the **DTCC *Trade Information Warehouse*** (TIW) that ensures that matches for **CDS** and equity derivatives established on triResolve are aligned with matches in the TIW.

Once the trades are matched, any discrepancies are highlighted and categorised into different types of classes and sub-classes for easy discrepancy reporting. The service also ages the discrepancies, so it is possible for management to keep track of aged issues. An example of trade statuses within the triResolve system is shown in Figure 31.2:

FIGURE 31.2   Screenshot of trade statuses within triResolve

---

*Note: besides just reconciliation of portfolios, it is common practice for subscribers to the triResolve service to also include their valuations of trades/positions, which triResolve compares alongside the portfolios submitted by each party. However, it is unlikely that the valuations submitted by each party to a trade will be identical, due to different sources of current rates/prices; consequently, triResolve has a standard tolerance level, within which trades are deemed to match. Should the difference exceed the cash tolerance amount, the trade is treated as matched with a difference, and is visible to both parties within that category.

The most common causes of non-reconciling trades identified by the system include:

- the trade is missing (e.g. late trade bookings, terminations, expired/exercised trades)
- incorrect counterparty (e.g. due to novations or incorrect bookings)
- double-bookings: a single trade has been entered twice in the system
- differing mark-to-market value, particularly where exchange rates are involved, and
- trades booked by both parties in the same direction.

Note that certain trade components (e.g. notional principal) that are found to be incorrect will also result in a mark-to-market discrepancy with the counterparty.

A subscribing firm can discover the latest matching status of trades by online enquiry on the triResolve website or may be notified by email as soon as a new match result is available. Furthermore, the service website provides the facility for subscribing firms to add trade comments, upload confirmations and a complete workflow to raise internal or external cases/tickets on exceptions for further investigation. An example of trade statuses within the triResolve system is shown in Figure 31.3:

FIGURE 31.3 Screenshot of trade statuses within triResolve

The triResolve service is used by a range of institutions, from firms that have fewer than 25 trades in their portfolios to major dealers with 1 million+ OTC derivative trades on their books.

The day-to-day internal users of triResolve within a subscribing financial institution can vary between different types of firm. For example, the Collateral Management Department is a typical user, but the larger *investment banks* have typically set up dedicated portfolio reconciliation teams and/or dispute teams that are responsible for investigating exceptions and for channelling identified issues to other teams within the bank (e.g. the *Operations Department* for trade booking issues and *Middle Office* or *Front Office* for valuation-related items).

The benefits of portfolio reconciliation have a broader reach in an institution than just the Collateral Management Department. The data in a firm's collateral management system can originate from a number of upstream systems. In generic terms, such a daily reconciliation process (as described earlier) is a very efficient way to detect and to prevent operational issues and valuation problems that may exist in such upstream systems. Consequently, the portfolio reconciliation process ensures that the firm's books & records are in order, as they are aligned with their counterparty's books & records.

31.6 CONCLUSION

In general terms, for a firm to act efficiently and to *mitigate* its risks, complete portfolio reconciliation should be performed with the same frequency as exposure calculation, daily in most cases. Within many firms, the monetary values of OTC derivative trades are typically extremely large with average trade sizes in the tens of millions of USD/ EUR/GBP.

Senior operations management within financial institutions remain very conscious of the need for ongoing risk mitigation; daily portfolio reconciliation provides the fundamental control in the OTC derivative collateral management process that leads to a firm properly mitigating its risk.

Since the 2008 *Global Financial Crisis*, regulators have identified portfolio reconciliation as a key control process for OTC derivatives and, as a result, it has become a mandatory process for many institutions relating to:

- *centrally cleared trades*, as part of the *Dodd-Frank Act*/CFTC rules in the US and *EMIR* rules in Europe; please refer to Chapter 47 'OTC Derivatives and Collateral Regulatory Change and the Future of Collateral – Centrally Cleared Trades', and to
- *non-centrally cleared trades*; please refer to Chapter 48 'OTC Derivatives and Collateral Regulatory Change and the Future of Collateral – Non-Centrally Cleared Trades'.

PART 4a

OTC Derivatives and Collateral – The Collateral Lifecycle – Throughout Lifetime of Trade – Marking-to-Market

This chapter describes the important step of discovering the current market price, of both OTC derivative trades and existing securities collateral, which forms an essential aspect of calculating daily exposures from which margin calls are made.

THE OTC DERIVATIVE COLLATERAL LIFECYCLE

1 **Pre-Trading**
Legal Documentation
Static Data

2 **Trading**
Trade Execution

3 **Post-Trading**
Trade Capture
Trade Confirmation/Affirmation
Trade/Portfolio Netting

4 **Throughout Lifetime of Trade**
Portfolio Reconciliation
Marking-to-Market
Exposure Calculation
Receiving Margin Calls
Issuing Margin Calls
Holding Collateral
Post-Trade Execution Events
Collateral Substitution
Income & Corporate Action Events

5 **Trade Termination**
Trade Termination

PART 4a

32.1 INTRODUCTION

At this point in the collateral lifecycle, a firm should have performed *portfolio reconciliation*, resulting in the firm having knowledge that it has an agreed population of *OTC derivative* trades with its various *counterparties*.

The next step is to apply *current market prices* to trades and positions, from which it can be determined whether *exposure* exists, and if so whether it is the firm or its counterparty that has the exposure and therefore which party should make the *margin call*.

The process of discovering current market prices and of applying such prices to underlying trades and positions is commonly known as *marking-to-market*. In plain English, this means applying (marking) the current market price to a trade or to an existing position.

The process of 'marking-to-market' (or 'mark-to-market') is highly generic as it is applicable to many types of financial product, including *securities* positions, OTC derivatives, and securities collateral.

In addition, current market prices are used by all types of financial institution, for example *investment banks*, *buy-side* firms, *central securities depositories*, *custodians* and OTC derivative *central counterparties*, for the purposes of, for example, risk management (i.e. trade valuation, collateral valuation), profit and loss calculation and client valuations.

Note: a similar term to marking-to-market is 'marking-to-model'. This is also a method of pricing a trade or position, but instead of gathering a price from an external market source, marking-to-model utilises internally derived prices for complex financial products for which external prices are unavailable.

32.2 GENERIC MARKING-TO-MARKET PRINCIPLES

As a general point, from an individual firm's perspective it is essential that the firm does not receive a margin call from its counterparty without the firm having the ability to verify the counterparty's call within a very short time frame. In order to avoid such a situation, the firm should conduct marking-to-market (MTM) with at least the same frequency as its counterparties.

It is important that the MTM process takes current market prices from one (or many) independent and neutral sources, otherwise the firm takes the risk of intentionally inflated or deflated prices.

Margin calls may be disputed by counterparties; this can be due to pricing differences in the MTM process. Beside the possibility of prices differing due to prices originating from different sources, another potential cause of such differences is that the two firms involved have gathered prices at different times of day.

In an attempt to avoid differences in valuations between firms, the sources of prices, the timing of gathering such prices, and any models to be used in the pricing of trades and positions should be aligned.

32.3 THE ORIGIN OF PRICES

From the perspective of the firm needing to perform MTM, current prices are normally available by subscription to *data vendors* such as Thomson Reuters, Bloomberg and SIX Financial Information. Most firms subscribing to data vendors receive pricing via electronic feeds, which are ideally updated automatically to a firm's various internal systems including collateral systems.

The current prices of most standard OTC derivative products are usually not difficult to locate; however, some **structured** OTC derivative products are more of a challenge and are more likely to be the cause of margin call disputes.

Where **bonds** have been previously given or taken as collateral, such assets must be marked-to-market at the agreed frequency. The current prices of most securities are normally not difficult to discover, although occasional problems may be encountered for securities in the less developed markets.

32.4 USES OF MARKING-TO-MARKET

Amongst a variety of uses, MTM is used under the following circumstances:

1. to value **securities lent and borrowed**
2. to value securities given or received as collateral in securities lending & borrowing
3. to value securities given or received as collateral in a **cash-based repo**
4. to value OTC derivative trades
5. to value securities given or received as collateral in an OTC derivative trade.

32.4.1 Securities Lent and Borrowed versus Cash or Securities Collateral

With regard to point 1, besides needing to MTM securities lent on trade date of the transaction, it is important to MTM every day. If MTM is not performed daily, the securities lender will not be aware if they have an exposure or not (whether the lent securities have risen or fallen in value). A rise in value of lent securities will potentially lead to a margin call on the counterparty; but this must take account of whether cash collateral or securities collateral was received from the counterparty. Where securities are lent against receipt of cash collateral, the only component with a price fluctuation possibility is the lent security, so if (for example) the security's price increases the securities lender may call its counterparty for more collateral. The counterparty (the securities borrower) will be able to call for return of some cash collateral where the security's price falls. These possibilities are reflected in Table 32.1:

TABLE 32.1 Cash collateral

Transaction Type	Increase/Decrease in MTM Value of Lent Security	Collateral Type	Collateral Impact
Securities Lending	Increase	Cash	Lender Due More Collateral
	Decrease		Lender Returns Some Collateral

Where securities have been lent against receipt of securities collateral, two components are subject to price fluctuation, namely a) the lent security, and b) the securities collateral; in this situation, the lent security could rise in value as could the value of the securities collateral, and so the securities lender's new exposure amount may be covered by the increase in value of the securities collateral. That and other situations are summarised in Table 32.2:

TABLE 32.2   Securities collateral

Transaction Type	Result of MTM on Lent Security	Result of MTM on Securities Collateral	Collateral Impact
Securities Lending	Increase	Increase by same value as lent security	No action
	Increase	Decrease	Lender Due More Collateral
	Decrease	Decrease by same value as lent security	No action
	Decrease	Increase	Lender Returns Some Collateral

32.4.2 Repo versus Securities Collateral

With regard to point 3 above, where securities have been given or received as collateral in a cash-based repo, only the securities collateral component has a price fluctuation possibility, so if (for example) the security's price decreases the cash lender may call its counterparty for more collateral (see Table 32.3).

TABLE 32.3   Repo versus securities collateral

Transaction Type	Increase/Decrease in MTM Value of Collateral	Collateral Type	Collateral Impact
Cash-Based Repo	Increase	Securities	Cash Lender Returns Some Collateral
	Decrease		Cash Borrower Gives More Collateral

32.4.3 The Value of OTC Derivatives

With regard to point 4 above, OTC derivative trades should be MTM in accordance with the frequency stated in the **Credit Support Annex**, typically every business day. It is important to remember that, unlike lending-type transactions which are directional (i.e. the lender of the asset has an immediate **exposure** if collateral is not received from the borrower), the current market value of an OTC derivative trade (which is not directional) may fall in favour of either party to the trade.

    If MTM is not performed daily, a party to a transaction will not be aware whether the trade's current market value has now moved in its favour or in the counterparty's favour.

32.4.4 OTC Derivatives versus Cash or Securities Collateral

With regard to point 5 above, besides needing to MTM the OTC derivative trade itself on a daily basis, a change in value of an underlying trade in favour of an individual firm will potentially lead to a margin call on the counterparty; but this must also take account of whether cash collateral or securities collateral has previously been given to or received from the counterparty. Where cash collateral has previously been given or taken in an OTC derivative trade, the only component that has fluctuation capability is the OTC derivative trade itself. Alternatively, where securities collateral has been given or taken previously, if (for example) the security's price moves in favour of one party, any collateral call must also take account of the direction of change in the MTM of the OTC derivative trade itself.

32.5 TRENDS IN MARKING-TO-MARKET FREQUENCY

There is a growing trend towards not just daily, but intraday MTM, exposure calculation and margin calls. Such frequency typically occurs in volatile market conditions, particularly in a central clearing (see below) environment, where exposures can fluctuate rapidly.

From an organisational standpoint, for firms practising intraday margin calls, their collateral staff must be in a position to react to margin calls received from counterparties within a very short time frame. This means that each firm must be capable of verifying an incoming margin call from a counterparty, then paying or delivering *eligible collateral* to the counterparty within the agreed deadline. Conversely, each firm must be capable of conducting MTM at the appropriate intraday frequency, with the ability to communicate such calls to counterparties within the agreed deadlines, and then to monitor receipt of the relevant collateral.

With the introduction of mandatory *central clearing* of OTC derivatives from 2015, intraday margin calls from *central counterparties* remain a real possibility under volatile market conditions. Please refer to Chapter 46 'OTC Derivatives and Collateral – Regulatory Change and the Future of Collateral – Introduction' and the two subsequent chapters.

PART 4a

OTC Derivatives and Collateral – The Collateral Lifecycle – Throughout Lifetime of Trade – Exposure Calculation

This chapter explains the critical process of identifying whether an exposure exists, and whether the exposure is callable by the firm on its counterparty, or vice versa.

THE OTC DERIVATIVE COLLATERAL LIFECYCLE

❶ Pre-Trading
Legal Documentation
Static Data

❷ Trading
Trade Execution

❸ Post-Trading
Trade Capture
Trade Confirmation/Affirmation
Trade/Portfolio Netting

❹ Throughout Lifetime of Trade
Portfolio Reconciliation
Marking-to-Market
→ Exposure Calculation
Receiving Margin Calls
Issuing Margin Calls
Holding Collateral
Post-Trade Execution Events
Collateral Substitution
Income & Corporate Action Events

❺ Trade Termination
Trade Termination

33.1 INTRODUCTION

At this point in the collateral lifecycle, a firm should have 1) performed *portfolio recon-ciliation* with its various counterparties, and 2) completed the *mark-to-market* process.
A number of components comprise the determination of:

1. whether an *exposure* exists 'today', and if so:
2. the party that is exposed (whether the firm itself or its counterparty), leading to:
3. issuance of a *margin call* by the *exposed party*.

The first two of these points are explored within this chapter, whilst the third point will be covered within the following two chapters.

33.2 CREDIT SUPPORT ANNEX

For OTC derivatives, each *Credit Support Annex* (CSA) that a firm has with its various counterparties is likely to contain details that, if not unique from one another, differ in many aspects. It is therefore essential that, for exposure calculation purposes, a firm ensures it utilises the exact information contained in the relevant CSA for each of its counterparties. For details comprising the CSA, please refer to Chapter 22 'OTC Derivatives and Collateral – Legal Protection – Credit Support Annex'.
In general terms, it is not essential to have daily access to the CSA itself; the salient parts from the CSA that affect daily exposure calculations can be captured within a dedicated collateral management system, from which daily exposure values can be determined.
However, risks exist at this point for the firm. If details extracted from the CSA fail to be captured accurately, or if certain components are not captured at all, errors in daily exposure calculations are likely to result. For *securities* collateral, if issuer ratings contained in the CSA are not captured accurately in the collateral management system, this may result in, for example, the firm *over-collateralising* the exposures of its counterparties.

33.3 DETERMINING EXPOSURE AMOUNTS AND DIRECTION

For each of its counterparties, at the required frequency as dictated by the applicable CSA (typically daily), a firm must determine:

- the exposure amount, and
- the direction of the exposure; whether the firm is to make a margin call on its counterparty, or vice versa, or whether no call can be made by either party.

Assume that Firm X and its counterparty, Firm P, have previously signed the necessary legal documentation including the CSA which in turn includes the following detail:

- Product Coverage: interest rate swaps, credit default swaps, cross-currency swaps, variance swaps
- Collateral Direction: bilateral
- Eligible Currency: USD, EUR, GBP
- Eligible Credit Support: USD cash, EUR cash, GBP cash, G10 government securities

- Valuation Percentage: cash in USD, EUR, GBP = 100%, G10 government securities = 99%
- Independent Amount: 6% of notional principal, in favour of Firm P
- Threshold: USD 1,000,000, bilateral
- Minimum Transfer Amount: USD 500,000, bilateral
- Rounding: round up to the nearest USD 50,000, bilateral.

Assume subsequently that Firm X had executed the OTC derivative trade shown in Table 33.1 (from the perspective of Firm X):

TABLE 33.1 OTC derivative trade record

OTC Derivative Trade Record	
Transaction Type	Credit Default Swap: Single-Name
Protection Buyer	Firm X
Protection Seller	Firm P
Notional Principal	USD 100,000,000.00
Price	126 *bppa*
Trade Date	12th June 2016
Scheduled Termination Date	20th June 2026
Reference Entity	Bond Issuer B

33.3.1 Exposure Amounts and Exposure Direction: Day 1

The components involved in determining the exposure amount and which party is exposed are a blend of 1) trade details and 2) CSA details, as per Table 33.2:

TABLE 33.2 Determining exposure #1

		Determining Exposure Amount & Exposure Direction: Calculation Day 1 (Perspective of Firm X)		
Item	Component	Component Origin	Example	Exposure Amount & Exposure Direction
1	Mark-to-Market Value of Trades/Positions	Pricing Department or Risk Department	USD 3,660,000.00 in favour of counterparty	– USD 3,660,000.00
2	Independent Amount	CSA	6% of trade notional in favour of counterparty	– USD 6,000,000.00
			Sub-total	– USD 9,660,000.00
3	Threshold	CSA	Bilateral fixed amount of USD 1,000,000.00	+ USD 1,000,000.00
4	Existing Collateral	Margin Calls on Prior Days	Nil	0.00
5	Collateral in Transit	Margin Calls on Prior Days	Nil	0.00
			Sub-total	– USD 8,660,000.00
6	Minimum Transfer Amount	CSA	USD 500,000.00	unaffected
			Sub-total	– USD 8,660,000.00
7	Rounding	CSA	Round up to nearest USD 50,000.00	– USD 40,000.00
8	**Margin Call Amount**			**– USD 8,700,000.00 in favour of Firm P**

PART 4a

The calculations shown within the above table are explained as follows:

- Item 1: in order to assess the current market value of the trade for exposure calculation purposes, at the frequency documented within the CSA the firm should perform **mark-to-market** following the close of the previous business day. In this example the current market value of the OTC derivative trade is USD 3,660,000.00 in favour of the counterparty (Firm P); in other words, Firm P has a **positive mark-to-market** and is the **exposed party**, whilst Firm X has a **negative mark-to-market** and is the **non-exposed party**
- Item 2: any **independent amount** agreed between the two parties, and in which party's favour, will be listed within the CSA. In this example, the independent amount has been agreed as being 6% of the trade's **notional principal**; as only one trade has been executed with this particular counterparty (Firm P), this calculation is simply 6% of USD 100,000,000.00
- Item 3: any **threshold** amount agreed between the two parties, and whether this is a bilateral arrangement or one way only, will be listed within the CSA. In this example, the threshold amount is bilateral to the value of USD 1,000,000.00 and is always applied
- Item 4: any collateral given or taken from margin calls on prior days must be taken into account. As there have been no prior days, no collateral exists between these two parties
- Item 5: any collateral that has left the control of the firm, but which is known to not (yet) have been received by the counterparty, is regarded as **collateral in transit**. As there have been no prior days, no margin calls have occurred previously, therefore there is no collateral in transit
- Item 6: any **minimum transfer amount** agreed between the two parties will be listed within the CSA. In this example, the minimum transfer amount, being considerably less than the exposure, means there is no impact and the exposure amount remains unaffected; such situations are referred to as 'No Move'
- Item 7: any **rounding** amount agreed between the two parties will be listed within the CSA. In this example, the rounding rule (round up to the nearest USD 50,000.00) has influence on the exposure amount resulting in USD 8,660,000.00 being rounded up by USD 40,000.00
- Item 8: the net result is that on this day, by Firm X's calculations, Firm P has an exposure of USD 8,700,000.00. Firm X awaits receipt of a **margin call notification** from Firm P.

In summary, as the mark-to-market value and the independent amount are both in favour of Firm P, Firm P is the exposed party and Firm X is the non-exposed party. Firm X must therefore provide collateral, in settlement of Firm P's margin call.

33.3.2 The Following Calculation Day: Day 2

The calculation frequency following the above calculation may be daily, weekly or monthly. Whatever the relevant period, now assume that on the very next occasion the mark-to-market valuation (from the previous business evening) revealed that the current market value of the trade had moved further in favour of Counterparty P. The components involved in this calculation are shown in Table 33.3:

TABLE 33.3   Determining exposure #2

			Determining Exposure Amount & Exposure Direction: Calculation Day 2 (Perspective of Firm X)		
Item	Component	Component Origin	Example	Exposure Amount & Exposure Direction	
1	Mark-to-Market Value of Trades/Positions	Pricing Department or Risk Department	USD 4,335,000.00 in favour of counterparty	– USD 4,335,000.00	
2	Independent Amount	CSA	6% of trade notional in favour of counterparty	– USD 6,000,000.00	
				Sub-total	– USD 10,335,000.00
3	Threshold	CSA	Bilateral fixed amount of USD 1,000,000.00	+ USD 1,000,000.00	
4	Existing Collateral	Margin Calls on Prior Days	USD 8,700,000.00 cash held by counterparty	+ USD 8,700,000.00	
5	Collateral in Transit	Margin Calls on Prior Days	Nil	0.00	
				Sub-total	– USD 635,000.00
6	Minimum Transfer Amount	CSA	USD 500,000.00	Unaffected	
				Sub-total	– USD 635,000.00
7	Rounding	CSA	Round up to nearest USD 50,000.00	– USD 15,000.00	
8	**Margin Call Amount**			**– USD 650,000.00 in favour of Firm P**	

The components within the above table are explained as follows:

- Item 1: the current market value of the OTC derivative trade is now USD 4,335,000.00 in favour of the counterparty (Firm P)
- Item 2: the independent amount is as per the CSA (6% of USD 100,000,000.00)
- Item 3: the threshold amount is as per the CSA (USD 1,000,000.00)
- Item 4: existing collateral amounts to USD 8,700,000.00, which results from the margin call on day 1
- Item 5: there is no collateral in transit as collateral relating to prior margin calls has been received by the collateral taker (as cash collateral movements are settled the same day)
- Item 6: as the sub-total prior to applying the minimum transfer amount exceeds the USD 500,000.00 MTA, the exposure amount remains unaffected
- Item 7: application of the rounding rule results in an increase of USD 15,000.00
- Item 8: by Firm X's calculations, Firm P has an exposure of USD 650,000.00. Firm X awaits receipt of a margin call notification from Firm P.

In summary, as the mark-to-market value has increased in the counterparty's favour, Firm X must provide further collateral, in addition to that provided previously.

33.3.3 The Following Calculation Day: Day 3

On this valuation date, the mark-to-market valuation (from the previous business evening) revealed that the current market value of the trade was still in favour of Counterparty P, but to a considerably lesser extent compared with the previous valuation date. The components involved in this calculation are shown in Table 33.4:

TABLE 33.4 Determining exposure #3

	Determining Exposure Amount & Exposure Direction: Calculation Day 3 (Perspective of Firm X)			
Item	Component	Component Origin	Example	Exposure Amount & Exposure Direction
1	Mark-to-Market Value of Trades/Positions	Pricing Department or Risk Department	USD 780,000.00 in favour of counterparty	– USD 780,000.00
2	Independent Amount	CSA	6% of trade notional in favour of counterparty	– USD 6,000,000.00
			Sub-total	– USD 6,780,000.00
3	Threshold	CSA	Bilateral fixed amount of USD 1,000,000.00	+ USD 1,000,000.00
4	Existing Collateral	Margin Calls on Prior Days	USD 9,350,000.00 cash held by counterparty	+ USD 9,350,000.00
5	Collateral in Transit	Margin Calls on Prior Days	Nil	0.00
			Sub-total	+ USD 3,570,000.00
6	Minimum Transfer Amount	CSA	USD 500,000.00	unaffected
			Sub-total	+ USD 3,570,000.00
7	Rounding	CSA	Round up to nearest USD 50,000.00	+ USD 30,000.00
8	Margin Call Amount			+ USD 3,600,000.00 in favour of Firm X

The components within the above table are explained as follows:

- Item 1: the current market value of the OTC derivative trade is now USD 780,000.00 in favour of the counterparty (Firm P).
- Item 2: the independent amount is as per the CSA (6% of USD 100,000,000.00)
- Item 3: the threshold amount is as per the CSA (USD 1,000,000.00)
- Item 4: existing collateral amounts to USD 9,350,000.00 (USD 8,700,000.00 on day 1 plus the margin call of USD 650,000.00 on day 2)
- Item 5: there is no collateral in transit as collateral relating to all prior margin calls has been received by the collateral taker (as cash collateral movements are settled the same day)
- Item 6: as the sub-total prior to applying the minimum transfer amount exceeds the USD 500,000.00 MTA, the exposure amount remains unaffected
- Item 7: application of the rounding rule results in an increase of USD 30,000.00
- Item 8: by Firm X's calculations, Firm X has an exposure of USD 3,600,000.00. Firm X issues a margin call notification to Firm P.

In summary, even though the mark-to-market value is still against Firm X, Firm P is now holding too much of Firm X's collateral; in other words, Firm X is over-collateralising. Consequently, the margin call will be made by Firm X in order to recover some of its collateral held by the counterparty (from prior margin calls).

33.3.4 The Following Calculation Day: Day 4

On this valuation date, the mark-to-market valuation (from the previous business evening) revealed that the current market value of the trade was still in favour of Firm P, but only just. The components involved in this calculation are shown in Table 33.5:

TABLE 33.5   Determining exposure #4

	Determining Exposure Amount & Exposure Direction: Calculation Day 4 (Perspective of Firm X)			
Item	Component	Component Origin	Example	Exposure Amount & Exposure Direction
1	Mark-to-Market Value of Trades/Positions	Pricing Department or Risk Department	USD 310,000.00 in favour of counterparty	– USD 310,000.00
2	Independent Amount	CSA	6% of trade notional in favour of counterparty	– USD 6,000,000.00
			Sub-total	– USD 6,310,000.00
3	Threshold	CSA	Bilateral fixed amount of USD 1,000,000.00	+ USD 1,000,000.00
4	Existing Collateral	Margin Calls on Prior Days	USD 5,750,000.00 cash held by counterparty	+ USD 5,750,000.00
5	Collateral in Transit	Margin Calls on Prior Days	Nil	0.00
			Sub-total	+ USD 440,000.00
6	Minimum Transfer Amount	CSA	USD 500,000.00	affected
			Sub-total	nil
7	Rounding	CSA	Round up to nearest USD 50,000.00	not applicable
8	**Margin Call Amount**			nil

The components within the above table are explained as follows:

- Item 1: the current market value of the OTC derivative trade is now USD 310,000.00 in favour of the counterparty (Firm P)
- Item 2: the independent amount is as per the CSA (6% of USD 100,000,000.00)
- Item 3: the threshold amount is as per the CSA (USD 1,000,000.00)
- Item 4: existing collateral amounts to USD 5,750,000.00 (USD 9,350,000.00 resulting from the day 2 margin call less the margin call of USD 3,600,000.00 on day 3)
- Item 5: there is no collateral in transit as collateral relating to all prior margin calls has been received by the collateral taker (as cash collateral movements are settled the same day)
- Item 6: as the sub-total prior to applying the minimum transfer amount is less than the USD 500,000.00 MTA, the exposure amount is affected
- Item 7: application of the rounding rule has no impact and results in a zero exposure amount
- Item 8: as no exposure exists, no margin call is made by either party.

PART 4a

In summary, the mark-to-market value has fallen compared with the previous valuation date, but by a relatively small amount, resulting in the exposure amount being less than the minimum transfer amount, therefore no margin call is applicable on this day.

33.3.5 The Following Calculation Day: Day 5

On this valuation date, the mark-to-market valuation (from the previous business evening) revealed that the current market value of the trade had moved in favour of Firm X. The components involved in this calculation are shown in Table 33.6:

TABLE 33.6 Determining exposure #5

		Determining Exposure Amount & Exposure Direction: Calculation Day 5 (Perspective of Firm X)		
Item	Component	Component Origin	Example	Exposure Amount & Exposure Direction
1	Mark-to-Market Value of Trades/Positions	Pricing Department or Risk Department	USD 1,600,000.00 in favour of Firm X	+ USD 1,600,000.00
2	Independent Amount	CSA	6% of trade notional in favour of counterparty	– USD 6,000,000.00
			Sub-total	– USD 4,400,000.00
3	Threshold	CSA	Bilateral fixed amount of USD 1,000,000.00	+ USD 1,000,000.00
4	Existing Collateral	Margin Calls on Prior Days	USD 5,750,000.00 cash held by counterparty	+ USD 5,750,000.00
5	Collateral in Transit	Margin Calls on Prior Days	Nil	0.00
			Sub-total	+ USD 2,350,000.00
6	Minimum Transfer Amount	CSA	USD 500,000.00	unaffected
			Sub-total	+ USD 2,350,000.00
7	Rounding	CSA	Round up to nearest USD 50,000.00	not applicable
8	**Margin Call Amount**			**+ USD 2,350,000.00 in favour of Firm X**

The components within the above table are explained as follows:

- Item 1: the current market value of the OTC derivative trade is now USD 1,600,000.00 in favour of Firm X
- Item 2: the independent amount is as per the CSA (6% of USD 100,000,000.00)
- Item 3: the threshold amount is as per the CSA (USD 1,000,000.00)
- Item 4: existing collateral amounts to USD 5,750,000.00 (unchanged due to zero exposure amount on the previous valuation date, day 4)
- Item 5: there is no collateral in transit as collateral relating to all prior margin calls has been received by the collateral taker (as cash collateral movements are settled the same day)
- Item 6: as the sub-total prior to applying the minimum transfer amount exceeds the USD 500,000.00 MTA, the exposure amount remains unaffected

- Item 7: application of the rounding rule has no impact as the pre-rounding sub-total is a valid exposure amount
- Item 8: by Firm X's calculations, Firm X has an exposure of USD 2,350,000.00. Firm X issues a margin call notification to Firm P.

In summary, the mark-to-market value has moved in favour of Firm X, but due to prior margin calls and the independent amount, Firm X requires the return of some of its collateral from the counterparty.

33.3.6 The Following Calculation Day: Day 6

On this valuation date, the mark-to-market valuation (from the previous business evening) revealed that the current market value of the trade had moved further in favour of Firm X. The components involved in this calculation are shown in Table 33.7:

TABLE 33.7   Determining exposure #6

Item	Component	Component Origin	Example	Exposure Amount & Exposure Direction
\multicolumn{5}{c}{Determining Exposure Amount & Exposure Direction: Calculation Day 6 (Perspective of Firm X)}
1	Mark-to-Market Value of Trades/Positions	Pricing Department or Risk Department	USD 7,955,000.00 in favour of Firm X	+ USD 7,955,000.00
2	Independent Amount	CSA	6% of trade notional in favour of counterparty	– USD 6,000,000.00
			Sub-total	+ USD 1,955,000.00
3	Threshold	CSA	Bilateral fixed amount of USD 1,000,000.00	– USD 1,000,000.00
4	Existing Collateral	Margin Calls on Prior Days	USD 3,400,000.00 cash held by counterparty	+ USD 3,400,000.00
5	Collateral in Transit	Margin Calls on Prior Days	Nil	0.00
			Sub-total	+ USD 4,355,000.00
6	Minimum Transfer Amount	CSA	USD 500,000.00	unaffected
			Sub-total	+ USD 4,355,000.00
7	Rounding	CSA	Round up to nearest USD 50,000.00	+ USD 45,000.00
8	**Margin Call Amount**			+ USD 4,400,000.00 in favour of Firm X

The components within the above table are explained as follows:

- Item 1: the current market value of the OTC derivative trade is now USD 7,955,000.00 in favour of Firm X
- Item 2: the independent amount is as per the CSA (6% of USD 100,000,000.00)
- Item 3: the threshold amount is as per the CSA (USD 1,000,000.00)
- Item 4: existing collateral amounts to USD 3,400,000.00 (USD 5,750,000.00 resulting from the day 3 margin call less the margin call of USD 2,350,000.00 on day 5)
- Item 5: there is no collateral in transit as collateral relating to all prior margin calls has been received by the collateral taker (as cash collateral movements are settled the same day)

- Item 6: as the sub-total prior to applying the minimum transfer amount exceeds the USD 500,000.00 MTA, the exposure amount remains unaffected
- Item 7: application of the rounding rule results in an increase of USD 45,000.00
- Item 8: by Firm X's calculations, Firm X has an exposure of USD 4,400,000.00. Firm X issues a margin call notification to Firm P.

In summary, the mark-to-market value has moved significantly further in favour of Firm X, consequently due to prior margin calls and the independent amount, Firm X requires both:

1. the return from Firm P of the USD 3,400,000.00 existing cash collateral given previously by Firm X, plus
2. delivery of the counterparty's own collateral in the amount of USD 1,000,000.00.

Many people find such calculations to be initially somewhat confusing. In order to avoid confusion and errors in such calculations, it is strongly recommended that positive (+) and negative (−) signs are applied to each calculation component, and that such signs are applied consistently from one set of exposure calculations to the next set. For example (from the Firm X perspective), where existing collateral is held by the counterparty and is shown with a positive sign (as in Table 33.6, Item 4), then the next exposure calculation must continue to be shown with a positive sign (as in Table 33.7, Item 4) providing the counterparty continues to hold the existing collateral. However, settlement of the margin call on Day 6 (as in Table 33.7, Item 8) would cause Firm X to show the existing collateral with a negative sign, as it is Firm X that is now in possession of the existing collateral (in an amount of USD 1,000,000.00).

Note: in the above exposure calculation example the independent amount and all other calculation components are combined, resulting in a single exposure amount on each calculation day. The two trading firms may instead agree to isolate the independent amount from the other components (including marking-to-market), in which case two margin calls will be issued.

33.4 CASH COLLATERAL VERSUS BOND COLLATERAL

In Section 33.3 'Determining Exposure Amounts and Direction', the form of collateral given or taken was always cash collateral.

If instead, bonds had been given or received as collateral, an additional significant step would have been necessary; both collateral giver and taker would need to independently calculate the current market value of such securities collateral. This adds a further dimension to the required calculation on each valuation date, with rises and falls in collateral values resulting in the following impacts:

- a rise in MTM value of the OTC derivative trades/positions, versus a greater rise in the value of existing bond collateral will mean a potential return of collateral to the *collateral giver*
- a rise in MTM value of the OTC derivative trades/positions, versus a lesser rise in the value of existing bond collateral will mean further collateral is to be provided by the collateral giver

- a fall in MTM value of the OTC derivative trades/positions, versus a lesser fall in the value of existing bond collateral will mean a potential return of collateral to the collateral giver
- a fall in MTM value of the OTC derivative trades/positions, versus a greater fall in the value of existing bond collateral will mean further collateral is to be provided by the collateral giver.

Unfortunately, such further calculations only increase the possibility of valuation disputes between parties. The mark-to-market process for bonds is conceptually similar to that for the underlying derivative trades or positions, and therefore prices gathered by the two trading parties may differ.

In addition, it must be remembered that the current value of an *interest-bearing bond* includes the current value of *accrued interest*. Interest-bearing bonds include *fixed rate bonds*, *floating rate notes* and *convertible bonds*, and exclude *zero coupon bonds*. Bond prices are quoted on either a *clean price* basis (to which the current value of accrued interest must be added), or on a *dirty price* basis (the 'all-in' price inclusive of accrued interest).

Furthermore, as bonds have *denominational values*, in order for a delivery of bonds to be successful at the *CSD* or *custodian*, a valid deliverable quantity must be instructed. If, for example, a particular bond has a single denominational value of USD 20,000.00, a *settlement instruction* requesting a delivery of, say USD 15,000.00, will be rejected by the CSD or custodian, as it is impossible to deliver such a quantity. Bond denominational values can be found in the issue *prospectus*.

33.5 EXPOSURES ON INDIVIDUAL TRADES VERSUS PORTFOLIOS

The above example of exposure calculation (within Section 33.3 'Determining Exposure Amounts and Direction') is based on a single trade. In reality, daily exposure calculation between a firm and its various counterparties is based on the entire portfolio of currently open and live OTC derivative trades.

33.6 CONCLUSION

The calculation of exposure amounts by a firm, whether *buy-side* or *sell-side*, at each appropriate valuation date, is an essential step for the firm in order to *mitigate* its risks with counterparties.

In the calculation of exposure amounts, the firm has risk when:

- the firm calculates that it has an exposure, and the calculated exposure value is in fact less than its true value, with a resultant risk that the firm's true exposure is not mitigated in full, and/or
- the firm calculates that the counterparty has an exposure, and the exposure value is in fact greater than its true value, with a resultant risk that the firm creates exposure for itself through over-collateralising.

It is therefore essential that great care is taken in the calculation of exposure amounts.

OTC Derivatives and Collateral – The Collateral Lifecycle – Throughout Lifetime of Trade – Receiving Margin Calls

This chapter lists and describes the various steps involved in a firm receiving a margin call from a counterparty, and the subsequent tasks necessary to mitigate the counterparty's exposure, without incurring risk for the firm. The processing steps for both cash collateral and bond collateral are described, as there are significant differences in the use and ongoing administration of such collateral forms.

THE OTC DERIVATIVE COLLATERAL LIFECYCLE

① **Pre-Trading**
Legal Documentation
Static Data

② **Trading**
Trade Execution

③ **Post-Trading**
Trade Capture
Trade Confirmation/Affirmation
Trade/Portfolio Netting

④ **Throughout Lifetime of Trade**
Portfolio Reconciliation
Marking-to-Market
Exposure Calculation
Receiving Margin Calls
Issuing Margin Calls
Holding Collateral
Post-Trade Execution Events
Collateral Substitution
Income & Corporate Action Events

⑤ **Trade Termination**
Trade Termination

34.1 INTRODUCTION

At this point in the collateral lifecycle, a firm should have completed (for each counterparty):

- *portfolio reconciliation*
- *marking-to-market*
- calculation of *exposure* amount, taking account of:
  - *CSA* components
  - existing collateral given or taken, including collateral in transit

in order to derive the firm's view as to whether an exposure exists, and accordingly whether a margin call is to be 1) made by the firm on the counterparty, or 2) made by the counterparty on the firm.

Assume that the firm's calculations show that the counterparty is the *exposed party*, and thus the firm is anticipating receipt of a *margin call notification* from the counterparty. Should the firm receive such a communication, and by the required deadline, and providing the firm agrees its contents, the firm will need to decide either to pay cash collateral or to deliver securities collateral (providing the particular CSA allows such a choice) to the counterparty on the agreed *value date*, in settlement of the margin call.

It is important to note that a firm that has calculated that its counterparty has an exposure has no legal obligation to alert the counterparty to make a margin call. However, in the particular circumstance where an *investment bank* has traded with its client (an *institutional investor*), and the investment bank's calculations reveal that the client has an exposure, for client relationship reasons the investment bank may choose to contact the client whenever such exposures arise.

Under the circumstances where the firm has established that its counterparty has an exposure, the *mitigation* of the counterparty's exposure is achieved by the procedural and sequential steps depicted in Figure 34.1:

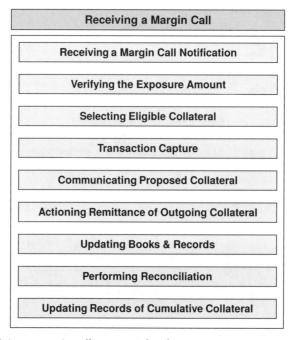

FIGURE 34.1   Receiving a margin call: sequential tasks

The following describes the individual processing steps required to process the incoming margin call successfully.

34.2 INCOMING MARGIN CALL: BOTH CASH AND SECURITIES COLLATERAL

The following steps must be taken regardless whether cash or securities collateral will ultimately be given to the counterparty, in settlement of the margin call.

34.2.1 Receiving a Margin Call Notification (MCN)

The typical content of an MCN is shown in Table 34.1:

TABLE 34.1   Margin call notification

Typical Content of a Margin Call Notification	
Message Purpose	Margin Call Notification
Message Issuer	Firm A
Message Receiver	Firm T
Message Issuer's Transaction Reference	MCN88827
Legal Agreement Date	2nd October YYYY
Valuation Date	15th January YYYY
Minimum Transfer Amount	EUR 500,000.00
Threshold Amount	EUR 500,000.00
Exposure Amount Claimed	EUR 1,200,000.00

There are two important aspects to the receipt of an MCN, namely the transmission method and the deadline. The method of transmission of the MCN is likely to include:

- email: for some firms email is their MCN transmission method, and it is clearly important that such communications arrive within a central 'Collateral Department' email account, as opposed to an individual staff member's account, otherwise the risk exists that the firm receives the MCN but does not act on it due to the absence of a staff member
- S.W.I.F.T.: via the MT503 'Collateral Claim' message type. S.W.I.F.T. is an acronym for the Society for Worldwide Interbank Financial Telecommunication. Many financial institutions around the globe subscribe to S.W.I.F.T., due to 1) its very high levels of security in which highly encrypted messages are transmitted between S.W.I.F.T. network subscribers, and 2) its highly structured message formatting facilitating automated generation and transmission of messages by the sender and automated system upload of messages by the recipient
- AcadiaSoft's '*MarginSphere*' system: this system for both *buy-side* and *sell-side* subscribers facilitates the electronic exchange of collateral messages, including the initiation of (and response to) margin calls.

PART 4a

One of the many components of the CSA is the Notification Time. This defines the deadline (within a particular day) by which the party issuing the MCN must notify its counterparty. It is very important to note that the recipient of an MCN received no later than the documented deadline is obliged to act upon the MCN on that business day, and conversely, for an MCN received beyond the deadline the recipient is not in any way obliged to act on that business day; instead a late-received MCN may be treated as though received the next business day. However, some firms apply the deadline very strictly, whereas other firms have a softer approach by taking the view that 'the counterparty is late today, but we may be late tomorrow'. If a counterparty misses the deadline they will be 1) contravening the terms of the legal agreement (contained within the CSA) and 2) by doing so on a regular basis causing persistent problems to the party receiving the MCN; such a situation may require a firm to have a discussion with the persistently late-running counterparty.

34.2.2 Verifying the Call (Exposure) Amount

When a firm is in receipt of an MCN, the counterparty's stated exposure amount must be verified by the firm against its own calculations, otherwise the risk of over-collateralising exists, through remitting a cash value or a securities quantity that is too large.

The counterparty's stated exposure is typically verified against the value calculated by the firm's system, and in addition, by a human check using the *four-eyes principle*.

It is important to note that agreement of exact exposure amounts between counterparties is unlikely due to the various sources of *current market prices* within the *mark-to-market* process. Despite that, the normal tolerance level is zero, and any differences in exposure amount between the firm and its counterparty are firstly subject to an internal assessment and approval, to identify (for example) whether a calculation error has been made by the firm. Such a situation may lead to the firm formally disputing the counterparty's margin call amount.

If the counterparty's stated exposure amount is regarded as adequately close to the receiving firm's calculations, the latter should proceed to the next stage of processing.

Conversely, if the counterparty's stated exposure amount is considerably greater than the receiving firm's calculations, it is normal practice for the receiving firm to pay the *undisputed amount* immediately, then to investigate (with the counterparty) the reason for the discrepancy. For example, Firm A calculates that its counterparty has an exposure of USD 6,000,000.00, and then receives an MCN for USD 8,000,000.00 from its counterparty; normal practice is for the MCN recipient to give collateral regarding the undisputed amount (USD 6,000,000.00) immediately, and then to investigate the reason for the difference without delay.

The most common circumstance of disputed call amounts stems from non-standard or 'structured' OTC derivative trades. At the first level, the trading parties will attempt to resolve between them the reason for calculation mismatch, but if this does not lead to agreement and if all other attempts to reconcile the exposure amount has failed, the *dispute resolution procedure* must be invoked.

The dispute resolution procedure, as stated within the CSA, involves the *valuation agent* performing its calculation, and the result is binding on both parties. Note that, in recent years, *ISDA* has introduced a Dispute Resolution Protocol which a firm and its various counterparties may choose to adhere to; this is a refinement to the procedure stated within the CSA.

34.2.3 Identifying Eligible Collateral

Once the recipient of the MCN has verified the call amount, the firm needs to decide whether to provide the counterparty with cash collateral or securities collateral.

Firstly, the details and components of the relevant CSA must be referenced in order to ascertain whether 1) only cash may be given, or 2) only bonds may be given, or 3) either cash or bonds may be given. The firm's Collateral Department has the choice of accessing the specific CSA directly, or more likely accessing static data held within a collateral system.

Assume the firm's CSA with the particular counterparty states that either cash or bonds may be given. Then, it must be decided by the firm whether to give cash or securities, or a combination. The following sections focus on the considerations in the selection of such collateral.

34.2.4 The Value Date of the Margin Call

Assuming the firm's proposed collateral is agreed by the counterparty, the next step is for the firm to now take the necessary action to ensure the collateral assets are in fact paid or delivered to the counterparty on the due date. The due date is known as the *value date*, and, in relation to the date the MCN is issued, is usually:

- for cash collateral: T+1 business day, meaning the very next business day
- for bond collateral: T+2 business days,

although in future the trend is likely to be earlier, including T+0. If and when same day (T+0) settlement of margin calls becomes the norm, it will be essential that all firms are able to act and react in such extremely short time frames.

Failure of the MCN recipient to settle the demand on its due date will mean that the exposed party's exposure will not have been mitigated when expected. Although an occasional failure by the MCN recipient may be tolerated by the exposed party, frequent failures are likely to be met with a stern warning. It is important to note that, within the ISDA master agreement, there is a 'Failure to Pay' clause which allows the aggrieved party to invoke close-out of the underlying transaction(s).

> *The next section of text refers to the procedure for paying cash collateral to the counterparty, followed by a section covering the procedure for delivering bond collateral to the counterparty.*

PART 4a

34.3 INCOMING MARGIN CALL: CASH COLLATERAL

Assume that the firm has checked the counterparty's MCN and agrees the call amount. Also assume that the firm has decided to give cash collateral to the counterparty, in settlement.

The firm will need to ensure it has adequate cash within the account (at its *cash correspondent* or *nostro*) from which payment is to occur, or to have the ability to borrow cash by use of an existing credit arrangement. Another possibility is that the return of funds is expected from a prior cash loan or other cash transaction (e.g. *repo*). If none of the aforementioned applies, the firm will need to arrange a cash borrowing from a third party.

For all firms, the cash amount payable forms a component part of the firm's overall treasury (also known as 'cash management') function, which is usually responsible for the firm's entire cash position, per currency, per value date. Typically, the individual amounts owed to counterparties (resulting from margin calls) are compiled by the Collateral Department, who must then liaise with the treasury function.

34.3.1 Transaction Capture

Within firms that have adequate functionality within their internal systems, at this stage a collateral transaction should be captured following which further processing steps can be triggered automatically.

34.3.2 Updating Internal Books & Records

Internal books & records must be updated to reflect the fact that cash will be given to the counterparty, in settlement of the margin call.

34.3.3 Communicating Proposed Collateral to Counterparty

As the counterparty needs to be made aware of the form of collateral the firm intends giving (to enable verification of its eligibility), a communication must be issued to the counterparty; this is usually achieved either by email or, for those that subscribe to it, via AcadiaSoft's MarginSphere system.

Alternatively, for S.W.I.F.T. subscribers, the MX series (rather than the traditional MT series, such as the MT504) is becoming increasingly popular. Under the MX series, a collateral proposal is a 'Colr.007'.

34.3.4 Instructing for Payment of Cash Collateral

The Collateral Department must now arrange for payment to be made to the counterparty on the due date; this is normally achieved in one of two ways according to each firm's internal procedures:

- issue an internal *payment instruction* to the firm's Treasury Department who will in turn generate and transmit their own *settlement instruction* to the firm's cash correspondent (or nostro), or
- issue a payment instruction direct to the firm's cash correspondent, the most common medium for which is *S.W.I.F.T.*, typically by use of an MT103.

Using either method, the content of such an instruction will include:

- the firm's account number (to be debited)
- payee's bank, location and account number (to be credited)
- *ISO currency code*
- payment amount
- *value date* (the due date of settlement)
- the firm's instruction reference number.

34.4 INCOMING MARGIN CALL: SECURITIES COLLATERAL

Assume that the firm has checked the counterparty's MCN and agrees the call amount. Also assume that the firm has decided to deliver bond collateral to the counterparty, in settlement.

34.4.1 Selecting Securities Collateral

Having decided to deliver bond collateral in order to satisfy the counterparty's margin call notification (MCN), the particular bonds to be delivered must now be identified.

A specific concern of any firm that chooses to give bond collateral is that, if a particular bond is selected for delivery in settlement of a margin call, but no account is taken of other transactions that the firm may have executed, in effect there may be internal competition for that same bond. Such a situation could result in the same bond holding being identified for use in two separate transactions (e.g. securities lending and OTC derivative collateral) simultaneously, resulting in one of such transactions failing to settle. Dependent upon the specific nature of their business, some firms have a very large inventory of securities from which to select. However, there remains the possibility of internal competition to utilise a particular bond (e.g. EUR 10,000,000 of City of Oslo 4.75% Bonds 1st October 2030) for a variety of purposes beside collateral in relation to an OTC derivative trade. For example, the bonds may be:

- sold and therefore must be delivered to the buying counterparty on the value date of the sale (otherwise the selling firm will not receive the sale proceeds on the due date and will incur loss of interest)
- lent and must be delivered to the borrowing counterparty
- delivered to a counterparty as collateral in a *repo* transaction.

Any failure to deliver the bonds as collateral to the exposed party on the value date has negative connotations; please refer to Sub-section 34.4.7 'Achieving Timely Delivery (Settlement)'.

In order to avoid such situations, a structured internal procedure is therefore necessary. Within some firms the responsibility for deciding whether to give either cash collateral or securities collateral to counterparties falls to the traders within the Front Office, as it is this area that is regarded as the internal owners of the firm's securities positions. Furthermore, in some firms, a certain set of bonds are identified periodically by the traders, which may be given as collateral by the Collateral Department; the internal procedure can then involve those bonds being transferred from the firm's account at the firm's relevant *custodian*, into a particular segregated account (entitled

PART 4a

PART 4a

'Outgoing Collateral Account' or similar) at the same custodian. The bonds will simply be held in the segregated account, with only the Collateral Department having access to the account. As and when the Collateral Department chooses to give bond collateral in settlement of margin calls, the Collateral Department will arrange deliveries of bonds from the segregated account, to the account of the relevant counterparty on a *free of payment* (FoP) basis.

In general terms, it is common practice to give bond collateral that meets the eligibility criteria as stated within the CSA, but without giving the highest quality collateral. For example, if the firm holds bonds of various types, ranked from AAA rated government bonds to corporate bonds and *mortgage-backed securities*, and a particular CSA lists AAA rated government bonds through to A– rated corporate bonds as *eligible collateral*, best practice is to provide the A– rated corporate bonds in settlement of an incoming margin call. By taking this 'bottom-up' approach, the higher rated bonds are retained and reserved for CSAs which list only AAA rated bonds as eligible collateral.

From the collateral giver's perspective, the negative aspect of utilising lower rated bonds is that greater levels of *haircut* are likely, resulting in the firm needing to provide a greater quantity of bonds in order for the *collateral value* of such bonds to be at least equal to the counterparty's exposure. If a greater quantity of an individual bond is not available to the collateral giver, a range of eligible bonds may need to be delivered, requiring greater operational effort at this point and also in ongoing tasks (e.g. marking-to-market). The haircut rate reflects the perceived risk to the investor of the bond *issuer* failing to meet its *contractual obligations*; the greater the haircut rate, the greater the differential between a bond's *market value* and its collateral value. In simple terms, if a collateral giver held USD 10,000,000 of Bond X and USD 10,000,000 of Bond Y, both of which have a current market price of 100%, the market value of both bonds would be USD 10,000,000 (excluding *accrued interest*). However, if both bonds were to be given as collateral, it is possible that (for example) Bond X has a haircut rate of 1.5%, while Bond Y has a haircut rate of 10%. This means that the same quantity (and same market value) of bonds could result in vastly differing collateral values. The particular aspects that require consideration are:

- Issue Type: bond types are categorised according to their perceived inherent riskiness; for example, bonds issued by *central banks* are regarded as less risky than *asset backed securities*; the greater the perceived risk, the greater the haircut rate
- Issuer Ratings: the credit ratings applied by *ratings agencies* refer to the perceived ability of an issuer to meet its financial obligations, per bond issue; the lower the rating, the greater the haircut rate
- Coupon Structure: bonds are issued with different types of coupon, primarily *fixed rate bonds, floating rate notes* and *zero coupon bonds*. Fixed rate bonds and floating rate notes are considered to be of lesser risk than zero coupon bonds; the latter therefore typically has a greater haircut rate applied
- Residual Maturity: the length of time between 'today' and the maturity date of a bond is known as its *residual maturity*. The greater the residual maturity, the greater the perceived risk and the greater the haircut rate

- Haircut: the haircut applied to bond collateral has the impact of reducing its (higher) market value to its (lower) collateral value. Therefore, the lower the haircut, the greater the 'value for money' the giver will enjoy.

The concept of haircut, and how haircut rates are derived, will be covered in Sub-section 34.4.2 'Valuing Securities Collateral'.

Another approach to the selection of bond collateral is to deliver eligible bonds that are less likely to be used for other purposes, possibly including relatively small bond quantities. The potential downside of this approach is that if this results in multiple pieces of collateral being delivered, as opposed to, say, a single piece of collateral, the operational effort (and associated cost) involved could outweigh any other benefit.

34.4.2 Valuing Securities Collateral

Having selected the (one or many) pieces of bond collateral to be delivered to the exposed party, the collateral must now be valued in order to ensure that their (combined) collateral value is at least the value of the counterparty's exposure.

The valuation process consists of applying:

- the *current market price* (*marking-to-market*)
- the current value of *accrued interest* (see the Marking-to-Market sub-section below), and
- the appropriate haircut.

Marking-to-Market   The purpose of marking-to-market is to apply a realistic current market price (and therefore current market value) to individual securities.

The various uses of marking-to-market of securities include:

- the calculation of *unrealised profit and loss* relating to securities trading
- the calculation of *net asset value* (NAV) by *mutual funds*, and
- the calculation of bond collateral values.

The process of marking-to-market involves the gathering of independently sourced bond prices; the requirement for independence is designed to prevent false prices being applied to bond positions, whether by accident or design.

Today, many financial services firms subscribe to the services of *data vendors* that specialise in the gathering of current securities prices. Examples of such firms include Bloomberg, ICE Data Services, SIX Financial Information and Thomson Reuters. Data vendors typically provide prices in electronic form to subscribing firms, enabling automated uploading of current prices to the internal systems of such firms.

It is important to note that bond prices are quoted in one of two ways:

- *'clean' price* – accrued interest must be added to such prices (see the next section)
- *'dirty' price* – the 'all-in' price, inclusive of accrued interest.

As an example, Table 34.2 depicts the mark-to-market 'clean' price of a bond, from which the market value and the collateral value are derived:

PART 4a

TABLE 34.2   Bond collateral value calculation #1 (Part 1 of 3)

USD 10,000,000 Issuer XXX 4.15% Bonds 15th April 2030		
Marked-to-Market 'clean' price	98.76%	USD 9,876,000.00
add Accrued Interest		
Total Market Value		
deduct Haircut		
Total Collateral Value		

Note: within the above table, the grey text is intentional. Both accrued interest and haircut are described within the upcoming pages and progressive versions of the table will be shown appropriately.

Accrued Interest   Interest-bearing bonds such as *fixed rate bonds* and *floating rate notes,* but excluding *zero coupon bonds*, accrue interest (commonly known as *coupon*) on a daily basis; in other words, a holder of an interest-bearing bond earns coupon each day, until the bond is sold. However, the bond *issuer* will pay coupon only on predefined dates throughout the bond's lifetime.

In terms of coupon payment frequency, the majority of fixed rate bonds pay coupons either annually or semi-annually (i.e. every 6 months, not every 2 years as that is bi-annual). Floating rate notes typically pay coupons semi-annually, quarterly or monthly. The details of when coupon payments are scheduled for a particular bond can be found in the issue *prospectus* and are also available from *data vendors*. (If a particular bond is already set up within the firm's static data, details of coupon rates and coupon dates should be included and be available for use.)

When an interest-bearing bond is bought and sold between coupon payment dates, market practice is for the buyer to pay the seller the value of coupon earned since the previous coupon payment date (i.e. the most recent date on which the issuer paid coupon). For example, if a bond pays interest at 4.15% annually on 15th April, and a quantity of USD 10,000,000 bonds were sold with a *value date* of 15th August, then 120 days of accrued interest is payable by the buyer to the seller upon settlement of the trade (assuming the applicable accrued interest convention is 30/360, meaning a day count of 30 days per month, and a divisor of 360). If, instead, the same quantity of bonds were sold with a value date of 27th January, then 282 days of accrued interest is payable by the buyer upon settlement of the trade. (Assuming that the buyer does not sell the bond until after payment of the next coupon, the buyer will receive compensation after another 78 days have elapsed when the buyer would be entitled to the coupon for the entire year, when the issuer makes the next scheduled annual coupon payment. The issuer will therefore pay 360 days of interest on the next 15th April.)

The calculation of accrued interest using the latter example above is as follows:

- bond quantity × coupon rate % / relevant divisor × accrued days = **value of accrued interest**
- USD 10,000,000 × 4.15% / 360 × 282 = **USD 325,083.33**

It is important to note the following:

- the method of counting accrued days is as follows: include the start date (the most recent date on which the issuer paid coupon), and exclude the end date (value date), taking account of the relevant *day count* convention. In the above example, 282 days is arrived at as follows:
  - 15th–30th April inclusive = 16 days
  - May–December = 8 months at 30 days per month = 240 days, and
  - 1st–26th January inclusive = 26 days
- accrued interest values are based upon the bond quantity (not the market value of the bond). This is because the issuer pays coupon based upon bond quantity, and accrued interest is the market's method of fairly distributing coupon amounts to the rightful party.
- different day count and *divisor* conventions exist according to bond type and issue currency. In the example above, the 30/360 convention is applicable as the bond is a USD-denominated fixed rate bond, where every month is counted as 30 days regardless of the actual number of days in the month and the divisor is always 360 (as opposed to actual/calendar days). Other conventions exist – see Figure 34.2:

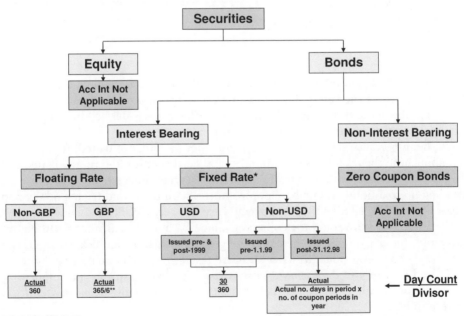

* including convertible bonds

**when coupon payment date falls in a leap year

FIGURE 34.2   Accrued interest conventions

For further detail regarding the subject of accrued interest, please refer to this author's book, *Securities Operations: a Guide to Trade and Position Management*, ISBN 0-471-49758-4, published by John Wiley.

The above-mentioned accrued interest concepts are applicable to both bond trades and to bond collateral values, as today's market value of a bond in fact incorporates the current value of accrued interest. Of course, each day that passes means a bond has accrued 1 additional day of interest (compared with the previous day); this will continue until the next coupon payment date, following which the bond will begin accruing interest all over again.

Continuing the example begun within the Marking-to-Market sub-section above, the value of accrued interest is added to the mark-to-market value which produces the total market value (from which haircut will need to be deducted subsequently in order to derive the total collateral value) – see Table 34.3:

TABLE 34.3   Bond collateral value calculation #2 (Part 2 of 3)

USD 10,000,000 Issuer XXX 4.15% Bonds 15th April 2030		
Marked-to-Market 'clean' price	98.76%	USD 9,876,000.00
add Accrued Interest	282 days	+ USD 325,083.33
Total Market Value		**USD 10,201,083.33**
deduct Haircut		
Total Collateral Value		

As stated earlier, the only exception to such rules occurs where a dirty price has been used, where the value of accrued interest is incorporated within the price; in the example above the dirty price is 102.0108%. This price is derived by simply dividing the bond quantity into the total market value.

The importance of accrued interest must not be underestimated; it is an essential component in the calculation of a bond's total market value and total collateral value. To provide a sense of the monetary value that accrued interest can reach, in the days leading up to a bond's annual coupon payment, with that bond paying 5% coupon, a quantity of EUR 100,000,000 bonds will carry an accrued interest value approaching EUR 5,000,000.00. Should the collateral value of a bond be calculated without taking account of accrued interest, the *collateral giver* is at risk of significantly undervaluing the bond's collateral value, which in turn will result in a greater quantity of bonds being delivered to *mitigate* the *exposed party's* risk. This will result in the collateral giver being unknowingly exposed, as they will have unintentionally *over-collateralised* the *counterparty*.

It is, however, absolutely normal to set up within a firm's securities *static data* the specific details of individual bonds in order to facilitate the automated calculation of accrued interest. However, automation does not remove the need for <u>correct</u> information to be set up within the firm's static data; incorrect information will produce incorrect calculations. In order to avoid use of incorrect information pertaining to accrued interest, it is strongly recommended that the details regarding a bond's interest characteristics are taken directly from the issue prospectus, for example:

- coupon payment date(s)
- coupon frequency: usually annual or semi-annual, but can be quarterly or monthly
- special coupon periods, such as *short first coupon* and *long first coupon*
- coupon rate(s); usually a single rate for the lifetime of the bond, but graduated rate bonds will have more than one coupon rate
- day count convention
- divisor convention.

Haircut (Valuation Percentage)   Haircuts are designed to account for the perceived risk of holding an asset (such as a bond). The haircut rate is directly associated with the perceived riskiness of the bond to be delivered as collateral. The risk relates specifically to the *creditworthiness* of the bond issuer.

Haircuts are applied so as to reduce the *market value* of a bond in order to derive its *collateral value*; regarding OTC derivative collateral, haircut rates are documented within the *Credit Support Annex*.

Examples of factors impacting bond haircut rates are contained within the following tables published by the European Central Bank (ECB) and which came into effect on 1st January 2011. Note: the following is used as a representative example of how haircut rates are derived.

Determining the relevant haircut for a particular bond involves a series of steps. Firstly, the liquidity category of a bond must be established by reference to Table 34.4:

TABLE 34.4   Liquidity categories for marketable assets

Liquidity Categories for Marketable Assets				
Category I	Category II	Category III	Category IV	Category V
Central government debt instruments	Local & regional government debt instruments	Traditional covered bank bonds	Credit institution debt instruments (uncovered)	Asset backed securities
Debt instruments issued by central banks	Jumbo covered bank bonds	Structured covered bank bonds		
	Agency debt instruments Supranational debt instruments	Multi-Cedulas Debt instruments issued by corporate and other issuers		

Source: ECB

Note: information listed is at summary level only – please refer to ECB for further details.

In the example covered in the two prior sections, assume that the bond issuer, namely XXX, is a corporate issuer, which falls within Category III.

Next, with reference to the landscape Table 34.6 'Levels of haircut percentages applied to eligible market assets', the bond in question has these characteristics:

- issuer rating: A–
- coupon structure: fixed rate
- *residual maturity*: greater than 10 years.

This reveals the relevant haircut rate to be 11% which, when deducted from the total market value (inclusive of accrued interest), produces a total collateral value of USD 9,078,964.16 (see Table 34.5).

TABLE 34.5   Bond collateral value calculation #3 (Part 3 of 3)

USD 10,000,000 Issuer XXX 4.15% Bonds 15th April 2030		
Marked-to-Market 'clean' price	98.76%	USD 9,876,000.00
add Accrued Interest	282 days	+ USD 325,083.33
Total Market Value		USD 10,201,083.33
deduct Haircut	11%	(USD 1,122,119.17)
Total Collateral Value		USD 9,078,964.16

Determining Haircut Percentage: Example Calculations   Using both the tables, firstly Table 34.4 'Liquidity categories for marketable assets' and secondly Table 34.6 'Levels of valuation haircuts applied to eligible market assets', calculate the answers to the following questions. (Note: some questions require an understanding of *bond denominational values* – see Chapter 2 'The Nature and Characteristics of Collateral Types'.)

Example #1   On 12th January 2012, a national central bank enters into a repurchase transaction with Counterparty B, in which the national bank purchases €71.9 million of Asset A, rated AA+. This asset is a supranational debt instrument with a 4.15% fixed coupon maturing on 15th October 2018. The market price of this bond is 101.09%, inclusive of accrued interest (i.e. a dirty price).

Question 1: what is the collateral value of the asset?

Answer: = *€69,412,943.05 (€71,900,000 × 101.09% = €72,683,710.00, less 4.5% = €3,270,766.95, final figure = €69,412,943.05).*

Explanation: Supranational debt instruments fall within Category II, with an AA+ rating and the fixed coupon bond in question having a residual maturity of 6 years, and because it has a fixed coupon, haircut of 4.5% is applicable.

Example #2   On 29th November 2012, a national central bank enters into a repurchase transaction with Counterparty G, in which the national bank purchases €52,250,000 of a European company's zero coupon bonds maturing on 1st April 2021, rated A–. The market price of this bond is 58.09%.

Question 2: what is the collateral value of the asset?

Answer: = €27,468,582.63 *(€52,250,000×58.09% = €30,352,025.00, less 9.5% = €2,883,442.38, final figure = €27,468,582.63).*

Explanation: Corporate bonds fall within Category III, with an A– rating and the bond in question having a residual maturity of greater than 8 years, and because it has a zero coupon, haircut of 9.5% is applicable.

Example #3   Counterparty T borrows €58 million cash from a national central bank on 21st October 2012 and owns Asset T (a central government bond with a 3.95% fixed coupon maturing 15th May 2025, rated AA). The market price of this bond is 97.81%, inclusive of accrued interest. The bond has a single denominational value of €100,000.00.

Question 3: what quantity of bonds (to the nearest €100,000.00) must be delivered to cover the cash borrowing?

Answer: = €62,800,000 *bonds (€62,800,000 × 97.81% = €61,424,680.00, less 5.5% = €3,378,357.40, final figure = €58,046,322.60).*

Explanation: Central government bonds fall within Category I, with an AA rating and the fixed rate coupon bond in question having a residual maturity of over 10 years, haircut of 5.5% is applicable.

*Suggested calculation method: 1) calculate the collateral value of 100,000 bonds (taking account of market price & haircut), namely 100,000 × market price × (100% less haircut %), then 2) divide that figure into the exposure amount in order to derive the bond quantity, followed by rounding up to the nearest €100,000.00.

Example #4   Counterparty P borrows €90 million cash from a national central bank on 7th August 2012 and owns Asset D (a credit institution debt instrument with a 4.65% coupon maturing 1st December 2016, rated BBB). The market price of this security is 100.09%, inclusive of accrued interest. The bond has a single denominational value of €100,000.00.

Question 4: what quantity of bonds (to the nearest €100,000.00) must be delivered to cover the cash borrowing?

Answer = €141,700,000 *bonds (€141,700,000 × 100.09% = €141,827,530.00, less 36.5% = €51,767,048.45, final figure = €90,060,481.55).*

Explanation: Credit institution debt instruments fall within Category IV, with a BBB rating and the fixed coupon bond in question having a residual maturity of 4+ years, haircut of 36.5% is applicable.

*Suggested calculation method: 1) calculate the collateral value of 100,000 bonds (taking account of market price & haircut), namely 100,000 × market price × (100% less haircut %), then 2) divide that figure into the exposure amount in order to derive the bond quantity, followed by rounding up to the nearest €100,000.00.

On a day-by-day basis, firms will need to refer to the details contained within the specific **Credit Support Annex** for the particular counterparty in order to identify the parameters for calculating haircut.

PART 4a

TABLE 34.6 Levels of haircut percentages applied to eligible market assets

Levels of Haircut Percentages Applied to Eligible Market Assets											
		Liquidity Categories									
		Category I		Category II		Category III		Category IV		Category V	
Credit Quality	Residual Maturity (years)	Fixed Coupon	Zero Coupon	Fixed Coupon	Zero Coupon	Fixed Coupon	Zero Coupon	Fixed Coupon	Zero Coupon	All	
AAA to A− (upper band)	0–1	0.5	0.5	1.0	1.0	1.5	1.5	6.5	6.5	16	
	1–3	1.5	1.5	2.5	2.5	3.0	3.0	8.5	9.0		
	3–5	2.5	3.0	3.5	4.0	5.0	5.5	11.0	11.5		
	5–7	3.0	3.5	4.5	5.0	6.5	7.5	12.5	13.5		
	7–10	4.0	4.5	5.5	6.5	8.5	9.5	14.0	15.5		
	>10	5.5	8.5	7.5	12.0	11.0	16.5	17.0	22.5		
BBB+ to BBB− (lower band)	0–1	5.5	5.5	6.0	6.0	8.0	8.0	15.0	15.0	Not eligible	
	1–3	6.5	6.5	10.5	11.5	18.0	19.5	27.5	29.5		
	3–5	7.5	8.0	15.5	17.0	25.5	28.0	36.5	39.5		
	5–7	8.0	8.5	18.0	20.5	28.0	31.5	38.5	43.0		
	7–10	9.0	9.5	19.5	22.5	29.0	33.5	39.0	44.5		
	>10	10.5	13.5	20.0	29.0	29.5	38.0	39.5	46.0		

The ECB's risk control framework for eligible marketable assets includes the following main elements:

- The haircuts are applied by deducting a certain percentage from the market value of the underlying asset. The haircuts applied to debt instruments included in categories I to IV differ according to the residual maturity and coupon structure of the debt instruments for eligible marketable fixed coupon and zero coupon debt instruments.
- Haircuts applicable to marketable debt instruments included in liquidity categories I to IV with variable rate coupons, excluding 'inverse floaters', will be those applicable to the 0–1 year maturity bucket of fixed coupon instruments in the corresponding liquidity and credit category.
- The assets are subject to daily valuation. On a daily basis, national central banks calculate the required value of underlying assets taking into account changes in outstanding credit volumes and the required valuation haircuts.
- The ECB may at any time decide to remove individual debt instruments from the published list of eligible marketable assets.
- (With effect from 1st January 2011, marketable debt instruments denominated in currencies other than the Euro (i.e. USD, GBP, JPY) and issued in the euro area, will no longer be eligible as collateral.)

Source: ECB (note: the above is not an exhaustive list of all elements quoted by ECB)

34.4.3 Transaction Capture

Having selected and valued the bond collateral which is to be delivered in order to satisfy a *margin call* from the *counterparty*, it is now necessary to formally record internally the details of the bonds to be given (i.e. delivered to the counterparty).

This is an essential step, albeit an internal one, in order for the firm to retain proper control over its assets.

Firstly, assume the following information was held within the firm's *books & records* prior to the firm's decision to deliver a specific quantity of these bonds as collateral to the counterparty (see Table 34.7).

TABLE 34.7 Books & records #1

Issuer XXX 4.15% Bonds 15th April 2030			
Ownership			Location
Trading Book 'A'	+15,000,000	-15,000,000	Custodian 'P'
	+15,000,000	-15,000,000	

Also assume that this information was fully *reconciled*, specifically that the Ownership position was successfully reconciled with the trading system and that the Location position was successfully reconciled with the statement of securities holdings issued by *Custodian* P.

Secondly, in order to settle a margin call, the firm now wishes to deliver to its counterparty, as collateral, a quantity of USD 10,000,000 of Issuer XXX 4.15% Bonds 15th April 2030.

In order for the firm's books & records to continue to reflect reality, it is essential at this point to record an internal transaction which results in securities accounting entries being passed. These entries must reflect the following:

- that the firm has selected these specific bonds (i.e. USD 10,000,000 Issuer XXX 4.15% Bonds 15th April 2030) to be delivered as collateral to the specific counterparty on the specific value date relating to the margin call (as shown in Table 34.8).

TABLE 34.8 Collateral transaction capture

Collateral Transaction Capture			
Component	Meaning	Example	
Transaction Type	*The type of transaction being recorded*	*Bond Collateral Delivery*	
Counterparty	*The name of the counterparty*	*Counterparty T, New York*	
Security Reference	*The security identifier code, e.g. ISIN*	*XX1234567891*	
Quantity	*The number of bonds intended to be delivered*	*USD 10,000,000*	
Value date	*The intended date of delivery*	*27th January*	
Current Market Price	*The current clean price of the bonds in the open marketplace*	*98.76%*	USD 9,876,000.00
Accrued Days/Interest	*The number of accrued days/value of accrued interest*	*282*	+USD 325,083.33
Total Market Value	*The total market value of the bond*		USD 10,201,083.33
Haircut	*The applicable haircut rate/value to be deducted*	*11%*	(USD 1,122,119.17)
Total Collateral Value	*The total collateral value of the bond*		USD 9,078,964.16

(continued)

PART 4a

TABLE 34.8 Collateral transaction capture (*continued*)

Component	Meaning	Example
Firm's Custodian*	*The firm's custodian/account number from which delivery will be made*	*Custodian 'P' account 12345*
Counterparty's Custodian*	*The counterparty's custodian account number to which delivery will be made*	*Custodian 'P' account 98765*
Settlement Method	*The method of bond delivery*	*Free of payment*

* *Firm's custodian and counterparty's custodian are commonly copied from* **standing settlement instructions** *(SSIs) held within the firm's static data repository*

Immediately following transaction capture, the settlement status of the transaction would be 'open'; it must remain as such until the custodian has advised that settlement has occurred (on the *value date* at the earliest). Note: premature recording within internal records that delivery has occurred will cause internal records to be incorrect and cause internal books & records versus the custodian's statement not to reconcile.

It is normal practice that the internal capture of such a transaction will produce a unique transaction reference number which should be used on all subsequent internal and external communication.

Such securities accounting entries can be achieved by:

- manual generation and manual input into the firm's books & records system, or
- booking of a collateral transaction within the firm's collateral system, which then creates the accounting entries (from predefined criteria held within the system) in the firm's books & records system.

The particular method of passing accounting entries within a firm will depend on the firm's level of automation relating to collateral. In modern systems, the recording of the collateral transaction results in the system generation of:

- a communication of proposed collateral to the counterparty, and
- a delivery instruction that will be automatically transmitted to the firm's custodian.

34.4.4 Communicating Proposed Collateral to Counterparty

At this stage, despite the fact that the firm has chosen to deliver bond collateral, the counterparty that has made the margin call is not aware of the specific bonds which the firm intends delivering in order to satisfy that call.

This step is important as it is the method by which the counterparty can validate that the collateral the firm is proposing to deliver (in advance of delivery):

- falls within the *eligible collateral* documented within the **Credit Support Annex** (CSA) between the two parties, and
- is of adequate value to cover the call amount, taking account of bond quantity, current market price, accrued interest and haircut.

The generic content of such a communication is shown in Table 34.9:

TABLE 34.9 Proposed collateral

Proposed Collateral	
From	*The name of the issuing firm*
To	*The name of the counterparty*
Attention	**The Collateral Department**
Subject	**Advice of Proposed Collateral**
Our Reference	*The issuing firm's collateral delivery reference number*
	Proposed Collateral
	Following receipt of your Margin Call Notification, we intend delivering the following bond:
Valuation Date	*The date on which the exposure has been determined*
Exposure Amount	*The value of exposure to which the margin call relates*
Security	*The full description of the bond proposed to be delivered*
Security Reference	*The security identifier code, e.g. ISIN*
Quantity	*The number of bonds intended to be delivered*
Value Date	*The intended date of delivery*
Current Market Price	*The current clean market price of the bond*
Accrued Days	*The applicable number of accrued days*
Accrued Interest	*The applicable value of accrued interest*
Haircut Rate	*The percentage haircut rate deducted from the current market value*
Current Collateral Value	*The collateral value of the bond, taking account of accrued interest and haircut*
	Settlement Details
Settlement Details	*The firm's custodian account number from which delivery will be made* *The counterparty's custodian account number to which delivery will be made*
Settlement Method	*The method of settlement (normally 'free of payment')*
Sign-off by the firm	*Full name and location of firm*
Transmission time	*A clear statement of the date and time of transmission*

The transmission methods employed to issue such a communication are:

- email, or
- AcadiaSoft's *MarginSphere* system (for subscribers), or
- *S.W.I.F.T.*; in particular an MT504 (Collateral Proposal).

Once the deadline for responses to the collateral proposal has passed and, providing the counterparty has not declined acceptance of the proposed bonds, the firm should proceed to arrange delivery of the bonds to the counterparty.

34.4.5 Instructing for Delivery of Securities Collateral

Having previously selected and valued the bonds to be delivered to the counterparty, and assuming the counterparty agrees, the considerations in issuing a *settlement instruction* for delivery of the bonds include:

- deciding from which custodian and custodian account the securities will be delivered, and
- deciding which transmission method should be used for communicating the settlement instruction to the custodian.

The normal content of a settlement instruction for delivery of collateral is shown in Table 34.10:

TABLE 34.10   Outgoing collateral delivery instruction

Outgoing Collateral Delivery Instruction		
Delivery Instruction Component	Origin of Information	Delivery Instruction Example
Our Transaction Reference Number	Allocated Manually or by System	Coll12121212
Firm's Account Number	Party Static Data; 'Our' SSI	12345
Counterparty Account Number	Party Static Data; 'Their' SSI	98765
Direction of Delivery	Agreement of Counterparty's Margin Call	Deliver
Quantity	Internal Books & Records &/or Custodian Statement	10,000,000
Security Identifier (ISIN)	Securities Static Data	XX1234567891
Value Date	Normal Collateral Delivery Cycle	27th January
Settlement Method	Normal Bond Collateral Settlement Method	Free of Payment

In a generic sense, for securities settlement two settlement methods exist, namely *delivery versus payment* (DvP) and *free of payment* (FoP). DvP requires an amount of cash to be moved in the opposite direction to the movement of the securities (for equivalent value), and is typically used for:

- the settlement of purchases and sales of securities, and for
- settlement of *cash-based repo* trades, and for
- settlement of *securities lending & borrowing* trades versus cash collateral.

Conversely, FoP requires zero cash to be moved when the securities are delivered. As settlement of an OTC derivative exposure requires the 'out-of-the-money' (i.e. *negative exposure*) party to remit value to the 'in-the-money' (i.e. *positive exposure*) party, the relevant method of settlement is FoP; common practice is that such FoP settlement instructions are issued by both parties and must match before settlement can occur.

A very popular method for the transmission of free of payment (FoP) securities settlement instructions (to either a *central securities depository*, or to a *custodian*), is S.W.I.F.T. Table 34.11 reflects the two types of FoP settlement instruction messages available for use by S.W.I.F.T. subscriber firms.

TABLE 34.11   S.W.I.F.T. message types

S.W.I.F.T. Securities Markets 'Free of Payment' Message Types		
MT	MT Name	MT Purpose
MT540	Receive securities on a free of payment basis	Receive securities without paying cash
MT542	Deliver securities on a free of payment basis	Deliver securities without receiving cash

Using S.W.I.F.T. for FoP settlement of a margin call requires the delivering party to transmit an MT542 instruction, whilst its counterparty transmits an MT540 instruction.

34.4.6 Achieving Matching Settlement Instructions

For actual delivery of bonds to occur between two parties, a firm's settlement instruction requires matching with the counterparty's settlement instruction. Matching of instructions is a control mechanism designed to ensure that the bonds are delivered to the correct account and for the correct quantity and value date; if the giver's instruction did not require to be matched, the giver would be at risk of delivering the securities to the account of a third party due to, for example:

- making an error when inputting the counterparty account number, or
- using an old (i.e. not current) counterparty *SSI*.

When the *collateral giver*'s instruction is received by the custodian, the custodian will perform a validity check to ensure that the security exists and the collateral giver's and the collateral taker's account numbers are valid, in force and usable. If any of these components are found to be invalid, the instruction will be rejected by the custodian. Should such a rejection occur, this must be investigated and resolved without delay otherwise the counterparty's exposure may not be *mitigated* within the required time frame.

Assuming the instruction passes such validity checks, the custodian will 1) record the detail of the settlement instruction, and 2) attempt to achieve a match of the instruction by searching for an equivalent instruction from the counterparty. Until a match

PART 4a

is achieved, a status of 'unmatched' will be applied to the collateral giver's instruction. Even after the collateral taker's settlement instruction has been received by the custodian, if any of the details differ compared with the collateral giver's instruction, the status of 'unmatched' will continue to be applied. If instructions are unmatched within 1 day of the value date, an increased status of 'urgent unmatched' will be applied; at this stage it is essential that the reason for the non-matching instruction is investigated and resolved. When all details match, the status of 'matched with a future value date' will be applied to both collateral giver's and collateral taker's instructions; this is the required status prior to value date, if the counterparty's exposure is to be mitigated on time.

Prior to value date, both instructions will retain a status of 'matched with future value date' (unless one of the parties cancels their instruction, in which case the status of the remaining instruction will revert to either 'unmatched' or 'urgent unmatched', dependent upon its proximity to value date).

34.4.7 Achieving Timely Delivery (Settlement)

The matching of instructions is an essential prerequisite for securities settlement. Following the matching of instructions, providing the securities are present within the collateral giver's account, there is no reason why settlement should not occur. Note: as the delivery of securities will occur on a *free of payment* basis, the collateral taker requires no cash to be present in its account; therefore a lack of cash in the taker's account is not a valid reason for delivery failure.

With matched FoP settlement instructions, the only reasons why the delivery of collateral should fail to occur is the giver having zero quantity of the bonds in its account, or a quantity of bonds which is less than the full delivery quantity. It is important to note that achieving a match of settlement instructions does not guarantee that settlement will occur on value date.

In order to ensure that the selected bonds are able to be delivered on time, the following steps should be taken by the giver of the collateral:

- select for delivery only those bonds which are known to be present at the custodian
- select for delivery only those bonds which cannot be accessed by other areas of the organisation; this may require segregation of bonds for use as collateral into a separate account at the custodian
- avoid selecting bonds for which an incoming delivery is yet to occur, as if there is a delay in receipt of such bonds, that will adversely affect the ability to deliver those bonds as collateral, in turn resulting in a failure to settle the counterparty's margin call in a timely manner.

In most (if not all) *central securities depositories* in the major financial centres, delivery from collateral giver to collateral taker will occur by a mechanism known as *electronic book entry*, resulting in the debit of securities from the collateral giver's account, and the simultaneous credit of the same to the collateral taker's account (without physical movement of securities).

The date that the delivery actually occurs is known as the *settlement date*. In most cases, because the vast majority of securities deliveries occur on their due date, settlement date and *value date* are the same date, in which case delivery is said to have occurred 'on time'. Where settlement date is later than value date, delivery is said to have 'failed', meaning that delivery has been delayed (not cancelled).

On value date, if *settlement failure* has occurred, the custodian will apply a *failed status* to both the collateral giver's and the collateral taker's settlement instruction. If the cause of settlement failure is the giver being deficient in the quantity of bonds, a status of 'deliverer insufficient' (or similar wording) will be applied to the settlement instruction of both parties. Both collateral giver and collateral taker will thereby become aware that the collateral taker's exposure has not been mitigated on the due date. The implications of such a failure are that the collateral taker has an unmitigated and ongoing exposure. What resultant action the collateral taker chooses is for the individual firm to decide; an occasional lapse by the collateral giver may be tolerated by the collateral taker, but frequent lapses are likely to be considered as very serious.

On whichever date settlement occurs, the custodian will issue an 'advice of settlement' which is a formal notification of delivery issued to both collateral giver and collateral taker; such a communication includes (see Table 34.12):

TABLE 34.12　Incoming advice of settlement

Incoming Advice of Settlement	
Delivery Instruction Component	Advice of Settlement Example
Our Transaction Reference Number	Coll12121212
Firm's Account Number	12345
Counterparty Account Number	98765
Direction of Delivery	Deliver
Quantity	10,000,000
Security Identifier (ISIN)	XX1234567891
Settlement Date	27th January
Settlement Method	FoP

In this example, the advice of settlement shows that delivery occurred on settlement date 27th January, the same date as the value date; therefore, delivery occurred 'on time' and consequently the collateral taker's exposure was mitigated 'on time'.

34.4.8　Updating Internal Books & Records Following Delivery

Now that an advice of settlement has been received, it is imperative that the collateral giver updates its internal *books & records* accurately and immediately with the following information (see Table 34.13):

- the removal of the specific quantity of bonds from the specific custodian account on the actual date that settlement occurred
- the specific quantity of bonds are now in the possession of the specific taker.

TABLE 34.13   Books & records #2

Issuer XXX 4.15% Bonds 15th April 2030			
Ownership		Location	
Trading Book 'A'	+15,000,000	–5,000,000	Custodian 'P'
		–10,000,000	Counterparty T, New York (Collateral)
	+15,000,000	–15,000,000	

Note that the Ownership position has remained the same as before (because the bonds have not been sold by Trading Book 'A'), but the Location position now reflects that some of those bonds are being held by the collateral taker.

Such record keeping is imperative for any firm to remain in proper control of its assets. Numerous benefits are derived from maintaining accurate books & records; three examples follow:

1. Should the collateral giver's trader wish to sell the bonds, the firm's *Operations Department* will identify (from the firm's books & records) that the bonds are not held at the custodian and cannot be delivered to settle the sale without first having the bonds returned by the collateral taker. This would be achieved by agreeing a *collateral substitution* with the collateral taker, following which the collateral giver will provide *replacement collateral* to the counterparty, in exchange for the return of the original bond (now sold).

2. Where a *coupon payment* on the bond falls due, the collateral giver's *Corporate Actions* Department will identify (from the firm's books & records) that the firm is entitled to the coupon on a total of USD 15,000,000 Issuer XXX 4.15% Bonds 15th April 2030. They will also see that USD 10,000,000 of the bonds are not held by the firm's custodian but are instead held by the collateral taker as at the *record date* of the coupon payment. Under such circumstances, the firm would be credited with the coupon payment by their custodian on only USD 5,000,000 bonds and would need to claim the coupon payment from the collateral taker on USD 10,000,000 bonds.

3. When the collateral giver conducts a *depot reconciliation* (a comparison of internal books & records of settled securities positions against the equivalent within the custodian's statement), there should be no reason why the reconciliation should not agree. This reconciliation is one of the most fundamentally important controls conducted by a firm on a day-by-day basis.

Without timely and accurate record keeping, the collateral giver's internal books & records will not reflect reality, and cash receipt in examples 1 and 2 above will not be achieved efficiently, potentially resulting in delayed cash receipt (a cost to the firm) as a minimum. Furthermore, each of the three examples above will require additional manpower to: a) identify the discrepancy, b) investigate the cause of the discrepancy, and c) take corrective action to resolve the discrepancy – all at additional cost to the firm.

Updating of books & records is typically achieved as follows. When the collateral transaction was captured earlier, a 'transaction record' would have been created showing the nature of the transaction and its component parts (e.g. counterparty, bond quantity, specific bond, value date). At the time of capture, the settlement status of the transaction would be 'open' (not yet settled). Once the advice of settlement is received from the custodian, the transaction record must be updated with the details of delivery (e.g. the quantity of bonds delivered, the settlement date). Once this update has occurred, the settlement status of the transaction should be changed to 'settled'. This formal updating of books & records therefore reveals that this delivery is no longer outstanding and that these bonds are not still to be delivered to the collateral taker.

34.4.9 Reconciliation

Following the updating of its books & records, proof that a firm is in control of its assets is evidenced through the process of reconciliation of internal books & records versus external statements.

Unfortunately, clerical errors do occur on occasions. Furthermore, a firm may experience attempts at internal or external fraud. Whether errors or fraud have occurred, a firm's best chance of identifying incorrect balances and/or missing assets is through regular (preferably daily) reconciliation.

Today, many firms utilise dedicated reconciliation software which compares the details of internal books & records versus external statements. The comparison process by such software typically takes a matter of seconds or minutes (rather than hours if performed manually). Any discrepancies are highlighted immediately, allowing investigation to begin without delay and resolution to be actioned very quickly. If fraud has been successful, at least the firm will become aware of it quickly and can then involve the relevant authorities while the trail is still 'hot'.

For cash, one of the foremost reconciliations is that of the ***nostro reconciliation***, which reconciles cash balances held at the firm's various ***cash correspondents***, otherwise known as ***nostros***.

The equivalent reconciliation for bonds is known as the ***depot reconciliation***, which reconciles securities balances held at the firm's various custodians, otherwise known as depots (in Europe) and depo (in the US).

34.5 CONCLUSION

Where a firm's various counterparties have ***exposures*** relating to a single OTC derivative trade, or a portfolio of OTC derivative trades, the firm has a legal responsibility to respond, in a timely manner, to ***margin calls*** received from such counterparties prior to the documented deadline.

Under such circumstances, the firm must ensure it acts appropriately in order to ***mitigate*** its counterparties' exposure within the normal market time frames (taking account of whether cash collateral or securities collateral is to be given). If the firm fails in this regard, particularly on a repeat basis, the firm is exposed to the risk that the counterparty (or counterparties) will treat such failure as being in ***default*** of the firm's ***contractual obligations***.

The firm must therefore ensure that it is equipped, under all circumstances (whether by use of modern systems or by experienced manpower, or preferably by a combination of both), to carry out its operational responsibilities within the legally documented time frames.

PART 4a

OTC Derivatives and Collateral – The Collateral Lifecycle – Throughout Lifetime of Trade – Issuing Margin Calls

The processing steps in making a margin call are broadly similar to those covered within the previous chapter (Receiving Margin Calls). However, there are certain specific aspects that relate only to making a call; this chapter highlights those processing aspects involved in successfully making a margin call, so as to mitigate the firm's exposure.

THE OTC DERIVATIVE COLLATERAL LIFECYCLE

1 **Pre-Trading**
Legal Documentation
Static Data

2 **Trading**
Trade Execution

3 **Post-Trading**
Trade Capture
Trade Confirmation/Affirmation
Trade/Portfolio Netting

4 **Throughout Lifetime of Trade**
Portfolio Reconciliation
Marking-to-Market
Exposure Calculation
Receiving Margin Calls
→ Issuing Margin Calls
Holding Collateral
Post-Trade Execution Events
Collateral Substitution
Income & Corporate Action Events

5 **Trade Termination**
Trade Termination

PART 4a

35.1 INTRODUCTION

By this stage in the collateral lifecycle, the following should have occurred. Note that these tasks are common to both receiving a margin call and making a margin call:

- *portfolio reconciliation*
- *marking-to-market*
- calculation of ***exposure*** amount, taking account of:
  - ***CSA*** components, per ***counterparty***
  - existing collateral given or taken.

In fact, all the above-mentioned tasks are essential in determining the monetary value of an exposure, and which party is exposed and therefore which party should make the ***margin call.***

Under the circumstances where the firm has established that it has an exposure, the ***mitigation*** of that exposure is achieved by the procedural steps depicted in Figure 35.1:

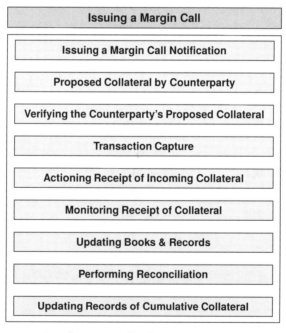

FIGURE 35.1   Issuing a margin call: sequential tasks

35.2 ISSUING A MARGIN CALL NOTIFICATION

The firm's ***margin call notification*** (MCN) must be issued to the counterparty, so as to be received by the counterparty no later than the deadline (Notification Time) stated within the relevant CSA.

Despite the fact that some counterparties do not apply the deadline strictly, the firm would be taking a risk if it relied upon such counterparties to treat each late-received MCN as though it had been received by the deadline. From a legal (CSA) standpoint and by default, MCNs received beyond the documented deadline are officially treated as late receipts and will be paid one day later or will be waived and recalculated the next day. Under such circumstances, in practice this is achieved by agreement with the counterparty.

35.2.1 Margin Call Notification: Counterparty's Agreement or Dispute

In relation to an MCN issued by a firm, either 1) the counterparty confirms its agreement, or 2) the counterparty disputes it. If the MCN is disputed, it is likely to be for one (or more) of the following reasons:

- difference in the population of OTC derivative trades*
- difference in mark-to-market*
- difference in records of existing collateral
- use of out-of-date CSA, for example revealing a different holiday calendar or valuation frequency
- miscalculation of CSA components, the most likely of which are independent amount, threshold, minimum transfer amount, and rounding.

35.2.2 Settlement of Undisputed Amount

Where the counterparty disputes the call amount, it is common practice to firstly settle the *undisputed amount*, then to attempt to resolve the monetary difference.

For example, if the firm issues a margin call of USD 3,000,000.00, but the counterparty calculates the exposure amount as USD 2,200,000.00, the latter amount (the undisputed amount) will be settled in the normal fashion. The residual amount of USD 800,000.00 (the *disputed amount*) will be investigated without delay; once the reason for the disputed amount has been identified, the result may mean that the *non-exposed party* will be required to pay additionally the full disputed amount, or a lesser amount, or a higher amount.

35.3 COLLATERAL PROPOSED BY COUNTERPARTY

Assuming the counterparty agrees the margin call amount, the counterparty must decide (where the CSA permits a choice) in which form the margin call is to be settled, whether by payment of cash or delivery of bonds.

---

*If prior portfolio reconciliation has been undertaken successfully, there should be no difference in the trade population, likewise for the marking-to-market of such trades. For further details, please refer to Chapter 31 'OTC Derivatives and Collateral – The Collateral Lifecycle – Throughout Lifetime of Trade – Portfolio Reconciliation'.

35.3.1 Receiving Advice of the Counterparty's Proposed Collateral

Having made the decision, the counterparty must then formally advise the firm as to the form of settlement it has chosen. The normal transmission method for such a communication is email or AcadiaSoft's '*MarginSphere*' system, and the deadline for its receipt by the firm is usually 24 hours after the MCN deadline. In practice, confirmation of the collateral proposed by the non-exposed party is usually received by the exposed party the same day as the MCN deadline, and in many cases within 3 hours (at the time of writing).

35.4 VERIFYING THE COUNTERPARTY'S PROPOSED COLLATERAL

The step of verifying the collateral proposed by the counterparty differs according to the nature of the collateral, whether cash or bonds; such differences are outlined below.

35.4.1 Cash Collateral

If the non-exposed party advises that they have chosen to provide cash collateral, the action for the exposed party is to ensure 1) that the currency of payment proposed by the counterparty is covered by the CSA, 2) that the cash amount claimed is accurate, and 3) that the counterparty will be paying such cash to the firm's correct *nostro* account. If the exposed party's nostro details are held incorrectly by the non-exposed party, the possibility exists that the firm's exposure may not be mitigated on its due date. In order for the exposed party to be aware as to the details of payment that the non-exposed party intends making, the exposed party's nostro account details should be communicated within the previously mentioned email. (The counterparty should be holding such information as a *standing settlement instruction* (SSI) within its *static data repository*, from information originally provided by the exposed party, although this is usually validated via a callback between the two firms.)

In addition, in order for the exposed party to receive '*good value*' on the incoming funds, the receiving nostro may require the receipt of a *funds preadvice* from the exposed party (the account holder); this communication provides the receiving nostro with a prior warning that funds are in process of being paid to it by another bank, in turn facilitating the receiving nostro updating its overall cash position. If the exposed party fails to issue a funds preadvice to its receiving nostro, the receiving nostro will still receive the funds but will not be expecting to receive them, and consequently the incoming funds will not have been 'positioned', meaning that the receiving nostro will not earn interest on this cash amount, and in turn the receiving nostro is unlikely to credit the exposed party with good value. On a normal week without a public holiday, a failure to receive good value between Monday and Thursday will lead to 1) exposure mitigation being delayed by one day, and 2) a loss of cash interest for one day (assuming a *positive interest rate* environment). Conversely, if the value date of the margin call is a Friday, a failure to receive good value will mean 1) that the exposed party's exposure has not been mitigated on its due date (Friday night) and for the following two nights (Saturday night, Sunday night), and 2) that the exposed party will suffer loss of cash interest for three nights. The loss of interest will be compensated via the claim process or via a correction in the interest calculation where the agreed date has been taken into account.

35.4.2 Bond Collateral

If, instead of cash, the non-exposed party elects to provide bond collateral, it is essential that the exposed party verifies the details as quickly as possible, primarily:

- that the particular bond does in fact legitimately fall within the bond eligibility criteria stated within the CSA, in particular covering the *issuer* type, *issue* type and the issuer's credit rating, and
- that the quantity of bonds proposed will in fact cover the exposure amount. The calculation components that determine this are represented within Table 35.1:

TABLE 35.1 Proposed bond collateral

Counterparty's Proposed Bond Collateral		
EUR 6,000,000 Issuer ABC 2.95% Bonds 1st July 2028		
Marked-to-Market price	101.73%	EUR 6,103,800.00
add Accrued Interest	44 days	EUR 21,633.33
Total Market Value		EUR 6,125,433.33
deduct Haircut	8%	(EUR 490,034.67)
Total Collateral Value		EUR 5,635,398.66

(In order to understand the component parts of this table, please refer to Chapter 34 'OTC Derivatives and Collateral – The Collateral Lifecycle – Throughout Lifetime of Trade – Receiving Margin Calls', and in particular, Sub-section 34.4.2 'Valuing Securities Collateral'.

If the exposed party's verification process reveals that, in the firm's opinion, either 1) the particular bond is not eligible under the terms of the CSA, and/or 2) the bond is eligible but the quantity of bonds proposed by the counterparty is inadequate, it is imperative that the exposed party communicates this immediately to the counterparty, and preferably in written form. Following such a communication, the non-exposed party may decide to provide a different eligible bond, a greater quantity of the same bond, or cash. When the non-exposed party submits its revised proposal to meet the firm's collateral demand, the exposed party should adopt the same procedure as for the originally proposed collateral. In summary, the exposed party is at risk of accepting ineligible bond collateral or an inadequate quantity (and consequently an inadequate value) of eligible bond collateral, therefore under any circumstances the firm must ensure its exposure is properly and fully *mitigated* by rigorous practice of such verification procedures.

The length of time required to carry out the process of verification by the exposed party can be greater than normal, in circumstances where the non-exposed party proposes delivery of multiple bonds to satisfy the firm's *MCN*. There is normally no restriction (stated within the CSA) regarding the number of different bonds that may be proposed by a *collateral giver*, to a *collateral taker*, other than that the bonds must be eligible under the terms of the CSA. Common practice is to apply an unofficial limit of five securities (*ISIN*s), although under exceptional circumstances the number of ISINs can be greater in order to cover the margin call. Clearly, the time and effort required to verify (say) five or ten different bonds, taking account of *marking-to-market, accrued interest* calculations and *haircut* percentage for each bond, will be significantly greater for the exposed party, compared with the non-exposed party's proposed delivery of a single bond; furthermore, if an exposed party has inadequate systems and therefore processing is performed manually, this aspect can account for significant amounts of time and effort. The exposed party's management should remain conscious of the potential impact of such extended time and effort, particularly if subsequent time-sensitive tasks are impacted. If the exposed party has not previously traded or held the particular bond proposed by the non-exposed party, it is entirely possible that the bond in question has not been set up within the firm's own *static data repository* and therefore no information about the bond is immediately available. Such missing information would include details about the bond's *coupon payment dates*, and the frequency of coupon payments; this in turn would impact the calculation of accrued interest. However, it is expected that subscribers to securities *data vendors* would be able to retrieve the details about the particular bond, although the speed at which such information is made available to the subscriber will depend on their *service level agreement* with the data vendor. A subscribing firm that receives a download of securities details from a data vendor (say) once per day at the end of each business day, is at risk of being unable to verify the non-exposed party's proposed bonds within an acceptable time frame.

35.4.3 Responding to the Counterparty's Proposed Collateral

Whether cash or bonds have been proposed by the counterparty, the exposed party, following its verification process, must respond to the non-exposed party's proposed collateral communication, with its own communication, stating that it either 1) agrees to the proposed collateral, or 2) disagrees. The method used for such communication is primarily email; however, such communication is logged systematically for users of AcadiaSoft's *MarginSphere* system.

In general terms, a failure of the exposed party to respond to the non-exposed party's proposal will leave the non-exposed party to assume the exposed party's agreement; best practice is to respond to the counterparty, whether the firm agrees or disagrees to the proposed collateral.

Where the exposed party disagrees, it is important that such a situation is followed up with the non-exposed party immediately, as any further delay may jeopardise the exposed party receiving collateral on the due date, thereby causing the exposed party's exposure to remain partially or fully unmitigated. In case resolution of a disagreement is considered to be taking too long, firms should be prepared to escalate the issue by calling the counterparty.

35.5 TRANSACTION CAPTURE

At this stage, if an exposed party is using a collateral management system, it is normal practice to capture the details of the particular collateral movement, including:

- the valuation (exposure) date
- the exposure amount

- operation (direction of call), either:
  - call by the firm (on the counterparty), or
  - call by the counterparty (on the firm)
- the particular counterparty
- the form and value of collateral:
  - if cash: currency and amount
  - if bonds: currency, unique identifier, quantity of each particular bond (whether one or many) and total collateral value
- value date of collateral movement (by default) either:
  - T+1 for cash, or
  - T+2 for bonds
- custodian account numbers (for bond collateral), for:
  - the firm, and
  - the counterparty
- the settlement method (for bond collateral):
  - usually *free of payment* (FoP).

As a result of such transaction capture, dependent upon the particular system some of the subsequent actions (see below) can be automated.

35.6 ACTIONING RECEIPT OF INCOMING COLLATERAL

Assuming the non-exposed party's proposed collateral is agreed by the exposed party, the next step is for the exposed party to now take the necessary action to ensure the collateral assets are in fact received from the counterparty on the due date. The due date is known as the *value date*, and, in relation to the date the MCN is issued, is usually:

- for cash collateral: T+1 business day, meaning the very next business day
- for bond collateral: T+2 business days,

although in future the trend is likely to be earlier, including T+0. If and when same day (T+0) settlement of margin calls becomes the norm, it will be essential that all firms are able to act and react in such extremely short time frames.

35.6.1 Cash Collateral

As mentioned earlier, the exposed party may need to issue a *funds preadvice*; otherwise the exposed party is required to issue nothing in order for the cash to be received (unlike securities, there is no pre-matching of cash in order for it to change hands), and the exposed party must monitor its account at the receiving nostro to ensure funds are in fact received on the value date.

35.6.2 Bond Collateral

In order for the exposed party to successfully receive the non-exposed party's bonds (as collateral), both parties must transmit an *FoP settlement instruction* to the place of settlement, either a *CSD* or *custodian*. This involves both parties generating and transmitting a securities settlement instruction, containing the information shown in Table 35.2:

TABLE 35.2   Settlement instruction components

Settlement Instruction Component	Exposed Party's Instruction	Non-Exposed Party's Instruction	Matchable Field?
The transmitting firm's account number at the relevant CSD	12345	98765	√
The counterparty's account number at the CSD (using the counterparty's SSI held in static data)	98765	12345	√
Internal Transaction Reference Number (unique to each firm)	Coll004469	ZZA 0177	x
The securities identifier (e.g. *ISIN*, or national code such as *CUSIP*)	ISIN XX1234567891	ISIN XX1234567891	√
The operation (direction of securities movement)	Receive	Deliver	√
The quantity of bonds	EUR 6,000,000	EUR 6,000,000	√
Value Date	dd/mm/yyyy	dd/mm/yyyy	√
Settlement Method	FoP	FoP	√

Note that most of the settlement instruction components must match exactly. The exceptions are 1) the direction of securities movement which must be opposing, and 2) the transaction reference numbers, as they are internal references for each firm.

The exposed party must transmit its settlement instruction to the destination CSD or custodian, whichever is applicable. The transmission method is extremely important, as there is a distinct external fraud opportunity if an inadequately secure transmission method is used; the sender should require the receiving party to verify the origin of the settlement instruction, and the receiving party should also want to verify the settlement instruction's authenticity for fear of acting upon a fraudulent instruction, and potentially being held liable for any loss the firm suffers. Thus, fax is regarded as very insecure, whilst *S.W.I.F.T.* is regarded as highly secure. The exposed party could generate and transmit settlement instructions automatically from its own systems via S.W.I.F.T. due to the highly structured and formatted message types.

It is important to note that the settlement instructions received by a CSD or custodian will firstly be subject to a validation process. The following are reasons why a securities settlement instruction may be rejected by a CSD or custodian:

- sender's account number does not exist or is inactive
- counterparty's account number does not exist or is inactive
- ISIN (or national code) does not exist or is inactive
- quantity is not a deliverable quantity according to *denominational values* of the bond issue
- value date is a non-business day.

PART 4a

Assuming that the exposed party's settlement instruction has been validated and accepted by the CSD or custodian, the instructions must match before the movement of bonds will occur. The CSD will repeatedly attempt to match the firm's settlement instruction against the non-exposed party's instruction. If the non-exposed party's instruction is missing, the exposed party's settlement instruction will be given a status of 'unmatched'; once the non-exposed party's instruction is received by the CSD, the attempt to match will reveal whether the instructions are in fact matched (status of both instructions updated to 'matched with a future value date'), or, due to one or more differences in the content of the instructions, both instructions will be given a status of 'unmatched'. Both parties are able to monitor the status of their instructions (typically online), and unmatched instructions should be investigated and resolved without delay. From the exposed party's perspective, if unmatched instructions are not resolved urgently, the risk remains of non-mitigation of their exposure on the due date.

Assuming that the exposed party's instruction has a status of 'matched', it is now a case of waiting for the value date to arrive. (Note: should the non-exposed party cancel their settlement instruction (for a reason unknown to the exposed party), the status of the exposed party's settlement instruction will revert to 'unmatched'; should this occur, the exposed party must communicate with the non-exposed party as a matter of urgency with a view to the non-exposed party's re-insertion of a settlement instruction.)

35.7 MONITORING RECEIPT OF COLLATERAL

Once the exposed party has taken appropriate action prior to the receipt of cash collateral or bond collateral, the exposed party can do no more but await being informed as to whether settlement has in fact occurred on the due date, or not.

35.7.1 Cash Collateral

For cash collateral, it is common practice for the exposed party to await the daily statement issued by its *nostro*, which confirms whether the funds have in fact been received, or not; for *S.W.I.F.T.* subscribers, the trend is for intraday messages to be received from their nostro.

Despite the fact that cash payments by the particular non-exposed party may have been successfully received by the exposed party on all such prior occasions, there is no guarantee whatsoever that the payment relating to the exposed party's current exposure will be received at the firm's nostro. Only if the non-exposed party has extremely strong internal controls can the non-exposed party hope that the exposed party's SSI (held within the non-exposed party's static data) will not have been altered, whether by accident or design. The exposed party will have no knowledge of the non-exposed party's internal control environment; consequently, the exposed party must remain extremely vigilant when expecting a payment from non-exposed parties.

If it transpires that the funds have been received by the exposed party, the exposed party's risk is considered to be mitigated. Should the funds fail to be received on the value date, the exposed party's Risk Department should be advised without delay; the non-exposed party may have breached the terms of the legal contract (the *ISDA Master Agreement*) with the firm as 'failure to pay' is classified as an *Event of Default*, however whether the exposed party takes any legal action is likely to be dependent upon the specific counterparty and the frequency with which such failures occur. As a minimum, the exposed party should at least make itself aware as to whether the funds have in fact been received on time or not; where not received on time, the next step the exposed party may choose to take is to discuss the situation with the non-exposed party, whether actioned by the exposed party's Trading Department, Risk Department or Operations Department.

The underlying reasons as to why the non-exposed party has failed to make the payment on the due date could be due to a one-off operational problem, or it may signify that the non-exposed party has more worrying issues. Where the latter appears to be the case, the exposed party may choose to gradually reduce their trades with the particular counterparty via *novation*, *unwind* or *offset* (refer to Chapter 37 'OTC Derivatives and Collateral – The Collateral Lifecycle – Throughout Lifetime of Trade – Post-Trade Execution Events – Introduction' and the subsequent three chapters), thereby reducing the likelihood of ongoing large exposures with that counterparty, in turn reducing the need for margin calls and collateral. The ultimate measure is the issuance of a default notification, and possibly the termination of the relationship.

35.7.2 Bond Collateral

For bond collateral, where settlement has occurred it is common practice for an advice of settlement to be issued by the exposed party's custodian; this communication will quote the exposed party's transaction reference number (as originally quoted on the exposed party's settlement instruction).

The earliest date that settlement (i.e. movement of the bonds from the non-exposed party's account to the exposed party's account) will occur is the *value date* of the settlement instruction; if settlement occurs on value date, the exposed party's risk will have been mitigated on the due date. Following the matching of settlement instructions, the cause of successful and timely settlement is the non-exposed party having an adequate quantity of the relevant bonds in its account, from which delivery is made to the exposed party's account on an *electronic book entry* basis; if this is not the case, settlement will fail, and the exposed party's risk will not have been mitigated on the due date.

If the non-exposed party is an active trader of bonds, the possibility remains that their purchase of bonds from another party has failed, in turn meaning that the non-exposed party cannot deliver to the exposed party. However, the underlying reasons why the non-exposed party has been unable to deliver the bonds are of no concern to the exposed party. What is of concern to the exposed party is the clear requirement for their exposure to be mitigated via receipt of collateral, from the non-exposed party, on the due date; in parallel with cash collateral, such failure may be classified as an 'event of default'. Under such circumstances and dependent upon timing, the non-exposed party could offer to settle the exposed party's margin call in cash (instead of bonds); this could mean that the exposed party's risk is mitigated that same day, particularly where the currency in question is a western currency (e.g. USD, CAD) as their banking day remains open for a number of hours beyond the European day and the Far East day.

35.8 UPDATING BOOKS & RECORDS

Following receipt of collateral, the firm must immediately update its *books & records*, which must show:

- the reason for the receipt of assets (e.g. collateral associated with an OTC derivative exposure)
- from which particular counterparty the collateral has been received
- the date the collateral was received, and
- the place of settlement, that is, in which particular nostro that cash collateral has been received, or in which particular custodian account bond collateral has been received
- the exact nature of the collateral; if 1) cash, the currency and cash amount (e.g. EUR 1,600,000.00), if bonds, the quantity of the particular bond received (e.g. USD 3,200,000.00 City of Oslo 4.25% bonds maturing 1st December 2029).

Table 35.3 illustrates one way of depicting receipt of bond collateral, within a firm's books & records:

TABLE 35.3   Books & records

Issuer ABC 2.95% Bonds 1st July 2028			
Ownership		Location	
	0	−6,000,000	Custodian 'P' Collateral Account
		+6,000,000	Counterparty T (OTCD Collateral)
	0	0	

Explanation of the above table:

- as the exposed party has received the bonds as collateral, but the exposed party has not purchased the bonds, although the exposed party has *legal ownership*, the exposed party has no *beneficial ownership* in the bonds (hence the Ownership position is zero)
- as the bonds are now held at the exposed party's custodian, this fact must be reflected so as to facilitate 1) *reconciliation* with *depot statements* received from the custodian, and 2) clarity as to which party is entitled to *coupon payments*
- as the bonds must eventually be returned to the non-exposed party (for example, if and when exposures reverse and the counterparty has a *positive exposure*), it is essential that the books & records show that the bonds are owed to Counterparty T, including the reason why (namely 'OTC Derivative Collateral').

35.9 PERFORMING RECONCILIATION

The passing of such entries over the exposed party's books & records provides a true statement of assets held (but not necessarily owned) by the exposed party, whilst also facilitating the process of proving that such records are accurate through the reconciliation of:

- cash against statements received from the firm's various nostros, via the ***nostro reconciliation*** process, and
- bonds against statements received from the firm's various custodians, via the ***depot reconciliation*** process.

Reconciliation is at the forefront of any firm's control environment. Firms should recognise all points of risk in their business, and conduct reconciliation at an adequate frequency (ideally daily) so as to ensure proper control is maintained.

If, for example, the exposed party has received bond collateral from a counterparty, and that collateral is supposed to be held in an account (of the exposed party) at a particular custodian, only by conducting a depot reconciliation daily can the exposed party be certain that the bonds remain under its control at the custodian. If, instead, the exposed party assumes on an ongoing basis that the bonds are held in the particular account at the custodian (but without proving so via reconciliation), it may eventually come to light that the bonds are in fact no longer in the account – and have been removed in an unauthorised fashion, possibly fraudulently. The exposed party will ultimately need to return such bond collateral to the non-exposed party, in which case the exposed party may have to purchase the bonds in the marketplace, at its own cost.

35.10 UPDATING RECORDS OF CUMULATIVE COLLATERAL

Whenever cash or bond collateral has been received, it is essential that the exposed party maintains accurate and timely records. Such records are used on a day-to-day basis, where the net margin call amount is impacted by 1) whether any collateral has been previously given or taken, and if so, 2) the current collateral value of such collateral. It is particularly important that the exposed party maintains a running (cumulative) balance of collateral received from and returned to each of its counterparties.

In terms of the impact of the cumulative collateral balance and the type of collateral received, there is a difference in treatment of cash collateral and bond collateral. Where a specific amount of cash collateral has been received by the exposed party in the past, its collateral value 'today' will be the same, as cash does not normally vary in value (***marking-to-market*** is irrelevant). For example, an amount of GBP 2,000,000.00 cash collateral received one week ago has the same collateral value today. However, a quantity of EUR 3,000,000.00 bonds received one week ago to cover an exposure at that time of EUR 3,200,000.00 may today have a collateral value of EUR 2,900,000.00; this is derived by multiplying the quantity of bonds held by the firm by today's market ***clean price*** (plus ***accrued interest***, less ***haircut*** percentage).

Table 35.4 depicts the same gross exposure amount and, utilising different prior collateral amounts resulting from collateral movements on prior days (held by the firm or by its counterparty), reveals the different impacts on net margin call amount calculations:

TABLE 35.4 Impact of existing collateral

	Example #1	Example #2	Example #3	Example #4	Example #5
	Impact of Existing (Cumulative) Collateral on Net Exposure Calculations				
Gross Exposure	USD 4,100,000.00 (firm's exposure)				
Prior Collateral	0.00	USD 1,800,000.00 held by the firm	USD 4,900,000.00 held by the firm	USD 2,300,000.00 held by cpty*	USD 5,200,000.00 held by cpty*
Net Exposure (Call Amount)	USD 4,100,000.00 firm's exposure	USD 2,300,000.00 firm's exposure	USD 800,000.00 cpty's exposure	USD 6,400,000.00 firm's exposure	USD 9,300,000.00 firm's exposure

*cpty = 'counterparty'

The differing impacts are explained as follows:

- Example #1: as there is no prior collateral, the net exposure is the same as the gross exposure
- Example #2: the firm's gross exposure value is reduced by the value of the counterparty's collateral held by the firm, and the firm need only issue a margin call for the difference
- Example #3: as the firm's gross exposure value is less than the value of the counterparty's collateral held by the firm, the firm should await a margin call from the counterparty, for the difference
- Example #4: the firm's gross exposure value is added to the value of the firm's collateral held by the counterparty, and the firm needs to issue a margin call for the combined amount
- Example #5: the firm's gross exposure value is added to the value of the firm's collateral held by the counterparty, and the firm needs to issue a margin call for the combined amount.

In summary, it is imperative to maintain accurate records of the cumulative value of assets received (and given) as collateral, otherwise the firm is at risk of:

- being under-collateralised through margin calls issued to counterparties being too small, and
- over-collateralising counterparties following receipt of margin calls that have not taken account of existing collateral.

For the same reasons, it is important that values of collateral given by the collateral giver, but not yet received by the taker (known as collateral *in-transit*), are incorporated into exposure calculations.

35.11 CONCLUSION

Where a firm has determined that it has exposures relating to one or many OTC derivative trades, the firm must ensure it communicates its margin calls to its various counterparties, so as to be received by such parties within the legally documented deadlines.

Then, the firm must follow up to ensure that 1) those counterparties agree the margin calls, 2) the form of collateral proposed by those parties is legally eligible, and 3) the necessary actions are taken to successfully settle such margin calls. Furthermore, the firm should monitor *nostro statements* received from cash correspondents (for cash collateral), and *depot statements* received from CSDs or custodians (for securities collateral), to ensure that the agreed collateral has in fact been received by the firm, as the exposed party.

Failure to complete the above-mentioned operational actions could easily result in the firm's exposures not in reality being mitigated. Conversely, proactive actions taken by operations personnel will result in positive knowledge that exposures have been mitigated, and identification of if and when a counterparty has failed to comply with their *contractual obligations*.

CHAPTER 36

OTC Derivatives and Collateral – The Collateral Lifecycle – Throughout Lifetime of Trade – Holding Collateral

This chapter describes the options for firms relating to the holding of collateral received from counterparties, as the legal status of the collateral impacts how the collateral should be held and whether the collateral taker may legally reuse the collateral in a subsequent transaction.

THE OTC DERIVATIVE COLLATERAL LIFECYCLE

1 Pre-Trading
Legal Documentation
Static Data

2 Trading
Trade Execution

3 Post-Trading
Trade Capture
Trade Confirmation/Affirmation
Trade/Portfolio Netting

4 Throughout Lifetime of Trade
Portfolio Reconciliation
Marking-to-Market
Exposure Calculation
Receiving Margin Calls
Issuing Margin Calls
Holding Collateral
Post-Trade Execution Events
Collateral Substitution
Income & Corporate Action Events

5 Trade Termination
Trade Termination

PART 4a

> *Please note that the contents of this chapter represent the author's own view of how the documentation produced by the International Swaps and Derivatives Association (ISDA) is normally used by financial institutions and is not an ISDA official guide of how to understand or to complete or to use such documentation. Readers are advised to take their own legal advice regarding the implementation and use of such documentation.*

36.1 INTRODUCTION

When a firm is in receipt of *collateral* (and in particular *securities* collateral), the way in which the firm holds such collateral can have significant implications.

Note that the primary focus of this chapter is on securities (primarily *bond*) collateral, which is *fungible* or interchangeable only within a specific securities *issue* or *ISIN*. Conversely, cash is regarded as fully fungible within a particular currency.

In order for the reader to be clear as to the role of each party, within this chapter the following terms will be used:

- 'transferor' – the *collateral giver*
- 'transferee' – the *collateral taker*.

36.2 LEGAL STRUCTURES IMPACTING THE HOLDING OF COLLATERAL

The way a transferee holds bond collateral received from a transferor is fundamentally dependent upon the legal arrangements in place between the two parties. Some types of legal arrangement give the transferee the automatic right to treat the collateral as their own and consequently to do whatever they choose to do with the collateral (including reusing it), whilst other types of legal agreement prevent automatic reuse of collateral.

It is imperative that both the transferor and the transferee remain conscious of what, in a legal sense, the transferee is permitted to do (or is prevented from doing) with the collateral. Such permissions (or denial of permission) have very important operational implications for both transferor and transferee.

From a legal standpoint, the common terminology that describes the basis on which the transfer of an asset (including collateral) is made is:

- *title transfer* basis; meaning that full legal title to the collateral passes from the transferor to the transferee, therefore the transferee is free to do with the collateral whatever it chooses
- *security interest* basis; meaning that the collateral remains in the beneficial interest of the transferor, and *rehypothecation* rights (see later) may or may not be granted.

The type of *Credit Support Annex* (CSA) signed between two parties governs the legal basis referred to above. (Please refer to Chapter 22 'OTC Derivatives and Collateral – Legal Protection – Credit Support Annex'.)

There are three main types of CSA:

- the English Law Credit Support Annex
- the New York Law Credit Support Annex, and
- the English Law Credit Support Deed.

For the avoidance of doubt, in each case the transferee has a *contractual obligation* to return *equivalent collateral* to the transferor.

36.2.1 The English Law CSA

The English Law CSA is a *title transfer* document. This means that full title to the collateral passes from the transferor to the transferee, exactly as it would if the transferee had purchased the bonds in the open marketplace. Legal title to the bonds will be registered to the transferee in the relevant clearing system (e.g. *Euroclear Bank* or *Clearstream International*). The <u>only</u> contractual obligation on the transferee is the requirement to return equivalent collateral.

Consequently, under this legal document the transferee owns the bonds and is entitled to do with those bonds whatever the transferee feels is appropriate, including the reuse of bonds (e.g. selling). From an operational (non-legal) standpoint, the transferee has not purchased the bonds in the normal manner but is in possession of them as they will be held by the transferee's custodian (unless reused in a different transaction); this point is explored further within Section 36.4 'Holding Bond Collateral with Reuse and Rehypothecation Rights'.

36.2.2 The New York Law CSA

In contrast to the English Law CSA, the New York Law CSA operates on a *security interest* basis. This means that collateral taken remains in the legal and beneficial ownership of the transferor, and there is a sharing of property rights between transferor and transferee.

To hypothecate is for Party A to grant an asset as security for a debt, to Party B, without transferring title; to rehypothecate is for Party B to re-grant those same assets as collateral, to Party C, in a separate transaction. The default position of the New York Law CSA gives the transferee the right to rehypothecate, providing the transferor consents to such an arrangement. Should the involved parties decide to exclude rehypothecation rights, the particular clause within the CSA must be switched off.

36.2.3 The English Law Credit Support Deed

In contrast to the English Law CSA, but in parallel with the New York Law CSA, the English Law Credit Support Deed operates on a *security interest* basis. As per the New York Law CSA, collateral taken remains in the beneficial ownership of the transferor and property rights are shared.

Regarding rehypothecation, the default position of the English Law CSD gives the transferee the right to rehypothecate, providing the transferor consents to such an arrangement. Should rehypothecation consent be granted, a bespoke provision must be added to the credit support deed.

Taking account of all three legal documents described above, a transferee needs to consider:

■ whether it has the legal right to reuse or to rehypothecate the collateral, and if so
■ whether (internally) it possesses the necessary controls to manage such collateral reuse or rehypothecation.

Consequently, the issues of 1) how the transferee holds the collateral at its CSD or custodian, and 2) whether the collateral may be reused or rehypothecated are extremely important in order for the transferee to avoid breaking legal contracts with its counterparties.

The implications of such legal matters are summarised in Figure 36.1:

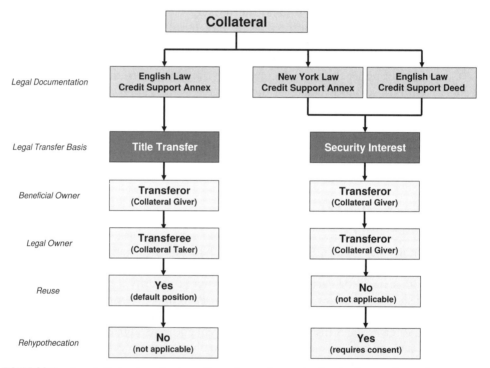

FIGURE 36.1   Legal distinctions in the collateral transfer methods of title transfer and security interest

To explain the content of the above diagram:

■ Legal Transfer Basis:
  ■ the English Law CSA (ELCSA) operates under the transfer method of title transfer, in which full legal title passes from transferor to transferee (the same transfer method applicable to buying and selling)
  ■ both the New York Law CSA (NYLCSA) and the English Law Credit Support Deed (ELCSD) operate under the transfer method of security interest, in which full ownership of the collateral is retained by the transferor

- Beneficial Owner:
  - beneficial ownership refers to the rights (benefits) accruing on bond collateral, such as coupon payments
    - under the ELCSA, the NYLCSA and the ELCSD, beneficial ownership is retained by the transferor
- Legal Owner:
  - legal ownership refers to the party that has an enforceable claim (or title) to the collateral
    - under the ELCSA, legal ownership is transferred from the transferor to the transferee (whilst the collateral is in possession of the transferee), due to title transfer
    - under the NYLCSA and the ELCSD, the transferor retains legal ownership, (although this is subject to surrender in case of enforcement of the security interest)
- Reuse:
  - reuse refers to the legal use of the collateral by the transferee, in a separate transaction, such as 1) the execution of a sale, 2) the loan of securities, 3) a sale & repurchase (repo), 4) as collateral in another OTC derivative trade
    - under the ELCSA, as the transferee becomes the legal owner, it is the transferee's automatic right to reuse the collateral if they so choose
    - under the NYLCSA and the ELCSD, due to the security interest transfer method, the term 'reuse' is not applicable
- Rehypothecation:
  - rehypothecation refers to the transferee being granted the right (by the transferor) to utilise the collateral in other (subsequent) transactions
    - under the ELCSA, the term 'rehypothecation' is not applicable, because the transferee is automatically the legal owner
    - under the NYLCSA and the ELCSD, the transferee may be specifically granted the right to rehypothecate by the transferor; for the avoidance of doubt, any such consent should be formally documented.

PART 4a

36.3 REUSE AND REHYPOTHECATION OF COLLATERAL: BENEFITS AND RISKS

Benefits can be gained by the transferee (where reuse or rehypothecation of collateral is permitted), but this is not without risk to the transferor. The following two sub-sections describe such benefits and risks.

36.3.1 Benefits of Collateral Reuse or Rehypothecation to the Transferee

Should the transferee be legally permitted to reuse or to rehypothecate bond collateral received from the transferor, and should the transferee choose to actually reuse or rehypothecate such collateral, the bonds could be used in the following ways, for example:

- selling the securities
- lending the securities to a borrowing counterparty, thereby earning additional revenue through receipt of a securities lending fee

- utilising the securities as collateral against the borrowing of cash under a *repo* transaction, thereby minimising the cost of borrowing cash
- using the securities as collateral for an 'out-of-the-money' OTC derivative trade.

Furthermore, if the transferee is an automatic lender of securities at one of the ICSDs (Clearstream International or Euroclear Brussels), the securities may be lent automatically; the transferee should consider whether such automated lending suits its purpose or not. Please refer to Chapter 12 'Securities Lending & Borrowing and Collateral – Accessing the SL&B Marketplace', Sub-section 12.1.3 'ICSDs' Failed Trade Management: Overview' for a description of automated securities lending via the ICSDs.

In all the above examples, the transferee is gaining a benefit, whether through gaining additional revenue or through minimising its costs.

Such reuse of bond collateral is depicted in Figure 36.2:

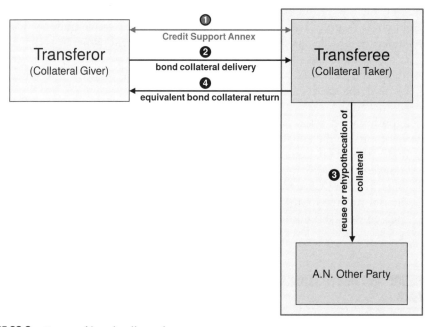

FIGURE 36.2   Reuse of bond collateral

Step 1: the legal documentation between the two trading parties permits reuse or rehypothecation of bond collateral

Step 2: following a margin call, bonds are received as collateral by the transferee

Step 3: the transferee chooses to reuse or to rehypothecate the collateral in a separate transaction (e.g. securities loan or repo)

Step 4: at a later date, the transferee will be required to return the bond collateral (equivalent collateral) to the transferor.

Imagine that, in this situation, the incoming bond collateral is held in the same custodian account as the transferee's proprietary securities positions; under these circumstances, the collateral is said to be ***commingled*** with the firm's own securities. This means there is every possibility that such collateral will be used (whether intended or not) in settlement of other transactions executed by the transferee.* For example, if the transferee had previously sold USD 3,000,000.00 IBRD 4.25% Bonds maturing 15th August 2030 (which is currently failing to settle due to insufficient securities), the receipt of USD 5,000,000.00 of the same bond (as collateral for an OTC derivative transaction) would facilitate settlement of that sale, enabling the transferee to receive the sale proceeds immediately.

Ultimately, when the transferee is required to return the collateral to the transferor (for reasons such as reduction in exposure, or the OTC derivative trade's *scheduled maturity date* having been reached), the transferee must ensure it can return equivalent collateral. If the transferee does not have possession of the relevant bonds to effect the return delivery to the collateral giver, the transferee's options include the borrowing of bonds, although there is no guarantee of being able to borrow.

36.3.2 Risks of Collateral Reuse and Rehypothecation for the Transferor

With specific regard to security interest arrangements (and not regarding title transfer arrangements), in a situation in which a transferor has delivered securities collateral directly to its counterparty (the transferee), and where the legal documentation denies the transferee the right of rehypothecation, it is recommended that the transferor periodically requests written confirmation from the transferee that the legal arrangements are being complied with and that the collateral remains in the possession of the transferee and has not been rehypothecated. If, in fact, the transferee has rehypothecated the collateral where it is not legally permitted to do so (whether unintentionally or by design):

- the transferee will have contravened the terms of the legal contract with the transferor, and
- the transferor's up-front efforts to negotiate the terms of the legal agreement will be of little benefit to the transferor, and
- should the transferee become insolvent, the return of the collateral to the transferor may take an inordinate length of time.

Therefore, under the circumstances described above, the transferor's attempts to ascertain whether rehypothecation has occurred (or not) are in its own interests. It is suggested that this topic is of concern to the transferor's Legal Department, its Compliance Department and its Risk Department. An alternative arrangement to the collateral being delivered by the transferor directly to the transferee, is for the collateral to be held by a neutral third-party custodian (in a bankruptcy remote fashion), on behalf of both the transferor and the transferee.

---

*Note: as securities are fungible it is not always possible to distinguish the collateral from the proprietary position once commingled, consequently it is not always certain whether collateral securities have been reused, or not.

In title transfer arrangements under the English Law CSA, a transferor of securities collateral ceases to have a proprietary right to the collateral itself and instead has a right against the transferee for the return of equivalent collateral. In one case, where securities collateral had been reused by the transferee followed by the transferee's insolvency, the collateral transferors formed part of the group of general unsecured creditors whose claims would be paid out after those of secured creditors (and to the extent that the assets realised in the transferee's estate would allow). The length of time taken in settling claims by transferors was caused by the considerable task of identifying the original owner of the securities, whether the collateral transferors or the (now insolvent) transferee. Title transfer contains the inherent risk that, if the transferee were to become insolvent, the collateral would either 1) not be returned at all, or 2) if returned, it may be for a relatively small proportion and potentially following a significant delay. Such risks mean that firms may consider the particular legal documentation in place with counterparties, whether the English Law CSA (full title transfer), the New York Law CSA (security interest) or the English Law Credit Support Deed (security interest), For firms having existing title transfer documentation in place with their counterparties, an option is to renegotiate to implement security interest documentation in order to prevent securities collateral reuse by the firm's counterparties.

Sections 36.4 and 36.5 focus on the options for transferees to hold incoming bond collateral, based upon whether reuse or rehypothecation is permitted or prevented.

36.4 HOLDING BOND COLLATERAL WITH REUSE AND REHYPOTHECATION RIGHTS

Where a transferee has title transfer documentation in place, and/or where rehypothecation rights are granted under a security interest arrangement, the transferee must decide whether it wishes to actually reuse or rehypothecate incoming bond collateral, or not. Despite the fact that a firm has the legal right to reuse or to rehypothecate, it may choose not to do so where, for example, the firm feels it does not have adequate internal controls in place to properly 1) track the movement of bonds, 2) update books & records following deliveries and receipts, and 3) reconcile. Only by successfully reconciling assets on a day-to-day basis can a firm validly claim to be in full control.

Under the English Law CSA, bond collateral which results from an exposure in an OTC derivative trade is received by the transferee under the legal transfer basis of title transfer. This is precisely the same legal transfer basis as occurs when a firm purchases a bond in the normal way (i.e. in the *secondary market*).

However, it is essential to appreciate that, just because bond collateral has been received, that collateral should not be treated in the same way as bonds that have been purchased in the normal way; it is only the legal transfer basis of title transfer that is common to both. To explain further, where a firm (Party A) chooses to invest in a particular bond (Bond X) in an 'outright' purchase, that investment is said to be a *trading position*; assume Party A has a trading position of EUR 10,000,000.00 of Bond X bonds. Completely unconnected, Party A has also executed an OTC derivative trade on which Party A has a *positive mark-to-market*, where that exposure has been *mitigated* by receipt of the same bond (EUR 3,000,000.00 of Bond X) from Party A's OTC derivative counterparty (Party B, the transferor). It is important to note that a trading position results from only buying and/or selling, and a trading position is adjusted only by further buying and/or selling; consequently, the giving or taking of collateral has no impact on a firm's trading position. Under such circumstances Party A has possession of Bond X for two underlying reasons, namely 1) it has a trading position, and 2) it holds Party B's collateral relating to an OTC derivative exposure. From Party A's perspective, despite the fact that they have possession of a total quantity of EUR 13,000,000.00 bonds, and that Party A has legal title to all EUR 13,000,000.00 bonds, there is a distinct difference in the way that the trading position and the collateral should be treated within the books & records of both firms.

For example, if a ***coupon payment*** falls due whilst Party A holds a quantity of EUR 13,000,000 bonds within their CSD or custodian account as at the close of business on ***record date*** of the coupon payment:

- Party A will be credited with the coupon payment on all EUR 13,000,000 bonds. Of that total amount:
  - Party A is entitled to the coupon payment on a quantity of EUR 10,000,000 bonds, because they have a positive trading position of this bond quantity – and should therefore retain this cash value, but
  - Party A is not entitled to the coupon payment on a quantity of EUR 3,000,000 bonds, because they have a zero trading position of this quantity of bonds. Party B is entitled to the coupon payment on a quantity of EUR 3,000,000 bonds, because they continue to have a positive trading position of this bond quantity (although they have lost possession of the bond temporarily). Party A is required to remit the equivalent cash value of the coupon payment to Party B.

In order for the correct actions to be taken at all times, it is essential that the books & records of both the transferor and transferee accurately reflect the reality of the situation on an ongoing basis, and that they be proven through ***reconciliation***.

To summarise the above, only the legal transfer basis is common to both 1) outright purchases, and 2) bond collateral received. Other than that aspect, the purchased bonds and the bond collateral received should be treated entirely separately.

If the transferee elects to reuse or to rehypothecate whenever possible, it may choose to hold the incoming bonds in its proprietary custodian account in order to make the greatest use of the collateral in an attempt to gain maximum benefit. Some firms may choose to reuse or to rehypothecate only under specific circumstances and may choose to hold such bonds either within its proprietary custodian account or within a segregated custodian account.

Conversely, the transferee may choose to act conservatively and to hold the bond collateral safely and securely, and not to reuse or to rehypothecate at all. Under these circumstances, and in order to prevent accidental reuse or rehypothecation, the transferee may choose to hold bond collateral received within a segregated account at its custodian.

36.5 HOLDING BOND COLLATERAL WITHOUT REHYPOTHECATION RIGHTS

Where consent to rehypothecate has not been granted under a security interest arrangement, the transferee must ensure that it does not rehypothecate bond collateral received from its counterparties; otherwise the transferee will be breaking the terms of the legal contract signed with the transferor.

Prevention of collateral rehypothecation can be achieved in the following ways:

1. set up one (or many) segregated accounts at the transferee's custodian (designated as 'collateral account(s)'), and ensure that incoming bond collateral is held and remains within such account(s), and is not held within the transferee's proprietary account at the custodian,
2. hold incoming bond collateral within the transferee's proprietary account at the custodian, but internally hold each bond within an internal *trading book*. This requires the transferee's bond traders, repo traders and Collateral Department to be sufficiently disciplined in their day-to-day activity so as not to utilise such bond collateral at all.

In the author's opinion, option 1 is the safer option as mistakes (such as unintentional rehypothecation) are less likely to occur due to the fact that only the Collateral Department should be aware of, and have access to, the securities in the segregated account(s).

36.6 HOLDING COLLATERAL AND OPERATIONAL CONTROL

It is entirely possible that a particular firm, as a transferee:

1. does not have the contractual right to rehypothecate incoming bond collateral with any of its counterparties, or
2. is contractually entitled to rehypothecate or to reuse bond collateral received from some counterparties, but not others.

Regarding point 1 above, operational control is simpler as the Collateral Department would need to ensure that all incoming bond collateral is held in one (or more) segregated account(s) at the custodian, where the account is designated as a 'counterparty incoming collateral' account (or similar meaningful title). Such a structure means that automatic rehypothecation of incoming collateral is prevented, in accordance with the legal documentation. The firm's books & records should be updated upon receipt of such incoming bond collateral, in turn facilitating frequent (preferably daily) reconciliation with the custodian's statements of the segregated account(s). The updating of books & records and regular reconciliation additionally mean that income events and *corporate actions* processing become much more straightforward, from an operational viewpoint.

Regarding point 2 above, operational control is more challenging and prone to error, as the destination custodian account must be determined according to the specific counterparty involved. This is particularly risky in a manual collateral environment. In an automated collateral environment, such control can be applied automatically through active use of static data.

In summary, a transferee will put itself at risk in a situation where rehypothecation is not permitted, but inadequate internal controls are applied regarding the destination account of incoming bond collateral. If the lack of control results in bond collateral being received into the transferee's proprietary account (rather than into a segregated account), the firm stands the risk that the bonds are inadvertently used in a different transaction. By so doing, the firm will be breaking the legal agreement with the counterparty.

One view of such activity by the transferee, from an operational perspective, is that such rehypothecation is fine providing that all incoming and outgoing movements of assets are accurately reflected within the firm's books & records at all times. If the firm is unable to capture all such movements, its books & records will prove not to reflect reality and as a result will be impossible to reconcile. This in turn means that fundamental control will have been lost, with the result that, for example, accurate funding of trading and settlement activity will be an extreme challenge, and accurate processing of income and corporate actions events will suffer, with monetary and reputational loss being the likely result.

Firms (as transferees) must decide whether this is a desirable situation for them; it's a trade-off between making money or saving money, versus maintaining internal control.

For firms that have been granted rehypothecation rights on incoming bond collateral, and who wish to actively rehypothecate, they will normally choose to receive such incoming collateral into their proprietary account at the relevant custodian.

For some firms, despite the fact that they have rehypothecation rights on incoming bond collateral from transferors, it is recognised by the firm's management that they have inadequate internal control mechanisms and so choose not to rehypothecate. Under these circumstances, it is suggested that such firms could adopt one of the following strategies:

- to receive and hold incoming bond collateral within a segregated account at the custodian, and apply internal operational controls preventing issuance of settlement instructions that would result in removal of such bonds for rehypothecation purposes. Note: settlement instructions will need to be issued over this account for the valid return of bond collateral to the transferor.
- to receive and hold incoming bond collateral within the firm's proprietary account at the custodian and reflect such collateral within a dedicated internal trading book. Although the bond traders may have sight of the bonds held within this trading book, internal trading level controls must be strictly applied in order to prevent rehypothecation.

36.7 BOND COLLATERAL

A number of conceptual points are important to appreciate in order to determine how a transferee should hold bonds received as collateral, and what constitutes good delivery when collateral must be returned to the transferor.

36.7.1 Bond Collateral Fundamental Concepts

Where a *Credit Support Annex* (CSA) permits, bonds are eligible as collateral. However, unlike cash, a giver of Bond A as collateral will require the return of Bond A, and not the return of a different bond.

Each individual security is uniquely identifiable by its *ISIN* code; within every ISIN, all deliveries of a bond are equal because they carry the same rights as one another and are therefore interchangeable (the bond is said to be *fungible*). Furthermore, each individual bond issue commands a different price in the marketplace, due to the difference in *issuer, coupon rate, maturity date* and (potentially) other characteristics such as bonds with a call option (*callable bonds*) and bonds with a put option (*puttable bonds*) which may apply to a particular bond issue.

To clarify, if Firm X receives a margin call from Counterparty P, and Firm X satisfies that margin call by the delivery of, for example, USD 5,000,000.00 of International Bank for Reconstruction and Development (IBRD) 4.25% Bonds maturing 15th August 2030, when at a later date the collateral must be returned to Firm X (e.g. the exposure may have reduced, or the underlying trade has reached its *scheduled maturity date*), the relevant quantity of the same bond issue must be returned by Counterparty P. Within the CSA, this is stated as *equivalent collateral*; this term covers the following situations:

- if the original bond issue received as collateral still exists and has not been replaced, then exactly the same bond issue must be returned to the transferor, but
- if the original bond issue received as collateral no longer exists and the bond issuer has replaced that bond issue with a different bond issue (as can result from a type of *corporate action* known as a *bond exchange offer*), then the replacement bond issue must be delivered to the transferor.

The following point is important from the perspective of both the transferor and the transferee. The transferor is the original owner of the bonds given as collateral, and at some prior point has acquired the bonds through buying in the marketplace. At the point when the bonds are selected to be given to satisfy a margin call, the transferor has not sold the bonds and as such has not received sale proceeds in fair exchange for such bonds. Consequently, the transferor retains *beneficial ownership* of the bonds from a trading and operational standpoint, and where the bonds were (let's assume) previously held by the transferor's custodian, they are now acting as collateral and are held by a counterparty. Should the transferor wish to sell the bonds in question, the bonds must be returned by the transferee and be substituted by another bond, or bonds, or by cash, or by a combination of bonds and cash collateral (assuming the counterparty's exposure remains). The subject of *collateral substitution* is covered within Chapter 42 'OTC Derivatives and Collateral – The Collateral Lifecycle – Throughout Lifetime of Trade – Collateral Substitution'.

Each bond issue involves one or more stated *denominational values*, which defines the valid deliverable quantities of the particular bond. For example, the denominational values of the (fictitious) IBRD 4.25% Bonds 15th August 2030 are stated as USD 20,000.00 and USD 100,000.00, meaning that quantities of this bond issue that can be validly delivered are a minimum of and multiples of USD 20,000.00. Both transferors and transferees of bond collateral must ensure that they identify valid deliverable quantities, if they are to avoid their settlement instructions being rejected by the CSD or custodian. The best way of applying a control to ensure only valid deliverable quantities are identified for a particular delivery of bond collateral, is to hold the relevant denominational values of the individual bond within the firm's internal *static data repository*, then to programme the relevant system to compare the intended delivery quantity with the denominational values held within the firm's static data.

From the transferee's perspective, bonds received as collateral from a counterparty will be received at the transferee's relevant custodian account, according to bond type. For example:

- US Treasury bonds are usually held within the *Fedwire* system
- UK Treasury bonds are usually held within the *Crest* system (operated by Euroclear)
- *Eurobonds* are usually held within the ICSDs *Euroclear Brussels* and *Clearstream International*
- Japanese Government bonds are usually held within the Bank of Japan.

The transferee must decide in which of their securities accounts (at the relevant CSD or custodian) the incoming bond collateral is to be held. This decision is critical for the transferee, as an incorrect decision can result in serious consequences. Clearly, whether the transferee has the legal right to reuse the collateral (under a title transfer arrangement) or has been granted rehypothecation rights (under a security interest arrangement) will play a major role in this decision-making.

36.7.2 Activities Associated with Holding Bond Collateral

The holding of bond collateral by a transferee requires certain activities to be performed. These activities should be regarded as best practice in order for the transferee to remain in full control of bonds received as collateral from transferors.

Whether the bonds are held by the transferee within its proprietary account (commingled) or within a segregated account, the following activities should be performed by the transferee:

- daily reconciliation of securities holdings between the custodian's statements of securities holdings and the transferee's books & records. This simple but highly effective reconciliation is designed to ensure that the bonds are in fact where they are supposed to be (within the transferee's account at the custodian), or not. If not, investigation should commence immediately in order to ascertain the reason for the discrepancy; such discrepancies may be due to timing differences, internal error or internal or external fraud. Financial assets, including cash and bonds, are desirable targets for thieves, and all holders of securities must take measures to prevent fraudulent activity, and to detect such activity as soon as possible after it has occurred; time is clearly an important factor. As the bonds are intended to be acting as collateral, and are therefore intended as a risk mitigator, if the bonds are no longer present in the transferee's account at the custodian, the transferee's risk is in fact not *mitigated*
- periodic calculation of *custody fees*. It is common practice for fees to be charged to account holders at the *ICSDs* and custodians, pertaining to the quantity of bonds held within each account. For example, Euroclear Brussels charges bond custody fees on a monthly basis. It is suggested that the transferee satisfies itself that such custody fees are reasonable, by performing its own calculation. (By the same token, the transferor will avoid being charged custody fees for the period the bonds are in the possession of the transferee.)

PART 4a

Additionally, in the case of bonds held as collateral, income and ***corporate action*** events may occur, for example:

- ***coupon payments***: in the case of ***fixed rate bonds*** the coupon rate and the coupon payment dates are known at the time of issue launch and are therefore predictable throughout the bond's lifetime. Such information should be found within the firm's securities ***static data***. In the case of ***floating rate notes***, the basis for calculation of the coupon rate (including the benchmark rate [e.g. ***Libor***] plus the defined premium or discount to be applied against the benchmark rate) is known at the time of issue launch
- ***restructuring events***: a bond issuer may decide to replace a number of their existing bonds with newly issued bonds, as a ***mandatory corporate action*** event
- bond tender offers: a bond issuer may invite bondholders to tender their bonds in exchange for another asset, as a ***voluntary corporate action*** event.

For all forms of income event and corporate action event, the transferee should proactively become aware of upcoming events, by 1) utilising existing information within the firm's internal static data repository and/or subscription to one or many ***corporate action data vendors***, and 2) comparison of each event with trades and positions within the firm's own books & records. Such activity is normally performed by the firm's Corporate Actions Department. When it is discovered that bonds are being held as collateral, the transferee will be required (by the transferor) to take appropriate action. For example, in the case of a coupon payment on a fixed rate bond, providing the bonds are being held by the transferee as at ***record date*** of the coupon payment, the transferee should be expecting to pay the coupon proceeds to the transferor, on the coupon payment date. Even where the transferee has reused or rehypothecated the bonds in settlement of another transaction, the transferee should behave proactively and pay the coupon amount to the transferor on coupon payment date. (By the same token, the transferor should be following a similar process internally and should be expecting receipt of the coupon proceeds on the coupon payment date. Indeed, in an attempt by the transferor to ensure that coupon proceeds are received on time, the transferee may receive a ***coupon claim*** from the transferor.) It should be noted that the task of managing coupon payments on bond collateral can be avoided if the particular bond is substituted for a different bond prior to record date of the coupon payment; this practice is frequently adopted by many firms.

36.8 CASH COLLATERAL

Cash is regarded as ***fungible***. This means that cash, within any particular currency, is truly interchangeable and able to be substituted for another of the same type, without detriment to the holder. A particular currency note (e.g. USD 1.00) provides neither an advantage nor a disadvantage to the holder when compared with any other USD 1.00 banknote.

A party lending EUR 5,000,000.00 in currency notes will not require the return of exactly the same notes upon closure of the loan, as all EUR currency notes have the same value as all other EUR currency notes.

Incoming cash collateral is no different. Therefore, the receipt of incoming cash collateral can be held together with the recipient's other cash balances in the same currency. Such cash would normally be lent by the recipient in order to generate interest income (in a *positive interest rate* environment). However, it is essential that the firm maintains accurate records of cash collateral received, within its internal books & records.

36.9 CONCLUSION

All transferors must remain aware of the risks associated with its bond collateral being delivered to and held by the transferee. Particularly for bond collateral where rehypothecation rights have not been granted to the transferee, in order to ensure that the terms of legal arrangements between the two parties are not being breached, the transferor should seek periodic confirmation (preferably written) that the bonds are in fact not being rehypothecated and that they are being held at the transferee's custodian.

OTC Derivatives and Collateral – The Collateral Lifecycle – Throughout Lifetime of Trade – Post-Trade Execution Events – Introduction

This chapter and the following four chapters are targeted at readers that have had no exposure or limited exposure to the events that can occur to OTC derivative trades, during their lifetime. Should one or more such events occur to a particular OTC derivative trade, there will be an impact on collateral management relating to such trades. This chapter and the following four chapters are designed to provide an overview of such events as they relate to OTC derivative trades.

PART 4a

THE OTC DERIVATIVE COLLATERAL LIFECYCLE

1 Pre-Trading
Legal Documentation
Static Data

2 Trading
Trade Execution

3 Post-Trading
Trade Capture
Trade Confirmation/Affirmation
Trade/Portfolio Netting

4 Throughout Lifetime of Trade
Portfolio Reconciliation
Marking-to-Market
Exposure Calculation
Receiving Margin Calls
Issuing Margin Calls
Holding Collateral
Post-Trade Execution Events
Collateral Substitution
Income & Corporate Action Events

5 Trade Termination
Trade Termination

Post-Trade Execution Events is an umbrella term that refers to any event that affects trades, following *trade execution* and prior to the trade's *scheduled maturity date*.

Within the world of *OTC derivatives*, such events include:

- Novation
- Unwind
- Offset
- Credit events (in the case of credit default swaps only).

The general background to such events relating to OTC derivatives is as follows; the contract that one party has in place with its *counterparty* may have a tenure of up to 50 years, from *trade date* through to the trade's *scheduled maturity date*. During the contract's lifetime, *exposures* will arise which require *mitigation* through the process of *collateral management*.

However, should one or more post-trade events occur during the contract's lifetime, such events will impact both *trade processing* and *collateral processing*.

The following four chapters focus on each of the above-mentioned events, including their purpose, how they arise, and their specific impact on collateral management.

OTC Derivatives and Collateral – The Collateral Lifecycle – Throughout Lifetime of Trade – Post-Trade Execution Events – Novation

This chapter describes the process of novation, whereby one party removes itself from an existing trade whilst a third party takes their place. Should this post-trade execution event occur to a particular OTC derivative trade or position, there will be a fundamental impact to the ongoing collateral management of that trade.

THE OTC DERIVATIVE COLLATERAL LIFECYCLE

❶ Pre-Trading
Legal Documentation
Static Data

❷ Trading
Trade Execution

❸ Post-Trading
Trade Capture
Trade Confirmation/Affirmation
Trade/Portfolio Netting

❹ Throughout Lifetime of Trade
Portfolio Reconciliation
Marking-to-Market
Exposure Calculation
Receiving Margin Calls
Issuing Margin Calls
Holding Collateral
→ Post-Trade Execution Events
Collateral Substitution
Income & Corporate Action Events

❺ Trade Termination
Trade Termination

38.1 INTRODUCTION

Where a firm has a live and current **OTC *derivative*** trade (or position) with a particular counterparty, at any point during its lifetime that trade or position may be subject to ***novation***.

Novation is a generic term meaning the legal act of replacing one participating member of a contract with another. The term is used in various situations involving the change of parties to a legal contract, and not just for OTC derivative trades.

Novation arises where one of the parties to a trade chooses to exit that trade, by introduction of a third party in its place. This situation is represented in Figures 38.1 and 38.2, the first of which represents the original parties to the trade, prior to novation:

FIGURE 38.1   Pre-novation parties

Following novation:

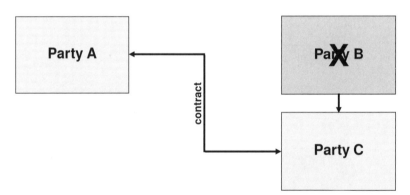

FIGURE 38.2   Post-novation parties

- Party A (the ***remaining party***) continues with the contract, but with a new counterparty
- Party B (the ***novation transferor***) has 'stepped out' of the trade
- Party C (the ***novation transferee***) has 'stepped in' to the trade.

Effecting novation involves firstly the transferor and the transferee agreeing terms, and secondly for the remaining party to agree to the novation by consenting to the change in counterparty. Obtaining the consent of the remaining party is clearly an essential aspect of such a fundamental change to the details (i.e. the counterparty) of an original trade.

Following novation, both the remaining party and the novation transferor are released from their *contractual obligations* under the original trade.

From the perspective of the remaining party, novation results in 1) the original contract being terminated and replaced by 2) a new contract with identical terms (including the *notional principal* and the *scheduled maturity date*), but with the novation transferee as counterparty.

Upon novation, the *current market value* of the trade is settled directly between the novation transferor and novation transferee; the remaining party is not involved in this action and remains unaffected. Any specific novation fee is negotiated between the novation transferor and novation transferee, without concerning the remaining party.

A formal novation process for OTC derivatives has existed for some years and was enhanced via the *ISDA Novation Protocol II*; to access details, please go to the website of the International Swaps and Derivatives Association (www.isda.org).

38.2 REASONS FOR NOVATION

A party to an OTC derivative trade may choose to exit a contract via novation for a variety of reasons, including:

- the original reason for the contract having altered (e.g. in a *credit default swap*, the *protection buyer* has sold the underlying bond)
- the trading limit with the original counterparty having been reached
- a desire to reduce exposure to certain products
- a takeover by a firm resulting in unacceptable levels of credit risk to the new (post-takeover) counterparty
- financial reasons in which a positive fee will be received as part of the novation.

A firm may choose to step in to an existing contract in order to gain some financial advantage, including:

- a desire to increase exposure to certain products and counterparties
- a belief that market prices will evolve in such a way that the profitability of the transaction may increase.

Novation may be effected for the total notional principal of a contract, or for a partial quantity. Partial novation can occur (for example) where, in the case of a *fund manager*, an original *block trade* has been subsequently split into multiple allocations relating to the fund manager's underlying funds. At any point during the contract, one of the underlying funds may choose to exit the contract; this situation is represented in Figure 38.3:

PART 4a

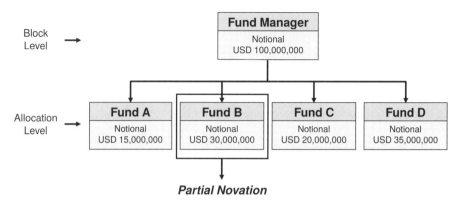

FIGURE 38.3   Partial novation

In the example above, just one of the underlying funds has chosen to exit the contract via novation, whilst the three other funds remain in their respective contracts.

38.3 IMPACT OF NOVATION ON BOOKS & RECORDS

Completed novations impact all three parties:

- for the remaining party; at the effective date of novation, the trade and exposure with the original (stepping-out) counterparty must be closed and the trade and exposure with the new (stepping-in) counterparty must be created
- for the stepping-out party; at the effective date of novation, the trade and exposure with the original (remaining) party must be closed
- for the stepping-in party; at the effective date of novation, the trade and exposure with the remaining party must be created.

The result of novation, from the perspective of each of the parties, is summarised in Table 38.1:

TABLE 38.1   Result of novation

Result of Novation			
Perspective of:	Ongoing Exposure?	Exposure With?	
		Original Counterparty	New Counterparty
Party A	√	x (exited from original trade)	√ (new to the original trade)
Party B	X	x (exited from original trade)	not applicable
Party C	√	√ (new trade)	not applicable

It is clearly essential that, once a novation has been completed, each of the parties updates its ***books & records*** appropriately and without delay, as ongoing activity for both ***trade processing*** and ***collateral processing*** will be impacted.

For example, the failure by the remaining party to update its books & records immediately can result in both trade processing and collateral processing being continued against the original counterparty rather than the stepping-in party (the novation transferee).

38.4 IMPACT OF NOVATION ON COLLATERAL MANAGEMENT

Following novation, providing the books & records of the remaining party, the novation transferor and the novation transferee have been updated correctly and in a timely fashion, the Collateral Departments within each firm will be aware of the updated situation and should begin the daily collateral process accordingly.

The process of ***portfolio reconciliation*** at the very start of the daily collateral lifecycle is intended to reveal whether the firm's trade population is the same as or different from the counterparty's records. This topic is covered within Chapter 31 'OTC Derivatives and Collateral – The Collateral Lifecycle – Throughout Lifetime of Trade – Portfolio Reconciliation'. Any novations should result in the firm's trade population being impacted in the appropriate manner, and the firm's current trade population being proven to be correct via the portfolio reconciliation process.

A particular risk for the remaining party relates to whether risk, associated purely with collateral management, is introduced following novation, where no such risk existed prior to novation. Such risks arise through, for example:

- collateral threshold differences
- collateral currency differences.

38.4.1 Collateral Threshold Differences

Differences in the thresholds applicable to a trade, due to the differences within a firm's CSAs with its various counterparties, can result in positive or negative consequences for the remaining party.

For example:

- prior to novation, due to zero threshold within the **CSA** with the original counterparty, the remaining party was able to make ***margin calls*** on the original counterparty without limit (with the exception of a ***minimum transfer amount***)
- following novation, due to a threshold of USD 1,000,000.00 within the CSA with the stepping-in counterparty, the remaining party is not able to make margin calls under that exposure amount.

Such negative consequences of novation to the remaining party are highlighted in Table 38.2:

PART 4a

TABLE 38.2 Negative consequences of novation

Negative Consequences of Novation on Threshold		
	Margin Calls...	
	... in Favour of Firm	... in Favour of Counterparty
Original Trade	**Zero Threshold** (firm's advantage: firm's exposures are fully mitigated)	**USD 1,000,000 Threshold** (firm's advantage: counterparty's exposures not fully mitigated)
Novated Trade	**USD 1,000,000 Threshold** (firm's disadvantage: firm's exposures not fully mitigated)	**Zero Threshold** (firm's disadvantage: counterparty's exposures are fully mitigated)

Conversely, the remaining party will benefit where its CSAs with the novation transferor and novation transferee differ, in the ways depicted in Table 38.3:

TABLE 38.3 Positive consequences of novation

Positive Consequences of Novation on Threshold		
	Margin Calls...	
	... in Favour of Firm	... in Favour of Counterparty
Original Trade	**USD 1,000,000 Threshold** (firm's disadvantage: firm's exposures not fully mitigated)	**Zero Threshold** (firm's disadvantage: counterparty's exposures are fully mitigated)
Novated Trade	**Zero Threshold** (firm's advantage: firm's exposures are fully mitigated)	**USD 1,000,000 Threshold** (firm's advantage: counterparty's exposures not fully mitigated)

It is recommended that a firm's OTC derivative traders consider the impact on collateral management when deciding whether to consent to a novation request.

38.4.2 Collateral Currency Differences

Differences in the currencies of cash collateral receivable following novation of a trade, due to the differences within a firm's CSAs with its various counterparties, can result in positive or negative consequences for the remaining party.

For example, a *pension fund* has executed an EUR OTC derivative trade with a US-based investment bank:

- prior to novation, where the pension fund has a *positive exposure* (following *marking-to-market*), the US investment bank pays USD cash collateral to the pension fund
- the US investment bank asks the pension fund to novate the trade to the bank's Frankfurt subsidiary

■ if the pension fund consents to the novation, positive exposures for the pension fund will mean that EUR cash collateral is received (based upon the CSA with the bank's Frankfurt subsidiary), which may in turn introduce exposure due to differences in interest rates between USD and EUR throughout the remaining duration of the contract.

38.5 CONCLUSION

Collateral management personnel should remain aware of the possibility of novation relating to current OTC derivative trades, and the impact of novation on ongoing counterparty exposures.

OTC derivative traders should have ongoing access to CSA details with each counterparty, in order to facilitate their decision-making regarding novation consent, and in particular the ongoing impact on collateral management.

PART 4a

OTC Derivatives and Collateral – The Collateral Lifecycle – Throughout Lifetime of Trade – Post-Trade Execution Events – Unwind

This chapter describes the process of unwinding a trade, whereby an original trade is closed out by a reversing trade. Should this post-trade execution event occur to a particular OTC derivative trade, there will be a fundamental impact to the ongoing collateral management of that trade.

THE OTC DERIVATIVE COLLATERAL LIFECYCLE

❶ Pre-Trading
Legal Documentation
Static Data

❷ Trading
Trade Execution

❸ Post-Trading
Trade Capture
Trade Confirmation/Affirmation
Trade/Portfolio Netting

❹ Throughout Lifetime of Trade
Portfolio Reconciliation
Marking-to-Market
Exposure Calculation
Receiving Margin Calls
Issuing Margin Calls
Holding Collateral
Post-Trade Execution Events
Collateral Substitution
Income & Corporate Action Events

❺ Trade Termination
Trade Termination

PART 4a

39.1 INTRODUCTION

Where a firm has a live and current **OTC *derivative*** trade (or position) with a particular ***counterparty***, at any point during its lifetime that trade or position may be subject to an ***unwind***.

Unwinds arise where both parties mutually agree to exit the trade. The specific characteristic of this method of exiting a contract from a particular firm's perspective is that it is the execution of an opposing trade to the existing trade, carried out with the same counterparty, the effect being to close (or to ***square-off***) the original trade resulting in no outstanding trade and no ongoing ***exposure***. This situation is depicted in Figure 39.1, which shows both the pre-unwind and post-unwind situation:

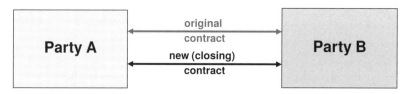

FIGURE 39.1 Pre- and post-unwind trade situations

Following unwind:

- Party A has no ongoing contract and therefore no exposure with Party B
- Party B has no ongoing contract and therefore no exposure with Party A.

Effecting an unwind involves one of the parties to a trade contacting its counterparty to request exiting the contract, specifically by unwinding. Upon execution of an unwind trade, the ***current market value*** of the trade is calculated in order to determine which party has a ***positive exposure***; settlement will then occur directly between the two parties, the party with the negative exposure being required to pay its counterparty in final settlement.

Unwind trades are also known as 'mutual early termination' trades or 'tear-up' trades.

For example, a ***buy-side*** firm (e.g. an ***insurance company***) executed a ***credit default swap*** trade 3½ years ago with ***Investment Bank*** D. The details of this contract, from the insurance company's perspective, are as shown in Table 39.1:

TABLE 39.1 Original trade details

Trade Component	Specific Trade Details
Transaction Type	Credit Default Swap
Operation	Protection Buyer
Counterparty	Investment Bank D
Trade Date	May 4th 2015
Notional Principal	USD 60,000,000.00
Scheduled Termination Date	June 20th 2028

To date, this (original) trade has been subject to **marking-to-market** from which exposures have been identified, resulting in **margin calls** and the need for the insurance company to either receive collateral from the investment bank, or to deliver collateral to the investment bank.

Now, the insurance company has decided it no longer has need of the contract and seeks to unwind the contract with the same investment bank. To clarify, unwinding a trade involves each party taking an economically equal and opposite position to their original trade; if they were a buyer in the original trade they would now need to be a seller, and vice versa for the counterparty. The investment bank agrees to the insurance company's request, resulting in the insurance company recording the unwind trade shown in Table 39.2 within its **books & records**:

TABLE 39.2   Unwind trade details

Trade Component	Specific Trade Details
Transaction Type	Credit Default Swap
Operation	Protection Seller (to Unwind)
Counterparty	Investment Bank D
Trade Date	November 8th 2018
Notional Principal	USD 60,000,000.00
Scheduled Termination Date	June 20th 2028

Once the counterparty agrees to execute the unwind trade, the traders within each firm must record the new trade specifically as an unwind trade, thereby indicating that the new trade is to close an existing trade. The failure to record an unwind trade in this way may result in non-**front-office** personnel treating the unwind trade as being a new trade (unconnected with and in addition to the original trade), with a subsequent failure to remove exposure with the counterparty.

Following the unwind, the fact that there will be no outstanding trade means that there is no ongoing exposure to either party, resulting (from that point forward) in there being no requirement to mark-to-market or to receive or to deliver collateral.

Should the counterparty be unwilling to execute such an unwind trade, the firm seeking to exit from a contract may choose an alternative exit method, via **novation** or **offset**.

Unwinds may be effected for the total **notional principal** of a contract, or for a partial quantity.

39.2 REASONS FOR UNWINDING

A party to an OTC derivative trade may choose to exit a contract via an unwind in preference to other methods, as the outcome of an unwind trade is that nothing remains of the original trade or position.

A party to an OTC derivative trade may choose to exit a contract via unwinding for a variety of reasons, including:

- the original reason for the contract has altered (e.g. in a credit default swap, the protection buyer has sold the underlying bond)
- a trading limit with the original counterparty has been reached
- a desire to reduce exposure to certain products
- a takeover by a firm resulting in unacceptable levels of credit risk to the new (post-takeover) counterparty
- cutting losses where the trade's mark-to-market is very negative.

This deserves comparison with the other contract exit methods, namely novation and offset. Following novation, a firm may have zero ongoing exposure, or alternatively exposure with a new counterparty; please refer to Chapter 38 'OTC Derivatives and Collateral – The Collateral Lifecycle – Throughout Lifetime of Trade – Post-Trade Execution Events – Novation'. Following offset, a firm will have ongoing exposure with two different counterparties; please refer to Chapter 40 'OTC Derivatives and Collateral – The Collateral Lifecycle – Throughout Lifetime of Trade – Post-Trade Execution Events – Offset'.

39.3 IMPACT OF UNWINDING ON BOOKS & RECORDS

Successful unwinds impact both the original parties to a trade:

- for the firm wishing to exit a contract; at the effective date of the unwind, the trade and exposure with its counterparty must be closed
- for that firm's counterparty; at the effective date of the unwind, the trade and exposure with its counterparty must be closed.

The result of an unwind, from the perspective of each of the parties, is summarised in Table 39.3:

TABLE 39.3 Result of unwind

Result of Unwind			
Party	Ongoing Exposure?	Exposure With?	
		Original Counterparty	New Counterparty
Party A	x	x	x
Party B	x	x	x

It is clearly essential that, once an unwind has been executed, each of the parties updates its *books & records* appropriately and without delay, as ongoing activity for both *trade processing* and *collateral processing* will be impacted.

For example, the failure by either party to update its books & records is likely to result in that party continuing both trade processing and collateral processing being actioned against the original trade, whereas in fact no exposure remains.

39.4 IMPACT OF UNWINDING ON COLLATERAL MANAGEMENT

As the intended result of an unwind trade is that zero exposure remains, and providing the books & records of both parties have been updated correctly and in a timely fashion, the Collateral Departments within each firm will be aware of the updated situation and should begin the daily collateral process accordingly.

The process of *portfolio reconciliation* at the very start of the daily collateral lifecycle is intended to reveal whether the firm's trade population is the same or different from the counterparty's records. This topic is covered within Chapter 31 'OTC Derivatives and Collateral – The Collateral Lifecycle – Throughout Lifetime of Trade – Portfolio Reconciliation'.

39.5 CONCLUSION

Collateral management personnel should remain aware of the possibility of unwinding relating to current OTC derivative trades, and the impact of unwind trades on ongoing counterparty exposures.

OTC Derivatives and Collateral – The Collateral Lifecycle – Throughout Lifetime of Trade – Post-Trade Execution Events – Offset

This chapter describes the process of offsetting a trade, whereby an existing OTC derivative position (with a particular counterparty) is reduced to a zero position via the execution of an opposing trade with a different counterparty. Should this post-trade execution event occur to a particular OTC derivative trade, there will be a fundamental impact on the ongoing collateral management of that trade.

PART 4a

THE OTC DERIVATIVE COLLATERAL LIFECYCLE

❶ Pre-Trading
Legal Documentation
Static Data

❷ Trading
Trade Execution

❸ Post-Trading
Trade Capture
Trade Confirmation/Affirmation
Trade/Portfolio Netting

❹ Throughout Lifetime of Trade
Portfolio Reconciliation
Marking-to-Market
Exposure Calculation
Receiving Margin Calls
Issuing Margin Calls
Holding Collateral
Post-Trade Execution Events
Collateral Substitution
Income & Corporate Action Events

❺ Trade Termination
Trade Termination

40.1 INTRODUCTION

Where a firm has a live and current *OTC derivative* trade (or position) with a particular *counterparty*, at any point during its lifetime that trade or position may be subject to an *offset*.

Offsets arise where one of the parties to a trade chooses to exit that trade. The specific characteristic of this method of exiting a contract, from a particular firm's perspective, is that it is the execution of an opposing trade to the existing trade, carried out with a different counterparty (to the original trade), the effect being to close overall *exposure* due to a zero overall position; however, exposure remains with both the original counterparty and the new counterparty. This situation is depicted in Figure 40.1, which shows both the pre-offset and post-offset situation:

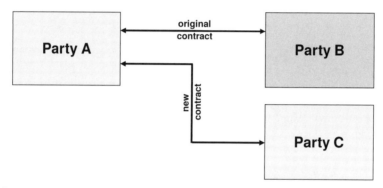

FIGURE 40.1   Pre-offset and post-offset situation

Following offset:

- Party A continues to have a contract with the original counterparty (Party B), plus an opposing contract with a new counterparty (Party C)
- Party B continues to have a contract with its original counterparty (Party A)
- Party C has a contract with a new counterparty (Party A).

Effecting an offset involves one of the parties to a trade contacting a counterparty to request exiting a contract, specifically by offsetting. (This would normally follow an unsuccessful attempt for the firm wishing to exit a contract, to have its original counterparty agree to an *unwind*.)

For example, a *buy-side* firm (e.g. an *insurance company*), executed a *credit default swap* 3½ years ago with *Investment Bank* D. The details of this contract, from the insurance company's perspective, are shown in Table 40.1:

TABLE 40.1   Original trade details

Trade Component	Specific Trade Details
Transaction Type	Credit Default Swap
Operation	Protection Buyer
Counterparty	Investment Bank D
Trade Date	May 4th 2015
Notional Principal	USD 60,000,000.00
Scheduled Termination Date	June 20th 2028

To date, this (original) trade has been subject to *marking-to-market* from which exposures have been identified, resulting in *margin calls* and the need for the insurance company to either receive collateral from the investment bank, or to deliver collateral to the investment bank.

Now, the insurance company has decided it no longer has need of the contract and seeks to unwind the contract with the same investment bank. However, Investment Bank D decides not to unwind the contract, and the insurance company contacts Investment Bank F who agrees to execute a new trade. The result for the insurance company is that its position in the CDS has been neutralised and its *market risk* has been *mitigated*, but (unlike the result of an unwind), the insurance company has ongoing exposure with two counterparties. The insurance company must record the new trade shown in Table 40.2 within its *books & records* (in addition to the original trade above):

TABLE 40.2   Offset trade details

Trade Component	Specific Trade Details
Transaction Type	Credit Default Swap
Operation	Protection Seller
Counterparty	Investment Bank F
Trade Date	November 8th 2018
Notional	USD 60,000,000.00
Scheduled Termination Date	June 20th 2028

Following the offset, the fact that there will be ongoing exposure with two counterparties will result in there being a requirement to mark-to-market both trades, to identify exposures on both trades, to issue and/or receive margin calls on both trades, and to receive collateral from or to deliver collateral to both counterparties.

Offsets may be effected for the total *notional principal* of the original contract, or for a partial quantity. Partial offsets occur where it may not be possible for the firm to hedge 100% of its exposure with another entity, and the firm may decide to leave some exposure open. For example, a firm buys protection originally for a notional principal of EUR 60,000,000.00, but now sells protection on a notional principal of EUR 50,000,000.00, thereby reducing their exposure.

40.2 REASONS FOR OFFSETTING

A party to an OTC derivative trade may choose to exit a contract via an offset, following an unsuccessful attempt to execute an unwind trade (which may have proven to be unacceptably costly).

An unwind trade may be regarded as being preferential to an offset trade, as the result of an unwind trade is that the counterparty exposure is removed in addition to zero exposure to the OTC derivative product being mitigated.

Note: from an investment bank's perspective, they would not enter into single trades which could result in open-ended losses. That is, a bank's trader is highly unlikely, for example in a credit default swap, to sell protection unless hedged elsewhere by buying protection in an offsetting trade.

40.3 IMPACT OF OFFSETTING ON BOOKS & RECORDS

Successful offsets impact all three parties:

- for the firm wishing to exit a contract: at the effective date of offset, the trade and exposure with its original counterparty must continue and the trade and exposure with the new counterparty must commence
- for that firm's original counterparty: the trade and exposure with its original counterparty must continue
- for the new counterparty: the trade and exposure with its (new) counterparty must commence.

The result of an offset, from the perspective of each of the parties, is summarised in Table 40.3:

TABLE 40.3 Result of offset

Result of Offset			
Perspective of:	Ongoing Exposure?	Exposure With?	
		Original Counterparty	New Counterparty
Party A	√	√ (remains in original trade)	√ (new trade)
Party B	√	√ (remains in original trade)	not applicable
Party C	√	√ (new trade)	not applicable

Internally, it may be regarded as beneficial for a firm to apply an indicator to an offset trade, with a cross-reference to the original trade which is the subject of the offset.

40.4 IMPACT OF OFFSETTING ON COLLATERAL MANAGEMENT

The result of an offset trade is that counterparty exposure is with two counterparties, and providing the books & records of all parties have been updated correctly and in a timely fashion, the Collateral Departments within each firm will be aware of the updated situation and should begin the daily collateral process accordingly.

The process of *portfolio reconciliation* at the very start of the daily collateral lifecycle is intended to reveal whether the firm's trade population is the same as or different from the counterparty's records. This topic is covered within Chapter 31 'OTC Derivatives and Collateral – The Collateral Lifecycle – Throughout Lifetime of Trade – Portfolio Reconciliation'.

40.5 CONCLUSION

Collateral management personnel should remain aware of the possibility of offset trades on current OTC derivative trades, and the impact of offset trades on ongoing counterparty exposures.

PART 4a

OTC Derivatives and Collateral – The Collateral Lifecycle – Throughout Lifetime of Trade – Post-Trade Execution Events – Credit Events

This chapter describes what credit events are, and how credit default swap contracts are impacted should a credit event occur. Should this post-trade execution event occur to a particular OTC derivative trade, there will be a fundamental impact to the ongoing collateral management of that trade.

THE OTC DERIVATIVE COLLATERAL LIFECYCLE

① **Pre-Trading**
Legal Documentation
Static Data

② **Trading**
Trade Execution

③ **Post-Trading**
Trade Capture
Trade Confirmation/Affirmation
Trade/Portfolio Netting

④ **Throughout Lifetime of Trade**
Portfolio Reconciliation
Marking-to-Market
Exposure Calculation
Receiving Margin Calls
Issuing Margin Calls
Holding Collateral
Post-Trade Execution Events
Collateral Substitution
Income & Corporate Action Events

⑤ **Trade Termination**
Trade Termination

Recommendation to Readers: as the subject of credit events relates directly to credit default swaps (CDS), it is recommended that readers that are not familiar with CDS should read Chapter 17 'OTC Derivatives and Collateral – Transaction Types – Credit Default Swaps' prior to reading this chapter.

41.1 INTRODUCTION

Where a firm has a live/current **OTC derivative** trade, specifically a **credit default swap** (CDS), at any point during its lifetime that trade may be subject to a **credit event**.

The term 'credit event' is a generic label given to a qualifying **event of default** by, for example, a **bond issuer** who, by the terms and conditions of the bond issue, must pay interest (coupon) to investors on scheduled dates and (typically) at a predetermined rate of interest, and who should repay capital to investors no later than the bond's **maturity date**. Should the bond issuer fail to make such payments, a credit event is deemed to have occurred, which triggers payout by the **protection seller** to the **protection buyer**, and immediate termination of the CDS trade.

When a CDS trade is executed, the particular events that will qualify as credit events are agreed between the two trading parties; amongst others, these typically include the bond issuer's:

- **bankruptcy**
- **failure to pay**, and
- debt **restructuring**.

Note that **ISDA** allows for a limited predefined set of credit events to be included within the contract.

At the outset of the CDS contract, there is no guarantee that a credit event will (or will not) occur, although the cost of protection (payable as a **premium** by the **protection buyer** to the **protection seller**) reflects the perceived likelihood of issuer default.

Should any one of the credit events listed within a particular trade actually occur during the lifetime of the CDS contract, the protection seller is required to settle the **notional principal** with the protection buyer.

Once settlement has occurred following a credit event, the CDS contract will automatically cease, and neither of the parties to the contract will suffer any ongoing exposure. This situation is depicted in Figure 41.1, which shows both the pre-credit event and post-credit event situation:

PART 4a

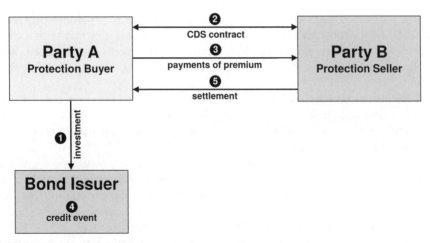

FIGURE 41.1   Credit default swap: pre- and post-credit event situation

Step 1: Party A invests in a bond

Step 2: Party A decides to seek protection against default by the bond issuer (known as the *reference entity* in a CDS) by choosing to enter into a credit default swap contract, and has become the *protection buyer*. Party B decides to provide protection to Party A, and has become the *protection seller*

Step 3: Party A remits premium payments (the cost of protection) to Party B periodically

Step 4: If the bond issuer undergoes a credit event, settlement of the CDS contract will be triggered

Step 5: The CDS contract is settled by the protection seller paying 100% of the notional principal, less an agreed recovery amount, to the protection buyer, at which point the contract is terminated with no ongoing exposure to either the protection buyer or protection seller. The recovery amount is derived from a recovery percentage which is set by an auction process; the recovery percentage reflects the market's expectation of how much a physical investor in a *senior unsecured bond* would likely receive after the issuer's bankruptcy process takes place.

Note: although the above-mentioned diagram and description depicts Party A having an investment in a bond which leads to a decision to execute a CDS contract, there is usually no requirement (legal, regulatory or otherwise) to be invested in a bond to become a party to a CDS contract. For example, Party B is providing protection to Party A and may choose to enter into an equal and opposite contract with a different counterparty where Party B becomes a protection buyer, thereby hedging their position. Under these circumstances, Party B has two CDS trades, but has no investment in the underlying bond issuer.

Events such as *novation*, *unwind* and *offset* are triggered by one party to a contract wishing to exit that contract. Conversely, credit events are triggered by, for example, the bankruptcy or default of an *obligor* (e.g. a bond issuer or reference entity) rather than by parties to the CDS contract.

Historically, disputes have arisen between protection buyer and protection seller, as to whether a qualifying credit event had in fact occurred, or not. During 2009, an *ISDA protocol* was introduced whereby regional determination committees (RDCs) were empowered to ascertain whether a credit event had occurred, or not. The RDC's decision is binding on all parties that have signed up to the protocol.

Following a credit event, the fact that there will be no ongoing exposure with the counterparty will result in there being no requirement to either *mark-to-market* the trade or to receive or to deliver collateral.

Credit events will impact the total *notional principal* of a contract; as a credit event impacts all outstanding CDS contracts (relating to the particular bond issuer or reference entity), no partial quantities will remain following a credit event.

41.2 IMPACT OF CREDIT EVENTS ON BOOKS & RECORDS

Should a credit event occur, both protection buyer and protection seller will be impacted:

- for the firm that has purchased protection, once they have received the settlement amount the contract and exposure with its counterparty must cease
- for the firm that has sold protection, once they have remitted payment of the settlement amount the contract and exposure with its counterparty must cease.

The result of a credit event, from the perspective of each of the parties, is summarised in Table 41.1:

TABLE 41.1 Result of credit event

Result of Credit Event			
Party	Ongoing Exposure?	Exposure With?	
		Original Counterparty	New Counterparty
Party A	X	not applicable	not applicable
Party B	X	not applicable	not applicable

Following a credit event, and once the protection seller has remitted payment to the protection buyer, both parties must ensure their *books & records* no longer show the trade as being live and valid.

41.3 IMPACT OF CREDIT EVENTS ON COLLATERAL MANAGEMENT

As the result of a credit event is that counterparty exposure no longer exists, and providing the books & records of both parties have been updated correctly and in a timely fashion, the Collateral Departments within each firm will be aware of the updated situation and should begin the daily collateral process accordingly.

The process of *portfolio reconciliation* at the very start of the daily collateral lifecycle is intended to reveal whether the firm's trade population is the same or different from the counterparty's records. This topic is covered within Chapter 31 'OTC Derivatives and Collateral – The Collateral Lifecycle – Throughout Lifetime of Trade – Portfolio Reconciliation'.

41.4 CONCLUSION

Collateral management personnel should remain aware of the possibility of credit events on current credit default swap contracts, and the impact of credit events on ongoing counterparty exposures.

OTC Derivatives and Collateral – The Collateral Lifecycle – Throughout Lifetime of Trade – Collateral Substitution

This chapter describes the circumstances under which existing securities collateral is substituted with other collateral, and the process of achieving substitution. The subject of collateral substitution is introduced within Sub-section 22.8.14 'Collateral Substitution' of Chapter 22 'OTC Derivatives and Collateral – Legal Protection – Credit Support Annex'; this chapter expands upon the concepts covered therein.

THE OTC DERIVATIVE COLLATERAL LIFECYCLE

1 **Pre-Trading**
Legal Documentation
Static Data

2 **Trading**
Trade Execution

3 **Post-Trading**
Trade Capture
Trade Confirmation/Affirmation
Trade/Portfolio Netting

4 **Throughout Lifetime of Trade**
Portfolio Reconciliation
Marking-to-Market
Exposure Calculation
Receiving Margin Calls
Issuing Margin Calls
Holding Collateral
Post-Trade Execution Events
→ Collateral Substitution
Income & Corporate Action Events

5 **Trade Termination**
Trade Termination

42.1 INTRODUCTION

In a situation in which *securities* (usually *bond,* unusually *equity*) collateral is being held by a *collateral taker*, the *collateral giver* may require return of that particular bond, in exchange for other collateral. The common term for such an exchange is 'collateral substitution' (see Figure 42.1).

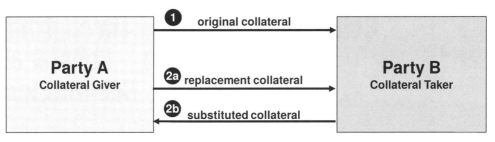

FIGURE 42.1   Collateral substitution

Providing the *replacement collateral* is eligible under the CSA with the particular *counterparty*, the replacement collateral may be:

- replacement bond or equity versus substituted bond or equity
- replacement bond or equity versus substituted cash
- replacement cash versus substituted bond or equity
- replacement currency versus substituted currency.

Furthermore, bond collateral used as replacement of existing collateral may be delivered using one particular bond (e.g. GBP 5,000,000 UK Government 3.75% bonds maturing 1st July 2030) or with multiple pieces, such as:

- GBP 2,000,000 Issuer X 3.95% bonds maturing 15th October 2028, plus
- GBP 2,200,000 Issuer Y 4.15% bonds maturing 1st February 2026, plus
- GBP 1,000,000 Issuer Z 4.25% bonds maturing 1st July 2032,

the total collateral value of which must cover the collateral taker's exposure.

42.2 REASONS FOR COLLATERAL SUBSTITUTION

The typical reason for a collateral giver wishing to substitute bonds is that the bonds are required for delivery purposes in another transaction, for example:

- sale of securities
- *securities lending*
- *repo*.

Another reason for substitution, in the interests of both parties, is to avoid holding bond collateral over a *record date* of a *coupon payment*, or equity collateral over a record date of a *dividend*. Such income payments may be subject to *withholding tax* which only complicates the treatment of such cash payments between collateral taker and collateral giver. (Withholding tax is a complex subject often involving tax reclaims where the incorrect rate of tax has been deducted; for further details, please refer to this author's book *Corporate Actions: a Guide to Securities Event Management* [ISBN 0470870664].) Note: within many financial institutions the personnel responsible for collateral management and *corporate actions* are within different sections or departments; when the Corporate Actions Department would prefer to have bond collateral returned prior to an upcoming coupon payment, the communication between the two areas can present an operational hurdle.

A further reason for substitution is that the collateral giver may have realised that the CSA with the particular counterparty allows bonds of a lower credit rating to be given as collateral (albeit typically with higher *haircut* percentages), and that taking back the higher rated bond will allow use of that bond as collateral in CSAs that have greater restrictions in terms of issuer credit ratings.

Substitution can also be applicable to existing cash collateral, where the collateral giver finds it advantageous to utilise securities collateral in replacement of cash collateral that is currently held by the collateral taker. Such substitutions can arise where the collateral giver chooses to utilise the cash (currently held by the collateral taker) for other purposes or where a differential in interest rates exists between money market rates and the interest rate stated within the CSA.

Yet another reason for substitution occurs where the bond issuer has suffered a *credit rating downgrade*, where the bond held by the collateral taker is no longer *eligible collateral* under the CSA. This scenario differs from most other collateral substitution scenarios, as under these circumstances substitution is in the best interest of the collateral taker, since their *exposure* is no longer *mitigated* due to the downgrade.

42.3 THE PROCESS OF COLLATERAL SUBSTITUTION

The following describes a scenario which triggers substitution of bond collateral, whilst also illustrating the steps in the process.

One week ago, following receipt of a *margin call*, in order to cover its counterparty's exposure at that time, Party A delivered to Party B a quantity of USD 10,000,000 International Bank for Reconstruction and Development 5.25% bonds maturing 15th May 2028.

Today, Party A's bond trader has sold all USD 10,000,000 bonds on a T+2 basis (i.e. for delivery in two business days from today). Party A's securities Settlement Department view their *books & records* in order to determine where the bonds are currently located, to discover the bonds are not held by Party A's *custodian*, but are currently acting as collateral and in possession of Party B.

At this point, Party A's Securities Settlement Department must contact their Collateral Department to advise of the sale and the need to have the securities returned from Party B (so as to facilitate timely delivery of the securities sold by Party A, thereby receiving the sale proceeds at the earliest time). Party A's Collateral Department must now select replacement collateral, either other securities or cash, which are eligible under the **Credit Support Annex** with the particular counterparty; USD 10,000,000 Inter American Development Bank 4.75% bonds maturing 1st October 2030 are selected. Party A's Collateral Department must now request substitution from Party B, by specifying both 1) the collateral to be substituted, and 2) the proposed replacement collateral. The normal method of communicating a substitution request is by email or by **S.W.I.F.T.**

Upon receipt of the substitution request, Party B's Collateral Department must satisfy themselves that the proposed replacement collateral falls within the **eligible collateral** parameters listed within the appropriate CSA. If so, Party B (being the **exposed party**) must ensure they remain collateralised at all times, and therefore should ensure they do not return the original collateral before receiving the replacement collateral.

The normal method of effecting delivery of the substituted original bonds and of the replacement bonds is by **free of payment** (FoP) delivery of each bond, on the same day, between the accounts of the collateral giver and the collateral taker, at the relevant **central securities depository** (CSD). The typical time frame for delivery of both bonds is T+1, where 'T' is the date of the substitution request issued by the collateral giver, and of agreement by the collateral taker.

The above-mentioned steps (and more) are represented within Figure 42.2:

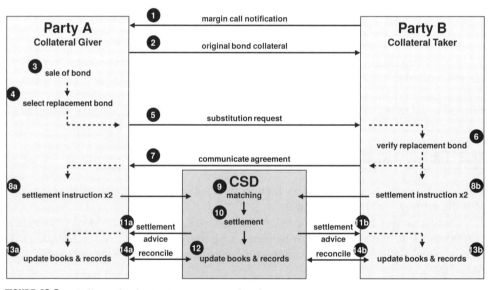

FIGURE 42.2   Collateral substitution: sequential tasks

The diagram is explained as follows:

Step 1: Party B (the exposed party) issues a margin call to Party A

Step 2: Party A agrees the margin call which is settled by delivery of a particular bond

Step 3: Party A sells the bond, currently in possession of Party B

Step 4: Party A identifies a different bond to be given as collateral to Party B

Step 5: Party A communicates a substitution request to Party B

Step 6: Party B verifies the eligibility (under the relevant CSA) of the proposed replacement bond

Step 7: Party B communicates its agreement to the substitution and to the replacement bond

Step 8: both parties issue two FoP settlement instructions to the CSD

Step 9: the CSD successfully matches instructions for 1) the original collateral, and 2) for the replacement collateral

Step 10: settlement of both deliveries occurs (non-simultaneously) on the value date of the substitution

Step 11: the CSD issues a settlement advice for each of the bond deliveries, to both parties

Step 12: the CSD updates its books & records resulting from the two deliveries

Step 13: internally, both parties update their respective books & records to reflect settlement of the two bond deliveries

Step 14: both parties attempt to reconcile their internal books & records of securities balances against the statements of securities holdings received from the CSD.

In summary, once agreement to substitute has been reached, from the perspective of both collateral giver and collateral taker, successful substitution involves:

- issuance of an FoP settlement instruction for the original bond
- issuance of an FoP settlement instruction for the replacement bond
- verification of each instruction by each party's CSD or custodian
- matching of both sets of settlement instructions prior to value date
- delivery of both bonds occurring on value date.

42.4 RISKS IN SETTLEMENT OF COLLATERAL SUBSTITUTION

The historic method of settling collateral substitutions, in particular the return of the original bond and replacement with a different bond, has been by two-way free of payment (FoP) settlement (as described earlier in this chapter). The concern regarding this settlement method is that the settlement of the bond delivered in one direction is conducted independently (and non-simultaneously) with the bond delivery in the opposite direction. If both deliveries do occur on the value date of the substitution (and in the same time zone), then neither party is at risk. Conversely, if only one of the deliveries occurs on the value date of the substitution, the party that still awaits delivery of the bond has a significant exposure.

By comparison with such non-simultaneous FoP settlement, common practice in major securities markets around the globe, for deliveries of securities versus cash (e.g. when settling purchases and sales), is the simultaneous exchange of securities versus cash by a mechanism known as *Delivery versus payment* (DvP). Due to its simultaneous exchange nature, DvP protects the assets of both parties; this means that delivery of bonds will not occur without simultaneous receipt of cash, and vice versa.

For the settlement of collateral substitutions involving the two-way delivery of securities, in order to mitigate the risks of FoP settlement described above, what is generically needed in the marketplace is simultaneous exchange of the two securities. In other words, ***delivery versus delivery*** (DvD). ***Target2 Securities*** (T2S), the pan-European settlement engine, provides users with the ability to link the settlement of one matched FoP settlement instruction with the settlement of another matched FoP settlement instruction, so that settlement of one delivery will occur only if both securities movements occur simultaneously. Stated in a different way, if the securities are not available to complete a delivery in one direction, the opposing delivery is prevented from occurring until both deliveries can occur; this settlement method is described as ***Effective DvD***. Note: in order to achieve true DvD (not just Effective DvD), the CSD needs to provide a single settlement instruction which contains the quantity of an ISIN in one direction and the quantity of the second ISIN in the opposing direction. Of course, such a settlement instruction would require matching by the counterparty's settlement instruction before settlement can occur. Also note that DvD would be of value not only for collateral substitution, but also for ***securities lending*** versus collateral in the form of securities.

42.5 URGENCY OF COLLATERAL SUBSTITUTION

Substitution is normally considered an urgent task, as the underlying reason for substitution typically has a financial consideration since it is time-dependent.

For example, from the collateral giver's perspective, any delay in the return of the original (substituted) bond is very likely to cause the collateral giver to suffer a monetary loss, where the securities have been sold. In such circumstances, the failure of the seller to deliver the securities to the buyer on the ***value date*** of the sale will mean the seller will not receive the sale proceeds at the earliest opportunity, causing loss of interest to the seller (assuming a ***positive interest rate*** environment). Therefore, collateral substitution is normally an urgent task for the collateral giver.

Where there has been a credit rating downgrade of the issuer of the substituted bond, the faster the collateral taker acts to effect substitution, the faster their exposure will be mitigated.

42.6 IMPACT OF COLLATERAL SUBSTITUTION ON THE COLLATERAL TAKER

From the perspective of the collateral taker (i.e. the exposed party), providing the replacement collateral is eligible collateral under the CSA, they are obliged to accept the substitution request from the collateral giver. However, the details of the substitution (e.g. value date, replacement ISIN, quantity of replacement ISIN) must be mutually agreed.

Furthermore, additional administrative effort by the collateral taker may be necessary in order to effect the substitution, in many cases for no obvious benefit. For example, the exposed party may never previously have needed to set up in its ***static data*** the bond which the collateral giver now wishes to deliver; such set-up requires operational effort (including *coupon rate*, coupon dates, coupon frequency, the applicable *accrued interest day count* and *divisor, maturity date*) to ensure errors do not arise. In addition, the counterparty's *standing settlement instructions* (SSIs) relating to the replacement collateral may be missing from the firm's static data. Not only does the set-up of such missing data require additional operational effort, but the fact that such data is missing can cause delays in processing; for example, the issuance of settlement instructions to effect movement of the collateral.

42.7 UNWANTED EXPOSURES IN COLLATERAL SUBSTITUTION

In attempting to effect substitution, both collateral giver and collateral taker must remain aware that unwanted exposures can be created.

The risks to the collateral giver when effecting a substitution include the following:

- failure of substituted bond receipt, in turn causing the failure to settle the underlying transaction (e.g. sale of bonds), resulting in monetary loss through delayed receipt of sale proceeds, caused by (for example):
  - the settlement instruction for the substituted bond failing to be transmitted to the relevant CSD or custodian by the necessary deadline
  - the settlement instruction failing to be matched by the necessary deadline
- counterparty exposure, where outgoing delivery of the replacement collateral has occurred on value date, but receipt of the substituted collateral has failed.

The risks to the collateral taker (exposed party) when effecting a substitution include the following:

- counterparty exposure, where outgoing delivery of the substituted collateral has occurred on value date, but receipt of the replacement collateral has failed.

Other situations that potentially cause exposure include the circumstances in which the collateral giver has delivered bond collateral to the collateral taker (the exposed party), but now the giver wishes to substitute the bond with cash in a particular currency. Of course, the currency must be permitted under the terms of the particular CSA between the two parties.

If the cash is in a different currency from the exposure, foreign exchange rate movements can cause the collateral taker to be under-collateralised, where previously the collateral taker's exposure was fully mitigated by possession of the bond. In particular, the time between agreeing a substitution request (and the exchange rate at that time) versus the point at which the funds are received may create an exposure for the collateral taker due to adverse movements in the exchange rate. Such a situation will only be exacerbated where bond collateral is returned to the collateral giver in advance of receipt of the cash amount as replacement collateral.

It is possible that a substitution between collateral giver and the collateral taker could trigger a chain of substitutions between a number of market participants, requiring all related movements of assets to occur on time if exposures are to be avoided.

42.8 UPDATING BOOKS & RECORDS

Once substitution has been effected successfully, the giver and taker must update their respective *books & records* in order to fully reflect reality.

Specifically, from the perspective of both parties, the substituted collateral must be shown as now being back in the possession of the collateral giver, and the replacement collateral must be shown as being in the hands of the collateral taker (the exposed party).

Correct books & records should be proven subsequently through the process of reconciliation; *nostro reconciliation* should be conducted for cash collateral, whilst *depot reconciliation* should be performed for bond collateral.

Furthermore, it is essential for a firm's accuracy of ongoing exposure calculations, that the cumulative collateral balance is updated following collateral substitution.

42.9 CONCLUSION

In order for a collateral giver (the non-exposed party) to avoid settlement losses, they must remain fully aware that newly executed transactions (including selling, repoing and securities lending) which demand delivery of securities on particular dates may require the return of such securities, via collateral substitution, from counterparties that are currently holding those securities as collateral relating to OTC derivative trades.

From the perspective of the collateral taker (the exposed party), following a collateral substitution request from the collateral giver they are at risk of returning the original collateral prior to receipt of the replacement collateral, thereby having an unmitigated exposure. Collateral takers should ensure they never suffer exposure resulting from collateral substitution.

OTC Derivatives and Collateral – The Collateral Lifecycle – Throughout Lifetime of Trade – Income & Corporate Action Events

This chapter describes the procedures between collateral giver and collateral taker when income events and corporate action events arise on securities collateral.

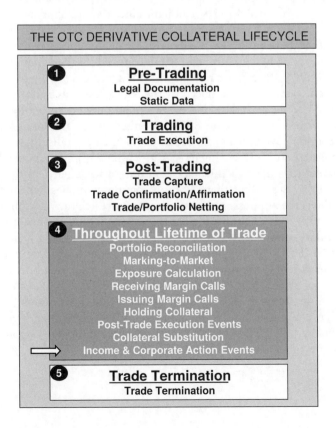

THE OTC DERIVATIVE COLLATERAL LIFECYCLE

① Pre-Trading
Legal Documentation
Static Data

② Trading
Trade Execution

③ Post-Trading
Trade Capture
Trade Confirmation/Affirmation
Trade/Portfolio Netting

④ Throughout Lifetime of Trade
Portfolio Reconciliation
Marking-to-Market
Exposure Calculation
Receiving Margin Calls
Issuing Margin Calls
Holding Collateral
Post-Trade Execution Events
Collateral Substitution
→ Income & Corporate Action Events

⑤ Trade Termination
Trade Termination

PART 4a

This chapter builds upon the Income and Corporate Actions sub-sections within Chapter 22 'OTC Derivatives and Collateral – Legal Protection – Credit Support Annex'. The management of income events and corporate action events is a major topic in its own right; this chapter focuses on those subjects as they pertain to bond collateral. (For further details, please refer to this author's book Corporate Actions: A Guide to Securities Event Management *[ISBN: 0470870664].)*

43.1 INTRODUCTION

Coupon payments are made by *bond issuers* to *bondholders* for most types of *debt* instrument (bonds), including *fixed rate bonds, floating rate notes* and *convertible bonds*. Coupon payments are not made on *zero coupon bonds.*

Coupon payments on certain types of bond are fully predictable in terms of the cash amount payable (based upon the coupon rate) and when payments are due (coupon payment dates), throughout the lifetime of the bond; both fixed rate bonds and convertible bonds fall within this category.

Floating rate notes (FRN) do not have a fixed rate of interest; instead their coupon rates are determined using a benchmark rate (e.g. Libor) which varies constantly. This means that a particular FRN that pays coupon (for example) every six months is extremely unlikely to pay a coupon at the same rate as the previous coupon payment.

Such differences between debt instruments with coupon rates and coupon payment dates that are fully predictable, as opposed to those debt instruments where the rate must be determined based upon a benchmark rate, require similar but not the same treatment operationally. All such coupon information must be set up within the firm's internal *static data*, but only those bonds with known coupon rates and coupon payment dates can be set up in final form and left unchanged for the remainder of the bond's life. However, for FRN, the coupon rate payable for a particular coupon date can only be set up within static data once announced by the issuer; that rate is normally announced either 2 days prior to the start date of the new coupon period, or on the start date itself (dependent upon currency). This means that (unlike fixed rate bonds and convertible bonds), FRN coupon payment details need to be updated periodically within static data.

The Corporate Actions Department (CAD) within a firm is responsible for calculation of *entitlement* to coupon payments. But in order to calculate entitlement, the CAD must firstly become aware that there is an upcoming coupon payment. The origin of such information is the bond issue's *prospectus*, from which the relevant coupon details are set up within the firm's own *static data repository*, which must be completely accurate and up-to-date at all times if coupon payments are not to be missed. Some firms choose to obtain details of individual bond instruments (including coupon rate and coupon payment date information) directly from *data vendors*, whilst others may utilise information available from *central securities depositories* and *custodians.*

If a firm's static data is inaccurate, the risks exist that, for example, 1) the firm fails to recognise that coupon income is due imminently and consequently is not expecting to receive payment, and 2) the firm will not receive the full value of coupon payments due to the coupon rate being incorrect.

43.2 BOND COLLATERAL AND COUPON PAYMENTS

Assuming that the firm's static data is accurate, the CAD should utilise such information to be alerted to upcoming coupon payments.

For example, approximately 1 week prior to the coupon payment date (e.g. 24th May), a report can be produced internally which lists all *interest-bearing bonds* with coupon payment dates of 1st June. (Many bonds pay interest either on the 1st of a month, or the 15th of a month.) Then, approaching the coupon payment date itself, the CAD could run a report to identify whether any trades or positions exist in such bonds; the fact that the firm holds static data regarding an individual bond does not guarantee that any trades or positions exist currently.

It is very important to note that, for an individual bond, the firm's *books & records* must clearly highlight where bonds have been given or taken for the purpose of collateralising *exposures*. In other words, the firm's books & records must clearly distinguish the transaction type underlying the delivery or receipt of the particular bond; therefore, in addition to highlighting the giving or taking of bond collateral, the firm's books & records must show other transaction types (e.g. buy/sell, repo/reverse, lend/borrow), to enable accurate identification of entitlement to each coupon payment.

Where trades or positions exist in a particular bond, it is possible that the firm has given or taken bond collateral. The relevant *central securities depository* (e.g. **Euroclear Bank** or **Clearstream International**) usually operates a *record date* system, whereby all holders of the particular bond that have a position in the bonds as at the close of business on record date will be credited with the coupon proceeds on the coupon payment date.

Because the *collateral giver* retains *beneficial ownership* of the bond (under a *title transfer* arrangement as is the case in the *English Law Credit Support Annex*), the collateral giver is entitled to the coupon payment. Where the *collateral taker* is credited with the coupon payment (but is not entitled to it), the collateral taker must remit the equivalent value of the coupon payment received to the collateral giver.

Where the firm has given bond collateral, and that collateral has been delivered from the firm's account at the CSD prior to the close of business on record date, this will in turn mean that the collateral taker has a record date position at the CSD. Consequently, the collateral taker will be credited with the coupon proceeds on coupon payment date and must remit the same cash amount to the collateral giver. The collateral giver must monitor this situation in order to ensure it receives payment from the collateral taker. The CSA states that the collateral taker is required to remit the equivalent value of the coupon payment to the collateral giver; in an attempt to ensure that the funds are received when due, the collateral giver may choose to issue a formal *coupon claim* to the collateral taker, as soon as possible after record date.

Many firms wish to avoid the administrative burden (for both collateral giver and collateral taker) of handling coupon payments on bond collateral, by effecting a *collateral substitution* of the original bond with a different (replacement) bond, or with cash, in advance of the record date.

PART 4a

43.2.1 Collateral Taker Holds the Collateral

In a situation where the collateral taker holds the bond collateral within its CSD or custodian account at close of business on record date (and does not *reuse* it or *rehypothecate* it in another transaction of its own), the collateral taker will be credited with the coupon payment by the CSD; the collateral taker is said to be the *legal owner* but is not entitled to the coupon payment. As the collateral giver is the *beneficial owner* of the bond, it is entitled to the coupon payment. Therefore, the collateral taker must remit the equivalent value of the coupon payment to the collateral giver. Such a situation is depicted in Figure 43.1.

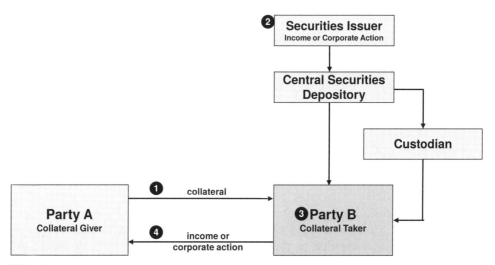

FIGURE 43.1 Coupon payment flow where collateral taker holds the collateral

43.2.2 Collateral Taker Reuses or Rehypothecates the Collateral

If, instead of holding the bond collateral, the collateral taker had reused or rehypothecated it in another transaction, the collateral taker is still obliged to remit the equivalent value of the coupon payment to the collateral giver. But whether the collateral taker can itself claim the coupon proceeds from the party with whom the collateral taker has executed a transaction (Party C in the diagram below) depends upon the transaction type executed between the collateral taker and Party C. Figure 43.2 illustrates such a situation.

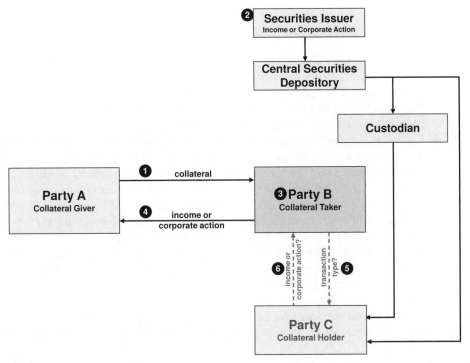

FIGURE 43.2   Coupon payment flow where collateral taker reuses or rehypothecates the collateral

From Party B's perspective when reusing or rehypothecating bond collateral, the usual choices of transaction type include the following:

1. executing a <u>Sale</u>; this means that Party B has sold the securities 'outright' to Party C, resulting in Party C becoming the owner of the securities
2. executing a <u>Repo</u>; this means that Party B has used the bond as collateral against the temporary borrowing of cash from Party C, resulting in Party C needing to return the bond to Party B upon closure of the repo transaction. *The subject of repo is covered within Part 2 'Sale & Repurchase (Repo) Trades and Collateral'*
3. executing a <u>Securities Loan</u>; this means that Party B has lent the bond temporarily to Party C, resulting in Party C needing to return the bond to Party B upon closure of the securities loan transaction. *The subject of securities lending is covered within Part 3 'Securities Lending & Borrowing and Collateral'*
4. <u>utilising the bond as collateral</u> as part of another transaction, in which Party B delivers the bond as collateral, for example in 1) another OTC derivative trade, or 2) as collateral against the borrowing of securities from Party C.

Each of the transaction types above will impact whether Party C owes the coupon payment to Party B, or not:

1. executing a <u>Sale</u>: as Party C has purchased the bond outright from Party B, Party C is entitled to the coupon payment (providing the value date of the trade is no later than the record date of the coupon payment)
   a. Party B will therefore not be entitled to the coupon payment and consequently should not claim the coupon payment from Party C
   b. Party B will, however, remain liable to remit the value of the coupon payment to Party A, meaning that Party B must pay the value of the coupon payment out of its own funds to Party A; this is known as ***manufactured income***
2. executing a <u>Repo</u>: as Party C has received the bond as collateral from Party B, Party C is not entitled to the coupon payment. As far as Party C is concerned, Party B is the beneficial owner and as such is entitled to the coupon payment
   a. Party B should claim the coupon payment from Party C
   b. Party B will, however, remain liable to remit the value of the coupon payment to Party A, meaning that the receipt of the coupon payment from Party C can be used to make payment to Party A.

The coupon payment impact on Party B when executing a securities loan (point 3 above), and when utilising the bond as collateral (point 4 above), is the same as for execution of a repo.

Note that Party A, regardless of the transaction type executed between Party B and Party C, is entitled to the coupon payment and is owed the value of the coupon payment by Party B.

43.3 BOND COLLATERAL AND CORPORATE ACTIONS

Whilst coupon payments on bonds are usually ***mandatory corporate action*** events, other types of corporate action are classified as ***voluntary corporate action*** events, which require an investment decision to be made. For example, a bond tender offer provides the opportunity for ***bondholders*** to accept the offer of cash in exchange for the bonds, by a specified deadline set by the bond issuer; bonds for which the offer is not accepted will remain outstanding on their original terms.

Where such a voluntary corporate action is announced, and where the bonds have been given as collateral, the party with the right to make the investment decision (i.e. whether to accept the offer, or not) is the collateral giver as the beneficial owner of the bond. Under such circumstances, the choices are:

- for the bonds to be returned to the collateral giver by the record date, so the collateral giver can communicate directly with its CSD should the collateral giver wish to accept the offer, or
- for the collateral giver to instruct the collateral taker either to accept the offer (on the collateral giver's behalf) or to not accept the offer.

Where the collateral giver instructs the collateral taker, this is best achieved in writing in case an error is made by the collateral taker.

43.4 CONCLUSION

In order for the Corporate Actions Department within any *buy-side* or *sell-side* firm to have a chance of ensuring that coupon payments (and other corporate action events) finish up in the correct hands, it is essential that:

- the firm's books & records:
    - at all times are completely up-to-date and reflect the reality of all trades and transaction types executed by the firm
    - are proven to be accurate through *reconciliation* of the component parts of the firm's books & records with, as a minimum, 1) the statements of securities holdings produced by the firm's CSDs or custodians, and 2) outstanding (open) trades with counterparties
- the firm's corporate actions personnel understand the implications of the various transaction types (including buy/sell, repo/reverse, securities lending/borrowing, giving/taking of bonds as collateral in OTC derivative trades) on income payments and corporate action events.

OTC Derivatives and Collateral – The Collateral Lifecycle – Trade Termination – Trade Termination

The Trade Termination section of the OTC Derivative Collateral Lifecycle covers the activity necessary when a trade reaches its scheduled maturity date, and ongoing exposures no longer exist.

This chapter describes what must happen when an OTC derivative trade reaches its scheduled maturity date, from a collateral management perspective.

THE OTC DERIVATIVE COLLATERAL LIFECYCLE

① Pre-Trading
Legal Documentation
Static Data

② Trading
Trade Execution

③ Post-Trading
Trade Capture
Trade Confirmation/Affirmation
Trade/Portfolio Netting

④ Throughout Lifetime of Trade
Portfolio Reconciliation
Marking-to-Market
Exposure Calculation
Receiving Margin Calls
Issuing Margin Calls
Holding Collateral
Post-Trade Execution Events
Collateral Substitution
Income & Corporate Action Events

⑤ Trade Termination
Trade Termination

OTC derivative trades may have very lengthy lifetimes; up to 50 years in some cases. The trade may fail to reach its **scheduled maturity date** for reasons such as trade/portfolio netting (**trade compression**), **novation**, **unwind** and **offset**. In the particular case of **credit default swaps**, the occurrence of a **credit event** will cause early termination of the trade.

However, if no such events arise, the trade will continue its life until the trade's scheduled maturity date is reached.

Beyond the scheduled maturity date the trade is no longer 'live', meaning that for a firm that's a party to such a trade, counterparty **exposure** has ceased (unless other OTC derivative trades with the same **counterparty** remain outstanding). This in turn means that any cash or bond collateral given or taken must be returned to the collateral giver.

(Conversely, imagine a situation in which a number of OTC derivative trades are validly outstanding with a particular counterparty, and one of those trades reaches its scheduled maturity date. Under such circumstances, the matured trade must be removed from the portfolio of outstanding trades and determining the exposure on the remaining trades must continue; therefore, associated collateral needs to be given or taken dependent upon the particular circumstances.)

For OTC derivative transaction types where settlement occurs shortly after the scheduled maturity date (e.g. **variance swaps**), a firm that is 'in-the-money' may choose not to return collateral until trade settlement has occurred.

It is important that internal systems treat trades that have reached their scheduled maturity date as being 'closed', as the trade is no longer 'open' with the counterparty. Any failure to close trades under these circumstances may mean that trades are treated by the system as still being 'live', with the result that a firm may still be calculating exposures and expecting to make or to receive **margin calls**. However, for those firms that use the **triResolve** system, the **portfolio reconciliation** process (see Chapter 31 'OTC Derivatives and Collateral – The Collateral Lifecycle – Throughout Lifetime of Trade – Portfolio Reconciliation') should identify such errors.

In general terms, systems offer the method of trade termination as both a manual process and an automated process. In some firms that utilise the manual termination method, the responsibility for closing the trade lies with the **traders**, or **Middle Office** or **Operations Department**. In other firms whose preference is for an automated termination process, the system is configured to close the trade following the trade's scheduled termination date.

– End of the OTC Derivative Collateral Lifecycle –

PART
4b

OTC Derivatives and Collateral – Legal Documentation

CHAPTER 45

OTC Derivatives and Collateral – Legal Documentation

The legal documentation that has historically been utilised in order to protect the interests of both parties in bilateral trading of OTC derivatives is:

- ISDA Master Agreement
- The Schedule, and
- The Credit Support Annex.

These documents are available from the International Swaps and Derivatives Association (ISDA); go to 'www.isda.org'.

OTC Derivatives and Collateral – Regulatory Change and the Future of Collateral

OTC Derivatives and Collateral – Regulatory Change and the Future of Collateral – Introduction

Part 4a of this book describes:

- *the essential nature of OTC derivative products*
- *the legal documentation which provides protection for both parties when trades are executed*
- *how exposures arise following trading*
- *the sequential steps in the collateral lifecycle designed to mitigate exposures, and*
- *post-trade execution events which can cause significant impacts on collateral processing.*

In summary, Part 4a focuses on trading and collateral management activities which have been executed directly between two parties, on a bilateral basis.

Part 4b refers to the set of ISDA legal documentation used for bilateral trading and collateral management of OTC derivative trades executed directly between two trading parties.

This Part of the book (4c) describes the far-reaching regulatory reforms introduced as a result of the 2008 Global Financial Crisis, which have very significant implications on the post-trade processing of OTC derivatives, and the management of exposures and collateral in particular.

This chapter provides an introduction and overview of such regulatory reforms, and the following two chapters describe at a more granular level what is involved both structurally in the marketplace, as well as how collateral management is impacted.

PART 4c

Recommendation: for those readers that have little or no prior awareness of OTC derivatives or their associated trade processing or collateral processing, it is strongly recommended that prior to reading Chapters 46, 47 and 48, such readers firstly familiarise themselves with Part 4a 'OTC Derivatives and Collateral' which is covered by Chapters 14–45, as those chapters provide a solid foundation of understanding, enabling readers to relate to the regulatory changes.

DISCLAIMER

The EMIR regulations relating to OTC Derivatives cover a significant amount of text and may be regarded as challenging to follow. Aligned with the author's aim for the entire book, the author's intention regarding the three chapters covering the EMIR regulations is to describe such regulations using plain English and written in a manner that is understandable to an operations readership; furthermore, the scale of the EMIR regulations has necessitated the author selecting for inclusion within those chapters the parts of the regulations that impact operations and collateral management personnel to the greatest extent. It is important to note that these chapters represent condensed versions of selected EMIR regulations, and the full EMIR regulations can be found within the various European Commission documents.

46.1 INTRODUCTION

The *Global Financial Crisis* in the autumn of 2008 highlighted the need for far greater levels of regulation than had been the case previously, regarding the trading of and ongoing management of *OTC derivative* trades.

During 2009, the G20 (the Group of Twenty Finance Ministers and Central Bank governors representing the world's 20 major economies) agreed a set of target measures designed to bring far greater structure and transparency to the OTC derivative marketplace.

The regulatory reforms are being spearheaded in Europe under the banner of the *European Market Infrastructure Regulation* (EMIR), and in the US by Title VII of the wide-ranging *Dodd-Frank Act*. Similar reforms are occurring in other regions including Australia, China, Hong Kong, Japan, Republic of Korea and Singapore.

This chapter introduces the most significant of such regulatory measures. It is important to note that the implications of those measures are so far reaching on *collateral management* that this chapter contains information at an overview level only. The two chapters that follow this chapter will delve into significantly greater detail on the implications on collateral management.

46.2 THE NEED FOR REGULATORY CHANGE

The background to and the reasons for these highly significant regulatory changes are stated within the following two communications, namely the European Commission's press release in September 2010 and the summary of measures issued by the US Senate in July 2010.

The European Commission

Press Release – Brussels, 15 September 2010

Making derivatives markets in Europe safer and more transparent

As part of its ongoing work in creating a sounder financial system, the European Commission has tabled today a proposal for a regulation aimed at bringing more safety and more transparency to the over-the-counter (OTC) derivatives market. In its draft regulation, the Commission proposes that information on OTC derivative contracts should be reported to trade repositories and be accessible to supervisory authorities. More information will also be made available to all market participants. The Commission also proposes that standard OTC derivative contracts be cleared through central counterparties (CCPs). This will reduce counterparty credit risk, i.e. the risk that one party to the contract defaults. The Commission's proposal, fully in line with the EU's G20 commitments and the approach adopted by the United States, now passes to the European Parliament and the EU Member States for consideration. Once adopted, the regulation would apply from end 2012.

Michel Barnier, Commissioner for Internal Market and Services said: 'No financial market can afford to remain a Wild West territory. OTC derivatives have a big impact on the real economy: from mortgages to food prices. The absence of any regulatory framework for OTC derivatives contributed to the financial crisis and the tremendous consequences we are all suffering from. Today, we are proposing rules which will bring more transparency and responsibility to derivatives markets. So we know who is doing what, and who owes what to whom. As well as taking action so that single failures do not destabilise the whole financial system, as was the case with Lehman's collapse.'

Key elements of the proposal:

Greater transparency: Currently, reporting of OTC derivatives is not mandatory. As a result, policy makers, regulators but also market participants do not have a clear overview of what is going on in the market. Under the Commission's proposal, trades in OTC derivatives in the EU will have to be reported to central data centres, known as trade repositories. Regulators in the EU will have access to these repositories, enabling them to have a better overview of who owes what and to whom and to detect any potential problems, such as accumulation of risk, early on. Meanwhile, the new European Securities and Markets Authority (ESMA) will be responsible for the surveillance of trade repositories and for granting/withdrawing their registration. In addition, trade repositories will have to publish aggregate positions by class of derivatives to give all market participants a clearer view of the OTC derivatives market.

Greater safety – Reducing counterparty risks: Under the current situation, participants in the OTC derivatives market do not sufficiently mitigate counterparty credit risk, which refers to the risk of loss arising from one party not making the required payments when they are due. Under the Commission's proposal, OTC

(continued)

PART 4c

(*continued*)

derivatives that are standardised (i.e. they have met predefined eligibility criteria), such as a high level of liquidity, would have to be cleared through central counterparties (CCPs). CCPs are entities that interpose themselves between the two counterparties to a transaction and thus become the 'buyer to every seller', as well as the 'seller to every buyer'. This will prevent the situation where a collapse of one market participant causes the collapse of other market participants, thereby putting the entire financial system at risk. If a contract is not eligible and therefore not cleared by a CCP, different risk management techniques must be applied (such as requirements to hold more capital). As CCPs are to take on additional risks, they will be subject to stringent business conducts and harmonised organisational and prudential requirements to ensure their safety – such as internal governance rules, audit checks, greater requirements on capital etc.

Greater safety – Reducing operational risk: The OTC derivatives market allows for a high degree of flexibility in defining the economic and legal terms of contracts. As a consequence, there are a number of highly bespoke and complex contracts in the market that still require significant manual intervention in many stages of the processing. This increases operational risk, i.e. the risk of loss due to, for example, human error. The Commission's proposal requires market participants to measure, monitor and mitigate this risk, for example by using electronic means for confirming the terms of OTC derivative contracts.

Scope: The proposal applies to all types of OTC derivatives. It applies both to financial firms who use OTC derivatives but also to non-financial firms that have large positions in OTC derivatives. It also applies to CCPs and trade repositories. However, when non-financial firms (such as manufacturers) who use OTC derivatives to mitigate risk arising from their core business activities ('commercial hedging' used to protect against exchange rate variations for example), they are exempt from the CCP clearing requirements.

Background

A derivative is a contract between two parties linked to the future value or status of the underlying to which it refers (e.g. the development of interest rates or of a currency value, or the possible bankruptcy of a debtor). An over-the-counter (OTC) derivative is a derivative not traded on an exchange but instead privately negotiated between two counterparts. The use of derivatives has grown exponentially over the last decade, with OTC transactions being the main contributor to this growth. At the end of December 2009, the size of the OTC derivatives market by notional value equalled approximately $615 trillion, a 12% increase with respect to the end of 2008. However, this was still 10% lower than the peak reached in June 2008.

The near-collapse of Bear Sterns in March 2008, the default of Lehman Brothers on 15 September 2008 and the bail-out of AIG the following day started to highlight the shortcomings in the functioning of the OTC derivatives market, where 80% of derivatives are traded. In a Communication on Driving European Recovery from

March 2009, the European Commission committed to deliver, on the basis of a report on derivatives and other complex structured products, appropriate initiatives to increase transparency and to address financial stability concerns.

More information:
   http://ec.europa.eu/internal_market/financial-markets/derivatives/index_en.htm

DODD-FRANK WALL STREET REFORM

Bringing Transparency and Accountability to the Derivatives Market

SUMMARY

US federal statute signed into law by President Barack Obama on July 21, 2010

Closes Regulatory Gaps:
Provides the SEC and CFTC with authority to regulate over-the-counter derivatives so that irresponsible practices and excessive risk-taking can no longer escape regulatory oversight.

Central Clearing and Exchange Trading:
Requires central clearing and exchange trading for derivatives that can be cleared and provides a role for both regulators and clearing houses to determine which contracts should be cleared.

Market Transparency:
Requires data collection and publication through clearing houses or swap repositories to improve market transparency and provide regulators important tools for monitoring and responding to risks.

Financial safeguards:
Adds safeguards to system by ensuring dealers and major swap participants have adequate financial resources to meet responsibilities. Provides regulators the authority to impose capital and margin requirements on swap dealers and major swap participants, not end users.

Higher standard of conduct:
Establishes a code of conduct for all registered swap dealers and major swap participants when advising a swap entity. When acting as counterparties to a pension fund, endowment fund, or state or local government, dealers are to have a reasonable basis to believe that the fund or governmental entity has an independent representative advising them.

http://banking.senate.gov/public/_files/070110_Dodd_Frank_Wall_Street_Reform_comprehensive_summary_Final.pdf

PART 4c

46.3 REGULATORY CHANGES: INTRODUCTION

The regulatory authorities have introduced the concept of *standardised OTC derivative* trades. This means that it has been determined, by an appointed authority, which component parts of (for example) an *interest rate swap* (IRS) trade, or a *credit default swap* (CDS) trade, are considered to be the most common, and hence 'standard'. The execution of standardised trades provides a number of benefits to trading firms, including the *multilateral netting* of trades; please refer to Section 46.5 'Central Clearing: Overview' within this chapter, and Chapter 47 'OTC Derivatives and Collateral – Regulatory Change and the Future of Collateral – Centrally Cleared Trades'.

The 'headline' objectives of the regulatory authorities relating to standardised OTC derivative trades are that they should be:

- traded on exchanges or *electronic trading platforms*
- centrally cleared via *central counterparties*, and
- reported to *trade repositories.*

It will continue to be possible to execute trades that do not conform to the standardised model; these are known as *non-centrally cleared trades,* and the regulatory objectives for such trades are that they should be subject to rigorous collateral and *capital requirements*.

Note: subsequent to this chapter:

- Chapter 47 'OTC Derivatives and Collateral – Regulatory Change and the Future of Collateral – Centrally Cleared Trades', describes the collateral-related implications of standardised trades with central counterparties, and
- Chapter 48 'OTC Derivatives and Collateral – Regulatory Change and the Future of Collateral – Non-Centrally Cleared Trades' describes the regulatory requirements relating to collateral management of trades which have (for example) non-standardised features and are therefore executed on a *bilateral* basis.

46.4 EXCHANGES AND ELECTRONIC TRADING PLATFORMS: OVERVIEW

This section refers solely to the act of *trade execution* pertaining to OTC derivative trades, under the regulatory initiative.

Prior to the new regulations, all OTC derivative trades were *privately negotiated* and were traded *bilaterally*, meaning directly between the two trading parties; in all cases such trades were tailored to suit the needs of the involved parties. Usually, the details of each trade were held (throughout the trade's lifetime) only by the two trading parties, with no other party being aware of the trade, including regulatory authorities.

Conversely, other types of derivative products such as *futures* and *options* have had a standardised structure and therefore lend themselves to being traded on exchanges ('*Exchange-Traded Derivatives*' *(ETD)*). Within derivative exchanges, members of the exchange place *orders* (electronically) to execute trades in standardised products, directly with the exchange; the exchange attempts to find a match of that order with opposing orders received from other exchange members. If a match is found, the order has been fulfilled and a trade has been executed. (Similar concepts are applicable at many electronic *stock exchanges*.) The standardised nature of ETD products facilitates speedy and transparent trade execution between members of the exchange.

The historic tailoring of OTC derivative trades to suit the needs of the two involved parties has not been conducive to standardisation and has been a barrier to achieving trading of such products within derivative exchanges.

Today, standardisation of certain types of OTC derivative products does exist; examples of this are *single name credit default swaps* (SN-CDS) and *fixed/floating interest rate swaps*. For instance, within a year of autumn 2008, major steps had been taken to standardise SN-CDS via the *Big Bang Protocol*, leading to a range of benefits enjoyed by buyers, sellers (and regulators) throughout the trade's lifetime; a key change was the introduction of *fixed coupons* which facilitates *portfolio compression*, whereby multiple gross trades are compressed resulting in a net position which represents the original pre-compressed trades. Such net positions result in both counterparty risk being reduced, and position maintenance costs being lowered. (For further details, please refer to Chapter 30 'OTC Derivatives and Collateral – The Collateral Lifecycle – Post-Trading – Trade/Portfolio Netting'.)

As for the new trading measures being required by regulators in the US and in Europe, recent years have seen a considerable expansion in the labels given to electronic trading platforms; for example, '*swap execution facility*' is just one of a range of labels given to sites where trade execution occurs.

In order to keep such labels generic in this book, from this point forward all references to electronic trading platforms will be referred to as *trade execution venues* (TEVs).

The common theme and primary regulatory requirement amongst all TEVs is that they bring together electronically parties that wish to execute trades, as per Figure 46.1:

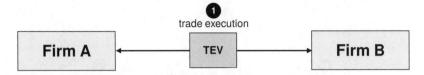

FIGURE 46.1 Trade execution via a trade execution venue

The types of firm permitted to participate directly with TEVs are banks (*sell-side* firms) and institutional investors (*buy-side* firms). As in the past, trades will continue to be executed:

- between sell-side firm and buy-side firm (dealer to client)
- between sell-side firm and sell-side firm (dealer to dealer).

Where a firm has executed an OTC derivative trade via a TEV, at trade execution the firm's counterparty will be, in some cases, a normal (bilateral) counterparty. In other cases, trades are executed via a TEV anonymously where, at trade execution, the firm's counterparty will be the TEV itself. Under the new measures, both trade execution methods will result in a trading firm's counterparty becoming the ***central counterparty***; see Section 46.5 'Central Clearing: Overview'.

Not all OTC derivative products are likely to be suited to electronic trading. The regulatory authorities (e.g. under EMIR, the ***European Securities and Markets Authority*** (ESMA)) must determine which OTC derivative types are subject to the mandatory trading requirement.

As trading is at the very start of the trade lifecycle, other measures being introduced such as ***central clearing*** and use of ***trade repositories*** should provide both pre-and post-trade transparency (and therefore a full audit trail) throughout the trade's lifetime, as required by the regulatory authorities.

46.5 CENTRAL CLEARING: OVERVIEW

Generically speaking, clearing is the process of managing exposures throughout the various steps through which a trade passes, from post-trade execution to pre-settlement, relating to trades in all financial products.

In the context of OTC derivative products, firstly central clearing pertains only to OTC derivative trades that are eligible for central clearing, whereby such trades executed via a trade execution venue (TEV) are of a standardised nature and are subsequently assigned to a central counterparty via the legal process of ***novation***, as depicted in Figure 46.2:

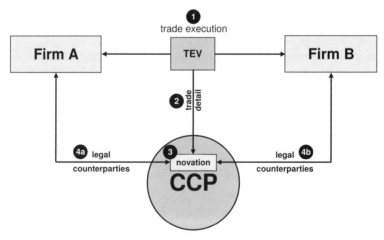

FIGURE 46.2   Post-execution, post-novation

The steps in the diagram are explained as follows:

Step 1: trade execution has occurred between two trading parties, via a TEV

Step 2: the TEV forwards the trade details to the appropriate CCP

Step 3: the CCP assesses the trade details and clearing limits, and (if accepted) the trade is novated

Step 4: novation results in two trades: 1) CCP versus Firm A, and 2) CCP versus Firm B.

This results in Firm A's counterparty being updated from 'Firm B' to the 'central counterparty' (*CCP*), meaning that the firm's ongoing exposure for the particular trade is with the CCP and not with Firm B.

(Note that, in addition to the OTC derivative product being subject to the *clearing obligation*, for a trade to be accepted by the CCP both the original trading parties must be subject to the clearing obligation under EMIR; this is described within Chapter 47 'OTC Derivatives and Collateral – Regulatory Change and the Future of Collateral – Centrally Cleared Trades'. If a party is not subject to the clearing obligation, the trade will not be centrally cleared unless that party voluntarily chooses to centrally clear the trade; otherwise the trade must be *bilaterally* cleared.)

Novation occurs from the perspective of both original trading parties; therefore, the ongoing counterparty from the perspective of Firm B is the same CCP. The CCP therefore interposes itself between the original trading parties; it becomes the seller to every buyer, and the buyer to every seller, thus eliminating traditional bilateral counterparty *exposures*.

It is important to note that before a trade is executed, a TEV must ensure that the trade is able to be cleared 1) by a particular CCP, and 2) on behalf of both parties to the trade. For this to occur, each party to the trade must:

- be a holder of a direct account at the particular CCP, namely
  - a '*clearing member*', or
- have use of *client clearing* services provided by a clearing member at the particular CCP, namely
  - a '*non-clearing member*' (sometimes referred to as 'indirect clearing member').

Following novation, central clearing involves the CCP managing trades, positions, collateral and the elimination of all risks. The CCP must remain *market risk neutral* at all times, meaning it must never take a position in an OTC derivative product for its own account, as, although the CCP will become counterparty in many thousands of trades, each pair of trades is offsetting, thereby leaving the CCP with a zero position.

A particular CCP is the focal point for many (if not all) eligible trades in a particular OTC derivative product; consequently one of the primary benefits of central clearing is that a firm that executes multiple buy and sell trades is likely to benefit from *multilateral netting*. Historically, if Firm T executed two purchases and one sale in the same OTC derivative product, with each of the three trades being executed with different bilateral counterparties, the netting of trades would not have been an option (as netting is achievable only with the same counterparty). Given the same three trades under a central clearing environment, Firm T's sole counterparty will be the CCP, and as such the CCP is in a position to see both sides of each trade it processes, meaning that Firm T could benefit greatly through the three individual trades being represented by a single (net) trade.

To extend those three example trades executed by Firm T, in the following table four parties execute a total of five trades bilaterally (refer to columns 1 to 5), followed by the effect of multilateral netting as would occur at a CCP (refer to columns 6 and 7):

TABLE 46.1   Multilateral netting at a central counterparty

Multilateral Netting at a Central Counterparty: Example						
1	2	3	4	5	6	7
Trade #	Firm	Cpty	Purchased	Sold	New Cpty	Net
1a	T	U	40m			+50m
2a		V	20m			
3a		W		10m		
1b	U	T		40m		-20m
4a		W	20m			
2b	V	T		20m		0
5a		W	20m			
3b	W	T	10m			-30m
4b		U		20m		
5b		V		20m		
					Total Net	0

(New Cpty column throughout: Central Counterparty)

Explanation of the table's content: following novation to the CCP, the CCP's multilateral netting process results in three firms each having a net position with the CCP, while the fourth firm (Firm V) has a zero net position. The CCP maintains a 'matched book' of offsetting trades resulting in the CCP having a post-netting position of zero, thereby remaining market risk neutral.

To take the CCP multilateral netting concept to a more detailed level, in the case (for example) of credit default swaps (CDS), an individual firm's trades would need to meet the following criteria in order for netting to occur on such trades:

- trades must belong to the same trading entity (e.g. Firm T), and
- trades must relate to the same *reference entity* (e.g. France Telecom), and

PART 4c

- trades must have the same *scheduled maturity date* (e.g. 20th June 2030), and
- trades must have the same *fixed coupon* (e.g. 100 *bppa*).

For a description of CDS, please refer to Chapter 17 'OTC Derivatives and Collateral – Transaction Types – Credit Default Swaps'.

Central counterparties are companies (not government utilities) which must be authorised to act in the role of CCP. It is therefore possible that for a particular OTC derivative product (e.g. interest rate swaps), two or more CCPs may be providing central clearing services in a particular geographic region. It is also possible that a single CCP may choose to focus on particular types of OTC derivative product (e.g. credit default swaps), but not other types (e.g. cross-currency swaps).

In summary, central clearing of OTC derivatives *mitigates* the traditional bilateral *counterparty risk* whilst reinforcing integrity of the market for investors and other participants. Additionally, centrally managed *trade processing* and *collateral processing* throughout the trade's lifetime is regarded as a benefit for all concerned. Furthermore, such high levels of transparency provide regulators with the ability to closely monitor new trades and existing positions.

Significantly greater detail of central clearing is provided within Chapter 47 'OTC Derivatives and Collateral – Regulatory Change and the Future of Collateral – Centrally Cleared Trades'.

46.6 TRADE REPOSITORIES: INTRODUCTION

A trade repository (TR) is in essence an electronic 'warehouse' for the storage and safekeeping of the details (terms) of individual OTC derivative trades and positions. TRs maintain details of trades reported to them by, or on behalf of, the parties to the trade. Regulatory authorities will access such trade information held by TRs in order to carry out their regulatory oversight responsibilities.

46.6.1 Reporting of Centrally Cleared Trades

Where trades have been novated to a CCP, the parties to each trade are 1) the CCP, and 2) one of the original parties to the trade. Trade details include both individual trades (not netted) and net positions resulting from multilateral netting by CCPs. As OTC derivative trades may have a tenor of (for example) up to 50 years, the ongoing maintenance of accurate and formal trade records is paramount.

As a party to a centrally cleared OTC derivative trade, the CCP has a reporting obligation. The CCP's counterparty (e.g. Firm A) also has a reporting obligation. Firm A is able to choose the method by which its trade is reported to the TR; Firm A may report directly to the TR or delegate the reporting task to the CCP. However, Firm A remains responsible for ensuring its trade details are received by the TR.

The flow of information by which a TR receives details of centrally cleared OTC derivative trades in which Firm A has delegated reporting to the CCP is depicted in Figure 46.3:

PART 4c

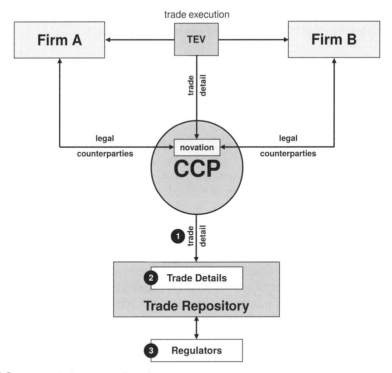

FIGURE 46.3   Central clearing and trade repositories

The steps in the diagram are explained as follows:

Step 1: the CCP sends a single electronic message containing trade details (for itself and for Firm A) to the TR

Step 2: the trade repository stores trade details using electronic records

Step 3: for regulatory oversight purposes, trade details are accessed by regulatory authorities.

In order to maintain direct control over reporting of trades, many of the larger trading (typically *sell-side*) firms that execute OTC derivative trades in greater volumes than other firms have developed their own reporting software systems. Firms executing lower volumes of CCP-eligible trades are more likely to delegate reporting to the CCP.

Similar to central counterparties, trade repositories are companies (not government utilities) which must be authorised to act in the role of TR. It is possible that a single TR receives trade details from one or more CCPs.

46.6.2 Reporting of Non-Centrally Cleared Trades

Where a firm executes a trade directly with a traditional counterparty (and the trade is not novated to a CCP), such trades are labelled '*non-centrally cleared*' or 'bilaterally cleared'.

(Note: the reasons why some trades are not centrally cleared are described within Chapter 48 'OTC Derivatives and Collateral – Regulatory Change and the Future of Collateral – Non-Centrally Cleared Trades' and include reasons such as the trade components being non-standard.)

For all such bilaterally cleared trades, the responsibility for reporting of trade details to the TR remains with each trading firm, and this direct reporting situation is depicted in Figure 46.4:

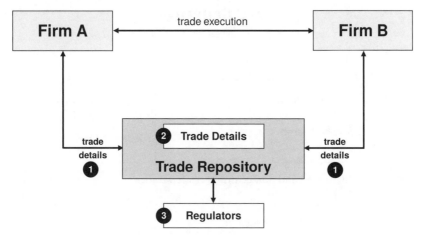

FIGURE 46.4   Bilateral clearing and trade repositories

It is important to note that both parties to a bilaterally cleared trade are responsible for ensuring that the details of each executed trade reach the TR. For example, a trade executed and cleared bilaterally between an ***investment bank*** and an ***institutional investor*** requires both the ***sell-side*** firm and the ***buy-side*** firm to report their trades to the TR. If the buy-side firm does not have the necessary infrastructure to action the reporting itself, that firm may enter into an arrangement whereby reporting is delegated to the sell-side firm, who would then report to the TR for both parties.

One of the most important regulatory measures is the requirement for regulators to have direct access to OTC derivative trade information, from a market transparency and oversight perspective. Through the integrity of their trade records, TRs will provide such information or make it available for retrieval by regulators.

Note: it must be re-emphasised that a trading firm is ultimately responsible for ensuring that the details of 100% of trades it executes are reported to a TR. As mentioned earlier, for trades which are centrally cleared, the CCP will pass gross or net trade details to the TR, on behalf of (and if required by) the trading firm. For trades which are not subject to central clearing ('non-centrally cleared' trades), it remains the responsibility of the trading firm to ensure trade details are sent to the TR; this may be achieved by direct reporting for which transmission options are available, including trade reporting services offered by some consulting firms.

At the time of writing, the reporting process within buy-side and sell-side firms is relatively new and will be improved by the future introduction of reconciliations to ensure the trade/position data reported to TRs is complete.

46.7 CENTRALLY CLEARED AND NON-CENTRALLY CLEARED TRADES

Under the regulatory initiative, each OTC derivative trade must be either centrally cleared via a central counterparty or be treated as non-centrally cleared with a traditional (bilateral) counterparty (see Figure 46.5).

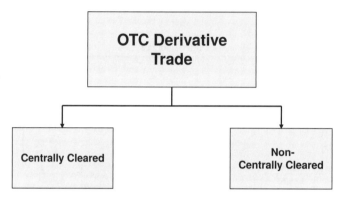

FIGURE 46.5   Centrally cleared and non-centrally cleared trades

The following two chapters describe:

1. for centrally cleared trades (see Chapter 47):
   a. the typical structure of CCPs and regulatory requirements pertaining to firms as both clearing members and non-clearing members
2. for non-centrally cleared trades (Chapter 48):
   a. the regulatory requirements for firms having trades with traditional bilateral counterparties.

OTC Derivatives and Collateral – Regulatory Change and the Future of Collateral – Centrally Cleared Trades

This chapter provides a description of central clearing of OTC derivative trades, possibly the most significant of the many regulatory reforms introduced as a result of the 2008 Global Financial Crisis; the introduction of mandatory central clearing has an extremely important impact on the post-trade processing of OTC derivatives, and the management of exposures and collateral in particular.

Please note: many aspects of the regulatory reforms are extremely technical in nature, consequently the descriptions of the regulatory concepts and related practices are intended to be suitable for an operations readership.

Further note: the chapter which follows this chapter describes non-centrally cleared trades.

Recommendation: for those readers that have little or no prior awareness of OTC derivatives or their associated trade processing or collateral processing, it is strongly recommended that prior to reading Chapters 46, 47 and 48, they firstly familiarise themselves with Part 4a 'OTC Derivatives and Collateral' which is covered by Chapters 14–45, as those chapters provide a solid foundation of understanding enabling readers to relate to the regulatory changes.

DISCLAIMER

The EMIR regulations relating to OTC derivatives cover a significant amount of text and may be regarded as challenging to follow. Aligned with the author's aim for the entire book, the author's intention regarding the three chapters covering the EMIR

(continued)

(continued)

regulations is to describe such regulations using plain English and written in a manner that is relevant to an operations readership; furthermore, the scale of the EMIR regulations has necessitated the author selecting for inclusion within those chapters the parts of the regulations that impact operations and collateral management personnel to the greatest extent. It is important to note that these chapters represent condensed versions of selected EMIR regulations, and the full EMIR regulations can be found within the various European Commission documents.

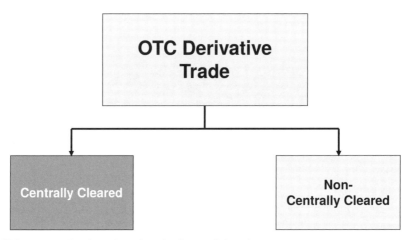

FIGURE 47.1   Centrally cleared trades: the focus of this chapter

47.1 INTRODUCTION

The highly publicised *Global Financial Crisis* in the autumn of 2008 highlighted the need for far greater levels of regulation and transparency regarding the trading and ongoing management of *OTC derivative* trades, on a global basis.

During 2009, the G20 (the Group of Twenty Finance Ministers and Central Bank governors representing the world's 20 major economies) agreed a set of target measures designed to bring far greater structure and transparency to the OTC derivative marketplace.

The regulatory reforms are being spearheaded in Europe by the *European Market Infrastructure Regulation* (EMIR), and in the US by Title VII of the wide-ranging *Dodd-Frank Act*. Similar reforms are occurring in other regions including Australia, China, Hong Kong, Japan, Republic of Korea and Singapore.

The introduction of *mandatory central clearing* of *standardised OTC derivative trades* involves each firm utilising the services provided by a *central counterparty* (CCP).

47.2 FUNDAMENTAL CENTRAL COUNTERPARTY CONCEPTS

The CCP becomes the common counterparty to all market participants, for all trades eligible for *central clearing* by the CCP. Such trades are standardised trades in that their features and components fall within predefined parameters for the particular type of OTC derivative product.

(Trades executed with features and components that are not classified as standard are not eligible for central clearing and must be managed on a bilateral basis with a traditional (bilateral) counterparty; see Chapter 48 'OTC Derivatives and Collateral – Regulatory Change and the Future of Collateral – Non-Centrally Cleared Trades'.)

To emphasise an important concept highlighted in the previous chapter, it is essential to remember that all CCPs must remain *'market risk neutral'*; this means that the CCP must never take a position for its own account under any circumstances. For example, when a trade has been executed between Party A and Party N, following which that trade is *novated* to the CCP:

- where Party A is the buyer, the CCP will become the seller, and
- where Party N is the seller, the CCP will become the buyer.

Therefore, once the original trade is novated to the CCP, the CCP is both a buyer and a seller of offsetting trades, leaving the CCP with a zero position.

In the past a firm (e.g. Party A) executing numerous OTC derivative trades may well have executed each trade with a different counterparty, as per Figure 47.2:

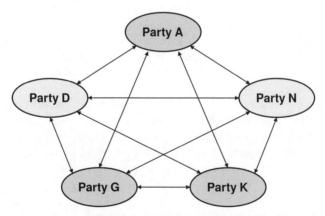

FIGURE 47.2   Bilateral trading and bilateral clearing

From a *collateral management* perspective, the (say) daily *mark-to-market* process would mean that Party A would be calculating *exposures* and potentially giving collateral to, or taking collateral from, each of the counterparties.

By comparison, in the central clearing world, those same trades (providing they were classified as standardised) would be executed with the same counterparties, but each trade would be *novated* to the CCP, as per Figure 47.3:

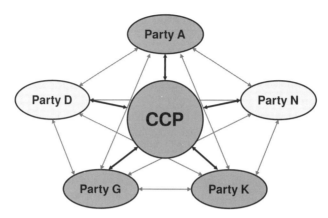

FIGURE 47.3   Bilateral trading and central clearing

From a collateral management perspective, the CCP would mark-to-market each of Party A's trades at least once per day (possibly multiple times per day), which would lead to Party A needing to give collateral to, or receive collateral from, the CCP.

When comparing the (historic) bilateral situation to the centrally cleared situation:

- bilaterally cleared:
  - a reasonably active firm could quite easily have (at least) hundreds of concurrent live OTC derivative trades that are validly outstanding over many years, with numerous counterparties
    - collateral management of such a situation would cause a large degree of human and system resources to *mitigate* the firm's risk with the various counterparties (and vice versa), on a daily basis, for the duration of each trade
- centrally cleared:
  - given the same trades (as executed above under a bilaterally cleared scenario), and providing that all such trades were executed with standard features, the firm's counterparty could be one single central counterparty
    - collateral management of such a situation could be with just one CCP, on a daily basis, for the duration of each trade.

47.3 CENTRAL COUNTERPARTY OPERATION AND SERVICES

Generically, CCPs provide the following services relating to OTC derivatives:

- product processing:
  - standardised product *trade processing* and *collateral processing*

- clearing:
  - novation of trades originally executed on a bilateral basis
  - identifying the financial obligations of trade parties
- trade netting:
  - wherever possible, reducing multiple gross trade obligations to a single net obligation through *multilateral netting*
- risk mitigation:
  - potential future exposures are mitigated via the CCP's risk assessment and resultant '*initial margin*' calls
  - current exposures are mitigated via the CCP's *marking-to-market* process and resultant '*variation margin*' calls
  - *clearing members* are required to contribute towards the CCP's *default fund*; in the event of *default* by any clearing member of the CCP, the default fund can be utilised to offset losses incurred by the defaulting member
    - Note: not all firms that execute trades in OTC derivatives will become clearing members of a CCP, requiring such firms to appoint a clearing member to act on its behalf at the CCP. Where a clearing member offers such *client clearing* services to its clients (usually *buy-side* firms), the CCP will not require the buy-side firm to contribute default funds, although the clearing member may attempt to recover a portion of its default fund contribution from its client(s).

47.4 CENTRAL CLEARING: ADVANTAGES & DISADVANTAGES

In general terms, the advantages that CCPs provide are:

- reduced counterparty risk:
  - a firm's counterparty becomes the CCP rather than a traditional (bilateral) counterparty; the CCP is generally regarded as a safer counterparty than a traditional counterparty
- net positions rather than multiple gross trades:
  - multilateral netting results in netting of exposures and net payments and receipts
- increased market integrity:
  - greater transparency as market activity and exposures are available to regulators.

Additionally, from the perspective of a firm that holds positions in CCP-eligible OTC derivatives, an advantage is that the firm needs to assess the creditworthiness of the CCP only, rather than the creditworthiness of all other bilateral trading parties with whom they would otherwise trade, and that all post-trade processing is conducted only with the CCP, including collateral management.

Conversely, it can be observed that the disadvantages of CCPs are that:

- initial margin is payable, compared with no equivalent under *legacy trades* executed bilaterally
- the *margin call* settlement period is shorter, compared with legacy trades executed bilaterally
- margin calls must be settled, compared with legacy bilateral arrangements in which a party in receipt of a margin call is able to dispute the call amount.

A trading party's risk does not vanish when having exposure with a CCP. As a firm's total exposure in a specific OTC derivative product could be with one particular CCP, a fundamental shortcoming is that of the CCP's potential failure.

47.5 CENTRAL COUNTERPARTY MEMBERSHIP AND NON-MEMBERSHIP

Some firms that trade in CCP-eligible OTC derivative products will choose to become members of a CCP, while others will choose not to do so.

Those firms that choose to become a member of a CCP are required to apply to the CCP; the CCP will assess the suitability of such firms before deciding whether the firm's application is successful. The CCP's assessment will include the applicant's:

- levels of available capital
- operational/administrative proficiency
- technical competency, and
- risk management capabilities.

Successful applicants remain subject to periodic monitoring by the CCP to ensure ongoing compliance with the CCP's various requirements.

The commonly used terms relating to membership (or otherwise) of CCPs are:

- Clearing members (CMs):
  - those firms that clear their own trades over their own account at the CCP
    - the majority of clearing members are typically *sell-side* firms
- Non-clearing members (NCMs):
  - those firms that choose not to become a CM will need to appoint a CM in order for their trades to be cleared at the CCP; from the CM's perspective this is known as client clearing
    - the majority of NCMs are typically buy-side firms and the smaller sell-side firms
    - NCMs are also known as 'indirect clearing members'.

NCMs are permitted to partake indirectly in the clearing of their trades via their appointed CM. Such an arrangement requires the NCM and the CM to sign the CCP's relevant legal agreement prior to the NCM being authorised to have their trades cleared by the CM. To clarify, NCMs are not permitted to clear their trades directly at the CCP, as the NCM does not hold the status of CM; only CMs are permitted to clear trades at the CCP. Furthermore, only a CM can be the CCP's counterparty in any particular transaction; legal relationships are between the CCP and a CM, and in turn between the CM and the NCM.

From the perspective of a CM, the accounts they hold at the CCP are:

- a house account, through which the firm's own trades (member clearing) will be processed
- client account(s), through which clients' trades (client clearing) will be processed (if the clearing member chooses to provide a client clearing service).

Note: Figures 47.4 and 47.5 depict use of CM's accounts at a CCP, following novation.

PART 4c

47.5.1 Clearing Member Accounts at the Central Counterparty

Figure 47.4 represents a situation in which both original parties to a trade are clearing members:

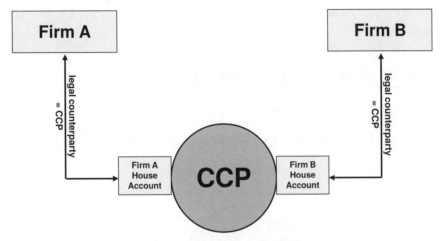

FIGURE 47.4 In this example, both parties to a trade are clearing members at the CCP

For clearing members, the activity that follows *trade execution* and *novation* (which will be described shortly) involves the CCP communicating directly with each CM.

47.5.2 Client Clearing Accounts at the Central Counterparty

Those firms choosing not to become a CM will need to set up a relationship with a CM who will clear trades on their behalf at the CCP. This situation is depicted in Figure 47.5, in which Firm C is a client of clearing member Firm M (whilst Firm A is a clearing member):

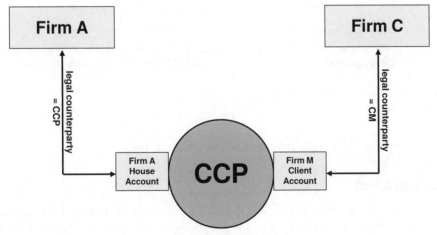

FIGURE 47.5 Firm A is a clearing member, whilst Firm C is a client of a clearing member

For non-clearing members, the activity that follows trade execution and novation (which will be described shortly) involves the CCP communicating directly with each CM. To clarify, for any trade activity over the CM's client account(s), the CCP will communicate only with the CM (and not with the client of the CM).

Further detail regarding the types of client account provided by CMs is covered within this chapter under Section 47.9 'Clearing Members and their Clients: Account Structures'.

47.6 CLEARING MEMBER MARGIN REQUIREMENTS

The risk management practised by CCPs includes both trade-related exposures and non-trade-related exposures, as per Figure 47.6. Non-trade-related exposures relate to default funds, whilst trade-related exposures consist of both initial margin and variation margin.

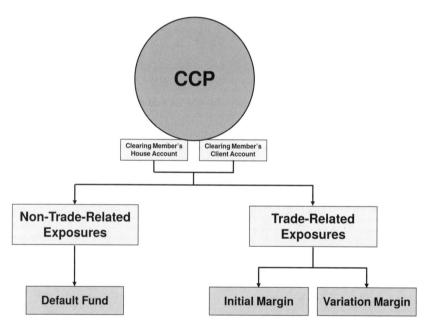

FIGURE 47.6 Clearing member margin requirements

All three types of margin are explained in what follows.

47.6.1 Default Funds

CMs are required to post collateral to the CCP's default fund; this is also known as a guarantee fund or clearing deposit and is a mandatory requirement. Over and above a minimum contribution, all CMs are required to maintain appropriate guarantee fund deposits at the CCP based upon their risk profile and historic trading volumes; a CM's risk profile is subject to periodic re-examination by the CCP.

Default funds are payable by each CM as their contribution towards the aggregate fund shared amongst the CMs and the CCP; this sharing is known as *mutualisation*. Default funds given by a CM are retained (held) by the CCP; such funds are not passed to any other CM, as depicted in Figure 47.7.

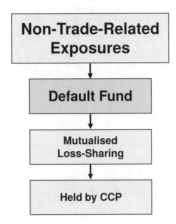

FIGURE 47.7   Default fund contributions

In the event of *default* by any CM, the CCP inherits that party's positions and attempts closeout of such positions (in order for the CCP to re-establish its *market risk neutral* position) through hedging or selling with the remaining (non-defaulting) clearing members, involving an auction process. If the defaulting CM is in a loss-making situation at the CCP, and if the CM's previously contributed initial margin (see next section) fails to cover the loss, the CCP will utilise a portion of the default fund to overcome the loss incurred.

A CM's default fund contribution may be payable as collateral to a CCP in an eligible currency or by delivery of eligible securities. Eligible securities are very likely to include bonds issued by a defined list of governments, which are of a minimum rating, and *residual maturity* will be applied in order to determine an appropriate *haircut*.

47.6.2 Initial Margin

Once a trade has been novated to the CCP (whether over the CM's house account or client account), the CM will receive a margin call from the CCP to provide initial margin (IM). IM is designed to protect the CCP against the maximum estimated loss (potential future change in the value of a trade),as depicted in Figure 47.8.

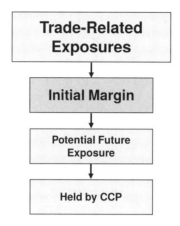

FIGURE 47.8   Initial margin

The amount of IM called by the CCP is dependent upon the complexity and tenor of the particular trade.

For non-clearing members (NCMs), it is important to note that the legal agreement between a CCP and the clearing member (CM) can be replicated between the CM and the NCM; such an agreement between CM and NCM is independent of the agreement between CCP and CM. Consequently, the posting of IM by the CM to satisfy the CCP's margin call is entirely separate and is not dependent upon the posting of IM by the NCM to the CM.

Many (if not all) CCPs require IM to be settled in either cash in a specified currency or highly liquid *securities* (e.g. AAA rated government bonds). IM is likely to be a one-off and up-front payment; however, over the course of time, it is possible that the CCP's IM calculations show that further IM is required from the CM.

Securities collateral given to satisfy an IM call will be subject to haircut (see Chapter 22 'OTC Derivatives and Collateral – Legal Protection – Credit Support Annex'). This has the impact of reducing the *current market value* of a security to its *current collateral value*, the applicable haircut rate being determined by a number of factors, including:

- *bond* type; e.g. *fixed rate, floating rate, zero coupon*
- *issuer* type; e.g. government, government agency, corporate
- *residual maturity*; the number of years from 'today' until the bond's *maturity date*. As a general rule, the shorter the residual maturity the lower the perceived risk and therefore the smaller the haircut percentage.

It is important to note that the current collateral value (as opposed to current market value) of collateral given must be at least equal to the IM required by the CCP. Securities received by the CCP as IM will be held by the CCP and can be liquidated to cover any loss suffered by the CCP in closing out the trade in the event that the CM defaults. CCPs are not permitted to *reuse* securities collateral received from CMs.

Under the central clearing model, the requirement for IM to be paid will be, for many market participants, an additional requirement from the traditional collateral requirement in the bilateral world, as historically only variation margin would have been payable. This is discussed further within the *collateral transformation* section of this chapter.

47.6.3 Variation Margin

In parallel with IM, once a trade has been novated to the CCP, the CM is required to provide or to receive variation margin (VM). Unlike IM, VM relates to current *exposures* of trades, and is calculated from the *mark-to-market* (MTM) process conducted by the CCP. CMs may choose to MTM their positions independently in order to validate the CCP's margin calls.

The frequency of the CCP's MTM and subsequent margin calls may vary greatly between different CCPs, for example ranging from once per day (at end of day) to multiple times per day (intraday).

VM is designed to protect the CM with a *positive exposure*. Protection is achieved by the CCP making a margin call on the CM with a *negative exposure*, and once settled the CCP passes the value of the margin call to the CM with the positive exposure.

VM given by a CM is not held by the CCP but is passed through to the CM with the positive exposure, as depicted in Figure 47.9.

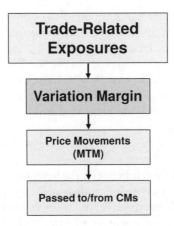

FIGURE 47.9 Variation margin

All CCPs are likely to require VM in the form of cash only, as VM must be highly *liquid* and *fungible* for it to be passed speedily between different CMs. Under normal circumstances, each CM is expected to *pre-fund* and hold adequate cash balances at its account(s) with the CCP, in order to facilitate the CCP accessing VM funds without delay. If inadequate funds are available in a CM's account to meet a margin call, the CM will be issued with a deadline for providing funds; if such deadlines are missed, the CM is at risk of being declared in default. Cash balances held by CMs at the CCP may attract some level of credit interest, dependent upon the particular CCP and the CM involved.

47.7 INITIAL MARGIN AND VARIATION MARGIN: IMPACT ON SELL-SIDE AND BUY-SIDE FIRMS

The CCPs' requirement to receive VM in the form of cash only (see Sub-section 47.6.3 'Variation Margin') will prove a significant challenge for some firms, and less of a challenge to others. The business models of different types of firm have different implications in this regard, for example:

- some *investment banks* may execute high volumes of OTC derivative trades, but due to their non-directional (offsetting) trading strategy, they typically sell what they buy and buy what they sell; this normally results in a zero position in a particular OTC derivative product. Under the CCP model, this trading strategy lends itself to high levels of netting at the CCP, meaning that (for a fully offset position at the same CCP) such firms will not be called for trade-related margin (neither IM nor VM)
- some buy-side firms (e.g. *mutual funds*) execute relatively low volumes of OTC derivative trades, but due to their directional (non-offsetting) trading strategy, they often hold what they buy; this typically results in a positive position in a particular OTC derivative product. Under the CCP model, this trading strategy does not lend itself to netting at the CCP, meaning that such firms will be called for trade-related margin (both IM and VM).

Firms having directional strategies are therefore unlikely to benefit from CCP trade netting. Any firm that conducts its OTC derivative business currently using a directional strategy, and that continues to operate in a similar manner in the central clearing environment, is likely to be extremely busy with managing IM and VM calls from its CM.

Where a firm holds little or no cash, where most or all investable funds have been invested in securities (primarily equity and bonds), for IM purposes such securities may or may not be CCP-eligible. Buy-side firms that hold highly rated government bonds may well find that such bonds are CCP-eligible, for IM purposes. Where a firm holds bonds issued by other issuer types, for example corporate bonds, such bonds are less likely to be CCP-eligible for IM purposes.

Where a firm has a poor match between the assets it owns and CCP-eligible assets, the process of collateral transformation is designed to supply the necessary collateral to the firm. From the sell-side perspective, the transformation of collateral for buy-side firms provides banks with the opportunity to offer a much-needed service to their clients. See Section 47.18 'Collateral Transformation' within this chapter.

47.8 CLEARING MEMBER REQUIREMENTS: OVERVIEW

For those firms wishing to become a clearing member (CM), becoming a CM will (or may) involve a range of activities:

- satisfying membership criteria; the CCP will evaluate applicants to ensure they meet joining criteria, such as minimum capital requirements and operational capability
- providing *default funds* to the CCP (see Sub-section 47.6.1 'Default Funds')

PART 4c

- performing *self-clearing*; the firm clears its own (proprietary) trades
- performing *client clearing* (if offered by the CM); the firm clears trades executed by its clients
- providing intraday *initial margin* (IM) and *variation margin* (VM) to the CCP, whether related to self-clearing and/or client clearing
- maintaining adequate VM levels at the CCP; when needing to call for VM the CCP would ideally have instant access to the CMs *pre-funded* account(s)
- modelling pre-trade margin calculations; the provision to clients of indicative costs of executing a particular trade
- validating the CCP's margin calculations; the firm is likely to want to satisfy itself that the CCP's *margin calls* are aligned with its own calculations
- calling clients for margin; for clients' trades, the calls received from the CCP will need to be mirrored to the client
- providing *collateral transformation* services to clients (see Section 47.18 'Collateral Transformation')
- reporting to *trade repositories* for both its own trading activity and on behalf of clients (if required)
- generating reports and trade-related information for clients, which are presented via a client portal or delivered via *S.W.I.F.T.* or email.

47.9 CLEARING MEMBERS AND THEIR CLIENTS: ACCOUNT STRUCTURES

The CCP has direct relationships only with clearing members (CMs); where a CM provides *client clearing* services, only the CM has direct relationships with its clients. It therefore follows that only the CM is responsible for responding to *margin calls* from the CCP. From the CM's perspective, for client business, the arrangements for mirroring such calls to its clients are a matter purely for the CM and the client; this is of no concern to the CCP.

Each CM that offers client clearing services provides its clients with fundamental choices as to how the client's OTC derivative positions and associated assets are held at the CCP, for example:

- omnibus client segregated account
  - a single account at the CCP within which positions and assets belonging to a particular client of the CM are *commingled* with positions and assets belonging to one or more other clients of the CM that have selected the omnibus client segregated account structure
- individual client segregated account
  - a single account at the CCP within which the positions and assets belonging to a particular client of the CM are held in a segregated fashion from the positions and assets of any other client of the CM.

It is important to note that the positions and assets that relate to the CM's own account are held within the CM's 'house' account at the CCP, and such positions and assets are therefore held at the CCP in a legally segregated account from those of the CM's clients.

PART 4c

The subject of client account structures offered by CMs is a legal and involved topic, the detail of which is beyond the scope of this book.

It should also be noted that the CCP will not perform netting of any client's positions and assets with those held within the CM's house account. Likewise, the CCP will not net positions and assets of clients which are held within an omnibus client segregated account, with those held within an individual client segregated account. However, the CCP is permitted to net positions and assets held within an omnibus client segregated account.

It is emphasised that the types of client account described above are fundamental choices only; different CMs may choose to offer a range of client account variations which may involve a mixture of account features and attributes.

A representative example of a CM's structure of accounts at a CCP is depicted in Figure 47.10:

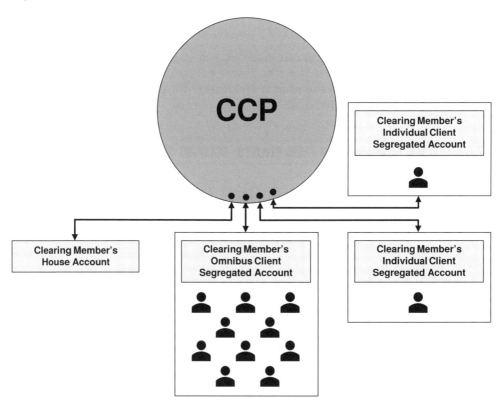

FIGURE 47.10 Possible structure of a clearing member's domain of accounts at a CCP

As the diagram shows, it is possible that:

- multiple clients opt for the omnibus client segregated account structure, and that
- one (or more) of the CM's clients may opt for an individual client segregated account.

47.9.1 Eligible Collateral

As described previously in this chapter under *initial margin* (IM) and *variation margin* (VM), CCPs will accept cash in specified currencies (both IM and VM) but only *securities* collateral in the form of highly rated government bonds (for IM) and not at all for VM.

For IM and VM calls made by the CCP to the CM relating to clients' OTC derivative *exposures*, the CM will in turn call for margin from clients. Each CM will determine the types of assets acceptable from its clients; such assets may be directly aligned with those required by the CCP, or the CM may allow its clients to provide a broader range of assets than is accepted by the CCP. Where a CM decides to accept a broader range of assets from clients to cover the CCP's margin calls, the CM may additionally provide a service to convert such assets received from clients into *CCP-eligible assets*; such a service is commonly known as *collateral transformation*. *Securities lending & borrowing* is one method by which a CM may transform collateral received from clients into assets accepted by a CCP; for details, please refer to Part 3 'Securities Lending & Borrowing and Collateral'.

47.9.2 Clearing Member Default: Handling Client's Assets

The primary significance of how the CM's client chooses to hold its positions and assets is realised if and when the CCP declares the CM to be in *default*. Under such circumstances, the CCP is required to transfer the positions and assets to a specific non-defaulting CM, generically known as a *backup clearing member* (BUCM), providing the client has appointed such a firm; the act of transferring positions and assets to the BUCM is known as *porting*. If the client has not appointed a BUCM, the CCP is required to either return the relevant positions and assets to the client directly, or to terminate any outstanding OTC derivative trades.

Where a client's original CM is declared in default by the CCP, the extent of segregation of the client's positions and assets (based upon the type of account) previously chosen by the client will impact whether porting to a BUCM is achievable, or not. For example, if the client in question has previously chosen to utilise the original CM's omnibus client segregated account, in the event of default by that CM, all of the CM's clients that utilise the omnibus client segregated account may (or will) need to agree to port their positions and assets to the same BUCM. Furthermore, the particular BUCM has the power to accept or to reject the entirety of positions and assets held within the omnibus client segregated account. Conversely, if a client has previously set up an individual client segregated account with the original CM, it will be the client's sole decision as to which BUCM to have their positions and assets ported to.

Following a CM's default, CCPs are allowed to stipulate a deadline by which a client's positions and assets must be ported to a BUCM, before the CCP takes action to mitigate its risk by terminating outstanding OTC derivative trades. Under such circumstances the termination value will be remitted to the client. Such deadlines are likely to vary from CCP to CCP.

47.10 THE CLEARING OBLIGATION

The term 'clearing obligation' refers to:

- those market participants that are required to clear their trades via CCPs, and
- those OTC derivative products that are required to be cleared via CCPs.

47.10.1 European Union (EU) Market Participants Subject to the Clearing Obligation: Overview

The clearing obligation relating to market participants is an involved subject in its own right. The intention of this part of the chapter is to provide an overview of which categories of EU market participants are required to centrally clear their trades, and which are not. Significantly greater detail is available on the website of ESMA (European Securities and Markets Authority).

The obligation for an EU firm to clear its OTC derivative trades via a central counterparty (CCP) is applicable providing the firm and its original counterparty are <u>both</u> subject to clearing their trades via a central counterparty.

CCPs must remain ***market risk neutral*** and it is therefore essential that the CCP becomes counterparty to both the original parties; with this in mind however, it is important to note that some firms are either temporarily or permanently exempt from the ***clearing obligation***. If one party (or both parties) to a trade is exempt from the clearing obligation, that fact will prevent the trade being centrally cleared, although the option exists for exempt parties to centrally clear their trades on a voluntary basis.

The clearing obligation is pertinent to all OTC derivative trades executed between any two EU parties that are classified as either 1) ***financial counterparties***, or 2) ***non-financial counterparties*** that surpass a defined ***clearing threshold***. Under ***EMIR***, these two party classifications are generally defined as follows:

- Financial Counterparties (FCs):
  - banks
  - ***insurance companies***
  - assurance companies
  - reinsurance companies
  - ***alternative investment funds***
  - investment firms
  - credit institutions
  - ***pension funds***
  - ***UCITS*** funds
  - sovereign wealth funds.

Note: the types of firm listed above must, in each case, be authorised under the appropriate regulation in order to be classified as an FC under EMIR.

Important note: an Alternative Investment Fund (AIF) is only classified as FC where it is managed by an AIF manager which is authorised / registered under the *Alternative Investment Fund Managers Directive* (AIFMD). All funds managed by a manager not authorised/registered under AIFMD are considered NFC (see below). Please refer to the full definition of FC/NFC in EMIR (art. 2(8) and 2(9)).

- Non-Financial Counterparties (NFCs):
  - under EMIR, all firms that execute OTC derivative trades but which are not classified as FCs will automatically be classified as an NFC
  - any NFC whose OTC derivative activity is below a defined clearing threshold is known as an NFC– and is therefore exempt from the clearing obligation
  - any NFC whose OTC derivative activity surpasses a defined clearing threshold is known as an NFC+ and is therefore subject to the clearing obligation.

At the time of writing, the defined clearing thresholds under EMIR are as shown in Table 47.1:

TABLE 47.1 NFC clearing thresholds

NFC Clearing Thresholds	
OTC Derivative Type	Threshold (in gross notional principal value)
Interest Rate	EUR 3 billion
Credit	EUR 1 billion
Equity	EUR 1 billion
Foreign Exchange	EUR 3 billion
Commodity and Other	EUR 3 billion

Source: ESMA

It is important to note that, where any OTC derivative trades executed by an NFC are classified as reducing risk relating to commercial or treasury financing activity, such trades should not contribute to the calculation of the NFC's clearing threshold. When the NFC's trading activity surpasses the clearing threshold for any of the OTC derivative types (listed above), the NFC becomes an NFC+, and as such the clearing obligation applies to that firm, until and unless the firm's trades fall beneath the clearing threshold. If and when the status of the NFC changes to NFC+ or to NFC–, it is the responsibility of the NFC to communicate that change in status to ESMA, and to each of its counterparties as it involves a change of obligations under EMIR.

The above text (relating to NFC Clearing Thresholds) is reproduced with the permission of ESMA. For further details, please see: https://www.esma.europa.eu/regulation/post-trading/non-financial-counterparties-nfcs.

PART 4c

The importance of the NFC classification (whether NFC+ or NFC−) should not be underestimated. From the perspective of the NFC itself:

- a classification of NFC+ means that the NFC is obliged to clear its trades via a *CCP*, report its trades to a *trade repository* and be subject to the same risk mitigation obligations as applies to *financial counterparties* (FCs)
- a classification of NFC− means that the NFC is required to report its trades to a trade repository whilst also being subject to specific risk mitigation obligations.

From the perspective of the counterparty to the NFC, they must remain very conscious of whether their counterparty is classified as NFC+ or NFC−, as this determines whether the trade is subject to *central clearing* or not. If not subject to central clearing, the trade must be treated as *non-centrally cleared*; please refer to Chapter 48 'OTC Derivatives and Collateral – Regulatory Change and the Future of Collateral – Non-Centrally Cleared Trades'. Under normal circumstances, the counterparty to the NFC must trust the classification as advised by the NFC. However, if the NFC's counterparty has reason to believe that the NFC's status has been incorrectly defined, the counterparty has the right to challenge it. OTC Answer 4 of the 'ESMA EMIR Questions and Answers' document (https://www.esma.europa.eu/file/21988/download?-token=fxp5Nz-J) states the following:

OTC Answer 4
NFCs which trade OTC derivatives are obliged to determine their own status against the clearing threshold. FCs should obtain representations from their NFC counterparties detailing the NFC's status. FCs are not expected to conduct verifications of the representations received from NFCs detailing their status and may rely on such representations unless they are in possession of information which clearly demonstrates that those representations are incorrect.

47.10.2 European Union (EU) Market Participants Exempt from the Clearing Obligation: Overview

Some types of market participant are (permanently or temporarily) exempt from the *clearing obligation*; therefore, all OTC derivative trades (including those that would otherwise be centrally cleared) that such firms execute whilst they have a valid exemption are treated as *non-centrally cleared trades* (unless such firms choose to centrally clear their trades on a voluntary basis).

The types of firm falling within the exempt category under *EMIR* are:

- Pension Funds:
  - as *pension funds* typically do not hold CCP-eligible assets, neither cash nor highly rated government bonds, the cost of *central clearing* for pension funds is seen as prohibitive, and would therefore have a detrimental effect on the investment returns achievable by pension funds, and in turn their pension payments to pensioners
  - were originally granted (under EMIR) a two-year exemption from the clearing obligation (expiring in August 2017), which was then extended by a year to August 2018, and subsequently extended once more until 2020

- Multilateral Development Banks:
  - MDBs are organisations focused on achieving economic equality and reducing severe poverty. They are international financial institutions that are supported by at least two countries for the purpose of promoting financial growth in specific regions. Also known as *supranational organisations*
  - are permanently exempt under EMIR regulations
- Non-Financial Counterparties (NFCs) rated NFC–:
  - any NFC whose OTC derivative activity is below a defined clearing threshold (see the NFC Clearing Thresholds table in the previous sub-section) is known as an NFC– and is therefore exempt from the clearing obligation.

Non-centrally cleared trades are described within the next chapter, namely Chapter 48 'OTC Derivatives and Collateral – Regulatory Change and the Future of Collateral – Non-Centrally Cleared Trades'.

As mentioned earlier in this chapter, firms that are exempt from the clearing obligation may voluntarily opt to centrally clear their OTC derivative trades.

47.10.3 The Clearing Obligation Relating to Non-European Union (EU) Market Participants: Overview

The aforementioned clearing obligation refers <u>directly</u> to EU market participants, whilst taking account of each participant's classification, whether financial counterparty (FC), or non-financial counterparty (NFC+ or NFC–).

It is very important, however, to note that EMIR obligations apply <u>indirectly</u> to non-EU market participants, as follows:

- when a non-EU entity trades with an EU entity, the non-EU entity is required to classify itself under EMIR as being either FC, NFC+ or NFC– 'as if it was established in the EU', or
- when a non-EU entity trades with another non-EU entity, where the trade has a direct, substantial and foreseeable effect within the Union; see Article 11 (12) of EMIR.

Additionally, the possibility exists that an EU market participant executes a trade with a non-EU market participant that is domiciled in a country or region having rules 'equivalent' to EMIR. Under such circumstances both firms have a challenge in determining which set of rules are applicable; to cater for such circumstances, some firms create decision trees or a set of specific rules.

47.10.4 OTC Derivative Products Subject to the Clearing Obligation: Overview

Similar to the clearing obligation for market participants described above, the clearing obligation relating to OTC derivative products is a complex topic in its own right. The intention of this part of the chapter is to provide an overview of how central clearing of OTC derivative products is being introduced. Significantly greater detail is available on the website of the European Securities and Markets Authority.

PART 4c

Following the *Global Financial Crisis* in 2008, one of the 'headline' objectives of the regulatory authorities related to *standardised OTC derivative* trades, and that such trades should be *centrally cleared* via *central counterparties.*

The standardisation of any financial product refers to the identification of the product's features and characteristics that are regarded as normal and regular. It is only by the execution of trades in standardised OTC derivative products that it is possible for any entity (including CCPs) to achieve netting of trades. Conversely, individual trades with special and unusual features makes achieving the netting of such trades extremely challenging, if not impossible; therefore, such non-standardised trades are not permitted to be novated and processed by CCPs and must be managed entirely separately (see Chapter 48 'OTC Derivatives and Collateral – Regulatory Change and the Future of Collateral – Non-Centrally Cleared Trades').

Under *EMIR*, the European Securities and Markets Authority (ESMA) is the body appointed to determine which particular OTC derivative products should be subject to the *clearing obligation*. For each OTC derivative product, ESMA assesses the features and characteristics of trades, in order to determine whether they meet the predefined criteria relating to:

- standardisation: to what extent trades are executed with normal and regular features
- liquidity: the speed and ease of finding a counterparty in order to trade, and
- pricing: the ease with which pricing information is available in the marketplace.

At the time of writing, EMIR has imposed the clearing obligation on the following combinations of OTC derivative product types and market participants. Note that interest rate derivatives are used here as an example of OTC derivative products that are subject to the clearing obligation:

Interest Rate Derivatives Included within this category, are those listed in Table 47.2:

TABLE 47.2 Interest rate derivatives

OTC Derivative Product Type	Denomination Currency						
	EUR	GBP	USD	JPY	NOK	PLN	SEK
Fixed-to-Floating Interest Rate Swaps*	√	√	√	√	√	√	√
Basis Swaps	√	√	√	√	x	x	x
Forward Rate Agreements	√	√	√	√	√	√	√
Overnight Index Swaps	√	√	√	√	x	x	x

*for a description of this OTC derivative product type, please refer to Chapter 16 'OTC Derivatives and Collateral – Transaction Types – Interest Rate Swaps'.

The EMIR-imposed deadline by which market participants are required to comply with the clearing obligation (relating to those interest rate derivatives listed above) is dependent upon the category of a firm and its counterparty. The four categories are:

- Category 1:
  - existing *clearing members* of a CCP
- Category 2:
  - *Non-clearing members* of a CCP whose group's aggregate month-end average of outstanding *notional principal* amount of OTC derivatives is above EUR 8bn (assessed over Jan/Feb/Mar of each year)
- Category 3:
  - Non-clearing members of a CCP whose group's aggregate month-end average of outstanding notional principal amount of OTC derivatives is below EUR 8bn (assessed over Jan/Feb/Mar of each year)
- Category 4:
  - *non-financial counterparties* (regardless whether *NFC+* or *NFC–*).

Furthermore, EMIR stipulates that two deadlines may apply for certain categories of market participant, namely a 'frontloading' deadline and the clearing deadline. The term 'frontloading' refers to the earlier capture and central clearing of trades rather than the formal mandatory deadline imposed under EMIR (see Table 47.3).

TABLE 47.3 Frontloading deadlines and central clearing deadlines

Interest Rate Derivatives denominated in EUR, GBP, USD and JPY: Frontloading Deadlines and Central Clearing Deadlines				
Deadline Type	For Trades Executed Between These Categories of Market Participants:			
	Category 1 with Category 1	Category 1 or 2 with Category 2	Category 1, 2 or 3 with Category 3	Category 1, 2, 3 or 4 with Category 4
Frontloading Deadline	February 21st 2016 for FCs	May 21st 2016 for FCs	*does not apply*	*does not apply*
Central Clearing Deadline	June 21st 2016	December 21st 2016	June 21st 2017	December 21st 2018

Source: ESMA

Note: the dates for the mandatory clearing (of IRS and CDS) of category 3 counterparties have been postponed to 21st June 2019, in accordance with regulation EU 2017/751 dated 16th March 2017.

Regarding frontloading, no requirement exists for market participants in category 3 or category 4.

The above text (including market participant categories and deadlines for frontloading and for central clearing) is reproduced with the permission of ESMA. For further details, please see: https://www.esma.europa.eu/.../public_register_for_the_clearing_obligation_under_emir.

In order to know whether the clearing obligation applies to a particular trade or not, individual firms must remain fully aware of their own 'current' category and that of each of their counterparties. Furthermore, firms must remain aware that the category applicable to themselves and of their counterparty is subject to periodic change; this specifically relates to firms in categories 2 and 3, where a group's aggregate month-end average of outstanding notional principal amounts could in some cases be above the EUR 8bn limit, and at other times below it.

Note that at the time of writing, no dates have yet been announced by EMIR/ESMA regarding the central clearing deadline for *single name credit default swaps* (CDS), although dates for central clearing of two types of *index CDS* have been announced.

47.11 TREATMENT OF LEGACY TRADES

For each OTC derivative product which is subject to the *clearing obligation*, it will be mandatory for all CCP-eligible trades to be *centrally cleared* from the effective date. (However, the possibility exists that differing effective dates may apply to the various categories of market participant; please refer to Sub-section 47.10.4 'OTC Derivative Products Subject to the Clearing Obligation: Overview'.)

With regard to trades executed prior to the effective date which have not reached their *scheduled maturity date* (*legacy trades*), in Europe and the US there is no mandatory requirement for such trades to be *novated* to a CCP.

However, it does remain possible for legacy trades to be novated to a CCP, providing both the original trade parties agree to do so. The term given to the movement of legacy trades from the original (*bilateral*) counterparty to a CCP is *backloading*. (Note: the term 'backloading' can be used in different ways, for example referring to the reporting of trades to a trade repository.)

Advantages of a firm backloading its legacy trades to a CCP are:

- reduction in outstanding notional principal amounts (via *portfolio compression*):
  - the inclusion of legacy trades, now novated to a CCP, in the portfolio compression process in which offsetting trades that contain the same details as an existing position in the same OTC derivative product are terminated (cancelled), resulting in a new net position. (Please refer to Chapter 30 'OTC Derivatives and Collateral – The Collateral Lifecycle – Post-Trading – Trade/ Portfolio Netting.)
- reduction in counterparty risk:
  - the replacement of the original (bilateral) counterparty with the *central counterparty*, thereby immediately reducing credit exposure for the firm
- reduction in outstanding notional principal amounts (via *multilateral netting*):
  - the opportunity to centrally clear legacy trades that might offset existing cleared trades, thereby maximising the benefits of multilateral netting through a CCP.

Therefore, for their legacy trades, firms may choose to either continue with bilateral clearing (direct with the original counterparty), or to backload trades via novation to a CCP.

PART 4c

47.12 CENTRAL COUNTERPARTIES AND INTEROPERABILITY

CCPs are usually companies (rather than utilities) which are owned by independent shareholders, and/or the members and/or an exchange.

In Europe, CCPs must seek authorisation to offer CCP services in the European Union under EMIR. A full list of authorised CCPs in Europe is available at: www.esma. europa.eu.

Each CCP must decide which OTC derivative product types it wishes to provide services for; it should be expected that more than one CCP will offer services in a particular OTC derivative product (e.g. interest rate swaps), but that not all CCPs will initially offer clearing in the same products, although that situation is likely to evolve over time. This means that, at least for some OTC derivative products, a trading firm is likely to have a choice as to which CCP it chooses to use.

47.12.1 Trade Parties Using the Same CCP

Assume Firm A is a *clearing member* (CM) of CCP1; when Party A executes a trade with Firm C (a client of clearing member Firm M) who is also a user of CCP1, there is no issue for CCP1 under these circumstances as CCP1 will, following *novation*, become the counterparty to both Firm A and Firm M, thereby allowing CCP1 to remain *market risk neutral*. This situation is depicted in Figure 47.11:

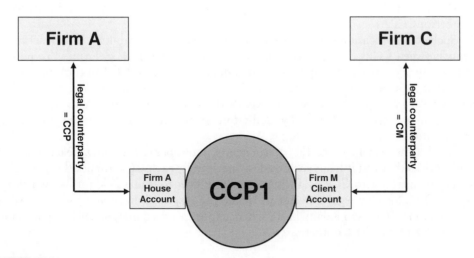

FIGURE 47.11   Both Firm A and Firm C (via Firm M) are users of the same CCP

(Note: exactly the same concepts apply when both the original trade parties are clearing members of the same CCP.)

47.12.2 Trade Parties Using Different CCPs

Assume that, in a separate trade, Firm A (still a user of CCP1), executes a trade with Firm D who is a user of CCP2. From the perspective of the two CCPs, it is of paramount importance that each remains market risk neutral; this neutrality is achieved by each CCP entering into a balancing trade which is a mirror image of the trade each CCP enters into with its own participant. This situation is depicted in Figure 47.12:

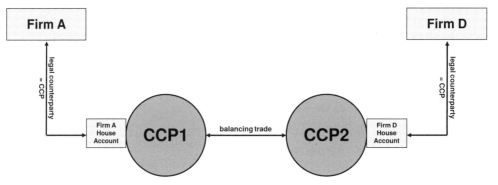

FIGURE 47.12   Firm A and Firm D are users of different CCPs

(Note: exactly the same concepts apply as if Firm D were a client of a clearing member of CCP2.)

Such communication between CCPs is known as 'interoperability'. If such arrangements between CCPs did not exist, this would require a firm (e.g. Firm A) to potentially set up accounts at multiple CCPs including its preferred CCP. In turn, this could mean that Firm A's OTC derivative positions would be fragmented amongst two or more CCPs. Interoperability between CCPs therefore allows Firm A to have all its trades at its preferred CCP, thereby facilitating Firm A reaping the benefits of netting maximisation.

Besides the benefit to market participants, interoperability allows each CCP to manage risks that result from such trades. Specifically, each CCP applies the same risk mitigation measures to CCP balancing trades as it does to trades held for its own clearing members. Specific legal agreements define the responsibilities and rights between interoperating CCPs. On a daily basis, where exposure exists margin calls will be made by one CCP to its CCP 'counterparty'.

47.13 PRODUCT, PARTY AND TRADE-RELATED STATIC DATA

Regulatory authorities around the globe demand the regulatory reporting of OTC derivative trades to *trade repositories* (TRs), and in order for such reporting to be executed effectively, common standards must be utilised. (For a description of trade repositories, please refer to Chapter 46 'OTC Derivatives and Collateral – Regulatory Change and the Future of Collateral – Introduction'.

In order to comply with the new regulations, additional *static data* must be managed by firms. Such new requirements can be quite challenging for many organisations as the static data is not created before or at *trade execution*, but rather as a post-trade process.

An example of static data usually set up prior to trade execution is as follows. The *Legal Entity Identifier* (LEI) uniquely identifies individual legal entities; it is an alpha-numeric 20-character code. The LEI is usually set up within a firm's counterparty static data at the very beginning of the firm's relationship with the counterparty, and ideally prior to execution of the first trade between the firms.

By comparison, in order to uniquely identify each individual trade *Unique Trade Identifiers* (UTIs) have been introduced; a specific methodology is used to assign such trade identifiers. As these identifiers will be permanently attached to the trade, they are considered to be static data. However, contrary to the traditional timing of static data set up, these identifiers result from both trade execution and from post-trade processing, and it is therefore not possible to set up such data prior to trade execution. This poses a unique challenge to registration and reconciliation of such static data. In some instances, the trading scenario may lead to the counterparty determining the UTI for the individual trade. Both parties to an individual trade are required to communicate transaction reports to TRs, who will attempt to reconcile the reporting from both trade parties. Consequently, each trade party must have processes in place to ensure the UTI data is exchanged, reconciled and stored with accuracy and in a timely manner. Failure to provide accurate reporting of UTIs may lead to sanctions from the supervisory body in the country where the firm is located.

Note: at the time of writing an alternative approach has been proposed: that the UTI is agreed between the two trading parties prior to trade execution. Normal market practice is for the *sell-side* firm to create the UTI, then to communicate it to the *buy-side* firm. *S.W.I.F.T.* messages have been updated to reflect the communication of the UTI.

In firms where static data is stored in a separate masterfile, the question of where to store these new static data elements arises. For example, should they be stored in the trading system or in the masterfile, with a reference to the trade? Such considerations pose new challenges as to how the data is processed internally, and specifically how to ensure the data is validated, before being stored.

47.14 OPERATIONAL IMPLICATIONS OF CENTRAL CLEARING: OVERVIEW

The operational implications of *central clearing* on *sell-side* firms (assuming such firms perform both *self-clearing* and *client clearing*), include:

- setting up relationships with one or many CCPs
- setting up house accounts and one or many client accounts at each CCP
- providing *default fund* contributions to each CCP
- providing trade-related collateral in response to *IM* and *VM* calls from CCPs
- providing or receiving VM in accordance with the frequency stated by each CCP on an ongoing basis
- *pre-funding* accounts at each CCP, for VM purposes

- verifying IM and VM calls from CCPs
- communicating with clients
- calling for IM and VM from clients
- monitoring receipt of IM and VM called from clients
- providing *collateral transformation* services to clients
- updating internal *books & records* whenever IM and VM is given or taken.

For *buy-side* firms, the implications of central clearing include:

- setting up clearing relationships with one or many CMs, including *backup* CMs
- providing trade-related collateral in the form of IM and VM
- utilising collateral transformation services provided by CMs
- providing or receiving VM in accordance with the frequency agreed with each CM on an ongoing basis
- verifying IM and VM calls from CMs
- monitoring receipt of VM called from CMs
- updating internal *books & records* whenever IM and VM is given or taken.

47.15 LEGAL DOCUMENTATION: OVERVIEW

To formalise obligations and responsibilities between a clearing member (CM) and a CCP, the CM is required to sign the CCP's Clearing Membership Agreement (CMA). The CMA typically includes the following:

- definitions of terms, including:
  - clearing member
  - contract
  - criteria for admission
  - default fund
  - default notice
  - default rules
  - exchange
  - rulebook
- clearing membership, including
  - written notice requirements following the CM's changing circumstances
- clearing member undertakings, including:
  - abiding by the CCP's rulebook
  - providing financial information required by the CCP
  - providing trade details to the CCP
- CCP's undertakings, including:
  - registration of trades
  - performance of obligations
  - trade record keeping
  - maintenance of accounts
  - CM's default: entitlement to effect appropriate action

- compensation arrangements, including
  - the CCP's entitlement to charge fees
  - fee increase notice period
- membership termination, including:
  - notice period
  - CM's termination of open trades
  - CCP's right to terminate the CM's trades
  - CCP's right to terminate the CM's membership.

The CMA is closely associated with the CCP's Rulebook, a large and detailed work which documents the obligations and rights of both the CCP and its clearing members.

Where a clearing member provides clearing services to its clients, the obligations and responsibilities of those two parties are typically formalised by the signing of a Client Clearing Agreement (CCA). In general terms, the CCA normally mirrors the documented arrangements between the CM and the (one or many) CCPs through which the CM clears. Figure 47.13 illustrates the parties involved in the CMA and the CCA:

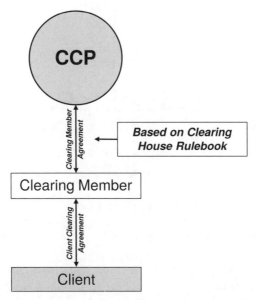

FIGURE 47.13 Clearing Member Agreement and Client Clearing Agreement

As a minimum, such arrangements allow the CM to communicate *margin calls* to its clients, aligned with the margin calls the CM itself receives from the CCP. CMs may choose to make margin calls on clients at the same frequency as received from CCPs (bearing in mind that CCPs may have differing margin call frequencies from one another), or less frequently.

PART 4c

47.16 STATUS OF INDIVIDUAL CENTRAL COUNTERPARTIES

Firms that have successfully applied to conduct business in the capacity of *central counterparty* (CCP) under *EMIR* are known as 'authorised' central counterparties.

The list of currently authorised CCPs and the classes of OTC derivative products for which each CCP is permitted to clear, can be found at ESMA's website (www.esma. europa.eu/).

47.17 CENTRAL CLEARING AND THE OTC DERIVATIVE COLLATERAL LIFECYCLE

The flow of trade details to a central counterparty (CCP), and the subsequent *initial margin* (IM) and *variation margin* (VM) movements are illustrated in Figure 47.14. (Assume the clearing members (CMs) shown have previously contributed to the CCP's default fund.)

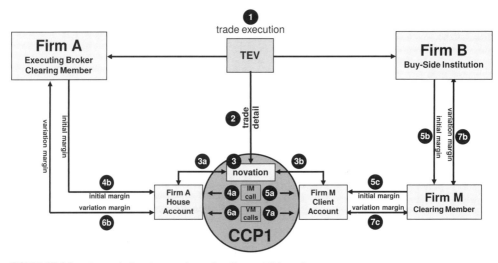

FIGURE 47.14   Central clearing trade and collateral lifecycle

The two original parties to the trade are:

- Firm A: the *executing broker* for the trade, and also a *clearing member* at CCP1
- Firm B: a *buy-side* firm that is not a clearing member, but utilises the client clearing service provided by clearing member Firm M at CCP1.

The steps shown within the diagram are explained as follows:

- Step 1. A trade is executed electronically via a *trade execution venue* (TEV), between two trading parties; the parties involved are a *sell-side* executing broker (Firm A) and a buy-side institution (Firm B)

- Step 2. Following trade execution, the TEV communicates trade details to a particular central counterparty (CCP1)
- Step 3. CCP1 steps in and *novates* the trade, thereby ensuring the CCP remains *market risk neutral*
- Step 3a. Novation results in a legal contract between CCP1 and Firm A
- Step 3b. Novation also results in a legal contract between CCP1 and clearing member Firm M who is acting on behalf of its client Firm B.
- Step 4a. CCP1, having calculated the potential future exposure relating to the trade with Firm A, issues an *initial margin* (IM) call to Firm A
- Step 4b. Firm A settles the IM call by providing cash or highly rated government bonds to CCP1, who holds those assets (they are not passed on by the CCP)
- Step 5a. In the same time frame as for Step 4a, CCP1 issues an IM call to Firm M
- Step 5b. Firm M communicates the IM call to Firm B, who settles the call with CCP-eligible assets appropriate to initial margin
- Step 5c. Firm M in turn settles the IM call by passing on to CCP1 the assets received from Firm B. CCP1 will hold those assets
- Step 6a. CCP1, having *marked-to-market* the trade from which current *exposure* is calculated, issues a variation margin (VM) call to Firm A, as Firm A has a *negative exposure* on this day
- Step 6b. Firm A settles the VM call by providing CCP-eligible cash to CCP1
- Step 7a. CCP1, having received the VM cash from Firm A, then passes that cash on to Firm M, who in turn passes that cash on to its client Firm B, as Firm M/Firm B have a *positive exposure* on this day. Note: margin call settlement timings may differ based on the agreement between Firm M and Firm B.

On a different day (or possibly intraday), if CCP1's current exposure calculations reveal that Firm M had a negative exposure, then:

- Step 7a: CCP1 issues a VM call to Firm M
- Step 7b. Firm M would pass on the VM call to Firm B. Firm B must settle the VM call by paying CCP-eligible cash to Firm M
- Step 7c: Firm M settles the VM call by providing CCP-eligible cash to CCP1, who then passes that cash on to Firm A (the party with the positive exposure).

Note that CCPs are very likely to calculate current exposure (leading to VM calls) at least once per day, with the possibility of multiple times per day in volatile market conditions; for example, one prominent CCP operates a total of eight current exposure runs during a business day. This can result, for example, in a firm that receives VM cash (due to a positive exposure) based on the 9:00am *mark-to-market*, being required to repay some, all or more VM cash (due to a negative exposure) based on the 2:00pm mark-to-market on the same business day.

47.18 COLLATERAL TRANSFORMATION

> *Further to the references (within the Central Clearing section of this chapter) regarding the inability of some buy-side firms to provide CCP-eligible collateral, this section describes how such firms can access the necessary collateral.*

This subject is not in itself a regulatory change, but it arises as a result of a regulatory change, namely the introduction of *central clearing*.

47.18.1 Collateral Transformation: Introduction

In the *bilateral* (pre-central clearing) world, firms have generally been required to give and to take collateral due to exposures resulting from the *mark-to-market* process, the equivalent of which in the *centrally cleared* world is known as *variation margin* (VM).

However, in addition to VM, CCPs will demand collateral for *initial margin* (IM) which relates to potential future exposures of the OTC derivative product.

Consequently, from the perspective of most firms that have historically traded in OTC derivatives, whereas VM with a CCP is the equivalent of *mark-to-market* (MTM) exposures with bilateral counterparties, IM is entirely new as collateral has not been traditionally required for potential future exposure in the bilateral world.

VM calls from CCPs are expected to be payable only in cash, for reasons of *fungibility* and speed of payment; when a CCP receives VM from a clearing member (CM) with a *negative MTM*, the VM payment received will be washed through the CCP to the CM having a *positive MTM*.

IM calls from CCPs are generally able to be settled either in cash or in a narrow set of eligible securities (principally highly rated government bonds); the CCP will hold such IM (and not pass it on as is the case for VM). For some *buy-side* firms that do not naturally hold such *CCP-eligible assets*, the payment or delivery of IM in CCP-eligible form is likely to prove problematic. Some types of buy-side firm (e.g. *insurance companies* and *pension funds*) invest in certain types of assets, but typically neither cash nor highly rated government bonds, as to invest in such products may adversely impact the firm's investment performance.

By way of an example, imagine that a *mutual fund* operates a corporate bond fund that primarily holds multiple bonds issued by corporate entities. The fund also executes OTC derivative trades, such as *credit default swaps*, in order to guard against the possibility of bond issuer default. Corporate bonds are not generally CCP-eligible for IM or for VM purposes. When the mutual fund's CM receives an IM or VM call from the CCP, the CM will in turn mirror the call with the mutual fund. Unless the mutual fund takes action, the mutual fund will be unable to satisfy the call if it does not hold CCP-eligible assets.

Collateral transformation is 1) a service offered by investment banks to its clients, and 2) a transaction involving the temporary exchange of an existing (non-CCP-eligible) asset for a CCP-eligible asset; it can be achieved by executing either:

- a *repo* (sale and repurchase) trade, or
- a *securities lending & borrowing* trade

with another party. That other party could be the buy-side firm's CM, or another bilateral counterparty. A number of large banks (that are likely to become CMs at CCPs) offer repo and/or securities lending trade capability to their clients as collateral transformation solutions.

47.18.2 Repo Trade: Overview

Imagine that Party A is a mutual fund holding only corporate bonds, which are non-CCP-eligible. In a repo, at the start of the trade Party A temporarily sells its corporate bond (as collateral) against receipt of cash from the counterparty; such cash can be used to satisfy the CCP's margin call on Party A. This is reflected in the upper part of Figure 47.15:

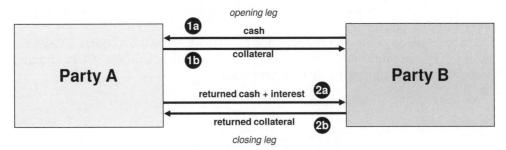

FIGURE 47.15 Repo trade for collateral transformation purposes

At the close of the trade, Party B will return to Party A the same corporate bond, in exchange for repayment of the borrowed cash, plus interest (assuming a *credit interest rate environment*). The cost to Party A is an agreed percentage (the *repo rate*) of the borrowed cash amount (which is itself based on the market value of the collateral given).

For further details regarding repo, please refer to Part 2 'Sale & Repurchase (Repo) Trades and Collateral'.

47.18.3 Securities Lending & Borrowing Trade: Overview

Imagine the same situation for Party A as described under 'Repo Trade: Overview' (above). In a securities lending & borrowing (SL&B) trade, at the start of the trade Party A borrows (receives) CCP-eligible securities against delivery of its corporate bond (as collateral) to the counterparty; the borrowed securities can be used to satisfy the CCP's margin call on Party A. This is reflected in the upper part of Figure 47.16:

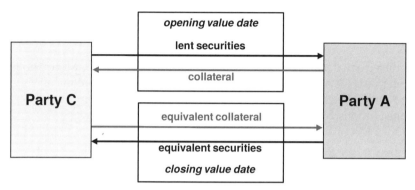

FIGURE 47.16   Securities lending & borrowing trade for collateral transformation purposes

At the close of the trade, Party C will return to Party A the same corporate bond, in exchange for the return of the CCP-eligible security from Party A. The cost to Party A is an agreed percentage of the market value of the borrowed security.

For further details regarding SL&B, please refer to Part 3 'Securities Lending & Borrowing and Collateral'.

In conclusion, collateral transformation facilitates firms that hold non-CCP-eligible assets to 1) maintain their normal investment strategy, and 2) satisfy the CCPs' demand for either cash or highly rated government bonds.

OTC Derivatives and Collateral – Regulatory Change and the Future of Collateral – Non-Centrally Cleared Trades

This chapter describes the operational and collateral management procedures relating to OTC derivative trades that are not centrally cleared; from a firm's perspective, their counterparty for such trades will be a traditional bilateral counterparty (rather than a central counterparty), although regulatory changes resulting from the Global Financial Crisis demand substantially different treatment of such trades compared with legacy bilateral trade practices.

Recommendation: for those readers that have little or no prior awareness of OTC derivatives or their associated trade processing or collateral processing, it is strongly recommended that prior to reading Chapters 46, 47 and 48, they firstly familiarise themselves with Part 4a 'OTC Derivatives and Collateral' which is covered by Chapters 14–45, as those chapters provide a solid foundation of understanding enabling readers to relate to the regulatory changes.

DISCLAIMER

The EMIR regulations relating to OTC derivatives cover a significant amount of text and may be regarded as challenging to follow. Aligned with the author's aim for the entire book, the author's intention regarding the three chapters covering the EMIR regulations is to describe such regulations using plain English and written in a manner that is relevant to an operations readership; furthermore, the scale of the EMIR regulations has necessitated the author selecting for inclusion within those chapters the parts of the regulations that impact operations and collateral management personnel to the greatest extent. It is important to note that these chapters represent condensed versions of selected EMIR regulations, and the full EMIR regulations can be found within the various European Commission documents.

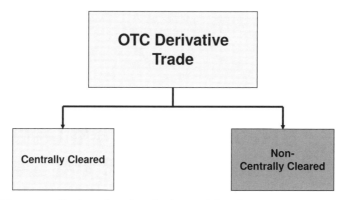

FIGURE 48.1   Non-centrally cleared trades: the focus of this chapter

48.1 INTRODUCTION

Following the regulations introduced as a result of the *Global Financial Crisis* in 2008, only those trades that conform to a defined standard and which are traded by market participants that are subject to the *clearing obligation* will be eligible for *central clearing* via *central counterparties* (CCPs). All other OTC derivative trades are classified as '*non-centrally cleared*' (see Figure 48.1), although the label '*bilaterally* cleared' may also be used.

Prior to the introduction of *mandatory central clearing*, the vast majority of OTC derivative trades were executed on a bilateral basis and were managed operationally (bilaterally cleared) by the Operations Departments and Collateral Departments of the two trading firms throughout the lifetime of the trade, utilising the set of legal documentation (*ISDA Master Agreement*, Schedule and *Credit Support Annex*) signed directly between the two parties. (This situation is described within this book under 'The OTC Derivative Collateral Lifecycle', from Chapter 24 'OTC Derivatives and Collateral – The Collateral Lifecycle – Introduction' to Chapter 44 'The OTC Derivative Collateral Lifecycle – Trade Termination'.) Within this book, such trades are labelled *legacy bilateral trades*. Although central clearing existed for certain types of OTC derivative product, it was not a regulatory requirement and was optional for the trading parties involved.

Since the Global Financial Crisis, regulatory authorities have mandated that every OTC derivative trade must be either 1) centrally cleared, but if central clearing is not possible, then 2) the trade must be non-centrally cleared and the trade must be subject to strict risk *mitigation* requirements (which are described later within this chapter) in order to reduce *counterparty credit risk*. Within this book, such non-centrally cleared trades are labelled *new bilateral trades*; however, some parties use the term regulatory bilateral trades.

Consequently, the similarities between legacy bilateral trades and new bilateral trades can be summarised as: trades bilaterally cleared throughout their lifetime, with each party carrying out operational tasks according to the set of legal documentation signed by the two parties. The difference can be summarised as follows:

- Legacy bilateral trades:
  - little or no regulatory requirements in terms of risk management

- New bilateral trades:
  - significant regulatory requirements in terms of risk management.

For all relevant firms, the mandatory posting of collateral for non-centrally cleared trades became effective from trade date 1st March 2017, requiring:

- *variation margin* (VM) to be posted with immediate effect for trades executed on the aforementioned trade date, and
- *initial margin* (IM) to be posted with effect from a series of dates, beginning 1st September 2017.

The regulatory requirements pertaining to new bilateral trades, the parties that are obliged to comply and the deadlines by which such parties must comply, for both VM and IM, are described subsequently within this chapter.

In brief, the risk management regulatory requirements for new bilateral trades are based on a defined set of rules, which include:

- specific margining practices must be applied to all non-centrally cleared trades
- the parties to a trade must exchange initial margin (IM), although exemptions exist
- IM should be exchanged by both parties without offsetting
- the parties to a trade must exchange variation margin (VM), although exemptions exist
- IM and VM calculation methods must be consistently applied
- assets used to settle IM and VM calls must be highly liquid to facilitate speedy encashment
- margin requirements should be phased in to ensure transition costs are manageable.

(Source: Bank for International Settlements, March 2015)

48.2 REASONS FOR THE EXISTENCE OF NON-CENTRALLY CLEARED TRADES

For firms of all types across differing industries, a variety of financial risks exist. In general terms, by use of suitable OTC derivative products, such risks can be mitigated.

For some types of risk, a firm can execute one or many trades which have standard features only and which provide a suitable offset (or hedge); such trades are able to be centrally cleared, providing both trade parties are subject to (not exempt from) the clearing obligation.

For other types of risk, a firm may find that trades with standard features will not adequately offset its underlying risk. Under these circumstances, such a trade will not be permitted into a centrally cleared environment and instead must be processed as a non-centrally cleared trade.

Because financial and other incentives (e.g. *multilateral netting*) exist for firms to execute trades that are centrally cleared, the firm may be tempted to execute trades having standard features, knowing that there is a mismatch between the underlying risk and the offsetting OTC derivative trade. Over time, the firm may discover that there is a growing and serious mismatch, due to the different financial make-up of the risk and of the offsetting trade.

Consequently, firms that continue to have specific risks which cannot be mitigated by standardised OTC derivative products are likely to continue executing trades which cannot be centrally cleared. (The alternatives are 1) for the firm to change its business model so that it does not incur such risks, or 2) to leave the risk unmitigated. Firms may consider neither of these alternatives to be acceptable.)

48.3 MARKET PARTICIPANTS EXECUTING NON-CENTRALLY CLEARED TRADES

The types of firm needing to manage their risks are typically *buy-side* institutions, therefore including mutual funds, pension funds, insurance companies and corporations.

In order to execute a non-centrally cleared trade, such firms will transact directly with a *sell-side* firm.

Unlike centrally cleared OTC derivative trades, there is no regulatory requirement to execute non-centrally cleared trades via a trade execution venue or electronic trading platform. However, firms are responsible for reporting 100% of their OTC derivative trading activity to a *trade repository*, whether such trades are centrally cleared or bilaterally cleared; the subject of trade reporting of non-centrally cleared trades is described in Section 48.7 'Non-Centrally Cleared Trades: Trade Reporting Regulations' later in this chapter.

48.3.1 European Union (EU) Market Participants Exempt from the Clearing Obligation: Overview

Some types of market participant are (permanently or temporarily) exempt from the clearing obligation; therefore all OTC derivative trades (including those that would otherwise be centrally cleared) that such firms execute whilst they have a valid exemption are treated as non-centrally cleared trades (unless such firms choose to centrally clear their trades on a voluntary basis).

The types of firm falling within the exempt category under EMIR are:

- Pension funds:
  - as pension funds typically do not hold CCP-eligible assets, neither cash nor highly rated government bonds, the cost of central clearing for pension funds is seen as prohibitive, and would therefore have a detrimental effect on the investment returns achievable by pension funds, and in turn their pension payments to pensioners
  - pension funds were originally granted (under EMIR) a two-year exemption from the clearing obligation (expiring in August 2017), which was then extended by a year to August 2018
  - it is important to note that pension funds are <u>not</u> exempt from the requirement to post initial margin (IM) and variation margin (VM) relating to non-centrally cleared trades

- Multilateral development banks:
  - MDBs are organisations focused on achieving economic equality and reducing severe poverty. They are international financial institutions that are supported by at least two countries for the purpose of promoting financial growth in specific regions. Also known as *supranational organisations*
  - MDBs are permanently exempt under EMIR regulations
- Non-financial counterparties (NFCs) rated NFC–:
  - under EMIR, all firms that execute OTC derivative trades, but which are not classified as a financial counterparty* will automatically be classified as an NFC
    - any NFC whose OTC derivative activity is below a defined clearing threshold is known as an NFC– and is therefore exempt from the clearing obligation
    - any NFC whose OTC derivative activity surpasses a defined clearing threshold is known as an NFC+ and is therefore subject to the clearing obligation
  - firms classified as NFC– are exempt from the requirement to post IM and VM relating to non-centrally cleared trades.

Firms that are exempt from the clearing obligation may voluntarily opt to centrally clear their OTC derivative trades (providing such trades are classified as *standardised OTC derivative* trades).

*For a list of financial counterparty and non-financial counterparty types, please refer to Chapter 47 'OTC Derivatives and Collateral – Regulatory Change and the Future of Collateral – Centrally Cleared Trades', and in particular Sub-section 47.10.1 'European Union (EU) Market Participants Subject to the Clearing Obligation: Overview', and Sub-section 47.10.2 'European Union (EU) Market Participants Exempt from the Clearing Obligation: Overview'.

At the time of writing, the defined clearing thresholds under EMIR are as follows:

TABLE 48.1   NFC clearing thresholds

NFC Clearing Thresholds	
OTC Derivative Type	**Threshold** (in gross notional principal value)
Interest Rate	EUR 3 billion
Credit	EUR 1 billion
Equity	EUR 1 billion
Foreign Exchange	EUR 3 billion
Commodity and Other	EUR 3 billion

Source: ESMA

It is important to note that, where any OTC derivative trades executed by an NFC are classified as reducing risk relating to commercial or treasury financing activity, such trades should not contribute to the calculation of the

NFC's clearing threshold. When the NFC's trading activity is below the clearing threshold for any of the OTC derivative types (listed above), the NFC is classified as an NFC–, and as such the clearing obligation does not apply to that firm, until and unless the firm's trades surpass the clearing threshold. If and when the status of the NFC changes to NFC+ or to NFC–, it is the responsibility of the NFC to communicate that change in status to ESMA, and to each of its *counterparties* as it involves a change of obligations under EMIR.

The above text (relating to NFC clearing thresholds) is reproduced with the permission of ESMA. For further details, please see: https://www.esma.europa.eu/regulation/post-trading/non-financial-counterparties-nfcs.

In very general terms, estimates are that the majority of OTC derivative trades will be centrally cleared, but it is expected that there will always be a minority ('a substantial fraction': source *Bank for International Settlements*) of trades that cannot be centrally cleared and so must be managed on a bilateral basis.

In parallel with centrally cleared trades, non-centrally cleared trades are required to be reported to a *trade repository*. Please see Section 48.7 'Non-Centrally Cleared Trades: Trade Reporting Regulations' later in this chapter.

48.4 NON-CENTRALLY CLEARED TRADES: MARGIN REGULATIONS

At the time of writing, the most recent publication of EMIR regulations came into effect on 4th January 2017 and is entitled 'Final Regulatory Technical Standards on risk mitigation techniques for OTC-derivative contracts not cleared by a CCP' (Final RTS).

Much of the information contained within this section is based upon the Final RTS, and is reproduced with the permission of The European Union; the English version of the Final RTS (document 2016/2251) is dated 4th October 2016 and is available at: http://eur-lex.europa.eu/legal-content/EN/TXT/?uri=uriserv%3AOJ.L_.2016.340.01.0009.01.ENG.

EMIR requires *financial counterparties* to have risk-management procedures in place that require the timely, accurate and appropriately segregated exchange of collateral with respect to non-centrally cleared OTC derivative trades. *Non-financial institutions* (NFCs) must have similar procedures in place if they are above the *clearing threshold*; the clearing thresholds are stated within this chapter under Section 48.3 'Market Participants Executing Non-Centrally Cleared Trades'.

Once a non-centrally cleared trade has been executed two forms of margin are required to be posted by the involved parties, namely:

- *initial margin* (IM), and
- *variation margin* (VM).

Both types of margin are applicable to centrally cleared and to non-centrally cleared trades. The following describes IM and VM which is applicable to non-centrally cleared trades.

> *The wording which follows has been selected from the Final RTS to be directly relevant to IM and VM and therefore of specific interest from a collateral management viewpoint. It should be noted that the Final RTS contains significantly more information than is applicable to reproduce in this book. For ease of reference, in many cases the Final RTS article number is quoted to enable the reader to look up directly the full wording.*

With regard to a firm's operational procedures and documentation, the Final RTS states: 'parties shall establish, apply and document risk management procedures for the exchange of collateral' (Article 2.1), including:

- agreement of terms (legal documentation) with all counterparties regarding the exchange of collateral, including:
  - *eligible collateral*
  - segregation of collateral
  - trades to be included in margin calculations
  - timing of *exposure* calculations, including revaluation of collateral
  - calculation of margins
  - *margin call notification* procedures
  - margin call settlement procedures relating to all eligible collateral types
  - events classified as *default* events and termination events
  - applicable law
- reporting of exceptions to senior management.

48.4.1 Eligible Collateral

The Final RTS states that the following asset types are included as eligible collateral for both IM and VM purposes:

- cash in any currency
- gold bullion
- *debt* securities (bonds) issued by:
  - EU central governments or *central banks*
  - EU regional governments or local authorities
  - EU public sector entities
  - *multilateral development banks*
  - third countries' governments or central banks
  - third countries' regional governments or local authorities
  - credit institutions or investment firms
  - corporations
- *convertible bonds*: convertible into *equity* comprising a main index
- equity comprising a main index
- shares or units in *UCITS* funds.

The complete list of eligible collateral is available in Article 4 of the Final RTS. A broad set of asset classes are permitted, but trade parties may choose to further restrict collateral which is acceptable between them; parties must agree the list of eligible collateral. (In practice, many firms prefer *cash collateral*, or they apply the same eligibility set as defined within their legacy legal agreements.)

The *haircuts* applicable to eligible collateral (as listed above) can be found in Annex II of the Final RTS.

48.4.2 Non-Centrally Cleared Trades: Initial Margin Regulations

In parallel with its purpose for centrally cleared trades, initial margin (IM) for non-centrally cleared trades is designed to protect both trade parties against the maximum estimated loss (potential future exposure) in the value of one (or more) individual trades which are currently live and outstanding.

From a collateral management perspective, the specific regulations (stated in the Final RTS) relating to IM in the non-centrally cleared trade environment include the following:

- both parties to a trade are required to post IM to its counterparty, without offsetting the amounts due (Article 11.2)
- IM may not be posted for the following OTC derivative transaction types (Article 27):
  - Foreign exchange forwards that are physically settled:
    - see Chapter 18 'OTC Derivatives and Collateral – Transaction Types – Foreign Exchange Swaps', and in particular Sub-section 18.2.2 '"Forward" Foreign Exchange'
  - *Foreign exchange swaps* that are physically settled:
    - see Chapter 18 'OTC Derivatives and Collateral – Transaction Types – Foreign Exchange Swaps'
  - *Cross-currency swaps* – exchange of principal:
    - see Chapter 19 'OTC Derivatives and Collateral – Transaction Types – Cross-Currency Swaps'
- Calculation method:
  - trade parties have the choice of utilising 1) a standardised approach, or 2) a calculation method agreed between the trade parties or provided by a third party agent, or 3) both methods (Article 11.1)
  - each trade party must agree on the calculation methods(s) used by its counterparty, but the parties are not required to use the same method (Article 11.5)
- Calculation frequency and timing:
  - IM must be calculated no later than the business day following one of these events, for example (Article 9.2):
    - execution of a new trade
    - trade reaching its *scheduled maturity date*
    - non-collateral-related payment or delivery
    - no IM calculated for the prior 10 business days
  - time zones (Article 9.3):
    - where both trade parties are located in the same time zone, calculations must be based upon the trade population as at the previous business day
    - where the trade parties are located in different time zones, calculations must be based upon the trade population prior to 4:00pm in the earlier time zone

- Form of collateral:
  - IM may be collected in the form of *cash collateral* or *non-cash collateral* (Article 4)
- Concentration limits:
  - *concentration limits* are applicable (Article 8.1)
- Threshold:
  - under particular conditions, a *threshold* of up to EUR 50 million can be applied between the trading firms (Article 29.1)
  - for intragroup trades, a threshold of up to EUR 10 million can be applied (Article 29.1)
- Minimum transfer amount (MTA):
  - an *MTA* may be agreed between trading parties (Article 25.2)
  - the MTA must not be greater than EUR 500,000.00 (Article 25.1)
  - it is permitted to have an IM MTA separate from a VM MTA, however, the sum of the two MTAs must not exceed EUR 500,000.00 (Article 25.4)
  - where an exposure amount exceeds the MTA, the full exposure amount should be called without deduction of the MTA (Article 25.3)
- Haircut:
  - cash collateral in the same currency as the exposure is subject to no *haircut* (Annex II)
  - cash collateral in a different currency from the exposure is subject to an 8% haircut (Annex II)
  - non-cash collateral is subject to a haircut according to the characteristics of the instrument (Annex II)
  - non-cash collateral in a different currency from the exposure is subject to an 8% haircut (Annex II)
- Timing of instructing:
  - the *collateral giver* must issue its *payment instruction* or delivery instruction within the business day of calculation (Article 13.2). (Firms need to agree with their counterparties whether *trade date* (T) or T+1 applies for the issuance of instructions. To clarify, this regulation does not refer to when settlement is due to occur.)
- Margin call disputes:
  - as a first step, the *undisputed amount* should be settled within the same business day (Article 13.3)
- Holding cash collateral:
  - if certain conditions apply, a firm is restricted to placing with a single *custodian* 20% of total collateral collected from a particular counterparty in the form of cash (Article 8.5)
  - can be held by a central bank or third party credit institution (Article 19.1)
  - is freely transferable to the *collateral giver* in the event of *default* by the *collateral taker* (Article 19.1)
  - reinvestment by a third party is permitted (Article 20.2)
- Holding securities collateral:
  - collateral received must be segregated (Article 19.4)
  - collateral must be revalued daily (Article 19.1)
  - if the collateral giver holds the collateral, it must be held in an insolvency-remote custody account (Article 19.1)
  - is transferable without regulatory or legal constraints (Article 19.1)

- Reuse and rehypothecation:
  - *reuse* or *rehypothecation* of collateral received is not permitted (Article 20.1)
  - *reinvestment* of cash collateral is permitted (Article 20.2)
- *Collateral substitution*:
  - existing assets held as collateral may be substituted (Article 19.2).

Market Participants Impacted (and Associated Implementation Deadlines) Whether a firm is impacted by IM requirements for non-centrally cleared trades is dependent upon their firm type. For a list of Financial Counterparty types, please refer to Chapter 47 'OTC Derivatives and Collateral – Regulatory Change and the Future of Collateral – Centrally Cleared Trades', and in particular Sub-section 47.10.1 'European Union (EU) Market Participants Subject to the Clearing Obligation: Overview', and Sub-section 47.10.2 'European Union (EU) Market Participants Exempt from the Clearing Obligation: Overview'.

Those European Union (EU) parties that <u>are</u> subject to the IM requirement for non-centrally cleared trades are:

- all *financial counterparties* (FCs)
- *non-financial counterparties* (NFCs):
  - *NFC+* (any NFC whose OTC derivative activity surpasses a defined *clearing threshold*),

providing that, with specific reference to non-centrally cleared OTC derivative trades, the above have an aggregate month end average *notional principal* amount of a minimum of EUR 8 billion. The deadlines for exchanging IM relate to the size of outstanding notional principal amounts at the group level, as depicted in the table below:

TABLE 48.2 Deadlines for exchanging initial margin

Non-Centrally Cleared Trades: Deadlines for Exchanging Initial Margin	
Both Parties Subject to the IM Requirement with AANA* in excess of:	**Trade Date from which New Trades Trigger IM Requirement**
EUR 3 trillion**	February 4th 2017
EUR 2.25 trillion	September 1st 2017
EUR 1.5 trillion	September 1st 2018
EUR 0.75 trillion	September 1st 2019
EUR 8 billion***	September 1st 2020

*AANA = Aggregate Average Notional Amount (gross notional principal outstanding amount)

**1 trillion = 1,000,000,000,000; one million million

***1 billion = 1,000,000,000; one thousand million

Source: Final RTS (Article 36)

Notes:

- calculation of AANA is defined further within Article 39 of the Final RTS
- the regulations apply only to new trades entered into from the dates specified in Table 48.2; *legacy bilateral trades* remain unaffected
- despite the fact that *pension funds* are temporarily exempt from the clearing obligation for centrally cleared trades, they are not exempt from the IM regulations relating to non-centrally cleared trades
- firms classified as NFC– are exempt from the requirement to exchange IM (Article 24)
- in a situation in which Firm A falls into the first deadline (i.e. February 2017), and its counterparty Firm B falls into the final deadline (i.e. September 2020), mandatory exchange of collateral for trades between Firm A and Firm B will begin from the less constraining deadline (i.e. September 2020)
- as stated within Chapter 47 'OTC Derivatives and Collateral – Regulatory Change and the Future of Collateral – Centrally Cleared Trades', in the case in which a non-EU entity would be classified as FC or NFC+ if it was established in the EU, that non-EU entity falls under the scope of EMIR for all the trades with EU entities which are FC or NFC+.

48.4.3 Non-Centrally Cleared Trades: Variation Margin Regulations

In parallel with its purpose for centrally cleared trades, variation margin (VM) for non-centrally cleared trades is designed to protect the trade party that has a *positive mark-to-market* relating to one (or many) OTC derivative trade which is currently live and outstanding.

From a collateral management perspective, the specific regulations (stated in the Final RTS) relating to VM in the non-centrally cleared trade environment include:

- on any one occasion where a *margin call* is made, only one of the trade parties must validly make a VM call, taking account of the *mark-to-market* of the OTC derivative trade(s) plus or minus the current value of any existing collateral (Article 10)
- Calculation method
  - trade parties are required to utilise the mark-to-market (M2M) method, but if market conditions prevent use of M2M, then utilise the *mark-to-model* method (Article 11.2 in Regulation No 648/2012)
- Calculation frequency and timing:
  - VM must be calculated at least on a daily basis (Article 9.1):
  - time zones (Article 9.3)
    - where both trade parties are located in the same time zone, calculations must be based upon the trade population as at the previous business day
    - where the trade parties are located in different time zones, calculations must be based upon the trade population prior to 4:00pm in the earlier time zone
- Form of collateral:
  - VM may be collected in the form of *cash collateral* or *non-cash collateral* (Article 4)

- Minimum transfer amount (MTA):
  - an *MTA* may be agreed between trading parties (Article 25.2)
  - the MTA must not be greater than EUR 500,000.00 (Article 25.1)
  - it is permitted to have a VM MTA separate from an IM MTA, however, the sum of the two MTAs must not exceed EUR 500,000.00 (Article 25.4)
  - where an exposure amount exceeds the MTA, the full exposure amount should be called without deduction of the MTA (Article 25.3)
- Haircut
  - cash collateral, whether in the same or different currency as the exposure, is subject to no *haircut* (Annex II)
  - non-cash collateral in the same currency as the exposure is subject to a haircut according to the characteristics of the instrument (Annex II)
  - non-cash collateral in a different currency from the exposure is subject to an 8% haircut (Annex II)
- Timing of instructing
  - the *collateral giver* must issue its *payment instruction* or delivery instruction within the business day of calculation (Article 12.1)
- Margin call disputes
  - as a first step, the *undisputed amount* should be settled within the same business day (Article 12.3)
- Holding securities collateral
  - must be revalued daily (Article 19.1)
  - is transferable without regulatory or legal constraints (Article 19.1)
- *Collateral substitution*:
  - existing assets held as collateral may be substituted (Article 19.2).

Market Participants Impacted (and Associated Implementation Deadlines) Whether a firm is impacted by VM requirements for non-centrally cleared trades is dependent upon their firm type. For a list of financial counterparty types, please refer to Chapter 47 'OTC Derivatives and Collateral – Regulatory Change and the Future of Collateral – Centrally Cleared Trades', and in particular Sub-section 47.10.1 'European Union (EU) Market Participants Subject to the Clearing Obligation: Overview', and Sub-section 47.10.2 'European Union (EU) Market Participants Exempt from the Clearing Obligation: Overview'.

Those European Union (EU) parties that <u>are</u> subject to the VM requirement for non-centrally cleared trades are:

- all *financial counterparties* (FCs)
- *non-financial counterparties* (NFCs):
  - *NFC +* (any NFC whose OTC derivative activity surpasses a defined *clearing threshold*).

The deadlines for exchanging VM relate to the type of firm involved, as depicted in Table 48.3:

TABLE 48.3 Deadlines for exchanging variation margin

Non-Centrally Cleared Trades: Deadlines for Exchanging Variation Margin	
Both Parties Subject to the VM Requirement with AANA* in excess of:	Trade Date from which New Trades Trigger VM Requirement
EUR 3 trillion**	February 4th 2017
All Other FC and NFC+	March 1st 2017

*AANA = Aggregate Average Notional Amount (gross notional principal outstanding amount)
**1 trillion = 1,000,000,000,000; one million million
Source: Final RTS (Article 37)

Notes:

- calculation of AANA is defined further within Article 39 of the Final RTS
- the regulations apply only to new trades entered into from the dates specified in the table above; *legacy bilateral trades* remain unaffected
- despite the fact that pension funds are temporarily exempt from the clearing obligation for centrally cleared trades, they are not exempt from the VM regulations relating to non-centrally cleared trades
- firms classified as NFC– are exempt from the requirement to exchange VM (Article 24).

48.4.4 Non-Centrally Cleared Trades: Initial Margin versus Variation Margin Regulations

Table 48.4 compares a number of components of initial margin (IM) and variation margin (VM) regulatory requirements, in order to provide an 'at-a-glance' guide to their similarities and differences:

TABLE 48.4 IM and VM regulations: similarities and differences

Non-Centrally Cleared Trades Initial Margin versus Variation Margin Regulations		
Margin-Related Component	Initial Margin	Variation Margin
Parties Subject to Regulation	FC and NFC+	
Implementation Deadlines	From February 4th 2017, and Phased-In up to 2020	From February 4th 2017, or from March 1st 2017
Party Responsible for Posting Margin	Both Parties	Non-Exposed Party (Per Call)
Is Margin Offsettable (Nettable)?	Not Permitted	Yes
Exposure Calculation: Method	Choice of Methods	*(see below)
Exposure Calculation: Frequency	Following Specific Events, at the latest following 10 business days	At Least Daily

(continued)

PART 4c

TABLE 48.4   IM and VM regulations: similarities and differences *(continued)*

Margin-Related Component	Initial Margin	Variation Margin
Exposure Calculation: Timing	No later than business day following the event	Unspecified
Form of Collateral	Cash or Non-Cash	
Concentration Limits	Applicable	Unspecified
Threshold	Up to EUR 50 million**, and up to EUR 10 million for intragroup trades	Unspecified
Minimum Transfer Amount	Up to EUR 500,000 combined	
Separate Minimum Transfer Amounts	Permitted	
Where Exposure Greater Than MTA	Call Full Exposure Amount	
Haircut: Cash Collateral: Same Currency	0%	
Haircut: Cash Collateral: Cross-Currency	8%	0%
Haircut: Non-Cash Collateral: Same Currency	Dependent Upon Instrument Characteristics	
Haircut: Non-Cash Collateral: Cross-Currency	8%	
Timing of Instructing	Within Business Day of Calculation	
Margin Call Disputes: First Step	Undisputed Amount To Be Settled Same Day	
Holding Cash Collateral By Custodian	Restriction Applicable**	Unspecified
Holding Cash Collateral By Third Party	Applicable	Unspecified
Holding Securities Collateral: Segregation	Applicable	Unspecified
Holding Securities Collateral: Revaluation	Daily	
Reuse and Rehypothecation	Not Permitted	Unspecified
Collateral Substitution	Permitted	

*marking-to-market is the preferred method, but if not available then use marking-to-model
**under certain conditions

Note: over and above the regulatory requirements stated above, trading parties may choose to apply further or additional parameters in the legal agreements that are set up between them; for example, a haircut may be applied to variation margin on cross-currency cash collateral.

48.5 NON-CENTRALLY CLEARED TRADES: LEGAL DOCUMENTATION

It is expected that the vast majority of *buy-side* and *sell-side* firms will have in place existing **Credit Support Annexes** (CSAs) with their various **counterparties**. Such legacy CSAs will contain either 1) the originally negotiated terms and conditions agreed between the two parties, or 2) in some cases amended or additional (in the form of an annex) terms and conditions following further negotiation in the past.

In order to produce a worldwide benchmark covering margin regulations for non-centrally cleared trades, a working group was formed by the **International Swaps and Derivatives Association** (ISDA), leading to the publication of a global policy document by the **Basel Committee on Banking Supervision** (BCBS) and the **International Organization of Securities Commissions** (IOSCO). This policy document has then been applied to regional jurisdictions, resulting in Europe in the Final Regulatory Technical Standards (Final RTS) described earlier in this chapter.

In order for trade parties to sign (and going forward, to operate by) standard legal documentation which reflects the margin regulations defined within the Final RTS (which entered into force in January 2017), ISDA has developed updated versions of jurisdiction-specific standard CSAs covering initial margin (the IM CSA) and variation margin (the VM CSA) separately. The Final RTS regulations for VM contain a similar set of conditions as those contained within legacy CSAs. However, the regulations covering IM in many cases did not exist within legacy CSAs, although in some trading relationships collateral was given or taken as an *independent amount*, in recognition of either a significant difference in the credit rating of the two firms, or because the OTC derivative product was regarded as riskier than normal.

The following are related points covering both the IM CSA and the VM CSA:

- IM received is required to be segregated, whereas VM received is not:
  - this significant difference in treatment of margin received gave rise to the creation of separate IM and VM CSAs, as to have both is regarded as operationally simpler
- a firm will need to put in place both an IM CSA and a VM CSA with each of its *bilateral* counterparties:
  - providing the firm and its counterparty are subject to the regulation
- where a firm and its counterparty have a legacy CSA in place, that CSA can be amended to take account of the terms and conditions contained within the regulation, or the new CSA can be signed instead:
  - please refer to the comment below regarding the ongoing treatment of legacy trades.

The introduction of the Final RTS and the related VM CSA gives rise to a decision to be made by individual firms and their counterparties. With effect from the relevant mandatory date (see Table 48.3 'Deadlines for Exchanging Variation Margin' and in particular 'Trade Date from which New Trades Trigger VM Requirement'), a firm is obliged to comply with the VM regulations stated within the Final RTS; compliance with that regulation requires the firm to have a bilateral legal agreement in place (either the VM CSA or an amended legacy CSA containing the terms and conditions in the Final RTS). Assuming the firm and its counterparty sign a VM CSA, together they must decide whether to go forward with:

- both the legacy CSA and the VM CSA concurrently, thereby requiring separate but parallel collateral management of trades according to their trade date:
  - the legacy CSA for trades executed prior to the relevant mandatory date, and
  - the VM CSA for trades executed on and after the relevant mandatory date, or
- only the VM CSA, wherein both legacy trades and new trades would all be subject to the terms and conditions in the VM CSA. Note that, if this is the chosen option, all legacy trades between the two trade parties must be included; an 'all or nothing' option.

The ISDA 2016 Variation Margin Protocol is a structured approach by which a firm and its counterparty are able to effectively amend their legacy CSA, in order to reflect the regulations detailed within the Final RTS. Frequently asked questions regarding the protocol can be found at: http://www2.isda.org/functional-areas/protocol-management/faq/29.

48.6 NON-CENTRALLY CLEARED TRADES: FURTHER RISK MITIGATION REGULATIONS

In addition to the *initial margin* (IM) and *variation margin* (VM) regulations described earlier in this chapter, a number of other risk mitigation regulations have been introduced relating to non-centrally cleared OTC derivatives.

The International Organization of Securities Commissions (IOSCO) was responsible for developing the regulations which pertain to all parties that execute trades in non-centrally cleared OTC derivatives. The primary risk mitigation regulations which impact collateral management are summarised as:

- *Trade confirmation*:
    - material details of trades must be communicated to *counterparties* as soon as possible following *trade execution*
- *Portfolio reconciliation*:
    - in an attempt to prevent *margin call* disagreements, trade parties should periodically reconcile each trade within a *portfolio*
- Trade valuation (*marking-to-market*):
    - for the purpose of identifying and mitigating exposures, the process and frequency of determining the value of trades should be agreed with counterparties
- *Portfolio compression*:
    - with a view to reducing the number of gross trades to a net position, trade parties should regularly assess their portfolio of trades
- *Dispute resolution*:
    - to minimise the impact of trade and/or valuation differences, trade parties should agree the process by which a margin call discrepancy is escalated to a dispute.

The following sub-sections expand upon each of the risk mitigation measures listed above, including the deadline(s) by which each are required to be implemented, and which trade parties (whether *FC*, *NFC+* or *NFC–*) are impacted.

Much of the information contained within this section is reproduced with the permission of:

- The European Union; the English version of 'Risk Mitigation Techniques for OTC Derivatives Contracts Not Cleared by a CCP', Commission Delegated Regulation (EU) No 149/2013 (dated 19th December 2012) and 2017/2155 (dated 22nd September 2017); these documents are available from http://eur-lex.europa.eu
- IOSCO, please see: http://www.iosco.org/library/pubdocs/pdf/IOSCOPD469.pdf.

48.6.1 Trade Confirmation Regulations

The reasons for and the essential elements of the *trade confirmation* process are described within Chapter 29 'OTC Derivatives and Collateral – The Collateral Lifecycle – Post-Trading – Trade Confirmation/ Affirmation'.

There is a risk that one or more discrepancies exist in any trade in the financial services industry which is executed on an *OTC* basis (as opposed to being exchange-traded); OTC trades occur in the *foreign exchange* market and in the *bond* market, as well as in the derivatives market. The involvement of human beings in the *trade execution* process frequently results in differences in trade details captured by the two trade parties; the trade confirmation/affirmation process is the primary mechanism used across the financial services industry to identify whether a firm's OTC executed trade details are the same as the *counterparty's* trade details, or are different.

For any trade executed on an OTC basis, but particularly important for OTC derivatives, if trade details between the two trading parties are not the same, numerous problems will result in the areas of *trade processing* and *collateral processing* throughout the trade's lifetime. The solution to such potential issues is to compare the trade details captured by both parties, via the trade confirmation or *trade affirmation* process.

Following trade execution, the speed with which trade details are compared between the trade parties is a critical factor; if the comparison of a counterparty's trade confirmation details with a firm's *books & records* takes an excessive amount of time (as was often the case prior to the mid-2000s), problems typically result. For example, if it takes 3 days (after *trade date*) for the trade parties to identify that a difference in a trade component (e.g. price or rate) exists, there is a distinct possibility that one of the trade parties will be very unhappy about amending their price or rate, particularly if market prices have moved against them over those 3 days.

The steps in the overall (non-electronic) process which results in a firm comparing its counterparty's trade confirmation against the firm's books & records are:

1. trade execution by the traders of Firm A and Firm B
2. trade capture by the traders of Firm A and by Firm B
3. generation and transmission of a trade confirmation by (say) Firm A
4. receipt of Firm A's trade confirmation by Firm B
5. comparison by Firm B of Firm A's trade confirmation versus Firm B's books & records
6. if Firm B discovers a discrepancy, communicating the fact to Firm A
7. investigation of the discrepancy between *operations* (or in some firms, *middle office*) personnel of both firms
8. dependent upon the discrepancy's nature, escalation of the issue to the traders of both firms
9. the traders of both firms resolve the issue between them
10. (say) Firm A's trader amends the price or rate of the trade captured originally, resulting in …
11. generation and transmission of an amended trade confirmation by Firm A
12. receipt of Firm A's amended trade confirmation by Firm B
13. comparison by Firm B of Firm A's amended trade confirmation versus Firm B's books & records.

As can be seen, there are a significant number of steps in the non-electronic trade confirmation process and a trade party that is due to receive a trade confirmation from its counterparty has usually had little control over the speed with which its counterparty acts, or the accuracy of its counterparty's trade confirmation. However, a control can be applied by *buy-side* firms where time limits (for the receipt of trade confirmations) are imposed on their *sell-side* counterparties. Another form of control can be applied where a regulatory procedure exists with time limits for comparison of trade details; for example, *ICMA* members were obliged to transmit electronically their bond trade details to ICMA's TRAX system within 30 minutes of trade execution, following which the matching status of trades was made available electronically to both trading parties.

Note: electronic trade confirmation platforms exist, and this is the faster and more efficient mechanism by which trade details are compared. However, in order to make use of such platforms, both trade parties must be members.

In conclusion, it is a fact that the longer it takes for a trade's details to be compared by one or both parties, the greater the risk of price or rate movement and of one of the parties incurring a loss. Furthermore, a trade which remains unconfirmed can result in interest payments (in an *interest rate swap*) or *premium* payments (in a *credit default swap*) made by a firm being unable to be agreed by its counterparty, and *margin calls* being disputed. Consequently, the introduction of this regulation is the authorities' underlining the importance of the trade confirmation/affirmation process.

The Regulations (Overview)   In brief, the regulations pertaining to trade confirmation relating to non-centrally cleared trades are:

- firms should implement procedures to ensure that trades are confirmed as soon as practicable following trade execution
- confirmations should be issued via electronic means whenever possible, otherwise in writing non-electronically
- deadlines for confirming trades will vary according to the types of parties involved; please refer to Table 48.5
- for *financial counterparties*, trades remaining unconfirmed beyond 5 business days must be reported to the appropriate regulatory authority, on a monthly basis.

(The full and final text is available from The European Union; the English version of 'Risk Mitigation Techniques for OTC Derivatives Contracts Not Cleared by a CCP', Commission Delegated Regulation (EU) No 149/2013 (dated 19th December 2012) and 2017/2155 (dated 22nd September 2017); these documents are available from http://eur-lex.europa.eu.)

Implementation Deadlines and Market Participants Impacted   At the time of writing, the deadline originally stated by the regulatory authorities, beginning in 2013, has passed. The final and current regulation is that firms of different types must meet the regulation as per Table 48.5:

TABLE 48.5   Trade confirmation regulations

Non-Centrally Cleared Trades Trade Confirmation Regulations	
Party Type	Final Deadline (By Close of Business)
Financial Counterparty (FC)	Trade Date + 1 Business Day (T+1)
Non-Financial Counterparty above clearing threshold (NFC+)	
Non-Financial Counterparty below clearing threshold (NFC−)	Trade Date + 2 Business Days (T+2)

Source: The European Union

Notes:

- the clearing thresholds for non-financial counterparties are stated within this chapter in Sub-section 48.3.1 'European Union (EU) Market Participants Exempt from the Clearing Obligation: Overview'. To clarify, the obligation to confirm non-centrally cleared trades is applicable to all firms, regardless whether a firm is above or below the clearing threshold
- when an FC or NFC+ trades with an NFC−, the less constraining obligations will apply: for timely confirmation, confirm within T+2.

48.6.2 Portfolio Reconciliation Regulations

The reasons for and the essential elements of portfolio reconciliation are described within Chapter 31 'OTC Derivatives and Collateral – The Collateral Lifecycle – Throughout Lifetime of Trade – Portfolio Reconciliation'.

The word 'portfolio' refers to the complete list of trades which a firm believes are validly live and outstanding with a particular counterparty. When it comes to *exposure* calculation which (in many cases) will lead to *margin calls* being made by the party with a *positive mark-to-market*, there is a significant likelihood of the margin call recipient disagreeing the margin call amount and/or direction, if the trade population on which exposures are calculated differs between the two parties.

In advance of either trade party issuing a margin call to its counterparty, performing a proactive comparison of the list of trades from both firms (*portfolio reconciliation*) is regarded as a sensible risk mitigation measure designed to avoid or to minimise the likelihood of margin call disagreements.

Events which can cause a firm's list of (what the firm believes are) validly live and outstanding trades to differ from their counterparty's list include:

- new trades captured by one trade party but not by the other
- new trades captured by one trade party against the incorrect counterparty
- bilateral *novation* captured by one trade party but not by the other
- *early termination* captured by one trade party but not by the other
- trade having reached its *scheduled maturity date* removed by one trade party but not by the other.

Given a choice, some firms may choose to conduct proactive portfolio reconciliation in recognition of its risk mitigation benefits, whereas other firms may prefer not to do so. The introduction of the regulation imposes portfolio reconciliation on firms of all types.

The Regulations (Overview)   In brief, the regulations pertaining to portfolio reconciliation relating to non-centrally cleared trades are:

- firms should document the agreed arrangements by which their trade portfolios are reconciled with each of their counterparties
  - this must be actioned prior to trade execution
- trade parties may perform the act of reconciling portfolios by themselves, or appoint a qualified third party to do so

PART 4c

- the reconciliation must include the primary trade details enabling unique identification of each trade, including:
  - underlying instrument
  - operation (direction) applicable to each party
  - price or rate
  - trade currency
  - *notional principal*
  - scheduled settlement dates
  - scheduled maturity date
- the reconciliation must also include the current valuation (*mark-to-market*) of each trade within the portfolio.

Note: additional trade components are expected to be added to the reconciliation as such trade components become part of the *transaction reporting* obligation. An example of this is the *unique trade identifier* (UTI).

(The full and final text is available from The European Union; the English version of 'Risk Mitigation Techniques for OTC Derivatives Contracts Not Cleared by a CCP', Commission Delegated Regulation (EU) No 149/2013 (dated 19th December 2012) and 2017/2155 (dated 22nd September 2017); these documents are available from http://eur-lex.europa.eu.)

Implementation Deadlines and Market Participants Impacted   At the time of writing, the deadline originally stated by the regulatory authorities, beginning in 2013, has passed. The final and current regulation is that firms of different types must meet the regulation as per Table 48.6:

TABLE 48.6   Portfolio reconciliation regulations

Non-Centrally Cleared Trades Portfolio Reconciliation Regulations		
Party Type	Number of Live and Outstanding Trades	Frequency of Reconciliation
Financial Counterparty (FC), and Non-Financial Counterparty above clearing threshold (NFC+)	500 or more	Each Business Day
	51 – 499 (at any time during the week)	Once per Week
	50 or less (at any time during the quarter)	Once per Quarter
Non-Financial Counterparty below clearing threshold (NFC–)	101 or more (at any time during the quarter)	Once per Quarter
	100 or less	Once per Year

Source: The European Union

Notes:

- the clearing thresholds for non-financial counterparties are stated within this chapter in Sub-section 48.3.1 'European Union (EU) Market Participants Exempt from the Clearing Obligation: Overview'. To clarify, the obligation to perform portfolio reconciliation of non-centrally cleared trades is applicable to all firms, regardless

whether a firm is above or below the clearing threshold. As can be seen from the table, only the reconciliation frequency differs
- as the above reconciliation frequency is usually difficult to implement with a large number of counterparties, and as it may change from time to time, market practice is to reconcile on a daily basis.

When this regulation came into effect on 15th September 2013, all live and outstanding trades were subject to the regulation; consequently, trades executed prior to that date (*legacy bilateral trades*) must be included within the portfolio for reconciliation purposes.

48.6.3 Trade Valuation Regulations

The reasons for and the essential elements of the trade valuation process are described within Chapter 32 'OTC Derivatives and Collateral – The Collateral Lifecycle – Throughout Lifetime of Trade – Marking-to-Market'.

From the perspective of a firm that has executed a trade in a non-centrally cleared OTC derivative, it is of paramount importance that the firm gathers the *current market price* accurately, and at an appropriate frequency. Only by so doing can the firm accurately identify when it is *exposed*, and therefore when it needs to issue a *margin call* to its *counterparty*. When it transpires that the counterparty has the exposure, the firm will still need to have determined the trade's current valuation so as to be in a position to assess the validity of the counterparty's margin call.

In the past, *bilateral* trade valuation differences relating to OTC derivative trades have been a common reason as to why margin call disagreements have arisen (which if not resolved will become margin call disputes). This is in addition to differences which may arise in the list of trades within a portfolio; see Sub-section 48.6.2 'Portfolio Reconciliation Regulations'.

Although current prices or rates relating to commonly traded OTC derivative products may be readily available, not all OTC derivative products will necessarily fall within that same category, in which case trade valuation may prove to be a significantly greater challenge. For this and previously stated reasons, the regulations require that a firm agrees the trade valuation arrangements with each of its counterparties in an attempt to minimise valuation differences.

The Regulations (Overview)   In brief, the regulations pertaining to trade valuation relating to non-centrally cleared trades are:

- *financial counterparties* and *non-financial counterparties* above the *clearing threshold* (NFC+) should *mark-to-market* all outstanding trades on a daily basis
- where marking-to-market is prevented due to market conditions, the *mark-to-model* method should be used.

(The full and final text is available from The European Union; the English version of 'OTC Derivatives, Central Counterparties and Trade Repositories', Commission

Delegated Regulation (EU) No 648/2012, dated 4th July 2012, (specifically Article 11.2); this document is available from http://eur-lex.europa.eu.)

At a more granular level, standards and key considerations relating to trade valuation has been provided by the International Organization of Securities Commissions (IOSCO), in their document 'Risk Mitigation Standards for Non-Centrally Cleared Trades', dated 28th January 2015. The following points are based on IOSCO's wording:

- for the purpose of exchanging margins, firms should document the agreed arrangements by which their live and outstanding trades are valued
    - from *trade execution* through to the *scheduled maturity date*, or *earlier termination*
- trade valuations may be determined internally or by third parties
- in order to take account of any changes in market conditions, firms should periodically review the previously agreed valuation process.

Implementation Deadlines and Market Participants Impacted At the time of writing, the deadline originally stated by the regulatory authorities, beginning in 2013, has passed. The final and current regulation is that firms of different types either are or are not subject to the regulation as per Table 48.7:

TABLE 48.7 Trade valuation regulations

Non-Centrally Cleared Trades Trade Valuation Regulations	
Party Type	Subject to Regulation? (Daily Marking-to-Market)
Financial Counterparty (FC)	Yes
Non-Financial Counterparty above clearing threshold (NFC+)	
Non-Financial Counterparty below clearing threshold (NFC−)	No

Source: The European Union

Note: the clearing thresholds for non-financial counterparties are stated within this chapter in Sub-section 48.3.1 'European Union (EU) Market Participants Exempt from the Clearing Obligation: Overview'. To clarify, the obligation to value non-centrally cleared trades on a daily basis is applicable only to firms classified as FC or NFC+, whereas the regulation does not apply to firms below the clearing threshold (NFC−).

48.6.4 Portfolio Compression Regulations

The reasons for and the essential elements of the portfolio compression process are described within Chapter 30 'OTC Derivatives and Collateral – The Collateral Lifecycle – Post-Trading – Trade/Portfolio Netting'.

In summary, trade/portfolio netting is the process of offsetting trades that contain the same details as an existing position in the same OTC derivative product, and updating that existing position to a new net position, whilst terminating (cancelling) the original trades. This netting process is commonly known as *portfolio compression*.

The holding of OTC derivative trades to their *scheduled maturity date*, especially when trades can have a lifetime of c.50 years, carries significant annual maintenance costs and risks, which can be either eliminated or minimised by reducing the number of trades to maintain, through the netting/compression process whereby 'unnecessary' gross trades are removed and/or replaced by an equivalent net trade.

Without netting/compressing multiple trades with a particular counterparty, the original trades will remain live and outstanding until their scheduled maturity date, requiring a significant amount of *trade processing* and *collateral processing* effort by both trade parties. Portfolio compression should therefore be regarded as a portfolio efficiency mechanism which positively impacts subsequent trade processing tasks and collateral management.

The Regulations (Overview)   In brief, the regulations pertaining to portfolio compression relating to non-centrally cleared trades are:

- with the aim of reducing *counterparty credit risk*, firms having 500 or more non-centrally cleared OTC derivative trades live and outstanding with a bilateral counterparty must regularly (at least twice per year) assess whether to compress their portfolio of trades
- firms having assessed their portfolio, but concluded that portfolio compression is not appropriate, must be prepared to explain their decision to the relevant regulatory authority.

(The full and final text is available from The European Union; the English version of 'Risk Mitigation Techniques for OTC Derivatives Contracts Not Cleared by a CCP', Commission Delegated Regulation (EU) No 149/2013 (dated 19th December 2012) and 2017/2155 (dated 22nd September 2017); these documents are available from http://eur-lex.europa.eu.)

Implementation Deadlines and Market Participants Impacted   At the time of writing, the deadline originally stated by the regulatory authorities, beginning in 2013, has passed. The final and current regulation is that firms of all types must meet the regulation as per Table 48.8:

TABLE 48.8   Portfolio compression regulations

Non-Centrally Cleared Trades Portfolio Compression Regulations	
Party Type	Subject to Regulation?
Financial Counterparty (FC)	Yes – providing the number of live and outstanding trades between the two firms is 500 or more
Non-Financial Counterparty above clearing threshold (NFC+)	
Non-Financial Counterparty below clearing threshold (NFC–)	

Source: The European Union

PART 4c

Note: the clearing thresholds for non-financial counterparties are stated within this chapter in Sub-section 48.3.1 'European Union (EU) Market Participants Exempt from the Clearing Obligation: Overview'. To clarify, the obligation to assess a portfolio for compression purposes is applicable to firms classified as FC, NFC+ and NFC– (therefore regardless whether a firm is above or below the clearing threshold), providing the number of trades live and outstanding with a bilateral counterparty is 500 or more. The regulation is not applicable to a firm that has fewer than 500 live and outstanding trades with a bilateral counterparty.

48.6.5 Dispute Resolution Regulations

In the context of this regulation, the word 'dispute' refers to as yet unresolved differences between a firm and its *bilateral* counterparty pertaining to non-centrally cleared trades, and in particular:

- the details of a newly executed trade, or
- the valuation (*mark-to-market*) of a trade, or
- the exchange of collateral via the *margin call* process.

The regulation demands that a pre-agreed framework is implemented between a firm and its counterparty, in order to resolve any disputes that may arise in relation to newly executed and existing trades between the trade parties. The framework is designed to prevent disputes remaining unresolved and causing firms to be *exposed* to further risks. Such a framework is an innovative concept, as no equivalent has typically existed in the past.

The Regulations (Overview)   In brief, the regulations pertaining to dispute resolution relating to non-centrally cleared trades are:

- prior to a firm executing trades with its counterparty, agreed detailed procedures must be in place pertaining to disputes in relation to:
  - the recognition of trades, and
  - the valuation of trades, and
  - the exchange of collateral
- the agreed procedures must cover the identification, recording and monitoring of disputes, including:
  - the identity of the counterparty
  - the period over which the dispute has remained unresolved
  - the nature (and value, if relevant) of the dispute
  - the resolution of disputes in a timely manner, with a specific process to resolve disputes outstanding longer than 5 business days
- *financial counterparties* must report disputes to a specified regulator known as their *National Competent Authority* (NCA):
  - for a value greater than EUR 15 million which has been outstanding for 15 or more business days.

(The full and final text is available from The European Union; the English version of 'Risk Mitigation Techniques for OTC Derivatives Contracts Not Cleared by a CCP', Commission Delegated Regulation (EU) No 149/2013 (dated 19th December 2012) and 2017/2155 (dated 22nd September 2017); these documents are available from http://eur-lex.europa.eu.)

Implementation Deadlines and Market Participants Impacted At the time of writing, the deadline originally stated by the regulatory authorities, beginning in 2013, has passed. The final and current regulation is that firms must comply with the regulation as per Table 48.9:

TABLE 48.9 Dispute resolution regulations

Non-Centrally Cleared Trades Dispute Resolution Regulations		
	Subject to Regulation?	
	At Trade Execution, Agreed Procedures Must Be in Place	Reporting of Disputes with Value Greater Than EUR 15 Million Outstanding 15 or More Business Days
Financial Counterparty (FC)		Yes
Non-Financial Counterparty above clearing threshold (NFC+)	Yes	No
Non-Financial Counterparty below clearing threshold (NFC–)		

Source: The European Union

Note: the clearing thresholds for non-financial counterparties are stated within this chapter in Sub-section 48.3.1 'European Union (EU) Market Participants Exempt from the Clearing Obligation: Overview'. To clarify, the obligation to have dispute resolution procedures in place between a firm and its counterparty is applicable to firms classified as FC, NFC+ and NFC– (therefore regardless whether a firm is above or below the clearing threshold). The obligation to report disputes with a value greater than EUR 15 million and which remain unresolved for 15 or more business days is applicable only to FCs (and not to firms classified as NFC+ or NFC–).

48.7 NON-CENTRALLY CLEARED TRADES: TRADE REPORTING REGULATIONS

The reporting of trade details to a *trade repository* (TR) is the primary mechanism by which regulators are able to assess risks and *exposures* relating to all OTC derivative trades. Aligned with the European Commission's press release dated 15th September 2010 (please refer to Chapter 46 'OTC Derivatives And Collateral – Regulatory Change and the Future of Collateral: Introduction'), it is also the principal means by which greater transparency is brought to the OTC derivatives market.

(For an introductory-level description of trade reporting via TRs, please see Chapter 46 'OTC Derivatives and Collateral – Regulatory Change and the Future of Collateral – Introduction', and in particular Section 46.6 'Trade Repositories: Introduction'.)

Whether trades are *centrally cleared* or *non-centrally cleared*, it is a regulatory requirement that 100% of trades executed by a firm must be reported to a TR; furthermore, it is the responsibility of the firm to ensure that their trade details successfully reach the TR.

However, as described within Chapter 47 'OTC Derivatives and Collateral – Regulatory Change and the Future of Collateral – Centrally Cleared Trades', options exist as to the route by which a firm's trade details are reported to a TR. Those options are:

- for a firm to report directly to a TR, or
- for a firm to delegate trade reporting to:
  - the counterparty, or to
  - a third party.

If the trade parties agree that one of the parties (whether the firm or its *counterparty*) should report on behalf of both parties, the reporting party is permitted to send a single report to the TR. Regarding use of a third party, the two trade parties can agree to delegate reporting to a common third entity which would submit a single trade report (to the TR) which must clearly identify that the report is issued on behalf of both trade parties. By taking either of these trade reporting routes, the firm will have fulfilled the requirement to report the trade to a TR.

Each of the parties to a trade is at liberty to choose to which TR they report their trades. Where a trade has been executed and where each trade party wishes to send their trade details to different TRs, the trade parties are firstly required to ensure that the common data is agreed between them. Furthermore, in order to ensure that the two TRs have certainty that the trade detail received is for one and the same trade, use of a *Unique Trade Identifier* is required.

In addition to the reporting of new trades, trade reporting is necessary following trade detail amendment or trade termination.

In order for the regulatory authorities to successfully monitor exposures on an ongoing basis, in addition to the requirement for firms to report newly executed trades, the regulation requires that OTC derivative exposures are reported to a TR. To begin with, the trade detail reported must include the details regarding the collateral given or taken by a firm, and subsequently the *mark-to-market* (or *mark-to-model*) valuation must be reported. However, firms have the choice of reporting collateral and exposures at an individual trade level or at a *portfolio* level. Note that *non-financial counterparties* classified as **NFC–*** are exempt from reporting collateral and mark-to-market or mark-to-model valuations.

---

*For a list of financial counterparty types, please refer to Chapter 47 'OTC Derivatives and Collateral – Regulatory Change and the Future of Collateral – Centrally Cleared Trades', and in particular Sub-section 47.10.1 'European Union (EU) Market Participants Subject to the Clearing Obligation: Overview', and Sub-section 47.10.2 'European Union (EU) Market Participants Exempt from the Clearing Obligation: Overview'.

(The full text is available from The European Union; the English version of 'Regulatory Technical Standards on the Minimum Details of the Data to be Reported to Trade Repositories', Commission Delegated Regulation (EU) No 148/2013, dated 19th December 2012; this document is available from http://eur-lex.europa.eu.)

On 19th October 2016, the European Union published an amendment to the above-mentioned regulation, including the following:

- trade valuations must be reported by trade parties using a common methodology
- the giving and taking of both *initial margin* (IM) and *variation margin* (VM) must be reported.

(The full and final amended text is available from The European Union; the English version of 'Regulatory Technical Standards on the Minimum Details of the Data to be Reported to Trade Repositories', Commission Delegated Regulation (EU) No 2017/104, dated 19th October 2016; this document is available from http://eur-lex.europa.eu.)

The amended details required to be reported to TRs are listed within the Annex of Regulation (EU) No 2017/104.

48.7.1　Implementation Deadlines and Market Participants Impacted

Please note the following: mandatory reporting of trades began on 12th February 2014, and mandatory reporting of valuation/collateral began 6 months later. The above-mentioned changes (as introduced in October 2016) are effective from 1st November 2017.

Parties to a trade are required to report their trade details to a TR no later than T+1 (i.e. the working day following trade execution); furthermore, amendments to trade details and trade terminations must be reported.

At the time of writing, the deadline originally stated by the regulatory authorities, beginning in 2012, has passed. The final and current regulation is that firms must comply with the regulation as per Table 48.10:

TABLE 48.10　Trade reporting regulations

Non-Centrally Cleared Trades Trade Reporting Regulations			
	Requirement to Report:		
Party Type	New, Amended or Terminated Trades	IM and VM Given and Taken	Mark-to-Market & Mark-to Model Valuations
*FC	Yes	Yes	Yes
**NFC+			
***NFC–		No	No

Source: The European Union
* Financial Counterparty
** Non-Financial Counterparty above clearing threshold (NFC+)
*** Non-Financial Counterparty below clearing threshold (NFC–)

Note: the clearing thresholds for non-financial counterparties are stated within this chapter in Sub-section 48.3.1 'European Union (EU) Market Participants Exempt from the Clearing Obligation: Overview'. To clarify, the obligation to report new, amended or terminated trades is applicable to firms classified as FC, NFC+ and NFC– (therefore regardless whether a firm is above or below the clearing threshold). The obligation to report 1) IM and VM given to or taken from a counterparty, and 2) mark-to-market and mark-to-model valuations, is applicable to firms classified as FC and NFC+ (and not to firms classified as NFC–).

An up-to-date list of registered TRs under EMIR can be found at: https://www. esma.europa.eu/supervision/trade-repositories/list-registered-trade-repositories.

Glossary of Terms

This glossary contains many of the terms mentioned within the book, but additionally contains frequently used terms not used within the book, but which may be of use to the reader. Words and phrases in *italics* within the description of terms indicate that an associated glossary item exists.

Terms are not only defined, but where appropriate the relevance to collateral management is described to enable the reader to place the term in its collateral management context.

Accrued Days	The number of days that have elapsed since the most recent *Coupon Payment Date*.
Accrued Interest	On *Interest-Bearing Bonds*, the accumulated interest since the most recent *Coupon Payment Date* and payable at the next coupon payment date. When a bond is used as *Collateral*, it's full market value must include the current value of accrued interest.
Agency Capacity	A method of trading in which a firm acts as an intermediary between two parties, typically charging *Commission* for its services. Also known as a *Broker*.
Agency Lending	See *Lending Agent*.
AIFMD	Acronym for *Alternative Investment Fund Managers Directive*
Alternative Investment Fund	In general terms, a collective investment scheme that invests in non-traditional asset types (e.g. *Derivatives*), and/or employs non-traditional investment strategies.
Alternative Investment Fund Managers Directive	European regulatory framework governing the activities of managers of *Alternative Investment Funds*. Commonly known as *AIFMD*.
American Depository Receipt	Documents that represent shares held in overseas companies and which enable US investors to invest in such securities in a tax efficient manner. ADRs are traded in their own right at a US Dollar price. See *Global Depository Receipts*.
Amortising Swap	A form of *Interest Rate Swap* in which the *Notional Principal* (on which all cashflows are based) reduces over time.
Annual General Meeting	A 12-monthly assembly of a company's board of directors and *Shareholders*, at which its future plans and performance are discussed, and voting opportunities arise.

Anti-Money Laundering	Legal procedures and controls designed to identify and report attempts to generate revenue illegally. See *Money Laundering*.
Asset-Backed Security	Generic term for a *Security* whose value is derived from a collection of *Underlying* assets. See *Mortgage-Backed Security*.
Asset Manager	An individual or organisation that manages the assets (normally *Securities* and cash) owned by its clients, with the general objective of maximising the return on the assets on behalf of the clients.
ASX Code	A 3-character number to uniquely identify individual *Equity* securities traded over the Australian Stock Exchange.
Asymmetrical Threshold	An amount of *Uncollateralised Exposure* applicable to one party only, where threshold is applicable to *Margin Calls* made by the weaker-rated party, but not to the stronger-rated party.
Back-to-Back Trading	*Trade Execution* in which a firm does not take a position, therefore any purchases are immediately sold, and vice versa. See *Market Risk Neutral*.
Backloading	1. The movement of *Legacy Trades* from the original (*Bilateral*) *Counterparty* to a *Central Counterparty*. 2. The reporting of existing trades to a *Trade Repository*.
BackUp Clearing Member	Where a *Non Clearing Member* (NCM) utilises the services of a *Clearing Member* (CM) at a *Central Counterparty*, a BackUp Clearing Member (BUCM) is appointed to transfer the NCM's positions to the BUCM in the event of default by the CM. See *Porting*
Bank for International Settlements	A Switzerland-based institution which supports numerous central banks and encourages international financial cooperation and stability.
Bank Interest	Cash interest which is payable or receivable on cash loans/deposits and *Repo* trades. The day count is actual (calendar) days, and the divisor is dependent upon the currency involved, either 360 (EUR/USD) or 365 (GBP).
Bankruptcy	The insolvency of a bond issuer in a *Credit Default Swap*. The occurrence of issuer bankruptcy will cause payout by the *Protection Seller* to the *Protection Buyer*. One type of *Credit Event*.
Base Currency	1. In a *Foreign Exchange* trade, a firm's existing currency that they wish to sell, resulting in the purchase of the *Quote Currency* at the agreed exchange rate. 2. In a *Credit Support Annex*, the currency into which *Exposures* and *Collateral* are converted.
Basel Committee on Banking Supervision	A worldwide organisation that sets standards for regulation and working practices of banks globally.
Basis Points Per Annum	A means of expressing a price or rate, where 1 basis point is 1/100th of 1%, therefore 0.01% (171 bppa = 1.71%).
Basket Default Swap	A *Credit Default Swap* in which multiple *Reference Entities* are applicable (as opposed to a single issuer as is the case in a Single Name *Credit Default Swap*).

BCBS	Acronym for *Basel Committee on Banking Supervision*.
Bearer Security	A *Security* issued in the form of physical paper *Certificates* which has no facility for the *Issuer* to record the owner of the security, and where proof of ownership is physical possession of the security certificate; historically, mainly *Bonds* rather than *Equity* were issued in bearer form. See *Bond Denominational Values*. For comparison, see *Registered Security*.
Beneficial Owner and Beneficial Ownership	In *Collateral*-related transactions executed under the *GMRA*, the *GMSLA* and the *English Law CSA*, the beneficial owner of securities collateral is the *Collateral Giver*. This means that all benefits that accrue on the *Securities* (e.g. *Coupon*, *Dividends* and other *Corporate Actions*) are owed by the *Collateral Taker* (the *Legal Owner*) to the collateral giver.
Big Bang Protocol	Relating to *Credit Default Swaps*, the introduction of a number of structural changes to standardise certain aspects of CDS trades, such as *Fixed Coupons*.
Bilateral	A term which indicates a financial transaction is executed directly between two firms, such as a *Buy-Side* firm trading with a *Sell-Side* firm. The term is not applicable to a trade in which a *Central Counterparty* is involved.
Bilateral CSA	A *Credit Support Annex* in which the stated terms are applicable to both parties. See *One-Way CSA*.
BIS	Acronym for *Bank for International Settlements*.
Block Trade	A financial transaction in which a *Fund Manager* executes a trade with a *Sell-Side* firm as *Counterparty*, but where the decision as to which of the fund manager's underlying funds the trade will be allocated is yet to be made. Once the decision is made, the 'block' trade will be replaced by the 'allocations' to the various underlying funds.
Bond	A type of *Security* that represents a loan of cash by an investor to a government, government agency, supranational organisation or company, for which the investor usually receives a fixed rate of interest periodically during the term of the loan, and receives repayment of capital at maturity of the bond, usually years later.
Bond Collateral	In *Collateral*-related transactions (*Repo*, *Securities Lending & Borrowing*, *OTC Derivatives*) the use of one or more bonds to mitigate the risk of the *Exposed Party*.
Bond Denominational Value	*Bonds* are normally issued in one (or more) denomination or quantity. For example, a bond issued to raise a total of EUR 1,000,000,000 may be issued in a single denomination of EUR 10,000, meaning that deliveries of that bond must be made in multiples of that denomination. (It is not possible to deliver a bond quantity that is not a multiple of the bond's smallest denomination.)
Bond Exchange Offer	An offer made by a *Bond Issuer* to the *Bondholders*, in which the existing bond may/will be exchanged for another bond or other asset. One form of *Corporate Action*.

Bond Repurchase Offer	An offer made by a bond issuer to the bondholders, in which the issuer offers to repurchase (buy) the bond at a defined price. One form of *Corporate Action*.
Bondholder	The owner of *Bonds*.
Bond Issue	An individual *Bond*.
Bond Issue Downgrade	The reduction in a *Rating Agency's* opinion (expressed as a lower rating) as to whether a *Bond Issuer* will make interest (*Coupon*) payments and *Capital Repayment*, when falling due; such revised ratings reflect the perceived risk of *Issuer Default*. For *Collateral* management purposes, such downgrades may cause the bond to be no longer classified as *Eligible Collateral*.
Bond Issuer	The entity that has issued a *Bond* and has received capital in exchange, from *Bondholders*.
Bonus Issue	The grant of additional *Shares* by an *Issuer* to its *Shareholders*, free of cost to the shareholders, typically at a fixed ratio of additional shares to original shares. One type of *Corporate Action*.
Book Entry	A method by which *Settlement* of trades is effected, whereby the exchange of *Securities* and cash involves no physical movement of securities, as both the seller and buyer use the same *Custodian*; under such circumstances, settlement results in a transfer of securities and cash between seller and buyer, within the custodian's books.
Books & Records	The internal record of an organisation's trading activity, positions in various financial instruments (e.g. *Securities*, *Derivatives*) and cash positions.
Books Closing Date	The date at which a company's *Share Register* is temporarily closed for the purpose of identifying, for example, the *Shareholders* to whom *Corporate Action* benefits, such as *Dividends* or *Bonus Issues*, will be paid. Also known as *Record Date*.
Borrower	An entity that issues *Bonds* as a means of raising cash is said to be the borrower of cash. Also known as the *Issuer*.
BPPA	Acronym for *Basis Points Per Annum*.
Broker	An organisation that executes trades on behalf of its clients (rather than on its own behalf), by finding buyers where clients wish to sell and finding sellers where clients wish to buy financial instruments. True brokers intend to not take *Trading Positions*, and therefore this form of trading is regarded as low risk. Such firms are said to act in an *Agency Capacity*. For comparison, see *Proprietary Trading*.
Buy-In	A formal procedure for a buyer to force the seller to deliver *Securities* owing, with associated costs payable by the seller; such procedures must be conducted under the rules of the *Stock Exchange* or market authority over which the trade has been *Executed*. For comparison, see *Sell-Out*.
Buy/Sell Back	A form of *Repo* transaction in which the *Opening Leg* and the *Closing Leg* are treated as two independent trades, whereas the two legs in a *Classic Repo* trade are linked to each other.

Buy-Side	Generic term to describe the *Institutional Investor* community that purchases financial instruments (e.g. *Equity*, *Bonds*, *OTC Derivatives*) from *Sell-Side* firms (*Investment Banks* or *Brokers*). Note that institutional investors also sell such financial instruments.
Call Option	A *Derivative* transaction in which the *Option* holder has the right (but not the obligation) to buy the *Underlying* product at a pre-agreed price (known as the *Exercise Price* or *Strike Price*), no later than the option's expiry date. See *Put Option*.
Callable Bonds	*Debt* instruments which have a feature permitting *Redemption* (by the *Issuer*) prior to the bond's *Maturity Date*. For comparison, see *Puttable Bonds*.
Capital Adequacy	Regulatory requirement for *Investment Banks* and other financial institutions to have sufficient capital (funds) available to meet their contractual obligations.
Capital Markets	Generic term for the financial marketplace in which *Equity* and *Bond Securities* are firstly brought to the marketplace (in the *Primary Market*) and then traded in the *Secondary Market*.
Capital Repayment	The return of capital by a *Bond Issuer* to *Bondholders*, scheduled to occur on the bond's *Maturity Date* but which can occur sooner in bonds that are redeemable earlier. See *Callable Bonds* and *Puttable Bonds*.
Capital Requirement	The value of assets a firm needs to set aside and avoid using, in recognition of the firm's risk. A regulatory prerequisite; also known as regulatory capital.
Cash-Based Repo	A *Repo* trade in which the primary motivation is for one party to borrow cash, requiring the cash borrower to provide collateral (normally in the form of *Bonds*) to mitigate the cash lender's risk of their cash failing to be returned. See *Stock-Based Repo*.
Cash Collateral	Collateral given or taken in the form of currency for the following transaction types: 1. *Securities Lending* may be collateralised by the *Securities Borrower* in the form of currency. 2. *OTC Derivative* exposures may be mitigated by the *Non-Exposed Party* providing currency.
Cash Collateral Reinvestment	Where an *Exposed Party* receives *Collateral* in the form of cash, the loan of such cash into the *Money Market*, with the aim of earning a superior interest rate to the rate agreed to be paid to the *Non-Exposed Party* (i.e. the *Rebate Rate*) at the close of the trade.
Cash Correspondent	The bank a firm uses to make outgoing cash payments, and to receive incoming cash payments. Some firms have a cash correspondent per currency, whereas other firms may utilise one cash correspondent (a single point of contact) that itself has a network of underlying banks per currency. Also known as *Nostro*, particularly in the world of securities operations.

Cash Dividend	The payment to *Shareholders* by an *Issuer*, of *Income* in the form of cash; whilst such payments are not guaranteed, many large companies pay cash dividends at regular intervals.
Cash Payment Risk	When paying cash by the traditional payment method (i.e. issuing a *Settlement Instruction* to a *Cash Correspondent*), the risk that payment is made to the incorrect recipient, due to there being no method of matching settlement instructions prior to payment being made. Risk is reduced if payment is made via *CLS Bank*.
Cash Settlement	In a *Credit Default Swap* and following a *Credit Event,* a settlement method whereby the *Protection Seller* pays a cash amount to the *Protection Buyer* in full and final settlement. For comparison, see *Physical Settlement*.
CCP	Acronym for *Central Counterparty.*
CCP-Eligible Assets	Financial assets used as *Collateral* (normally cash in specified currencies and highly rated *Bonds*) that are acceptable to *Central Counterparties*, as defined under *EMIR. See Non-CCP-Eligible Assets.*
CDS	Common abbreviation for *Credit Default Swap.*
Central Bank	A national institution that regulates banks and executes *Monetary Policy*, with the aim of controlling inflation and stability of the nation's currency.
Central Bank Money	Coins and notes of a particular currency that have been introduced by a *Central Bank* (as opposed to commercial bank money). Additionally, the holding and movement of such cash only within the books of the central bank.
Central Clearing	The act of a *Central Counterparty* becoming *Counterparty* to both the original buyer and the original seller, then performing *Trade Processing* and *Collateral Processing* with the original buyer and original seller throughout the lifetime of the trade. The benefit to both the original buyer and the original seller is that *Counterparty Risk* is reduced due to the strength and risk mitigation techniques of the central counterparty.
Central Counterparty	An organisation that places itself between the original parties to a trade, becoming the *Counterparty* to both seller and buyer; the resultant contractual obligation is between seller and central counterparty, and buyer and central counterparty. Due to various risk mitigation measures utilised by central counterparties, as a firm's counterparty they are considered to be low risk. Such organisations practice *Multilateral Netting.*
Central Securities Depository	The ultimate storage location of *Securities* within a financial centre, in which the record of ownership is typically maintained electronically (by *Book Entry*). Settlement (delivery of securities and payment of cash) of trades and *Collateral* movements occur following the CSD's receipt of *Settlement Instructions* from the account holders. A type of *Custodian* organisation.

Centrally Cleared Trade	For *OTC Derivatives* under *EMIR*, trades which comply with the regulatory requirement to be *Novated* to a *Central Counterparty*. The requirement relates to 1) standardised trades, and 2) both original parties must be subject to the *Clearing Obligation*. See *Non-Centrally Cleared Trades*.
Certificate	Document of ownership in a *Security*; certificates have historically been issued in *Registered* or *Bearer* form. In many financial centres today, certificates are not issued and proof of ownership is held electronically within *Book-Entry* systems at *Central Securities Depositories*.
CET	Acronym for Central European Time.
Cheapest to Deliver	Where assets are owed by one party to another, but where no specific asset is stated, the delivering party may choose which specific asset to deliver in settlement. Such situations allow the delivering party to acquire and then deliver the asset that is least expensive.
CHESS	Clearing House Electronic Subregister System; the normal place of *Settlement* for *Equity* traded in Australia. CHESS effects settlement for its account holders on a *Book-Entry* basis.
Classic Repo	A popular form of *Repo* transaction in which the *Opening Leg* and the *Closing Leg* are treated as one transaction (with two connected legs). See *Buy/Sell Back*.
Clean Price	The price of a *Bond*, excluding *Accrued Interest*; the total *Market Value* and *Collateral Value* of a bond includes its current value of accrued interest, therefore accrued interest must be added to the clean price. The alternative is *Dirty Price*.
Clearing House	An alternative name for a *Central Counterparty*.
Clearing Member	A firm that holds one or more accounts directly at a *Central Counterparty*. Such account holders are typically *Sell-Side* firms, which may offer *Client Clearing* services.
Clearing Obligation	Under *EMIR*, any *OTC Derivative* trade executed from the effective date must be cleared by a *Central Counterparty*, providing the involved parties are either a *Financial Counterparty* or a *Non-Financial Counterparty* whose trading activity surpasses the defined *Clearing Threshold*. See *NFC+* and *NFC–*.
Clearing Threshold	Under *EMIR*, a level of trading activity in *OTC Derivatives* above which a *Non-Financial Counterparty* (NFC) is obliged to clear their trades via a *Central Counterparty*, and below which an NFC is exempt. See *NFC+* and *NFC–*.
Clearstream International	Located in Luxembourg, one of the two *International Central Securities Depositories* (ICSDs) offering custody and *Settlement* services to its participants; the other ICSD is *Euroclear*.
Client Clearing	A service offered by some *Clearing Members* (CM) of a *Central Counterparty*, whereby the CM holds trades and positions for and on behalf of *Non-Clearing Members* in one or more accounts that are segregated from the CM's own trades and positions.

Close Out Netting	Should a firm's *Counterparty* experience an *Event of Default*, the current *Market Value* of all *Open Trades* is determined, following which the positive and negative trade values are *Set Off* (netted) into a cash amount payable by either the firm or its counterparty.
Closing Leg and Closing Value Date	In a two-sided transaction (e.g. *Repo* and *Securities Lending & Borrowing*), the date at which the re-exchange of assets is intended to occur.
CLS Bank	A cash *Settlement* system which facilitates the payment and receipt of cash in multiple currencies for its members, avoiding the traditional risk associated with non-matching of payment instructions. Settlement of *Foreign Exchange* trades is achieved on a simultaneous exchange basis, whilst one-way currency payments are also catered for. See *Herstatt Risk*.
Collateral	Where a transaction (e.g. *Repo*, *Securities Lending & Borrowing*, *OTC Derivative*) is executed between two firms, and where *Exposure* arises for either firm, assets which must be provided by the *Non-Exposed Party* to the *Exposed Party* in order to mitigate the exposed party's risk, in accordance with a signed legal agreement. Collateral assets are typically cash or *Bonds*.
Collateral Basket	Predefined categories or groupings of *Collateral* for delivery in order to satisfy an *Exposure*. See *DBV Basket*.
Collateral Call	A communication issued by an *Exposed Party* to the *Non-Exposed Party*, to claim *Collateral* assets. More commonly known as a *Margin Call*.
Collateral Giver	The party (the *Non-Exposed Party*) that has given *Collateral* to the *Exposed Party* in order to mitigate the exposed party's risk. Also known as *Transferor*. See *Collateral Taker*.
Collateral In Transit	Assets given as *Collateral* by a *Non-Exposed Party*, but which have not yet been received by the *Exposed Party*.
Collateral Management	Identification of *Exposure* in certain types of financial transaction, and utilisation of financial instruments in order to mitigate such exposures. *Exposures* arise for lenders of assets, such as the cash lender in a *Repo*, and the securities lender in a *Securities Lending & Borrowing* trade. Exposures also arise for parties to *OTC Derivative* trades, due to changes in the current *Market Value* of a trade.
Collateral Processing	For *OTC Derivatives*, a generic term given to the area (within *Buy-Side* and *Sell-Side* firms) responsible for the management of trade *Exposures* through the giving and receipt of *Collateral*. The alternative is *Trade Processing*. Each trade creates the need for both collateral processing and trade processing.
Collateral Substitution	In a *Collateral*-related transaction (*Repo*, *Securities Lending & Borrowing*, *OTC Derivative*), the exchange of an asset that is currently being used as collateral for a different asset.
Collateral Taker	The party (the *Exposed Party*) that has received *Collateral* from the *Non-Exposed Party* in order to mitigate the exposed party's risk. Also known as *Transferee*. See *Collateral Giver*.

Collateral Transformation	The act of temporarily exchanging *Non CCP Eligible Assets* to *CCP-Eligible Assets*, in order to satisfy *Margin Calls* received from a *Central Counterparty*.
Collateral Value	The value of a financial asset given/taken in order to mitigate an *Exposure*; such value is derived by taking the *Current Market Value* of the asset, then deducting any applicable *Haircut*.
Collateralised Cash Borrowing	The borrowing of cash against the delivery of another financial asset in order to mitigate the cash lender's risk and therefore to minimise borrowing costs. The alternative is *Unsecured Cash Borrowing*.
Commingle	Generically speaking, to blend or to amalgamate. From a *Collateral Taker's* perspective, to hold *Securities Collateral* received in the same *CSD* or *Custodian* account as the taker's own securities.
Commission	Amount charged by a *Broker* to its client, for execution of a purchase or sale of securities on the client's behalf.
Common Stock	The standard description of *Shares* issued by companies in the United States. See *Ordinary Shares*.
Comparative Advantage	The benefit that one party can gain (e.g. when borrowing cash) in comparison with another party, due to the type of firm involved or their geographic location.
Competitive Blind Auction	A bidding process in which the bidders make their bids based upon their own valuation of the product on offer, and without being aware of the details of bids made by other bidders.
Concentration Limit	A restriction placed on the type of assets receivable as *Collateral* from a *Counterparty* in order to mitigate an *Exposure*. For example, no more than 50% of the total exposure amount can be mitigated by collateral issued by a single *Bond Issuer*.
Contract Specification	In an *Exchange-Traded Derivative* (including *Futures* and *Options*), definition of the derivative product's trading terms (i.e. features and characteristics) as defined by the exchange, and tradable under such terms by the exchange members.
Contractual Obligations	Actions and responsibilities that are documented within legal agreements. A party that fails to comply with such responsibilities is said to be in *Default*.
Contractual Settlement	The crediting or debiting of *Securities* and/or cash to reflect settlement on *Value Date*, regardless when the exchange of securities and cash actually occurs.
Contractual Settlement Date	The intended date of exchange of *Securities* and cash between buyer and seller. Another term for *Value Date*.
Convertible Bond	A *Bond* issued by a company that pays a fixed *Coupon* and gives the *Bondholder* the right to convert the bond into another of the *Issuer's* assets, (usually) a fixed quantity of the issuer's *Equity*.
Corporate Action	The distribution (by an *Issuer*), of benefits to existing *Shareholders* or *Bondholders*, or a change to the structure of an existing security.
Corporate Action Data Vendor	An organisation that supplies information to subscribers regarding the detail of *Corporate Actions* as and when announced, typically on an electronic basis.

Counterparty	The opposing entity with which a firm executes a financial transaction.
Counterparty Credit Risk	See *Counterparty Risk*.
Counterparty Onboarding	The multi-faceted and regulatory procedure by which a firm assesses the potential counterparty's suitability as a true counterparty with which the firm is prepared to enter into transactions.
Counterparty Risk	The risk that the *Counterparty* to a trade will fail to honour its *Contractual Obligations* (e.g. to pay cash or deliver *Securities*), as and when such obligations fall due.
Coupon	On *Interest-Bearing Bonds*, historically *Bond Certificates* were issued with paper coupons attached; each coupon represents interest due on one specified *Coupon Payment Date*. Although today bonds are usually issued in electronic form, the nickname of 'coupon' continues to be used to describe interest payments on bonds.
Coupon Claim	A communication issued by one party to its *Counterparty*, requesting remittance of the value of a *Coupon Payment*.
Coupon Paying Agent	An organisation appointed by an *Issuer* to collect *Coupons* from *Bondholders*, verify the validity of the coupons and to make coupon payments to the bondholders on behalf of the issuer.
Coupon Payment	The payment of interest by a *Bond Issuer* to *Bondholders* in accordance with the *Issue* terms, whether a *Fixed Rate Bond*, a *Floating Rate Note* or a *Convertible Bond*.
Coupon Payment Date	The scheduled date of a *Coupon Payment*.
Coupon Period	The period of time between each payment of interest on a *Bond*.
Coupon Rate	The rate of interest payable by the *Bond Issuer* to the *Bondholders*.
Covered Short	A sale of *Securities* which are not owned by the seller (a *Short Sale*), for which the relevant securities have been borrowed thereby facilitating settlement of the sale. The alternative is a *Naked Short*.
Credit Default Swap	A type of *OTC Derivative* trade in which one party (*Protection Buyer*) pays a regular *Premium* to its *Counterparty* (*Protection Seller*) who provides financial protection in the event of bond *Issuer Default*. Should the issuer default during the lifetime of the CDS trade, the protection seller must pay the protection buyer. Credit Default Swaps can also be applied to cash loans.
Credit Derivative	An umbrella term covering a family of *Derivative* products, all of which are designed to transfer the risk of cash borrower default from a cash lender to another party (except the cash borrower). Credit Derivatives include *Credit Default Swaps* and *Index CDS*.
Credit Event	The term given to an *Event of Default* by a *Reference Entity* in a *Credit Default Swap*; this triggers payout by the *Protection Seller* to the *Protection Buyer*.
Credit Interest Rate Environment	The general conditions in the *Money Market* in which loans of cash result in the cash lender receiving interest on the cash amount lent. Conversely, in a debit/negative rate environment, the cash lender pays interest to the cash borrower.

Credit Line	An overdraft limit provided by a bank to its customer.
Credit Rating Downgrade	See *Bond Issue Downgrade*.
Credit Risk	The possibility that a party that is borrowing an asset will *Default* on its contractual obligation to return such asset on the due date.
Credit Support Annex	A legal document that defines the *Collateral* arrangements between two parties, relating to *OTC Derivatives*. Commonly known as *CSA*.
Creditworthiness	An assessment of an entity's ability to repay cash borrowed, and therefore the likelihood of *Default*. See *Ratings Agencies*.
CREST	The system name of the *Central Securities Depository* for the UK and Ireland, operated by *Euroclear* UK and Ireland. The normal place of *Settlement* for *Equity* traded in those countries.
Cross-Currency Swap	A type of *OTC Derivative* trade in which two parties exchange principal amounts in different currencies at the start of the trade, with the reverse exchange occurring at the close of the trade, and with the exchange of interest payments in different currencies periodically. For comparison, see *Foreign Exchange Swap*.
CSA	Acronym for *Credit Support Annex*.
CSD	Acronym for *Central Securities Depository*.
Currency Derivative	A collective term for a range of financial *Derivative* products which have *Foreign Exchange* rates or foreign currency cashflows as their *Underlying* asset. Can be traded as an *Exchange-Traded Derivative* or as an *OTC Derivative*.
Currency Option Dividend	A type of *Dividend* on *Equity*, in which the *Issuer* provides *Shareholders* with payment in one currency, unless the shareholder elects to receive payment in a specified alternative currency.
Current Collateral Value	The up-to-date cash worth of a financial instrument used as *Collateral* (usually a *Bond* or *Equity* security) in the open marketplace.
Current Market Price	The up-to-date price of a financial instrument in the open marketplace.
Current Market Value	The up-to-date cash worth of a trade or position in a financial instrument in the open marketplace.
CUSIP	Committee on Uniform Securities Identification Procedures; an organisation that provides standardised and unique reference numbers (CUSIP numbers) for individual *Securities* traded in the United States and Canada, enabling unambiguous identification of the *Issue* being traded and delivered. See *ISIN*.
Custodian	An organisation that specialises in holding *Securities* and cash and effecting movements of securities and cash on behalf of its account holders. Custodians are normally members of their country's *Central Securities Depository*.
Custody Fees	Periodic charges made by a *CSD* or *Custodian* for the safekeeping of *Bond* and/or *Equity Securities*, charged to the account holder.
Data Scrubbing	The process of comparing and cleansing data (e.g. *Securities* or *Corporate Actions* data) received from two or more sources.

Data Vendors	Firms that specialise in the collection of information regarding *Securities*, and *Current Market Prices* of securities, and (in some cases) *Corporate Actions* relating to securities.
Day Count (Convention)	With the overall aim of determining an interest amount payable or receivable in a specific trade, the particular method used to determine the number of days in the period. Such conventions include 'actual' (calendar) days, and 30-day months. See *Divisor*.
Daylight Exposure	Incurring a risk due to an intraday timing difference between the giving of one asset and the receipt of a contra asset from a *Counterparty*.
DBV	Acronym for *Delivery By Value*.
DBV Basket	Predefined categories or groupings of *Collateral* for delivery against the borrowing of cash within *CREST*. See *Delivery By Value*.
Debt	The issuance of *Bonds* signifies that the *Issuer* is in debt to the investors; a 'debt issue' is synonymous with the term 'bond issue'.
Default	Failure by a bond *Issuer* to make payments of interest and/ or repayments of capital at the scheduled time, or failure by a *Counterparty* to comply with its *Contractual Obligations*.
Default Funds	An up-front contribution by each *Clearing Member* of a *Central Counterparty*, for the purpose of sharing any loss incurred if the default of any clearing member should arise. See *Mutualisation*.
Defaulting Party	In a financial transaction between two parties, the party that fails to honour its contractual obligations.
Delivery By Value	A collateralised cash borrowing. The input of matching *DBV Settlement Instructions* within the *CREST* system results in the transfer of the cash amount and the delivery of one or many pieces of pre-agreed securities *Collateral* in order to mitigate the cash lender's risk.
Delivery versus delivery	The delivery of a *Bond* or *Equity* security against the simultaneous receipt of another security; such settlement can occur only if both securities are available to be delivered. From a *Collateral* management perspective, as *DvD* mitigates delivery risk, it is valuable in *Collateral Substitution* and in *Securities Lending & Borrowing* where securities are given as collateral. Commonly known as *DvD*. See *Effective DvD*.
Delivery versus payment	The simultaneous, irrevocable and risk-free exchange of *securities* and cash between seller and buyer (or their custodians). The normal method utilised for settling the *opening leg* and *closing leg* of a *Repo* trade. Commonly known as *DvP*.
Denominational Value	See *Bond Denominational Value*.
Depot	An organisation that holds *Securities* and effects *Settlement* of trades on behalf of its account holder; also known as *Custodian*.
Depot Account	The specific account held by a *Depot* or *Custodian* in which *Securities* are held.
Depot Reconciliation	Within *Buy-Side* and *Sell-Side* firms, the internal process of comparing its *Books & Records* of securities holdings at *CSDs* and *Custodians* versus securities holdings stated on the CSD's or custodian's statement, known as a *Depot Statement*.

Depot Statement	A formal list of *Bond* and *Equity* securities held within a specific account at a *CSD* or *Custodian*. Such statements are normally available at the close of each business day, and list the quantity of securities and the *ISIN* code (or a national securities identifier such as a *SEDOL* or *CUSIP* code).
Derivative	A range of financial products, the value of each being derived from an associated (*Underlying*) asset. A derivative trade is a contract containing specific terms between a firm and its *Counterparty*, involving either no upfront payment or a relatively low percentage of the underlying asset's value.
Dirty Price	The price of a bond, inclusive of *Accrued Interest*. The alternative is *Clean Price*, which requires the addition of accrued interest to derive the bond's total *Market Value* and *Collateral Value*.
Discount Factor	Taking a known cash amount that is payable or receivable on a known future date, the rate used to determine 'today's' value of that same cash amount, through the process of discounting. See *Present Value* and *Time Value of Money*.
Dispute Resolution	Where the issuance of a *Margin Call Notification* is disagreed by the receiving party, if attempts at resolving the disagreement fail, dispute resolution is a documented procedure designed to overcome such disagreements, by the involvement of a neutral third party.
Disputed Amount	Following receipt of a *Margin Call Notification*, the disagreement of part of its value. The remainder is known as the *Undisputed Amount*.
Dividend	The distribution of earnings by a company to its *Shareholders*, whether in the form of cash or *Securities*.
Dividend Payment	Following a decision by an *Equity Issuer's* board of directors, the payment of cash to *Shareholders* as a reward for investment. Such payments usually relate to profits made in a defined trading period.
Divisor (Convention)	With the overall aim of determining an interest amount payable or receivable in a specific trade, the particular method used to determine the amount of interest per day, prior to multiplying by the number of days of interest. Such conventions include '360' and '365'. See *Day Count (Convention)*.
Dodd-Frank Act	Following the *Global Financial Crisis* in 2008, the legislation passed in the United States in 2010, designed to reduce risk in the financial marketplace. Amongst other aspects, the legislation requires *OTC Derivatives* to be *Centrally Cleared*. The equivalent in Europe is *EMIR*.
Double-Entry Bookkeeping	A basic accounting principle whereby each accounting entry is offset by a contra (debit or credit) entry.
Double Taxation Agreement	An arrangement between two countries, whereby residents of one country that invest in *Securities* issued by *Issuers* within the other country will have *Withholding Tax* deducted at a lower rate than the statutory (standard) rate payable by investors. Also known as a *Treaty*.
DTC	Depository Trust Company; the normal place of *Settlement* of *Equity*, corporate and municipal bonds traded in the United States. DTC effects settlement for its account holders on an *Electronic Book-Entry* basis.

DTCC Trade Information Warehouse	An organisation that provides a range of services relating to *Credit Derivatives*, including holding the current version of trades, plus post-trade processing, plus associated payment services.
DvD	Acronym for *Delivery versus delivery*.
DvP	Acronym for *Delivery versus payment*.
Early Termination	In an *OTC Derivative* trade, the closure of the trade prior to its *Scheduled Maturity Date*; this can be caused by a *Default* event documented under an *ISDA Master Agreement*.
Effective DvD	Within *Target2 Securities*, the simultaneous exchange (delivery) of one *Security* versus a different security, achieved by the linking of one matched *Settlement Instruction* with another matched settlement instruction with the same *Counterparty*. Following such linking, the delivery of one security will occur only if the opposing security is also available for delivery. See *Delivery versus delivery*.
Electronic Book Entry	The normal method by which *Securities* and cash are transferred between participant accounts at a *Central Securities Depository*. When assets are moved to effect *Settlement* at the *CSD*, no physical movement usually occurs and the result of settlement is updated electronically within the CSD's *Books & Records* by debiting one party and crediting the other.
Electronic Trade Confirmation	The process of comparing a seller's and a buyer's trade details electronically, shortly after *Trade Execution*, where one of the parties is an *Institutional Investor*. A method of achieving *Trade Agreement*.
Electronic Trading Platform	A generic term describing software systems that facilitate *Trade Execution*, involving the matching of buyers with sellers.
Eligible Collateral	Financial assets that are agreed by the involved parties to be acceptable as *Collateral* for the purpose of *Mitigating* risk. Such assets typically include cash in one or more major currency and highly rated government *Bonds*; blue chip *Equity* may also be included.
Eligible Currency	One or more currency that is agreed by the involved parties to be acceptable as collateral for the purpose of mitigating risk. See *Eligible Collateral*.
EMIR	Acronym for *European Market Infrastructure Regulation*.
Encryption	A secret coding system designed to prevent unauthorised access to important and/or sensitive data.
English Law CSA	The *Credit Support Annex* written under English Law. Of the many features contained therein, one of the most important is that the collateral transfer method is *Title Transfer*. For comparison, see *New York Law CSA*.
Entitlement	The right of ownership relating to certain types of *Corporate Action*.
Entitlement Date	A generic term to describe the date used to determine whether seller or buyer is entitled to a *Corporate Action*. See *Ex-Dividend Date*.
EONIA	Euro OverNight Index Average. A *Floating Benchmark* interest rate which is the average rate quoted by a number of banks for a duration of 1 day, for EUR. See *Euribor* and *Libor*.

Equity and Equity Collateral	An alternative description for the term *Shares*; an 'equity issue' is synonymous with the term 'share issue'. Of limited popularity when used as *Collateral* due to their historic volatility, particularly when compared with *Cash Collateral* and *Bond Collateral*.
Equity Issuer	The entity that has issued *Equity* and has received capital in exchange, from *Shareholders*.
Equivalent Collateral	For trades in Securities Lending & Borrowing and in *OTC Derivatives*, where *Securities Collateral* has been delivered to the *Collateral Taker*, that party is obliged to return to the *Collateral Giver* the same *ISIN* or (if the original ISIN has been replaced due to a *Corporate Action*), the replacement ISIN.
Equivalent Security	In a *Repo* trade, the cash lender is obliged to return to the cash borrower the same *ISIN* or (if the original ISIN has been replaced due to a *Corporate Action*), the replacement ISIN. In a Securities Lending & Borrowing trade, where securities have been lent to a *Securities Borrower*, that party is obliged to return to the *Securities Lender* the same ISIN or (if the original ISIN has been replaced due to a Corporate Action), the replacement ISIN.
ESMA	Acronym for *European Securities and Markets Authority*.
Eurex	A financial markets exchange offering electronic trading services in a variety of products, including *Derivatives*.
Eurex Clearing	Incorporated in Germany, a *Central Counterparty* for multiple asset classes, including *Repo* and *OTC Derivatives*.
Eurex Repo	An electronic trading venue for *Repo*.
Euribor	Acronym for 'Euro Interbank Offered Rate'. A *Floating Benchmark* interest rate which is the average rate quoted by a number of banks, for EUR. See *EONIA* and *Libor*.
Eurobond	A type of *Bond* that is usually sold to investors outside the country relating to the currency of issue. No *Withholding Tax* on income is payable by investors.
Euroclear Bank	Located in Brussels, one of the two *International Central Securities Depositories* (ICSDs) offering *Safe Custody, Settlement* and *Collateral Management* services to its participants; the other ICSD is *Clearstream International*.
European Market Infrastructure Regulation	The primary suite of regulatory measures introduced in Europe relating to *OTC Derivatives*, following the *Global Financial Crisis* in 2008. The foremost measures include stringent risk management of trades, including the mandatory use of *Central Counterparties* for standardised trades, and reporting of trades to *Trade Repositories*. Commonly known as *EMIR*.
European Securities and Markets Authority	An EU authority whose focus is the preservation of the strength of the financial system in the European Union, achieved by improving investor protection and promoting well organised financial markets. Commonly known as *ESMA*.
Event of Default	A predefined and legally documented set of circumstances (e.g. *Bankruptcy*) which, if they occur during the lifetime of a trade, enable a *Collateral Taker* to legally cover its *Exposure* by selling the *Collateral*.

Ex-Dividend Date	The date used to determine whether seller or buyer has *Entitlement* to certain types of *Corporate Action* on (primarily) *Equity Securities*.
Exchange Rate Risk	Where an investor holds cash in a foreign currency, or holds *Securities* denominated in a foreign currency, the risk that adverse exchange rate movements will result in a loss.
Exchange-Traded Derivative	*Derivative* products that are available for trading on formal derivative exchanges, where only exchange members are permitted to execute trades directly. *Futures* and *Options* products are usually tradable, on standardised terms. For comparison, see *OTC (Over-the-counter) Derivative*.
Exchange-Traded Funds	A collective investment scheme (similar to a *Mutual Fund*) that invests in *Equity* and *Bonds* but which is tradable on *Stock Exchanges*.
Executing Broker	From the perspective of a *Buy-Side* firm that has executed a trade in a financial asset, the *Counterparty* to the trade.
Execution	The agreement to trade between two parties, whether buying or selling, lending or borrowing, etc. See *Trade Execution*.
Exercise	The process of converting a *Security* to an associated (or *Underlying*) security.
Exercise Price	The price at which an *Option* holder is entitled to buy (*Call Option*) or sell (*Put Option*) the underlying asset. Also known as *Strike Price*.
Exposed Party	The party to a financial transaction that has an *Exposure* during the lifetime of the trade, due to changes in the current *Market Value* of the assets involved. Such parties will issue a *Margin Call* to their *Counterparty*, following which the *Exposed Party* will receive *Collateral* in order to mitigate that risk. See *Non-Exposed Party*.
Exposure	The extent to which a firm has risk relating to executed transactions. In a *Repo*, the difference in value between the cash lent and the current *Market Value* of the *Collateral* received. In *Securities Lending & Borrowing*, the difference in value between the current market value of *Securities* lent versus the current market value of the collateral received. In *OTC Derivatives*, the difference in value between the original terms of the trade and the *Replacement Cost*, taking account of any existing collateral.
Failed Status	As advised by a *CSD* or *Custodian*, the current condition of a *Settlement Instruction* which reflects the fact that *Settlement* has not occurred on *Value Date*. In addition, a reason for the settlement delay is provided.
Failed Settlement	See *Settlement Failure*.
Failure to Pay	A term given to a specific *Event of Default* in a *Credit Default Swap*. Specifically, if a *Bond Issuer* does not pay *Coupon* or maturity proceeds to the *Bondholders* when falling due (normally taking account of a grace period), such non-payment is regarded as a Failure to Pay, therefore an Event of Default has occurred which will trigger payout by the *Protection Seller* to the *Protection Buyer*. One type of *Credit Event*.

FC	Acronym for *Financial Counterparty*.
Federal Funds Rate	In the United States, the *Floating Benchmark* interest rate at which institutions lend USD cash to one another on an overnight basis.
Fedwire	In the United States, an electronic real-time USD payment and securities transfer system operated by the Federal Reserve.
Financial Counterparty	Under *EMIR*, financial counterparties are banks, insurance companies, assurance companies, reinsurance companies, alternative investment funds, investment firms, credit institutions, pension funds, *UCITS* funds, sovereign wealth funds. In order to be classified as an FC under EMIR, firms must be authorised under the appropriate regulation. See *Non-Financial Counterparty*.
Fixed Coupon	In a *Credit Default Swap*, the standardised premium amounts introduced after the *Global Financial Crisis* to facilitate firms benefitting from *Portfolio Compression*.
Fixed-for-Floating Interest Rate Swap	A type of *OTC Derivative* trade designed to mitigate the risk of adverse movements in interest rates. One party pays an agreed fixed rate of interest at an agreed frequency (e.g. every 6 months) whilst the counterparty pays a floating rate of interest based upon a *Floating Benchmark* rate (e.g. *Libor*) over the same time period. Whilst the fixed rate remains constant throughout the lifetime of the trade, the floating rate will almost certainly differ on each occasion. *Settlement* occurs on a net basis (the difference in rates between the fixed rate and the floating rate).
Fixed Rate Bond	A *Bond* which pays the same fixed rate of interest at regular and predefined intervals (e.g. every 12 months or 6 months) on predefined *Coupon Payment Dates*.
Fixing Date	A generic term that describes the date on which the interest rate of a *Floating Benchmark* rate (e.g. *Euribor*, *Libor*, *EONIA*) is reset, as occurs in a *Floating Rate Note* and in an *Interest Rate Swap*.
Floating Benchmark	A generic term for interest rates that are not fixed, but instead fluctuate in accordance with current *Money Market* rates, examples of which are *EONIA*, *Euribor*, *Federal Funds Rate* and *Libor*.
Floating Rate Note	A form of *Bond* that pays variable rates of interest, as opposed to the majority of bonds that have a fixed rate of interest throughout their lives.
FoP	Acronym for *Free of payment*.
Foreign Exchange	The part of the financial services industry which deals with the buying and selling of currencies.
Foreign Exchange Risk	A potential *Exposure* for a firm where a financial transaction has been executed in a currency which differs from a firm's base currency, where exchange rate fluctuation could negatively impact the firm.
Foreign Exchange Swap	A type of *OTC Derivative* trade in which two parties exchange principal amounts in different currencies at the start of the trade (at one exchange rate), with the reverse exchange occurring at the close of the trade (at a different exchange rate). For comparison, see *Cross-Currency Swap*.

Forward Exchange Rate	In a *Foreign Exchange* trade, the rate at which a trade is executed for *Settlement* on an agreed future *Value Date*. For comparison, see *Spot Exchange Rate*.
Four Eyes Principle	The practice of having work verified by a second person prior to acceptance into a system or acting on the information.
Free of payment	The separate (non-simultaneous) exchange of *Securities* and cash between seller and buyer (or their *Custodians*). In *Collateral Management*, settlement of *Margin Calls* using *Bonds* is normally actioned free of payment. Commonly known as *FoP*.
FRN	Acronym for *Floating Rate Note*.
Front Office	A general term within *Buy-Side* and *Sell-Side* firms, which refers to the department in which *Traders* reside. Within sell-side firms, can also encompass *Relationship Managers*.
Fund Manager	A type of *Buy-Side* organisation that usually operates a range of funds in which end investors place their cash; the fund manager decides how to invest the cash in order to maximise the return on investment or to maximise regular income, in accordance with the objective of each fund operated by the fund manager. Also known as *Mutual Fund*.
Funding	The act of minimising the cost of borrowing cash, and maximising the benefit of lending cash. This usually involves borrowing and lending cash in a number of currencies on a *Secured* (*Collateralised*) and *Unsecured* basis, over varying periods of time.
Funds Pre-Advice	A communication issued by a firm to a *Cash Correspondent* (or *Nostro*), formally advising that a specific incoming cash amount is expected to be received on a specified *Value Date*. Failure to issue such a communication is likely to result in delayed crediting of cash.
Fungible and Fungibility	Assets (e.g. a currency or a *Security*) which are equivalent to, interchangeable with and substitutable by assets of the same type.
Fungible Securities	Two securities (issued by the same *Issuer*) that have become equal in all respects, where at the time of issue each security carried different rights. For example, the holders of the first security may have been entitled to a dividend, whereas the holders of the second security were not entitled to that particular dividend.
Futures	An *Exchange-Traded Derivative* product; the investor buys or sells an *Underlying* asset for delivery and payment on a specific date. The exchange provides a range of futures products which contain standardised terms relating to quantity, quality and *Value Date*.
G-7 and G-10	Both the G-7 and G-10 are unofficial groups of industrialised nations that meet periodically to debate monetary and other issues.
GC Pooling	An electronic, anonymous and multicurrency *Repo* trading platform utilising standardised baskets of *General Collateral*. Trades are cleared via *Eurex Clearing*.
General Collateral	In a *Cash-Based Repo*, although the *Collateral* provided by the cash borrower must be of a minimum quality, no specific security (*ISIN*) is required by the cash lender. Such collateral is therefore interchangeable (able to be substituted) during the lifetime of the trade. Commonly known as 'GC'. See *Collateral Substitution*.

General Creditor	A cash lender that has not secured the loan by taking any assets as *Collateral* from the cash borrower.
Gilt	Commonly used term for *Bonds* issued by the UK government. Historically, when certificates in such bonds were issued, the certificates had a gilt (gold) edging and such bonds became known as 'gilt-edged' securities, or 'gilts' for short.
Global Custodian	An organisation that offers a broad range of services to its clients, including the holding of *Securities* and other financial instruments, the holding of cash in various currencies, the *Settlement* of trades and the collection of *Corporate Actions*. Global custodians typically operate a network of sub-custodians (located in a variety of the world's financial centres) that hold such assets on its behalf. For comparison, see *Local Custodian*.
Global Depository Receipts	Documents that represent *Shares* held in overseas companies and which enable investors located in a different country to invest in such *Securities*. See *American Depository Receipts*.
Global Equity	*Equity* issued in various countries around the globe, and which is generally available to investors.
Global Financial Crisis	A common term for the highly negative and worldwide impact of a series of events (e.g. homeowners defaulting on residential mortgages, the bailout of American International Group, and the bankruptcy of *Investment Bank* Lehman Brothers) which culminated during September 2008. This crisis resulted in a loss of trust between firms in financial markets, and a dramatic increase in the importance of *Collateral* as a primary mechanism for mitigation of *Counterparty Risk*.
Global Master Repurchase Agreement	The standard legal document used in Europe which states the contractual terms and conditions applicable to the parties to *Repo* trades; produced by *ICMA* and *SIFMA*. Once signed, all subsequent repo trades between the parties fall under the *GMRA's* terms and conditions.
Global Master Securities Lending Agreement	The standard legal document which states the contractual terms and conditions applicable to the parties to *Securities Lending & Borrowing* trades; produced by *ISLA*. Once signed, all subsequent securities lending & borrowing trades between the parties fall under the *GMSLA's* terms and conditions.
Global Note	A legal document which represents the entirety of a *Bond* issue. For comparison, see *Bearer Security*.
GMRA	Acronym for *Global Master Repurchase Agreement*.
GMSLA	Acronym for *Global Master Securities Lending Agreement*.
Good Value	At a *Cash Correspondent* (or *Nostro*), the crediting of funds due to a firm on *Value Date*, without delay. See *Funds Pre-Advice*.
Grey Market Trading	Buying and selling *Securities* that are in course of being brought to the marketplace, when it is still possible that the *Issue* may be withdrawn and not come to fruition. See *Primary Market*.
Gross Exposure	In a *Repo*, the differential between the current value of *Securities Collateral* and the current value of the cash lent/borrowed, prior to taking account of any *Minimum Transfer Amount* or *Threshold*.

Haircut	A percentage reduction from the *Market Value* of an asset (e.g. a *Bond*), in order to derive the asset's *Collateral Value*. Haircut is the perceived risk of loss resulting from the asset's fall in value; the haircut's size reflects the perceived risk and *Liquidity* of the asset.
Hedge Fund	An organisation that invests its clients' funds, but which is subject to fewer restrictions than other funds (such as *Mutual Funds*); typically, hedge funds indulge in speculative investments, including but not limited to *Securities*. Such speculation may earn hedge fund investors large profits, at the risk of large losses.
Hedging	Investing in *Securities* (or other financial instruments) as a safeguard against loss in the event of adverse price movements in other investments.
Herstatt Risk	Relates to foreign exchange trades in which one currency is sold whilst a different currency is bought, for settlement on the same *Value Date*. The risk of loss exists for a firm where the currency sold is paid to the *Counterparty* without receiving the currency bought. Named after Bank Herstatt which (in 1974) received payments in Deutsche Marks prior to entering into *Bankruptcy* and prior to making payments to its counterparties in USD.
High Quality Liquid Assets	Financial assets that are issued by highly rated *Issuers* and which are easily and immediately converted into cash.
HQLA	Acronym for *High Quality Liquid Assets*.
ICMA	Acronym for *International Capital Market Association*.
ICSD	Acronym for *International Central Securities Depository*.
ICSD Auto-Lending/ Borrowing	Service provided by *ICSDs* in which participants can automatically lend their securities to the ICSD, who in turn lend the same securities to those participants that are automatic borrowers. See *Securities Lending* and *Securities Borrowing*.
Illegality	The condition of being outside the laws of a particular authority or jurisdiction.
IM	Acronym for *Initial Margin*.
Income	Within the world of *Securities*, *Dividend Payments* on *Equity* and *Coupon Payments* on *Bonds*.
Independent Amount	In *OTC Derivatives*, a cash amount or percentage of *Notional Principal* given by a firm to its higher rated *Counterparty*.
Index CDS	A *Credit Derivative* product which enables investors to take a position in a number of *Reference Entities* (as opposed to one entity as occurs in a *Single Name Credit Default Swap*).
Index Tracking Fund	A form of *Mutual Fund* whose investment objectives are to mirror the companies which comprise a specified market index.
Individual Segregated Account	An account owned by a *Clearing Member* (CM) at a *Central Counterparty*, in which trades and positions that are owned by one specific client of the CM (*Non-Clearing Members*) are held, as part of the CM's *Client Clearing* service. See *Omnibus Account*.

Initial Margin	In *Repo*, a percentage reduction from the *Market Value* of an asset (e.g. a *Bond*), in order to derive the asset's *Collateral Value*. An amount of additional collateral given by the cash borrower to the cash lender. Similar to *Haircut*, although the calculation method differs.
	In *OTC Derivatives* under *EMIR*, a form of *Margin Call* made by a *Central Counterparty* which reflects potential future exposure.
Initial Public Offering	A method of bringing a new *Equity Issue* to the *Securities* marketplace, whereby the general public is given the opportunity to apply for shares in the issue. A term used in the United States; the equivalent of an *Offer for Sale* in the UK.
Institutional Investors	A generic term given to end-investors that are organisations, as opposed to individuals; such investors include *Fund Managers*, *Hedge Funds*, *Insurance Companies* and *Pension Funds*. Also known as the '*Buy-Side*'.
Insurance Companies	A type of *Buy-Side* organisation that invest the insurance premiums (received from policyholders) in the stock market. A type of *Institutional Investor*.
Inter-Dealer Broker	In the *Capital Market*, a firm that executes trades as middleman between *Investment Banks*, earning commission for providing such a service.
Interest-Bearing Bond	A *Bond* which pays interest (*Coupon*), including *Fixed Rate Bonds*, *Floating Rate Notes* and *Convertible Bonds*, but excluding *Zero Coupon Bonds*.
Interest Claim	A claim for missing cash interest resulting from a delay in receipt of such cash. For *Securities*, a request by a seller to the buyer for reimbursement of missing cash interest, where the seller was able to deliver securities (on or after the *Value Date*) but the buyer was unable to pay.
Interest Rate Derivative	An umbrella term covering a family of financial products whose value changes according to fluctuations in interest rates, an example of which is a *Fixed-for-Floating Interest Rate Swap*.
Interest Rate Swap	See *Fixed-for-Floating Interest Rate Swap*.
International Capital Market Association	An organisation that represents its members, particularly in the fields of market practices relating to the international *Bond* and *Repo* markets. Its members are located in over 60 countries, including both *Buy-Side* and *Sell-Side* firms. Commonly abbreviated to *ICMA*.
International Central Securities Depository	A *Central Securities Depository* that holds overseas *Securities* and which usually facilitates *Settlement* of trades in numerous currencies. Euroclear (Brussels) and Clearstream International (Luxembourg) are two recognised ICSDs.
International Organization of Securities Commissions	An institution that develops and promotes international standards relating to *Securities* regulation.
International Securities Lending Association	An independent organisation that represents the *Securities Lending & Borrowing* marketplace, whose aim is to promote a competitive, efficient and orderly securities lending & borrowing environment.
	Commonly abbreviated to *ISLA*.

International Swaps and Derivatives Association	An industry body that is focused on the safety and efficiency of the global derivatives market, through encouraging wide-ranging risk management practices, amongst other activities. Both *Buy-Side* and *Sell-Side* firms comprise over 850 members. Commonly abbreviated to *ISDA*.
Investment Bank	A type of *Sell-Side* firm which provides a wide range of financial services to its *Buy-Side* clients, including trading in *Bonds*, *Equity*, *Foreign Exchange*, *Derivatives*, plus corporate finance expertise including capital raising activities plus mergers & acquisitions services. Investment banks also trade with other sell-side firms. An organisation that practices *Proprietary Trading*, involving the buying, selling and holding of financial instruments for its own account. Typically known as *Broker* by buy-side firms.
Investor	An individual or institution that has purchased and owns *Securities*, or has invested in *Derivatives*. See *Institutional Investors*.
IOSCO	Acronym for *International Organization of Securities Commissions*.
IPO	Acronym for *Initial Public Offering*.
IRS	Acronym for *Interest Rate Swap*
ISDA	Acronym for *International Swaps and Derivatives Association*
ISDA Master Agreement	A commonly used global standard for documenting the legal arrangements between two parties that intend trading with one another in a variety of *OTC Derivative* product types, such as *Interest Rate Swaps* and *Credit Default Swaps*. Produced by *ISDA*.
ISDA Novation Protocol II	An *ISDA* standard procedure designed to ensure that the three parties involved in a *Novation* of an *OTC Derivative* trade, follow the documented procedure so as to achieve a legally binding novation.
ISDA Protocol	A standard document (representing for example, a change to a particular procedure or existing legal document) issued by the *International Swaps and Derivatives Association* which facilitates ISDA members agreeing to abide by the terms stated within that document. Firms are required to sign an adherence letter to formally signify their agreement to the protocol.
ISDA Regional Determination Committee	Where a party to a *Credit Default Swap* trade believes that a *Credit Event* may have occurred, *ISDA* instructs the appropriate determination committee to investigate and to pronounce whether a credit event has occurred. Their decision is binding.
ISIN	Acronym for International Securities Identification Number; a uniform global standard providing unique reference numbers (ISIN numbers) for individual securities, enabling unambiguous identification of the issue being traded and delivered. See *CUSIP, SEDOL Code, WKN Code*.
ISLA	Acronym for the *International Securities Lending Association*.
ISO Currency Codes	A set of internationally recognised three-digit codes representing each of the world's currencies.
Issue	An individual *Security*.

Issuer	The originating entity that supplies *Securities* to the marketplace in order to raise cash; such entities include companies, sovereign entities, governments, government agencies and *Supranational Organisations*.
Issuer Default	The failure of a *Bond Issuer* to make interest (*Coupon*) payments and *Capital Repayment* when falling due.
Know Your Customer	An internal process within financial institutions designed to properly identify new clients and *Counterparties*, with the aim of preventing *Money Laundering*. The process requires firms to comply with strict regulation.
KYC	Acronym for *Know Your Customer*.
Legacy Trades and Legacy Bilateral Trades	Relevant to *OTC Derivatives*, trades executed on a *Bilateral* basis prior to the mandatory *Central Clearing* of trades under *EMIR*.
Legal Entity Identifier	A coding system to uniquely identify individual entities involved in financial transactions. Commonly known as *LEI*.
Legal Owner and Legal Ownership	In *Collateral*-related transactions executed under the *GMRA*, the *GMSLA* and the *English Law CSA*, the legal owner of securities collateral is the *Collateral Taker* whilst the collateral is in that party's possession. The *Collateral Giver* retains *Beneficial Ownership*.
Legal Title	Ownership of an asset which is able to be proven through legal enforceability. See *Title Transfer*.
LEI	Acronym for *Legal Entity Identifier*.
Lending Agent	A firm that acts as an intermediary between *Securities Lenders* and *Securities Borrowers*.
Libor	Acronym for 'London Interbank Offered Rate'. A *Floating Benchmark* interest rate which is the average rate quoted by a number of banks, for a range of currencies for a variety of time periods. Used in the calculation of *Coupon* on *Floating Rate Notes* and in *OTC Derivative* trades such as *Fixed-for-Floating Interest Rate Swaps*. See *Euribor* and *EONIA*.
Liquid, Liquid Assets and Liquidity	Financial assets which are quickly and easily convertible into cash.
Liquidation	From a *Collateral Management* perspective, the process of converting an asset into cash.
Local Custodian	An organisation that specialises in holding *Securities* and cash and effecting movements of securities and cash on behalf of its account holders, and which is typically a member of the *Central Securities Depository* in the financial centre in which it is located. For comparison, see *Global Custodian*.
Long First Coupon	A term given to the first payment of interest after a *Bond* has been issued, specifically where the elapsed time between issuance of the bond and the first *Coupon Payment Date* is greater than the normal *Coupon Period* for that bond. See *Short First Coupon*.

Long Form Confirmation	Relating to an *OTC Derivative* trade where no *ISDA Master Agreement* is in place between the two parties, a legal document issued by a firm to its *Counterparty* that specifies the full terms of an individual trade. See *Short Form Confirmation*.
Mandatory Central Clearing	The requirement (as stated under *EMIR*) that all trades in standardised *OTC Derivatives* must be cleared via a *Central Counterparty*, providing that both the original trade parties are subject to the *Clearing Obligation*.
Mandatory Corporate Action	An event in the lifetime of an *Equity* or *Bond* security which is normally triggered by the *Issuer*, where a benefit (e.g. additional cash or securities) is available to holders, or the security is reorganised (e.g. *Stock Split*). The compulsory nature of such events means that no choice of outcome is available to holders. See *Optional Corporate Action* and *Voluntary Corporate Action*.
Manufactured Coupon and Manufactured Dividend and Manufactured Income	Where a firm owes an *Income* amount to its *Counterparty,* and where such funds are not receivable from any other party, the payment by the firm from its own funds. For example, where *Securities* have been lent, the *Securities Borrower* must remit (to the *Securities Lender*) income that falls due on the borrowed securities; typically the borrower will not be in possession of the borrowed securities and will therefore not receive the income from the Issuer.
Margin Call	Additional *Collateral* requested by a firm (from its *Counterparty*) to avoid being under-collateralised. In the event that collateral (used to secure the borrowing of cash or *securities,* or to mitigate exposures in *OTC Derivative* trades) loses its value due to a reduction in its market price, additional collateral may need to be given to the *Exposed Party*. Margin calls can also be made by the *Collateral Giver* (where the market price of the collateral increases), in order to avoid over-collateralising.
Margin Call Notification	A communication issued by an *Exposed Party* to the *Non-Exposed Party* which, if agreed, will result in the non-exposed party providing *Collateral* in settlement of the margin call thereby mitigating the exposed party's risk.
MarginSphere	A mechanism for the electronic communication of *Margin Calls* and *Collateral Substitution* between market participants including *Buy-Side* and *Sell-Side* firms.
Mark-to-Market	Revaluation of a trade or position in a financial instrument (e.g. *Equity*, *Bond*, *Derivative*) to the *Current Market Price*; used when determining *Exposures*, including the current value of *Collateral*. Also known as 'MTM' or 'M2M'.
Mark-to-Model	Revaluation of a trade or position in a financial instrument based upon prices calculated using a financial model. For comparison, see *Mark-to-Market*.
Market	An environment within which trades in financial instruments (e.g. currency, *Equity*, *Bonds*, *Derivatives*, commodities) are *Executed*, for example the US Treasury bond market, the *Foreign Exchange* market, the *OTC Derivative* market.

Market Maker	An *Investment Bank* (or *Broker*) that publishes the price at which it is prepared to buy and sell specific *Securities*, and which is obliged to trade at the publicised price. Firms wishing to act in this capacity are required to operate to strict rules laid down by the relevant *Stock Exchange* or market authority.
Market Price	The price of a financial instrument in the open marketplace.
Market Risk	The risk of loss due to adverse movements in the *Market Price* of a financial instrument.
Market Risk Neutral	A trading strategy involving an organisation intentionally avoiding taking a position in a financial instrument. Where a firm buys (temporarily taking a position), they will immediately sell (thereby reducing the position to zero). Position taking exposes the firm to potential losses resulting from adverse price movements (*Market Risk*). *Central Counterparties* employ such a strategy.
Market Value	The current cash value of a financial asset (which is subject to fluctuation in value) in the open marketplace, including *Bonds*, *Equity* and *OTC Derivatives*. (Cash is not subject to fluctuation as it retains 100% of its value.)
Matched Settlement Instruction	See *Settlement Instruction*. Following receipt of a settlement instruction, the *CSD* compares the details with the *Counterparty's* settlement instruction details and if they agree, are reported as 'matched'. Normally, *Settlement* cannot occur at the CSD without settlement instructions being matched.
Maturity Date (Bond)	The date at which capital invested by *Bondholders* is scheduled to be repaid by the *Bond Issuer*. Beyond this date, the bond is no longer live and valid.
Mid-Market Quotation	The average of the current buy price and the current sale price, as quoted by *Market Makers*.
Mid Price	The average of the bid (to buy) and offer (to sell) prices.
Middle Office	A section (or department) of people within some *Buy-Side* and *Sell-Side* firms, that are typically responsible for supporting the trading department (e.g. profit & loss calculation, risk management) and for communication between the trading department and the *Operations Department*.
Minimum Transfer Amount	An amount agreed between two trading firms, below which no *Margin Call* will be made. Commonly abbreviated to MTA.
Mitigate	To reduce or to lessen an *Exposure*.
Monetary Policy	The mechanism used by *Central Banks* to influence various aspects of a country's economy, including inflation and interest rates.
Money Laundering	A criminal activity involving disguising the true origin of funds obtained through illegal means. See *Know Your Customer*.

Money Market	The environment in which cash is lent and borrowed, typically with a maximum duration of 12 months. *Floating Rate Notes* are regarded as money market Instruments as their interest rates track current money market interest rates. *Repo* trades are also classified as money market instruments, as the primary motivation for such trades is the lending and borrowing of cash.
Money Market Divisor	The denominator used to determine a currency interest amount per day. Specifically, 360 for EUR and USD, 365 for GBP. Used for *Money Market* trades, including *Repo*.
Moody's Investors Service	An issuer *Ratings Agency* that publishes its view of an *Issuer's* ability to repay *Debt*.
Mortgage-Backed Security	A financial instrument that represents loans of cash, for example residential mortgages. Loans with similar characteristics are pooled then *Securitised* into a *Security* which is available for purchasing by investors.
MTA	Acronym for *Minimum Transfer Amount*.
Multilateral Development Banks	Organisations focused on achieving economic equality and reducing severe poverty. International financial institutions supported by at least two countries for the purpose of promoting financial growth in specific regions. Also known as *Supranational Organisations*.
Multilateral Netting	Generically speaking, a number of parties involved in an arrangement whereby each party agrees to reduce their gross trades to a net position (which is representative of the gross trades). More specifically, for *Standardised OTC Derivatives* under *EMIR*, the *Central Counterparty* operates such netting with all of its *Clearing Members*. *Counterparty Risk* is reduced as a result.
Mutual Fund	See *Fund Manager*.
Mutualisation	Within a *Central Counterparty*, the sharing of *Counterparty Risk* amongst its *Clearing Members*.
Naked Short	A sale of *Securities* which are not owned by the seller (a *Short Sale*), for which the relevant securities have not been borrowed; under these circumstances the sale will remain unsettled. The alternative is a *Covered Short*.
National CSD	A *Central Securities Depository* that holds domestic *Securities* and which typically facilitates *Settlement* of trades in the domestic currency on an *Electronic Book Entry* basis.
National Competent Authority	An organisation having been granted the legal power to perform a particular function.
NAV	Acronym for *Net Asset Value*.
NCA	Acronym for *National Competent Authority*.
Nearest Integer	The nearest whole number. A rounding rule which defines whether a figure less than a whole number should be rounded up or rounded down. The general rule is: 1) if the number is less than '5', then round down, and 2) if the number is '5' or above, then round up.
Negative Exposure	This term has the same meaning as *Negative Mark-to-Market*.

Negative Interest Rate	An interest rate in which the cash lender pays interest to the cash borrower. See *Positive Interest Rate*.
Negative Mark-to-Market	Resulting from the (normally daily) revaluation process, the *Current Market Value* of an asset having moved against one of the parties to a trade. In *Collateral*-related trades, this results in a *Margin Call* being received by that party from its *Counterparty*. See *Positive Mark-to-Market*.
Negative Trading Position	A firm's trade-dated balance in a financial instrument where a greater quantity of sales (compared with purchases) have been *Executed*. The resultant impact of *Short Selling* on a firm's *Trading Position*.
Net Asset Value	Relevant to *Exchange-Traded Funds* and *Mutual Funds*, the value of the fund's assets after deduction of the value of its liabilities.
Net Exposure	In a *Repo*, the differential between the current value of *Securities Collateral* and the current value of the cash lent/borrowed, after taking account of any *Minimum Transfer Amount* or *Threshold*.
New Bilateral Trades	Relevant to *OTC Derivatives*, trades executed on a *Bilateral* basis following the mandatory *Central Clearing* of trades under *EMIR*. Specifically, trades which cannot be centrally cleared. Also known as Regulatory Bilateral Trades. For comparison, see *Legacy Bilateral Trades*.
New York Law CSA	The *Credit Support Annex* written under New York Law. Of the many features contained therein, one of the most important is that the collateral transfer method is *Security Interest*. For comparison, see *English Law CSA*.
NFC+	Under *EMIR*, a *Non-Financial Counterparty* whose *OTC Derivative* activity is above a regulatory-defined level known as the *Clearing Threshold*. Such firms are obliged to clear their trades via a *Central Counterparty*.
NFC–	Under *EMIR*, a *Non-Financial Counterparty* whose *OTC Derivative* trading activity is below a regulatory-defined level known as the *Clearing Threshold*. Such firms are exempt from the requirement to clear their trades via a *Central Counterparty*.
Non-Cash Collateral	Assets given or taken as *Collateral* in a form other than *Cash Collateral*. Theoretically, this can include assets such as precious metals (e.g. gold) or valuable oil paintings. Under normal circumstances, such collateral is in the form of *Securities* (*Bonds* or *Equity*).
Non-CCP-Eligible Assets	Financial assets used as *Collateral* that are not acceptable to *Central Counterparties*, as defined under *EMIR*. See *CCP-Eligible Assets*.
Non-Centrally Cleared Trade	For *OTC Derivatives* under *EMIR*, trades which do not comply with the requirement to be *Novated* to a *Central Counterparty*. If the trade has non-standard features, or if one (or both) parties is not subject to the *Clearing Obligation,* the trade must be non-centrally cleared. See *Centrally Cleared Trades*.
Non-Clearing Member	A firm which has chosen not be become a *Clearing Member* at a *Central Counterparty*, and instead utilises the services provided by a *Clearing Member* that offers *Client Clearing* services.

Non-Exposed Party	A firm that is a party to a financial transaction has no risk (currently), but its *Counterparty* is at risk due to changes in the *Current Market Value* of the assets involved. The counterparty (the *Exposed Party*) will issue a *Margin Call Notification*, following which the firm is obliged to give *Collateral* in order to mitigate the counterparty's risk.
Non-Financial Counterparty	Under *EMIR*, all firms that execute *OTC Derivative* trades but which are not classified as a *Financial Counterparty* are automatically classified as an NFC. Dependent upon whether an NFC's trading activity is above or below a defined *Clearing Threshold* will determine whether the NFC is exempt or not from the requirement to clear their trades via a *Central Counterparty*. See *NFC+* and *NFC–*.
Nostro	See *Cash Correspondent*.
Nostro Account	The specific account held by a *Nostro* in which cash is held on behalf of the account holder.
Nostro Reconciliation	Within *Buy-Side* and *Sell-Side* firms, the internal process of comparing its *Books & Records* of cash balances held at *Cash Correspondents*, *CSDs* and *Custodians* versus cash balances stated on the statements received from cash correspondents, CSDs and custodians, known as a *Nostro Statement*.
Nostro Statement	A formal list of individual cash movements and cash balances within a specific account at a *Cash Correspondent*, *CSD* or Custodian. Such statements are normally available at the close of each business day.
Notional Principal	Relevant specifically to *OTC Derivatives*, the quantity or value on which all trade calculations are based. Note that true derivative trades do not involve the up-front payment or receipt of the notional principal: it can therefore be described as a theoretical *Underlying* quantity.
Novation	1. On an individual trade, the replacement of an individual *Counterparty* with a *Central Counterparty*. 2. On an individual *OTC Derivative* trade, the reassignment of the contract from the (original) *Bilateral* counterparty to a replacement bilateral counterparty.
Novation Transferee	In an *OTC Derivative* trade where *Novation* has occurred, the party that has 'stepped in' to the trade. See *Novation Transferor*.
Novation Transferor	In an *OTC Derivative* trade where *Novation* has occurred, the party that has 'stepped out' of the trade. See *Novation Transferee*.
Obligor	An entity that is contractually required to make payment; for example a *Bond Issuer* who is required to pay *Coupon* and to make *Capital Repayment*.
Offset	The execution of an opposing trade to an existing *OTC Derivative* trade in order to negate the position, and carried out with a *Counterparty* other than the original counterparty. For comparison, see *Unwind*.
Omgeo's CTM (Central Trade Manager)	A system that facilitates the critically important post-*Trade Execution* step (known as *Trade Confirmation*) of comparing trade details between *Buy-Side* and *Sell-Side* firms to ensure accuracy, prior to settlement. Covering trades in *Equity* and *Bonds*, plus the transaction type of *Repo*.

Omnibus Account	An account owned by a *Clearing Member* (CM) at a *Central Counterparty*, in which trades and positions that are owned by multiple clients of the CM (*Non Clearing Members*) are held, as part of the CM's *Client Clearing* service. See *Individual Segregated Account*.
One-Way CSA	A *Credit Support Annex* in which the stated terms (particularly exposure management) are in favour of one of the parties. See *Bilateral CSA*.
Open Market Operations	*Repo* and/or *Securities Lending & Borrowing* activity undertaken by a *Central Bank*, in which the central bank lends cash to an entity that provides an asset (typically *Bonds*) as *Collateral*. A means by which *Monetary Policy* is implemented by central banks.
Open Trade	1. A *Securities* trade for which *Settlement* has not yet occurred, whether *Value Date* is in the future or in the past. 2. A *Securities Lending & Borrowing* trade executed without (yet) specifying the *Closing Value Date*. 3. An *OTC Derivative* trade which has not yet reached its *Scheduled Maturity Date*.
Opening Leg and Opening Value Date	In a two-sided transaction (e.g. *Repo* and *Securities Lending & Borrowing*), the date at which the initial exchange of assets is intended to occur.
Operations Department	A department or division within a *Buy-Side* or *Sell-Side* firm that is responsible for the timely processing of trades *Executed* by the firm's *Traders*. Trades can be of one type only or of a range of types, such as *Equity*, *Bond*, *Foreign Exchange*, *Exchange-Traded Derivatives*, *OTC Derivatives* and commodities. Such processing tasks typically include issuance and receipt of *Trade Confirmations* to *Counterparties*, issuance of cash-related and *Securities*-related *Settlement Instructions*, *Settlement* of trades, processing of *Corporate Actions*, the updating of *Books & Records* and multiple types of *Reconciliation*. The *Collateral* Department is normally part of the Operations Department.
Optional Corporate Action	An event in the lifetime of an *Equity* or *Bond* security which is normally triggered by the *Issuer*, where a benefit (e.g. additional cash or securities) is available to holders. The optional nature of such events means that a choice of outcome is available to holders (e.g. cash dividend with an option to take *Securities* rather than cash). See *Mandatory Corporate Action* and *Voluntary Corporate Action*.
Options	An *Exchange-Traded Derivative* product; giving the investor the right (but not the obligation) to buy or to sell the *Underlying* asset at a fixed price (*Exercise Price* or *Strike Price*), for exercise no later than the option's expiry date. See *Call Option* and *Put Option*.
Order	1. A request issued by a member of a *Stock Exchange* or Derivative Exchange to execute a trade. 2. A request (issued by an investor to an *Investment Bank* or *Broker*) to buy or to sell *Securities*, typically at a specified price or at the *Current Market Price*.
Ordinary Shares	The standard description of *Shares* issued by companies in various parts of the globe, including Australia, India and the UK. See *Common Stock*.

OTC	Acronym for *Over-the-counter*.
OTC Derivative	Shortened form of *Over-the-counter Derivative*.
Over-Collateralisation	The effect of *Haircut*. A *Collateral Giver* is required to cover its *Counterparty's* exposure by providing *Collateral* with a *Collateral Value* that is no less than the *Exposure* amount, meaning that over-collateralisation has occurred by the value of the haircut. Also, the effect of a *Non-Exposed Party* undervaluing collateral given to the *Exposed Party*, resulting in a greater value of collateral being given than is necessary to cover the *Exposure*.
Over-the-counter	A generic term which describes a method of *Trade Execution*, in which trades are executed *Bilaterally* and directly between two parties (and not via an exchange, such as a *Stock Exchange* or derivative exchange). Financial products traded in this way include *Bonds*, *Foreign Exchange* and *OTC Derivatives*.
Over-the-counter Derivative	A *Derivative* trade in which the two involved parties executed the trade directly with one another, on a *Bilateral* basis. Synonymous with the term *Swap*. Commonly abbreviated to *OTC Derivative*.
Overnight Index Swap	Similar to an *Interest Rate Swap*, a type of *OTC Derivative* involving a fixed rate of interest versus an overnight rate index.
Par	A *Bond* price of 100%.
Par Value	The face value of an *Equity Security*. Also known as 'nominal value'.
Partial Settlement	The exchange of a quantity of *Securities* and a pro-rata amount of cash that are less than the full quantity and cash value of the trade.
Partial Unwind	The execution of an opposing trade to an existing *OTC Derivative* trade in order to reduce (not remove) the position, and carried out with the original *Counterparty*. For comparison, see *Unwind*.
Pass Through Securities	A type of security (e.g. a *Mortgage-Backed Security*) in which the periodic (e.g. monthly) flow of cash received from the mortgagees, representing the repayment of capital and interest and any *Prepayments*, is forwarded (i.e. passed through) to the investors.
Payment Instruction	An alternative name for a cash-only *Settlement Instruction*.
Payment versus Payment	The simultaneous exchange of two currencies, as practised within *CLS Bank*.
Pension Funds	Organisations that typically invest pension contributions in *Securities* and *Derivatives*, in order to maximise future pension payments. A type of *Institutional Investor*.
Physical Settlement	In a *Credit Default Swap* and following a *Credit Event*, a *Settlement* method whereby the *Protection Buyer* delivers *Bonds* to the *Protection Seller* in order to receive payout in full and final settlement. For comparison, see *Cash Settlement*.
Pledge	One method of securing (collateralising) a loan. Where an asset has been lent, the lender takes possession of *Collateral* but does not have legal ownership of the collateral unless the borrower *Defaults*. Should borrower default occur, the lender has the legal right to sell the collateral to recover the value of the lent asset.

Pool Factor	Relevant to *Mortgage-Backed Securities*, a number representing the amount by which the initial capital amount must be adjusted in order to determine the current capital amount outstanding, following capital repayment and *Prepayment* by the mortgagees.
Portfolio	A list of *Securities*, or of 'live' *Derivative* trades.
Portfolio Compression	The process of offsetting trades that contain the same details as an existing position in the same *OTC Derivative* product, and updating that existing position to a new net position, whilst terminating (cancelling) the original trades. See *triReduce*.
Portfolio Reconciliation	For collateral management purposes, the comparison of a firm's list of trades with a *Bilateral Counterparty*, in an attempt to ensure that the trade population is the same to increase the likelihood of *Exposure* amounts and *Margin Calls* being agreed between the two parties. See *triResolve*.
Porting	Where a firm holds its *OTC Derivative* assets at a *Clearing Member* (of a *Central Counterparty*), and that clearing member *Defaults*, the firm's assets are ported (transferred) to a specific non-defaulting clearing member, generically known as a *BackUp Clearing Member*.
Positive Exposure	This term has the same meaning as *Positive Mark-to-Market*.
Positive Interest Rate	An interest rate in which the cash borrower pays interest to the cash lender. See *Negative Interest Rate*.
Positive Mark-to-Market	Resulting from the (normally daily) revaluation process, the *Current Market Value* of an asset having moved in favour of one of the parties to a trade. In *Collateral*-related trades, this results in a *Margin Call* issued by that party to its Counterparty. See *Negative Mark-to-Market*.
Positive Trading Position	A firm's trade-dated balance in a financial instrument where a greater quantity of purchases (compared with sales) have been executed. See *Negative Trading Position*.
Post-'Trade-Execution' Event	An 'umbrella' term that refers to any event that affects *OTC Derivative* trades following *Trade Execution* and prior to the trade's *Scheduled Maturity Date*, including *Novation*, *Unwind*, *Offset* and *Credit Events*.
Power of Attorney	Authority given by the owner of *Securities* and cash to an individual or company to remove those assets from their place of safekeeping, on behalf of the owner of the assets.
Pre-Collateralise	The provision of *Collateral* by a *Collateral Giver* (e.g. a *Securities Borrower*), in advance of receiving the *Collateral Taker's* opposing asset.
Pre-Funding	Inserting funds into a cash account in anticipation of such an account being debited, as (for example) can occur at a *Central Counterparty* when a *Clearing Member* is required to pay *Variation Margin*.
Premium	The cost of insurance; the regular payment of an agreed amount by an insured party to the insurer. Applicable in *Credit Default Swaps*.
Prepayment	Generically, payment of an obligation prior to its official repayment date. Specifically relating to *Mortgage-Backed Securities*, the unscheduled repayment of capital by mortgagees, which can typically be made at any time and which impacts the amount of capital outstanding on the security. See *Pool Factor*.

Present Value and Present Valuing	'Today's' value of a cash amount that is payable or receivable on a known future date, achieved by applying a *Discount Factor*. See *Time Value of Money*.
Primary Market	A generic term to describe the issuance of and trading in *Securities* that are in course of being brought to the marketplace. See *Secondary Market*.
Prime Broker	A division within an *Investment Bank* that provides a broad range of services to its *Hedge Fund* clients.
Privately Negotiated	An alternative term used to describe financial transactions which are traded *Bilaterally* (on an *Over-the-counter* basis).
Proprietary Positions	A position in a financial instrument which is owned by the firm, typically an *Investment Bank*. See *Positive Trading Position* and *Negative Trading Position*.
Proprietary Trading	A method of trading in financial instruments where a firm (e.g. *Investment Bank*) executes trades for its own account, which can result in the firm having a *Positive Trading Position* or *Negative Trading Position*; such position taking means that the firm is *Exposed* to fluctuations in value of the financial instrument, and is therefore considered to be a high risk activity. Note: the Volcker Rule (US) prevents certain types of firm from indulging in proprietary trading. For comparison, see *Broker*.
Prospectus	A document issued by (or on behalf of) a *Securities* issuer, that details the terms and conditions applicable to the individual security.
Protection Buyer	In a *Credit Default Swap* trade, the party that seeks cover against the *Default* of the *Reference Entity*; the payer of *Premium* to the *Protection Seller*.
Protection Seller	In a *Credit Default Swap* trade, the party that provides cover against the *Default* of the *Reference Entity*, to the *Protection Buyer*; the receiver of *Premium*.
Purchase Date	Alternative term for the *Opening Value Date* in a *Repo* trade.
Put Option	A *Derivative* transaction in which the *Option* holder has the right (but not the obligation) to sell the *Underlying* product at a pre-agreed price (known as the *Exercise Price or Strike Price*), no later than the option's expiry date. See *Call Option*.
Puttable Bonds	*Debt* instruments which have a feature permitting *Redemption* (by the *Bondholder*, and in some cases by the *Issuer*) prior to the bond's *Maturity Date*. For comparison, see *Callable Bonds*.
Quick Code	A 4-character number to uniquely identify individual securities traded in Japan.
Quote Currency	In a *Foreign Exchange* trade, the currency a firm purchases by the sale of an existing currency at the agreed exchange rate. See *Base Currency*.
Ratings Agencies	Organisations that publish their view of an *Issuer's* ability to repay *Debt*. Such views (typically expressed as an alphabetical rating) are used in the assessment of risk associated with buying and selling *Bonds*, and in the use of bonds as *Collateral*. See *Moody's Investors Service* and *Standard & Poor's*.

Ratings Downgrades	The reduction, by a *Ratings Agency*, of the perceived creditworthiness of an entity (whether a corporation, government or government agency).
Ratings Upgrades	The increase, by a *Ratings Agency*, of the perceived creditworthiness of an entity (whether a corporation, government or government agency).
Realised Profit & Loss	Actual profit or loss following sales and purchases of *Securities*. See *Unrealised Profit & Loss*.
Rebate Rate	Where a *Non-Exposed Party* gives *Collateral* in the form of cash to the *Exposed Party*, the agreed rate of interest that the exposed party will pay to the non-exposed party at the close of the trade, to enable the non-exposed party to earn some return on the cash collateral given. See *Cash Collateral Reinvestment* and *Reinvestment Rate*.
Recall (Securities Lending)	In a *Securities Lending & Borrowing* trade that is executed on an *Open* basis, the request by the *Securities Lender* to the *Securities Borrower* to return the lent securities, usually because the securities lender has a delivery commitment relating to a separate transaction. See *Return (Securities Borrowing)*.
Reconciliation	A primary and critically important control for all financial services firms; the comparison of internal *Books & Records* (of trade details or *Trading Positions* or *Settled Positions* or *Open Trades*, and cash balances) versus statements from external entities.
Record Date	*Equity*: the date at which a company's *Share Register* is temporarily closed for the purpose of identifying the shareholders to whom *Corporate Action* benefits, such as *Dividends* or *Bonus Issues*, will be paid. Also known as *Books Closing Date*. *Bonds*: the date at which a custodian identifies its account holders to whom *Coupon Payments* will be made. Note that for equity and bonds, the recipient of a payment is not necessarily entitled to the benefit (due to settlement failure). See *Entitlement*, *Entitlement Date* and *Ex-Dividend Date*.
Redemption	The repayment of capital by an *issuer* to *Bondholders*.
Reference Entity	The formal title of the *Bond Issuer* in a *Credit Default Swap*.
Reference Entity Database	For *Credit Default Swaps*, a coding system that uniquely identifies *Bond Issuers* (*Reference Entities*) and their *Bonds* (*Reference Obligations*).
Reference Obligation	A formal term given to an individual *Bond Issue*, within a *Credit Default Swap*.
Register	The list of holders of a *Registered Security*, maintained by a *Registrar* acting on the *Issuer's* behalf; this allows direct communication (for example, payments of income) by the issuer with the registered owners of the security.
Registered Security	A *Security* where a *Registrar* (acting on the *Issuer's* behalf) maintains a record of owners of the security; this requires that when securities are sold, the seller's name is replaced by the buyer's name on the register. Typically, *Equity* rather than *Bonds* are issued in registered form. See *Bearer Security*.

Registered Shareholder	For *Equity*, the individual or organisation in whose name shares are held on the *Register* of shareholders maintained by a *Registrar* on behalf of the *Issuer*.
Registrar	An organisation appointed by an *Issuer* of a *Registered Security* to maintain the *Register* of holders of that security. Also known as transfer agent in the US.
Registration	The act of updating the *Issuer's* register of owners (of a *Registered Security*) in order to reflect transfer of ownership.
Regulator	An entity that is responsible for the monitoring and controlling of activities within a financial marketplace, to ensure compliance with rules and regulations.
Regulatory Bilateral Trades	An alternative label for *New Bilateral Trades*.
Regulatory Reporting	The provision of information (to a *Regulator*) by *Buy-Side* and *Sell-Side* firms regarding trading activity and *Securities* and *Derivative* positions.
Rehypothecation	Under a *Security Interest* arrangement (as is the case for the *New York Law CSA*), the *Collateral Taker* has no automatic right to reuse *Securities Collateral*. However, the *Collateral Giver* may choose to grant the collateral taker the right to rehypothecate. The term 'rehypothecation' under security interest has a similar (but not the same) meaning as the term 'reuse' under *Title Transfer*. For comparison, see *Reuse of Securities Collateral*.
Reinvestment	1. Instead of a *Securities* investor choosing to receive *Dividends* or *Coupon* in the form of cash, the cash receivable is used to purchase more securities (providing the *Issuer* allows that choice). 2. Where cash *Collateral* is received, the loan of that cash into the *Money Market* in order to earn a positive return.
Reinvestment Rate	Where *Cash Collateral* has been received and that cash has been reinvested (loaned) into the *Money Market*, the interest rate applicable to such reinvested cash. For comparison, see *Rebate Rate*.
Reinvestment Risk	Where *Cash Collateral* has been received, the risk that the interest rate earned (by the *Collateral Taker*) on such cash is less than the *Rebate Rate* that must be paid to the *Collateral Giver*.
Relationship Manager	An individual (for example, within an *Investment Bank*) that is the primary point of contact for clients. Responsible for maintaining relationships with existing clients, and for nurturing relationships with new clients. Also known as a salesperson.
Remaining Party	In an *OTC Derivative* trade where *Novation* has occurred, the party that continues to be involved in the trade, albeit with a new *Counterparty*. See *Novation Transferee* and *Novation Transferor*.
Reorganisation	A term normally applied to the restructuring of a company's issued *Share Capital*, for example via a form of *Corporate Action* known as a *Stock Split* or *Reverse Split*.
Replacement Collateral	As part of the *Collateral Substitution* process, the (new) collateral that replaces the original collateral.

Replacement Cost	With reference to an existing and live *OTC Derivative* trade, the cost of replacing the trade at the *Current Market Price* (in the event that the *Counterparty Defaults*).
Replacement Trade	In *Portfolio Compression*, an alternative approach to the notional change method resulting in the same outcome in terms of net position. Where two trades have been executed, 1) a *Notional Principal* of USD 100m and 2) a notional principal of USD 60m in the opposing direction, instead of adjusting the notional principal to USD 40m, both trades would be fully compressed and a new (replacement) trade for a notional principal of USD 40m would be created between the original parties. Also known as 'replacement swap'.
Repo	A financial transaction in which one party borrows cash against delivery of *Securities* (usually *Bonds*) as *Collateral*. The collateral is intended as a guarantee to the cash lender that the full value of the cash lent is recoverable in the event of *Default* by the cash borrower. Common abbreviation for *Sale & Repurchase Trade*. See *Reverse Repo*, *Classic Repo* and *Buy/Sell Back*.
RepoClear	An organisation that provides *Central Clearing* of European *Bonds*, including normal buy and sell trades and *Repo* trades.
Repo Interest	The amount of cash interest payable or receivable in a *Repo* trade.
Repo Rate	The negotiated percentage interest rate payable by the cash borrower in a *Positive Interest Rate* environment, or by the cash lender in a *Negative Interest Rate* environment.
Repurchase Date	Alternative term for the *Closing Value Date* in a *Repo* trade.
Required Collateral Value	The minimum monetary value of *Collateral* that a *Counterparty* must provide, after deduction of any applicable *Haircut* from the collateral's *Market Value*.
Reset Date	In an *Interest Rate Swap*, the date at which the floating interest rate for an upcoming period becomes effective, and therefore the date from which calculations should commence for that new rate.
Residual Maturity	For *Collateral Management* purposes (specifically for determination of *Haircut*), the period of time from 'today' until the maturity date of a *Bond*, usually expressed in years.
Restructuring Event	A change in the terms of a *Bond* issue during the bond's lifetime, triggered by the *Issuer*. One or many existing bond issues may be replaced by one or more replacement securities. One form of *Corporate Action*. May be included as a qualifying *Credit Event* in a *Credit Default Swap*.
Return (Securities Borrowing)	In a *Securities Lending & Borrowing* trade that is executed on an *Open* basis, the return delivery of securities from the *Securities Borrower* to the *Securities Lender*, where the lender requires the return of the lent securities or the borrower no longer has the requirement to borrow. See *Recall (Securities Lending)*.
Reuse of Securities Collateral	Under a *Title Transfer* arrangement (as is the case for the *English Law CSA*, the *GMRA* and the *GMSLA*), the *Collateral Taker* has the legal right to reuse securities collateral in any way of their choosing. For comparison, see *Rehypothecation*.

Reverse Repo	A *Repo* transaction viewed from the perspective of the cash lender. *Securities* are initially received from the *Counterparty* (against payment of cash), and will require to be returned to the counterparty on the *Closing Value Date* of the trade.
Reverse Split	With the *Issuer's* intention of increasing the *Current Market Price* of a share, the replacement of an *Equity* issue having a particular *Par Value* (e.g. USD 1.00), with an equivalent quantity of a higher par value security (e.g. USD 2.00), at an effective date. One type of *Corporate Action*. See *Stock Split*.
Rights Issue	An offer by an *Issuer* (that wishes to raise further capital) to the existing *Shareholders* to purchase additional *Shares* in proportion to their existing shareholding; in order to entice the shareholders to take up the offer, the price of the rights is typically offered at a discount to the *Current Market Price* of the existing shares. Care: the issuer imposes a deadline for the receipt of cash from shareholders wishing to subscribe. One type of *Corporate Action*.
Rounding	The process of increasing (rounding up) or decreasing (rounding down) a number or cash value, in accordance with an agreed method. This is common practice when issuing *Margin Calls*.
Safe Custody	The holding of *Securities* in safekeeping on behalf of the owner of the assets, and the provision of associated services, such as the collection of income payable to the owner.
Sale & Repurchase Trade	A form of *Securities Financing* transaction. Commonly abbreviated to *Repo*.
Salesman	An employee of an *Investment Bank* that is the liaison point with *Institutional Investors* and the investment bank's traders.
Scheduled Maturity Date	The final day that an *OTC Derivative* trade is live and valid. Once this day has passed, as no *Exposure* exists for the parties to the trade, all *Collateral* must be returned to the original owner.
Secondary Market	A generic term to describe the marketplace where existing *Securities* are traded (as opposed to those securities that are in course of being brought to the marketplace, within the *Primary Market*).
Secure File Transfer Protocol	A method of accessing and transferring data in a secure manner.
Secured Cash Borrowing	The borrowing of cash against the delivery of *Collateral*, in order to mitigate the cash lender's risk (of not having the cash returned). Also known as *Collateralised Cash Borrowing*. The alternative is *Unsecured Cash Borrowing*.
Securities	Financial instruments that may be purchased and sold, repo'd and reverse repo'd, lent and borrowed, and used as *Collateral*. The most common forms of securities are *Equities* and *Bonds*.
Securities Borrowing	In the event that *Securities* sold cannot (yet) be delivered to the buyer, the practice of borrowing securities from a *Shareholder* or *Bondholder* at a cost, in order to settle the sale, thereby enabling the seller to receive the sale proceeds at the earliest opportunity. See *Securities Lending*.

Securities Data Vendors	Organisations that supply detailed information concerning individual *Securities*, usually electronically, to those that subscribe to the service.
Securities Delivery Risk	Where *Securities* are due to be delivered against receipt of an asset of equivalent value, the risk that the asset given by the deliverer is delivered on a non-simultaneous basis, where the possibility exists that the deliverer will have possession of neither asset. See *Delivery versus payment* and *Free of payment*.
Securities Industry and Financial Markets Association	An organisation which promotes effective and efficient operation of *Capital Markets*, and which represents *Investment Banks*, Broker-Dealers and *Asset Managers* in the United States. Commonly abbreviated to SIFMA.
Securities Financing	An 'umbrella' term for any transaction type in which *Securities* (i.e. *Equity* and/or *Bonds*) are used to borrow cash, and where cash is used to borrow securities, and where securities are used to borrow other securities. Applicable to *Repo*, *Buy/Sell Back* and *Securities Lending & Borrowing*.
Securities Lending	The practice of a *Shareholder* or *Bondholder* loaning its securities to a borrower for a fee, in order to enhance the lender's return on its investment. See *Securities Borrowing*.
Securities Lending & Borrowing	Generic name for the practice in which securities are temporarily delivered (by lenders) to parties needing temporary use (borrowers) of such securities. Collateral is provided by borrowers to mitigate the lender's risk of their asset failing to be returned by the borrower.
Securities Safekeeping Fees	Charges made by *Central Securities Depositories* and *Custodians* to *Shareholders* and *Bondholders* for holding *Securities* safely and securely. Equity-related fees are typically based on *Market Value* of the securities held, whereas *Bond*-related fees are typically based on the bond quantity held.
Securitised and Securitisation	The process of transforming one or more financial assets (e.g. a collection of loans) into a tradable *Security*. See *Mortgage-Backed Security*.
Security	A negotiable financial instrument (specifically *Equity* and *Bonds*) which is tradable between investors, and whose price fluctuates according to the laws of supply and demand. *Securities* are brought to the marketplace within the *Primary Market*, and are subsequently tradable within the *Secondary Market*. Each security is uniquely identifiable via its *ISIN*.
Security Interest	The legal method of transfer of *Collateral* under the *New York Law CSA*. The *Collateral Giver* retains *Legal Ownership*, although this is subject to surrender in case of *Default* by that party. *Rehypothecation* is not permitted automatically. For comparison, see *Title Transfer*.
SEDOL Code	Acronym for 'Stock Exchange Daily Official List'. A coding regime that identifies UK and Irish securities.
Self-Clearing	The administration of a firm's *Operations* and *Settlement* activity by the firm that has executed the trade. (The alternative being to outsource such activity.)

Sell-Out	A formal procedure for a seller to force the buyer to pay for *Securities* it is owed, with associated costs payable by the buyer; such procedures must be conducted under the rules of the *Stock Exchange* or market authority over which the trade has been *Executed*. For comparison, see *Buy-In*.
Sell-Side	Generic term which describes the community of *Investment Banks* and *Brokers* that execute trades (in financial instruments of various types) for and with *Buy-Side* firms. Note that the sell-side also buys such financial instruments.
Senior Unsecured Bond	A *Debt* security issued by a corporation which, in the event of the *Issuer's* bankruptcy, will repay such *Bondholders* prior to repaying other forms of debt.
Service Level Agreement	Generically speaking, a formal contract between a service provider and its client, which is designed to clearly document the agreed level of service. In a financial services environment, one use of such agreement is between a *Central Securities Depository* or *Custodian* and its account holder.
Set-Off	The legally documented netting of *Repo* or *OTC Derivative* trades, resulting from an *Event of Default* by a firm or its *Counterparty*.
Settled Position and Settled Securities Position	The quantity of *Securities* held in the account of an account holder, at a *CSD* or *Custodian*; differences in the settled position and *Trading Position* are usually due to one or many *Open Trades*.
Settlement	1. *Securities*: the act of buyer and seller (or their agents) exchanging securities and cash in order to fulfill their contractual obligations. 2. *Derivatives*: payment (or receipt) of monies falling due periodically throughout the lifetime of a trade; e.g. quarterly *Premium* in a *Credit Default Swap*. 3. *Collateral*: payment of cash or delivery of *Securities* to satisfy a *Margin Call*.
Settlement Cycle	The standard or default period of time between *Trade Date* and *Value Date* of *Securities* trades, within a marketplace. (At the time of writing, the settlement cycle in Europe and the USA is T+2 (trade date plus 2 business days).) Also applicable in *Spot Foreign Exchange* trades.
Settlement Date	The date the actual exchange of *Securities* and cash has been effected; this date is known only after *Settlement* has occurred. For comparison, see *Value Date*.
Settlement Failure	Trades where *Securities* and cash have not been exchanged on *Value Date* (the *Contractual Settlement Date*); *Settlement* is therefore delayed.
Settlement Instruction	A message issued by an account holder to its *CSD* or *custodian* (or *Nostro* in the case of cash) that requests the delivery or receipt of *Securities* and/or payment or receipt of cash, on a specified date (the *Value Date* of the trade).
Settlement Netting	Instead of settling each *Open Trade* independently, the *Settlement* of two or more trades may be effected by the single delivery (or receipt) of the remaining quantity of *Securities* and the single receipt (or payment) of the remaining amount of cash.

Settlement Status	The condition of a *Securities Settlement Instruction* reported by a *CSD* or *Custodian* to its account holder; typical statuses are unmatched with counterparty, matched with counterparty, settled, and failed.
Settlement Tolerance	A predefined cash limit (set by a *CSD* or *Custodian*), within which differing cash amounts on seller's and buyer's *Settlement Instructions* are deemed to match; such tolerances avoid small cash differences from preventing *Settlement* occurring.
Settlement Write-Off	Internally within a *Buy-Side* or *Sell-Side* firm, the clearance of an open cash balance of an individual trade, where the open cash amount is transferred to an internal account leaving no cash amount to be paid to or received from the *Counterparty*.
Share	That which represents *Equity* ownership in a company.
Share Buy-Back	The offer by an *Equity Issuer* to purchase the *Shareholders'* shares at a specified price per share. One type of *Voluntary Corporate Action*.
Share Capital	The total *Par Value* of issued *Shares* in a company.
Share Register	The list of *Registered Holders* of *Equity*, maintained by a *Registrar* on behalf of the *Issuer*.
Shareholder	The owner of *Shares* in a company.
Short First Coupon	A term given to the first payment of interest after a *Bond* has been issued, specifically where the elapsed time between issue of the bond and the first *Coupon Payment Date* is less than the normal *Coupon Period* for that bond. See *Long First Coupon*.
Short Form Confirmation	Relating to an *OTC Derivative* trade where an *ISDA Master Agreement* is in place between the two parties, a legal document issued by a firm to its *Counterparty* that specifies the basic terms of the trade. See *Long Form Confirmation*.
Short Sale and Short Selling	A sale of securities which are not owned by the seller. See *Covered Short* and *Naked Short*.
SIFMA	Acronym for *Securities Industry and Financial Markets Association*.
Single-Name Credit Default Swap	A *Credit Default Swap* in which the *Reference Entity* is a single issuer (as opposed to multiple issuers as is the case in a *Basket Default Swap*).
SONIA	Acronym for 'Sterling OverNight Index Average'. A *Floating Benchmark* interest rate which is the average rate quoted by a number of banks for a duration of 1 day, for GBP. See *Euribor* and *Libor*.
Special Collateral	A *Security* which is in extraordinarily high demand, particularly when compared with the demand for other securities. See *Special Repo*.
Special Repo	A type of *Repo* transaction (a *Stock-Based Repo*), in which the motivation for the trade is that one party wishes to borrow the *Security*. In return, the securities borrower (*Collateral Taker*) provides cash to the *Collateral Giver*, for which either 1) a low rate of credit interest may be payable by the collateral giver, or 2) the collateral taker is required to pay debit (i.e. negative) interest.
Spot Exchange Rate	In a *Foreign Exchange* trade, the rate at which a trade is executed for immediate *Settlement* on the 'spot' *Value Date*, which (for most currency combinations) is *Trade Date* + 2 business days. For comparison, see *Forward Exchange Rate*.

Square-Off	In an existing *OTC Derivative* trade, the closure of that trade by the execution of an equal and opposite trade with the same *Counterparty*, resulting in no outstanding trade and no ongoing exposure. The effect of an *Unwind*.
SSI	Acronym for *Standing Settlement Instruction*.
Standard & Poor's	An *Issuer Ratings Agency* that publishes its view of an issuer's ability to repay *Debt*.
Standardised OTC Derivative	Under *EMIR*, an *OTC Derivative* trade which is deemed to have only normal (standard) characteristics; only trades such as this are eligible for clearing via a *Central Counterparty*. Trades with abnormal or additional characteristics are not permitted to be cleared via a central counterparty, and are classified as *Non-Centrally Cleared Trades*.
Standing Settlement Instruction	A firm's and its *Counterparties'* account numbers (at *CSDs* and *Cash Correspondents*) held within the firm's *Static Data Repository*, so as to facilitate *Straight Through Processing* of trades. Commonly abbreviated to *SSI*.
Static Data and Static Data Repository	An internal store of information pertaining to trading companies, *Counterparties*, *Securities* and currencies which is used repeatedly in the processing of *Trades*, position management and *Corporate Actions*.
Static Data Defaulting	The automatic process of 1) locating (from a *Static Data Repository*) of relevant account numbers and cash values, and 2) attachment of the same to basic trade details, according to predefined set of rules.
Stock-Based Repo	A *Repo* trade in which the primary motivation is for one of the parties to borrow securities; the alternative is *Cash-Based Repo*.
Stock Dividend	A *Dividend* paid by an *Issuer* to its *Shareholders* in the form of *Securities*; also known as 'Scrip Dividend'.
Stock Exchange	Historically, a physical meeting point for buyers and sellers, where *Equity* securities were traded. Today, some financial centres continue to operate in such a manner whilst others operate on an electronic basis.
Stock Split	With the *Issuer's* intention of reducing the *Current Market Price* of a share, the replacement of an *Equity* issue having a particular *Par Value* (e.g. USD 1.00), with an equivalent quantity of a lower par value security (e.g. USD 0.50), at an effective date. Also known as a 'Forward Split'. One type of *Corporate Action*. See *Reverse Split*.
STP	Acronym for *Straight Through Processing*.
Straight Through Processing	An objective of *Buy-Side* and *Sell-Side* firms, suppliers of communications software, *CSDs*, *Custodians*, etc., to manage the entire *Trade Lifecycle* in an automated and seamless manner, without the need for review or repair. The intended benefit of straight through processing is reduced costs and the ability to process high volumes of trades in a secure and risk-free manner. Commonly abbreviated to *STP*.
Stressed Market	A financial market which is undergoing increased or extreme volatility, typically caused by unusual external events.
Strike Price	See *Exercise Price*.

Structured Trade	A transaction that has been created to meet an investor's particular needs, by the amalgamation of a number of features over and above those of standardised financial products.
Supranational Organisations	Entities that issue *Bonds* but which are not associated with a specific country; such entities include the International Bank for Reconstruction & Development (World Bank), the Inter-American Development Bank (IADB), and the European Coal & Steel Community (ECSC). See *Multilateral Development Banks*.
Swap	A *Derivative* trade in which the two involved parties *Execute* the trade directly with one another, on a *Bilateral* basis. The word 'swap' refers to the exchange of cashflows which occurs in such trades. Synonymous with the term *OTC (Over-the-counter) Derivative*.
Swap Execution Facility	An electronic trading platform via which those parties that wish to execute *OTC Derivative* trades can be matched with one another.
S.W.I.F.T.	Acronym for 'Society for Worldwide Interbank Financial Telecommunications'. A worldwide organisation providing secure message transmission between subscribing parties. Message types include *Trade Confirmation, Settlement Instructions, Securities* and cash statements and *Corporate Actions*.
Systemic Risk	The threat of complete failure of a financial marketplace or of the global financial system.
T2S	Acronym for *Target2 Securities*.
Target2 Securities	The European Commission's pan-European *Settlement* platform, designed to harmonise cross-border securities settlement. Clients of participating *CSDs* in Europe can utilise their CSD as a single point of contact for settlement of movements in European securities, utilising *Central Bank Money*. Commonly abbreviated to *T2S*.
Tax Avoidance	Legal strategies designed to minimise the amount of tax owed to tax authorities. See *Tax Evasion*.
Tax Evasion	Unlawful practices designed to avoid taxes payable to tax authorities. See *Tax Avoidance*.
Tax Event	Relating to *OTC Derivatives*, an event that results in termination of a trade. Specifically, a change in tax law causing either party to pay a tax amount or additional tax amount.
Threshold	An amount of *Uncollateralised Exposure* which two parties may agree and document. Where a firm has an *Exposure* and a threshold is applicable, that firm's *Margin Call* on its *Counterparty* must exclude the threshold amount.
Time Value of Money	The concept that a cash amount received today is worth more than that same cash amount receivable in future, assuming that credit interest can be earned on that cash. See *Discount Factor* and *Present Value*.
Time Zone Difference	The difference in the time of day between one time zone and a different time zone.

Title Transfer	The legal method of transfer of *Collateral* under the *English Law CSA*. Full legal title to *Securities* collateral passes from the *Collateral Giver* to the *Collateral Taker* whilst the collateral is in the taker's possession, consequently *Reuse of Securities Collateral* is permitted automatically. For comparison, see *Security Interest*.
Trade	An agreement to exchange financial products on a permanent or temporary basis, between two parties, whether buying or selling, lending or borrowing, etc. This term is applicable to *Equity*, *Bonds*, currencies, *Derivatives* and commodities.
Trade Affirmation	A communication of the details of a *trade* from a *Sell-Side* firm to its *Buy-Side* client, following which the latter responds to the former to affirm (agree to) the details presented. This is a sequential process. A means of achieving *Trade Agreement*.
Trade Agreement	Following *Trade Execution*, the act of one party gaining agreement to the details of a *Trade* with its *Counterparty*, whether by electronic or manual means.
Trade Capture	The act of recording the components of a trade internally, following *Trade Execution*.
Trade Confirmation	A communication of the details of a *Trade* from one party to its *Counterparty*; various media are used for the communication method, including *S.W.I.F.T.* A means of achieving *Trade Agreement*.
Trade Date	The date the parties to a *Trade* agree to trade; the date of *Trade Execution*.
Trade Execution	The agreement to *Trade* between the *Traders* of two parties (e.g. a *Buy-Side* firm and a *Sell-Side* firm). Applicable to buying or selling, *Repo* and *Reverse Repo*, *Securities Lending* and *Securities Borrowing*, *OTC Derivatives*, etc.
Trade Execution Venue	For *OTC Derivatives* under *EMIR*, an 'umbrella' and generic term representing systems that facilitate *Trade Execution*.
Trade Lifecycle	A series of sequential steps through which a financial transaction passes, beginning with *Trade Execution* and finishing with the updating of *Books & Records,* following *Settlement*. Applicable to all product types (e.g. *Equity*, *Bonds*, currency, *OTC Derivatives*) and all transaction types including buy/sell, *Repo/Reverse Repo*, *Securities Lending/Securities Borrowing*).
Trade Matching	The process of comparing a seller's and a buyer's *Trade* details electronically, shortly after *Trade Execution*. A means of achieving *Trade Agreement*.
Trade Processing	For *OTC Derivatives*, a generic term given to the area (within *Buy-Side* and *Sell-Side* firms) responsible for the *Settlement* of trades (e.g. periodic payment or receipt of premium in a *CDS*). The alternative is *Collateral Processing*. Each trade creates the need for both trade processing and collateral processing.

Trade Repository	For *OTC Derivatives* under *EMIR*, an electronic 'warehouse' for the storage and safekeeping of the terms of individual trades and positions. *Regulators* will access such trade information in order to carry out their regulatory oversight responsibilities.
Trade Time	The hour and minute (within a *Trade Date*) that *Trade Execution* occurred.
Trader	An individual responsible for *Trade Execution* within a *Buy-Side* firm or a *Sell-Side* firm. This term is applicable to trading in *Equities*, *Bonds*, currencies, *Derivatives* and commodities.
Trading Book	A subdivision of a trading department within an *Investment Bank* in which trading in a specific grouping of *Securities* (for example) is conducted and kept separate from the business of other trading books.
Trading Position	A positive or negative trade-dated balance (holding) in a particular financial instrument. For comparison, see *Settled Position*.
Transaction Reporting	The regulatory requirement for firms to report each individual trade they execute to a *Regulator*. In the case of *OTC Derivatives* under *EMIR*, trades must be reported to a *Trade Repository*.
Transferee	The receiver of Collateral. Also known as *Collateral Taker*. See *Transferor*.
Transferor	The payer (cash) or deliverer (*Bonds* or *Equity*) of *Collateral*. Also known as *Collateral Giver*. See *Transferee*.
Treaty	A common abbreviation for *Double Taxation Agreement*.
Tri-Party Agent	An organisation (such as an *ICSD*), that provides trade lifecycle administration services for *Collateral*-related transactions.
Tri-Party Repo	A *Repo* trade in which the two trading parties utilise the services of a *Tri-Party Agent* to administer the trade throughout its lifetime.
triReduce	A *Portfolio Compression* service for firms wishing to net their trades with a particular *Counterparty*. Submitted trades are assessed for full or partial compression and the results are presented as compression proposals.
triResolve	A *Portfolio Reconciliation* system that (for *Collateral Management* purposes) compares *OTC Derivative* trades executed under legal agreements between two parties, and provides matching results.
UCITS	Acronym for 'Undertakings for Collective Investment in Transferable Securities'. A type of *Mutual Fund* which is listed in Europe and which permits investors within and outside of Europe to invest in a diversified manner.
Uncollateralised Exposure	An *Exposure* amount for which no *Collateral* is given or taken. For example, an amount of exposure which the *Exposed Party* is not permitted to include within a *Margin Call* issued to the *Counterparty*, in accordance with the *Credit Support Annex* in place between the two parties. See *Threshold*.

Underlying	The financial (or other) asset which is associated with a trade in a *Derivative* product. For example, a stock *Option* is a derivative product, the associated asset being (for example) IBM Corporation shares. The price of the derivative product relates directly to the price of the underlying asset.
Undisputed Amount	Following receipt of a *Margin Call Notification*, the agreement (by the recipient party) of part of its value. The remainder is known as the *Disputed Amount*.
Unique Trade Identifier	A coding mechanism designed to uniquely identify individual *OTC Derivative* trades, for transaction reporting to *Trade Repositories*. Commonly abbreviated to *UTI*.
Unmatched Settlement Instruction	A *Settlement Instruction* issued to a *CSD* or *Custodian* to deliver or to receive *Securities* (typically versus payment or receipt of cash) that has no direct equivalent issued by the *Counterparty* to the trade. For comparison, see *Matched Settlement Instruction*.
Unrealised Profit & Loss	Theoretical profit or loss on a positive or negative securities *Trading Position* following revaluation of the position. For comparison, see *Realised Profit & Loss*.
Unsecured Cash Borrowing	The borrowing of cash without supplying *Collateral* to the cash lender; the rate of interest payable by the borrower is usually higher than for *Secured Borrowing*, to reflect the lender's risk.
Unsecured Cash Lending	The loan of cash without the lender having the security of the borrower's *Collateral*.
Unsecured Creditor	A cash lender that has not secured the loan by taking any assets as *Collateral* from the cash borrower.
Unwind	The execution of an opposing trade to an existing *OTC Derivative* trade in order to negate the position, and carried out with the original *Counterparty*. For comparison, see *Offset*.
UTI	Acronym for *Unique Trade Identifier*.
Valuation Agent	Within the *Credit Support Annex*, the party (or parties) responsible for carrying out valuation of *Open Trades* in relevant *OTC Derivative* products and any previously delivered *Collateral*.
Value Date	The intended date of exchange of *Securities* and cash between buyer and seller. Also known as *Contractual Settlement Date*.
Variance Swap	A type of *OTC Derivative* which provides an investor with direct *Exposure* to changes in the future volatility of an *Underlying* asset such as a stock or an index. Returns are based on difference between expected volatility level and actual volatility level.
Variation Margin	For *OTC Derivative* trades and positions held at a *Central Counterparty*, the giving and taking of *Collateral* resulting from the *Mark-to-Market* process.
VM	Acronym for *Variation Margin*.

Voluntary Corporate Action	An event in the lifetime of an *Equity* or *Bond* security which is normally triggered by the *Issuer*, in which a financial opportunity is presented to holders. For example, whether to convert a *Convertible Bond*, or to subscribe in a *Rights Issue*. The voluntary nature of such events means that no action will be taken unless the holder elects to take action. See *Mandatory Corporate Action and Optional Corporate Action*.
Withholding Tax	Tax deducted in the issuer's country of residence, on income paid by *Issuers* to investors, whether on *Equities* or *Bonds*. Investors resident in certain countries may be subject to a lower rate of withholding tax, if the issuer's country and the investor's country have a *Double Taxation Agreement* (or *Treaty*) in place.
WKN Code	A coding regime that identifies German securities.
Zero Coupon Bond	*Debt Securities* that do not pay interest, but which are issued at a deep discount and are typically redeemed at their full face value on the bond's *Maturity Date*.

Useful Websites

The author recommends the following websites for further information relating to collateral management, and for contact details.

Website Address	Organisation	Role/Responsibility
www.bis.org	Bank for International Settlements	Support for Central Banks
www.bmeclearing.es	BME Clearing	Central Counterparty
www.clearstream.com	Clearstream International	International Central Securities Depository
www.cls-group.com	CLS Bank	Foreign Exchange Settlement
www.eseclending.com	eSecLending	Securities Lending Agent
www.eurexclearing.com	Eurex Clearing AG	Central Counterparty
www.euroclear.com	Euroclear Bank	International Central Securities Depository
www.ec.europa.eu	European Commission	European Market Infrastructure Regulation
www.esma.europa.eu	European Securities and Markets Authority	Authorised Central Counterparties
		Registered Trade Repositories
www.eurexrepo.com	GC Pooling	Electronic Trading Platform for Repo
www.theice.com	ICE Clear Europe	Central Counterparty
www.icmagroup.org	International Capital Market Association	Trade Association for Capital Markets
www.isla.co.uk/	International Securities Lending Association	Trade Association for Securities Lending
www.isda.org	International Swaps and Derivatives Association	Trade Organisation for OTC Derivatives
www.lch.com	LCH Ltd	Central Counterparty
www.acadiasoft.com	MarginSphere	Electronic Margin Call Platform

(continued)

(continued)

Website Address	Organisation	Role/Responsibility
www.markitserv.com	MarkitSERV	OTC Derivative Electronic Trade Confirmation
www.moodys.com	Moody's Investors Service	Credit Ratings Agency
www.mtsmarkets.com	MTS Repo	Electronic Trading Platform for Repo
www.dtcc.com	Omgeo Central Trade Manager	Automated Trade Confirmation/ Affirmation
www.regis-tr.com	Regis-TR S.A.	Trade Repository
www.sifma.org	Securities Industry and Financial Markets Association	Industry Trade Group for Capital Markets (USA)
www.six-financial-information.com	SIX Financial Information	Data Vendor
www.standardandpoors.com	Standard & Poor's	Credit Ratings Agency
www.swift.com	S.W.I.F.T.	Secure Financial Messaging Between Subscribers
www.ecb.europa.eu	Target2 Securities	Pan-European Securities Settlement Platform
www.trioptima.com	triOptima	Portfolio Compression (via triReduce)
		Portfolio Reconciliation (via triResolve)
www.lseg.com	UnaVista Limited	Trade Repository

Further Reading

In order to enhance the readers' understanding of matters relating to collateral management, the author recommends the following books.

Book Title	Author(s)	ISBN
Securities Operations: A Guide to Trade and Position Management	Michael Simmons	978-0-471-49758-5
Corporate Actions: A Guide to Securities Event Management	Michael Simmons Elaine Dalgleish	978-0-470-87066-2
Trading the Fixed Income, Inflation and Credit Markets: A Relative Value Guide	Neil Schofield Troy Bowler	978-0-470-74229-7

Index